STATISTICS

FOR BUSINESS AND ECONOMICS

USING MICROSOFT EXCEL 97

STATISTICS

FOR BUSINESS AND ECONOMICS

USING MICROSOFT EXCEL 97

William E. Becker

INDIANA UNIVERSITY

S. R. B. Publishing

Printed in the United States of America

ISBN: 0-9658576-0-3

Managing Editor: Suzanne Becker
Production Coordinator: Julie Marker
Printer: Metropolitan Printing Service, Inc.
Cover Art: David Suter
Reprinted from *The Wall Street Journal* (May 17, 1994), with the permission of David Suter.

Library of Congress Cataloging–in–Publication Data

Becker, William E.
Statistics for business and economics using Microsoft Excel 97 / William E. Becker.
p. cm.
Includes bibliographical references and index.
ISBN 0-9658576-0-3
1. Statistics. 2. Commercial statistics. 3. Economics-
-Statistical methods. I. Title.
Library of Congress Catalog Card Number: 97–93693

S. R. B. Publishing
Bloomington, Indiana

Contents

10 Two-Sample Hypothesiss Testing 357

11 Chi-Square Test of Independence 369

12 Correlation and Regression Analysis within a Sample 377

13 The Two-Variable Population Model 433

14 Multiple Regression 475

Credits

About the Author

William E. Becker is Professor of Economics at Indiana University, Bloomington. He is editor of the *Journal of Economic Education* and also serves on the editorial board of the *Economics of Education Review.* Before joining the faculty of Indiana University in 1979 he was a tenured faculty member at the University of Minnesota, where he returned for the academic year of 1988 to serve as acting director of the Management Information Division. During the summers of 1987 and 1988, he was a visiting fellow at Princeton University. In the fall of 1990, he toured Indonesia consulting for the World Bank Midwest Universities Consortium for International Activities. In the spring of 1993 he visited Spain, consulting for the Universidad Carlos III. For the second half of 1995, he was a visiting professor of economics at the Universities of Adelaide, Melbourne, and South Australia. He now holds an adjunct professorship at the University of South Australia and was in residence there for some of the work on this book between May and June 1997.

Professor Becker's research appears in the *American Economic Review, American Statistician, American Journal of Agricultural Economics, Econometric Theory, Education Researcher, Economic Inquiry, Journal of Economic Literature, Journal of Finance, Journal of Human Resources, Journal of Risk and Insurance, Monthly Labor Review, Research in Higher Education, Review of Economics and Statistics*, and numerous other journals. In addition to writing commissioned monographs on the value of human capital, and giving expert statistical and econometric testimony in Minnesota, Illinois and Indiana courtrooms, he has been a paid consultant for the United States Department of Justice, Ford Motor Company, Chrysler Corporation, Nissan, Westinghouse, as well as many smaller firms and individuals. He is the author of *Statistics for Business and Economics* (International Thomson Publishing), coauthor of *Business and Economics Statistics* (Addison-Wesley), and coeditor of *Academic Rewards in Higher Education* (Ballinger), *Econometric Modeling in Economic Education Research* (Kluwer-Nijhoff), *The Economics of American Higher Education* (Kluwer) and *Higher Education and National Growth* (Kluwer). His most recent volume, coedited with William Baumol, *Assessing Educational Practices: The Contribution of Economics*, is a 1996 publication of the MIT Press.

Dr. Becker earned a bachelor's degree in mathematics from the College of St. Thomas, a master's degree in economics from the University of Wisconsin, and a doctorate in economics from the University of Pittsburgh. In 1987, he received the Henry H. Villard Research Award for his work in education.

PREFACE

This book is designed for the first-semester course in statistics for business and economics students, as taught at Indiana University, Bloomington. To ensure real-life applicability, it employs numerous examples and exercises with information from news and business publications, government documents, and scholarly journals. Whenever possible the original source material is cited. Data analysis is conducted primarily with Microsoft Excel 97, although other popular statistical computer packages are occasionally featured.

The text makes extensive use of firm-specific data as well as aggregate economic data. Data sets, together with relevant statistics, are based on actual situations described in the academic and business press. These examples, case studies, and exercises were chosen from business publications such as *Business Week (BW),* and *The Wall Street Journal (WSJ),* government publications such as the *Monthly Labor Review, Economic Report of the President,* and *Federal Reserve Bulletin,* and scholarly journals that publish quantitative studies in business and economics. Available to students at Indiana University are over 170 data files that the students can download from the World Wide Web site at http://www.indiana.edu/~statist/e270.htm and then read directly into EXCEL as ASCII files with data in fixed widths columns. All of the smaller data sets and a few of the large ones as well are also provided within the pages of this book. They are designed to provide students with activities that will make them aware of statistical procedures for solving problems in business, and to enable them to use these procedures in actual data analysis.

The theory underlying these data applications is classical inferential statistics. Drawing from my two-semester book (*Statistics for Business and Economics*, International Thomson Publishing, 1995), a wide range of concepts and topics are considered in both specific applications and full chapter coverage. The historical developments of statistical techniques and ideas are considered throughout the text. Special features include Queries, which are problems similar to those an instructor might assign as exercises or give on an exam. Through worked-out solutions to these Queries, students are able to see how to prepare their work.

Problem Solving with Data

Each chapter opens with an introduction that describes various economic and business applications of the techniques to be covered in that chapter. Short cases present the data that are used throughout the chapter to solve problems related to accounting, law, marketing, economics, finance, personnel, operations and production, and administration. New situations and data are introduced in each chapter and are used to demonstrate how statistical concepts build, with more in-depth data analysis resulting in more precise solutions. Whenever possible, real data from clearly identified sources are employed, but in some cases artificial data had to be created. Any hypothetical data, however, were constructed to closely mimic the application described in an actual situation.

Topics and Content

Cases provided throughout the book describe contemporary problems that face managers within firms and government agencies. For example, Chapter 1 analyzes technological developments in small versus large firms. Examples involving executive pay are introduced in Chapters 1 and 2. Chapters 3 and 4 introduce probability and random variables. Chapter 4 emphasizes the use of expected values and sums of random variables in financial decisions. Chapters 5 and 6 extend the coverage of probability to specific distributions for discrete and continuous random variables.

Cases and examples that deal with selected topics in sampling, estimation, testing, modeling, and forecasting are employed throughout the book, but there are also separate chapters devoted to these topics, as seen in Chapters 7 through 14. Extensive attention is given to estimation (Chapter 8), hypothesis testing (Chapters 9, 10, and 11), and the relationship between the two. Resampling techniques are demonstrated in the chapters on sampling distributions (Chapter 7) and estimation (Chapter 8). Chapter 9 reviews the controversy surrounding the usefulness of hypothesis testing in business decisionmaking. Because of the central role of regression analysis in data analysis, three chapters are devoted to this topic (Chapters 12 through 14). Special attention is given to prediction, estimation, and hypothesis testing within the regression framework.

Theory

Although this book is oriented to applications, it is rooted in the theory of classical inferential statistics. For brevity, the alternative theoretical views found in Bayesian and nonparametric literature are not presented here. Discussion of these alternatives to classical inference can be found in my two semester textbook. At all times, the focus of this book is the inferential techniques of classical statistics and their application to real-life problem solving. Theory is discussed only to the extent required in the actual situations and cases under consideration. Some mathematical derivations and more in-depth presentations of theory are provided for the highly motivated student in endnotes. Calculus is used in only a very few places and can be ignored by students who want only a basic understanding and working knowledge of statistics.

This book is designed to teach the application of statistical theory to problems encountered in business and economics. It is not a cookbook for data manipulation in EXCEL or any other computer package. Function commands found in EXCEL and a few other computer packages are presented only after the rationale and calculation procedures have been discussed and demonstrated. Computer programs are not treated as magical boxes into which data are poured and answers mysteriously emerge.

Historical Perspective

In the spirit of the works of Glenn Shafer, Stephen Stigler, and Theodore Porter, this book describes how the statistical way of thinking developed in business and economic analysis. In Chapters 3 and 4, for example, students get a sense of the importance of alternative interpretations of probability. In the study of regression (Chapters 12, 13, and 14), students learn that Carl Friedrich Gauss was their age when he developed the idea of least-squares estimation. They learn how Nobel Laureate economist Milton Friedman as a young scholar used multiple regression (which required weeks of calculations without a computer) to design a metal alloy for aircraft engines during World War II. Similar historical tidbits throughout the book convey a sense of history in the development of statistical ideas.

Q&A

In addition to the case studies that introduce each chapter, other empirical examples are used to develop and demonstrate the statistical way of thinking. These "Queries" and "Answers" are employed regularly to show students how exercises and exam questions should be answered. They are often used to show how computer programs are used in data analyses. Although emphasis is given to EXCEL, other programs are employed when they provide an advantage over EXCEL and to demonstrate that EXCEL is not the only vehicle for statistical analysis.

Definitions and Formulas

Definitions of key terms are presented in the margins. Formulas and key equations are highlighted and numbered for easy identification; derivations are provided when needed in endnotes and appendices. Although this book does not emphasize hand calculations using computational formulas, a complete understanding of statistics is not possible without at least an awareness of the mathematics on which statistics is founded. Thus, students are shown basic calculations using small data sets before they are shown the procedures and output from EXCEL and other computer programs.

Illustrations

Students often have difficulty grasping the basic ideas of statistical analysis when those ideas are presented only through algebra and verbal explanations. This is especially true in drawing distinctions among population parameters, their estimators, and specific estimates. In this book, numerous graphs, charts, diagrams and other illustrations are used to help students visualize difficult concepts. Throughout this book, diagrams and graphs show the relevant components of estimation and testing procedures. These illustrations are typically based on small data sets that students can use to easily replicate calculations.

Exercises

At key points in each chapter there are exercises for students to try. These exercises are based on material from the immediately preceding sections of the chapter. At the end of each chapter there are additional exercises that require students to draw on material from the entire chapter. Exercises are of two types: (1) problem-solving exercises that present questions using business and economic situations and data, and (2) drill exercises that emphasize the procedures and algebraic manipulations that are critical to an operational understanding of statistical principles. Chapters often have over 50 exercises, many with multiple parts. Abridged answers to most even-numbered exercises are provided at the back of this book, with detailed answers available in a student solution manual that also includes practice tests. Detailed answers to all exercises appear in a manual restricted to circulate only to instructors.

Acknowledgments

This book benefits greatly from the editorial and research assistance of my wife, Suzanne Becker. Sue is the assistant editor of the *Journal of Economic Education*, where she has invested years making scholars' works readable. I have benefitted from her expertise. If there are errors or poorly worded passages in this book, they likely reflect another case in which I did not listen to Sue.

As with the *Journal of Economic Education,* assisting in the preparation of this manuscript was Julie Marker. I gratefully acknowledge Julie's patience, precision, and promptness in the production of a manuscript that was pieced together from numerous documents, electronic files, and programs. Julie has been a loyal friend and I thank her for her support in this project.

My thanks go to the many students and fellow instructors at Indiana University whose work with earlier versions of this material gave rise to comments and suggestions that have helped make this a better book. Of particular note among instructors are James Isaac (Ike) Brannon, Choong-Geun Chung, Mousumi Duttaray, Robert Hooper, Sergey Kovalyou, Sandy Latal, Kaushik Mukhopadhaya, Brian Peterson, Robert Toutkoushian, and Kevin Stroupe. Students deserving special recognition include Erin Dingman, Elon Danon, Spencer Hays, Andrei Levchenko, Mark Partia, Mike Tonkosley, and Rebecca Vanosdol.

Professors Daniel Maki and Wayne Winston deserve special acknowledgment for involving me in the "Mathematics Throughout the Curriculum" project at Indiana University. This National Science Foundation (DUE 9555408) initiative is providing financial support for the development and pilot testing of many of the activities contained in this book as implemented in the teaching of business and economics statistics at Indiana University.

Finally, my appreciation goes to Indiana University and the National Council on Economic Education for the support they have provided me over the years. The University of South Australia deserves thanks for the support it provided while I was in residence during 1997.

William E. Becker
Department of Economics
Indiana University
Bloomington, Indiana
47405
email: beckerw@indiana.edu
Fax: 812-855-3736

Chapter 1

Collection and Presentation of Data

The age of chivalry has gone. That of sophisters, economists, and calculators has succeeded; and the glory of Europe is extinguished for ever.

Edmund Burke
1729–1797

1.1 Introduction

Statistician Stephen Fienberg tells us that 400 years ago problems involving coins, cards, dice, and the drawing of balls from urns were curiosities pursued by mathematicians trying to solve puzzles in probability. One hundred years later, concepts in probability were applied to data (measurements) from astronomy, demography, biology, and genetics---statistical analysis was born. By the 19th century, statistical analysis had spread to economics and the other social sciences. In the early 1990s, newspaper columnist Chuck Stone lamented that "we have become a nation of numbers-crunching arithmomaniacs." (September 5, 1992) As demonstrated by Cynthia Crossen in *Tainted Truth: The Manipulation of Fact in America* (1994), if for no other reason than to protect yourself from the misuse of statistics, it is essential to have a knowledge of statistical application.

Advances have been made in the use of statistics within the social sciences, but in its most general form statistics continues to be a study of collecting, organizing, presenting, describing, summarizing, and interpreting data. Unlike probability, which continues to be a central branch of mathematics, statistics is an area of inquiry that is not central to mathematics. Statistics has a methodology closely tied to the discipline in which it is applied.[1] In this book, we will study statistics within the context of economics, accounting, finance, sociology, psychology, and other social science and business-related areas.

Today successful decision makers in both the public and private sectors must have a working knowledge of statistics—not as a general tool of data analysis but as a specific method for addressing issues and questions in their daily business environments. Although an arithmetic average is the same in medicine and accounting, a discussion of average accounts receivable is more pertinent and enlightening to those majoring in business and public policy areas than a discussion of average blood pressure.

As an example of the statistical way of thinking in business- and economics-related areas, consider a topic that is regularly addressed by the popular and business press: Are corporate chief executive officers of energy companies overpaid? A question from an economics perspective would be: Overpaid relative to whom and by how much? Information provided in a *Wall Street Journal* (April 22, 1992) article will help answer these questions in a statistical analysis. The *WSJ* details are for the compensation of a subset of managers taken from a survey of the country's biggest companies conducted by Towers Perrin, a compensation-consulting company. The *WSJ* used this information (sample data) to make a statement (inference) about the pay of all executives (population data).

As another example, consider the debate over sources of economic growth, technological change, and the role of patents. Harvard University economist Zvi Griliches concluded in a *Journal of Economic Literature* article that "the appearance of diminishing returns (to patents) at the cross-sectional level is due, I think, primarily to two effects: selectivity and the differential role of formal R & D and patents for small and large firms." Griliches calls attention to a problem in drawing conclusions about a population when the selected sample may provide a biased representation of the population.

This book emphasizes the collection, presentation, description, and interpretation of sample data for decision making about a population. A large share of the text is aimed at **statistical inference,** the process of making statements about a population based on sample data. Unlike books on statistics in biology, engineering, medicine, or other derivatives of the natural sciences, the populations of interest and the problems of sampling that we consider will deal with real-world situations in economics and other business areas.

Statistical Inference
The process of making statements about a population based on a sample.

This chapter introduces a way of thinking that should enable you to distinguish between a sample and a population, retrieve data from different sources, discuss alternative methods for obtaining data, display data in tabular and graphical form, and recognize problems in making statements about a population on the basis of sample information. By the end of this chapter, you will have a sense of how data are obtained, presented, and used in business and economic decision making.

1.2 Population and Sample Data

Population
The set or collection of all the observations or measurements of interest to a decision maker.

Sample
A subset of measurements taken from the population of interest to the decision maker.

Quantitative Data
Measurements that are expressed numerically, where the number has meaning on a number line (such as inches on a ruler).

Qualitative Data
Information in the form of an attribute or characteristic that is not numerical.

A **population** is the set or collection of all the observations or measurements of interest to a decision maker. The specific characteristics of a population are generally unknown. To make statements about things of interest in the population (for example, the compensation of CEOs versus other lower-level executives or the number of patents at small versus large firms), sample information can be used. A **sample** is a subset of measurements taken from the population. The process of making statements about a population on the basis of information provided in a sample is called statistical inference. Figure 1.1 illustrates the relationship between a population, a sample, and a statistical inference.

Population and sample information can be either quantitative or qualitative. **Quantitative data** are measurements that are expressed numerically, where the number has meaning on a number line, such as a ruler. For quantitative data, the arithmetic functions of addition and multiplication give sums and products that can be interpreted on the same number line as the original values. Baseball and basketball jerseys have numbers, but those numbers have no meaning on a number line; they cannot be added and subtracted in a meaningful way. Unlike quantitative data, baseball jersey numbers simply identify a player; they are like names. On the other hand, the salaries professional baseball players receive are quantitative data; all the players' salaries on a team can be added, with the sum being the total player salary budget of the team.

Qualitative data are information that is nonnumerical. A survey might ask whether the respondent has a job; whether the respondent is a male or female; and whether he or she is married. The responses to these inquiries would all be qualitative information. As we will see in later chapters, qualitative information can sometimes be coded to make it appear quantitative. For example, a male or female response can be coded 0 if male and 1 if female. If the underlying attribute (gender, in this case) has no meaning on a number line, then the assignment of numerical values is arbitrary. However, some

FIGURE 1.1 A Population, a Sample, and an Inference

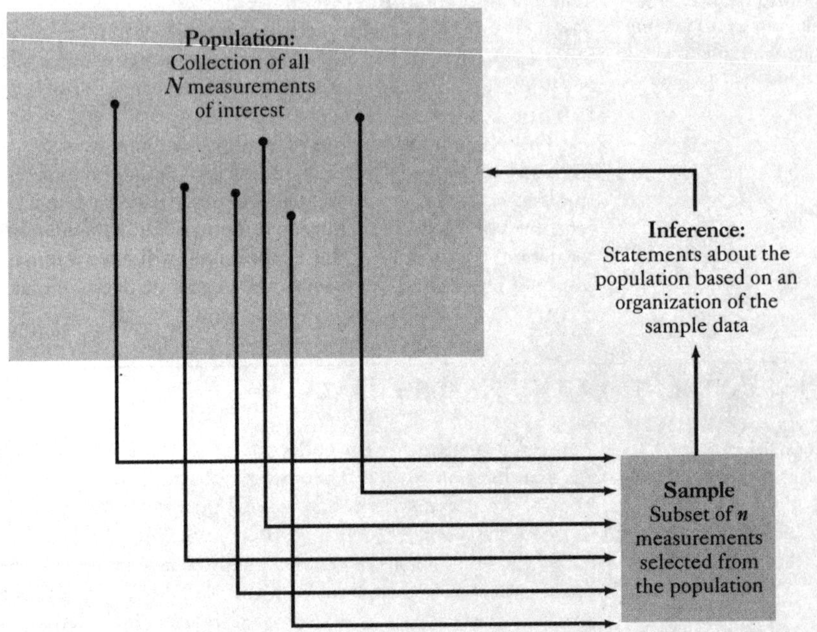

types of qualitative information can have meaning on a number line. For example, the letter grades of A, B, C, D, and F are typically coded 4, 3, 2, 1, and 0 to calculate a grade point average. Here the grade of A is clearly better than that of B, which is better than C. Thus, the numerical value given to A must exceed that given to B and C but the numerical amounts by which A exceeds B and B exceeds C are arbitrary. The measurement scale must preserve order, but the ratio by which one value exceeds the other is arbitrary. For example, a prior grading policy at Purdue University made a grade of A worth 6 points, a B worth 5, and a C worth 4.

Unlike samples, which are always finite, populations can be either finite in size or infinite. If the population has a fixed and limited size, that size is designated by the uppercase letter *N*. Populations that have unlimited size must be viewed as hypothetical or conceptual; after all, by definition they are not observable in a finite span of time. Shakespeare's characters, Rosencrantz and Guildenstern, as portrayed in Tom Stoppard's play, would have had to flip the coins an infinite number of times to actually observe 50 percent of the tosses resulting in heads. The idea that a coin has a 0.50

probability of coming up heads is based on the idea of an infinite number of flips that can never really be observed. Similarly, the mathematician's probabilities for card and dice tricks are based on the idea of an infinite number of attempts. Notions of probability based on infinite populations are discussed in Chapters 3, 4, 5, and 6.

In many real-world problems, a finite population can be treated as if it were infinite if the size of the sample is a small proportion of the size of the population. Sample size is designated by the lower case letter n. Ignoring the cost of acquiring the sample, bigger samples are always preferred to smaller samples. As the sample size increases, the probability that the sample represents the population increases. Sampling is not costless, however; each additional observation typically adds to the cost. As discussed in Chapters 7 and 17, when cost is considered, a smaller sample may be preferred to a larger one.

As discussed in Chapters 6, 7, 8, and 9, if relatively small samples are randomly drawn from relatively large (infinite) populations, then probability theory can be used to make inferences about the population, even though we do not know if the sample is representative of the population. This ability to make probabilistic statements about a population based on relatively little sample information is the essence of statistics.

1.3 Sampling and Statistical Analysis

If a sample was a perfect representative of the population from which it was drawn, it would be a perfect small-scale replica. Typically, however, it is impossible to know exactly how well a sample represents a population because the characteristics of the population are unknown. In some cases, however, the importance of sample selection can be assessed.

Griliches reproduced a **line chart** that originated in the research of John Bound. (See Figure 1.2.) The vertical axis is the number of patents per million dollars of research and development (R & D) expenditures. As we move up the vertical axis the number of patents increases. The horizontal axis is the size of the R & D program measured on a logarithmic scale that will be discussed in Chapter 6. For now, it is enough to recognize that firm size increases as we move from left to right along the horizontal axis.

The line chart in Figure 1.2 shows smaller firms (those with smaller R & D programs) as more efficient, receiving a larger number of patents per R & D expenditure. As firm size increases, the number of patents falls off quickly and becomes effectively constant as the size of the firm continues to increase.

Griliches argues, however, that this diagram was not constructed from sample observations that were selected by rules of probability. Rather, this sample is an "opportunity sample" based on other criteria. It consists of all manufacturing firms listed on the New York and American Stock Exchanges and also on the over-the-counter market. Almost all large firms are listed on the New York, American, or over-the-counter market. To be listed on one of these markets, a small firm has to be more successful, be more interesting to investors, or have some special appeal. A small firm listed on one of these exchanges would likely have more patents than one not listed.

FIGURE 1.2 Patents per Million R & D Dollars by R & D Size Class for Firms with both R & D and Patents

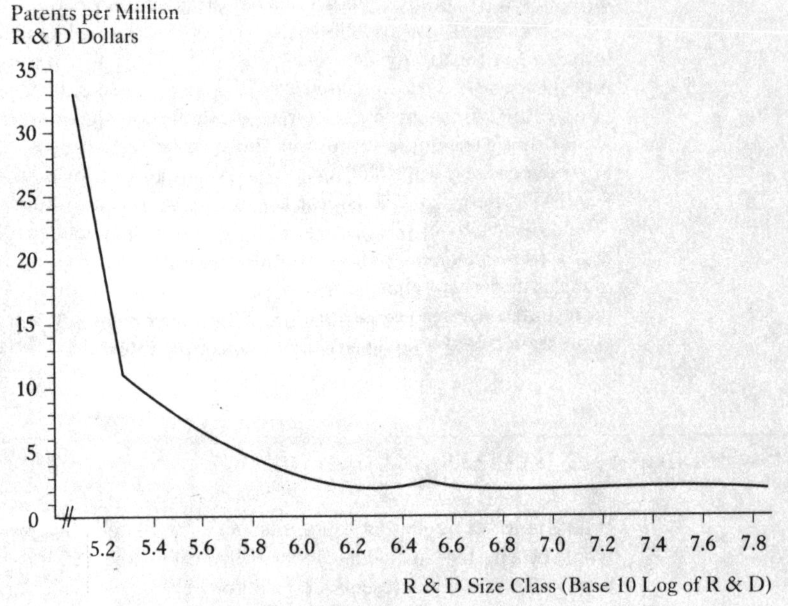

Frequency Distribution A presentation of the number of times different values (or classes of values) in a data set occur.

Frequency The number of times an observation (or observations in a class) occurs.

Griliches compared the number of small firms in this sample with all firms counted by the U.S. Bureau of the Census (see Table 1.1). Table 1.1 is a **frequency distribution** that shows the number of firms classified by the number of employees. There are four classes: firms with fewer than 10 employees, firms with 10 to 99 employees, firms with 100 to 999 employees, and firms with more than 1,000 employees. There were 24 firms in the sample with fewer than 10 employees, 301 with 10 to 99 employees, 952 with 100 to 999 employees, and 1,267 with more than 1,000 employees. These are the frequencies of each class. The **frequency** of the *i*th class is written f_i so the $f_1 = 24, f_2 = 301, f_3 = 952$ and $f_4 = 1{,}267$. The class frequencies must sum to the sample size, which is written $n = 2{,}544$.

The **relative frequency** of a class is the proportion (or percentage) of the total number of observations in the sample that are in that class. The relative frequency of "fewer than 10" is 0.00943, because 24 of the 2,544 firms in the sample were in this class (i.e., the relative frequency of the first class is $f_1/n = 24/2544 = 0.00943$). The other three relative frequencies (0.11832, 0.37421, and 0.49803) are shown in Table 1.1. Notice that the sum of the relative frequencies is 1.00.

TABLE 1.1
Selectivity of Firms

Class i	Number of Employees	Number of Firms in the Sample f_i	Relative Frequency of Firms in the Sample f_i/n	Number of Firms in the Census f_i	Relative Frequency of Firms in the Census f_i/N
1	< 10	24	0.0094340	16000	0.3883495
2	10 – 99	301	0.1183176	14300	0.3470874
3	100 – 999	952	0.3742138	9000	0.2184466
4	1,000 +	1267	0.4980346	1900	0.0461165
	Column Sum =	2544	1.0000000	41200	1.0000000

Sources: Sample is from Bound et al. (1984), and Census is from U.S. Bureau of the Census (1981), with frequencies presented in Zvi Griliches, "Patent Statistics as Economic Indicators: A Survey," *Journal of Economic Literature*, December 1990, p. 1677.

Relative Frequency
The proportion (or percentage) of the total number of observations in a data set that take a specific value (or class of values).

Relative Frequency of a class is the proportion of the total number of observations in the distribution that are in that class.

Relative frequency $= f_i/N$, for a population of size N. (1.1a)

Relative frequency $= f_i/n$, for a sample of size n, (1.1b)

where f_i is the frequency of the ith class.

Census
A survey that attempts to capture all of the items or elements in the population.

Also reported in Table 1.1 are the number of firms in the census of enterprises classified by the number of employees. Unlike a sample, a **census** is a survey that attempts to capture all of the items or elements in the population. Compiling a census is more costly than sampling. According to the U.S. General Accounting Office, for instance, the cost of counting each housing unit (in 1980 dollars) rose from \$5 in 1950 to \$12 in 1980, and it exceeded \$17 in 1990. In many problems, a census is not possible. In a production process, for example, the durability of all items cannot be tested because such testing implies the destruction of each item.

Compared to the relative frequency of small firms in the population, small firms are underrepresented in the Bound et al. sample. About 39 percent of the census is small firms, but less than 1 percent (0.9434%) of the sample is small firms. Unfortunately, as stated by Griliches, we have no information on the firms not in the sample and, hence, cannot make an appropriate sample selectivity adjustment.

Current patents are likely to be more important to small firms than to large firms. The near-term existence of large firms is insured by their past patents, while the existence of small firms may be tied directly to their current prospects for patents. To establish a position, small firms must pursue patents more quickly and more aggressively than larger firms. Yet, small firms can be expected to report less expenditure on R & D, because research and development at small firms is an informal activity. Thus, the ratio of patents per millions of R & D dollars is driven up at small firms by the need to patent and the lack of reporting of expenditures on R & D.

Even if inventiveness rates were equal between small and large firms, the opportunity sample employed and the use of the number of patents per dollar of expenditure as the measure of inventiveness would give the impression that small firms are more efficient at inventing. Given this empirical assessment, Griliches turned to economic theory and concluded that, "This is not surprising, after all. If there were such diminishing returns, firms could split themselves into divisions or separate enterprises and escape them." (p. 1677) It is this injection of economics into the analysis that distinguishes the use of the statistics (population, sample, and relative frequencies) by an economist from that of an engineer looking at the same problem.

The purpose of the analysis is of primary importance when deciding what type of sample is needed to make an inference about a characteristic of the population. A classic example that demonstrates inappropriate sampling for the task at hand is a 60-year-old study by the now-defunct *Literary Digest*. The *Literary Digest* sent questionnaires to more than 2 million people whose names were selected from telephone directories and automobile registrations. From the responses, it predicted that Alf Landon would win the 1936 U.S. presidential election with an overwhelming victory. Instead, Franklin Roosevelt won by a substantial margin. The responses received by the *Literary Digest* were not random and could not have been representative of the population of relevant voters. They were from predominantly wealthy people who owned cars and telephones at a time when ownership of such items was beyond the reach of most people.

A more contemporary example of problems arising from sample selectivity is the debate over the employment effect of the 1992 change in the New Jersey minimum wage law, as evident in the exchange of viewpoints and reader reactions found in *Business Week* (April 24 and May 15, 1995). At the center of the debate was an *American Economic Review* article by Princeton University researchers David Card and Alan Krueger. These researchers used a data set based on a telephone survey of 410 fast food restaurants associated with four chains. They concluded that after New Jersey raised its minimum wage, employment rose in its restaurants, while employment fell in neighboring Pennsylvania where the minimum wage did not change. Michigan State professor David Neumark and Federal Reserve economist William Wascher acquired what they claimed were the actual payroll data from 71 restaurants in two of the chains and found that Pennsylvania employment rose relative to New Jersey after the change in the New Jersey minimum wage. Card and Krueger were faulted for using data for which there was no control over the providers of the phone information. The work of Neumark and Wascher was suspect, according to Card, because their data were for a select group of franchises collected by the Employment Policy Institute, an organization funded by business contributions and opposed to minimum wages.

To see that problems of sample selectivity and information gathering are not restricted to economics, business, and politics, consider the controversy that arose over an article in the *New England Journal of Medicine* (October 14, 1992) reporting on the lack of special benefits of oat bran products in lowering cholesterol. In addition to questions about the size of the sample (20 men and women), the study was criticized for using mostly dieticians: subjects not representative of the general population of the United States.

Deciding on the type and amount of sample data that are needed, and how these data can best be gathered is a major decision in the inference making process. The nature of the sampling will greatly affect the cost of the study. Searching existing data banks is usually the least expensive way to find useable information; the trick is knowing where to look. Although a business brainstorming session seldom passes without someone suggesting a survey as a means for collecting information, conducting surveys or running experiments that result in meaningful data are usually expensive ways to get information. Poorly conceived and less than adequately controlled surveys typically yield data that suffer from sample selectivity problems that make inference difficult if not impossible.

1.4 Data Sources

Data can be obtained from primary sources or secondary sources. They can represent a situation at a point in time or a flow of information over time. The results that can be drawn from statistics always depend on the quality of the data.

Primary Data
Data that are published or made available from the person (or agency) responsible for collecting the data.

Primary data are observations obtained from the original generator of the data; primary source data are always preferred and are often the only data acceptable in legal proceedings. Annual reports, technical manuals, personnel files, computer files of accounting data, and other routinely filed information within a corporation may be the source of primary data on a corporation. Table 1.2, for example, illustrates the source of sales revenue of the Ford Motor Company as obtained from Ford's 1987 annual report and submitted as a deposition exhibit in a wrongful death case filed against Ford.

As corporations have moved to centralized information systems and computerized information networks, primary source data have become more easily and efficiently obtained. Production schedules, inventory levels, sales history and forecasts, and employee data are among the vast amounts of information typically found in corporate computers.

The government also collects and disseminates primary data. In addition to internal corporate data, information about a wide variety of subjects is available from numerous external sources. Consider just a few examples:

- Monthly economic indicators, such as the Consumer Price Index, housing starts, and industrial production, are available from the U.S. Bureau of Labor Statistics.
- Weekly monetary indicators, such as the money supply, banks' business loans, and free reserves, are provided by the 12 Federal Reserve Banks and the Board of Governors of the Federal Reserve System in Washington, D.C.

- A variety of business and economic indicators are published by Standard and Poor's, Moody's, Dun & Bradstreet, and numerous federal and state agencies. Almost all of this information is available on magnetic tape or on disks.
- Demographic data on the U.S. population have been collected every 10 years since 1790 by the Bureau of the Census.

Secondary Data
Data that are published or made available by someone other than the one who collected the data.

Data are also available from many **secondary data** sources. *Business Week,* for example, uses internal corporate data when it puts together its annual "Corporate Scoreboard" issue each spring. The source for the corporate data published by *Business Week* is Standard & Poor's Compustat Services, Inc. The *Business Week* publication of these data is a secondary source. It is thus not as acceptable in legal proceedings as the primary source data; its accuracy can be questioned.

TABLE 1.2
Ford Motor Company Annual Report Information

Total Sales Revenue (in millions)	1986	1985	1984
United States	$50,034	$43,526	$42,829
Canada	9,782	9,073	8,231
Europe	13,609	9,566	9,083
Latin America	3,286	3,107	2,764
All other (primarily Asia-Pacific)	2,046	2,028	2,590
Elimination of intercompany sales	(16,041)	(14,526)	(13,131)
Total Sales	$62,716	$52,774	$52,366

Source: December 31, 1986, Financial Report of Ford Motor Company, Coopers & Lybrand Auditors' Opinion, February 10, 1987, p. 35.

One of the best secondary sources for annual summary data on national income, expenditures, population, employment, productivity, production, wages, business activity, prices, money stock, credit, finance, profits, agriculture, and international statistics is the *Economic Report of the President,* which is issued every February. Later in the spring of each year the *Statistical Abstract of the United States* becomes available with some 1,500 tables covering everything from the amount of chicken Americans consume to the number of persons over age 40 who wear glasses. Both the *Economic Report of the President* and the *Statistical Abstract of the United States* are excellent data sources, although not always the primary source of data. Economic journalist Robert J. Samuelson, for example, stated that, "The *Statistical Abstract* has endless uses. . . . The sheer variety of statistics on so many subjects is chastening." (*Newsweek* June 1, 1987, p. 49) Both the *Economic Report of the President* and *Statistical Abstract of the United States* can be purchased from the Superintendent of Documents, U.S. Government Printing Office, Washington, D.C., 20402.

The Organization for Economic Cooperation and Development (OECD) provides international data on developing countries on computer disk and in hard copy form. These data include statistics on health, education, bank profitability, employment, productivity, and other economic indicators for Eastern and Western European, North American, and Pacific countries. This information is available from OECD, 2001 L Street, N.W., Suite 700, Washington, D.C., 20036-4910.

Besides business and government publications, trade associations, such as the American Bankers Association and the U.S. Chamber of Commerce, provide information about their areas of interest. Similarly, union and professional organizations, such as the AFL-CIO and the American Medical Association, provide information of interest to members. Numerous testing and research companies also provide data on specific products. One of the best listings of information available from associations, periodicals, libraries, companies, and other agencies—with capsule descriptions of each—is *Who Knows What: The Essential Business Resource Book* by Daniel Starer. The Federal Reserve Bank of Richmond also makes available a useful manual titled *Macroeconomic Data: A User's Guide* (1994), edited by Ray H. Webb.

Data from national pollsters can also be used to investigate a diverse range of demographic, behavioral, and attitudinal topics. For example, J.D. Powers and *Consumer Reports* are famous for their survey results on consumer satisfaction with automobiles. The Roper Center and the Louis Harris Data Center are major sources of public-opinion polls. The Roper Center adds more than 500 files a year to its collection of more than 11,000 data files that cover social and political preferences and political opinions dating from 1930. Harris polls have been conducted since 1956, surveying opinions categorized into 24 topics and numerous subtopics. The Gallup Poll, which is familiar to many people, regularly contributes data files to the Roper Center. Many other public-opinion polls, such as those sponsored by the news media, contribute to the Roper Center files. The largest service for social science data is the Inter-University Consortium for Political and Social Research (ICPSR), which is a collection of more than 18,000 data files housed at the University of Michigan.

Internet surfers have also learned that the World Wide Web is a source of data. Major media services, government agencies, and businesses maintain home pages and links to each other. For instance, the large data bases maintained by the Bureau of the Census can be accessed at "http://www.census.gov". This Census site enables users to download data following self-explanatory menus and FTP transfers. A starting point to search for financial data is the site of the Wall Street News, at "http://wall-street-news.com/forecast". This site provides links to such resources as the Chicago Mercantile Exchange's information on commodity trading as well as university and research lab sites like the financial economics servers at the University of Texas and Ohio State University. A few of the hundreds of other useful WWW data sources are:

CIA factbook at http://www.odci.gov/cia/publications/95fact/
Commerce department at http://www.stat-usa.gov/BEN/Brochures/stat.html
Dun & Bradstreet at http://www.dnb.com
ESRC Data Archive at http://dawww.essex.ac.uk
Mead Data Central Lexis/Nexis at http://www.meaddata.com
Nikko Securities at http://www.nikko.co.jp
Standard & Poor's News Service at http://www.quote.com/info/spnews.html

These existing data files may provide the user with standardized items, a census, or at least samples that are representative of the entire nation and can be used as a basis for comparison. As discussed earlier, Griliches demonstrated this in his use of U.S. census data to show the

Cross-Section Data Data that are collected across geographical regions or individuals, at a single point in time.

Time-Series Data Data collected over time.

sample selectivity problem in assessing small-firm efficiency in research and development. Griliches' comparisons of sample frequencies with those in the census were for one time period. When data are compared across geographical regions or among individuals at a point in time, the study is called **cross-section** analysis. On the other hand, if observations from a time period are compared with prior or subsequent time periods, then the study is called a **time-series** analysis. As demonstrated in later chapters, in a time-series analysis that covers many years it is essential to determine how important concepts are defined, how the data collection methods and the sample base may have changed over time, and how observations in one period might be connected to the next.

Griliches compared a national sample with a national census. National data can also be used to infer things about individual situations. For instance, in the lawsuit against Ford cited earlier, the plaintiff's expert witness stated that according to the *Statistical Abstract of the United States*, Table 1.3, the median weekly earnings of workers in the United States was $358 in 1986. This witness argued that a $2 parking ticket would inflict only a 0.55866 percent [= (2/358)(100%)] hardship on such a worker. Imposing a similar hardship on Ford would imply punitive damages of $6.738 million [= (62,716/52)(0.0055866)], assuming that the worker's weekly earnings in Table 1.3 are comparable to Ford's weekly earnings as calculated from the annual data in Table 1.2.

The author of this book, representing Ford Motor Company, questioned whether a worker's earnings should be compared to Ford's earnings in establishing punitive damages. In essence, we do not base damages and punish an entire family for an alleged misdeed of one of its members. Why, then, would we consider basing damages on the entire worldwide Ford family for an alleged misdeed at one of its transmission plants? If quantitative comparisons are made, they must be made on a like basis.

Although data exist on a wide array of topics, locating the exact types of data needed for a particular analysis and to make a particular point is always difficult. The format in which the data is available can also pose problems. Some agencies and researchers may be reluctant to share their data. In all cases, the user of existing data must check the methods by which the data were collected, recorded, and classified. Indeed, caution is needed when using any data, regardless of whether they are primary or secondary, manual or computer stored, government or privately generated. A statistical analysis can be no better than the data on which it is based. Always keep in mind the old and proven adage: garbage in, garbage out (GIGO).

TABLE 1.3
Earnings of Full-Time Wage and Salary Workers

	Median Weekly Earnings		
	1985	1986	1987
All workers	$343	$358	$373

Source: *Statistical Abstract of the United States*, 1989, p. 406.

1.5 Experiments and Randomization

Despite the existence of burgeoning data files, the questions, problems, and circumstances facing decision makers may change too quickly to allow extensive use of existing data sources. For example, final adjusted and detailed 1990 U.S. census data were scheduled to be available sometime in 1992. In 1994 the U.S. Circuit Court of Appeals reversed Commerce Secretary Robert Mosbacher's 1991 decision not to adjust raw counts for estimated undercounting of minorities. The adjustment increased the nation's 1990 population by about 5 million, to nearly 255 million. Such adjustments make studies linking census demographics and dollars with specific regions of little use for business. When confronted with new situations for which there is no data available to guide in the decision-making process, government agencies and corporations are forced to collect their own data via surveys and experiments.

Surveys are typically associated with field studies, which are like opportunity samples because there is little attempt to control who gets into the sample. Market researchers use surveys to determine how products are used and how they perform, and to identify new markets. For instance, a sample survey might involve stopping people in a shopping mall to ask them what brand of soft drink they prefer. Governmental units use surveys for determining employment conditions, travel patterns, and for planning purposes. As discussed in a *Business Week* article (Sept. 5, 1994) on "Data Base Marketing" some 85 percent of marketing managers in Donnelley Marketing Inc.'s annual survey believe they need data based marketing in which customers are regularly surveyed about product needs.

In experiments, behavior is observed under controlled conditions. An **experiment** is a method of data collection in which the researcher makes every attempt to eliminate or to control for aspects of the test that are not important, or that might influence the experiment one way or another. For example, an early 1990s Chrysler Corporation advertising campaign reported the results of studies comparing several models of Chrysler Corporation cars with the Honda Accord and Civic and with Toyota's Tercel and Camry. In these ads, Lee Iacocca, then Chrysler CEO, proudly stated that the Chrysler cars were judged as better than the Honda and Toyota cars by a vast majority of likely import-car buyers. The actual study used two test panels of 25 respondents each. Half of the test panel did the exterior/interior appearance, convenience, and comfort portion of the test first, followed by the riding/driving portion. The other half reversed this order. Similarly, the order of the test vehicle assigned to each respondent was rotated, as was the order of riding and driving. In this manner, the effect of order (if any) was controlled and the marketing people at Chrysler argued that they had a controlled experiment.

Experiments are designed to control for undesired effects, with subjects selected on a random basis. Simple random-sampling techniques are designed to insure that each element (and in turn, each subgroup of elements) in a population has an equal probability of being included in the sample. With simple random sampling, every sample of n elements selected from a population of N elements has an equally likely probability of being selected, and each of the n elements has a probability of $1/N$ of being selected.

As discussed in detail in Chapter 7, simple random sampling may be done by a blind-draw approach (putting numbers in a hat and then drawing them out, for exam-

Random Number
A number (often a digit between 0 to 9) where there is no pattern to the numbers (each number is as likely to occur as any other number).

Simple Random Sample
A sample collected using techniques designed to insure that each element (and in turn each subgroup of elements) in a population has an equal probability of being included in the sample.

ple), a random number table (in which there is no pattern to numbered population items to be selected), or computer programs that generate **random numbers**. As you will see throughout later chapters, **simple random sampling** plays a critical part in statistical analysis. Any one sample obtained by simple random sampling may not give a perfect representation of the population. However, Chapter 7 will show that across many samples the average characteristics of these samples will represent the corresponding characteristics in the population. Chapters 3, 4, 5, and 6 provide the necessary concepts from probability theory to define when sample characteristics are close to those of the population.

Other than the pure chance factor in random sampling, an experiment will control for all other factors that can influence the results. Unfortunately, an experiment that controls for all factors other than chance is often impossible or too expensive. Econometrician Edward Leamer in "Let's Take the Con Out of Econometrics," argued that, "No one has ever designed an experiment that is free of bias, and no one ever can." (p. 33) The difference between experiments and field studies is a difference in degree, but not kind. There are always tradeoffs in considering the controls to design into a study. For instance, Chrysler ignored geographical location (possibly because it thought that preference for cars is not influenced by location); hence, it only selected participants from the greater Los Angeles area. If, however, location is important, then inferences from the Chrysler sample will yield systematic biases.

1.6 Other Types of Samples

Traditional test marketing of products calls for the introduction of a new product in a small town—such as Duluth, Erie, Indianapolis, Charleston, or Fresno—that closely matches desired aspects of U.S. census data. For example, *American Demographics* (January 1992) found Tulsa, Oklahoma to best typify the age, racial makeup, and housing value of the 555 U.S. cities with populations of at least 50,000.

Once a typical town has been identified, researchers swarm over the area collecting data on consumer and retailer reaction to the new product while they modify the package and the promotion. As stated in a *Business Week* (August 10, 1992) article, "The 12-to-18-month process can cost more than $1 million, but it's a lot better to bomb in test than in a coast-to-coast flameout. These days, though, fewer companies are bothering to see how their fledgling products play in Peoria. Instead, consumer-goods marketers such as Lever Brothers, Colgate-Palmolive, and General Mills want newer, faster, and cheaper ways to test their offerings." (See Table 1.4.)

Listening to "buyer focus groups" is a popular approach to pretesting. In this approach, a group of potential buyers are brought together and their opinions about a product are solicited. For instance, the *Wall Street Journal* (September 16, 1992) reported on the home buyers' focus groups that Marketing Directions conducted in 12 cities. From these groups, Marketing Directions learned that today's home buyers say that in houses "every inch of space has to count . . . (if a) closet is bigger than their kid's bedroom they don't like it."

TABLE 1.4
Skipping the Test

SKIPPING THE TEST
Some alternatives to the traditional 12- to 18-month market test:
PRETESTING Show a few consumers samples of new products along with ads to gauge probable response
COMPUTER MODELING Use historical data on similar products to turn small samples of data into sales projections
ROLLING THE DICE Introduce a new product region by region, fixing ads and promotions along the way to going national
FOREIGN FLING The lead country concept calls for trying out a product in an overseas market, then rolling it out globally

The participants in a focus group might be shown a new product, view its ads, or just have a product concept explained. Prior to entering a focus group, recruits are asked to provide information about themselves. Once in the group, participants typically interact under the guidance of a facilitator. Finally, group members might complete a questionnaire or they might be called a few weeks later and asked about their reactions to product samples they were given. Researchers then incorporate this information, along with historical data, to form a computer-simulated market in which sales can be projected. Most data collection done through focus groups and many mail and telephone surveys do not employ the simple random-sampling techniques required for experiments.

Stratification
The act of dividing a population into subgroups that share a given characteristic or attribute.

Throughout this book, we assume that the data can at least be thought of as coming from experiments. In social research, however, simple random sampling may not be feasible or may not be efficient. In such cases, alternative sampling techniques are preferred to no controls at all. As discussed in Chapter 7, these other sampling techniques might involve the drawing of every 10th item in the population (systematic selection) or the division (**stratification**) of the population into groups with known characteristics, from which sampling then takes place. There are also a number of other techniques that may give rise to samples from which information can be packaged to make inferences about an unknown population.

EXERCISES

1.1 How do a sample and a census differ?

1.2 Is it possible for a group of students in a university to be viewed as a sample for one purpose and as a population for another? Give an example.

1.3 Give a situation in which a sample would be drawn because all the elements in a population could not be tested.

1.4 Here is the breakdown of owner-occupied housing in Monroe County (*HT*, July 2, 1993).

Housing Value	Number of Owner Occupied
Less than $25,000	513
$25,000-$99,999	12,173
$100,000-$199,999	2,642
$200,000-$299,999	331
$300,000-$399,999	65
$400,000 and above	24

a. Construct a relative frequency distribution of owner-occupied housing in Monroe County.

b. Is this distribution based on sample or population data? Explain.

1.5 Construct a frequency and relative frequency distribution for the following information on medical claims from a *Wall Street Journal* (June 17, 1994) article on employer health plans. " A survey of 461,208 employees at private companies shows that 31% (0.3099990) of employees had no medical claims and another 50% (0.5000000) had claims of less than $1,000. Another 14% (0.1399997) of employees had claims from $1,000 to $5,000 ... Of the 461,208 employees, only 32 had big ticket claims greater than $300,000.

1.6 Unlike baseball and basketball jerseys, the numbers on football jerseys are assigned on the basis of the position played. In the National Football League, quarterbacks are assigned 1 through 19, running backs 20 through 49, and offensive linemen 50 through 79. A student in Professor Becker's class observed that these jersey numbers may have meaning on a number line, and thus, represent quantitative data. To what measurement was the student referring?

1.7 Find a library source where the most recent data can be obtained for each of the following.

a. The yield on constant maturity three- and ten-year U.S. Treasury securities.

b. Money earning for full-time and part-time workers in the United States by years of school completed.

c. Changes in productivity and related data on the business sector of the U.S. economy.

d. The U.S. monthly unemployment rates by age.

e. The U.S. rate of inflation as measured by changes in the Consumer Price Index (CPI).

f. Business failures in the United States per year.

g. The sales and profits of U.S. corporations classified by major business type.

1.8 What is the difference between a comparison of profitability of U.S. corporations among different major business types in 1994, and a comparison of profitability of U.S. corporations from 1983 to 1994?

1.9 Go to the library and locate copies (either electronically or off the shelves) of the following journals. State relevant reference information for each publication including the publisher, how often it is published, the most recent issue, and three examples of topics covered in the most recent issue.

- *Monthly Labor Review*
- *American Economic Review*
- *Survey of Current Business*
- *Federal Reserve Bulletin*
- *Business Condition Review*
- *Moody's Industrial Manual.*

1.10 Go to the library and select any yearly volume of the *American Economic Review*. Excluding the May papers and proceedings issue, how many articles in the remaining four issues can be classified as reporting on quantitative data? Of those, how many use time-series data? How many use cross-sectional data? How many use a combination of time-series and cross-sectional data? What can you conclude about the nature of data used in economic research?

1.11 A *Wall Street Journal* article (August 28, 1990) reported on the results of a survey of 167 companies by the American Society for Training and Development. According to the *Wall Street Journal*, "Some 92% of companies consider it critical to teach employees new skills, but just 23% do that to 'a great or very great extent.'"

a. What fallacy in surveying does this result highlight?
b. Why might one be suspicious of these results?

1.12 In an evaluation of pension and life insurance needs, an accountant estimated life expectancy by averaging the ages of individuals at the time of their deaths as reported on randomly selected days in the obituary column of his local newspaper. Comment on the appropriateness of this sampling and estimation procedure.

1.13 An article titled "The Science of Polling," in *Newsweek* (September 28, 1992) stated:

> Ensuring a random sample also requires something beyond statistics. During Ronald Reagan's 1984 re-election campaign, his internal 'tracking' polls showed him well ahead of Walter Mondale—except on Friday nights. 'They went into a panic every week until they figured it out,' says Frank Luntz, a political-science professor at the University of Pennsylvania . . . . The explanation: registered Republicans, on average more flush than their Democratic counterparts, were more likely to go out on the town Friday nights and not be home to answer the pollster's phone call. (p. 38)

a. This is an example of what kind of problem in sampling?
b. Instead of writing, "Ensuring a random sample . . . . " should the author have written "Ensuring a representative sample . . . ?" Explain the difference.

1.14 According to former Indiana University Kinsey Institute director June Reinisch, the 1948 Kinsey Report was based on a survey of about 5,000 men. About 10 percent of those reported having homosexual contact with another man during the previous three years. Yet, in a more recent study by the Battelle Human Affairs Research Center in Seattle, published in *Time* magazine, only about 1 percent of 3,321 men surveyed reported having sex exclusively with other men during the past 10 years. In an Associated Press release (*HT*, April 26, 1993), Reinisch said these were not comparable results because approximately

30 percent of Battelle's initial group refused to be interviewed when they were asked for their social security number and place of work. To what was she alluding?

1.15 ABC's 20/20 television broadcast on July 16, 1993 reported on a study in which individuals who had lived to be 100 years of age or more were queried in the hope of finding common characteristics. The implication was drawn that if a younger person worked at acquiring the characteristics shared by these centenarians, then the probability of reaching such an old age increased. Why was this study design inappropriate for the implication drawn?

1.7 Organizing, Condensing and Presenting Quantitative Data

Once quantitative data are collected, they must be organized and condensed so they can be reported in a way that facilitates interpretation. Griliches used a frequency distribution to organize, describe, and compare the sample and population data on firm size shown in Table 1.1. Here we address the construction of frequency distributions from the original, or raw, data collected in a sample. We will also consider the presentation of data in graphical form.

Frequency Distributions

There are four steps to organize and condense original, or raw, data into an easily understood frequency distribution:

Class Interval
A grouping of data, which occurs along a continuum, that is identified by boundary or limiting values.

Class Boundaries
The values that serve as the delineators of classes in a frequency distribution.

1. Determine the number of classes.
2. Establish the **class interval** or width for each class.
3. Set the **class boundaries** or values that form the beginning and end of each of the classes.
4. Count the number of values in the data set that fall into each class.

From just looking at raw data, the number of classes that will best represent the data may not be apparent. Wand discusses alternative rules of thumb for determining the number of classes for a frequency distribution; worth special mention is that proposed by Terrell and Scott:

The approximate number of classes is the integer that just exceeds $2(\text{number of values in data set})^{(0.3333)}$ (1.2)

To illustrate, consider the compensation of the chief executive officers (CEOs) of 20 energy companies surveyed by *The Wall Street Journal* (April 22, 1992). (See Table 1.5.) Comparable data were obtained on only 18 of those CEOs (see note below the table). Thus, the approximate number of classes to be employed in a frequency distribution is

$$2(18)^{(0.3333)} = 2(2.62) = 5.24$$

TABLE 1.5 Compensation of CEOs of Energy Companies

	Company	Executive	1991 Salary/ Bonus (in thousands)	% Change from 1990	Long-Term Comp. (in thousands)	Total Direct Comp. (in thousands)
1.	Amerada Hess	Leon Hess	300.0	N/A	0.0	300.0*
2.	Amoco	H. Laurance Fuller	1302.2	N/A	236.3	1538.5
3.	Ashland Oil	John R. Hall	1038.0	–6	0.0	1038.0
4.	Atlantic Richfield	Lodwrick M. Cook	1673.9	–26	2008.9	3682.8
5.	Baker Hughes	James D. Woods	916.0	–27	393.1	1309.1
6.	Chevron	Kenneth T. Derr	1385.6	2	363.8	1749.4
7.	Coastal	James R. Paul	813.8	N/A	913.4	1727.2
8.	Dresser Industries	John J. Murphy	1070.6	–3	578.7	1649.3
9.	Exxon	Lawrence G. Rawl	1812.8	17	7453.0	9265.8
10.	FINA	Ron W. Haddock	476.3	N/A	0.0	476.3
11.	Halliburton	Thomas H. Cruikshank	1200.0	9	401.5	1601.5
12.	Kerr-McGee	F.A. McPherson	542.0	–32	129.4	671.4
13.	Mobil	Allen E. Murray	2040.0	9	2624.9	4664.9
14.	Occidental	Ray R. Irani	2324.0	N/A	147.1	2471.1
15.	Pennzoil	James L. Pate	650.0	–2	0.0	650.0
16.	Sun Co.	Robert McClements Jr.	1001.1	3	0.0	1001.1
17.	Texaco	James W. Kinnear	1667.0	–14	1658.8	3325.8
18.	USX	Charles A. Corry	1313.2	–18	840.2	2153.4
19.	Unocal	Richard J. Stegemeier	1054.7	N/A	0.0	1054.7*
20.	Valero	William E. Greehey	1097.4	12	352.5	1449.9

*Salary/Bonus data not valid for comparison (e.g., partial year data).

Source: *Wall Street Journal,* April 22, 1992.

where $(18)^{(0.3333)}$ is the cube root of 18, 2.62. The number of classes to be employed in the frequency distribution is then 6, which is the integer value that just exceeds 5.24.

The second step in constructing a frequency distribution is to establish class interval widths. Often this is achieved by simply finding the highest and lowest values in the data set and dividing their difference (the range) by the number of classes.

$$\text{Approximate width of each class, after an adjustment for outliers} = \frac{\text{highest value} - \text{lowest value}}{\text{adjusted number of classes}} \tag{1.3}$$

Outlier
An extreme value.

If, however, the data set has a few extreme values, called **outliers**, then these values are best treated as special cases or as classes unto themselves. For example, among the 18 CEOs, Lawrence Rawl's compensation of $9,265,800 at Exxon is an outlier. Because this value is far above the others, it will be difficult to include in a class with lower values. It is best treated as a class of its own. The next highest compensation is that of Allen Murray's at Mobil, $4,664,900. It is nearly one-half that of Rawl's. The remaining compensations are more closely spaced down to the lowest of $476,300 for Ron Haddock at FINA. The subrange for these 17 compensations is $4,188,600.

Allocating one class to the outlier $9,265,800 leaves us with five classes to be divided into a subrange of $4,188,600. Each of these five classes is thus $837,720. Arbitrarily rounding up to the nearest $10,000 gives a class width for these five classes of $840,000. (As will be seen in a moment, this rounding up is done to insure that the classes are sufficiently wide to cover the data of interest.)

The third step is to set the class boundaries. Class boundaries are set so that the classes include all the values. The lowest boundary that begins the lowest class will typically be an arbitrary, but convenient, value slightly below the lowest value in the data set. For example, in the case of CEO compensation, the lowest compensation is $476,300. Rounding down to the nearest $10,000 gives an arbitrary lower boundary for the first class of $470,000. The upper boundary for the lowest or first class is set by adding the class width to the lower boundary. Thus, the first class includes all values from $470,000 to $1,310,000. Similarly, the upper boundary for the second class is obtained by adding the class width to the upper boundary for the first class. The second class has a lower boundary of $1,310,000 and an upper boundary of $2,150,000. Likewise, the boundaries of the third class are $2,150,000 and $2,990,000 and so on up to $4,670,000 with $9,265,800 being a special case, as shown in Table 1.6.

To include the outlier of $9,265,800 in the distribution, the prior class of $3,830,000 to $4,670,000 may be left open as $3,830,000 and higher. Ideally, open-ended classes should be avoided because of the loss of information. Sometimes they cannot be avoided conveniently, as apparently was the case for Griliches in constructing Table 1.1, where the fourth case is "1000 +."

Class Limits
The lowest and highest attainable values in a class interval.

Class boundaries must be set so that each value falls into one and only one class. The boundaries cannot overlap and must be distinct. Ideally, boundaries are set at values that do not occur in the data set, with the observed values tending to fall toward the middle of the classes. For large data sets, with values that could occur anywhere along a number line, it is critical to know the **limiting value of a class;** that is, whether the class includes the boundary value or not. We must know to which class the actual boundary value belongs. In the case of the CEO compensation, we will define the lower boundary value to belong to that class and the upper boundary value to belong to the next class. Thus, we can write the classes as:

Class 1: At least 0.470 but less than 1.310 million

Class 2: At least 1.310 but less than 2.150 million

Class 3: At least 2.150 but less than 2.990 million

Class 4: At least 2.990 but less than 3.830 million

Class 5: At least 3.830 but less than 4.670 million

Outlier: 9.2658 million

or in a shorthand notation as in Table 1.6.

Table 1.6 Frequency Distribution of Energy Company Chief Executive Officers

i	Compensation of Energy Company CEOs (in millions of $)	Frequency f_i	Relative Frequency f_i/n
1	0.470 to 1.309999	6	0.3333
2	1.310 to 2.149999	6	0.3333
3	2.150 to 2.989999	2	0.1111
4	2.990 to 3.829999	2	0.1111
5	3.830 to 4.669999	1	0.0555
	Outlier 9.265	1	0.0555
		18	1.000

If the data set consists of items that have only distinct value, as with the integer value for the number of employees in Griliches' Table 1.1, then the limiting values of the class are the lowest and highest attainable integer values in the class. The class boundaries, however, must be placed between these class limits. The class boundary that separates the class intervals given by "10–99" and "100–999" in Table 1.1 is, thus, 99.5 even though no firm could have a fractional employee.

The fourth step in constructing the frequency distribution is to count the number of observations in each class. These counts for the CEO compensation case are shown in Table 1.6. From this frequency distribution, it can be seen easily that there are six CEOs with compensation of at least $470,000 but less than $1,310,000, six CEOs with compensation of at least $1,310,000 but less than $2,150,000, and so on.

As already demonstrated for the frequency distribution of firms prepared by Griliches, Table 1.1, relative frequencies are obtained by dividing each class frequency by the total number of observations in the data set. The relative frequencies for the CEO compensation data are shown in the third column of Table 1.6. For example, the classes with the highest relative frequencies are the first and second classes ($i = 1$ and 2) that include values equal to or greater than $0.470 million but less than $2.150 million. Each of these classes have relative frequencies of 0.333, which is calculated as $f_1/n = 6/18$.

In summary, when constructing a frequency distribution, several general principles must be kept in mind. First, an observation must fall in one and only one class; classes cannot overlap. This first principle can never be violated. Second, classes should have widths that are the same. Sometimes data are so spread out that maintaining equal class widths is difficult; in these cases outliers should be identified and treated as special cases. Third, in deciding how many classes to have, try to avoid empty classes or classes that contain an overly large percentage of the data. Fourth, the **midpoint** (middle) of each class should be representative of the observations in that class. Ideally, observations would be distributed evenly around the class midpoint, although this ideal is seldom achievable. Finally, try to avoid open-ended intervals. As demonstrated in Table 1.1, however, this is an ideal that often is not realized.

Midpoint
The middle value of a class in a frequency distribution.

FIGURE 1.3 Histogram of Energy Company CEO Compensation

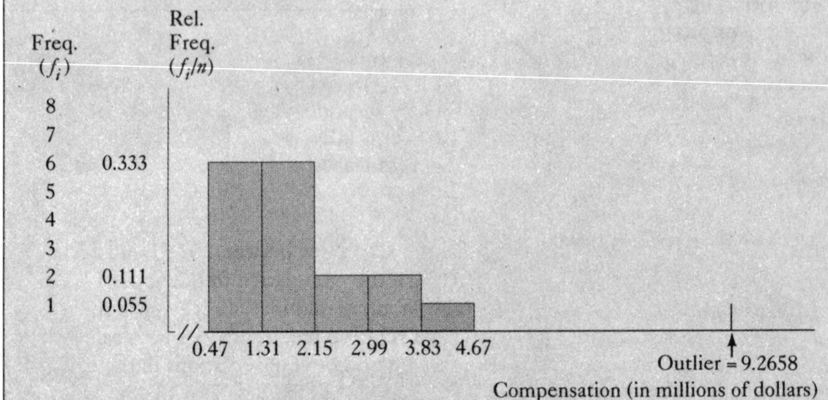

Histograms

Histogram
A graph of a frequency distribution, where class intervals are represented on a horizontal axis and the class relative or absolute frequencies are represented vertically.

The quantitative data in frequency distributions can be portrayed graphically in histograms. A **histogram** has a horizontal axis that is scaled to show all values of the measurements—in this case the compensation of energy company CEOs. It is also segmented to identify class boundaries with a vertical bar rising to the height of the frequency (or relative frequency) for each class at the identified boundary value. Figure 1.3 shows the histogram for the 18 CEOs in the sample. Notice in this figure that both the highest and lowest values in the data set are identified to eliminate any confusion about the location of these values.

Cumulative Frequency Distributions

Cumulative Frequency Distribution
A presentation of an entire set of cumulative frequencies.

Cumulative Frequency
The number of observations that have values less than or equal to a specified number.

Knowledge of the number of observations that lie below a certain value is often desired. For instance, in assessing CEO compensation, knowing the compensation level achieved by the majority of CEOs would be helpful. A **cumulative frequency distribution** shows the total number of observations that are less than a specified value. When data are in classes like those in Tables 1.1 and 1.6, the specified values are the class boundaries (10, 100, and 1,000 employees in Table 1.1 and \$0.47, \$1.31, \$2.15, \$2.99, \$3.83, and \$4.67 million in Table 1.6).

The **cumulative frequency** of \$1.31 million for the compensation data in Table 1.6, as shown in Figure 1.3, is six, since there are six observations that are less than \$1.31 million. The cumulative frequency for \$2.15 million is 12: the six values less than

Table 1.7 Cumulative Frequency of Energy Company CEO Compensation

CEO Compensation (in thousands of dollars)	Cumulative Frequency	Cumulative Relative Frequency
less than 1310	6	0.33333
less than 2150	12	0.66667
less than 2990	14	0.77778
less than 3830	16	0.88889
less than 4670	17	0.94444
less than 9266	18	1.00000

$1.31 million plus the six values between $1.31 and $2.15 million, and similarly up to $4.67 million for which the cumulative frequency is 17. The cumulative frequency for the entire distribution, up to and including $9.2658 million, is 18.

Cumulative Relative Frequency
A ratio calculated by dividing a cumulative frequency by the total number of observations in the data set.

The **cumulative relative frequency** is a ratio calculated by dividing a cumulative frequency by the total number of observations in the data set. For example, the cumulative relative frequency for 2.15 is 0.6667 (= 12/18). Thus, we know that approximately 66.67 percent of the CEOs have compensation of less than $2.15 million. Both the cumulative frequencies and cumulative relative frequencies are shown in Table 1.7.

A graph of cumulative relative frequencies provides a good visual impression of how the data accumulate. The cumulative relative frequency function shown in Figure 1.4 was constructed from the CEO cumulative frequency distribution in Table 1.7. In Figure 1.4, the height of each bar shows the percentage of data less than the upper boundary of the class. Thus, the bar for the class "2.15" shows that 66.7 percent of these CEOs make less than $2.15 million.

Ogive
A series of lines connecting the lower boundaries of each class in a cumulative relative frequency distribution.

An **ogive** is sometimes used to smooth the graph of cumulative relative frequencies. An ogive is formed by lines connecting the lower-right corner points of the bars that make up the cumulative relative frequency graph. It is typically drawn as a smooth arching curve, as in an architectural arch of the same name. At each of these points, the ogive shows the amount of the distribution that is less than the value on the horizontal axis. Figure 1.4 is the ogive for the CEO compensation data. The ogive will be used in the next chapter to find hypothetical values that might lie within given class intervals.

Query:

For all eight industrial groups in the *Wall Street Journal* (April 22, 1992) data set on CEO total pay—including salary, bonus, and long-term incentives—construct a frequency distribution and a histogram to give a visual display of the data. Also, provide the cumulative frequencies associated with the frequency distribution you construct. Is there a big difference between this distribution and that of the CEOs of energy companies?

Answer:

Because this data set is large, a histogram cannot be constructed easily without a computer program. With a statistics package such as EXCEL, this data set can be managed quickly. The compensation of the 317 CEOs can be retrieved by down-

FIGURE 1.4 Cumulative Frequency and the Ogive

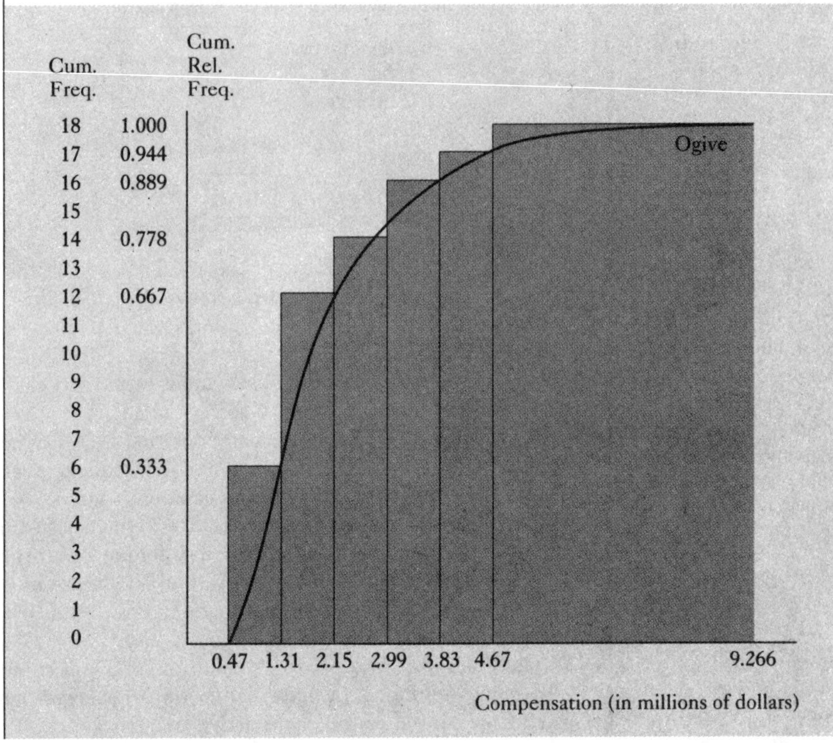

loading the data sets found on the E270 World Wide Web site at

http://www.indiana.edu/~statist/e270.htm

The downloading procedures are located at this Web site. You need only a MSDOS formatted 1.44K disk in the A drive of the host computer. Once the data sets are downloaded and on the disk in the A drive (or transferred to your hard drive) open EXCEL and do the following to load the CEO compensation data into EXCEL:

1. Click on the "File" menu at the top left-hand corner of the EXCEL screen, and click on "Open."
2. Within the "Open" screen, set the "Files of Type" to "All Files" and set the drive to "A:" (or to another drive containing the data). (You must set "file type" to "all" because the files on the data disk are "ASCII." These are generic "text" files that can be read by any computer program.) Your screen display should now look like that is Chart 1.1.
3. Select the "queries" subdirectory by double clicking on it or highlighting it and clicking on "Open". The queries subdirectory will appear.

CHART 1.1 EXCEL Open Screen Display Set to Show All Files on the A: Drive

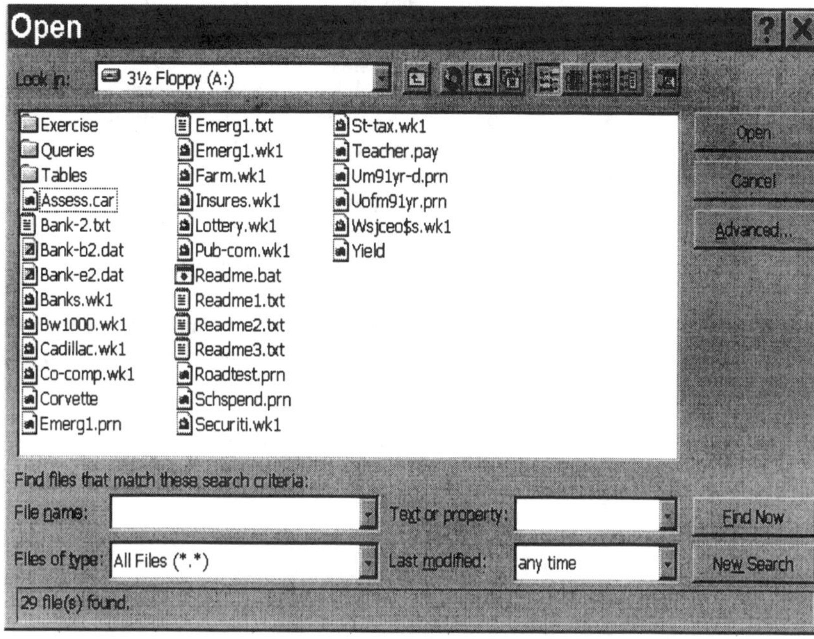

4. Highlight the "que1.prn" file and select it by clicking "Open." The "Text Import Wizard - Step 1 of 3" screen display will appear, which will show the first few CEO compensations in the lower, left-hand corner.
5. Click on "Next" in the lower right-hand corner to pass through both the "Step 1 of 3" and "Step 2 or 3" screen displays. At the "Step 3 of 3" screen display click on "Finish." The 317 CEO compensations (in $1,000 units) will appear in cells A1 through A317, as partially shown here:

	A
1	74799.7
2	22563.2
.	.
.	.
317	100.0

We can either let EXCEL automatically construct a histogram or we can set the classes ourselves, as demonstrated below.

CLASS BOUNDARIES SET AUTOMATICALLY BY EXCEL.

EXCEL labels classes in histogram "bins," and the difference between the class boundaries are referred to as "bin ranges." If we do not specify the bin ranges, EXCEL automatically creates a set of evenly distributed bins from the minimum value to the maximum value. To see this demonstrated, do the following:

1. With the CEO data in cells A1 through A317, click on the "Tools" menu at the top of the EXCEL screen. A list will appear, and at the bottom of this list is "Data Analysis." (If "Data Analysis" is not on the bottom of the Tools menu, the "Analysis Tool Pack" needs to be added to the "Tools" menu, which is done via the "Add In" within the "Tools" menu.)
2. Clicking on "Data Analysis" leads to a menu from which "Histogram" is selected. The Histogram submenu will pop up.
3. In the Histogram submenu, for the "input range" enter "$A$1:$A$317." To have EXCEL automatically create a histogram for these 317 CEO compensations, leave all other entries blank with the exception of the "output range," for which "B1" can be entered. A click on "OK" yields the frequency distribution:

	B	C
1	Bin	Frequency
2	100.0	1
3	4494.1	290
4	8888.2	17
5	13282.3	4
6	17676.4	3
7	22070.5	0
8	26464.6	1
9	30858.7	0
10	35252.8	0
11	39646.9	0
12	44041.0	0
13	48435.1	0
14	52829.2	0
15	57223.3	0
16	61617.4	0
17	66011.5	0
18	70405.6	0
19	More	1

There are 19 classes (bins) created by EXCEL for these 317 data points. The resulting frequency distribution is not very good. It has too many empty classes. Formula 1.2 suggests that we need only about 14 classes to represent these data.

$$2(317)^{0.33333} = 2(6.817) = 13.6$$

But that number of classes might not allow a good comparison with Table 1.6, where only seven classes were employed.

SETTING CLASS BOUNDARIES IN EXCEL

To facilitate comparison of the small data set of 18 CEOs in Table 1.6 and the entire 317 CEO compensation list, the class boundaries of Table 1.6 must be used. This requires a specification of the bin range. After loading the "que1.prn" file into an EXCEL spreadsheet, as directed earlier, the desired upper bin limits (highest attainable values in a class interval from Table 1.6), are entered into cells B1 to B6:

	A	B	C
1	74799.7	469.999	
2	22563.2	1309.999	
3	16913.2	2149.999	
4	16778.9	2989.999	
5	13812.7		
6	12178.0		
⋮	⋮		

Next, use the "Tools" menu to get to "Data Analysis" and then the "Histogram" screen. Fill in the Histogram submenu as follows:

1. Enter "$A$1:$A$317" for the "input range."
2. Enter "$B$1:$B$6" for the "bin range."
3. Enter $B$8 for the "output range."
4. Click the box for "Cumulative Percentage."
5. Click the box for "Chart Output."

Your screen display should now look like that in Chart 1.2. Finally, clicking "OK" yields the Chart 1.3 screen display:

CHART 1.2 EXCEL Histogram Screen Display Set for Specific Class Limits

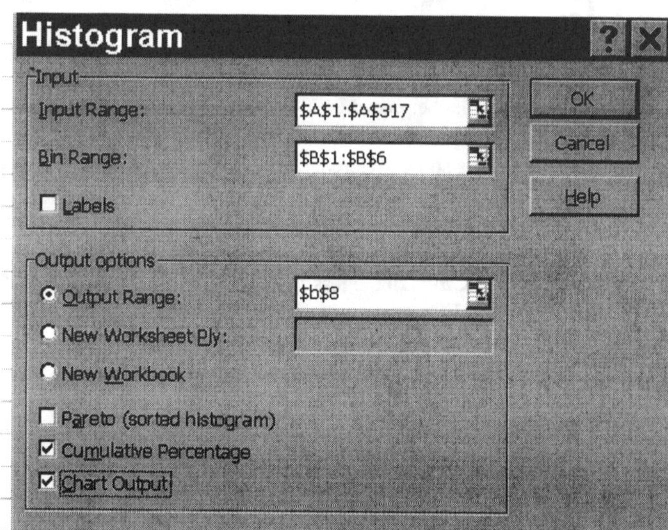

CHART 1.3 EXCEL Histogram Results

74799.7	469.999		
22563.2	1309.999		
16913.2	2149.999		
16778.9	2989.999		
13812.7	3829.999		
12178	4669.999		
11436.2			
9725.9	Bin	Frequency	Cumulative
9265.8	469.999	11	3.47%
7620	1309.999	142	48.26%
7211.8	2149.999	72	70.98%
6654.9	2989.999	33	81.39%
6411.4	3829.999	17	86.75%
6299.5	4669.999	17	92.11%
5955.8	More	25	100.00%
5829.7			
5630			
5497.3			

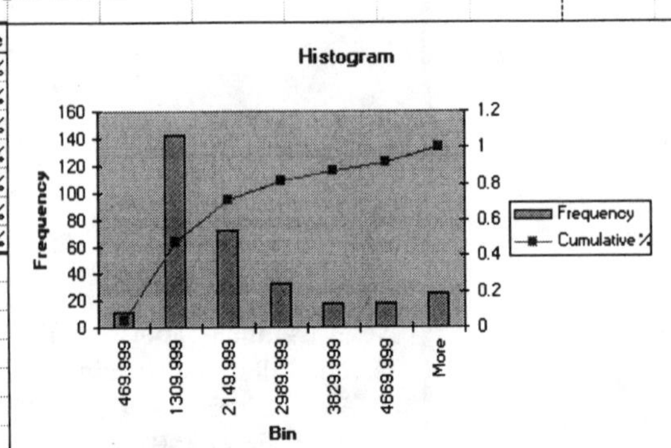

EXCEL requires that all classes (bins) have an upper limit, with the exception of the last class that appears as "More," for "More than $4,669,999" in the EXCEL printout of CEO compensation. Thus, an observation of $4,670,000 would go in this last class (bin). An observation of $470,000 would go in the class (bin) that is represented as $470,000 to $1,309,999 in Table 1.6. (Different programs require that upper or lower limits or boundaries be specified in certain ways. The important point is to know how the program handles observations at these beginning and ending points.)

Notice that EXCEL gives the cumulative relative frequencies but not the relative frequency of observed values in each class. Relative frequencies are easily calculated. For example, between $470,000 and $1,309,999 there are 142 observed values so the relative frequency for this class is 142/317 = 0.44795.

There is some difference between the compensation of CEOs in general and those of the energy companies. For example, none of the energy company CEOs make less than $0.47 million per year while the distribution of all CEOs shows 11, or 3.47 percent, making less than $0.47 million. In addition, 71 percent [(11 + 142 + 72)/317] of the 317 CEOs make less than $2.15 million while only 67 percent of the 18 energy company CEOs make less than $2.15 million. Before concluding that energy company CEOs are among the highest paid CEOs, however, notice that at the high end of the compensation distribution, 7.89 percent of the 317 CEOs make more than $4.67 million, while only 5.56 percent of the 18 energy company CEOs do. Energy company CEOs are not among the lowest-compensated CEOs, but they are not among the highest-compensated ones either.

1.8 CLOSING COMMENTS

Today computer programs are readily available to manage and manipulate data and create different types of diagrams to summarize data. For now it is sufficient to recognize how data are collected, organized, condensed, and reported in histograms and other frequency forms. The next chapter introduces summary measures that can be employed in describing the central location and variability of data. Spreadsheet programs such as EXCEL will compute most of these summary measures and create diagrams to show results. The use of these programs will be demonstrated throughout this book.

CHAPTER EXERCISES

1.16 In the process of auditing the "petty cash box" of a local construction firm for the past week you found 40 "IOUs" in the following amounts.

$7.10 $5.80 $6.60 $11.90 $5.50 $4.50 $6.10 $4.50
$8.40 $6.80 $9.10 $4.70 $10.20 $7.60 $6.30 $5.50
$5.20 $6.90 $7.50 $1.00 $6.50 $6.60 $3.50 $7.00
$7.80 $8.50 $3.20 $6.30 $5.50 $5.50 $4.60 $2.20
$6.90 $8.40 $7.20 $10.70 $9.60 $5.80 $4.70 $6.10

Using EXCEL, describe these data in
a. A frequency distribution
b. A histogram
c. A cumulative relative frequency distribution

1.17 A candy shop has declared bankruptcy with the following amounts owed to suppliers, in hundreds of dollars (i.e., 3.02 represents $302.00)

3.02 2.95 2.94 2.78 3.12 3.18 2.86 2.24 2.30 3.41
2.30 3.13 3.28 3.42 3.04 2.65 2.50 2.63 2.68 3.17
3.01 3.05 3.14 3.25 2.78 2.95 3.36 3.02 2.86 3.02
3.55 3.36 3.27 3.02 3.21 3.13 2.82 3.50 3.11 2.86
2.95 2.87 3.52 3.05 3.12 2.86 2.85 3.34 2.75 3.06

Your task is to describe these data to the courts. Using EXCEL, construct a frequency distribution and draw a histogram to describe these data.

1.18 Construct a histogram for the breakdown of owner-occupied housing in Monroe County as shown in Exercise 1.4.

1.19 Construct an ogive for the breakdown of owner-occupied housing in Monroe County as shown in Exercise 1.4.

1.20 Census Bureau data for 1989 show that the poorest 20 percent of the population of married couples with children had a cash income under $22,700; the next 20 percent had income under $34,100; the middle 20 percent had income under $45,500; the next 20 percent had income up to $62,200; and the richest 20 percent had income over $62,200. Draw the ogive for this distribution.

1.21 For the data in Exercise 1.17, construct a cumulative frequency distribution.

1.22 Do you prefer your histogram (Exercise 1.18), or the ogive (Exercise 1.19) representation of the breakdown of owner-occupied housing in Monroe County? Explain.

1.23 The following percentages from the National Highway Traffic Safety Administration show the relative speed involved in U.S. automobile accidents in 1993. (Notice that the class boundaries appear to confuse the limiting values, but these values can be discerned from a careful examination of the first and sixth classes.) To which class does a 30 mph accident belong? Draw a histogram for these data. Does your histogram suggest that it is safer to drive at higher speeds? Explain.

Class	Speed	Relative Frequency
1	20 mph or less	2.0%
2	20 to 30 mph	29.7%
3	30 to 40 mph	30.4%
4	40 to 50 mph	16.5%
5	50 to 60 mph	19.2%
6	more than 60 mph	2.2%

1.24 A 1994 Roper report (*HT*, February 12, 1995) showed survey respondents saying that at least $25,000 was needed "just to get by," $40,000 was needed to "live in reasonable comfort," and more than $100,000 was required to "fulfill all their dreams." From the below 1993 Census Bureau histogram of U.S. household income, approximately what percentage of families actually fulfill each of these three living standards?

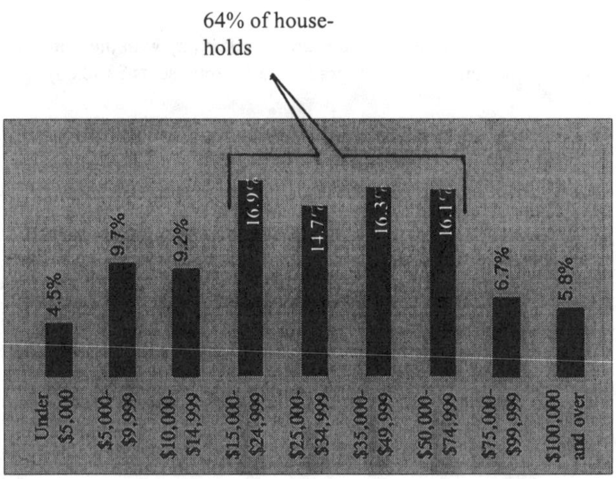

1.25 Below are the profits per partner in the 20 law firms identified in a *Wall Street Journal* (June 29, 1993) article on pay at elite law firms. Construct a histogram for these data.

Law Firm (city)	Profit per partner (In thousands of dollars)
Baker & McKenzie (Chicago)	415
Skadden Arps (New York)	885
Jones Day (Cleveland)	310
Gibson, Dunn & Crutcher (Los Angeles)	505
Weil, Gotshal & Manges (New York)	725
Shearman & Sterling (New York)	680
Sullivan & Cromwell (New York)	1080
Davis Polk & Wardell (New York)	1020
Cleary Gottlieb (New York)	880
Sidley & Austin (Chicago)	410
O'Melveny & Myers (Los Angeles)	605
Latham & Watkins (Los Angeles)	455
Morgan, Lewis & Bockius (Philadelphia)	365
Mayer, Brown & Platt (Chicago)	330
Pillsbury Madison & Sutro (San Francisco)	345
Fried Frank (New York)	905
Fulbright & Jaworski (Houston)	355
Cravath, Swaine & Moore (New York)	1385
Simpson, Thacher & Bartlett (New York)	960
Morrison & Foerster (San Francisco)	235

1.26 The computer ASCII file "EX1-49.PRN" contains the 51 average salaries for teachers by state and the District of Columbia. Make up a frequency distribution, and draw the histogram for these salaries.

1.27 Below is a *Business Week* (August 9, 1993) breakdown of the general population and voters by age. Draw two histograms: one for the general population and one for the other voters. What do your histograms show?

	Relative Frequencies	
Age	Population	Voters
18–29	24.0%	18.0%
30–44	32.5	32.0
45–54	15.0	17.5
55–64	11.5	13.5
65 +	17.0	19.0

1.28 The article "Resort Ads Caught Snowing the Ski Set" (*WSJ*, December 22, 1992), reported on Killington Ski Resort's hiring of an engineering firm to measure its skiterrain and that of other New England ski areas in an attempt to show that "dishonesty and hype are rampant." The aerial survey conducted by W. Byrd LaPrade Inc. for Killington showed that while Killington "over-reported its mileage by some 9%," the other areas had "degrees of hype" much greater, as shown. Demonstrate why the "degree of hype" should be even greater than reported if it is a measure of over-reporting of the actual miles of trails.

Ski Area	Actual Miles of Trails	Miles Claimed by Resort	Degree of Hype
Killington	70	77	9%
Sugarbush	46	53	13%
Sunday River	29	36	19%
Sugarloaf	36	45	20%
Okemo	25	32	22%
Smuggler's Notch	22	32	31%

1.29 According to an article in the *Herald Times* (September 5, 1990), titled "Statistics Switch Blurs Census Data," Bloomington, Indiana, between the 1980 and 1990 census, grew by 11.5 percent by one set of figures and 15 percent by another. In 1980 the official population count was 52,044, but between 1980 and 1990 the city annexed an area that, in 1980, had a population of 1,152 people. In addition, 619 people needed to be added to the 1980 base because of an error in the 1980 count. The 1990 census figure for Bloomington was 59,998.

a. Show how the 11.5 percent and 15 percent growth rates were obtained.
b. Which percentage more accurately reflects population growth in Bloomington?

1.30 In sex and race discrimination cases, considerable courtroom time is usually devoted to defining the preselection pool (population) from which potential employees might be hired. Typically, plaintiffs (those bringing suit against an employer) argue that the appropriate preselection pool should be the entire U.S. working-age population. Defendants (employers) argue for a much more restrictive preselection pool, for example, only those in the local community who have obtained a specific education level. Why do the plaintiffs and defendants argue in this way over the appropriate preselection pool?

1.31 A *New York Times* News Service release on December 3, 1989 stated: The 117 executives surveyed told Runzheimer (the survey firm) they preferred the Taurus, followed by GM's Celebrity . . . . The highest rated foreign auto was a Toyota, which was selected as the most desirable by 6 percent of the managers.

a. From this quote we know that Toyota was selected by how many of the managers?
b. What else would you like to know about this sample before drawing a conclusion about the car that managers consider the most desirable?

1.32 In its second annual ranking of female-owned businesses, *Working Woman* (May 1993) reported that the number of such companies grew 20 percent in the past year to 6.5 million. Why might you question the magnitude of this increase based on data-collection considerations?

1.33 A study by Scott Smith and Kim Lloyd in the *American Sociological Review* (February, 1995) reported on "Spousal Alternatives and Marital Dissolution." In the article it is reported that 50 percent or less of the white survey respondents resided in "a marriage market" having 128 unmarried men in their twenties per 100 unmarried women of the same age. Additional cumulative relative frequencies are given below:

Ratio of unmarried men per 100 unmarried women	Cumulative Relative Frequency (Percentage)
105	10
115	25
128	50
137	75
162	90

For these data construct an Ogive.

1.34 A relative frequency distribution for U.S. home sales by price in the first quarter of 1990 as prepared by the *Chicago Tribune* (reported in *HT*, June 24, 1990) is shown below.

a. Construct the histogram for this relative frequency data.
b. Construct the cumulative relative frequency for this relative frequency data.

U.S. home sales by price in the first quarter of 1990

Under $69,000	11%
$70,000-79,999	9%
$80,000-89,999	8%
$90,000-99,999	8%
$100,000-119,000	12%
$120,000-149,999	17%
$150,000-199,999	17%
$200,000 and more	18%

1.35 An article in the *Wall Street Journal* (February 25, 1997) on the need to revise the Consumer Price Index (CPI) reported on the views of 320 academic economists when asked how well the CPI reflects the cost of living.

Generally accurate or understates	13%
Overstates by 0.1 to 0.59 percent	23%
Overstates by 0.6 to 1.0 percent	35%
Overstates by more than 1.0 percent	21%
No opinion	8%

a. How many of the 320 economists responded in each of the five classes?
b. Construct a histogram to represent the frequency distribution.

1.36 According to a *Herald Times* (June 23, 1990) article, between 8 p.m. on June 17th and 5 p.m. on June 21st, 20 Indiana state troopers stopped 561 trucks and ticketed most of them to collect $42,985 in fines. Why would you be suspicious about conclusions drawn from this information regarding weight and number of violations of "the typical type of truck," on the highways?

1.37 A consultant says owners of private companies with annual sales below $100 million earned a median salary of just $51,000 in 1989. Those with sales of $20 million to $100 million have a median salary of $231,000 compared with $508,000 for heads of big public companies. The conclusion according to Business Week (April 16, 1990): "If you want a huge salary don't start your own business." Why doesn't this information imply that starting your own business yields small rewards?

1.38 A note in *The Wall Street Journal* (October 8, 1992) reported "About 86% of U.S.units of foreign firms support the arts in the U.S. . . . says a survey by the Business Committee for the Arts. The result is based on 44 responses to the 115 survey forms sent out."

a. How high could this percentage have been had the response rate been 100 percent?

b. How low could this percentage have been had the response rate been 100 percent?

1.39 In sailboat racing, rule violations are handled by the local yacht club. Those involved in protests who are not satisfied with the results at the local level may appeal to the U.S. Sailing Association. Below are the frequency distributions for the time needed to process those appeals in 1989, 1990, and 1991, from *American Sailor* (September 1992). Draw the histogram for each year of data. What does a comparison of these histograms show?

Time to Process an Appeal

Time in weeks	FY 89	FY 90	FY 91	Total
0 to < 5	5	2	4	11
5 to < 10	1	8	1	10
10 to < 15	9	4	1	14
15 to < 20	7	8	2	17
20 to < 25	3	3	3	9
25 to < 30	4	0	3	7
30 or more	0	1	4*	5
Total	29	26	18	73

*Only two appeals received before 10/31/91 were still open as of 4/30/92, and in both cases the Committee is waiting for information from the protest committee. Both will have taken more than 30 weeks to process and are included in the statistics.

Academic References

Clogg, Clifford. "The Impact of Sociological Methodology on Statistical Methodology." *Statistical Science*, May 1992, pp. 183–195.

Crossen, Cynthia. *Tainted Truth: The Manipulation of Fact in America.* New York: Simon & Schuster, 1994.

Fienberg, Stephen. "A Brief History of Statistics in Three and One-Half Chapters: A Review Essay." *Statistical Science*, May 1992.

Fisher, Ronald. *Statistical Methods for Research Workers*. New York: Hafner Publishing Company, 1970.

Griliches, Zvi. "Patent Statistics as Economic Indicators: A Survey." *Journal of Economic Literature*, December 1990, pp. 1661–1707.

Leamer, Edward. "Let's Take the Con Out of Econometrics." American Economic Review, March 1983, p. 33.

Starer, Daniel. *Who Knows What: The Essential Business Resource Book*. New York: Henry Holt, 1993.

Terrell, George R. and David W. Scott. "Oversmoothed Nonparametric Density Estimates." *Journal of the American Statistical Association*, Vol. 80, March 1985, pp. 209–214.

Wand, M.P. "Data-Based Choice of Histogram Bin Width." *American Statistician*, Vol. 51, February 1997, pp. 59-64.

Webb, Ray H. (Ed.) *Macroeconomic Data: A User's Guide*. Richmond: Federal Reserve Bank of Richmond, December 1994.

Endnotes

1. Sir Ronald Fisher, in the 1970 14th edition of possibly the most influential book in statistics, *Statistical Methods for Research Workers*, wrote:

   > The science of statistics is essentially a branch of Applied Mathematics, and may be regarded as mathematics applied to observational data. (p. 1)
   >
   > Statistical methods are essential to social studies, and it is principally by the aid of such methods that these studies may be raised to the rank of sciences. This particular dependence of social studies upon statistical methods has led to the unfortunate misapprehension that statistics is to be regarded as a branch of economics, whereas in truth methods adequate to the treatment of economic data, insofar as these exist, have mostly been developed in biology and the other sciences. (p. 2)

   Fisher's view, although traceable to the first version of his book in 1925, is still held today by many scholars in the natural sciences and departments of mathematics. Econometricians (economists who apply statistical methods in economics), psychometricians, cliometricians, and other "metricians" in the social sciences have different views of the process by which statistical methods have developed. Given that Fisher's numerous and great contributions to statistics were in applications within biology, genetics, and agriculture, his view is understandable, although it is refuted by sociologist Clifford Clogg (1992) and the numerous commenters on his article.

FORMULAS

- Relative frequency $= f_i/N$, for a population of size N.
- Relative frequency $= f_i/n$, for a sample of size n where f_i is the frequency of the ith class.
- The approximate number of classes is the integer that just exceeds 2 (number of values in data set)$^{(0.3333)}$.
- The approximate width of each class is highest value number of classes.

CHAPTER 2

DESCRIPTION AND SUMMARY OF DATA

The purpose of computing is insight, not numbers.

Richard Hamming
b. 1915

2.1 INTRODUCTION

Frequency distributions alone cannot tell the whole story about a data set. We need more information to describe the central values, variability, and shape of the distribution, whether population or sample. The following situations depict problems encountered in business and economics that require knowledge of data position and data dispersion.

- A *Wall Street Journal* (April 22, 1992) article showed that "median CEO total pay—including salary, bonus and long-term incentives—came to $1.3 million in 1991." But what is the mean total pay for these chief executive officers? A stockholder of an energy company may ask, "What do these values imply about overcompensation or undercompensation of my company's CEO?"
- A *Wall Street Journal* (September 23, 1991) article on bank closings reported that, "A House Banking Committee study found that regulators kept critically ill banks open an average of 10 to 12 months before failure." Is this average correct? Why might it be misleading?
- According to journalist Joyce Lain Kennedy, in a syndicated column on merit pay policies that appeared in the *Herald Times* (February 26, 1989), a *Newsweek* survey showed that roughly 80 percent of American workers believe they are above average in merit. She quotes a Hays management consultant who said Americans suffer from the "Lake Woebegone myth," where all the children are above average. Is it possible for nearly everyone to be above the average? Or must 50 percent be above and 50 percent be below the average?
- A *Wall Street Journal* (November 15, 1996) article stated that "The nation's continuing economic expansion, now 67 months old, has far surpassed the previous postwar average (50 months) and few see the party ending anytime soon." Does the word "average" pertain to the median or mean and what difference does it make?
- A *Washington Post* (January 29, 1995) syndicated article reported that "Risk is a fuzzy concept, but it's possible to put a number on it." For instance, suppose a corporate stock has yielded a net quarterly mean return of $100 per $1,000 invested, with a standard deviation of $50. Moreover, the distribution of the net return has been bell shaped (or normal). If we assume the future will be like the past, what is the likelihood that an investor of $1,000 will lose money on this investment?

By the end of this chapter, you will be able to calculate and use the three measures of central location—mean, median and mode—and other measures of location, such as percentiles and quartiles. You also will be able to compute and interpret three measures of dispersion—the range, the variance, and the standard deviation. Using the mean and standard deviation, you will be able to make statements about the proportions of a distribution that are associated with deviations from the mean.

2.2 Descriptive Summary Measures

For large data sets, a listing of the data in the original order of collection (the raw data) or even a frequency distribution representation may provide too much information to identify the "middle" of the data and their "spread." What we need are summary measures that represent a typical middle value and typical deviations from that middle value. These descriptive summary measures are of two types: measures of central tendency and measures of dispersion.

Measure of Central Tendency or Central Location
A value that identifies the middle of a distribution; it is a measure of the "typical" value.

Measures of central tendency or central location are numbers that represent the typical or middle values in a distribution. To illustrate, consider the issue of CEO compensation introduced in the first chapter. Table 2.1 reproduces the compensation of the 20 CEOs of the energy companies surveyed by *The Wall Street Journal.* We want to know the distance of each CEO's total compensation (salary and bonus) from the typical compensation, but first, the "typical" must be defined. The typical, middle, or central compensation can be defined in different ways, depending on the purpose of the inquiry and the nature of the data, as discussed in Sections 2.3 through 2.10.

Table 2.1 Compensation of CEOs of Energy Companies

	Company	Executive	1991 Salary/Bonus (in thousands)	% Change from 1990	Long-Term Comp. (in thousands)	Total Direct Comp. (in thousands)
1.	Amerada Hess	Leon Hess	300.0	N/A	0.0	300.0*
2.	Amoco	H. Laurance Fuller	1302.2	N/A	236.3	1538.5
3.	Ashland Oil	John R. Hall	1038.0	–6	0.0	1038.0
4.	Atlantic Richfield	Lodwrick M. Cook	1673.9	–26	2008.9	3682.8
5.	Baker Hughes	James D. Woods	916.0	–27	393.1	1309.1
6.	Chevron	Kenneth T. Derr	1385.6	2	363.8	1749.4
7.	Coastal	James R. Paul	813.8	N/A	913.4	1727.2
8.	Dresser Industries	John J. Murphy	1070.6	–3	578.7	1649.3
9.	Exxon	Lawrence G. Rawl	1812.8	17	7453.0	9265.8
10.	FINA	Ron W. Haddock	476.3	N/A	0.0	476.3
11.	Halliburton	Thomas H. Cruikshank	1200.0	9	401.5	1601.5
12.	Kerr-McGee	F.A. McPherson	542.0	–32	129.4	671.4
13.	Mobil	Allen E. Murray	2040.0	9	2624.9	4664.9
14.	Occidental	Ray R. Irani	2324.0	N/A	147.1	2471.1
15.	Pennzoil	James L. Pate	650.0	–2	0.0	650.0
16.	Sun Co.	Robert McClements, Jr.	1001.1	3	0.0	1001.1
17.	Texaco	James W. Kinnear	1667.0	–14	1658.8	3325.8
18.	USX	Charles A. Corry	1313.2	–18	840.2	2153.4
19.	Unocal	Richard J. Stegemeier	1054.7	N/A	0.0	1054.7*
20.	Valero	William E. Greehey	1097.4	12	352.5	1449.9

*Salary/bonus data not valid for comparison (e.g., partial year data).

Source: *Wall Street Journal,* April 22, 1992.

Measure of Dispersion
A value that indicates how "spread out" the distribution is.

Measures of dispersion are numbers that represent the spread or variability of values in a distribution. The distance of each CEO's compensation from a measure of central tendency, for instance, reflects the dispersion of the distribution. A measure of dispersion, however, is a single summary number that reflects these deviations. Several summary measures of dispersion will be presented later in this chapter. As introduced in Section 2.11 and the sections that follow, the choice of a specific measure of dispersion will depend on the goal of the inquiry and type of data considered.

2.3 The Mean as a Measure of Central Tendency

Mean
A measure of central location defined by the arithmetic average, which is the sum of the values in a data set divided by the number of values.

The arithmetic average is also called the **mean.** For the mean to be useful, all the data used in its calculation must be comparable. For instance, Table 2.1 reports different forms of pay for 20 CEOs of the energy companies, but comparable data are available for only 18 of those CEOs. The mean total direct compensation for those 18 CEOs is \$2,245,861, which is calculated from the data in Table 2.1 in thousands of dollars as

$$\frac{1538.5 + 1038.0 + \ldots + 2153.4 + 1449.9}{18} = \frac{40425.5}{18} = 2245.861$$

Because it is inconvenient to list all 18 comparable compensations that form the sum 40425.5, the notation 1538.5 + ... + 1449.9 is used to indicate that all of the 18 comparable compensations from 1,538.5 to 1,449.9 in the last column of Table 2.1 are included in the sum of 18 compensations. In a more general form, the calculation of the mean of the 18 comparable values is written

$$\text{Mean} = \frac{x_1 + x_2 + \ldots + x_{17} + x_{18}}{18}$$

where x_1 is the value of the first observation (that is, $x_1 = 1538.5$), x_2 is the second value ($x_2 = 1038.0$), and so on, until the final value ($x_{18} = 1449.9$).

Even more compact sigma notation can be used to represent the sum of x_1 to x_{18}. Capital sigma Σ is used to indicate a summation, and the symbol x_i indicates the variable over which the addition is to occur. The subscript i identifies the ith value in a string of values. For instance, in the energy companies' CEO compensation, $i = 1$, or $i = 2$, or any number to $i = 18$. The beginning and ending x_i to be added are identified by a starting number of i below the sigma and the stopping number above the sigma. Thus, the notation

$$\sum_{i=1}^{18} x_i$$

symbolizes the summation of values from x_1 to x_{18}; that is,

$$\sum_{i=1}^{18} x_i = x_1 + x_2 + \ldots + x_{17} + x_{18}$$

Using this sigma notation, the mean of the CEO energy company compensation is written

$$\text{Mean} = (1/18)\sum_{i=1}^{18} x_i = (1/18)(x_1 + x_2 + \ldots + x_{17} + x_{18})$$

As discussed in Chapter 1, observable data sets consist either of all N values in the population of interest or an n observation sample (or subset) of those N values. Hypothetical populations obviously can be of infinite size but observed data must be countable. Here we are concerned with only observable data sets that are either a sample or a population.

Population Mean (μ) A parameter of the population that is the arithmetic average; it is the measure of central location identified by the Greek letter "mu," μ.

The **population mean** is typically designated by the Greek letter μ (verbalized "mu"), or μ_x (verbalized "mu sub-ex"). If the population values are labeled y, then the mean of y would be designated μ_y. The x and y subscript identifiers are helpful when comparing means from different populations but they may be deleted when there is no confusion about the population to which the mean applies.

The **population mean** of x is the sum of the N x values divided by N. In shorthand notation this population mean is designated μ_x and is calculated as

$$\mu_x = \frac{1}{N}\sum_{i=1}^{N} x_i = (1/N)(x_1 + x_2 + \ldots + x_N) \quad (2.1a)$$

For an n observation sample of x values, the **sample mean** is written $\bar{x}$, which is read "ex bar." A sample of y values would have a mean identified by $\bar{y}$, and likewise for any other letter capped with a bar to identify a sample mean.

The **sample mean** of x is the sum of the n x values divided by n. In shorthand notation, this sample mean is designated $\bar{x}$ and is calculated as

$$\bar{x} = \frac{1}{n}\sum_{i=1}^{n} x_i = (1/n)(x_1 + x_2 + \ldots + x_n) \quad (2.1b)$$

As a general rule, Greek letters are used to identify population measures and Roman letters are used to signify sample measures. Whether a data set is a population or a sample depends on the type of data and the use to which they are to be put. For instance, if we are only interested in comparing how far any given energy company CEO's compensation is from the mean of the 20 CEOs who head energy companies, then the 20 compensation values are a population. But we do not have the 20 compensations; we have only 18 comparable values. We thus have a subset of all 20 CEOs; these 18 usable records are a sample.

Even if *The Wall Street Journal* had complete information on all 350 companies in its survey, the resulting data set would not be a population if we are interested in all corporations in the United States. Typically, smaller data sets are samples from larger sets, but even large data sets may be samples of still larger sets of data. Remember, only a complete census of the group of interest will yield the population.

QUERY 2.1:
In reviewing the salary increases of six employees at a small firm, the office manager noticed that the mean percentage increase (4.46 percent) was not equal to the percentage increase in the mean salary (4.63 percent). Does this suggest a mistake in the calculation of the means?

	1992 Salary	Percentage Increase	1993 Salary
	\$60,000	4.26%	\$62,557
	60,000	4.26%	62,557
	58,000	12.07%	65,000
	52,883	1.94%	53,908
	51,250	2.00%	52,275
	45,800	2.24%	46,825
Mean	\$54,656	4.63%	\$57,187
Mean percentage increase in salaries		4.46%	

ANSWER:
No mistake was made in the calculation of the means. The percentage increase in the mean salary (4.63 percent) is the same as the actual percentage increase in the total budget for the six employees:

6(\$54656) = \$327936
6(\$57187) = \$343122
(343122 – 327936)/327936 = 0.0463

although it was calculated on the basis of the change in the mean salary in each year

\$54656)
\$57187)
(57187 – 54656)/54656 = 0.0463

The mean percentage increase (4.46 percent) was calculated as the average of the six percentage increases in salaries.

$$\frac{4.26\% + 4.26\% + 12.07\% + 1.94\% + 2.00\% + 2.24\%}{6} = 4.46\%$$

The mean percentage increase has no relationship to the actual budget for the six employees. It can be decreased, for example, by giving larger dollar raises to the higher-paid employees and smaller dollar raises to the lower paid. It is an artifact of the way in which dollar raises are allocated.

2.4 The Weighted Mean

Data are often reported in frequency distributions. If the frequency of each value in the original data set is not known, and only the frequencies of class intervals are provided, then the mean may be approximated by "weighting" representative class values by their respective frequencies. If, however, the frequency or relative frequency of each value in the data set is known, then the exact mean may be calculated by weighting actual values by their respective relative frequencies.

Approximation Method

Once values are grouped into class intervals, their individual identities are lost. This can be seen in Table 2.2, where risky banks were grouped by the time interval before they failed. For instance, 92 banks failed in the 10- to 12-month interval after being placed on the high-risk list. Although we know the frequency of bank failures for the 10- to 12-month interval, we cannot determine the exact length of time before each of the 92 banks failed because of the grouping. *The Wall Street Journal* did not provide the original data, and we can work only with the frequency distribution provided.

For data that are grouped in a frequency distribution, a true mean cannot be calculated if the actual values are unavailable. An approximate mean can be calculated by assuming that the observations in each class fall evenly throughout the class. This assumption enables us to use a class midpoint to represent the average value in the class. For instance, if the 92 banks failed evenly between 10 and 12 months, then the class midpoint of 11 months is the average time to failure for these 92 banks.

TABLE 2.2
Lingering Death

Length of time banks with "extremely high" risk of failure stayed open before failing, January 1, 1985 to May 10, 1991

Months	Number of Banks
0–3	74
4–6	53
7–9	62
10–12	92
13–18	95
19–30	51
31–58	10

Source: *Wall Street Journal*, September 23, 1991.

Table 2.2 shows seven classes, so $i = 1, 2, \ldots$ or 7. In general, the maximum number of classes is designated by c (in Table 2.2, $c = 7$). Let the ith class midpoint be m_i. The 10- to 12-month class is then the fourth class, and the midpoint of this class is $m_4 = 11$. The frequency of each m_i midpoint is denoted by f_i, so the frequency of the fourth class is $f_4 = 92$. The frequency f_i is the weight given to the class midpoint value m_i in the calculation of the data set mean. An approximate **weighted mean** may be calculated by multiplying each midpoint value (m_i) by its frequency weight (f_i). The sum of these c products is then divided by the sum of frequencies (which is the total number of observations, N or n).

A general statement of the population weighted mean for grouped data is

Population weighted mean

$$\mu_x = \frac{1}{N}\sum_{i=1}^{C} f_i m_i = (1/N)(f_1 m_1 + f_2 m_2 + \ldots + f_C m_C) \qquad (2.2a)$$

The sample weighted mean for grouped data is, likewise

Sample weighted mean

$$\bar{x} = \frac{1}{n}\sum_{i=1}^{C} f_i m_i = (1/n)(f_1 m_1 + f_2 m_2 + \ldots + f_C m_C) \qquad (2.2b)$$

The bank failure data in Table 2.2 might be viewed as population data because they represent all 437 banks that failed between January 1, 1985, and May 10, 1991. On the other hand, this is but a slice of time, so that bank failures during this period are only a subset of all such bank failures that could have occurred to the present day. Since we will be interested in making statements about all bank failures, these data will be treated as a sample because they do not include every bank failure to the present or into the future.

The data and calculations required for the approximate weighted mean in the case of bank failures are given in tabular form in Table 2.3, where all calculations were done using the computer spreadsheet program LOTUS 1-2-3. These calculations could have been done with any other computer spreadsheet (such as EXCEL or QUATTRO) or a hand-held calculator. The relevant quantities also can be arranged in algebraic form:

$$\bar{x} = (1/437)\sum_{i=1}^{7} f_i m_i = (1/437)[1.5(74) + 5.0(53) + 8.0(62) + 11.0(92) + 15.5(95) + 24.5(51) + 44.5(10)] = 11.55835$$

In some cases, we may not even know the size of the data set but we may know the relative frequencies of the classes. In such cases, alternatives to Formulas (2.2a) and (2.2b) can be employed. These alternatives are based on the relative frequency of each class. For the population, this formula is

Table 2.3 Calculation of a Weighted Mean for the Bank Failure Data

m_i Class Midpoints (months)	(f_i) Frequency of Banks Failing (number)	$f_i m_i$ Product of Frequency Times the Midpoint
1.5	74	111.0
5.0	53	265.0
8.0	62	496.0
11.0	92	1012.0
15.5	95	1472.5
24.5	51	1249.5
44.5	10	445.0
	$n = \Sigma f_i = 437$	$5051.0 = \Sigma f_i m_i$

Mean = 11.55835 = $\Sigma f_i m_i / n$

Population weighted mean

$$\mu = \sum_{i=1}^{c}(f_i/N)(m_i) = [(f_1/N)(m_1) + (f_2/N)(m_2) + \ldots(f_c/N)(m_c)] \quad (2.3a)$$

For the sample weighted mean, the frequency formula is

Sample weighted mean

$$\bar{x} = \sum_{i=1}^{c}(f_i/n)(m_i) = [(f_1/n)(m_1) + (f_2/n)(m_2) + \ldots(f_c/n)(m_c)] \quad (2.3b)$$

Notice that each term in these formulas already contains a division by the total number of observations because the relative frequency is the weight; thus, no additional division by N or n is involved after summing the c terms. As demonstrated later, to use these alternative formulas, we do not need to know the number of observations in the data set.

Comments on Approximating a Mean

The data in Table 2.2 and the weighted mean of 11.56 months in Table 2.3 support the House Banking Committee study that found that "regulators kept critically ill banks open an average of 10 to 12 months before failure," as reported in *The Wall Street Journal.* Our calculation is not exact, however.

First, we had to assume the boundaries of the class intervals, since they were not given. The class intervals are not of equal width, so the boundaries cannot be equally spaced. Assuming that the class boundaries are at the half-month points between identified class values implies that the boundaries of the "0–3" month class are –0.5 to 3.5 months, and the next "4–6" month class has boundaries of 3.5 to 6.5 months, and so on. In the case of the first class, however, this looks a bit strange, since –0.5 is not possible. On the other hand, if we assume that the bank failures occurred only at the monthly integer values in the classes, then these class boundaries are irrelevant. But why would bank failures occur only in exact monthly intervals?

Either of the above sets of assumptions are consistent with the 11.56-month average as an approximation of the mean that could be calculated with the raw data. As long as the data are only reported in frequency form, as they were in *The Wall Street Journal*, the correctness of any assumption regarding the placement of the data remains open to question.

Second, even if the House Banking Committee had access to the raw data, an average calculated from bank failures would be for those banks that failed within 58 months. We do not know what happened after 58 months. We do know from *The Wall Street Journal* article that "90% of the banks that received extended credit failed," but what about the other 10 percent? They are not included in the calculation of length of time before failure because they did not fail within the 58 months. But what if some of them failed at 158 months, and some at 258 months, and . . . ? This would greatly raise the average time to failure, yet the House Banking Committee study's average of 10 to 12 months before failure does not reflect these extremes.

Many widely cited averages involving data collected over time suffer from a truncation of the data before the underlying process has exhausted all possibilities. The average duration of unemployment, the expected life span, the mean time to complete a college education, and the mean time before tire failure are all examples of averages calculated from data for which the length of time or duration in a given condition may be cut off before extreme values are realized. Econometrician Nicholas Kiefer (1988) discusses problems in calculating means and other descriptive statistics when time-series data are "censored" by beginning the study period after the spell or process has started, by making observations at time intervals too wide to observe the spells, or by ending the study prior to the completion of spells. Means calculated with such data are always susceptible to these sampling problems.

Exact Method

If the actual values in a data set are reported with their respective frequencies or relative frequencies, then an exact mean may be calculated by weighting values by their respective relative frequencies. As an example, consider an instructor who assigns grades so that the top 13 percent of the students get A's (4 points), the next 25 percent get B's (3 points), the next 50 percent get C's (2 points), and the bottom 12 percent equally split D's (1 point) and F's (0 points).

The number of students who will finish the course is unknown in the first week of classes, so the mean grade at the end of the course cannot be calculated with frequencies as in Formula (2.2a). Because the relative frequencies of grades are known,

TABLE 2.4 Weighted Mean of Grades

Letter Grade	Numerical Grade (m_i)	f_i/N	$(f_i/N)m_i$
A	4	0.13	0.52
B	3	0.25	0.75
C	2	0.50	1.00
D	1	0.06	0.06
F	0	0.06	0.00
			Mean = 2.33

however, the mean grade can be determined by the alternative Formula (2.3a), where the calculations are

$$\mu = \sum_{i=1}^{5}(f_i/N)m_i = (.13)(4)+(.25)(3)+(.50)(2)+(.06)(1)+(.06)(0) = 2.33$$

Or, if done in a spreadsheet, they would appear as in Table 2.4.

No matter whether 100, 200, or 1,000 students complete the course, the average numerical grade will be 2.33. Furthermore, as long as the A, B, C, D, and F letter grade equivalents of 4, 3, 2, 1, and 0 do not represent midpoints of intervals (brought about by + and – letter grades), 2.33 is the exact mean.

EXERCISES

2.1 In what ways do the population parameter μ and sample statistic $\bar{x}$ differ?

2.2 What is the mean profit per partner in the 20 law firms identified in *The Wall Street Journal* (June 29, 1993) article cited in Exercise 1.25?

2.3 An August 4, 1992, article in *The Wall Street Journal* reported that "although there haven't been any major accidents since the Valdez disaster, about 4,700 gallons of oil or other liquids considered hazardous have been spilled along the (Alaskan pipe) line in 351 minor mishaps, according to data compiled by Alaska's Department of Environmental Conservation." What is the average spill per mishap? Why shouldn't information on the average spill be of great interest to environmentalists? What should they be interested in?

2.4 A *Wall Street Journal* (August 25, 1992) article reported that of the 17,000 members surveyed by the Texas State Teachers Federation, the average amount of their own money spent to buy classroom supplies the prior year was $242. What was the total size of the subsidy these teachers contributed for classroom supplies?

2.5 According to an article in *Business Week* (July 18, 1994), the American Medical Association is going to "include the salaries of 86,468 medical residents when figuring the average doctor's salary. Residents earn $20,000 to $30,000 a year, so that should lower the average physician's $177,000 salary considerably. Above the resident level, there are 564,000 doctors." This new AMA mean calculation is going to yield what approximate average value?

2.6 In its second annual ranking of women-owned businesses, *Working Woman* (May 1993) reported that there are 6.5 million such companies and that these women-owned businesses employed 12 million people, which is more than the roughly 11.7 million employed by the Fortune 500 companies.
   a. What is the mean workforce of the women-owned companies?
   b. What is the mean workforce of the Fortune 500 companies?

2.7 According to an article in the *Baltimore Sun* (January 8, 1995), Consumer Loan Advocates of Lake Bluff, Illinois, audited 14,442 adjustable home mortgages (ARMs) across the United States and discovered several different types of errors in half of them (ranging from inconsequential typos to recording and mathematical errors). "Among these errors, about two-thirds were overcharges, with an average of about $1,500."
   a. Errors were discovered in how many of the surveyed ARMs?
   b. How many of the surveyed ARMs involved no overcharges?
   c. If those with no overcharges were charged correctly, then what is the mean overcharge for all those surveyed?
   d. If those with no overcharges were charged correctly, then could the shape of the distribution of (exact or over) charges be bell shaped and symmetric? Explain.

2.5 THE MEDIAN AS A MEASURE OF CENTRAL TENDENCY

Median
The value that divides an ordered set of data into two parts, with the values of at least half of the data being less than or equal to the median and at least half of the data being greater than or equal to the median.

Most American workers believe they are better than average, according to Kennedy's column cited at the beginning of this chapter. Is it possible for more than 50 percent be above the mean? To answer this question, we must look at another summary measure of central location: the median.

The most common method of locating the median involves an ordering of the data from lowest value to highest. The median is then the middle value that splits the data into two equal halves. For example, suppose we want to find the middle value of the following seven observations:

9.0 lb, 2.5 lb, 5.5 lb, 6.0 lb, 2.0 lb, 1.5 lb, and 2.0 lb

The first step is to order the data from lowest to highest values:

1.5, 2.0, 2.0, 2.5, 5.5, 6.0, 9.0

The middle value in this ordered array is the fourth number, 2.5; thus, 2.5 lb is the median because three observations are less than 2.5 lb and three observations are greater than 2.5 lb.

The middle value can always be found by adding one to the total number of observations in the set of data and then dividing by two. That is, if there are N observations, the middle observation is $(N + 1)/2$. For $N = 7$, the middle observation is the fourth value in the ordered array since $(7 + 1)/2 = 4$.

For an *even* number of observations, there is no unique middle value. For an eight-observation set of data, for example, the middle observation would be the 4.5th, which does not exist; any value between the fourth and the fifth ordered value could work. In the ordered data set \$1, \$2, \$2, \$6, \$7, \$8, \$9, \$10, any value between \$6 and \$7 could serve as a median, even though there is no actual observation there. The value halfway between the two values that flank the median (\$6.50) is typically picked.

In both of the above examples, the medians of 2.5 lb and \$6.50 split their respective data sets into two equal pieces. The means of these data sets, however, do not equal these medians. In the first example, the mean is 4.07 lb, which is greater than the median. In the second example, the mean is \$5.625, which is less than the median. Thus, in the first example the majority of observations (four out of seven) are below the mean, and in the second the majority of observations (five out of eight) are above the mean. Clearly, the majority of observations (50 percent or more) can be above or below the mean if the median and mean are not the same value.

If the mean exceeds the median, the majority of observations will have values lower than the mean. If the median exceeds the mean, then most of the values will be greater than the mean.

The median is not well suited to describing the central location of some small data sets. For instance, the data set \$1, \$1, \$3 does not have a median that splits the data into two equal halves, although \$1 fulfills the definition of a median. At least half the values are equal to or less than \$1, and at least half the values are greater than or equal to \$1. Computer programs will force a median onto a data set even when the efficacy of imposing a median is dubious. Users of these programs are left with the problem of making sure the concept of the median is meaningful before attempting to compute one.

QUERY 2.2:

What is the median for the CEO compensation data in Table 2.1? How does it compare to the mean? Why might the median be preferred as a measure of the "typical" compensation?

ANSWER:

With the 18 company numbers and compensations (Total Pay) entered in columns A and B, and using the data sort command in EXCEL, the 18 comparable values are quickly ordered from lowest to highest.

Company #	Total Pay (in thousands of \$s)
10	476.3
15	650.0
12	671.4
16	1001.1
3	1038.0

(continued)

Company #	Total Pay (in thousands of $s)
5	1309.1
20	1449.9
2	1538.5
11	1601.5
8	1649.3
7	1727.2
6	1749.4
18	2153.4
14	2471.1
17	3325.8
4	3682.8
13	4664.9
9	9265.8

← 1625.4 Approximate Median

The two middle ordered values are 1601.5 and 1649.3; the median could be any value in between. We can therefore consider 1625.4, which is midway between, as the median compensation for CEOs of the energy corporations. A median salary of $1,625,400 is well below the mean of $2,245,900 for these CEOs. The majority of CEOs make less than the mean compensation of $2,245,900 because the mean is being pulled up by a few very high compensation packages, such as the $9,265,800 total paid to Lawrence G. Rawl at Exxon. For this reason, the median might be preferred to the mean as a measure of the typical compensation of these CEOs.

QUERY 2.3:
As a check on how your statistics computer program responds to a command for the median, request the descriptive statistics for the extremely small data set $1, $1, and $3.

ANSWER:
To get descriptive statistics from the MINITAB computer program, for example, enter the following statements (as given in lowercase after each uppercase prompt from MINITAB).

```
MTB> set c1
DATA> 1 1 3
DATA> end
MTB> describe "c1"

        N      MEAN    MEDIAN    TRMEAN    STDEV    SEMEAN
C1      3     1.667     1.000     1.667    1.155     0.667
      MIN       MAX        Q1        Q3
C1  1.000     3.000     1.000     3.000
```

In this printout, we have not yet discussed the STDEV (standard deviation) = 1.155, and the SEMEAN (standard error of the mean) = 0.667; these will be considered later in this chapter. The TRMEAN is the "trimmed mean," a mean that MINITAB calculates after discarding the top 5 percent and bottom 5 percent of the data to mitigate the effect of extreme values. This data set is so small, however, that this feature is not operational as seen by the equality of the TRMEAN and the MEAN = 1.667. Similarly, the program did not produce meaningful quartiles (Q1 and Q3), which will be discussed later in this chapter as the values that place 25 percent and 75 percent below them. The median produced by the program, MEDIAN = 1.000, is likewise of little value because the data set is so small. Ideally, half the values would be above and half the values below the median, but here no values are smaller than $1 and one value ($3) is larger.

2.6 LOCATING THE MEDIAN IN GROUPED DATA

Median Class
The first class to have a cumulative relative frequency of 50 percent or more; it is the class that contains the median.

Determination of a median can be especially trying if only frequency distributions are available and the original raw data values cannot be retrieved. A **median class** in a frequency distribution is easy to find; it is the first class to have a cumulative relative frequency of 50 percent or more. Determining the actual median value within the median class, however, is impossible without the original values; it must be approximated.

In the case of unemployment duration shown in Table 2.5, the median class is five to 15 weeks. This class is the first interval for which the cumulative relative frequency is 50 percent or more (78.12 percent of the distribution is below 15 weeks). That is, the five- to 15-week class contains the middle value, which is between the 3,437th and 3,438th ordered observation [(N+1)/2 = (6874 + 1)/2 = 3437.5].

The actual median value that is buried within the median class interval in Table 2.5 is not apparent because the original values are not given. By assuming that the values are spread evenly throughout the median class, however, we can approximate a median by algebraic interpolation. An alternative procedure to approximate the median is to use the ogive graph. Both these procedures are illustrated.

Algebraic Approximation of the Median

The cumulative frequency up to the lower boundary of the median class was 3,169 persons (or 46.1 percent of the data). The median, as already determined, is the value of

TABLE 2.5 Unemployment Duration in 1990 (thousands of persons)

Duration	Frequency of Duration	Relative Frequency of Duration	Cumulative Relative Frequency of Duration	
less than 5 weeks	3169	0.461012	0.461012	
5 to 15 weeks	2201	0.320192	0.781204	← Median Class
15 to 27 weeks	809	0.117689	0.898894	
27 weeks and over	695	0.101105	1.000000	
	6874	1.000000		

Source: *Economic Report of the President*, February 1992, p. 342.

the 3,437.5th observation. Thus the median value must be 268.5 observations (that is, 3,437.5 – 3,169) into the median class. There are 2,201 observations in the median class of five to 15 weeks. If these 2,201 observations are evenly distributed within the class, then the median is 12.2 percent (268.5/2201) of the way into the median class. Because the median class is 10 weeks wide (15 – 5), the approximate median is found about 1.22 weeks (that is, 0.122 × 10) into the median class. An approximate median is thus 6.22 weeks (5 + 1.22).

From this example a formula can be derived for finding the median in grouped data:

$$\text{Median} \cong L + (o_1/o_2)(U - L) \tag{2.4}$$

where L is the low boundary of the median class (e.g., 5 weeks),
U is the upper bound of the median class (e.g., 15 weeks),
o_1 is the number of observations into the median class until the median is found (e.g., 268.5), and
o_2 is the number of observations in the median class (e.g., 2201).

To assess the magnitude of error in using Formula (2.4), compare the approximate median of 6.2 weeks with the actual median duration of unemployment of 5.4 weeks as reported by the Department of Labor, U.S. Bureau of Labor Statistics. The difference between this reported median calculated from raw data and the approximation from Formula (2.4) reflects the critical nature of the assumption that the observations within the median class (o_2) are evenly distributed. In the case of unemployment duration, apparently they are not; the observations in the median class must be more concentrated at the lower end.

Graphical Approximation of the Median

Instead of assuming an even distribution of observations within the median class, an alternative graphical method is to use the cumulative relative frequency distribution and its ogive. From a starting point at 0.5 on the vertical axis, a horizontal line is drawn to the ogive with a vertical line then drawn to the horizontal axis. The connecting value on the horizontal axis is the approximate median. This procedure is shown in Figure 2.1, where the approximate median value read from the horizontal axis is about 5.4.

There are other methods of approximating medians when the data are in frequency form. If extremely accurate measures of the median are required, however, the analyst should get the original raw data.

QUERY 2.4:
The Wall Street Journal article on bank failures summarized at the beginning of this chapter reported that "90% of the banks that received extended credit failed" within a 58-month time period; the frequency of failures is given in Table 2.2. Construct a frequency distribution showing the number of months before failure of all the troubled banks that received extended credit. What are the mean and the median of

FIGURE 2.1 Median Location on the Ogive for the Distribution of Unemployment Duration

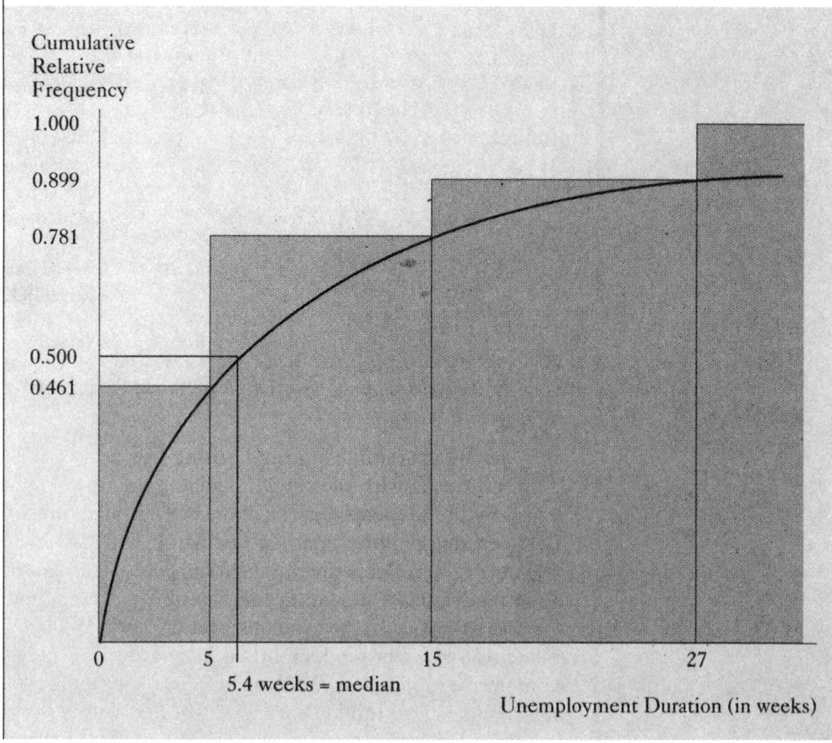

this distribution? Why is one of these measures of central tendency preferred to the other in this case?

ANSWER:

Because 437 banks represent 90 percent of all these troubled banks, there must have been some 486 such banks ($0.9x = 437$, so $x = 437/0.9 = 485.55$). Because the actual number and time until failure of the 49 banks that had not failed in 58 months is unknown, the mean cannot be approximated for all 486 banks. Thus, the mean is not relevant in this case. The complete frequency distribution, the portion of the cumulative frequency distribution needed to approximate the median, and the approximate median are

Months to Failure	Number of Banks	Cumulative Frequency	
0–3	74	74	
4–6	53	127	
7–9	62	189	
10–12	92	281	← Median class: The median is the value of the 243.5 observation [(486+1)/2]. Assuming an even distribution of data within this class, the approximate median is located 59.2 percent of the way into the class. The approximate median is 11.3 months [(0.592)(12.5 – 9.5) + 9.5].
13–18	95		
19–30	51		
31–58	10		
59 or more or never failed	49		
	486		

From this frequency distribution, we know that about 50 percent of all the troubled banks failed within 11.3 months after being designated as troubled and receiving emergency extended credit.

QUERY 2.5:

Acting under the Oil Pollution Act of 1990, the National Oceanic and Atmospheric Administration invited six economists, including two Nobel Prize winners, to assist in writing damage-assessment rules for oil spills. The economists concluded that contingent-value measures of passive use of the environment by those who may never see or use an affected area (such as Prince William Sound prior to the Exxon Valdez oil spill) can produce initial estimates for a judicial process of damage assessment. As reported in *The New York Times* (September 6, 1993), the state of Alaska commissioned a $3 million survey of 1,043 randomly selected people in 50 states to see what Americans would pay to avoid a repeat of the 1989 Valdez disaster. The sample median response was $31, from which the state of Alaska inferred that all households in the United States collectively would be willing to pay $2.8 billion—the damages it ascribed to Exxon. The sample mean of $94, implied even higher damages of $8.6 billion. Although this contingent survey was never tested in the courts, because the liability suit was settled for $1 billion before the survey was introduced as evidence, what is the difference in the interpretation that can be given to the median and mean in these damage calculations?

ANSWER:

Interpreted as the answer to a popularity survey or a referendum, the $2.8 billion inferred median represents the amount that the majority of U.S. households would vote to pay to prevent another oil spill. Interpreted as a market survey or market outcome, and the mean suggests that households would collectively pay $8.6 billion to buy a spill-free environment for Prince William Sound.

2.7 The Mode as a Measure of Central Tendency

Mode
The mode is the most frequently occurring value.

The **mode** is a third measure of central tendency or central location of the data. It is the value that occurs most frequently. It provides the answer to questions such as: What fan belt size is most often requested in an auto parts store? What is the most common teaching load at the University of Wisconsin? What is the customary workweek for a real estate agent?

In the set of data 9.0 lb, 2.5 lb, 5.5 lb, 6.0 lb, 2.0 lb, 1.5 lb, and 2.0 lb, the mode is 2.0 lb because it occurs most often. For this seven-item data set, the median is 2.5 lb and the mean is 4.07 lb; thus, the mode is less than the median, which in turn is less than the mean. As will be shown later in this chapter, this is the anticipated ordering of these three measures of central tendency for large data sets, with continuous measurements along a number line where there is only one modal value and only a few high values pull up the mean. If a few low values are pulling the mean down, then the mean is expected to be less than the median, which in turn is expected to be less than the mode.

For data sets with discrete values, as in all the data sets described so far in this chapter, or for those with more than one mode, the position of the mode(s) relative to the median and mean need not be consistent with the above anticipated pattern. In the data set $1, $2, $2, $6, $7, $8, $9, $10, a median is $6.50 and the mean is $5.625. Although the mean is being pulled down by a few low values, those two low values of $2 happen also to be the mode.

Because the mode does not take account of the magnitude of the values involved, it is not a good indication of the middle of a set of data. In the above two data sets, the number 2 was the mode in each even though its relative contribution to the sum of the eight values was different in the two sets. Reporting the mode by itself can be misleading. For instance, in the spring of 1992, an administrator at the University of Wisconsin told a legislator that the most frequent teaching load on the Madison campus was two courses a semester. Such a fact could be consistent with a mean and median teaching load well above or below two courses a semester.

Unimodal Distribution
A distribution with one mode.

Bimodal Distribution
A distribution with two modes.

Trimodal Distribution
A distribution with three modes.

Distributions that have a single mode are called **unimodal.** Those with two modes are **bimodal,** and those with three modes are **trimodal.** A frequency distribution can have only one mean but there is no limit to the number of modes that it may have. Some data sets do not even have one well-defined mode. For instance, the CEO compensation data in Table 2.1 does not have a well-defined mode because each value occurs only once.

Modal Class
The class in a frequency distribution with the most occurrences in it.

Finally, if data are grouped into classes, a **modal class** is defined as that with the greatest frequency. In Table 2.2, for example, 95 banks failed in 13 to 18 weeks, which is the interval with the highest frequency and is thus the modal class. Without having the raw data, however, we cannot know if this interval contains the exact mode or if there are one, two, three, or even more modes.

Historical Perspective

Strange as it may seem today, arithmetic and graphical techniques for describing data once had a terrible reputation. They were viewed as tools used by social reformers to denigrate the doctrines of free will and individual responsibility and by scoundrels to mislead and obscure truth.

According to Stephen Stigler (1986, pp. 169–172), one of the most controversial concepts has been "the average man," or, as his creator Adolphe Quetelet labeled him, "l'homme moyen." Quetelet was born in Belgium in 1796; he became a mathematician, an astronomer, and then a sociologist. He created the notion of the "average man" in 1835 as a fictional being, never imagining that this idea would take on a life of its own and live on in newspaper headlines and corporate board rooms. It has become the means to disguise the identity of individuals. More important for the social sciences, Quetelet provided the key notion and framework for separating the fixed (that felt in common by all) from the random (individual) determinants of behavior.

William Playfair (1759–1823) introduced and developed the fundamental rules for graphical representation of quantitative data. His goal was to replace tables of numbers with visual representations of his "linear arithmetic." However, graphing involves many diverse skills. The visual needs of art, the accuracy of drafting, the rigors of mathematics, and the fuzziness of social science concepts did not mix well in the minds of established scholars of the time.

Famed nursing pioneer and hospital reformer Florence Nightingale (1820–1910) was a leading advocate of Quetelet's "social physics" and Playfair's visual representation of data. She invented the "coxcomb" diagram, the forerunner of a pie chart, in which the magnitude being represented is proportional to the area of a wedge in a circular diagram. To her, average mortality rates in the general public were the measures against which average death rates in the military should be compared. She used data and graphs in defiance of the prevailing doctrine of John Stuart Mill and Charles Dickens, who viewed statistics as dehumanizing and characteristic of "a deadly statistical clock" that was an anathema of individualism.

The proper use of numbers and graphs to represent social phenomena continued to be debated well into the twentieth century. As reflected in the popular book by Darrell Huff, *How to Lie With Statistics* (1954), much of post-World War II academic interest in descriptive statistics and graphs focused on debunking false calculations and improperly drawn graphs that were designed to fool naive readers. Descriptive statistics and graphs were viewed as devices either for showing the obvious to the ignorant or obscuring the truth from the informed. Credit for demonstrating the absurdity of these myths goes to world-renowned statistician John Tukey.

In the 1970s, Tukey demonstrated how graphs can be used as tools of analysis, and he created new types of graphs to explore large and complex data sets. The advent of inexpensive computer programs in the 1980s enabled the further development of graphical techniques in data analysis. Today, descriptive statistics and graphical analysis are key components in the use of nonparametric statistical techniques, a few of which are introduced in later chapters of this book.

In the world of manufacturing, W. Edwards Deming used histograms and quality control charts demonstrated in this chapter to convince Japanese engineers and executives that statistical methods could be used to overcome the post-World War II belief that "made in Japan" meant "cheap junk." Deming was a statistician on the faculty at New York University when he advanced the process control tools that helped Japanese manufacturers achieve a new reputation. Curiously, however, major U.S. manufacturers were not willing to follow the example of Japan until the late 1980s. For years, Japanese firms have been competing among themselves to win the annual Deming Medal. It wasn't until 1988 that American firms began competing for the Malcolm Baldrige National Quality Award, given annually to the company making the greatest advances in improved product quality and customer satisfaction.

Total Quality Management (TQM) is no longer viewed as a panacea by which companies can dash past their competitors, as reflected in numerous articles with titles like "The Cost of Quality: Faced with hard times business sours on 'Total Quality Management'" (*Newsweek*, September 7, 1992). Florida Power & Light, winner of Japan's Deming Prize for quality management slashed its program because of excessive paperwork. Less than two years after winning the 1990 U.S. Commerce Department's Baldrige award, the Houston oil-supply company Wallace Co. filed for Chapter 11 bankruptcy protection. These disappointments have not discouraged the numerous quality control gurus who continue to crisscross the United States selling their total quality management techniques to large and small firms alike. Clearly, a knowledge of statistics is required to ferret out the useful from the wasteful business practices being advanced in the name of TQM.

2.8 Percentiles, Deciles, and Quartiles

pth Percentile
The pth percentile is the value of the observation for which p percent of the observed values are equal to or less than it.

First Quartile (or lower quartile)
The 25th percentile defines the lowest quartile of a distribution; the value for which one quarter of the values are equal to or lower.

Third Quartile (or upper quartile)
The 75th percentile of a distribution.

Second Quartile
The 50th percentile is the second quartile of a distribution.

The use of proportions in the description of data is not restricted to qualitative data. We already have seen that cumulative relative frequencies describe the proportion of quantitative observations up to a numerical value. Percentiles, deciles, and quartiles identify special values by their relative positions in the set of data. The **pth percentile** is the value for which p percent of the data set is less than or equal to the value. The typical percentiles cited in research are the 25th, 50th, and the 75th percentiles. These three percentiles are referred to as the quartiles. The **first quartile** is the 25th percentile; the **third quartile** is 75th percentile. The **second quartile** is the 50th percentile, which for large data sets is also the approximate median. Although not commonly reported, **deciles** are defined by the 10th, 20th, 30th, . . . and 90th percentiles.

Like the median, the percentile, decile, and quartile values for small data sets and grouped data may not be unique and well defined. For example, Table 2.6 gives the relative frequencies and cumulative relative frequencies for the U.S. Census age groups in Figure 2.2. The 25th percentile (and first quartile) can be seen to be an age of slightly less than 18 years, because the cumulative relative frequency up to age 18 years is 0.255737. The 50th percentile (fifth decile and second quartile), as with the median, is in the age interval 25 to 45 years, but we cannot determine it exactly because the original data are camouflaged by the grouping. (From other current population reports of census data, the median age in 1990 is known to be 32.9 years.) Similarly, the 75th percentile (third quartile) is in the 45–55 age interval, but without the original data

Table 2.6
1990 U.S. Census by Age

Age Group	1990 Population	Relative Frequency	Cumulative Relative Frequency
less than 5	18,354,443	0.073798	0.073798
5 to 18	45,249,989	0.181938	0.255737
18 to 25	26,737,766	0.107505	0.363243
25 to 45	80,754,835	0.324694	0.687938
45 to 55	25,223,086	0.101415	0.789353
55 to 65	21,147,923	0.085030	0.874384
65 to 75	18,106,558	0.072801	0.947186
75 to 85	10,055,108	0.040429	0.987615
85 +	3,080,165	0.012384	1.000000
	248,709,873	1.000000	

Decile
The first decile is the value that puts one-tenth of the values at or below it; the second decile puts two-tenths of the values at or below it, etc.

we can only approximate it by making an assumption about the position of observations within this class (as evenly distributed or following an ogive, for example).

Query 2.6:
Find the first, second and third quartiles, for the CEO compensation data in Table 2.1, and assess their distances from the median.

Answer:
Using the data sort command in LOTUS 1-2-3, the 18 comparable observations on CEO compensation can be ordered quickly.

Original Company #	Total Pay (in thousands of $s)	
9	9265.8	
13	4664.9	
4	3682.8	
17	3325.8	
14	2471.1	← Third Quartile
18	2153.4	
6	1749.4	
7	1727.2	
8	1649.3	
11	1601.5	← Second Quartile
2	1538.5	
20	1449.9	
5	1309.1	
3	1038.0	← First Quartile
16	1001.1	
12	671.4	
15	650.0	
10	476.3	

The median, as determined in Query 2.2, is $1,625,400, which is also the 50th percentile and second quartile. The 25th and 75th percentiles are the values of the 4.5 and 13.5 observations, which of course do not exist. As approximations, either $1,019,550 or $1,038,000 may be specified as the first quartile and $2,312,250 or $2,471,100 may be set as the third quartile.

2.9 Skewness

Skewness
A measure of the degree of asymmetry of a distribution.

Positively (or right) Skewed Distribution
An asymmetric distribution in which the mean is greater than the median.

Negatively (or left) Skewed Distribution
An asymmetric distribution in which the mean is less than the median.

Symmetric Distribution
A distribution in which the mean and median are the same value.

Knowing all three measures of central tendency can suggest the shape of a frequency distribution. A relationship between the measures of central location and the shape of the distribution is described by **skewness.** In general, distributions that have a mean value greater than the median are **positively (or right) skewed** and those with a mean value less than the median are **negatively (or left) skewed.** If the mean is the same value as the median, the distribution is said to be **symmetric.**

If a data set is large (infinite) with no breaks in the data (continuous), and if the distribution is right-skewed, with only a single mode, then the mean will exceed the median, and both the mean and median will be greater than the mode. As stated earlier, the mean exceeds the median because a few large values, in the upper tail pull up the mean. Such a right-skewed distribution is Figure 2.2, panel a. For a left-skewed unimodal distribution, the mean will be less than the median and the mode will exceed both the mean and median. The mean is less than the median because a few low values in the lower tail pull the mean down, as depicted in Figure 2.2, panel b. Because the median is not influenced by extreme values in the tails, it is often preferred to the mean as a measure of central tendency for highly skewed data sets.

A unimodal, continuous, and symmetric distribution will have a bell shape for which the mean, median, and mode will all be equal, as shown in Figure 2.2, panel c. For symmetric distributions, whether the mean or median is used as the measure of central tendency is irrelevant since they are the same value.

Exercises

2.8 When are the mean, median, and mode the same value?

2.9 What assumptions are necessary when calculating the mean and median with grouped data?

2.10 In a sample of nine job qualifying exams, applicants scored 50, 35, 40, 65, 80, 90, 95, 85, 70.
   a. What is the mean score?
   b. What is the median score?
   c. What is (are) the mode(s)?

FIGURE 2.2 Measures of Central Tendency and Skewness

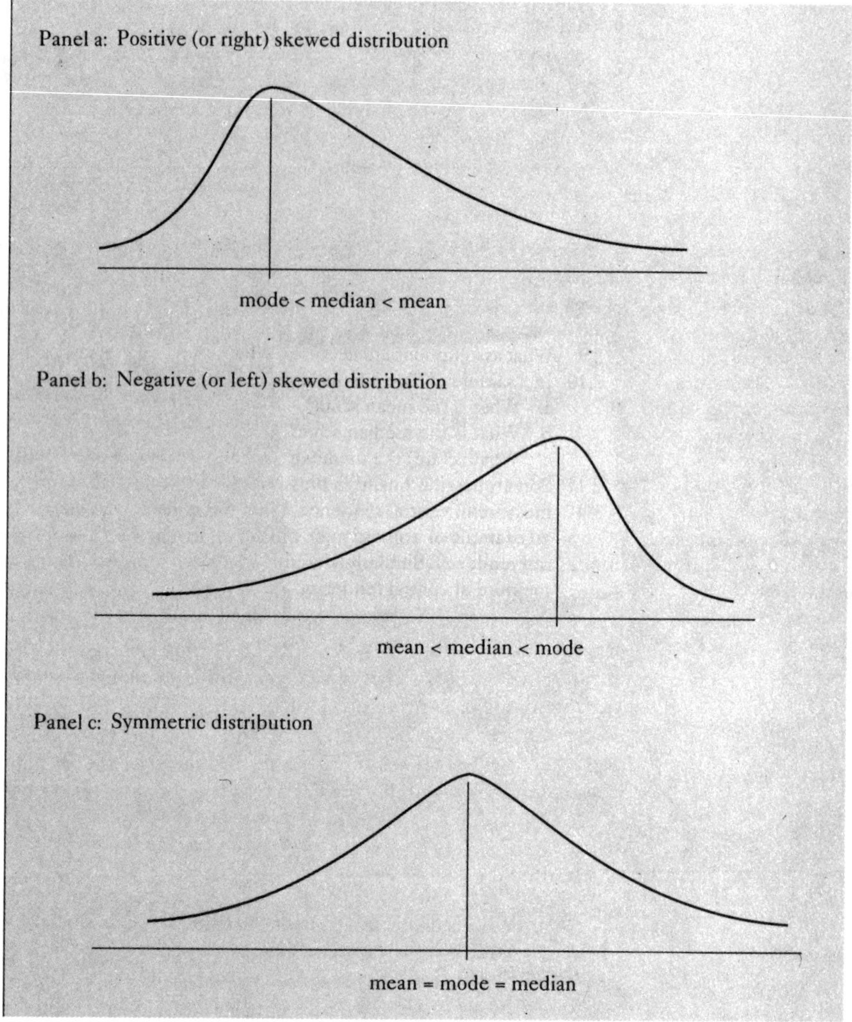

2.11 In an article titled "Maybe They Should Call them 'Scammers,'" *Business Week* (January 16, 1995) reports that an official with the Morris County Office of Weights & Measures found mistakes at the electronic checkout scanning system at Bradlees, Inc., store in East Hanover, N.J. "In all, six of 17 items in his cart have the wrong price in the scanner, resulting in an overcharge of $12.30 on a $161.85 total purchase." These overcharges where identified as

	Advertised	Charged	Difference
Tiger Trail Nail Trimmer	$6.99	$ 7.99	$1.00
Harper's Beefhide Bone	3.99	4.49	0.50
Friskies Frisbie Rawhide	3.49	3.99	0.50
Allison Key Holder	1.29	2.39	1.10
Parker 2"x2" Adhesive	1.49	2.69	1.20
Criterion Queen Sheet Set	21.99	29.99	8.00

a. What is the mean overcharge for the 6 items?
b. What is the median overcharge for the 6 items?
c. What is the mode overcharge for the 6 items?
d. What is the mean overcharge for 17 items?
e. Why does the notion of a median for all 17 items have little meaning?

2.12 A salesperson for a large corporation had the following credit card balances on her different cards at the indicated interest rate.

Amount of Loan	Interest Rate
$ 250	19.0%
425	18.5%
1,200	17.0%
235	16.5%
110	16.0%
750	15.5%
935	15.0%

a. What is the mean and the median interest rate paid by this person?
b. What is the shape of the distribution of interest rates?

2.13 The *DeVoe Report* (June 2, 1980) quoted then U.S. President Jimmy Carter as saying "half the people in this country are living below the median income—and this is intolerable." What is disputable and what is true in this quote?

2.14 In sailboat racing, rule violations are handled by the local yacht club. Anyone involved in a protest who is not satisfied with the results may appeal to the U.S. Sailing Association. The frequency distributions for the time to process appeals in 1989, 1990, and 1991 are in Exercise 1.39. Approximate the median time to process appeals for each of the three years. What does a comparison of medians show? Why wouldn't a comparison of means be appropriate or even possible from these data?

2.15 Below is information on supermarket sales and market share for the leading sports drinks, from *The Wall Street Journal* (September 29, 1992). What are the mean and median sales for these 11 products? Which is a better representation of sales of a representative product in the sports drink market? Explain.

Sports Drink	Sales 52 Weeks to 7/12/93 (millions)	Market Share 52 Weeks to 7/12/92	Sales Growth 1/1/92–7/12/92
Gatorade	$288.3	85.2%	+7%
Gatorade Light	14.6	4.3	+ 16
10-K	12.2	3.6	—
PowerBurst	6.7	2.0	–72
Private label	4.2	1.2	–19
1st Ade	2.6	0.8	–1
All Sport	1.7	0.5	+451
Joggin' in a Jug	1.6	0.5	+138
Enduro	1.2	0.4	–45
Body Works	0.9	0.3	+6
Spike	0.4	0.1	+182

Source: Information Resources Inc.

2.16 On the following page is a Computer Associates' advertisement that appeared in *PC Magazine* (June 30, 1992). Determine a median for each of the three spreadsheets. Why is the median better than the mean as a measure of central tendency for this data?

2.17 *The Wall Street Journal* (October 27, 1992) reported that of the 94 patients treated for skin cancer (melanoma lesions), "the average time from their surgery and injection to the recurrence of melanoma was 30 months." Is it clear whether "the average time" pertains to the mean or the median? Why might the mean time from injection to recurrence be higher than 30 months, regardless of whether "the average time" pertains to the mean or the median? Why might the median time before recurrence be a better measure of successful treatment than the mean?

2.18 *The Wall Street Journal* (October 27, 1992) article on skin cancer quoted Dr. Donald L. Morton as saying "that of the 136 patients who were vaccinated, half have survived for 23 months or longer compared with an average survival of 7.3 months for unvaccinated melanoma patients in similar advanced states of the disease." Do you suspect that Morton is using the "average survival" wording to refer to the mean or median survival?

2.19 Exercise 1.20 required the drawing of the ogive for the Census Bureau data showing that in 1989 the poorest 20 percent of the population of married couples with children had cash income under $22,700; the next 20 percent had income under $34,100; the middle 20 percent had income under $45,500; the next 20 percent had income up to $62,200; and the richest 20 percent had income over $62,200. Use this ogive to estimate the median income.

VARBUSINESS Spreadsheet Report Card

	CA-SuperCalc	Lotus 1-2-3	Microsoft Excel
Ease of use	7.30	6.50	7.11
Memory Requirement	7.00	5.41	6.14
Ease of programming	6.48	5.86	6.26
Ability to manipulate data	7.31	6.71	7.00
Sorting capabilities	7.50	6.64	6.68
Provision for software security	6.96	5.25	5.10
Report writing capabilities	6.78	5.33	6.17
Ease of use of interface	7.45	6.19	6.77
Software integration capabilities	7.30	6.23	6.78
Ease of data retrieval	7.50	6.78	7.00
Satisfaction with product profitability	6.81	5.75	6.42
Overall quality of product	7.70	7.18	7.53
Provision for customer support	7.52	5.79	6.22
Charges for training time	6.43	5.60	5.71
Provision for technical support	7.34	5.55	5.95
Provision for marketing support	6.69	5.71	5.93
Documentation & product information	6.90	6.70	6.98
Frequency of updates & revisions	6.59	5.75	6.15
OVERALL AVERAGE	7.09	6.05	6.44

2.10 Measures of Dispersion

As already discussed in assessing skewness, differences in the mean, median, and mode convey information about the distribution. The distance between certain data points and an average measure of dispersion is relevant for decision makers. In fact, a 1992 television ad for the Lexus automobile portrayed the uniformity of the distance between the fenders and trunk lid, engine hood, and the doors by having a marble roll around the car as the car was turned in a giant vise. Because the assembly process of the Lexus is near perfect, very little variation in the clearance was evident as the marble moved.

Obviously, door-fender and hood-fender clearances do not have to be as precise as on a Lexus for daily operation. At some point, however, the width of these clearances on even the cheapest car could be too wide or too narrow to permit the doors, hood and trunk lid to operate easily. The Lexus ads make it clear that Lexus management has decided to make the width of the door-fender, hood-fender, and trunk lid-fender clearances and their variability an important part of overall Lexus quality assessment.

Data width can be measured in several different ways; two such ways are the distance between two points and the average dispersion. The remaining sections of this chapter consider two types of distance measures (range and interquartile range) and two types of average dispersion (variance and the standard deviation).

2.11 THE RANGE

The simplest measure of variability is the range. The range is the difference between the largest and smallest values in a set of data. After the data are ordered from lowest to highest, the range is the difference between the two extremes. In the energy company CEO pay example, Table 2.1, the lowest comparable yearly compensation was that of Ron W. Haddock of FINA ($476,300) and the highest compensation was received by Lawrence G. Rawl of Exxon ($9,265,800). Thus, the range of comparable compensation packages was $8,789,500.

FIGURE 2.3 **Same Range with Different Dispersions**

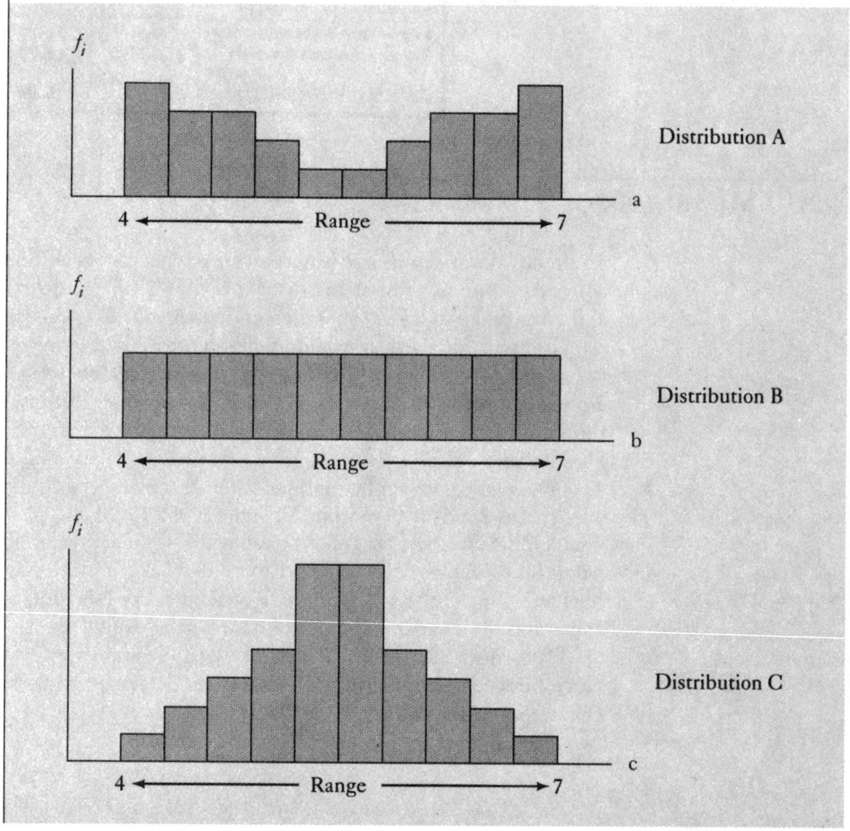

Although the range is easy to calculate, it is not used much outside of quality control work. One reason why the range is often ignored is that distributions may have the same range but yet appear different in terms of observable dispersion. All three distributions in Figure 2.3, for instance, have the same mean ($\mu = 5.5$) and the same range ($7 - 4 = 3$). Yet, distribution A appears to be more "variable" or "spread out" or "diverse" than distribution B, and distribution B appears more diverse than distribution C.

A second reason why the range is not used extensively is that it is sensitive to the sample size, as noted earlier. As the sample size increases, the range tends to grow, as well. The influence of sample sizes may be removed by dividing the range by the sample size n. As discussed in the next sections, however, the range divided by the sample size is not a common measure of average dispersion. It is still sensitive to extreme values and insensitive to other values.

2.12 The Interquartile Range and the Box Plot

Another measure of distance between data points is the interquartile range, which is the difference between the third and first quartiles. Because the third quartile is the 75th percentile and the first quartile is the 25th percentile, the interquartile range gives the middle 50 percent of the data. An advantage of using the interquartile range is that it can be calculated from frequency data that have open-ended class intervals, whereas the range can not. For instance, Figure 2.4 contains a histogram from the *Occupational Outlook Handbook* (first published by the U.S. Bureau of Labor Statistics). It shows that

Figure 2.4

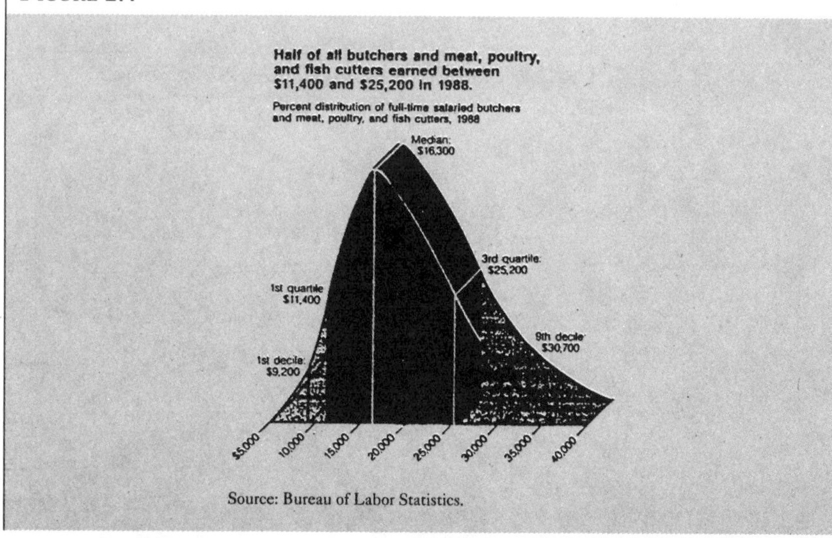

Source: Bureau of Labor Statistics.

"half of all butchers and meat, poultry, and fish cutters earned between $11,400 and $25,000 in 1988."

The *Handbook* also uses interquartile ranges to show how annual salaries differ across and within occupations. For instance, Figure 2.5 provides a *Handbook* box plot that shows the interquartile range of salaries for eight levels of engineers, five levels of

FIGURE 2.5 Box Plot for Salaries

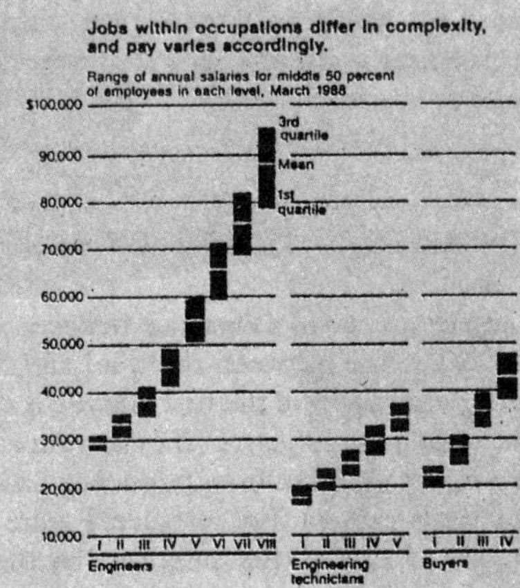

Source: Bureau of Labor Statistics.

FIGURE 2.6 Box Plot for CEO Compensation

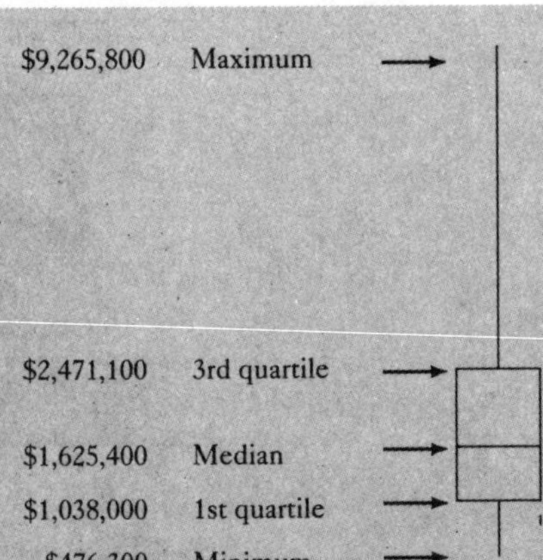

engineering technicians, and four levels of buyers. These interquartile salary levels, as indicated by each boxed area, reflect differences in experience, starting with entry-level jobs and continuing up the career ladder to the most complex and responsible supervisory positions within the occupation.

Because the mean is pulled in the direction of the extreme tail values, box plots are often centered on the median. In fact, in 1952 when Mary Eleanor Spear invented the "range bar," which John Tukey popularized as the box plot, she used the median as the center of the data. This more standard box plot is shown in Figure 2.6 for the CEO compensation data for which we derived the quartiles in Query 2.6. The right skewness of these data is apparent in the long "whisker" extending from the top of the box and the median being closer to the first quartile than to the second quartile in the box.

2.13 Variance and Standard Deviations

Variance
The average of squared differences between values and their mean.

The most common average measures of dispersion are the **variance** and the standard deviation. Although the conceptual definition of a variance is the same for populations and samples, the method of calculation is slightly different. Calculation of both population and sample variances begins by subtracting the mean from each value in the data set; those individual differences, which are called deviations, are then squared and summed. For the population, the sum of squared deviations is divided by the population size (N). For a sample, the sum of squared deviations is divided by the sample size minus one ($n - 1$). The reason for the division by $n - 1$ for sample data versus division by N for population data will be addressed briefly in this chapter but in more detail in Chapter 8.

To illustrate the calculation of a variance, consider the 18 comparable values of CEO compensation in Table 2.1. The mean of this data set was calculated to be $2,245,861, or, in the units of measurement used in *The Wall Street Journal,* 2245.861 thousands of dollars; thus, the 18 deviations from the mean are

$x_i - \bar{x}$		
1538.5	− 2245.861 =	−707.361
1038.0	− 2245.861 =	−1207.861
3682.8	− 2245.861 =	1436.939
1309.1	− 2245.861 =	−936.761
1749.4	− 2245.861 =	−496.461
1727.2	− 2245.861 =	−518.661
1649.3	− 2245.861 =	−596.561
9265.8	− 2245.861 =	7019.939
476.3	− 2245.861 =	−1769.561
1601.5	− 2245.861 =	−644.361
671.4	− 2245.861 =	−1574.461
4664.9	− 2245.861 =	2419.039
2471.1	− 2245.861 =	225.239

(continued)

$x_i - \bar{x}$ (continued)
650.0 − 2245.861 = −1595.861
1001.1 − 2245.861 = −1244.761
3325.8 − 2245.861 = 1079.939
2153.4 − 2245.861 = −92.461
1449.9 − 2245.861 = −795.961
0.000

Because of the magnitude of these chief executives' compensation, the 18 deviations from the mean cannot be easily calculated with a hand-held calculator. A spreadsheet program, such as LOTUS 1-2-3 or EXCEL, is best suited to confirm the above arithmetic. Notice that as a check of the arithmetic, the sum of deviations from the mean must sum to zero, assuming no rounding error. That is,

$$\text{Sum of deviations} = \sum_{i=1}^{18}\left(x_i - \bar{x}\right) = \left(1538.5 - 2245.861\right) + \ldots$$
$$\ldots + \left(1449.9 - 2245.861\right) = 0$$

Because the sum of deviations is always zero (regardless of the shape of the distribution), this sum is not meaningful as a measure of dispersion. Squaring each of these deviations, however, removes the negative signs. Therefore, summing the *squared* deviations from the mean does provide a measure of variability that will differ from distribution to distribution—the more variability in the distribution, the larger the sum of squared deviations from the mean. As shown in Table 2.7, the sum of squared devia-

Table 2.7 Sample Variance of the Energy Companies CEO Compensation

	x_i	$(x_i - \bar{x})$	$(x_i - \bar{x})^2$
	1538.5	−707.361	500359.742
	1038.0	−1207.861	1458928.464
	3682.8	1436.939	2064793.370
	1309.1	−936.761	877521.379
	1749.4	−496.461	246473.635
	1727.2	−518.661	269009.348
	1649.3	−596.561	355885.159
	9265.8	7019.939	49279542.004
	476.3	−1769.561	3131346.526
	1601.5	−644.361	415201.242
	671.4	−1574.461	2478927.790
	4664.9	2419.039	5851749.146
	2471.1	225.239	50732.557
	650.0	−1595.861	2546772.686
	1001.1	−1244.761	1549430.224
	3325.8	1079.939	1166268.004
	2153.4	−92.461	8549.057
	1449.9	−795.961	633554.090
Column sum =	40425.5	0.000	72885044.423

Variance of x = 72885044.423/17 = 4287355.554

tions from the mean for the CEO compensation data is 72885044.423; again, this is a sum easily obtained with a computer spreadsheet program:

$$\text{Sum of squared deviations} = \sum_{i=1}^{18}(x_i - \bar{x})^2 = (1538.5 - 2245.861)^2 + \ldots + (1449.9 - 2245.861)^2 = 72885044.423$$

Sample Variance (s^2)
The average of squared deviations of values in a sample that are free to vary after the sample mean is fixed at its value in a specific sample; a statistic designated by a letter s squared, s^2.

Population Variance (σ^2)
The average of squared deviations of population values from the population mean for a population; a parameter designated by the Greek letter "sigma" squared, σ^2.

Parameter
A numerical value that describes a characteristic of a population (e.g., the mean (μ) is a parameter that gives central location).

Sample Mean ($\bar{x}$)
The arithmetic average of a sample; a measure of central location identified by the symbol "ex-bar," $\bar{x}$.

Statistic
A numerical value describing a characteristic of a sample as a function of the sample values.

Finally, the sample variance is obtained by dividing the sum of squared deviations by 17 (that is, by $n - 1$):

$$\text{Sample variance} = \frac{\text{Sum of squared deviations}}{\text{Sample size minus one}} = \frac{72885044.423}{17} = 4287355.554$$

Unlike the variance of the population that has a single and fixed mean μ, the mean of a sample $\bar{x}$ varies from sample to sample. That is, two samples from the same population need not have the same mean. As demonstrated in Chapter 8, when the sample mean is treated as a unique value within a single sample, only $n - 1$ of the values in that sample can be treated as if they were freely determined.

A **sample variance** is designated by s^2. The **population variance** is identified by the symbol σ^2, which is the square of the lowercase Greek letter sigma. They are calculated as

$$\text{Population variance}: \ \sigma^2 = \frac{1}{N}\sum_{i=1}^{N}(x_i - \mu)^2 \tag{2.5a}$$

$$\text{Sample variance}: \ s^2 = \frac{1}{n-1}\sum_{i=1}^{n}(x_i - \bar{x})^2 \tag{2.5b}$$

The population variance is calculated the same way as the sample variance, except that the sum of squared deviations around the mean μ is divided by the population size N. Because the population is all of the values of x, μ does not vary; its one value is the population **parameter** that characterizes a central tendency of the population data. Similarly, the σ^2 has one and only one value that represents a characteristic of the population; it is a parameter of the population that measures dispersion. On the other hand, as $\bar{x}$ varies from sample to sample, so does s^2. The **sample mean** and sample variance are called sample **statistics** because they give the status of the sample at hand; sample statistics report different values from sample to sample even though the samples are all drawn from the same population. In the case of the CEO compensation, the one sample variance we calculated is written

$$s^2 = 4287355.554 \text{ (thousands of dollars squared)}$$

If we randomly selected another sample of CEO compensation, s^2 would be a different value; it is a sample statistic.

The variance is measured in square units. It is thus not possible to relate it directly to the original units of measurements. To return to the original units of measure, the positive square root of the variance is typically reported. The positive square root of the variance is called the **standard deviation.**

Standard Deviation
Square root of the variance.

The **standard deviation** is the positive square root of the variance.

The population standard deviation is $\sigma = +\sqrt{\sigma^2}$ (2.6a)

For the sample, the standard deviation is $s = +\sqrt{s^2}$ (2.6b)

For the energy company CEO compensation data, the sample standard deviation is 2.070593 million dollars.

$$s = \sqrt{4287355.554} = 2070.593 \text{ thousands of dollars}$$

What should be apparent from Formulas (2.5) and (2.6) is that the variance and standard deviation are larger for distributions with many values far away from their mean (such as in Figure 2.3a) than for distributions with many values close to their mean (as in Figure 2.3c). Notice also that while the variance is an "average squared deviation," there is no simple verbal definition for the standard deviation. The best we can say is that the standard deviation relates directly to the proportion of values that are grouped around the mean, as will be shown later in this chapter.

QUERY 2.7:
The weights of a sample of seven pennies were measured and reported to the nearest 0.02 gram to be 3.11, 3.03, 3.05, 3.15, 3.11, 2.99, and 3.01 grams. First, use a statistical computer program to construct a cumulative relative frequency distribution for each value and produce a box plot showing the range, and quartile distances. With reference to the cumulative frequency, show how the quartile distance is calculated in the construction of the box plot. Second, use the statistical computer program to obtain the mean and standard deviation for these seven penny weights. Use Formulas 2.1b, 2.5b, and 2.6b to confirm that the computer program calculated the mean and standard deviation correctly. Finally, why can't an exact mean and standard deviation be calculated from these data regardless of the method employed?

ANSWER:
First, these seven values can be typed or read into a statistics package such as SPSS for WINDOWS. SPSS for WINDOWS (clicking along the path: "Statistics" to "Summary" to "Frequency" to "Select Variable") yields the following cumulative relative frequencies of penny weights in the last column of the printout.

Label Value	Frequency	Percent	Valid Percent	Cum Percent
2.99	1	14.3	14.3	14.3
3.01	1	14.3	14.3	28.6
3.03	1	14.3	14.3	42.9
3.05	1	14.3	14.3	57.1
3.11	2	28.6	28.6	85.7
3.15	1	14.3	14.3	100.0
	--	-------	-------	-------
Total	7	100.0	100.0	

The box plot in Chart 2.1 is obtained following the SPSS path "Graphic" to "BoxPlot," selecting "Simple," and "Summary of separate variables."

CHART 2.1 SPSS Box Plot of Penny Weights

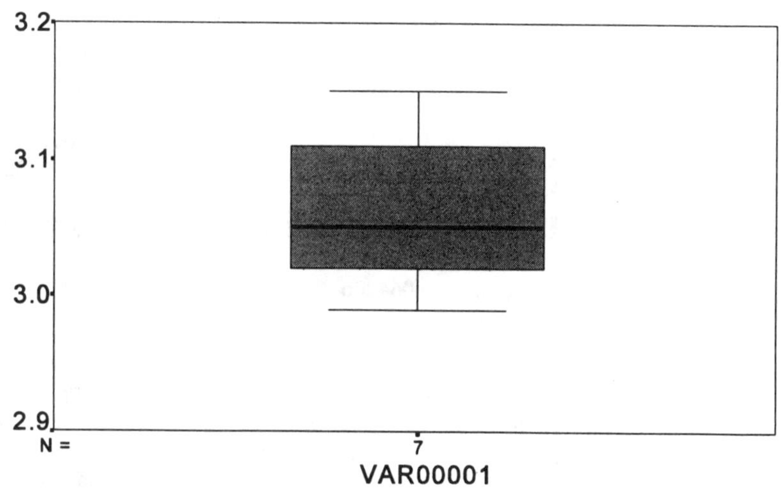

The first quartile (25th percentile) may be approximated by assuming hypothetical data evenly spaced between the lowest observed value (2.99, which is at the 14.286 percentile = 1/7) and next value (3.01, at the 28.571 percentile = 2/7). That is, the hypothetical value that corresponds to the 25th percentile is 3.005.

$$2.99 + \frac{25.000 - 14.286}{28.571 - 14.286}(3.01 - 2.99) = 3.005$$

Similar calculations yield an approximate median of 3.04, and a third quartile of 3.11. These values are illustrated in the SPSS box plot.

Second, the mean and standard deviation can be automatically calculated in SPSS using the "statistics" menu under the subtitle "Summary."

Variable	Mean	Std Dev	Minimum	Maximum	N
VAR00001	3.06	.06	2.99	3.15	7

As a check on the mean, variance and standard deviation calculated by SPSS, the seven penny weights were typed into the A1 through A7 cells of EXCEL and recalculated using Formulas 2.1b, 2.5b, and 2.6b and appropriate EXCEL commands (e.g., "=sum(A1:A7)" in cell A8, "=sum(A1:A7)/7" in cell A9,"=A1-$A$9" in cell B1, "=B1^2" in cell C1, "=C8/6" in C9, "=sqrt(C9)" in C10, and the copy/paste routine) to produce:

Penny Weights	Deviations from mean	Deviations Squared
3.11	0.04571	0.002090
3.03	-0.03429	0.001176
3.05	-0.01429	0.000204
3.15	0.08571	0.007347
3.11	0.04571	0.002090
2.99	-0.07429	0.005518
3.01	-0.05429	0.002947
Sum =21.45		0.021371 = Sum
Mean = 3.064286		0.003562 = Sample variance
		0.059682 = Sample standard deviation

Alternatively, the mean and standard deviation along with other summary measures for a sample can be obtained easily using the Descriptive Statistics routine in EXCEL for WINDOWS. (This descriptive statistics routine is part of the "Analysis Tool Pack" that must be added to the "Tools" menu via the "Add In" submenu within the "Tools" menu.) After bringing up EXCEL, do the following:

1. Type the seven penny weights into the cells A1 through A7, or bring them in from the disk file that accompanies your textbook.
2. Click on the "Tools" menu. (At the bottom of the "Tools" menu will be a submenu "Data Analysis...", if the Analysis Tool Pack has been properly installed.)
3. Clicking on "Data Analysis..." will lead to a menu that includes "Descriptive Statistics."
4. Select "Descriptive Statistics" by pointing at it and clicking twice, or by highlighting it and clicking on the "Okay" button.

5. Within the Descriptive Statistics submenu,

a. for the "input range" enter "A1:A7", assuming you typed the seven penny weights into cells A1 to A7.

b. for the "output range" enter "C1:C16".

c. with a click on the Summary Statistics box, your screen display of "Descriptive Statistics" will look like Chart 2.2;

d. finally, a click on "Okay" yields the summary information in Chart 2.3, where the C column was expanded with a click on its border with column D at the top of the spread sheet area.

CHART 2.2 EXCEL Interim Screen Display for Descriptive Statistics

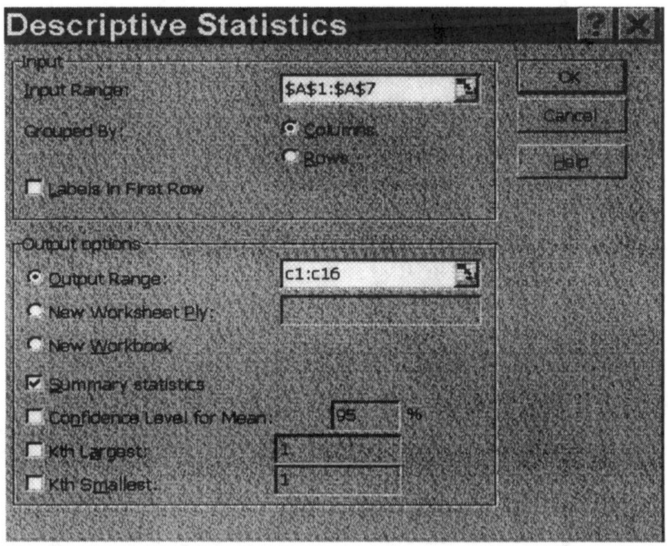

Finally, these computer printouts suggest that the mean is exactly 3.064286 grams and the standard deviation is 0.059682 grams. Although the mean and standard deviation are reported here to six decimal places, they are not totally accurate because the original data were rounded to the nearest 0.02 grams. Computer results are no more accurate than the data fed in. (Many of the other descriptive statistics contained in this printout that have not yet been introduced will be discussed in later chapters of the textbook.)

CHART 2.3 EXCEL Printout of Summary Measures for Penny Weights

A B	C	D
3.11	Column 1	
3.03		
3.05	Mean	3.064286
3.15	Standard Error	0.022558
3.11	Median	3.05
2.99	Mode	3.11
3.01	Standard Deviation	0.059682
	Sample Variance	0.003562
	Kurtosis	-1.60138
	Skewness	0.227947
	Range	0.16
	Minimum	2.99
	Maximum	3.15
	Sum	21.45
	Count	7

QUERY 2.8:
Treating the eight industrial groups in *The Wall Street Journal* (April 22, 1992) data set on CEO total compensation as the population, what are the mean and standard deviation of the CEO compensation? Is this distribution skewed?

ANSWER:
Before attempting to obtain the desired population parameters, notice that the data set is too large to easily type into a computer package. The compensation of the 317 CEOs can be retrieved easily after you download all of the data sets on the E270 World Wide Web site and import the "que1.prn" file into EXCEL, as described in the first "Query" in the first chapter of this book. As in the latter part of the answer to Query 2.7, EXCEL can be made to automatically calculate descriptive statistics for the 317 values read into EXCEL through the "Tools" and "Data Analysis" menus, where the input range is "A1:A317" and the output range is "C1:C16". The resulting summary statistics appear in an EXCEL printout, Chart 2.4.

CHART 2.4 EXCEL Summary Measures for 317 CEO Compensations

A	B	C	
74799.7		Column1	
22563.2			
16913.2		Mean	2325.647003
16778.9		Standard Error	267.5671969
13812.7		Median	1325.3
12178		Mode	3067.6
11436.2		Standard Deviation	4763.898503
9725.9		Sample Variance	22694728.94
9265.8		Kurtosis	171.6088504
7620		Skewness	11.76422022
7211.8		Range	74699.7
6654.9		Minimum	100
6411.4		Maximum	74799.7
6299.5		Sum	737230.1
5955.8		Count	317

From this computer printout, we see that for the 317 CEOs, the lowest compensation level is $100,000 and the highest is $74,799,700. Because the formula for the mean involves the same calculations for both population and sample data, the mean compensation for this population of 317 CEOs is $2,325,647.

This computer printout, and most others produced by statistical packages, automatically calculates sample statistics. If population data are read in, the program does not recognize this and makes incorrect calculations of the variance and standard deviation. To convert to population values reference must be made to the formulas employed. To get the population standard deviation, we must retrieve the sum of square deviations from the 4763.8985 figure given in the printout. To facilitate this with a hand calculator, we first put the standard deviation in millions of dollars as 4.7639. The computer made the following calculation, which we need to reverse by hand.

$$\sqrt{\frac{\sum(x_i - mean)^2}{(n-1)}} = \sqrt{\frac{\sum(x_i - mean)^2}{316}} = 4.763899$$

By multiplying both sides of this expression by $\sqrt{316}$ and then squaring both sides we get the sum of squared deviations

$$\sum(x_i - \text{mean})^2 = 7171.54$$

Now dividing this sum of squared deviations by the population size 317 gives the variance of the population.

$$\frac{\Sigma(x_i - \text{mean})^2}{N} = \frac{7171.54}{317} = 22.62315$$

and the population standard deviation is 4.75638 million dollars. Because the data set is large, whether the standard deviation formula for a sample or population was used is of little consequence here (4.7639 versus 4.75638 million). For a small data set, however, such is not the case. We must know whether a data set is a population or a sample and how our computer program is treating it.

A box and whisker plot can be produced showing the information on the quartiles, expressed below in millions of dollars:

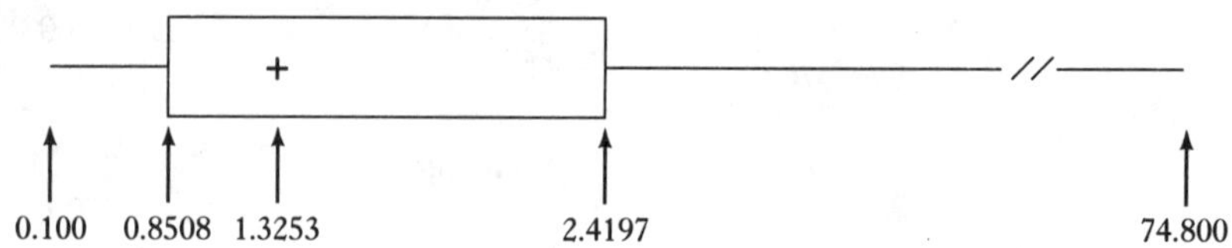

Clearly this distribution is highly right skewed, with the median compensation 1.3253 million dollars closer to the first quartile, 0.8508, than to the third, 2.4197. It is much more skewed than the sample of 18 energy company CEOs, where the box and whisker plot given in Figure 2.6 is reproduced here for scale comparison:

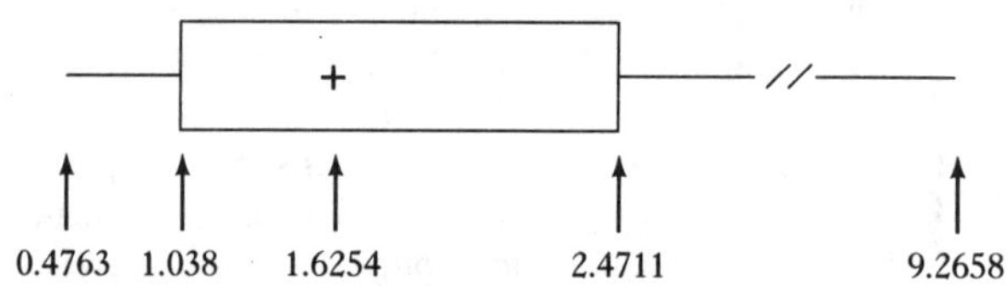

The right or positive skewness of the population of all 317 CEOs is also reflected numerically in the "coefficient of skewness" of 11.764, which was reported earlier in the computer printout in the row titled "Skewness." We will not go into the details of the coefficient of skewness here. It is sufficient to know that a positive coefficient of skewness indicates a distribution that is skewed right and a negative value indicates left skewed.[1]

2.14 The Variance and Standard Deviation in Frequency Form

The procedures for calculating a variance after data have been grouped into a frequency distribution are similar to those for the ungrouped raw data except the value or class midpoint (m_i) at which multiple observations occur is used instead of x_i, and deviations of m_i from the mean are weighted by the respective frequencies (f_i). Formulas (2.7a, b and c) give formulas for determining the variances for population and sample data after the original values have been placed in a frequency distribution.

Weighted variances for grouped data:

Population variance:

$$\sigma^2 = \frac{1}{N}\sum_{i=1}^{c} f_i (m_i - \mu)^2 \qquad (2.7a)$$

where μ is the mean of the population, m_i is the value or class midpoint at which multiple observations occur, f_i is the frequency of the ith class, c is the number of classes, and N is the number of items in the population $N = \Sigma f_i$

Alternative population variance:

$$\sigma^2 = \sum_{i=1}^{c} (f_i / N)(m_i - \mu)^2. \qquad (2.7b)$$

where f_i/N is the relative frequency of ith class

Sample variance:

$$s^2 = \frac{1}{n-1}\sum_{i=1}^{c} f_i (m_i - \bar{x})^2 \qquad (2.7c)$$

where $\bar{x}$ is the sample mean and the sample size is $n = \Sigma f_i$

Notice that the Formula (2.7b) for the population variance is simply Formula (2.7a) rewritten in terms of the relative frequencies. By focusing on the relative frequency, we do not need to know the actual population size; only the relative frequencies of occurrences are needed. As in our discussion of mean calculations, Formulas (2.7a, b, and c) give approximate variances if the data have been grouped and placed in frequency form. As in the approximation of the mean, if we do not know the original values, we simply assume that the class midpoint represents the class.

As with the calculation of a mean, if we are fortunate and have the frequencies or relative frequencies of each of the original values in the population, then Formula (2.7a) or its alternative (2.7b) can be used to get the exact variance of the population. Table 2.8 illustrates the calculation of the true population variance for the population grade distribution in Table 2.4. The population variance is

$$\sigma^2 = \sum_{i=1}^{5} (f_i / N)(m_i - 2.33)^2 = 0.9611$$

and the population standard deviation is

$$\sigma = \sqrt{\sigma^2} = \sqrt{0.96} = 0.980357$$

Table 2.8 Weighted Population Variance Calculation of Grades

Letter Grade	Numerical Grade (m_i)	f_i/N	$(f_i/N)m_i$	$(m_i-\mu)$	$(m_i-\mu)^2$	$(f_i/N)(m_i-\mu)^2$
A	4	0.13	0.52	1.67	2.7889	0.362557
B	3	0.25	0.75	0.67	0.4489	0.112225
C	2	0.50	1.00	−0.33	0.1089	0.054450
D	1	0.06	0.06	−1.33	1.7689	0.106134
F	0	0.06	0.00	−2.33	5.4289	0.325734
			$\mu = 2.33$			$0.9611 = \sigma^2$

Table 2.9 Weighted Sample Variance Calculation of Grades in One Course Offering by an Instructor Who Has Taught Many Courses

Letter Grade	Numerical Grade (m_i)	f_i	$(f_i)m_i$	$(m_i-\bar{x})$	$(m_i-\bar{x})^2$	$(f_i)(m_i-\bar{x})^2$
A	4	13	52.00	1.67	2.7889	36.2557
B	3	25	75.00	0.67	0.4489	11.2225
C	2	50	100.00	−0.33	0.1089	5.4450
D	1	6	6.00	−1.33	1.7689	10.6134
F	0	6	0.00	−2.33	5.4289	32.5734
			233.00			96.110
			$\bar{x} = 2.33$			$s^2 = 96.11/99$
						$= 0.970808$

For sample data, there is no corresponding relative frequency form of Formula (2.7b), because the division of the sum of squared deviations is by $n - 1$ and not by n. For instance, if at the end of a semester, 100 students complete a course for which 13 receive an A grade, 25 a B, 50 a C, six a D, and six an F, and if this course is viewed as a subset of all the courses this instructor has taught, then grades in this one course are a sample of all grades given in all of this instructor's courses. As such, the variance must be calculated by Formula (2.7c), as shown in Table 2.9. This sample variance is

$$s^2 = \frac{1}{99}\sum_{i=1}^{5} f_i\left(m_i - 2.33\right)^2 = 96.11/99 = 0.970808$$

and the sample standard deviation is

$$s = \sqrt{s^2} = \sqrt{0.970808} = 0.985296$$

Exercises

2.20 According to an article in *The Wall Street Journal* (May 3, 1988), advertisers bought \$1.59 billion of commercial time on network sports programs in 1987, a 10 percent increase from 1986. The top 10 advertisers are given below, where advertising expenditures are in millions of dollars and identified by the variable "ADVERTISE."

General Motors	111.400	AT&T	34.300
Anheuser-Busch	102.000	Tandy	30.600
Phillip Morris	78.600	IBM	29.400
U.S. Air Force	42.200	Sears	27.800
Chrysler	37.600	Ford	27.000

Interpret the following computer output by showing how the identified quantities were calculated for this data

Variable	Mean	Standard Deviation	S.E. of Mean	Cases
ADVERTISE	52.09000	32.54380	10.29125	10

How much time did the other advertisers buy on network sports programs in 1987?

2.21 Is there skewness in the data in Exercise 2.20 dealing with advertising expenditures on network sports programs?

2.22 Calculate the mean and variance for the following two samples:

Set A is \$1, \$4, –\$6, and \$2.

Set B is \$100, \$400, –\$600 and \$200.

What is the relationship between the means of these sets and the relationship between the variances? Would this relationship be different if these were population data?

2.23 A larger sample than that reported in Query 2.7 about the weight of newly minted pennies was undertaken by W. J. Youden, as reported by S. B. Vardeman, ("What About the Other Intervals?" *American Statistician*, August 1992, p. 195). The weight of 100 pennies was measured to the nearest 10^{-4}g but reported to the nearest 0.02g. What is the approximate mean and standard deviation?

Penny weight	Frequency
2.99	1
3.01	4
3.03	4
3.05	4
3.07	7
3.09	17
3.11	24
3.13	17
3.15	13
3.17	6
3.19	2
3.21	1

2.24 In a study of used car prices, a sample of dealerships in a large city showed a wide discrepancy in final sales prices. For 50 cars of identical specifications, the following prices were recorded.

Prices	Relative Frequency
At least \$9,800 but under \$10,000	.10
At least \$9,600 but under \$ 9,800	.20
At least \$9,400 but under \$ 9,600	.40
At least \$9,200 but under \$ 9,400	.30

Approximate the mean and standard deviation for this sample.

2.25 Is there skewness in the distribution of car prices in Exercise 2.24?

2.26 The three distributions in Exercise 2.14 deal with the time to process appeals in 1989, 1990, and 1991, from *American Sailor* (September 1992). In which of the three years is the distribution of time to process an appeal most skewed? Why?

2.27 An article in *The Wall Street Journal* (October 12, 1992) reported the mean compensation of CEOs in seven countries. An earlier *WSJ* (September 24, 1992) article reported information on the world's 100 largest public companies. Below are summary data on CEO compensation and number of headquartered companies in the identified countries.

	CEO Compensation	Number of Headquarter Companies in Country
United States	\$717,237	49
France	\$479,772	2
Italy	\$463,009	1
Britain	\$439,441	16
Canada	\$416,066	0
Germany	\$390,933	4
Japan	\$390,723	23
Other	not avail	5

a. What are the mean and standard deviation of CEO compensation per country, ignoring the number of headquarters?

b. What are the mean and standard deviation of number of headquartered companies per country for the seven identified countries?

c. What are the approximate mean and standard deviation of CEO compensation for the 95 companies, ignoring the country?

d. How does your answer in part b influence the difference in your answers in parts a and c?

2.28 For the data on CEO compensation and company headquarters per country, in Exercise 2.27, as the number of headquartered companies deviates from its mean what tends to happen to deviations in CEO compensation? What can you conclude from this?

2.15 Data Location and the Standard Deviation

Rule of Thumb for Bell-Shaped Distributions
For most bell-shaped distributions, the interval $\mu \pm \sigma$ contains about 68 percent of the distribution, $\mu \pm 2\sigma$ contains about 95 percent of the distribution and $\mu \pm 3\sigma$ contains nearly all of the distribution.

In later chapters, we will examine exact probability calculations associated with several different distributions.[2] For now, it is helpful to see how the standard deviation relates to the area on either side of the mean of a symmetric bell-shaped distribution. The **rule of thumb** for these bell-shaped distributions, such as those in Figure 2.7, is that

about 68 percent of the distribution is between

$$\mu - 1\sigma \text{ and } \mu + 1\sigma$$

about 95 percent falls between

$$\mu - 2\sigma \text{ and } \mu + 2\sigma$$

nearly all of the distribution is between

$$\mu - 3\sigma \text{ and } \mu + 3\sigma$$

FIGURE 2.7 Rule of Thumb for Bell-Shaped Distributions

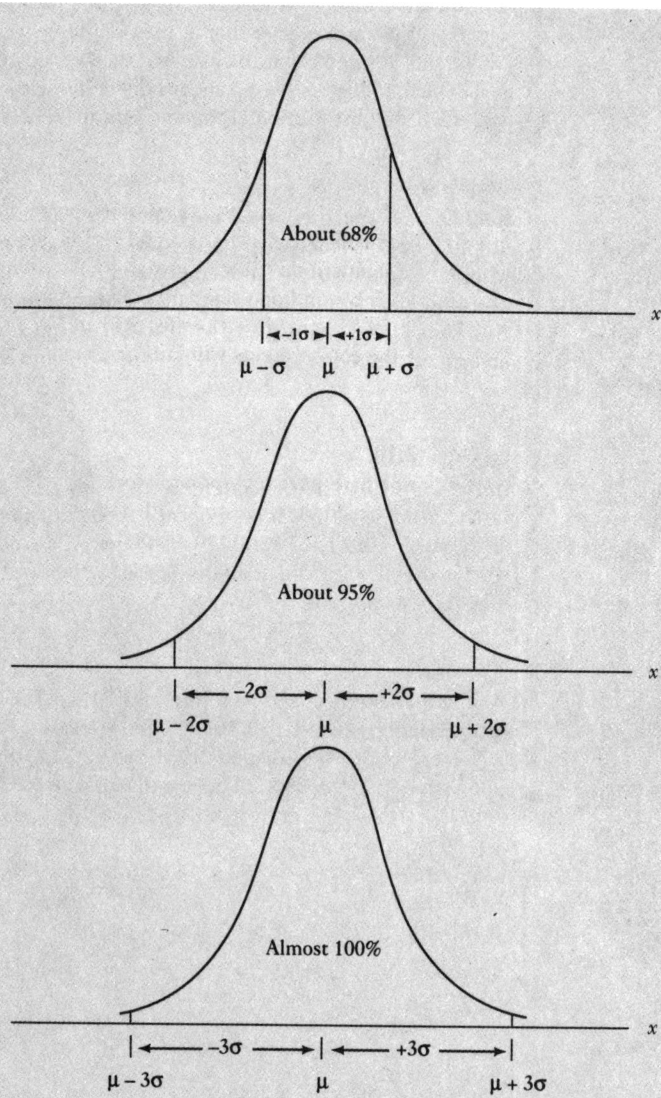

The rule of thumb for bell-shaped distributions:
between $\mu - 1\sigma$ and $\mu + 1\sigma$ is about 68 percent of the distribution;
between $\mu - 2\sigma$ and $\mu + 2\sigma$ is about 95 percent of the distribution;
and nearly all of the distribution is between $\mu - 3\sigma$ and $\mu + 3\sigma$.

QUERY 2.9:
An executive training firm wants to design a CPA review study course that is of a length sufficient to ensure that at least 84 percent of the participants will pass the CPA exam. It knows that the average review study time required to pass this exam is 40 hours, with a 9.5 hour standard deviation. How much time should be devoted to study if the distribution of time is "approximately bell shaped"?

ANSWER:
If 40 hours is specified, then only 50 percent will pass the exam. From the rule of thumb for bell-shaped distributions, we know that 68 percent of the distribution is within one standard deviation above and below the mean. Thus, 32 percent of the distribution is beyond one standard deviation of the mean, with 16 percent in each tail. Thus, if 49.5 hours [$\mu + \sigma = 40 + 9.5$] are specified for the study course, only 16 percent of the course takers will fail the exam and 84 percent will pass.

QUERY 2.10:
In the immediate past, a corporate stock has yielded a net semiannual average return of $100 per $1,000 invested, with a standard deviation of $50. If the distribution of the net return has been bell shaped, then assuming the future is like the past, what is the likelihood that an investor of $1,000 will lose money on this investment if held for a half year?

ANSWER:
Between $100 return and no return at all is two standard deviations, since each standard deviation is worth $50. In each tail beyond two standard deviations of the mean is 2.5 percent of a bell-shaped distribution. Thus, this investment will result in losses 2.5 percent of the time. (The return also will exceed $200 about 2.5 percent of the time.)

QUERY 2.11:

A *Wall Street Journal* (November 15, 1996) article, from which the following data where extracted, stated that "The nation's continuing economic expansion, now 67 months old, has far surpassed the previous postwar average (50 months) and few see the party ending anytime soon."

Beginning to End of U.S. Expansion	Duration (in months)
Oct-45 to Nov-48	37
Oct-49 to Jul-53	45
May-54 to Aug-57	39
Apr-58 to Apr-60	24
Feb-61 to Dec-69	106
Nov-70 to Nov-73	36
Mar-75 to Jan-80	58
Jul-80 to Jul-81	12
Nov-82 to Jul-90	92
Mar-91 to Present	67

Data Source: National Bureau of Economics Research

First, does the "50-month average" pertain to the mean or median of the length of U.S. expansions since WWII? Second, what is your best estimate of the standard deviation of duration of U.S. expansions that occurred since WWII? Third, use the EXCEL program to construct a diagram to show the range of values within one standard deviation of the mean length of U.S. expansions since WWII. Has the latest 67 month spell "far surpassed the previous postwar average?"

ANSWER:

First, in November 1996, *The Wall Street Journal* could not have included the then current expansion in calculating the mean duration of expansions since WWII because that expansion had not yet come to an end. That is, the length of the expansion still underway as of November 15, 1996, was unknown; we only know that it had been underway for 67 months up to November. After entering the 10 duration values into A1 through A10 of an EXCEL spreadsheet, the "Descriptive Statistics" routine, which is accessed through the "Tools" menu described in Query 2.7, can be used to get the descriptive statistics for the input range to "A1:A9." With the output range set to "C1," the resulting summary statistics appear as follows:

CHART 2.5 EXCEL Summary Measures for Duration of Expansion Data

A	B	C	D
37		Column1	
45		----------------------	-----------
39		Mean	49.88888889
24		Standard Error	10.27056804
106		Median	39
36		Mode	#N/A
58		Standard Deviation	30.81170413
12		Sample Variance	949.3611111
92		Kurtosis	0.080068248
67		Skewness	0.955462191
		Range	94
		Minimum	12
		Maximum	106
		Sum	449
		Count	9

Notice that although cell A10 contains the 67-month value for the most recent expansion, only the prior 9 expansions were used in the EXCEL calculations of descriptive statistics. The mean duration of these 9 expansions is approximately 50 months (49.88888889), as reported in *The Wall Street Journal*. The median for these 9 completed spells of expansion is 39 months but a median for all 10 expansions can be determined even though the exact length of the last spell was not known. The median of all 10 spells is between 39 and 45 months regardless of how long the final expansion might last. Setting the median at 42 months shows five durations shorter and 5 durations longer than 42 months no matter how long the last expansion. Although *The Wall Street Journal* did not report it, for duration data the median is often the preferred measure of central tendency because it is less sensitive to the completion of spells.

Second, the standard deviation for duration of U.S. expansions since WWII can only be calculated for the first nine spells. From the EXCEL printout we see that this standard deviation is 30.8117 months. Thus, plus or minus one standard deviation from the mean duration covers a range from approximately 19.1 months to 80.7 months.

Third, the EXCEL program can be used to construct a diagram to show the range of values within one standard deviations of the mean length of U.S. expansion since WWII. This requires a click on the ChartWizard. The following "Steps" then appear:

1) At Step 1 of 4 highlight "XY (Scatter)" and click on "Next."
3) At Step 2 of 4 for "Data range" enter "A1:A9" and click on "Next."
4) At Step 3 of 4 click "Next."
5) At Step 4 of 4 click "Finish."
6) A scatter plot will emerge with the nine data points appearing as blue diamonds. Double click on any one of the blue data points with black surrounding boxes and the "Format Data Series" screen appears.
7) In the "Format Data Series," click on "Y Error Bars" at top of screen.
8) Click on the subscreen box for "Both" to highlight vertical error bar.
9) Click on bottom for "Standard deviation," and leave indicator set at one.
10) With a click on "OK" the Chart 2.6 appears:

CHART 2.6 EXCEL Error Bar Diagram for Duration of Expansion Data

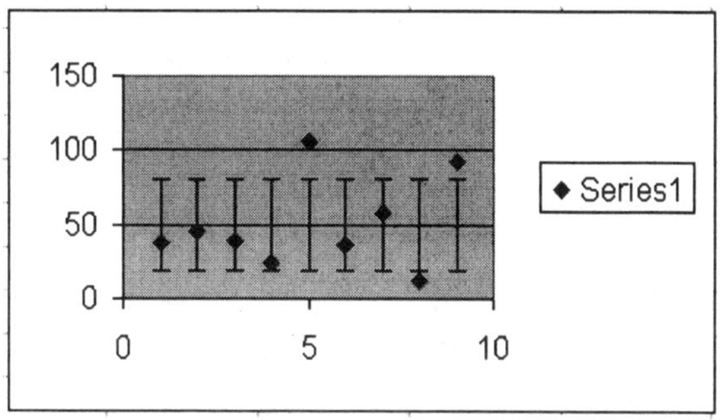

As can be seen in this diagram one standard deviation from the mean extends from approximately 20 to 80 months. Only three of the previous expansions were outside this range. The expansion that was 67 months old and still underway in November of 1996 was nowhere near the upper 80 month limit and thus has not "far surpassed" the previous postwar average of 50 months. In general, for an observation to be considered "far away from the mean," it must be at least one standard deviation from the mean. Later in this book we will refine what is meant by "far away from the mean."

EXERCISES

2.29 A study of the loss payment per insurance claim by homeowners showed an average of \$810, with a standard deviation of \$90.

a. If the distribution of loss payments is bell shaped, then what percentage of payments is above \$990? What percentage of payments is below \$720?

b. *If the shape of the distribution of loss payments is unknown, then what percentage of payments is above \$990? What percentage of payments is below \$720?

2.30 According to a note in *The Wall Street Journal* (December 30, 1987), telephone calls that are put on hold average 55 seconds on hold. If the standard deviation is 15 seconds, what is the smallest number of calls that are handled within 25 and 85 seconds, assuming a bell-shaped distribution?

2.31 How, if at all, would your answer in Exercise 2.30 change if you now learned that the distribution of hold time in the above question was not bell shaped?

2.32 *According to a fact sheet in *The Wall Street Journal* (September 10, 1993), the minimum, maximum, and average salary of students in executive training programs in 1992 were approximately \$20,000, \$400,000, and \$80,000. If the standard deviation of this distribution was \$40,000, what proportion of students had salaries above \$140,000? (*see Endnote 2.)

2.16 LOOKING AHEAD

Many key concepts and important ideas for almost any statistical analysis have been surveyed in this chapter. The remaining chapters in this book continue to come back to these basic notions and greatly expand on them. Of particular importance is recognition that the median may be preferred to the mean as a measure of central location if a distribution is skewed. For measures of dispersion, the standard deviation is usually preferred to the range.

Essential throughout this book is the notion that randomness and chance are inherent in sampling. Both the measures of central location and the measures of dispersion vary from sample to sample. Chapters 7 and 8 deal explicitly with the implications of chance for estimating population parameters. To appreciate the implications of the errors in estimation that may result from random chance events, an understanding of probability, expected values, and probability distributions is required.

The basics of probability and expected value calculations are discussed in Chapters 3 and 4, and specific probability distributions (including the binomial, normal, and other discrete and continuous distributions) are considered in Chapters 5 and 6. If you have already had a course in probability, you may be able to skip over Chapters 3 through 6 and go directly to the application of descriptive statistics in estimation and hypothesis testing, Chapters 7, 8, and 9. In the absence of such a course, however, Chapters 3 through 6 are necessary before you continue your study of inferential statistics.

CHAPTER EXERCISES

2.33 For the sample of 40 petty cash observations in Exercise 1.16,

a. Calculate the median.

b. Calculate the first and third quartiles.

c. Calculate the mean and standard deviation.

d. Are these data skewed? Explain.

2.34 Below are data on average delivery times after 8 a.m. for a *Business Week* (June 6, 1988) experiment involving the sending of 12 letters via each of seven overnight delivery services. Can the mean, median, and mode delivery time for all 84 letters be determined from this data? Can the standard deviation and variance be determined? If possible, do so.

Emery Worldwide	1 hour, 31 minutes
Federal Express	1 hour, 44 minutes
Airborne Express	2 hours
DHL Worldwide	3 hours, 2 minutes
Purolator Courier	3 hours, 12 minutes
U.S. Postal Service Express Mail	3 hours, 15 minutes
United Parcel Service	3 hours, 31 minutes

2.35 The following distribution is the word processing speed of a large pool of clerical workers:

Words Per Minute	Frequency
35–44	1
45–54	7
55–64	12
65–74	15
75–84	6
85–94	3
95–104	4
105–114	1

a. What is the mode? b. What is the median?

c. What is the mean? d. What is the variance?

e. What is the standard deviation? f. What is the range?

g. What proportion of the clerical workers type 64 or fewer words per minute?

h. Do your calculations in parts a through f depend on whether these are population or sample data? In what type of problem might these be population data, and in what type of problem might these be sample data?

2.36 A *Wall Street Journal* (August 10, 1992) article attempted to show that "High-Priced Stocks Are Hardest Hit." The followng table shows the percentage of stocks, within a "P/E decile grouping of stocks," whose price fell by 30 percent or more. For example, in the tenth decile the median price/earnings ratio was 80.5, and about 35 percent of the stocks in this highest decile had price drops of 30 percent or more. From this diagram, what are the 5th, 15th, 25th, . . . 95th percentiles for the P/E ratios?

Median P/E										
Ratio	7.8	10.7	12.7	14.3	16.4	19.0	22.3	27.5	38.5	80.5
Decile	1st	2nd	3rd	4th	5th	6th	7th	8th	9th	10th
Decline	27%	22%	12%	20%	20%	24%	26%	24%	48%	35%

2.37 Regarding the life of new nickel-metal hydride batteries, a Scripps Howard News Service (*HT*, July 19, 1992) press release stated that, "Most passenger cars don't need a range of much more than 300 miles," with an average range of maybe 350 miles. "If the battery can be charged in 15 minutes, that's about the time it takes to get a snack and stretch your legs." What do you know about the distribution of battery life range from these statements?

2.38 A *Washington Post* syndicated article (January 29, 1995) reported that "Risk is a fuzzy concept, but it's possible to put a number on it ... a risk measure called 'standard deviation.'" Five sample percentage annual returns were reported for American Heritage Mutual Fund (31, 96, 19, 41, and 35) and Valley Forge Mutual Fund (6, 8, 9, 17, and 6). The article also reported that as "the risk" goes up "the average return" also goes up.

a. What are the mean and median annual percentage returns for each fund?
b. Are each of these data sets symmetric or skewed? Explain.
c. What is the range of the annual percentage return for each fund?
d. What is the standard deviation of the annual percentage return for each fund?
e. What relationship between "average return" and "risk" is suggested by these sample data? Explain.

2.39 The following frequency distribution from *Business Week* (September 21, 1992) shows the share of credit card accounts being charged the indicated interest rates. The accompanying article also stated that "only 2% are paying under 12%."

a. What percentage of card holders are paying less than 16 percent but at least 12 percent?
b. Assuming that the mean rate paid by those who are paying less than 12 percent is 6 percent, and that 25 percent is the mean for those paying more than 19 percent, what is the approximate overall mean rate? What is the approximate standard deviation?

Card Rate	Share of Accounts
Over 19%	36%
18–19	8
17–18	15
16–17	12
Less than 16	29

2.40 For the information in Exercise 2.39 on the rates charged card holders, what is the approximate median rate? What did you have to assume to calculate this median?

2.41 An A&E television special, "First Flights" (May 19, 1993), featured astronaut Neil Armstrong saying that "in the early years of World War II, the average number of missions B17 bombers survived was the unlucky 13." He also said that "200 planes per week were lost during the major campaigns of World War II." Comment on the appropriateness of these averages.

2.42 A survey conducted by American Sports Data found that "people who ski fewer than 12 times a year, for example, account for half of all ski sales. People who play tennis fewer than 25 times a year buy nearly half of all rackets. And people who golf fewer than 25 times a year make up about half of the market for golf club sets."(*WSJ*, June 2, 1993) From this quote, what, if anything, do you know about the approximate mean, median, or modal number of times per year people who a) buy skies ski, b) buy rackets play tennis, or c) buy golf clubs play golf?

2.43 "Most of Indiana's top officials spend less than one-tenth of what President Clinton paid ($200) to have his hair cut and styled last month in Los Angeles," according to an Associated Press article (*HT*, June 1993). From this quote, can you provide an approximate mean, median, or modal value for the amount paid by Indiana's top officials for haircuts and stylings?

2.44 In reporting on health care costs, *Business Week* (March 15, 1993) stated, "Only 5.7% chose such coverage (low-cost but high-satisfaction health care plans), while 54.2% are in plans with above-average premiums." Is there a mistake here? How can 54.2 percent be above the average? Explain.

2.45 The information in Exercise 2.39 from *Business Week* (September 21, 1992) on the rates charged card holders, was from a survey of the top 100 institutions in the credit card industry, by the *Nilson Report*, a Santa Monica, California, newsletter firm that tracks the industry. These top 100 institutions account for 139 million card accounts.

a. In calculating the variance of rates from these data, is the population or sample size 100 or 139 million?

b. Should the population or the sample variance formula be used?

c. Why wouldn't it make much difference if the population or sample formula were used to calculate the variance?

2.46 Below are the automobile output plans for the fourth quarter of 1991 and 1992, as reported in *The Wall Street Journal* (October 8, 1992):

	1992	1991	% Change
GM	647,000	674,000	–4.0
Ford	307,000	251,000	+22.3
Chrysler	118,837	151,000	–21.3
Honda	100,000	112,174	–10.9
Mazda	64,000	47,000	+36.2
Nissan	60,000	34,000	+76.5
Toyota	58,903	47,000	+25.3
Nummi	43,000	51,000	–15.7
Diamstar	32,500	39,712	–18.2
Sub-ISU	14,000	15,000	–6.7

What is the mean output of automobiles from these 10 companies in each year? What is the median in each year? Why aren't the mean and median equal in 1992? Why aren't they equal in 1991?

2.47 In Exercise 2.46 what is the average percentage change in output? What is the percentage change in average output? Why aren't these two measures of change the same?

2.48 In Exercise 2.46, which is a better measure of change: the percentage change in the median or the percentage change in the average? Explain.

2.49 A syndicated *Washington Post* (January 24, 1997) article titled "Working Class Posts Gains in Wealth, Fed Study Finds" stated that net worth - the value of assets minus debt - for the typical family in the United States changed little in inflation-adjusted terms from 1989 to 1995. In what sense is this true? Family net worth (in thousands of 1995 dollars), as provided by the *Federal Reserve Bulletin* cited in the article, are in the following table. In this table, the entry 1.6 indicates that in 1989, families with income of less than $10,000 per year (of which there were 15.4 percent) had a median net worth of $1,600 (in 1995 dollars), and the 1465.2 entry indicates that families with incomes in excess of $100,000 per year (or which there were 6.1 percent) had a mean net worth of $1,465,200 in 1995.

	1989			1995		
Income	Net Worth Median	Net Worth Mean	Percent of families	Net Worth Median	Net Worth Mean	Percent of families
(1995 dollars)						
All families	56.4	216.7	100.0	56.4	205.9	100.0
Less than $10,000	1.6	26.1	15.4	4.8	45.6	16.0
$10,000 - 24,999	25.6	77.9	24.3	30.0	74.6	26.5
$25,000 - 49,999	56.0	121.8	30.3	54.9	119.3	31.1
$50,000 - 99,999	128.1	229.5	22.3	21.1	256.0	20.2
$100,000 and more	474.7	1372.9	7.7	485.9	1465.2	6.1

Source: *Federal Reserve Bulletin*. Washington, D.C.: Board of Governors, January 1997.

a. Did the rich or poor gain or lose between 1989 and 1995? That is, in what sense is the *Washington Post* article right or wrong?
b. James Heckman and Jeffrey Smith (*Journal of Economic Perspectives*, Spring 1995, p. 89) call attention to problems in using the median to measure change. Why isn't the median a good measure of change here?

2.50 The 125th edition of the *World Almanac and Book of Facts* (Pharos Books, 1993) tells of British doctors recommending that beer mugs be made of tougher glass, so they do less damage in bar fights. "Mugs are the weapon of choice in 3,400 to 5,400 bar fights a year in England and Wales."(*Parade*, October 25, 1992) Which of the following can be determined from this quote?
a. The median is 4,400.5 fights.
b. The mean is 4,400 fights.
c. The range is 2,000 fights.
d. If the number of times mugs are selected in fights is approximately normal, the approximate standard deviation is 285.7 fights.

2.51 An article in *The Wall Street Journal* (November 13, 1992) reported, "Airlines Wage Fare Battle City by City, Spreading Confusion as Well as Bargains." The following table was provided to support the text:

	American	Continental	Delta	NorthWest	United
Phoenix-St. Louis	$400	$248	$400	$400	$228
Austin-Los Angeles	248	258	360	340	248
Detroit-Kansas City	164	113	280	113	113

For which city is there the largest dispersion in price? Is your answer sensitive to the measure of dispersion used? Explain.

2.52 Which airline has the median price for the three cities identified in the above exercise?

2.53 An article in *The Wall Street Journal* (November 25, 1992) reported that "women doctors in private practice earned median incomes 34% less than male colleagues in 1991, according to *Medical Economics* magazine." To check this statement and related issues, samples of 100 female and 200 male doctors were selected. Below are computer-generated descriptive statistics and worksheet calculations made from these data, where the mean earnings are reported in thousands of dollars for FEMALES and MALES. Use these printouts to answer the next eight questions.

Variable	Mean	Standard Deviation	S.E.Mean	Cases
FEMALE	117.180	89.17444	.89174	100
MALE	185.730	143.3742	.71687	200

Some worksheet calculations:

		Female: n = 100				Male: n = 200			
Earnings: thousands of dollars	mid pt m	Rel Frq (f/n)		(f/n)m	$f(m-\bar{x})^2$	Rel.Frq. (f/n)		(f/n)m	$f(m-\bar{x})^2$
400 plus	700.000	0.01		7.0	334546.6	0.05		35.0	521220.5
300–400	350.000	0.01		3.5	52166.6	0.06		21.0	51520.5
200–300	250.000	0.10		25.0	164865.6	0.21		52.5	73205.0
100–200	150.000	0.36		54.0	29036.2	0.43	158.13	64.5	112338.0
60–100	80.000	0.33	97.575	26.4	57108.5	0.18		14.4	791356.5
below 60	30.000	0.19		5.7	159420.6	0.07		2.1	966729.5
		1.00		121.60	797144	1.00		189.50	2516370

a. The mean earnings of the 100 female doctors is ________?

b. The median earnings of the 100 female doctors is ________?

c. If each female doctor who is above the median earnings level for female doctors in the sample had her earnings increased by $60,000, then what would happen to the median earnings of the 100 female doctors?

d. If each female doctor who is above the median earnings level for female doctors in the sample had her earnings increased by $60,000, then what would happen to the mean earnings of the 100 female doctors?

e. If each female doctor who is above the median earnings level for female doctors in the sample had her earnings increased by $60,000, then what would happen to the mode earnings of the 100 female doctors?

f. What proportion of the total earnings of these 300 female and male doctors goes to the female doctors?

g. What is the variance of the earnings of the 100 female doctors?

h. Is the distribution of female earnings skewed?

2.54 (Use a computer spreadsheet and the data file "EX2–54.PRN" for this problem.) An Associated Press story (July 31, 1992) reported on the number of farms by state, as given below. Calculate three measures of central location and three measures of dispersion for these farm data. What difference does it make in your calculation of each of the measures of central location and each measure of dispersion if you treat these data as a population versus sample? What would determine whether they are population or sample data?

State	Number of Farms
Alabama	46,000
Alaska	540
Arizona	8,000
Arkansas	46,000
California	81,000
Colorado	25,500
Connecticut	3,900
Delaware	2,700
Florida	39,000
Georgia	46,000
Hawaii	4,500
Idaho	21,000
Illinois	81,000
Indiana	65,000
Iowa	102,000
Kansas	67,000
Kentucky	91,000
Louisiana	30,000
Maine	7,100
Maryland	15,600
Massachusetts	6,900
Michigan	54,000
Minnesota	38,000
Mississippi	38,000
Missouri	107,000
Montana	24,600
Nebraska	56,000
Nevada	2,500
New Hampshire	2,900
New Jersey	8,500
New Mexico	13,500
New York	38,000
North Carolina	60,000
North Dakota	33,000
Ohio	78,000
Oklahoma	71,000
Oregon	37,500
Pennsylvania	52,000
Rhode Island	700
South Carolina	24,500
South Dakota	35,000
Tennessee	88,000
Texas	183,000
Utah	13,200
Vermont	6,900
Virginia	44,000
Washington	38,000
West Virginia	20,000
Wisconsin	79,000
Wyoming	9,200
TOTAL	2,095,740

2.55 (Use a computer spreadsheet and the file "EX2–55.PRN" for this problem.) For the following data on different types of taxes paid by tax-payers, calculate the average tax across the states paid in each of the four categories. Add up the averages for the four categories. Calculate the average tax for the total paid within a state. Why is there a difference between the sum of the averages across the four categories and the average of the total? (Data are from *USA Today* October 10, 1991.)

State	Sales Tax	Indiv. Income	Gas Tax	Tags	Total Tax
Alabama	257	278	73	31	945
Alaska	0	0	75	37	2811
Arizona	523	290	91	63	1194
Arkansas	357	314	93	33	962
California	458	565	46	36	1459
Colorado	251	407	99	33	932
Connecticut	743	186	94	53	1603
Delaware	0	685	95	35	1696
Florida	633	0	60	37	1027

(continued)

State	Sales Tax	Indiv. Income	Gas Tax	Tags	Total Tax
Georgia	407	443	68	12	1093
Hawaii	1062	627	48	18	2107
Idaho	381	400	107	56	1131
Illinois	357	375	80	54	1128
Indiana	460	377	102	32	1101
Iowa	340	458	120	78	1193
Kansas	352	346	91	39	1077
Kentucky	295	328	98	40	1156
Louisiana	299	175	95	17	968
Maine	415	473	112	39	1271
Maryland	329	599	94	31	1349
Massachusetts	325	816	50	42	1557
Michigan	343	422	80	52	1220
Minnesota	427	658	105	73	1559
Mississippi	423	167	120	24	931
Missouri	371	350	69	39	965
Montana	0	350	140	46	1073
Nebraska	322	314	133	36	959
Nevada	667	0	93	56	1317
New Hampshire	0	37	73	46	537
New Jersey	426	382	54	44	1350
New Mexico	552	238	109	67	1329
New York	334	850	30	30	1591
North Carolina	267	511	120	34	1186
North Dakota	362	165	105	60	1060
Ohio	331	380	90	36	1054
Oklahoma	268	318	105	85	1105
Oregon	0	643	83	76	980
Pennsylvania	356	271	63	36	1113
Rhode Island	396	425	73	40	1229
South Carolina	415	396	103	22	1128
South Dakota	359	0	115	29	719
Tennessee	481	21	129	31	870
Texas	449	0	89	42	866
Utah	410	375	77	24	1026
Vermont	242	446	95	66	1183
Virginia	219	498	101	40	1067
Washington	919	0	99	36	1525
West Virginia	426	288	116	41	1243
Wisconsin	406	537	108	33	1341
Wyoming	358	0	83	93	1348

2.56 A *Wall Street Journal* article (April 18, 1988) reported the following percentage of time that managers spent in development programs and how much time they thought they should be spending.

Workdays Per Year	Percent Who Currently Spend	Percent Who Prefer To Spend
0	10	2
1–2	34	6
3–5	39	48
6–10	13	39
11+	4	5

a. What are the approximate means and medians for the two distributions? How do they differ?
b. Why isn't the above data in a proper form for a frequency distribution? What are the implications of this for the approximation of the mean and median?
c. Is the approximate mean or median the preferred measure of central location for the above data? (Explain, using your answer in part b.)

2.57 Surveys to determine product quality are extremely popular. Consider, for example, the following evaluation data for two automobiles. The results are based on new purchaser's response to the survey question.

"The overall quality of your new car is ________ ?"

9 8 7 6 5 4 3 2 1 0
High Low

Summary Data	Car A	Car B
Number of new purchasers in survey	360	300
Number responding	60	50
Mean response value	4.0	5.0
Standard deviation of responses	1.0	2.0
Median response value	5.0	4.0

a. What are the response rates for each car as a percentage of new purchasers surveyed?
b. If there had been a 100 percent response rate, how high could each car's mean score have been?
c. About how many new purchasers who responded rated car A between 7 and 1?
d. A salesperson reviewed this data and decided that car B is clearly better. This person argued, "The majority of new car buyers gave car B an average score higher than A. The higher variability in car B's rating is more than made up by the higher mean score of car B. The majority of new car buyers cannot be wrong; thus, I am confident in the superiority of car B." Point out at least four errors or shortcomings in this reasoning.

2.58 *Business Week* (August 31, 1992) reported the following costs for a "night at home," which included McDonald's Quarter-Pounders with cheese for two, a six-pack of either Budweiser or Miller Lite, and a new Monopoly board game.

City	Cost
New York City	$27.44
Anchorage	$26.69
Tulsa	$18.42
Orlando	$17.97
Cleveland	$17.57

What are the mean and median? What are the variance and standard deviation for this sample data?

2.59 Below are data on the percentage of gross domestic product that each industrialized nation spent on education, according to the Organization for Economic Cooperation and Development publication "Education at a Glance (1992)," which are also in the ASCII computer file "EX2–59.PRN." Use a computer statistics package to determine the mean, median, and mode of the total column. Comment on the appropriateness of each of these measures as a description of the central tendency of these data.

School Spending

Country	Total
Denmark	6.9
Finland	6.8
Norway	6.6
Canada	7.2
Netherlands	6.6
Belgium	6.1
Luxembourg	6
Ireland	6.2
Sweden	5.7
Austria	5.6
Switzerland	5.1
France	5.7
United States	5.7
Australia	4.8
Italy	4.8
United Kingdom	4.7
Portugal	4.9
Germany	6.2
Spain	5
Japan	4.9

2.60 Below are data on Corvette sales, from *Corvette Quarterly* which are also in the ASCII computer file "EX2–60.PRN" that accompanies this text. Use a computer spreadsheet program or computer statistics package to check if the average yearly production run for each body style has increased since the Corvette's introduction in 1953. Why would or wouldn't this be relevant information in planning the introduction of a new body style in 1997?

	Type of Production			Body
Year	Convertible	Coupe	Total	Style
1953	300	0	300	1
1954	3640	0	3640	1
1955	700	0	700	1

(continued)

Year	Type of Production		Total	Body
	Convertible	Coupe		Style
1956	3467	0	3467	2
1957	6339	0	6339	2
1958	9168	0	9168	2
1959	9670	0	9670	2
1960	10261	0	10261	2
1961	10939	0	10939	2
1962	14531	0	14531	2
1963	10919	10594	21513	3
1964	13925	8304	22229	3
1965	15376	8186	23562	3
1966	17762	9958	27720	3
1967	14436	8504	22940	3
1968	18630	9936	28566	4
1969	16633	22129	38762	4
1970	6648	10668	17316	4
1971	7121	14680	21801	4
1972	6508	20496	27004	4
1973	4943	25521	30464	4
1974	5474	32028	37502	4
1975	4629	33836	38465	4
1976	0	46558	46558	4
1977	0	49213	49213	4
1978	0	46776	46776	4
1979	0	53807	53807	4
1980	0	40614	40614	4
1981	0	40606	40606	4
1982	0	25407	25407	4
1983	0	43	43	4
1984	0	51547	51547	5
1985	0	39729	39729	5
1986	7315	27794	35109	5
1987	10625	20007	30632	5
1988	7407	15382	22789	5
1989	9749	16663	26412	5
1990	7630	16016	23646	5
1991	5672	14967	20639	5
1992	5875	14604	20479	5
1993	5692	15898	21590	5
1994	NA	NA	23330	5
1995	4971	15711	20742	5

style code:
1: introductory model
2: side panel insert model
3: original Stingray model
4: shark shape model
5: wide stance model

2.61 The data set from *The Wall Street Journal* (September 24, 1992) on the world's 50 largest insurers is in the spreadsheet file "EX2–61.WK1," which is readable by any LOTUS compatible computer spreadsheet. Use a spreadsheet program to calculate 1) the average capital asset ratio and 2) the ratio of average capital to average assets. Why aren't these the same?

2.62 The data set from *The Wall Street Journal* (September 24, 1992) on the world's 100 largest banks is in the spreadsheet file "EX2–62.WK1," which is readable by any LOTUS compatible computer spreadsheet. Use a spreadsheet program to calculate 1) the average capital asset ratio and 2) the ratio of average capital to average assets. Why aren't these the same?

2.63 The data set from *The Wall Street Journal* (September 24, 1992) on the world's 25 largest security firms is in the spreadsheet file "EX2–63.WK1," which is readable by any LOTUS compatible computer spreadsheet. Use a spreadsheet program to show how the capital growth rates of 0.8 percent, 23.2 percent, 0.9 percent and 10.7 percent were calculated respectively for Japan, the United States, the other countries, and the top 25 average.

2.64 The data set from *The Wall Street Journal* (September 24, 1992) on the world's 100 largest public companies is in the spreadsheet file "EX2–64.WK1," which is readable by any LOTUS compatible computer spreadsheet. Use a spreadsheet program to show how the sales and profit growth rates compare for the Netherlands/United Kingdom, the United States, Japan, Germany, France, Italy, Switzerland, and the other countries.

2.65 In a television show "The Birth of Europe," A&E Journey (August 11, 1991), the commentator stated that "during World War I (1914), the average survival rate of an English flier was two weeks." Why should you suspect that this was an incorrect statement of the facts? What did the two weeks most likely pertain to?

2.66 Using the salary data on the men and the women bank executives at the midwestern bank in the data file "EX2–66.PRN," calculate the mean and median salaries for each. Are women receiving much less than men? By what measure and by how much? If the 10 highest paid women each received $50,000 raises, what would happen to your measures of discrimination? Which measure of central tendency is best for assessing the cost of removing salary differences between men and women?

2.67 An article in *The Wall Street Journal* (January 30, 1995) reported on "Mobil's five types of Gasoline Buyers: Road Warriors (high mileage drivers, 16% of buyers, with average annual expenditures of $1,200), True Blue (loyal to the brand, 16% of buyers, with average annual expenditures of $1,075), Generation F3 (for fuel, food, and fast, 27% of buyers, with average annual expenditure of $950), Homebodies (use gas station along route of travel, 21% of buyers, with average annual expenditures of $825), and Price Shoppers (buy lowest priced gas, 20% of buyers, with average annual expenditures of $700)." What is the mean expenditure of a Mobil gasoline buyer? Is this an exact mean? Can exact medians and standard deviations be determined for expenditures of Mobil gasoline buyers? Explain.

2.68 A question to Marilyn vos Savant, *Parade Magazine* (June 11, 1995) asked how it is possible, based on a sex survey, to report that "the typical male has six sexual partners in his life and the typical female has two?" Assuming the typical male is heterosexual, what is your answer?

2.69 The computer ASCII file "EX1–49.PRN" was introduced in Exercise 1.49. The Scripps Howard News Service (HT, April 23, 1993) article that accompanies this data stated that the average teacher's salary for the 50 states and District of Columbia was $35,334. What is the average salary for teachers in the data set? Why don't these averages agree?

2.70 Calculate the median and first and third quartiles for the population of 50 candy shop accounts payable in Exercise 1.17.

2.71 According to a *Wall Street Journal* article (June 17, 1994), "a survey of employees at private companies shows that 31% of employees had no medical claims, and another 50% had claims of less than $1,000. Another 14% of employees had claims ranging from $1,000 to $5,000."

a. Assuming there were no claims of exactly $5,000, what is the proportion of surveyed employees with medical claims greater than $5,000?

b. If the values are evenly distributed within each class, then what is the median of medical claims of surveyed employees?

c. Why can't the mean be calculated?

ACADEMIC REFERENCES

Deming, W. Edwards. *Out of the Crisis*. Cambridge, Mass.: MIT Center for Advanced Engineering Study, 1986.

Kiefer, Nicholas. "Economic Duration Data and Hazard Functions." *Journal of Economic Literature*, June 1988, pp. 646–681.

Spear, Mary Eleanor. *Charting Statistics*. New York, McGraw-Hill, 1952.

Stigler, Stephen. *The History of Statistics*. Harvard University Press, 1986, pp. 169–172.

Tukey, John. *Exploratory Data Analysis*. Reading, Mass., Addison-Wesley, 1977.

Tukey, John. "Some Graphic and Semigraphic Displays," in T. A. Bancroft, ed., *Statistical Papers in Honor of George W. Snedecor*. Ames, Iowa: Iowa University Press, 1972, pp. 293–316.

Tukey, John and Martin Wilk. "Data Analysis and Statistics: Techniques and Approaches," in Edward R. Tufte, ed., *The Quantitative Analysis of Social Problems*. Reading, Mass.: Addison-Wesley, 1970, pp. 370–390.

ENDNOTES

1. Computer programs typically calculate the coefficient of skewness for sample data as

$$\frac{\dfrac{\Sigma\left(x_i - \text{mean}\right)^3}{n-1}}{\left[\dfrac{\Sigma\left(x_i - \text{mean}\right)^2}{n-1}\right]^{(3/2)}}$$

   For population data, this formula would have to be rewritten for divisions by N instead of n – 1. Regardless of whether the data are for a population or a sample, the denominator of the coefficient of skewness is always positive; the numerator dictates the sign of skewness. If low values of x are close to the mean, while high values extend far beyond the mean, then the coefficient of skewness will be positive; in this case, "right skew" and "positive skew" are used as synonyms. If the distribution is skewed left (mean < median), then the coefficient of skewness will be negative, and "left skew" and "negative skew" are used as synonyms. If a distribution is symmetric (mean = median), then the coefficient of skewness will be zero.

2. If the shape of the distribution is unknown, then the percentage of values contained within a distance of $\pm k$ standard deviations of the mean will be at least $[1 - (1/k)^2]$, as determined by Russian mathematician Pafnuty Chebychev more than a century ago. Unfortunately, Chebychev's theorem does not convey much information . For instance, within two standard deviations of the mean (an interval $\mu \pm 2\sigma$) we know only there are at least 75 percent $[1 - (1/2)^2]$ of the observations. If $k = 2.5$, then at least 84 percent $[1 - (1/2.5)^2]$ is inside the interval $\mu \pm 2.5\sigma$. If $k = 3$, then at least 88.9 percent $[1 - (1/3)^2]$ of the values fall in the interval $\mu \pm 3\sigma$.

FORMULAS

- Population mean of x is the sum of the N x values divided by N. In shorthand notation, this population mean is designated μ_x and is calculated as

$$\mu = \frac{1}{N}\sum_{i=1}^{N} x_i = (1/N)(x_1 + x_2 + \ldots + x_N)$$

- Sample mean of x is the sum of the n x values divided by n. In shorthand notation, this sample mean is designated $\bar{x}$ and is calculated as

$$\bar{x} = \frac{1}{n}\sum_{i=1}^{n} x_i = (1/n)(x_1 + x_2 + \ldots + x_n)$$

- Population frequency weighted mean

$$\mu = \frac{1}{N}\sum_{i=1}^{c} f_i m_i = (1/N)(f_1 m_1 + f_1 m_2 + \ldots + f_c m_c)$$

or

$$\mu = \sum_{i=1}^{c}(f_i / N)(m_i)$$

- Sample frequency weighted mean

$$\bar{x} = \frac{1}{n}\sum_{i=1}^{c}(f_i m_i) = (1/n)(f_1 m_1 + f_2 m_2 + \ldots + f_c m_c)$$

- Population relative frequency weighted mean

$$\mu = \sum_{i=1}^{c}(f_i / N)(m_i) = [(f_1 / N)(m_1) + (f_2 / N)(m_2) + \ldots + (f_c / N)(m_c)]$$

- Sample relative frequency weighted mean

$$\bar{x} = \sum_{i=1}^{c}(f_i / n)(m_i) = [(f_1 / n)(m_1) + (f_2 / n)(m_2) + \ldots + (f_c / n)(m_c)]$$

- Median ~ L + (o_1/o_2)(U – L)
  where L is the low boundary of the median class
  U is the upper boundary of the median class
  o_1 is the number of observations into the median class until the median is found, and
  o_2 is the number of observations in the median class.
- Population variance

$$\sigma^2 = \frac{1}{N}\sum_{i=1}^{N}(x_i - \mu)^2$$

- Sample variance

$$s^2 = \frac{1}{n-1}\sum_{i=1}^{n}(x_i - \bar{x})^2$$

- Population standard deviation

$$\sigma = +\sqrt{\sigma^2}$$

- Sample standard deviation

$$s = +\sqrt{s^2}$$

- Weighted population variance:

$$\sigma^2 = \frac{1}{N}\sum_{i=1}^{c} f_i \left(m_i - \mu\right)^2$$

where μ is the mean of the population, m_i is the value or class midpoint at which multiple observations occur, f_i is the frequency of the ith class, c is the number of classes, and N is the number of items in the population $N = \Sigma f_i$

- Alternative weighted population variance

$$\sigma^2 = \sum_{i=1}^{c} \left(f_i / N\right)\left(m_i - \mu\right)^2$$

- Weighted sample variance:

$$s^2 = \frac{1}{n-1}\sum_{i=1}^{c} f_i \left(m_i - \bar{x}\right)^2$$

where $\bar{x}$ is the sample mean and the sample size is $n = \Sigma f_i$

- Coefficient of skewness

$$\frac{\dfrac{\Sigma\left(x_i - \text{mean}\right)^3}{n-1}}{\left[\dfrac{\Sigma\left(x_i - \text{mean}\right)^2}{n-1}\right]^{(3/2)}}$$

CHAPTER 3

PROBABILITY

Chance is a nickname for Providence.

Sebastien Roch Nicolas Chamfort
1741–1794

3.1 INTRODUCTION

Data collection, summary, and presentation, as discussed in the first two chapters, are essential for reducing the guesswork in decision making. But risk and uncertainty in decisions cannot be avoided completely. The following represent the different types of problems involving chance events that are considered in this chapter.

- A firm hires three people from a labor force that is 50 percent female. What is the probability that this firm hires no women, if its hiring process is equivalent to a random draw? If the firm is observed hiring no women, then what could we conclude about the hiring process?
- The "morning line" or starting odds appear in local newspapers wherever there is horse racing. These odds represent the best guess of experts (handicappers) about horses' relative chances of winning that day. A handicapper's "8" means that the horse has an eight to one chance of winning and a "5–2" means that the horse has a five to two chance of winning. But what do these odds imply about the probability of a horse winning?
- In state lotteries, there are typically more than one type of game, but at least one game is designed to identify winners and losers quickly while others are more involved and ongoing games. In the Indiana state lottery, for example, "based on the 75 million tickets available for each six- to eight-week game, the odds of winning an instant cash prize are:
  - $1, 1 in 12.50 tickets
  - $2, 1 in 31.25
  - $5, 1 in 64.94
  - $10, 1 in 135.14
  - $25, 1 in 384.62
  - $500, 1 in 7,692.00
  - $5,000, 1 in 100,000.00"(*HT*, October 8, 1989).

  What is the probability of having a winning ticket in this instant cash game?
- A company that tests athletes and prospective employees for drugs, announces that its test is "95 percent accurate," by which it means that 95 percent of drug users are accurately identified and 95 percent of nondrug users are accurately identified. From government statistics, we know that approximately 5 percent of the adult population in a community are drug users. A human resource manager of a large firm in this community wants to know whether it would be a good idea to start testing prospective employees.
- According to a story in *Newsweek* (June 8, 1992), promoting drugs in medical journals is big business, with American drug companies spending $350 million a year for advertising. A study by UCLA researchers showed 100 of 109 ads in medical journals had factual errors in areas where the Food and Drug Administration (FDA) has established explicit standards. The FDA checks only about 15 percent of all these drug ads. What is the probability of the FDA finding deficiencies?

Subjective Probability Probability that is based on personal belief or judgment.

Objective Probability Probability that at least in some sense is based on observable relative frequencies.

Each of these problems involves chance factors that requires the determination of probabilities of uncertain events. By the end of this chapter, you will be able to identify other economics and business situations in which probability calculations are needed. You will be able to distinguish between **subjective** and **objective probabilities** and give a historical perspective on their developments. You will know the implication of dependent, independent, and mutually exclusive events, and know how to calculate the probabilities of unions and intersections of events. Using the basic rules of probability, you will be able to make probability calculations for everyday business and economic decisions involving compound probabilities.

3.2 Relative Frequency and Probability

Before addressing the problems identified at the beginning of this chapter, let's make sure we have an idea of what probability is. One way to do this is to flip a coin 10 times, record the results, and then flip it 20 times, record the results, and, finally, flip it 40 times and record the results. You can record your results as in Table 3.1, where both the frequency and relative frequencies are calculated for each of the three sample sizes of $n = 10$, $n = 20$, and $n = 40$. You should recall from Chapter 1 that the randomness inherent in sampling should make your results different from those in Table 3.1.

Probability The long-term relative frequency with which a single outcome (or set of outcomes called an event) occurs.

Notice in Table 3.1 how the relative frequency of heads is approaching or converging to 0.50. If we could continue to flip the coin in samples of $n = 80$, $n = 160$, $n = 320$ and so on, then as we devoted more and more time to generating larger and larger samples, this relative frequency would settle down on the limiting value 0.50. This long-term limit to which relative frequency converges is called a **probability**.

3.3 Experiments, Outcomes, and Probability

The occurrence or realization of a result, a "head" or a "tail" in Table 3.1, is called an outcome. For a coin toss, these are the only two outcomes, and each is equally likely. For the roll of a die there are six outcomes: a face value of 1, 2, 3, 4, 5, or 6, and each is equally likely. In the lottery's instant cash game discussed at the beginning of this chapter there are eight outcomes: No instant cash, \$1, \$2, \$5, \$10, \$25, \$500, and \$5,000, but each of these outcomes is not equally likely.

Table 3.1
Outcome of Coin Toss

Outcome	Frequency	Relative Frequency	Frequency	Relative Frequency	Frequency	Relative Frequency
Heads:	3	0.3	12	0.6	21	0.525
Tails:	7	0.7	8	0.4	19	0.475
$n =$	10		20		40	

The calculation of probability requires knowledge of how the outcome is determined. For instance, shaking a die in a cup for two seconds and then dumping it on the table is an experiment in which each face value (an outcome) has an equal one in six chance of occurring. As introduced in Chapter 1, an **experiment** is a situation that can be repeated a large (infinite) number of times, with the random chance factor being the only source of difference in outcomes for each running of the experiment.

Experiment
Trials or testing situations that can be repeated a large (infinite) number of times where the chance factor is the only source of difference in outcomes for each administration.

In the state lottery instant cash game, the experiment entails the identification of winning contestants (tickets). This experiment may be replicated month after month with many different contestants or with the same people entering the lottery over and over. In other experiments, actual replication may not take place or it may not be perfect. For example, the conditions under which robberies take place are not identical, but yet they may be viewed as experiments that give rise to a randomly determined outcome: the dollar value of things taken.

Many uncertain events involve outcomes that are not numerical. Whether or not a lottery contestant or a slot machine player has a match on three out of six "windows" is an event that may be deemed a success or a failure with no regard to the dollar value of the outcome. Whether a statistics test is "passed" or failed; whether a job applicant is rated unacceptable, satisfactory, or excellent; or whether a customer likes or does not like the service are all examples of outcomes that are not quantitative. They are qualitative attributes that are determined with a chance factor (guessing on the exam, for example). As we will see, probability calculations can be made on any attribute that occurs by chance.

In the lottery's instant cash game the prizes are: No instant cash, \$1, \$2, \$5, \$10, \$25, \$500, and \$5,000. These are the only eight outcomes that are possible in one administration of a game in which there are 75 million equally likely ways these outcomes could occur. This is the **sample space** or **outcome set** for the experiment that determines the "immediate redemption value of ticket."[1] The sample space includes all the outcomes and ways in which they could occur in an experiment.

Sample Space (or Outcome Set)
The set of all possible outcomes in an experiment.

One of the outcomes in the sample space must occur as an outcome of an experiment, but which one is uncertain. Before running an experiment, any one of the elements could be selected. After the experiment, however, the outcome selected is known with certainty. The amount of a winning ticket in last month's lottery was observed and is public knowledge, but the amount of a winning ticket eight weeks from now is in doubt. Identification of the sample space and the nature of the chance factor that determines the outcomes are the keys in our work to determine probability.

In the instant cash state lottery, the chance of winning is based on the 75 million tickets. This qualifier and the stated chances of winning show how the probability is related to the different ways the outcomes in the sample space can occur and their relative frequency of occurrences. In Chapter 1, relative frequencies were defined in terms of the number of times outcomes had actually been observed. The concept of probability pertains to the relative frequency of outcomes that have not yet occurred but that would occur over a large (infinite) number of future experiments that could be conducted in a sufficiently long (infinite) time period.

In the instant cash lottery game, if one in 12.5 tickets is worth \$1 and there are 75 million tickets, then we know that there must be six million of the \$1 tickets

(= 75000000/12.5) per running of the game. This *does not say* that a contestant who plays the game 25 times (where each play is in a new lottery) will get two tickets worth $1 each. It *does not say* that a contestant who plays the game 50 times (in a new lottery) will get four tickets worth $1 each. A chance or probability of 0.08 (=1/12.5) says that if a contestant plays the instant cash game an extremely large (infinite) number of times, then 8 percent of the time he or she will win $1, where each play is a new lottery.

For the $2 prize, the chance of winning is one in 31.25, which for 75 million tickets implies 2.4 million tickets worth $2 per running of the lottery. Again, this does not say that a contestant who plays the game 125 times will get four tickets worth $2 each. A likelihood or probability of 0.032 (=1/31.25) says that if a contestant plays the instant cash game an extremely large (infinite) number of times, then 3.2 percent of the time he or she will win $2. And similarly for the other prizes shown in Table 3.2, where the probability of a winning amount is calculated as the number of equally likely ways an outcome may occur divided by the number of equally likely ways all outcomes may occur.

$$\text{Probability of an outcome} = \frac{\text{Number of equally likely ways the outcome may occur}}{\text{Total number of equally likely ways all outcomes may occur}} \quad (3.1a)$$

Exhaustive Outcomes
All of the possible outcomes; all of those outcomes that make up the sample space.

There are several things to be emphasized in Table 3.2. First, the chance of winning must be interpreted as an average win per number of occurrences (for example, a $1 winning ticket occurs an average of once in 12.5 tickets). There are no assurances that one winning dollar ticket will appear in 12.5 tickets; this only happens on average. Similarly, the decimals in the probability column must be interpreted as a relative frequency over a large (infinite) number of plays. Finally, notice that the probabilities of all eight outcomes in the sample space sum to one, as with relative frequency. The eight outcomes are **exhaustive** since there are no other possible outcomes.

TABLE 3.2
Chances of Winning the Instant Cash Lottery

Prize	Number of winning tickets in 75 million	Chance of winning	Probability of winning
$ 0	64,684,610	1 in 1.1595	0.862461
$ 1	6,000,000	1 in 12.50	0.080000
$ 2	2,400,000	1 in 31.25	0.032000
$ 5	1,154,912	1 in 64.94	0.015399
$ 10	554,980	1 in 135.14	0.007400
$ 25	194,998	1 in 384.62	0.002600
$ 500	9,750	1 in 7,692.0	0.000130
$5,000	750	1 in 100,000	0.000010
	75,000,000		1.000000

Source: *HT*, October 8, 1989.

Mutually Exclusive Outcomes or events that cannot occur together.

The outcomes that form the sample space must also be **mutually exclusive;** they cannot occur together. That is, one outcome (ticket value) cannot be both a $1 and a $5,000 winner at the same time.

The sample space must be formed by outcomes that are mutually exclusive and exhaustive so that the probabilities of all the outcomes sum to one. For example, in a coin toss

$$P(\text{head}) + P(\text{tail}) = (1/2) + (1/2) = 1.00$$

For the throw of a die,

$$P(1) + P(2) + P(3) + P(4) + P(5) + P(6) =$$
$$(1/6) + (1/6) + (1/6) + (1/6) + (1/6) + (1/6) = 1.00$$

And in the instant cash game,

$$P(\$0) + P(\$1) + P(\$2) + P(\$5) + P(\$10) + P(\$25) + P(\$500) + P(\$5{,}000) =$$
$$0.862461 + 0.080000 + 0.032000 + 0.015399 + 0.007400 + 0.002600 +$$
$$0.000130 + 0.000010 = 1.000000$$

3.4 Events and Probability

Event A subset of the sample space that is formed by outcomes that share an attribute of interest.

In addition to the probability of an outcome, the probability of a subset of the sample space can be defined. The subset of outcomes of interest is called an **event**; it can consist of one or more outcomes in the sample space. In the instant cash game, we form the event "contestant wins some instant cash" with seven of the eight outcomes ($1, $2, $5, $10, $25, $500, and $5,000); this event is fulfilled if any one of these seven outcomes occurs.

The probability of an event is the sum of the probabilities of the outcomes that form the event. For example, the probability that a contestant has a ticket that turns out to be an instant winner is the sum of the probabilities that the contestant receives $1, $2, $5, $10, $25, $500, or $5,000:

$$P(\text{win } \$\text{s}) = P(\$1) + P(\$2) + P(\$5) + P(\$10) + P(\$25) + P(\$500) + P(\$5000) =$$
$$0.080000 + 0.032000 + 0.015399 + 0.007400 + 0.002600 + 0.000130 + 0.000010 =$$
$$0.137539$$

This adding-up process gives rise to another formula for the probability of an event: the number of equally likely ways that the outcomes making up an event may occur divided by the total number of equally likely ways all outcomes may occur.

Probability of an event

= Sum of the probabilities of the outcomes in the event

$$= \frac{\text{Number of equally likely ways outcomes in an event may occur}}{\text{Total number of equally likely ways all outcomes may occur}} \qquad (3.1b)$$

Because the eight outcomes \$0, \$1, \$2, \$5, \$10, \$25, \$500, and \$5,000 are exhaustive in the instant cash game with 75 million equally likely tickets, the events "win no instant dollars" and "win some instant dollars" are also said to be exhaustive. They are also mutually exclusive because they share no outcomes and cannot occur together; that is, one ticket cannot be both a "loser" and a "winner." If events are mutually exclusive and exhaustive, then their probabilities must sum to one. In the instant cash game,

$$P(\text{win \$s}) + P(\text{win no \$s}) = 0.137539 + 0.862461 = 1$$

EXERCISES

3.1 Probability may be referred to as relative frequency in the long term. What does this mean?

3.2 What is the difference between an outcome and an event in the calculation of probability?

3.3 The National Basketball Association used to flip a coin to determine which of the two worst teams would get the first draft choice. For many years, heads dominated, and sportscasters began to question the fairness of the process. How could heads keep coming up if this was a fair procedure?

3.4 An article in *The Wall Street Journal* (August 6, 1992) on risk analysis stated that, Risk analysis begins with scientific studies . . . . The data from the studies are then run through computer models of bewildering complexity, which produce results of implausible precision . . . risk analysis of the space shuttle showed a chance of failure so miniscule that it could probably fly every day for 300 years without an accident. Then the Challenger blew up." Comment on the reporter's understanding of probability.

3.5 With the notable exception of problems involving dice, coins, card tricks, and the drawing of balls from urns, why are the conditions of classical probability seldom fulfilled?

3.6 If the probability is 0.2 that an event will occur and if in four attempts we do not observe the event, then do we know how many times it will occur in the next six attempts? Explain.

3.7 If the probability is 0.1 that an event will occur and if in nine attempts the event is not realized, then what will happen on the next attempt?

3.8 A denigrating statement about the creative genius of artists sometimes heard at business meetings and dinner parties is that "if you had 700 monkeys with 700 typewriters, in 700 years at least one of them would have typed a play by Shakespeare." This statement is false, but it is true that "there is almost a 100 percent chance that if you had an infinite number of monkeys and typewriters for an infinite number of years, then at least one of them would type a play by Shakespeare." What is the difference between these two statements? Why is one false and the other true?

3.9 From the following probabilities $P(A_1) = 0.62$, $P(A_2) = 0.09$, $P(A_3) = 0.29$, $P(A_1 \,\&\, A_2) = 0.24$, determine if A_1, A_2, and A_3 are mutually exclusive and exhaustive.

3.5 DETERMINING THE SAMPLE SPACE

Determination of the sample space and its subsets is not always straightforward. A tree diagram may be helpful in identifying the different ways in which outcomes occur. To see this, consider a firm hiring three people. Assume that the firm sequentially and randomly draws these three people from a labor force that continually renews itself so that it is always 50 percent female. That is, each time a woman (or a man) leaves the labor force, a like woman (or man) enters so the probability of drawing a woman on the first hiring draw is 0.50; the probability that the second draw is a woman is 0.50, and the probability that the third is a woman is also 0.50. Also assume that each hiring situation is identical and unrelated to the previous one or the subsequent one. (Cases in which these probabilities and hiring situations change from hire to hire are considered later in this chapter and in more detail in following chapters.)

A tree diagram shows the likelihood of the hiring outcomes. It is thus a model or description of the way in which hiring may progress. Starting on the left, the first branch in Figure 3.1 represents the first hire, where either a woman (W) or man (M) may be hired. Movement up the top branch represents a woman hired; movement down the bottom branch represents a man hired. At each of the three branching positions, the same routing is followed. Each of the eight paths, from the left starting point to the stopping point on the right, represents an outcome. Because each of these eight paths is equally likely, we know the probability of each path is 1/8 = 0.125.

The outcome WMW, for example, is the path marked in Figure 3.1. The probability of the outcome WMW can be visualized by starting at the left-most point. Although we are interested only in one firm, to visualize probability here it is advantageous to think of 40 firms starting at this left-most point. We would expect 20 of these 40 firms to get a women on the first draw (assuming a continually updated labor force that is always 50 percent women). Of those 20, only 10 would get a man on the second draw and

FIGURE 3.1 A Tree Diagram as a Model of Hiring

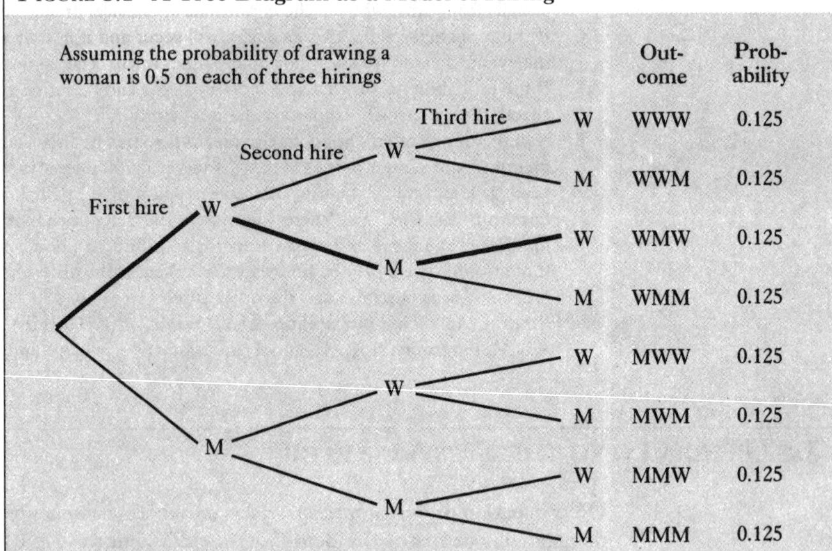

of those 10, only five would get a woman on the third. Thus, only five of the original 40 firms (or one-eighth) would have the outcome WMW.

In general, tree diagrams provide a good way to represent sequential experiments. If an experiment can be described in a tree diagram as a sequence of s steps, in which there are k outcomes on each step, then the total number of outcomes for the experiment is k^s. That is, the total outcomes in an s sequence of k items is k^s.

QUERY 3.1:
Give two different representations of the outcome set for a coin toss involving one flip of a nickel and a flip of a dime. Show the probability of each outcome.

ANSWER:
Below are a tree and a rectangular or tabular array of the outcomes and probabilities associated with the two coin tosses.

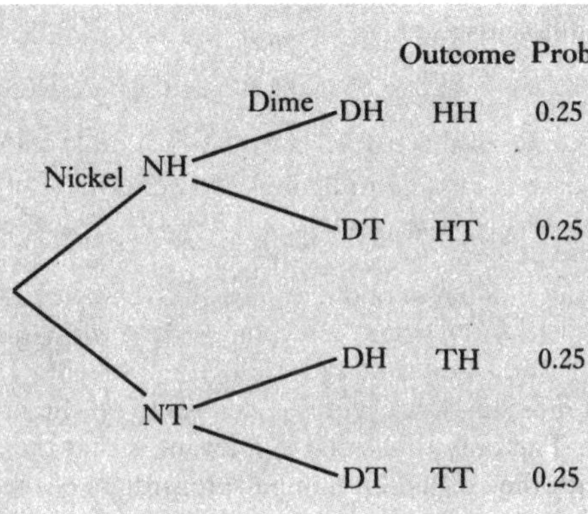

		Nickel	
		Heads	Tails
Dime	Heads	HH (.25)	HT (.25)
	Tails	TH (.25)	TT (.25)

3.6 Counting Techniques

Basic rules of counting also may be helpful in determining the sample space and its subsets. In the instant cash lottery example, the total number of ways all possible outcomes occur was given as 75 million, the sample space. If a winning ticket number were selected, but no one had purchased the identified ticket number, the game would still end and a new one would begin with no change in future cash prizes or the probabilities.

In big, ongoing lotteries, the total number of ways all outcomes can occur is determined by a fixed number of draws from a known population. These big games differ from the instant cash game because the payoffs are not immediate; they accumulate into big amounts (multimillion-dollar pots) until there is a winner, and they are shared by anyone holding a purchased ticket with the correct numbers.

Permutation
Any one of the different sequences of numbers that can be formed from a set of numbers.

Most big lotto games involve the random selection of six numbers from a pool of about 40 to 54 numbers. If the six numbers are selected from 54, without replacement, each sequence of six numbers is called a **permutation.** The sequence 1,2,3,4,5,6 is a permutation; the sequence 6,5,4,3,2,1, is another. Similarly, 16,51,4,32,22,1 is a permutation, as is 51,16,32,4,1,22. For permutations, the order matters.

The first number in a permutation of six numbers can be any one of the 54 numbers that can be drawn from the population. The second number, however, is restricted to the 53 numbers that were not chosen on the first selection. Thus, for any number selected on the first draw, there are 53 that could be matched with it on the second. Thus, the number of permutations of two numbers that can be selected from 54 is 2,862 = (54)(53). If a third number is restricted to the 52 numbers not selected on the first and second draws, the number of permutations of three numbers that can be selected from 54 is 148,824 = (54)(53)(52). By the sixth selection, there are only 49 numbers left in the population. Thus, the number of permutations of six numbers that can be selected from 54 numbers is

$$18{,}595{,}558{,}800 = (54)(53)(52)(51)(50)(49)$$

Thus, the probability of there being a winner in a multimillion-dollar lotto of this type would be only

$$1/18595558800 = 0.000000000053776$$

In general, the number of permutations of x items that can be selected from n items is $n(n-1)(n-2)\ldots(n-x+1)$, where selection is made without replacement and the order in which items are selected is meaningful.

Winning in most big lotto games is not based on the order in which the six numbers are drawn. The only thing that is relevant is that the six numbers on a winning ticket match with the six chosen numbers, regardless of the order. If the ordering in a selection of objects is not relevant, then what we need is the number of combinations that can be formed. That is, while AB and BA are two permutations of A and B, they are a single combination. The number of different ways of selecting x items from n items, ignoring the order of selection, is the number of **combinations** that can be formed from n items taken x at a time. This number of combinations is

Combination
A group of elements or items selected from a set with no regard to the order in which they are selected.

$$\frac{n(n-1)(n-2)\ldots(n-x+1)}{x(x-1)(x-2)\ldots(2)(1)}$$

An equivalent for this combination count can be written

$$\frac{n(n-1)(n-2)\ldots(2)(1)}{[x(x-1)(x-2)\ldots(2)(1)][(n-x)(n-x-1)(n-x-2)\ldots(2)(1)]}$$

Factorial of n ($n!$)
$n! = n(n-1)(n-2)\ldots(3)(2)(1)$

A shorthand notation for the product $n(n-1)(n-2)\ldots(2)(1)$ is the **factorial $n!$.** For example, $5! = 5 \cdot 4 \cdot 3 \cdot 2 \cdot 1$, where $0! = 1$. Using the factorial notation, the number of combinations of x items selected from n items is identified by $C(n,x)$ and calculated as

Combination of x items selected from n items is

$$C(n,x) = \frac{n!}{x!(n-x)!} \tag{3.2}$$

For $n = 54$ and $x = 6$,

$$C(n,x) = \frac{n!}{x!(n-x)!} = C(54,6) = \frac{54!}{6!48!}$$

$$= \frac{54 \cdot 53 \cdot 52 \cdot 51 \cdot 50 \cdot 49}{6 \cdot 5 \cdot 4 \cdot 3 \cdot 2 \cdot 1}$$

$$= \frac{18595558800}{720} = 25,827,165$$

So there are 25,827,165 different ways of randomly drawing six numbers from 54, with no regard to the order of selection. (Inexpensive hand calculators will not be accurate in the above division. They will show 18595558800/720 approximately equal to 25827.16+, where the + may be any digit depending on the manner in which the calculator does rounding. The number on the screen (25827.16+) must be multiplied by 1,000 to approximate the correct answer. A spreadsheet program, such as LOTUS 1-2-3, can be programmed to accurately do this division.)[2]

Only one combination of six numbers on a purchased ticket will match the six selected numbers. The appropriate probability of winning this big jackpot in which the order of selected numbers does not matter is thus 1/25827165 = 0.0000000387189, which is far greater than the probability of winning when order matters.

QUERY 3.2:
If a briefcase has a three-wheel lock, with each wheel numbered from 0 to 9, how many different ways are there to arrange the numbers on the three wheels? Is it unlikely that such a locked briefcase could be opened?

ANSWER:
There are 1,000 ways to order the numbers on the three wheels ($k^s=10^3$). With only 1,000 different orderings, it would be possible to try them all. Even by the chance, the probability of finding the correct ordering on the first try is 0.001, which is not extremely unlikely.

QUERY 3.3:

If a technician tests four computers per hour, with three of four expected to work properly, what is the probability of any two in a batch of four computers selected at random working properly? Determine your answer algebraically and show the outcome set.

ANSWER:

If the sequence in which the computers are tested is not important, the size of the sample space is

$$C(n,x) = \frac{n!}{x!(n-x)!} = C(4,2) = \frac{4!}{2!2!} = 6$$

Let G_1, G_2, and G_3 be the good computers and B_1 the bad one. The outcome set, assuming that sequencing is irrelevant, is then the six combinations

$$\{G_1G_2,\ G_1G_3,\ G_2G_3,\ G_1B_1,\ G_2B_1,\ G_3B_1\}$$

Again, if the sequence in which the computers are tested is unimportant, there are three outcomes that form the event "two good," namely:

$$\{G_1G_2,\ G_2G_3,\ G_1G_3\}$$

Algebraically, these three outcomes are calculated as

$$C(n,x) = \frac{n!}{x!(n-x)!} = C(3,2) = \frac{3!}{2!1!} = 3$$

Thus, the probability of selecting two of four computers at random and having both work properly on the first try is 3/6 = 0.5. (Note: If the effects of sequencing were to be considered, then the outcome set would be twice as large, with 12 permutations, and the event space would be twice as large, with six permutations, but the probability of two of four computers working properly would still be 0.5.)

QUERY 3.4:

When the "Big Ten Conference" accepted Penn State as the eleventh college in the conference, the question was asked "If each of the 11 schools played the other teams twice, how many games would there be?"

ANSWER:

If each of the 11 schools plays the others twice, then the number of games is 110, which is determined by the permutation

$$n(n-1)(n-2) \ldots (n-x+1) = (11)(10) = 110$$

(Note: The answer is 110 and not 220, as some might expect, because when one team plays another it counts for both.)

EXERCISES

3.10 Two portable computers are to be selected from a pool of five. Unknown to the potential users is that computer number one is defective. It is known that computers one (A_1) and two (A_2) are the same make and model (A) and computers three (B_1), four (B_2), and five (B_3) are the same make and model (B), which is different from that of computers one and two. Use a tree diagram to show the possible outcomes in the sample space.

3.11 If each of the 20 outcomes in Exercise 3.10 is equally likely, what is the probability that at least one of the two selected computers is defective and that at least one of the computers is a make and model A?

3.12 A department consists of 10 members. Three are to be selected for different jobs. The order in which assignments are made is important, because the three jobs are viewed as being of different status. In how many different ways can the jobs be assigned?

3.13 From the information in Exercise 3.12, if the assignment order is not important (all three jobs are considered of equal status, for example), then in how many different ways can the jobs be assigned?

3.14 It is sometimes argued that one of the consequences of affirmative action legislation is that hiring becomes random. If six applicants for a position are not of equal ability but, unknown to the prospective employer, could be ranked from most able (1) to least able (6), then if two of these applicants are hired at random what is the probability that the most able is hired?

3.15 There are three private contractors competing for two government contracts. The government agency could assign each contract to any one of the contractors or assign them both to the same contractor. If all outcomes are equally likely, what is the probability that both contracts go to the third contractor? (Identify the contractors and show the possible ways in which the contracts could be assigned.)

3.16 A specialty shop can produce five engines per day. If the selection of each is equally likely, what is the probability that the selection of two engines will result in both starting on the first try if only three of the five are properly timed to start?

3.17 A preselection pool consists of seven applicants for two jobs. If applicants are of equal ability and the jobs are the same, then in how many ways can the jobs be assigned?

3.18 A feature on the *Insider* TV show (Feb. 15, 1995) quoted a New York city official saying that no more than one percent of the cars that are towed off city streets and impounded have objects inside stolen. The TV show put four cars on streets where they would get towed; one had stuff inside taken by the tow truck operator. Assuming the probability of theft is 0.01 for each car, use a tree diagram to show the probability of 0, 1, 2, 3, and 4 cars being burglarized.

3.7 MULTIPLE EVENTS

Multiple sets of outcomes may be of interest to decision makers. For instance, if 50 percent of the available labor force is female, the U.S. Employment and Equal Opportunity Commission (EEOC) might be suspicious of a firm that hires fewer than two women for three jobs or one that hires all three of the same sex. This event can be written as

Compound (or Joint) Event
Events that must occur together.

"fewer than two women *or* all the same sex"

The EEOC and an employer will definitely be interested in the probability of this **compound** or **joint event**. Compound or joint events are formed by two or more events in one of two ways: either as a union of two or more events or as an intersection of two or more events. Below we consider such compound events together with complements and conditional statements involving multiple events.

Unions and Intersections

Union of Two Events
All of the outcomes that make up the two events.

The probability calculation for "fewer than two women *or* all the same sex" is referred to as the probability of a **union of the two events** "fewer than two women" and "all the same sex." From Figure 3.1, it can be seen that there are four outcomes that have "fewer than two women": WMM, MWM, MMW, and MMM. This event is represented by the shaded area in Figure 3.2, panel a. There are two outcomes that have "all the same sex": WWW and MMM, as represented by the shaded area in Figure 3.2, panel b. Panel c shows the five outcomes that make up the compound event "fewer than two women or all the same sex." (Notice that adding the caveat "or both events" to the description of this compound event would not change the shaded area in panel c or the probability of this compound event.)

The probability of fewer than two women or all the same sex is five-eighths, or 0.625. This probability cannot be obtained by simply adding the probability of "fewer than two women" and the probability of "all the same sex" because these two events are not mutually exclusive; they share the outcome MMM. This double counting must be eliminated by subtracting it from the sum of the probability of these two events. That is,

$$\begin{aligned}&P(\text{fewer than two women or all the same sex})\\&= P(\text{fewer than two women}) + P(\text{all same sex})\\&- P(\text{fewer than two women and all same sex})\\&= \frac{4}{8} + \frac{2}{8} - \frac{1}{8} = \frac{5}{8} = 0.625\end{aligned}$$

Intersection of Two Events
The outcomes that fulfill the conditions for both events.

In general, if A or B are the two events of interest, then the probability of A or B is the probability of the union of A or B. The probability of A or B is calculated as the probability of A plus the probability of B minus the probability of A and B. The probability of the **intersection**, $P(A \text{ and } B)$, is subtracted from the sum of the probability of A and the probability of B because it is included in each of these probabilities and it cannot be counted twice, so one of the intersection probabilities is removed by subtracting it from the total.

Probability of ***A*** or ***B***

$$P(A \text{ or } B) = P(A) + P(B) - P(A \text{ and } B) \tag{3.3}$$

Complement of an Event
The set of outcomes that is not in the event.

Complements

If we define the event "all of the same sex" as event A, then those outcomes that are not in A are called the **complement** of A. The complement of A in the hiring case is represented by the unshaded area in Figure 3.2, panel b: WWM, WMW, WMM, MWW, MWM, and MMW. The complement of any set A is written Ā and is the set of all outcomes not in A.

Because the outcomes in A and the outcomes in Ā make up 100 percent of the sample space, $P(A) + P(\bar{A}) = 1.00$, we have the formula for the probability of the complement of A given by

Probability of the Complement of *A*

$$P(\bar{A}) = P(\text{not } A) = 1 - P(A) \tag{3.4}$$

The probability that not all hires are of the same sex is thus 0.75 (= 6/8). As another example, let event B be "fewer than two women." The complement is then "two or more women," which is the unshaded area in Figure 3.2, panel a. The probability of the complement of *B* is thus 0.50 (= 4/8).

FIGURE 3.2 Venn Diagrams for Events in the Hiring of Men and Women

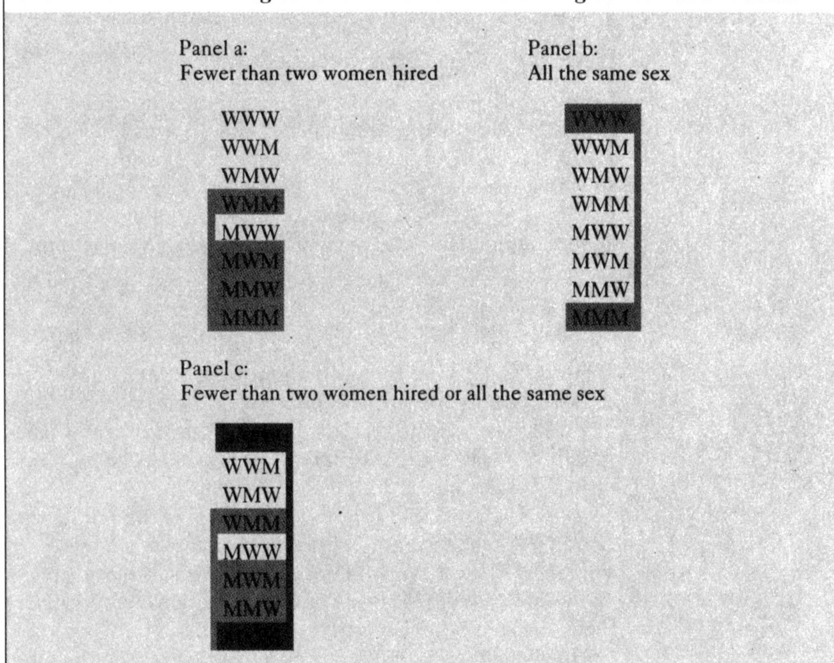

QUERY 3.5:
A firm has only six applicants (three men and three women) for three jobs. If hiring is random, what is the probability of at least one woman being hired? Why does your answer here differ from that obtained from Figure 3.1?

ANSWER:
First, the size of the sample space is

$$C(n,x) = \frac{n!}{x!(n-x)!} = C(6,3) = \frac{6!}{3!3!} = 20$$

Second, notice that the probability of at least one woman is the complement of all men hired. Thus,

$$P(\text{at least one woman}) = 1 - P(\text{all three men})$$

Only one of the outcomes involve the hiring of all three men.

$$C(n,x) = \frac{n!}{x!(n-x)!} = C(3,3) = \frac{3!}{3!0!} = 1$$

Thus, the probability of selecting at least one woman is

$$P(\text{at least one woman}) = 1 - (1/20) = 19/20 = 0.95$$

In Figure 3.1, the probability of hiring at least one woman was 0.875 (= 1.000 – 0.125), because the probability of hiring a woman on each trial was assumed fixed at 0.5. This assumption was reasonable as long as the pool from which individuals were drawn was extremely large or renewed over the sequence of hiring. In this query, that is not the case since the number of applicants is only six and there is no replacement. Thus, the probability of hiring a woman must change from trial to trial.

Conditional Probability

Conditional Probability
The likelihood of one event given that another event occurs.

Decision makers are often interested in the probability of one event given another. This is a **conditional probability**. For example, the EEOC might have documentation of an employer saying that it would hire "at most one woman." It might then ask the question: What is the probability of no woman being hired given that at most one woman is to be hired?

Suppose again that Figure 3.2, panel a, is the relevant sample space for this employer. We can see that there are four outcomes that make up the event "at most one woman": WMM, MWM, MMW, and MMM. Of these, only one constitutes the event "no women hired," MMM. Thus the conditional probability of no women hired, given that at most one woman is to be hired, is 1/4 or 0.25.

In general terms, if A is one event and B another, then the probability of A given B is calculated by the formula

Conditional probability of A given B

$$P(A \mid B) = \frac{P(A \text{ and } B)}{P(B)} \tag{3.5}$$

where $P(B) > 0$

The formula for conditional probability facilitates the determination of the probability of the intersection. In many problems, the decision maker will need to know the probability of the intersection (A and B) but he or she will only know a conditional probability and the probability of the event on which the conditional probability is based. As demonstrated by the next Query 3.6, Formula (3.5) provides the key to solving for the intersection of the two events.

QUERY 3.6:

According to a story in *Newsweek* (June 8, 1992), promoting drugs in medical journals is big business, with American drug companies spending $350 million a year for advertising. A study by UCLA researchers showed 100 of 109 ads in medical journals had factual errors in areas for which the Food and Drug Administration (FDA) has established explicit standards. The FDA checks only about 15 percent of all drug ads. What is the probability of the FDA checking and finding an error for which it has standards?

ANSWER:

Let the probability of finding an error if checked be

$$P(\text{error} \mid \text{check}) = 100/109 = 0.917431$$

The probability of FDA checking is $P(\text{check}) = 0.15$. Thus, the probability of the FDA checking and finding an error is 0.1376. From a rewriting of Formula (3.5)

$$\begin{aligned} P(\text{error and check}) &= P(\text{error} \mid \text{checked})*P(\text{check}) \\ &= (0.917431)(0.15) \\ &= 0.137615 \end{aligned}$$

QUERY 3.7:

A drug-testing company claims that its screening tests are 95 percent accurate, meaning that 95 percent of drug users are accurately identified and 95 percent of those who don't use drugs are accurately identified. From government statistics, we know that approximately 5 percent of the adult population in a community are drug users. A human resource manager of a large firm in this community asks if it would be a good idea to start testing prospective employees.

ANSWER:

Unless the manager wants to waste company resources, these tests should not be purchased. If a prospective employee is identified as a drug user (tests positive), there is only a 0.5 probability that he or she is actually a drug user. This can be seen by constructing the following table:

	Drug user	Nondrug user	
test positive	0.0475	0.0475	0.0950
test negative	0.0025	0.9025	0.9050
	0.0500	0.9500	1.0000

where $P(\text{test positive} \mid \text{drug use}) = 0.95$, as claimed by the drug company, and $P(\text{drug use}) = 0.05$, as found in government records for your community, imply that $P(\text{test positive and drug use}) = (0.95)(0.05) = 0.0475$ and $P(\text{test negative and nondrug use}) = (0.95)(0.95) = 0.9025$, from which the other two intersections are obtained by subtracting from the relevant column probabilities at the bottom of the table. The probability of someone actually being a drug user given that he/she tests positively is now calculated as

$$P(\text{drug user} \mid \text{positive}) = P(\text{drug user and positive})/P(\text{positive})$$
$$= 0.0475/0.095 = 0.5000$$

Thus, there is only a 50-50 chance (as in a coin toss) that someone in the community who tests positively for drugs is actually a drug user. A manager thus has little reason to make use of the drug tests.

3.8 INDEPENDENCE

Two events are independent if information about the occurrence of one does not affect the probability of the other occurring. Coin tosses are typically independent: Whether a head or tail occurs on the first toss has no influence on a head or tail on the second. The probability that a tennis player wins a tennis tournament, however, is likely related to the seed or ranking assigned prior to the tournament; winning is not independent of seed.

If two events A and B are independent then

$$P(A \mid B) = P(A)$$

That is, the probability of A given B is the same as the probability of A; the occurrence of B does not affect the probability of A. From the definition of conditional probability, we also know that independence must imply that

$$\frac{P(A \text{ and } B)}{P(B)} = P(A)$$

Multiplying both sides of this expression by the probability of B gives

$$P(A \text{ and } B) = P(A)P(B)$$

which is a helpful formula for calculating the probability of the intersection of two **independent events.**

Independent Events
Two events that do not influence each other so that the probability of the first occurring, given that the second occurs, is the probability of the first in isolation.

QUERY 3.8:
The probability of rolling a one with either of two dice is one-sixth. What is the probability of rolling snake eyes (two ones with a pair of dice)?

ANSWER:
The outcomes of the dice rolls are independent; thus, the probability of snake eyes is 1/36 [=(1/6)(1/6)].

QUERY 3.9:
G. Howard (1987) describes a system that was alleged to be able to "beat" big, ongoing lotto games such as that in Pennsylvania. It is based on the so-called balanced game theory, which says that numbers that occur randomly should have their sums distributed approximately as a bell-shaped distribution. A lotto game that involves the selection of six numbers out of 54, for example, should yield a sum of those six numbers that is bell shaped with a mean, median, and mode of 165. [The median of the 54 numbers is 27.5; with six numbers drawn, the numbers with the highest probability must thus sum to 165 = (6)(27.5).] With the sum of the six selected numbers forming a bell-shaped distribution around a mean, median, and mode of 165, feasible ranges of values for the sum of the six selected numbers can be calculated using the rule of bell-shaped distributions. For example, a 68 percent interval could be computed with the explanation that 68 percent of all sums will fall within this range of values. If a ticket with a sum of the six numbers is chosen outside this range, then those numbers have only a 32 percent chance of being selected. This is alleged to imply that tickets with numbers that sum to 165 should be purchased. Is this theory correct?

ANSWER:
R. Paulson (1992) provides a good answer. He states that the information about sums being approximately bell shaped around a theoretical mean is correct, as discussed in Chapter 7 when the Central Limit Theorem is introduced. Paulson also states, however, that it is irrelevant in the prediction of future lottery winning numbers. As we will see in Chapter 7, the Central Limit Theorem explains the mathematics of what is expected to happen, but it doesn't tell a person which particular combination that adds up to a given sum will occur.

The balanced game system ignores the quantity of various combinations of numbers that all add up to the same total. Paulson considers a lottery game in which six numbers are selected from 40, so the most probable sum for those six numbers is 123 [=(6)(40+1)/2]. The probability of winning, however, is not altered by having your chosen numbers add up to 123. There are 56,512 different combinations that sum to 123, and there are 3,838,380 possible combinations for this particular game. Let the event *A* be the winning numbers sum to 123; let event *B* be your ticket numbers sum to 123, and event *C* is you win. If your numbers sum to 123, then your probability of winning is $P(A \cap C) = P(C \mid A)P(A)$, or (1/56,512)(56,512/3,838,380) = 1/3,838,380. The following conditional probabilities show that the probability of winning is not affected by the ticket numbers summing to 123:

$$P(C|B) = \frac{P(B \cap C)}{P(B)} = \frac{P(B|C)P(C)}{P(B)}$$

$$= \frac{(56{,}512/3{,}838{,}380)(1/3{,}838{,}380)}{56{,}512/3{,}838{,}380}$$

This is the same as your probability of winning if your numbers do not add up to 123; events B and C are independent.

QUERY 3.10:
The briefcase in Query 3.2 had only one three-wheel combination lock, where each wheel was numbered from 0 to 9. If the briefcase had two of these locks, with each requiring a different three number sequence to open, what would be the probability of opening it by chance?

ANSWER:
If the briefcase has two three-wheel locks, where each wheel is numbered 0 to 9 and each lock operates independently, then the chances are one in million of opening the case by chance. That is,
P(both open) = *P*(lock one opens) × *P*(lock two opens) = (0.001)(.001) = 0.000001

QUERY 3.11:
According to an article in *The Wall Street Journal* (September 9, 1993), in a typical shift a telephone sales rep for DialAmerica Marketing Inc. of Mahwah, N.J. will speak to the person he or she is trying to reach "about half the time and will 'convert' about 15% of those who hear the 'presentation.'" What proportion of the people on a rep's list to call are reached and not converted?

ANSWER:
We can determine that about 7.5 percent of those on a rep's list are reached and converted,

$P(C \text{ and } R)/P(R) = P(C|R) => P(C \text{ and } R) = P(R)R(C|R) = (.5)(.15) = 0.075$

Thus, 42.5 percent of those on a rep's list to call are reached and not converted, 0.500 - 0.075 = 0.425.

The Best of Marilyn on Conditional Probability

The following are excerpts from Marilyn vos Savant's column "Ask Marilyn," in *Parade Magazine*.

QUERY 3.12:

I'll come straight to the point. In the following question and answer, you blew it!

"Suppose you're on a game show and you're given a choice of three doors. Behind one door is a car; behind the others, goats. You pick a door—say, No. 1—and the host, who knows what's behind the doors, opens another door—say, No. 3—which has a goat. He then says to you, 'Do you want to pick door No. 2?' Is it to your advantage to switch your choice?"

You answered, "Yes, you should switch. The first door has a 1/3 chance of winning, but the second door has a 2/3 chance."

Let me explain: If one door is shown to be a loser, that information changes the probability to 1/2. As a professional mathematician, I'm very concerned with the general public's lack of mathematical skills. Please help by confessing your error and, in the future, being more careful.

—Robert Sachs, Ph.D.
George Mason University
Fairfax, VA
December 2, 1990

You blew it, and you blew it big! I'll explain: After the host reveals a goat, you now have a one-in-two chance of being correct. Whether you change your answer or not, the odds are the same. There is enough mathematical illiteracy in this country, and we don't need the world's highest IQ propagating more. Shame!

—Scott Smith, Ph.D.
University of Florida
December 2, 1990

Your answer to the question is in error. But if it is any consolation, many of my academic colleagues also have been stumped by this problem.

—Barry Pasternack, Ph.D.
California Faculty Association
December 2, 1990

You are utterly incorrect about the game-show question . . . . How many irate mathematicians are needed to get you to change your mind?

—E. Ray Bobo, Ph.D.
Georgetown University
February 17, 1991

I am in shock that after being corrected by at least three mathematicians, you still do not see your mistake.

—Kent Ford
Dickinson State University
February 17, 1991

Answer:

Good heavens! With so much learned opposition, I'll bet this one is going to keep math classes all over the country busy on Monday.

My original answer is correct. But first, let me explain why your answer is wrong. The winning odds of 1/3 on the first choice can't go up to 1/2 just because the host opens a losing door. To illustrate this, let's say we play a shell game. You look away, and I put a pea under one of three shells. Then I ask you to put your finger on a shell. The odds that your choice contains a pea are 1/3, agreed? Then I simply lift up an empty shell from the remaining two. As I can (and will) do this regardless of what you've chosen, we've learned nothing to allow us to revise the odds on the shell under your finger.

The benefits of switching are readily proved by playing through the six games that exhaust all the possibilities. For the first three games, you choose No. 1 and switch each time; for the second three games, you choose No. 1 and "stay" each time, and the host always opens a loser. Here are the results (each row is a game):

DOOR 1	DOOR 2	DOOR 3
AUTO Switch and you lose.	GOAT	GOAT
GOAT Switch and you win.	**AUTO**	GOAT
GOAT Switch and you win.	GOAT	**AUTO**
AUTO Stay and you win.	GOAT	GOAT
GOAT Stay and you lose.	**AUTO**	GOAT
GOAT Stay and you lose.	GOAT	**AUTO**

When you switch, you win two out of three times and lose one time in three; but when you don't switch, you only win one in three times.

You can play the game with another person acting as host with three playing cards—two jokers for the goats and an ace for the auto. Doing it a few hundred times to get valid statistics can get a little tedious, so perhaps you can assign it for extra credit—or for punishment. (*That'll* get their goats!)

— Marilyn vos Savant
December 2, 1990

. . . I'm receiving thousands of letters, nearly all insisting that I'm wrong, including one from the deputy director of the Center for Defense Information and another from a research mathematical statistician from the National Institute of Health! Of the letters from the general public 92% are against my answer, and of the letters from universities, 65% are against me . . . . But math answers aren't determined by vote . . . . The original answer is still correct . . . .

— Marilyn vos Savant
February 17,1991

Maybe women look at math problems differently than men...I still think you're wrong. There is such a thing as female logic.

—Don Edwards
Sunriver, OR
February 17 and July 7, 1991

You are the goat!

—Glenn Calkins
Western State College
February 17, 1991

You're wrong, but look at the positive side. If all those Ph.D.s were wrong, the country would be in very serious trouble.

—Everett Harman, Ph.D.
U.S. Army Research Institute
February 17, 1991

You are indeed correct. My colleagues at work had a ball with this problem, and I dare say that most of them—including me at first—thought you were wrong!

—Seth Kalson, Ph.D.
Massachusetts Institute of Technology
February 17, 1991

I put my solution of the problem on the bulletin board in the Physics Department office here, following it with a declaration that you were right. All morning I took a lot of criticism and abuse from colleagues, but by late in the afternoon most of them came around. I even won a free dinner from one overconfident professor.

—Eugene Mosca, Ph.D.
U.S. Naval Academy
Annapolis, MD
July 7, 1991

After considerable discussion and vacillation here at the Los Alamos National Laboratory, two of my colleagues independently programmed the problem, and in one million trials, switching paid off 66.7% of the time. The total running time on the computer was less than one second.

—G.P. DeVault, Ph.D.
Los Alamos National Laboratory
Los Alamos, NM
July 7, 1991

Now fess up. Did you really figure all this out, or did you get help from a mathematician?

—Lawrence Bryan
San Jose, CA
July 7, 1991

NOTE: *The New York Times* gave front-page coverage to this "Let's Make a Deal" controversy. Outside her column, however, Marilyn vos Savant responded only to an article in the *American Statistician* (November 1991). Her letter to the authors (J.P. Morgan, N.R. Chagantry, R.C. Dahiya, and M.J. Doviak) and their rejoinders demonstrate that issues of probability depend critically on the nature of the question asked and the sample space defined.

EXERCISES

3.19 Identify the following as either the probability of an event, a joint event (unions or intersections), or a conditional event.

a. The probability the next president of the United States is under 50 years of age and female.

b. The probability it rains tomorrow given that it rained today.

c. The probability that the stock market rises and the prime interest rate declines next week.

d. The probability a person earns a grade of B in a statistics course if he or she earned a B in microeconomics.

e. The probability that either of two machines in a production process produces a defect.

f. The probability that a real estate agent is a member of the "ten million dollar club" and is under 35 years old.

g. The probability that an unidentified executive is earning more than $100,000 per year regardless of his or her age.

3.20 State whether each of the following is true or false and give your reason.

a. If $P(A_1 \mid A_2) = 0$, then A_1 and A_2 are independent.

b. If $P(A_1 \mid A_2) = 0$, then A_1 and A_2 are mutually exclusive.

c. If A_1 and A_2 are independent, then $P(A_1) = P(A_2)$.

3.21 Two independent machines produce plastic decals, with defect rates of 0.015 and 0.025. If 100 decals are produced, what is the probability of three or fewer defects?

3.22 A *Business Week*/Harris Poll (June 15, 1992) of 400 female executives at companies with $100 million or more in sales found that 27 percent had been harassed, but of those who had been harassed, only 25 percent reported it to their employers. What is the probability of a female executive having been harassed and reporting it?

3.23 Purdue University Cooperative Extension Service reports that 50 percent of fatal tractor accidents are from tractor rollovers and 18 percent are from run overs. "Indeed, tractor accidents are the leading cause of farm-related fatalities in Indiana, accounting for 53 percent of all farm-related deaths, according to the American Society of Agricultural Engineers."(*HT*, June 14, 1992)

a. Given a fatal farming accident, what is the probability it was from a tractor rollover?

b. Given a fatal farming accident, what is the probability it was from something other than tractor rollover or tractor run over?

3.24 A *WSJ* (July 15, 1992) article reported that institutional investors are getting more assertive in an attempt to curb excessive executive pay. Of the 56 institutions surveyed, 66 percent (37 of 56) said they favored the creation of compensation committees to review or even set executive pay. In addition, 50 percent said such committees should have the power to hire and pay compensation consultants directly. From this information, can you calculate the probability that an institutional investor would favor the creation of a compensation committee that has the power to hire and pay compensation consultants? Why or why not? Explain.

3.25 A *Wall Street Journal* article (August 11, 1992) reported that "Most American men—eight out of 10—use a hair dryer, according to industry estimates . . . . And while men purchase just 20 percent of the 20 million hair dryers each year, Frank Lindsey, vice president of marketing for Conair Corp., a leading maker of blow dryers, says that's not important." If use and purchase of hair dryers are independent, what is the probability that a man does not buy but uses a hair dryer?

3.26 A *Wall Street Journal* (July 14, 1992) article, suggested that "Only 7%" of companies have a "very complete" understanding of the Americans With Disabilities Act. A *WSJ* (August 11, 1992) article reported that "76% worry" about possible lawsuits under this new disability law. What is the probability of a company being worried and having a complete understanding of this act, assuming independence?

3.27 An arms dealer accepts or rejects shipments of bullets on the basis of testing a few bullets sampled from boxes selected from the shipment. Suppose we know that an inspector has accepted 99 percent of all good shipments and has incorrectly rejected 1 percent of the good shipments. In addition, the inspector accepts 94 percent of all shipments. It is also known that 10 percent of all shipments are of inferior quality. Find the probability that a shipment is

a. rejected.
b. good.
c. good and accepted.
d. inferior or rejected.
e. inferior if it is accepted.
f. good if it is rejected.

3.28 A financial analyst states that the probability "a real estate stock rises is 0.75, if the stock market rises." The probability that the stock market will rise is 0.2. What is the probability of both the stock market in general rising and the real estate stock rising?

3.29 Steven C. Salop, in "Evaluating Uncertain Evidence With Sir Thomas Bayes: A Note For Teachers," *Economic Perspectives* (Summer 1987), provides a discussion of the reliability of evidence in a wrongful injury suit against the Blue Cab Company for a hit-and-run accident alleged to involve one of its blue taxis. Salop states that the eyewitness was ". . . 80 percent reliable in identifying the color of taxi. That is, he was able to identify the correct color of taxis 80 percent of the time . . . ." Salop provided the following "matrix" to show how many of the city's 15 blue taxis and 85 green taxis this eyewitness could be expected to identify correctly—12 of the 15 blue and 68 of the 85 green. Salop stated: "Therefore, when the eyewitness testifies that a particular taxi is blue, the likelihood that the taxi is blue in fact is only 12/29, or 41 percent . . . the plaintiff should have sued the Green Cab company, on the strength of the Registrar's testimony (of 15 blue and 85 green cabs in the city)." In coming to this conclusion, Salop made a major error confusing conditional with unconditional probability. What is his error, and what are its implications for the analysis?

		Color Perceived by Eyewitness		
		Blue	Green	Total
Color in fact	Blue	12	3	15
	Green	17	68	85
	Total	29	71	100

3.30 A computer manufacturer uses disk drives from two suppliers. The first supplier accounts for 80 percent of the drives. It is known that 5 percent of all drives are defective and that 6 percent of the drives supplied by the first supplier are defective. If a disk drive is found to be defective, what is the probability it came from the first supplier?

3.31 In a retirement community, 60 percent of the population are coffee drinkers and 30 percent are smokers. Moreover all the smokers are coffee drinkers. What is the probability that a randomly selected person from the community would be a smoker, given that the person is a coffee drinker?

3.32 Three students were late for an exam and said the car in which they were riding had a flat tire. The instructor agreed to giving them extra time conditional on their agreeing to answer one additional question and to taking the exam in separate rooms. The added question was: What tire was it - driver's side front or rear, or passenger's side front or rear? What is the probability that all three would name the same tire by chance?

3.9 SUBJECTIVE AND OBJECTIVE ODDS AND PROBABILITY

Odds
A statement of chance that gives the number of times an event will occur versus the number of times it will not occur over a large (infinite) number of trials.

The words **odds**, probability, chance, and likelihood are typically used as synonyms. But they may have different meanings in different circumstances.

"Chance" and "likelihood" are typically used to describe the probability of an event. In the random flip of a coin, the chance of a "head" may be given as 1 out of 2, or 1 in 2, for a probability of 0.50. The "odds" of a head, however, describe the probability of a head versus the probability of a tail. For the coin toss, the odds of heads are 1 to 1, which is written 1:1. The odds of getting a face value of four in a single, six-sided dice toss is 1:5, for a probability of $1/6 = 0.1667$. More generally, mathematical odds give the probability of an event A relative to its complement.

$$\text{Mathematical odds of event } A = \frac{P(A)}{1 - P(A)}$$

To complicate the interpretation of the word "odds," as used in mathematics, it is used differently in gambling. In horse racing, for example, the "morning line odds" (or simply morning line) on a horse are written as "5-2" or "5:2." But these <u>do not</u> say that the expert handicapper believes this horse will win the race 5 of 7 times. These odds pertain to the money wager: according to the handicapper's prediction (educated guess) if you bet \$2.00 on this horse to win and it does, then you will get \$7.00 back - the \$2.00 bet plus \$5.00 net return. Alternatively, if this horse could run a large (infinite) number of races against the same field, and each time you bet \$2.00 on it to win, 5 of 7 times you would get nothing back; 2 of 7 times you would get \$7.00 back. That is, the handicapper is predicting that only 2 out of 7 times will this horse win, on the average, for an approximate probability of winning of 0.2857. Similarly, if the odds on a horse are given as "9:1" or simple "9," then the predicted probability of this horse winning is only 0.10. In general, gambling odds are expressed as the probability of not winning relative to the probability of winning when money is wagered on the outcome.

$$\text{Gambling odds of wager} = \frac{1 - P(\text{winning})}{P(\text{winning})}$$

Recognize that a handicapper's odds of a horse paying off need not be based on a direct reference to any relative frequency distribution. The handicapper's odds are his or her best guess about the probabilities of a horse "being in the money." Similarly, when stock market forecasters predict what is going to happen to stock prices, they need not be basing their likely scenario of a rise or fall on actual past data.

The handicapper's odds and the forecaster's likely scenario are not the same as statements about probabilities in the state-run lotteries, wheels of chance (e.g., a 38-number roulette wheel or a 360-number wheel of fortune), dice games (e.g., craps or Yahtzee), card games (e.g., blackjack or stud), or flipping coins. In those games of chance, the likelihoods of outcomes are fixed in accordance with physical, time, or rule constraints. Because a roulette wheel is numbered one through 38, the number 15 will come around once each turn of the wheel. Once in 38 spins, on the average, the ball will land on number 15. It makes sense to talk about repeated spins of the wheel. The imagination is stretched, however, in thinking about replicating horse races at Churchill Downs, and days at the New York Stock Exchange.

In the case of the stock market, horse racing, or other investment opportunities involving uncertain events that cannot be replicated, the relative frequentist's interpretation of probability can be approximated by finding groups of comparable stocks or horses to see what fraction of them had price appreciation or actually won races under like conditions. The obvious question is how to find groups of comparable stocks or horses.

Peter Asch and Richard Quandt (1991, p.111) demonstrated how race-time odds can be used to group horses. Race-time odds, unlike the handicapper's morning odds, are calculated as the amount bet on a horse divided by the total amount bet on all horses in the race. This relative frequency measure is still a subjective probability measure, because it is based on the opinions of the betting public, but it may be viewed as "more objective" because it reflects what racetrack patrons are betting. The "most objective measure" of the probability of winning might be to count how many horses in each group actually won as a percentage of the total number of horses in the group. Even this measure, however, is not truly objective in the sense that it represents a count of replicable results; it overlooks events that might have taken place during the races that may have influenced the results in a nonreplicable way. Similarly, in studies of the stock market, identical daily replications are not possible.

The notion that there is a truly objective probability that can be interpreted as a long-term relative frequency is an idea that may not be fully realized in the real world.

Historical Perspective

As demonstrated by questions asked of Marilyn vos Savant, the concept of probability is not easily applied to everyday problems. Part of the reason for this is that the issues are difficult to formulate and are open to different interpretations. Another is that the definition and meaning of probability are not unique and universally accepted. There is no universally accepted and fully adequate definition of probability.

Galileo (1564–1642), mathematician and astronomer, may have been the first to formally attempt and apply a definition of probability. In his high-paying academic position at the University of Pisa, Galileo had no explicit duties other than to answer queries from his Highness Cosimo II of Tuscany. Cosimo, an avid dice player, reportedly had noticed that throwing three six-sided dice resulted in a sum of nine less often than a sum of 10; yet, he reasoned that there are six outcomes (3 + 3 + 3, 5 + 3 + 1, 4 + 3 + 2, 5 + 2 + 2, 6 + 2 + 1, and 4 + 4 + 1) that sum to nine and six that yield 10 (4 + 3 + 3, 4 + 4 + 2, 5 + 4 + 1, 5 + 3 + 2, 6 + 3 + 1, and 6 + 2 + 2), suggesting that the sum of nine and 10 should have the same number of occurrences. What is amiss, he asked Galileo?

Galileo responded that the six outcomes identified by Cosimo are not each equally likely. There are 216 (= 6 · 6 · 6) ways of forming a sum from the outcomes on the faces of three dice; of these, 25 form a sum of nine and 27 sum to 10. Galileo then formulated the classic definition of probability:

> The probability of an outcome (or event) is the number of ways an outcome may occur divided by the total number of ways all outcomes may occur; thus,

$$P(9) = 25/216 = 0.11574 < P(10) = 27/216 = 0.125$$

This classical definition of probability suffers from two shortcomings. First, the concept is defined in terms of its measurement (circularity). Second, it cannot easily handle a large (infinite) number of outcomes and large (infinite) number of ways of obtaining those outcomes. Jacques Bernoulli (1654–1705) evaded the circularity problem by defining probability as a "degree of confidence" that may vary from person to person but could be objectively determined by looking at observable frequencies. This frequency approach was later placed on an axiomatic footing (in which generalities are deduced from assumptions) when John Venn defined probability as the limiting value of the percentage of favorable outcomes in an infinite sequence of independent replications (Richard von Mises, 1964).

The axiomatic definition of probability suffers from three weaknesses. First, an exact replication is impossible—if the rolling of a die is replicated perfectly, then wouldn't it always result in the same outcome? Second, because infinity is never realized, probability is never a precise or exact number; it is always an estimate. Third, and possibly most important in applications, the sample space is typically unclear. When taking a road trip, is the objective probability of your car crashing determined by your experiences on all prior trips? Your trips only to the same location? The trips of all other drivers? Or only those drivers with your kind of car; or, . . . ?

Economist John Maynard Keynes (1921) and mathematician Harold Jeffreys (1948) advanced a third definition of probability. Although Jeffreys tried to distance himself from Keynes, they both set out an approach to probability based on personal degrees of belief and linked those to the notion of utility. Both approaches view objective probability as a measure of the strength of the connection between a set of evidence and the truth of some hypothesis, when viewed by a "rational person." However, the establishment of the hypothesis believed true (e.g., person is innocent) against which the probability of another hypothesis is assessed (person is guilty) requires a prior subjective judgment so the resulting probability calculation cannot be uniquely objective.

Finally, there is the subjective or personal school of probability, as codified by Leonard Savage (1954). Subjective or Bayesian probabilities can be degrees of beliefs about one-time events (e.g., the introduction of a new series of Cadillacs or the destruction of the center structure of the Golden Gate Bridge in an earthquake) or events that can be replicated. The only requirement is that the belief system is consistent, so that multiple bets cannot be made with the agent winning under all outcomes. The question to be raised, however, is: How are these consistent subjective probabilities formulated by the agent?

As pointed out by Paul Schoemaker (1982) in his review of different types of probability, "The important point is that probability is not a simple construct . . . . Its measurement is obviously difficult in real-world settings." Casual students of statistics and serious scholars alike have learned that there may be no unique and unquestionable answer to complex problems involving probabilities.

QUERY 3.13:
The following letter was circulated by the Indiana State Lottery. How does its use of the word "odds" relate to the probability of winning?

Dear Lotto Cash player,

Thank you for your interest in the Hoosier Lottery's Lotto Cash game. You indicated that you had a question about how odds are calculated for the game. Hopefully the following will provide you with the information you need.

The general formula for calculating lotto odds is as follows:

$$\text{Odds}(m) = \frac{\binom{f}{p}}{\binom{p}{m}\binom{f-p}{p-m}}$$

Where f = field size, p = player picks, and m = number of matches.

The factors in the form of (x/y) are called binomial coefficients and are evaluated as follows:

$$\binom{x}{y} = \frac{x!}{y!\,(x - \hat{y})\,!}$$

A binomial coefficient provides a means of calculating the number of ways there are to draw *y* objects from a set of *x* objects (in this case the objects are lotto balls).

x! means x factorial and is evaluated as x(x-1)(x-2)...1. For example, 5!=5 ×4×3×2×1=120. Zero factorial is evaluated as 1.

In the case of the Hoosier Lottery's Lotto Cash game, the field size **f** is 44, the player picks **p** is 6 and the number of matches **m** may be 6, 5, 4, 3, 2, 1 or 0, depending on how many of the balls drawn by the lottery the player matches.

Using our formula for 6 matches, (the 6 of 6 grand prize) we get, Odds of 6 matches:

$$=\frac{\binom{44}{6}}{\binom{6}{6}\binom{44-6}{6-6}}=\frac{\frac{44!}{6!(44-6)!}}{\frac{6!}{6!(6-6)!}\ \frac{38!}{0!(38-0)!}}=\frac{\frac{44\times43\times42\times41\times40\times39}{6\times5\times4\times3\times2}}{1\times1}=7{,}059{,}05$$

If we perform the calculations for matching 5 of 6 and 4 of 6, we get odds of winning of 30,960.75 and 669.42 respectively.

To calculate overall odds, add the probabilities of each of the above prize levels and divide into 1 to convert back to odds, thus:

Overall Odds = 1/ (7,059,052 + 1/30,960.75 + 1/669.42) = 655.19

We hope this has helped you with your calculations.

HOOSIER LOTTERY

ANSWER:

The "mathematical odds" of six matches is not 7,059,052. This is the size of the sample space, which is the denominator for the probability of winning with six matches. The probability of the prize associated with six matches is 1/7,059,052, as acknowledged later in the letter. The "gambling odds" of six matches is also not 7,059,052, although they are close. The gambling odds are

$$\frac{7{,}059{,}051/7{,}059{,}052}{1/7{,}059{,}052}=7{,}059{,}051$$

or 7,059,051:1, which is a real "long shot."

3.10 Concluding Comments

This chapter provided an introduction to the application of probability for decisions involving outcomes and events associated with experiments. You now know how to define uncertainty in the context of these outcomes and events and their associated probabilities. You are able to distinguish between subjective and objective probabilities and give a historical perspective on their developments. With the basic rules of probability, you are able to make probability calculations for everyday business and economic decisions involving unions and intersections of events, complementary events, and independent events. You know how to work with conditional probability and relate this concept to the idea of independence. The next chapter extends these concepts and procedures to similar topics involving random variables.

Academic References

Asch, Peter, and Richard E. Quandt. *Racetrack Betting: The Professors' Guide to Strategies.* New York: Praeger, 1991.

Howard, G. "Balanced Game Theory." *Gambling Times,* January 1987, pp. 36–39.

Keynes, John Maynard. *A Treatise on Probability.* London: Macmillan, 1921.

Jeffreys, Harold. *Theory of Probability.* Oxford: Clarendon Press, Second Edition, 1948.

Von Mises, Richard. *Mathematical Theory of Probability and Statistics.* New York: Academic Press, 1964.

Morgan, J.P., N.R. Chagantry, R.C. Dahiya, and M.J. Doviak. "Let's Make a Deal: The Player's Dilemma." *American Statistician,* November 1991.

Paulson, R. "Using Lottery Games to Illustrate Statistical Concepts and Abuses." *American Statistician,* August 1992, pp. 202–204.

Savage, Leonard. *The Foundations of Statistics,* New York: John Wiley, 1954.

Schoemaker, Paul. "The Expected Utility Model: Its Variants, Purposes, Evidence and Limitations." *Journal of Economic Literature,* June, 1982.

Endnotes

1. The Indiana state lottery has six window tickets that are scratched open by contestants. Three matching windows wins the holder $1 to $5,000 in "instant cash." There is also a more involved and ongoing game in which 150,000 ticket purchasers out of 75 million get a chance to be on television, if they mail their tickets with the matching three windows that identify them as entrants. Of those 150,000 tickets, about 75 are planned for selection to be on the TV show. Each week, six finalist TV contestants pick unmarked doors for $3,000 to $30,000 prizes; the big prize winner also tries for $1 million. "But the odds of a person winning one of the $1 million jackpots are about 1 in 24 million." (*HT,* October 8, 1989)

2. To appreciate how a hand calculator does arithmetic with large numbers, try one with the typical eight-digit display. Enter the number 4321, which gives a calculator display of 00004321. Depressing the "x square" key gives a display that reads 18671041. Depressing the x square key again gives an error message, if the calculator does not use scientific notation. If the calculator uses scientific notation, then 3.4861 14 appears, which is scientific notation for 3.4861 times 10^{14}. Only five digits are presented accurately. when a number gets too large to be displayed, calculators that use scientific notation automatically shift to powers of ten. Statistical programs typically use floating point calculations when working with extremely large or small numbers. Floating point is similar to scientific notation except that it is based on powers of two instead of 10.

FORMULAS

- Probability of an outcome

$$= \frac{\text{Number of equally likely ways the outcome may occur}}{\text{Total number of equally likely ways all outcomes may occur}}$$

- Probability of an event

$$= \text{Sum of the probabilities of the outcomes in the event}$$

$$= \frac{\text{Number of equally likely ways the outcome in an event may occur}}{\text{Total number of equally likely ways all outcomes may occur}}$$

- Total outcomes in an s sequence of k items is k^s

- Combination of x items selected from n items is

$$C(n,x) = \frac{n!}{x!(n-x)!}$$

- Probability of A or B

$$P(A \text{ or } B) = P(A) + P(B) - P(A \text{ and } B)$$

- Probability of the complement of A

$$P(\overline{A}) = P(\text{not } A) = 1 - P(A)$$

- Conditional probability of A given B

$$P(A \mid B) = \frac{P(A \text{ and } B)}{P(B)}$$

CHAPTER 4

RANDOM VARIABLES

I shall never believe that God plays dice with the world.

Albert Einstein
1879–1955

4.1 Introduction

When working with outcomes that can be denominated in dollars, or any other quantifiable unit of measurement, knowledge of the event probabilities, as presented in the previous chapter, is not sufficient. We also need to have a central or expected value and a gauge of variability around that expected value. We need a concept that can represent all the values that might occur, along with their probabilities of occurrence. The following situations describe business and economics situations in which such knowledge will prove helpful, if not financially profitable:

- An article in *Newsweek* (December 9, 1991) on "fame and filthy lucre" reported that the average take in heists in the previous year was \$3,244 but that 85 percent of the robbers were caught. What is the expected return from a robbery? What magnitude of retribution would be a deterrent to would-be thieves?
- According to an article in *Business Week* (June 29, 1992), Cadillac is having trouble capitalizing on its award-winning Seville STS. "Part of the problem is that Cadillac misjudged the market. It thought 75% of Hamtramck's production would be the Seville's sister car, the two-door Eldorado (retailing at \$35,500), 15% would be the basic Seville (at \$37,000), and only 10% would be the STS, which retails for \$38,500. Instead 58% of the output is the Seville, half of that the STS." (p. 88) What is the probability distribution of projected retail sales of these new Cadillacs? What is the value of retail sales originally expected? Why and by how much does this differ from what was realized?
- During the 1992 America's Cup yacht race in San Diego, American industrialist Bill Koch and Italian tycoon Raul Gardini had to assess how much the other was spending on the race. Each took a different strategy in trying to throw off the other. Gardini was quoted as saying "whatever it takes," while Koch was forever complaining about cost. If Gardini is believed to be spending \$165 million, what is the probability that Koch is spending \$100 million?
- CNN MoneyLine (July 1, 1992) featured a story on failing interest in and falling state revenues from lotteries because of too few winners and rising administrative costs. In response, a social activist proposes an alternative to the Indiana instant cash game that he claims would raise the payout and prizes without adding to the administrative cost because it would make use of the existing structure. Instead of only a fraction (one in 24 million) of nonwinners in the instant cash game being eligible to enter the bigger but more distant \$1 million prize game, he proposes that each of the 75 million ticket holders have an independent chance at winning \$1 million.[1] If the chance of winning a \$1 million jackpot is one in 24 million and if the games are independent drawings from the same ticket pool, what is the probability that a ticket is a winner in either? What is the overall expected win for a ticket in these combined games?
- An article in *The Wall Street Journal,* "Putting Together Right Mix of Funds in Your Portfolio," stated "the idea is to own a variety of funds that tend to do well at different times, so that the overall value of your portfolio doesn't jump around too much." The question is: How does diversification reduce the risk of price fluctuation?

By the end of this chapter, you will be able to define a random variable to represent all of the chance values that are relevant to a situation. You will distinguish discrete random variables from continuous random variables. You also will be able to work with sums of random variables in economics and business situations where probability calculations are to be made. You will be able to calculate and interpret the expected value and variance of sets of discrete random variables and to relate these measures to risk assessment. You will know how to use the variance, covariance, and coefficient of variation in the assessment of the uncertainty associated with random variables.

4.2 Random Variables and Probability

Random Variable
A mapping or function that assigns one and only one numerical value to each outcome in an experiment.

When an experiment gives rise to numerically valued outcomes that occur by chance, those numerical values are said to be the realizations of a **random variable.** This and later chapters are devoted to the properties of random variables. At this stage, however, four points must be made clear:

- The notion of a random variable requires that an experiment can be conducted, with outcomes determined by chance.
- The outcomes of the experiment constitute a sample space, where the outcomes are both mutually exclusive and exhaustive.
- The outcomes are identified by unique numerical values that occur in accordance with a probability distribution.
- The numerical values are either discrete numbers or a continuous range of values along a number line.

Thus, a random variable is a rule for assigning numbers to outcomes that occur in an experiment by chance. Although experiments that give rise to nonnumerical outcomes are not associated with random variables, we can often transform qualitative outcomes into meaningful quantitative outcomes, and the experiments thus can be associated with a random variable. The rating of job candidates, for example, can be represented by the discrete numerical scale: 0 = unacceptable, 1 = satisfactory, and 2 = excellent. Pass/fail, success/failure, and yes/no outcomes and the like can be quantified by arbitrarily assigning the number one to the first option (pass, success, yes) and a zero to the other (fail, failure, no).

In the case of employment, the hiring of one type of person (say a woman) might be assigned the number 1 and the hiring of another type (a man) the number 0. Each hiring can now be viewed as a random variable resulting in either a 1 or 0. In addition, we might be interested in the total number of women hired in n hires, in which case the hiring of x women in n tries is a random variable that equals 0, 1, 2, 3, 4, . . . n, as discussed further in Chapter 5. For now, consider the small sample hiring situation depicted in Figure 3.1. Three people were to be hired by random draw, where the probability of selecting (hiring) a woman was fixed at 0.50 on each attempt. How many women might be hired in three attempts? The answer to this question can be interpreted as the outcome or realization of a random variable, denoted by the letter x.

$$x = \text{number of women hired}$$

The values of x are $x = 0$, 1, 2, and 3. The likelihood of each of these four values can be determined from the sample space in Figure 3.1, reprinted in Figure 4.1. The probability of each of the eight outcomes in the sample space is (0.5)(0.5)(0.5) = 0.125; thus, the probability of each of the four values of the random variable are

$$P(x=0) = P(\text{MMM}) = 0.125$$

$$P(x=1) = P(\text{WMM}) + P(\text{MWM}) + P(\text{MMW})$$

$$= 0.125 + 0.125 + 0.125 = 0.375$$

$$P(x=2) = P(\text{WWM}) + P(\text{WMW}) + P(\text{MWW})$$

$$= 0.125 + 0.125 + 0.125 = 0.375$$

$$P(x=3) = P(\text{WWW}) = 0.125$$

These probabilities make up the probability distribution of x, as shown on the right-hand side of Figure 4.1.

The sample space on the left-hand side of Figure 4.1 is written more compactly as the probability distribution on the right. The original sample space on the left is required to obtain the probabilities shown for each of the values of the random variable x on the right. Once the probability distribution $P(x)$ is obtained, however, the original sample space of male and female outcomes can be disregarded because the probability distribution contains all the information required to answer probability questions about the values of x. In Figure 4.1, the random variable x is a rule that maps each outcome in the original sample space into a numerical value x.

Discrete Random Variable
A random variable that has only a finite number of specific and distinct values.

In this chapter and the next, random variables that give rise to discrete values (as in $x = 0$, 1, 2, 3) are emphasized. Such a random variable is called a **discrete random variable,** because it can take only distinct values along a number line. In contrast to a discrete random variable is a continuous random variable, which is one that can have any value along a number line. For example, the continuous random variable x might

FIGURE 4.1 Sample Space and Probability Distribution

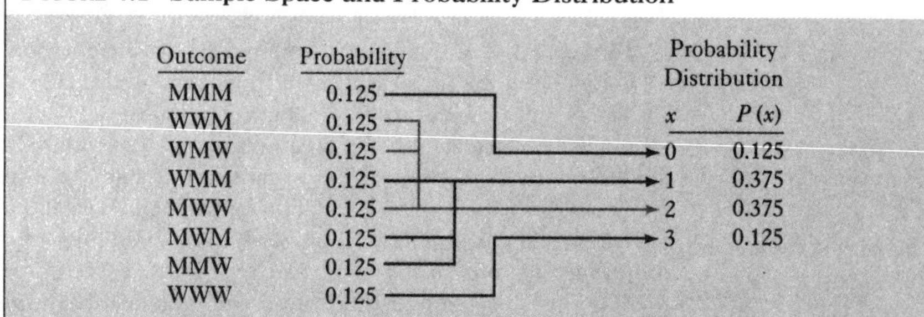

be the height of students in a dorm and its realization x might be any value between four feet and eight feet. Chapter 6 has a detailed discussion of continuous random variables.

In the case of horse racing, slot machines, lotteries, and similar experiments where the names of the winners are the basic outcomes, a discrete random variable can be defined as the dollar value of the winning prize. Remember, in these games of chance, it is the dollar value that defines the random variable and not the name of the winner. Random variables are always defined in terms of their numerical values and the probability of the occurrence of those values.

4.3 Probability Mass

In Chapter 1, relative frequency distributions were presented in tabular lists and in histograms. In a like manner, tables and diagrams can be used to present the probability associated with given values of a random variable. These tables and diagrams are called "probability distributions." When drawn as in a histogram, the vertical height at each discrete random variable value is the probability of that value.

In the case of Cadillac production at the Detroit-Hamtramck plant, according to *Business Week*, GM executives planned on 75 percent of production to be Eldorados (retailing at $35,500), 15 percent basic Sevilles (at $37,000), and 10 percent Seville STSs (at $38,500). The probability distribution for the random variable "retail price of Hamtramck-produced Cadillac" is shown in Figure 4.2, where each vertical bar is one dollar wide. The vertical bar at $35,500, for instance, has a height of 0.75 and an implied width from $35,499.50 to $35,500.50. The mass of this bar is its height (0.75) times the one unit horizontal distance, which is just the (long-term) relative frequency 0.75 given by the height. Because this bar actually represents an area, even though we need only know its height, it is called the **probability mass** at $35,500. The probability mass is 0.15 at $37,000 and 0.10 at $38,500. Although a diagram such as that in Figure 4.2 is commonly called a "probability function," it is more appropriately referred to as a "probability mass function."

Probability mass function (p.m.f.)
A tabular list, a graph, or a formula that gives the probability for each possible value of a discrete random variable, where the sum of probability masses is one.

An alternative representation of probability mass is shown as a list in Table 4.1 for the instant cash lottery game introduced in Chapter 3. These probabilities were formed by the first and last columns of Table 3.2. The probability of a winning $1 instant cash ticket is written

$$P(x = 1) = P(1) = 0.08,$$

of a $2 ticket is

$$P(x = 2) = P(2) = 0.032,$$

and so on.

The probabilities in this lottery example are not easily represented in a diagram because of the wide range in x values from $0 to $5,000. A diagram is a helpful way to visualize probabilities only if there is not a lot of dispersion in the random variable.

FIGURE 4.2 **Probability Mass Function of Retail Prices of Hamtramck-Produced Cadillacs**

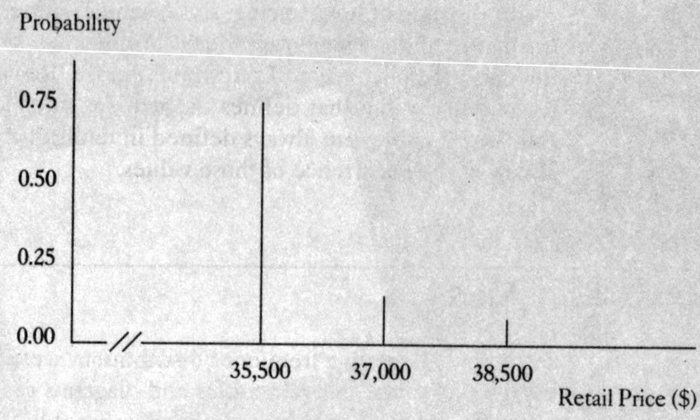

TABLE 4.1
Probability Mass Function of Instant Cash Lottery

Prize won (x)	Probability of winning $P(x)$
$ 0	0.862461
$ 1	0.080000
$ 2	0.032000
$ 5	0.015399
$ 10	0.007400
$ 25	0.002600
$ 500	0.000130
$5,000	0.000010
	1.000000

4.4 THE EXPECTED VALUE OF A RANDOM VARIABLE

Calculations of probabilities associated with a random variable say nothing about the cost and benefit of making an investment, placing a bet, or making a decision in any other uncertain situation. One possible question is: How much money can we expect to make or lose as the result of an action?

In Chapter 2, the mean was calculated to describe the central location of a set of numbers. Calculations were made on the relative frequency of the observed values. A random variable represents a set of numerical values whose occurrences are determined by probability. These probabilities can be used as long-term relative frequencies in the calculation of a mean. The mean of a random variable is called its **expected value.** The expected value will provide an answer to questions about how much can be won or lost in uncertain investments and games of chance.

Expected Value of x, $E(x)$
Mean (μ) of the random variable x.

As with any population mean μ, the expected value of a random variable x is calculated by multiplying each value x by its (long-term) relative frequency, and then these products are summed, $\Sigma xP(x)$. Unlike any other weighted mean calculations in Chapter 2, however, the use of the expected value designation indicates that the relevant relative frequency is the probability of x, which is $P(x)$. Thus, we have Formula 4.1.

Expected value of x

$$E(x) = \mu = \Sigma_x xP(x) \tag{4.1}$$

where $P(x)$ is the probability of an x value,

$\sum_x xP(x)$ is the sum of x and $P(x)$ products, for all the values of x,

$E(x)$ is the expected value of x, and

μ is the mean of x.

Formula (4.1) is similar to Formula (2.2a) for a mean calculated with relative frequencies, except that here each value of x is weighted by its probability. Formula (4.1) provides a way of computing the mean of x based on the long-term relative frequencies. Notice that the summation is over all the values of x and their respective probabilities, which is indicated by the x under the sigma summation sign. As an example, consider Table 4.2; the first column again contains the x values for the instant cash lottery, and the second gives their probabilities. The third column is formed by the products $xP(x)$. The sum of the eight entries in the third column is the expected value of x,

$$E(x) = \sum_x xP(x) = 0.475$$

TABLE 4.2
Calculation of the Expected Value in the Instant Cash Lottery

Prize won (x)	Probability of winning $P(x)$	$xP(x)$
0	0.862461	0.000
1	0.080000	0.080
2	0.032000	0.064
5	0.015399	0.077
10	0.007400	0.074
25	0.002600	0.065
500	0.000130	0.065
5000	0.000010	0.050
		$0.475 = \Sigma xP(x) = E(x) = \mu$

The expression $E(x) = 0.475$ says that, prior to knowing if a ticket is a winner or loser, each ticket has an expected win of $0.475 in the instant cash lottery game.[2] That is, for a large number of ticket purchases, the mean amount received per ticket will be 47.5 cents in this game. No contestant will actually receive 47.5 cents from any one ticket, since this value isn't even possible; 47.5 cents is an average value.

A contestant who could buy all 75 million tickets in one administration of the game would get an average return of 47.5 cents per ticket. Alternatively, if he or she bought one ticket every time the game was run (every six to eight weeks), then he or she could expect to receive 47.5 cents per ticket over a long (infinite) period of time. No matter which interpretation is used, the average return to a contestant is 47.5 cents per ticket in this instant cash lottery game.[3]

QUERY 4.1:
In the early 1990s, *Newsweek* reported that "average take" for bank robberies was $3,244 but 85 percent of the robbers were caught. Assuming 60 percent of those caught lose their entire take and 40 percent lose half, graph the probability mass function using EXCEL. Calculate the expected take from a bank robbery. Does it pay to be a bank robber?

ANSWER:
Construction of the probability mass function for bank robberies first requires the defining of the random variable x, bank robbery take. If the robber is not caught $x = 3,244$. If the robber is caught and manages to keep half, $x = 1,622$. If the robber is caught and loses it all, then $x = 0$. The associated probabilities for these x values are 0.15 (= 1 - 0.85), 0.34 (= 0.85×0.4), and 0.51 (= 0.85×0.6) After entering the x values in cells A1, A2 and A3 and the associated probabilities in B1, B2, and B3, the following steps lead to the probability mass function:

1) Click on the ChartWizard. The "ChartWizard - Step 1 of 4" screen will appear.
2) Highlight "Column" at "ChartWizard - Step 1 of 4" and push "Next."
3) At "ChartWizard-Step 2 of 4 - Chart Source Data," enter "=B1:B3" for "Data range," and push "column" button for "Series in." A graph will appear. Click on "series" toward the top of the screen to get a new page.
4) At the bottom of the "Series" page is a rectangle for "Category (x) axis labels:" Click on this rectangle and then highlight A1:A3.
5) At "Step 3 of 4" move on by clicking on "Next," and at "Step 4 of 4" click on "Finish." Your screen should now look like that in Chart 4.1.

CHART 4.1 Probability Mass Function for Bank Robberies Within the EXCEL SpreadSheet

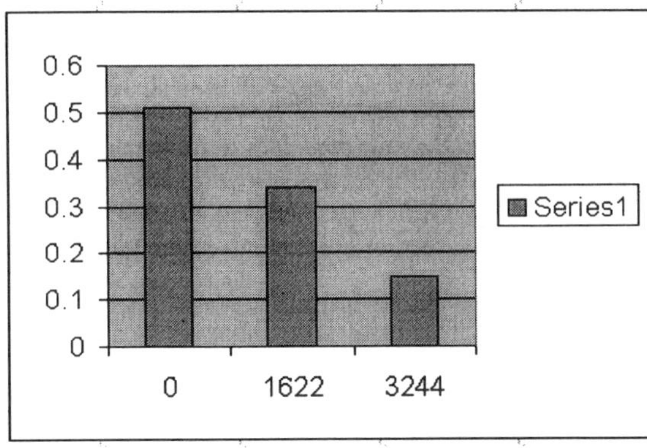

The expected value of a robbery is \$1,038.08.

$$E(x) = \sum xP(x) = (0)(0.51) + (1622)(0.34) + (3244)(0.15)$$
$$= 0 + 551.48 + 486.60 = 1038.08$$

The expected return to bank robbery is positive - on average, bank robbers get \$1,038.08 per heist. If criminals make their decisions strictly on this expected value, then it pays to rob banks. A decision rule based only on an expected value, however, ignores the risks or variability in the returns. In addition, our expected value calculations do not include the cost of jail time, which could be viewed by criminals as substantial.

QUERY 4.2:

In the case of Cadillac production at the Detroit–Hamtramck plant, according to *Business Week* (June 29, 1992), GM executives planned on 75 percent of production to be Eldorados (retailing at \$35,500), 15 percent basic Sevilles (\$37,000), and 10 percent Seville STSs (\$38,500). As it turned out, 58 percent of the output was in the Seville, 29 percent in the STS, and 13 percent in the Eldorado. Why did the expected and actual percentages differ, and what are the consequences in terms of expected and actual return per car?

ANSWER:

Initially the executives could only be working with subjective probability, since they had no experience with this new series of Cadillacs. However even if they had a more objective notion of probability based on long-term relative frequencies, there is no reason why the initial year of production should match those long-term values. The expected value of the initial retail returns (x), based on probabilities $P(x) = 0.75$, 0.15, and 0.10, from the Cadillac production is \$36,025 per car. The actual retail returns (y), with realized relative frequencies $f/n = 0.13$, 0.58, and 0.29, was \$37,240 per car. Thus, on the average, Cadillac retail sales are \$1,215 per car more than what was initially expected.

x	$P(x)$	$xP(x)$
35500	0.75	26625
37000	0.15	5550
38500	0.10	3850
		$\mu_x = 36025$

y	f/n	$y(f/n)$
35500	0.13	4615
37000	0.58	21460
38500	0.29	11165
		$\mu_y = 37240$

EXERCISES

4.1 What is the difference between the information in the sample space and outcome set and that in a random variable?

4.2 *New York Times* syndicated columnist Marilyn Geewax, in an article titled "Financial plight of aging Catholic nuns should be lesson for all women"(*Saint Paul Pioneer Press*, June 3, 1993), stated that the median age of a U.S. nun is 65 years. What is the approximate probability of selecting a nun at random who is 65 years or older?

4.3 In Exercise 4.2, if three nuns are selected at random, what is the implied probability mass function of the number of nuns 65 years or older? Use a tree diagram to show the determination of the relevant probabilities.

4.4 How does the notion of an expected value differ from that of an arithmetic average calculated with relative frequency data?

4.5 A *Business Week* (March 12, 1984) article described a violent crime insurance policy that costs \$210 and pays \$50,000 to a victim. If police records in your community suggest a one in a 1,000 chance of being victimized, what is your expected return in buying this policy? What did you assume in your calculations?

4.6 Would you buy the violent crime insurance described in the above question? Why or why not?

4.7 In the summer of 1992, the author of this text received an "Application for Service Protection Plus" from General Electric for insurance on a television set to cover the cost of major service work. The television set cost about \$500, and the service insurance was being offered at "the special 20% discount." The cost was listed at \$119.95 for one year's coverage, less \$23.99 for a discounted one-year contract price of \$95.96. Ignoring the use that is obtained from the TV set prior to a claim, what would have to be the probability of total destruction to break even on this policy?

4.8 Why would someone buy the General Electric service insurance policy described in Exercise 4.7?

4.9 An open-air theater promoter is considering taking out an insurance policy to cover possible losses if it rains. If the event in question is a complete failure because of rain, the promoter feels that a loss of \$80,000 will be incurred. If it is moderately successful, with a little drizzle occurring, a loss of \$25,000 would be incurred. Insurance actuaries have determined that the probabilities of total failure or moderate success are 0.01 and 0.05, respectively. Assuming the promoter would be willing to ignore all other possible losses, what premium should he be willing to pay the insurance company for the policy?

4.10 The local Schwinn dealer has three models of men's 27-inch bicycles: a \$220 model, a \$240 model, and a \$260 model. The Schwinn dealer makes a profit of \$35 on the first model, \$45 on the second model, and \$60 on the third model. For the coming year, the Schwinn dealer estimates that for customers who buy the 27-inch size, 60 percent will want the lowest-priced model, 30 percent will purchase the \$240 model, and 10 percent will buy the \$260 model. Thus, the probability of each profit is:

$$P(\$35 \text{ profit}) = 0.60,\ P(\$45 \text{ profit}) = 0.30, \text{ and } P(\$60 \text{ profit}) = 0.10$$

a. Define the random variable for this situation.
b. Find the expected value of this random variable.
c. Find the variance of this random variable.
d. What are the expected profits for selling 100 of the 27-inch bikes?

4.5 The Dispersion of a Random Variable

Variance of a Random Variable
The mean squared deviation of outcome values from the mean of the random variable, where each squared deviation is weighted by its probability.

Just as the expected value of a random variable is a long-term average value, measures of dispersion around this mean can be defined in probability terms. The **variance of a random variable** is a measure of the spread of the distribution. The variance of a random variable is the mean squared deviation of values from their mean. Unlike the sample variance discussed in Chapter 2, however, now probability is used for the weighing of those squared deviations. The variance of a random variable x is thus the expected squared deviation of the values of x around the expected value of x. In shorthand notation,

$$\text{Var}(x) = \sigma^2 = E[x - E(x)]^2 = E(x - \mu)^2$$

As with any finite population variance σ^2, the variance of a random variable x is calculated by multiplying each squared deviation of values of x from their mean by the associated (long-term) relative frequency $P(x)$, and then summing these products, $\Sigma(x - \mu)^2 P(x)$. Thus, we have the formula.[4]

Variance of random variable x

$$\sigma^2 = E\left[x - E(x)\right]^2 = E(x - \mu)^2 = \sum_x (x - \mu)^2 P(x) \tag{4.2}$$

where $P(x)$ is the probability of an x value,

$\sum_x (x - \mu)^2 P(x)$ is the sum of products, of squared deviations multiplied by respective probabilities, for all the values of x,

$E(x)$ is the expected value of x, which is also the mean of x.

Formula (4.2) is similar to Formula (2.7a), with the exception that probability or long-term relative frequency is used for weighting the squared deviations. A variance calculated by Formula (4.2) starts with the mean of x, as calculated in Table 4.2 and re-

TABLE 4.3 Calculation of the Variance in the Instant Cash Lottery

x	$P(x)$	$xP(x)$	$x-\mu$	$(x-\mu)^2$	$(x-\mu)^2P(x)$
0	0.862461	0.000	–0.475	0.2256	0.1945874
1	0.080000	0.080	0.525	0.2756	0.0220506
2	0.032000	0.064	1.525	2.3256	0.0744207
5	0.015399	0.077	4.525	20.4757	0.3153016
10	0.007400	0.074	9.525	90.7258	0.6713464
25	0.002600	0.065	24.525	601.4760	1.5638187
500	0.000130	0.065	499.525	249525.2323	32.4395778
5000	0.000010	0.050	4999.525	24995250.2926	249.9525029
	1.000000	0.475			285.2336060
		‖			‖
		μ			$\sum_x (x-\mu)^2P(x)$

peated in Table 4.3, followed by the calculation of deviations from this mean, as shown in the fourth column of Table 4.3. Next, the deviations from the mean are squared, as in column five, and multiplied by the probability of getting this squared deviation, column six. Finally, the probability weighted squared deviations are added, with the resulting variance of $\sigma^2 = 285.233606$.

Standard Deviation of a Random Variable x
The standard deviation of random variable x is the positive square root of the variance.

As with the data sets in Chapter 2, the **standard deviation of a random variable x** is the positive square root of the variance. So for the instant cash lottery, the standard deviation is \$16.89.

$$\sigma = \sqrt{\sum_x (x-\mu)^2 P(x)} = \sqrt{285.233606} = 16.89$$

Standard deviation of random variable x

$$\sigma = \sqrt{E[x - E(x)]^2} = \sqrt{E(x-\mu)^2} = \sqrt{\sum_x (x-\mu)^2 P(x)} \tag{4.3}$$

If there was no variability in x (it was not a random variable and had only one value), then the variance and the standard deviation would be zero. On the other hand, if x can take values far away from its mean with great likelihood, then the variance and standard deviation will be large because both factors of the product $(x-\mu)^2P(x)$ will then be large.

QUERY 4.3:
In the case of Cadillac production at the Detroit-Hamtramck plant, where GM executives planned on 75 percent of production to be Eldorados (retailing at \$35,500), 15 percent basic Sevilles (\$37,000), and 10 percent Seville STSs (\$38,500), but realized 58 percent of the output in the basic Seville, 29 percent in the Seville STS, and 13 percent in the Eldorado, what is the difference in variability in actual retail prices from what was expected initially?

ANSWER:

The expected value of the initial retail returns (x) from the Cadillac production is \$36,025 per car. The actual retail returns (y) average \$37,240 per car. As a measure of variability around these means, the initial standard deviation based on probabilities is \$980.75, and the standard deviation based on realized relative frequencies is \$942.02. Thus, there is more variability in actual sales than what was expected initially.

x	$P(x)$	$xP(x)$	$(x-\mu)^2$	$(x-\mu)^2P(x)$	
35500	0.75	26625	275625	206718.75	
37000	0.15	5550	950625	142593.75	
38500	0.10	3850	6125625	612562.50	
		$\mu_x = 36025$		961875.00	$980.75 = \sigma_x$

y	f/N	$y(f/N)$	$(y-\mu)^2$	$(y-\mu)^2(f/N)$	
35500	0.13	4615	327600	393588	
37000	0.58	21460	57600	33408	
38500	0.29	11165	1587600	46404	
		$\mu_y = 37240$		887400	$942.02 = \sigma_y$

4.6 RISK ASSESSMENT

The standard deviation is often used in finance as a measure of the riskiness of an investment. For instance, if two investments each have the same expected monetary return, but the first has a standard deviation smaller than the second, then the first is less risky than the second. To see the implications of these two different standard deviations and their ramifications for risk, we consider a bell-shaped distribution of returns.

Standard Deviation Comparison

From the rule of bell-shaped distributions introduced in Chapter 2, if monetary returns are bell shaped, then approximately 68 percent of the time dollar returns will be within one standard deviation (either direction) of the expected dollar return; about 95 percent of the time those returns will be within two standard deviations (either side) of the expected return. Thus, for two investments, if the standard deviation of the second is twice the magnitude of the first, then within the same dollar bounds the second (with the larger standard deviation) has about 68 percent of its returns and the first (with the smaller standard deviation) will have about 95 percent of its returns.

As an illustration, consider two corporate stocks that both have an expected net return (dividend and price appreciation) of \$150 on a \$1,000 investment. From historical records, suppose that the standard deviation of the net return of the first stock is calculated to be \$20, and the standard deviation of the second is \$40. Assume returns are bell shaped, as in Figure 4.3. From the rule of normality, 95 percent of the time the first stock will have a net return between \$110 and \$190, because for this stock the distance from \$150 to \$110 or from \$150 to \$190 is two standard deviations below and two standard deviations above the mean. Because the distance from \$150 to \$110 or from \$150

FIGURE 4.3 Probability Distributions of Net Returns to Two Stocks With Different Standard Deviations

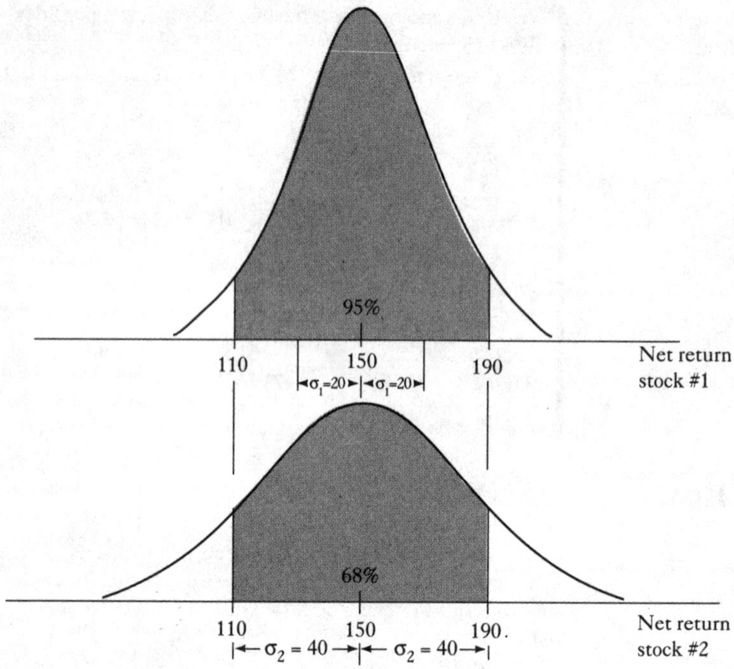

to \$190 represents only one standard deviation below and one standard deviation above the mean in the second stock, only about 68 percent of the net return for this stock will be within the \$110 and \$190 interval. Clearly, for stocks expected to have similar net returns, the more risky stock will have the larger standard deviation.

Coefficient of Variation Comparison

Coefficient of Variation
Ratio of the standard deviation of a random variable to its mean.

To compare riskiness among distributions that have different means and standard deviations, a measure often employed is the coefficient of variation. The **coefficient of variation** is calculated by dividing the standard deviation by the expected value. Because the standard deviation typically gets larger as the magnitude of values involved in its calculation get larger, an unadjusted comparison of standard deviations between stocks with greatly different expected returns is not a meaningful way to assess risk. Dividing standard deviations by their respective means results in the cancellation of the units of measurement and removes the influence of the size of the variable's values. The coefficient of variation is a measure of dispersion free of the measurement unit of the original values.

Coefficient of variation
The coefficient of variation is a ratio of the standard deviation to the expected value or mean of a variable.

$$C = \frac{\sqrt{E\left[x - E(x)\right]^2}}{E(x)} = \frac{\sqrt{E(x-\mu)^2}}{\mu} = \frac{\sigma}{\mu} \tag{4.4}$$

From Table 4.3, we know that the expected value and standard deviation of the instant cash game are \$0.475 and \$16.89. Suppose we must make a choice between this lottery and a dollar bet on a "wheel of fortune" that has 360 numbers on which a clicker might rest after the wheel is spun; it pays \$325 if the wheel stops on your number. Which should we choose? Table 4.4 provides the calculation of the expected value and standard deviation for this wheel of fortune.

Table 4.4 shows the expected value for the wheel to be \$0.903, which exceeds the \$0.475 expected value for the instant cash lottery. If we are not concerned with risk and only care about what will happen on the average, then the wheel is preferred.

It is worth recognizing that the chance to play either the lottery or the wheel of fortune is not costless. If each were offered at \$1 per entry, then the expected net win for the lottery would be a negative \$0.525 and that of the wheel would be a negative \$0.097 (= 1 – 0.903). That is, if we paid a dollar to enter each of these games a large (infinite) number of times, then each time we would pay a dollar but on average we would get back only 47.5 cents in the lottery and 90.3 cents on the wheel. Most times we will get nothing back in either game, but sometimes we will win the amounts specified in accordance with the odds given—for the lottery, on average, one in 1 million times you will even win \$5,000, but on average you will lose 52.5 cents per entry.

If we are concerned with the risk of winning or losing, then we must consider the dispersion around the expected value. The standard deviation of the wheel (\$17.11) exceeds that of the lottery (\$16.89), suggesting that the wheel of fortune is more risky. But after deflating the standard deviations by the magnitudes of the expected value involved, the lottery continues to show itself as more risky. The coefficient of variation for the lottery is

$$C = \sigma/\mu = \$16.89/\$0.475 = 35.56$$

The coefficient of variation for the wheel is only

$$C = \sigma/\mu = \$17.11/\$0.903 = 18.95$$

TABLE 4.4
Mean, Variance, and Standard Deviation for a 360-Number Wheel of Fortune that Pays \$325 on One Number

x	$P(x)$	$xP(x)$	$x-\mu$	$(x-\mu)^2$	$(x-\mu)^2P(x)$
0	0.997222	0.000	–0.903	0.8150	0.8127438
325	0.002778	0.903	324.097	105039.0095	291.7750263
	1.000000	$0.903 = \mu$			$292.5877701 = \sigma^2$
					$\sigma = 17.10519717$

Further consideration of risk and investors' behavior toward risk are provided in later chapters. The analysis of risk has become a critical part of government regulations. For instance, U.S. Presidential Executive Order 12291 (*Federal Register*, 1981, pp. 13193–98) states that all federal regulatory action must be accompanied by a cost/benefit analysis that includes risk assessments. Modern-day financial analysis is founded on cost/benefit risk analysis. Liability considerations in product development require risk analysis. The pricing of insurance policies is based on expected payout and risk of disaster. In short, all decision making should incorporate an assessment of expected gains and losses and the risks involved.

QUERY 4.4:

A raffle costs \$2.00 to enter. Winning entries are determined with the following probabilities for the identified gross payouts.

$P(x)$	.7	.2	.1
x	0	\$3.00	\$5.00

a. What is the modal net payout per entry based on this population of returns?
b. What is the mean net payout per entry?
c. What is the variance for the net payout?
d. How often will the net payout be more than two standard deviations above its mean level?

ANSWER:

a. The modal gross payout is 0; thus, the modal net payout is -\$2.00 per entry.
b. The expected gross payout is
   $E(x) = .7(0) + .2(3) + .1(5) = \$1.10$
   Thus, the expected net payout is -\$0.90, because the raffle gets \$2.00 per entry. That is, over a large (infinite) number of entries the mean gain to the raffle is 90 cents per entry and the mean loss to the entrant is 90 cents.
c. The variance of the net payout is
   $$E[x - E(x)]^2 = .7[-2.0 - (-0.9)]^2 + .2[1.0 - (-0.9)]^2 + .1[3.0 - (-0.9)]^2$$
   $$= 3.09 \text{ sq. dollars}$$
d. A standard deviation of the net payout is approximately \$1.76; thus, two standard deviations above the expected value of -\$0.90 is approximately \$2.62. Only the gross payout of \$5.00, which occurs with a 10 percent probability, will result in a net payout above \$2.62.

QUERY 4.5 :
The following three investments (U, V, and W) are available for a one year $1,500 investment.

Investments:	U	V	W
Expected net return	$100	$200	$300
Median net return	$100	$210	$300
St. dev. of net return	$ 20	$ 25	$ 30
Range of net return	$200	$250	$234

a. An investor who does not care about risk (and is said to be risk neutral) and is only interested in getting the highest average net return over an long time period would select which investment?

b. According to James Glassman, writing for the *Washington Post* (January 29 1995), "Risk is a fuzzy concept, but it's possible to put a number on it." How do economists and financial analysts measure risk? Are the rankings of these three investments in terms of "riskiness" sensitive to the measure of "riskiness" employed?

ANSWER:

a. An investor who does not care about risk but is only interested in getting the highest net return will select investment W, as it has the highest expected net return.

b. Riskiness could be defined by any measure of dispersion. Here it appears that the standard deviation rises with the expected net return while the range does not, which gives rise to different "risk rankings" based on the standard deviation and the range. The coefficient of variance is a measure of risk that adjusts the standard deviation for the magnitude of values involved. The coefficients of variation for U, V and W are 0.2, 0.125, and 0.10, which would suggest that investment W is the least risky after adjusting for random dispersion in the net return.

EXERCISES

4.11 The following investments are available at a price of $10,000 each:

Investment:	x	y
Expected net returns:	$ 1,000	$ 900
Standard deviation	$ 1,000	$ 450

a. What are the coefficients of variation for the returns of x and y?

b. If the distributions of returns of both x and y are continuous and bell shaped, what is the probability that x is less than zero and what is the probability that y is less than zero?

c. How do your answers in parts a and b relate?

4.12 Graph the probability mass function associated with the random variable x:

x	0	1	2	3	4	5	6
$P(x)$	.02	.09	.23	.32	.23	.09	.02

a. What is the expected value of x?
b. What is the standard deviation of x?
c. What proportion of the distribution of x is within two standard deviations of the expected value of x?
d. Is your answer in part c consistent with the "rule of thumb" for a bell-shaped distribution?

4.13 These three investments are available at a price of $12,000 each.

Investments:	*A*	*B*	*C*
Expected net returns	$ 1,000	$ 1,500	$ 2,000
Standard deviation	$ 500	$ 700	$ 1,150

Which investment has the least risk? By what measure?

4.14 If you ignore risk, which one of investments *A*, *B*, and *C* is the preferred purchase in Exercise 4.13? Why?

4.15 The following investments are available at a price of $100,000 each:

Investment:	*A*	*B* (in thousands of dollars)
Expected net returns	10	15
Standard deviation	3	4

Which investment has the more risk? By what measure?

4.16 If an investor ignores risk, and will purchase only one of the investments in Exercise 4.15 but not both, which one should he or she buy? Why?

4.17 One of the following investments is available to you at a price of $10,000 each:

Investment:	x	y
Expected net returns	$ 2,000	$ 1,500
Standard deviation	$ 1,000	$ 750

If you ignore risk, which investment would you make? Which of the above investments of $10,000 in x or y is the least risky? By what measure?

4.7 Multiple Random Variables

In the instant cash game discussed in the previous chapter, the random variable was the immediate redemption value of a ticket (No instant cash, $1, $2, $5, $10, $25, $500, and $5,000). Experiments may involve more than one variable, however. For example, a variation of the Indiana state lottery, introduced at the beginning of this chapter, has two random variables associated with each ticket: one for the instant cash game (which we have analyzed) and another for the millionaire game (which we will consider in the next section). An insurance company interested in the age, gender, education level, and marital status of a driver with a propensity to be involved in accidents provides another example of a multivariable probability situation in which accidents are divided into four random variables for age, gender, education, and marital status.

The remainder of this chapter focuses on questions related to situations involving multiple random variables. First, the key role of independence is shown in the calculation of the probability of joint occurrence of two random variables. Next, attention is given to expected values and variances of multiple random variables. Consideration is given to the role of the variance in risk assessment. The importance of the covariances is demonstrated in investment decisions.

4.8 Joint Probability Distributions

Analysis of multiple random variables often requires the construction of joint probability distributions that show the probabilities of combined sets of the variables. As a special case, consider the construct of a bivariate probability distribution for analysis of two discrete random variables. A table for a bivariate probability distribution contains the probabilities of all combined outcomes of the two random variables. For instance, what we know about the two random variables in the proposed millionaire and instant cash lotteries is represented in the bivariate probability distribution in Table 4.5.

The probabilities in the instant cash game, from Table 3.2 and Table 4.1, are shown down the right-hand margin, $P(x)$. The chances of winning (one in 24 million) and losing in the proposed millionaire game are given across the bottom margin of the table, where

$$P(y = 0) = 0.99999995833 \text{ and } P(y = 1000000) = 0.00000004167$$

Table 4.5
Incomplete Bivariate Probability Distribution for Instant Cash and Millionaire Games

		Proposed Millionaire Game (y): no million $0	Proposed Millionaire Game (y): win million $1,000,000		
Instant Cash Game (x)	$ 0			0.86246146270	Probability of winning in the Instant Cash Game $P(x)$
	$ 1			0.08000000000	
	$ 2			0.03200000000	
	$ 5			0.01539882969	
	$ 10			0.00739973361	
	$ 25			0.00259996880	
	$ 500			0.00013000520	
	$5,000			0.00001000000	
		0.99999995833	0.00000004167	1.00000000000	
		Probability of winning in this Millionaire Game $P(y)$			

Marginal Probability
The sum of joint probabilities over all values of one variable in a multivariate probability distribution.

In keeping with their placement in this table, $P(x)$ and $P(y)$ are called **marginal probabilities;** as in Chapter 3, they represent probabilities of the occurrence of values for one random variable with no regard to the other variable. Notice that each marginal probability is between zero and one and that the marginal probabilities for each random variable sum to one.

Missing in Table 4.5 are the joint probabilities that reflect the likelihood that the values of one variable will occur with the values of the other variable. For instance, the first empty cell in Table 4.5 is the probability that a ticket is worth nothing in the instant cash game *and* worth nothing in the millionaire game. It must be a probability between the row marginal probability 0.86246146270 and the column marginal probability 0.99999995833. The last empty cell in the lower right-hand corner is the probability that a ticket is worth $5,000 in the instant cash game *and* $1 million in the millionaire game. It must be a probability between 0.000010 and 0.00000004167. All 16 cells in the table will be exhaustive, mutually exclusive, and have probabilities that sum to unity.

Before attempting to determine these joint probabilities, we need to address how the two variables are related. The social activist's proposals for the millionaire game as given at the beginning of this chapter call for a contestant's winning or losing in the instant cash game to not affect his or her chances of winning or losing in the millionaire game. Winning tickets in the instant cash game are chosen randomly, and winners in the millionaire game are selected randomly from the 75 million tickets: outcomes in the two games are independent. As in the previous chapter, Section 3.8, independence means that if a contestant did not win in the instant cash game, the probability of winning the million dollars is not influenced; or, a contestant winning $1 instant cash does not alter the probability of winning the million; or, given that a contestant won $5,000 does not change the probability of winning the million, and similarly for the other instant cash winnings. This critical assumption of independence between the two games is summarized in the following statements of conditional probabilities.

$$P(y = 1000000) = P(y = 1000000 \mid x) = 0.00000004167$$

which says the probability of winning the million is equal to the probability of winning the million given x in the instant cash game.

$$P(y = 0) = P(y = 0 \mid x) = 0.99999995833$$

which says the probability of not winning the million is equal to the probability of not winning the million given x in the instant cash game.

where x =\$0, \$1, \$2, \$5, \$10, \$25, \$500, and \$5,000

In this enumeration $P(y = 0) = 0.99999995833$ and $P(y = 1000000) = 0.00000004167$ are the two probability masses that make up the two marginal probability distributions $P(y = 0)$ and $P(y = 1000000)$. There are eight conditional random variables of the form "$y \mid x$"—one for each of the eight values of x in the instant cash game. For each of those values of x, y is either 0 or 1000000, with probabilities determined by the conditional probabilities $P(y = 0 \mid x)$ or $P(y = 1000000 \mid x)$. But because of independence, these conditional probabilities are equal to their marginal probabilities, regardless of the value of x.

Independent Random Variables
Random variables y and x are independent if the conditional probability distribution of y, given any value of x, is the same as the marginal probability distribution of y, and if the conditional probability distribution of x given any value of y is the same as the marginal probability distribution of x.

If all occurrences of the two random variables x and y are **independent**, then the two random variables are said to be independent. Two random variables are independent if and only if the marginal and conditional probability distributions are identical, as is the case above.

If two variables are independent, then the joint probability of any pair of occurrences from the two variables is the product of the two marginal probabilities. The reason for this can be seen by considering the breakdown of the 75 million tickets as given in Table 4.1. There are 64,684,610 tickets that yield nothing in the instant cash game, but one in 24 million of these will be a winner in the proposed millionaire game. That is, the number of tickets, on the average, that will result in \$0 in the instant cash game *and* \$1 million in the millionaire game are 2.695 out of 75 million tickets:

$$\text{Frequency of } x = 0 \text{ and } y = 1000000 = (64{,}684{,}610)(1/24{,}000{,}000) = 2.695192$$

The joint probability of \$0 in the instant cash game *and* \$1 million in the millionaire game is thus 0.00000003594 = 2.695192/75000000. Or in terms of probability

$$\begin{aligned} P(x = 0 \text{ and } y = 1000000) &= (64{,}684{,}610/75{,}000{,}000)(1/24{,}000{,}000) \\ &= (0.8624614627)(0.00000004167) \\ &= P(x = 0) \times P(y = 1000000) \\ &= 0.00000003594 \end{aligned}$$

Similarly, by multiplying the marginal products for the other 15 y and x pairs in Table 4.5, the associated joint probabilities can be obtained. For instance, the joint probability of \$5 in the instant cash game *and* \$0 in the proposed millionaire game is 0.01539882905:

$$\begin{aligned} P(x = 5 \text{ and } y = 0) &= P(x = 5) \times P(y = 0) \\ &= (0.01539882969)(0.99999995833) \\ &= 0.01539882905 \end{aligned}$$

as shown in Table 4.6.

Notice in Table 4.6 that the joint probability of winning \$5,000 in the instant cash game *and* \$1 million in the millionaire game is given as zero. This probability is not zero; it is just smaller than the decimal places shown. It can be expressed, however, in scientific notation as 4.167×10^{-13}, which is 4.167 in 10 trillion:

$$\begin{aligned} P(x = 5000 \text{ and } y = 1000000) &= P(x = 5000) \times P(y = 1000000) \\ &= (0.000010)(0.00000004167) \\ &= 0.0000000000004167 = 4.167 \times 10^{-13} \end{aligned}$$

Marginal probabilities can be multiplied together to determine joint probabilities only if the variables are independent. If the variables are dependent, then from a rewriting of Formula (3.5), we know only that a joint probability can be expressed as the product of a conditional probability times the associated marginal probability. That is, rewriting Formula (3.5) yields: $P(A \text{ and } B) = P(A|B) \times P(B.)$ If the random variables are independent, however, then $P(A \text{ and } B) = P(A) \times P(B)$.

TABLE 4.6
Bivariate Probability Distribution for Instant Cash and Proposed Millionaire Games

		Proposed Millionaire Game *(y)*: no million \$0	win million \$1,000,000	Probability of winning in the Instant Cash Game *P (x)*
Instant Cash Game *(x)*	\$ 0	0.86246142676	0.00000003594	0.86246146270
	\$ 1	0.07999999667	0.00000000333	0.08000000000
	\$ 2	0.03199999867	0.00000000133	0.03200000000
	\$ 5	0.01539882905	0.00000000064	0.01539882969
	\$ 10	0.00739973330	0.00000000031	0.00739973361
	\$ 25	0.00259996869	0.00000000011	0.00259996880
	\$ 500	0.00013000519	0.00000000001	0.00013000520
	\$5,000	0.00001000000	0.00000000000	0.00001000000
Probability of winning in this Millionaire Game *P (y)*		0.99999995833	0.00000004167	1.00000000000

QUERY 4.6:
Below is a bivariate probability distribution for the amounts of money America's Cup competitors Bill Koch and Raul Gardini were alleged to be spending. These probabilities were obtained from a cursory review of what TV commentators, journalists, and yachting experts were saying the two were spending. They are thus subjective probabilities. What does treating these probabilities as objective imply about the independence of spending? If Gardini is believed to be spending $165 million, what is the probability that Koch is spending $100 million?

Probabilities of Expenditures by the Challenger and Defender in 1992 America's Cup

Bill Koch's spending on the defense	Raul Gardini's spending on the challenge				
	$105,000,000	$135,000,000	$165,000,000	$195,000,000	
$ 50,000,000	0.00	0.01	0.01	0.00	0.02
$ 75,000,000	0.01	0.19	0.20	0.09	0.49
$100,000,000	0.00	0.17	0.24	0.08	0.49
	0.01	0.37	0.45	0.17	1.00

ANSWER:
If Bill's spending of $50 million and Raul's spending of $105 million were independent, then

$$P(\text{Bill spends } 50) \times P(\text{Raul spends } 105) = (.02)(.01) = 0.0002$$

which would have to equal

$$P(\text{Bill spends 50 and Raul spends 105 million dollars}),$$

but this is not the case; the latter probability is zero. These two variables are dependent. None of the joint probabilities are equal to the products of the respective marginal probabilities. It only takes one inequality to show dependence, while all of the joint probabilities must equal the products of their respective marginal probabilities for independence. Finally, from a rewriting of Formula (3.5), if Raul Gardini is believed to be spending $165 million (***b***), the probability that Bill Koch is spending $100 million (***a***) is 0.533.

$$P\left(A = \text{a} \middle| B = \text{b}\right) = \frac{P\left(A = \text{a and } B = \text{b}\right)}{P\left(B = \text{b}\right)} = \frac{0.24}{0.45} = 0.5333$$

QUERY 4.7:

A stock analyst predicts that the stock price of a new startup pharmaceutical corporation, currently selling at $100, may rise by $30 if the corporation's diet drug is approved by the FDA, but may fall by $30 if it is not. On questioning by the interviewing TV host, the analyst stated that the probability of the $30 increase in the next six months is 60 percent, the likelihood of a price decrease is 30 percent, and the chance of no noteworthy price change is 10 percent. For comparison, the analyst also stated that $100 worth of a mature pharmaceutical corporation's stock would likely rise in value by $15 with a 40 percent chance, fall by $15 with a 10 percent chance, and not change with a 50 percent chance. From these probabilities, determine the bivariate probability distribution of the price change of the startup and the mature corporation, assuming independence. Is this assumption of independence reasonable?

ANSWER:

The bivariate probability distribution is

		Startup Corp.			
		$ –30	0	30	
	$ 15	0.12	0.04	0.24	0.40
Mature Corp.	0	0.15	0.05	0.30	0.50
	–15	0.03	0.01	0.06	0.10
		0.30	0.10	0.60	1.00

The assumption of independence is reasonable if the new startup is to be unaffected by the same economic forces that influence the mature corporation. This might be true if the new startup's patent is truly unique and revolutionary, but, in general, all stock prices in an industry tend to move together.

4.9 ADDITIVE PROBABILITY

In the consideration of a single random variable, we calculated the probabilities that an instant cash contestant wins $1, $2, $5, $10, $25, $500, or $5,000: $P(x > 0) = 0.137539$.

TABLE 4.7
Abridged Probability Table for Instant Cash and Proposed Millionaire Games

		Proposed Millionaire Game (y)			
		no million $0	win million $1,000,000		
Instant Cash Game (x)	No $s	0.86246142676	0.00000003594	0.86246146270	Probability of winning in Instant Cash Game $P(x)$
	Some $s	0.13753853157	0.00000000573	0.13753853730	
		0.99999995833	0.00000004167	1.00000000000	
		Probability of winning in this Millionaire Game $P(y)$			

We also know the probability that a contestant wins $1 million in the millionaire game: $P(y = 1000000) = 0.00000004167$. We can now ask and answer the question: What is the probability of winning in either the instant cash game or the proposed millionaire game?

Again, because there are two random variables involved, a bivariate probability table is needed, Table 4.7. As in Table 4.6, the joint probabilities in Table 4.7 were calculated as products of the marginal probabilities, because the two games represent independent random variables.

In essence, calculation of the probability of winning in either game is the same as the calculation of the probability of a union presented in the previous chapter. As in our discussion of the probability of the union of two events in Formula 3.3 (where the probability of the intersection of the two events is subtracted from the sum of the two event probabilities), here both marginal probabilities include the joint occurrence of the values, so one of the joint probabilities is removed by subtracting it from the sum of the two marginal probabilities.

The probability of winning in either the instant cash or the millionaire game is

$$\begin{aligned} P(x > 0 \text{ or } y = 1000000) &= P(x > 0) + P(y = 1000000) - P(x > 0 \text{ and } y = 1000000) \\ &= 0.13753853730 + 0.00000004167 - 0.00000000573 \\ &= 0.13753857324 \end{aligned}$$

This says that in fewer than 14 out of 100 times will a contestant win some amount in either of these two independent lottery games. In a like manner, other additive probabilities associated with these two games can be determined.

QUERY 4.8:

Using the information on the joint probabilities of Bill Koch's and Raul Gardini's spending on the 1992 America's Cup yacht race, what is the probability that either one is spending at their respective maximum ($100 million for Koch or $195 million for Gardini)?

ANSWER:

Let Koch's spending be $\boldsymbol{a}$ and Gardini's $\boldsymbol{b}$. The probability of either spending at his maximum is 0.58.

$$\begin{aligned} P(\boldsymbol{a} \text{ or } \boldsymbol{b}) &= P(\boldsymbol{a}) + P(\boldsymbol{b}) - P(\boldsymbol{a} \text{ and } \boldsymbol{b}) \\ &= 0.49 + 0.17 - 0.08 = 0.58 \end{aligned}$$

4.10 Linear Functions of Random Variables

Instead of being independent, two random variables might be related linearly. A random variable y is a linear function of another random variable x if

$$y = \alpha + \beta x$$

where α (alpha) and β (beta) are constants and y and x are realized in matched pairs. For instance, y might be annual profits of a car dealership and x might be number of cars sold. Ian Ayers (1991) reports on how car dealerships extract different premiums per car sold, depending on the size of the dealership, type of car, and the age, race, and sex of the customers and salespersons. Thus, the number of cars sold x is a random variable that influences dealership profits y.

If the number of cars sold in a fixed time period is a random variable with a known expected value, then the expected profit per car is likewise known and written as[7]

$$E(y) = \alpha + \beta E(x)$$

Continuing the car dealership example, suppose the fixed cost of the dealership is \$220,000 per year. The gross profit from each car sold is the selling price less the variable cost associated with the car (invoice plus shipping, preparation, salesperson's commission, etc.); say this gross profit is \$800. The number of cars sold through the dealership is a random variable with an expected value of 300. The expected value of this dealership's annual profit is \$20,000: $y = -220000 + 800x$, so

$$E(y) = -220000 + 800(300) = 20000$$

In Chapter 6 on the normal distribution, a linear transformation of one random variable is introduced to create another normal random variable. In Chapters 12, 13, and 14, regression analysis is introduced to do much more with the linear relationships that exist among economic and business variables. For now, it is sufficient to recognize that models such as $y = \alpha + \beta x$ can be constructed and that the distribution of y is a function of that of x.

EXERCISES

4.18 For the following bivariate probability table,

	A_1	A_2	A_3
B_1	0.12	0.03	0.10
B_2	0.21	0.02	0.18
B_3	0.11	0.09	0.14

a. give the six marginal probabilities.
b. find $P(A_1 \text{ and } B_1)$.
c. determine $P(A_1 \text{ or } B_2)$.
d. calculate $P(A_1 \mid B_1)$.
e. are A_1 and B_2 independent or dependent?

4.19 Northwest Airlines runs a commuter service from Chicago to Minneapolis, with several flights per day. In the winter months, bad weather influences arrival time. Let $y = 1$ if the flight is on time and 0 otherwise. Let $x = 1$ if the flight is made during bad weather and 0 if not. The bivariate probability distribution for y and x is as follows:

		x (weather)	
		0 (good)	1 (bad)
y (arrival)	0 (late)	0.02	0.14
	1 (on time)	0.80	0.04

a. What are the marginal probabilities?
b. Are weather conditions and arrival times independent?

4.20 According to an article in the *WSJ* (February 24, 1993), only 0.9 percent of some 113,829,200 tax returns get audited. Only about 20 percent of those audited get a field audit, in which an agent comes to the taxpayer's home or place of business. The article states, however: "When the IRS goes looking for a problem, it usually finds one . . . .The average payment: \$15,801 after a field audit, and \$2,348 after an office audit." If a taxpayer is notified that he or she is going to be audited but does not yet know whether it will be a field or office audit, what is the additional payment that he or she can expect?

4.21 Using only the information in Exercise 4.20, what is the additional payment that any individual taxpayer can expect after completing his or her return if auditing is random? Why doesn't this expected value have much meaning for low-income students?

4.11 Expected Value and Variance of Sums of Random Variables

Random variables can be related in many different ways. Thus, multiple variable analysis is tricky but essential to business and economic problem solving. Later chapters are devoted to multivariate analysis in a linear equation (regression) setting; what is important here is to grasp how random variables interact in the calculation of measures of central tendency and dispersion in the sums and differences of the variables.

Consider Query 4.7, involving a stock analyst's predictions. The analyst states that the stock price of a new startup pharmaceutical corporation, currently selling at \$100, may rise by \$30 if the corporation's diet drug is approved by the FDA, but may fall by \$30 if it is not. The analyst also states that the probability of the \$30 increase is 60 percent; the likelihood of a price decrease is 30 percent, and the chance of no noteworthy price change is 10 percent. On the other hand, the analyst states that \$100 worth of a mature pharmaceutical corporation's stock would likely rise in value by \$15 with a 40 percent chance, fall by \$15 with a 10 percent chance, and not change with a 50 percent chance. The query involved the joint probability distribution of price changes for the two stocks. Now we ask about the expected value of the price change in these two stocks.

We already know how to calculate the expected values of the net returns to the two stocks (\$9 for the startup and \$4.50 for the mature pharmaceutical corporation) and the standard deviations (\$12.41 and \$3.82).

$$\text{Startup}: \quad \mu_s = E(s) = \sum sP(s) = 9.00$$

$$\sigma_s = \sqrt{\sum (s-\mu_s)^2 P(s)} = \sqrt{729} = 27$$

$$\text{Mature}: \quad \mu_m = E(m) = \sum mP(m) = 4.50$$

$$\sigma_m = \sqrt{\sum (m-\mu_m)^2 P(m)} = \sqrt{92.25} = 9.605$$

Is there any advantage in splitting an investment by putting, say, 50 percent in the startup and 50 percent in the mature corporation? That is, is there any advantage to diversification?

If, instead of putting \$100 into the startup or \$100 into the stock of the mature corporation, \$50 was placed in each, then the expected net return for this diversified portfolio would be \$6.75.

$$E(0.5s + 0.5m) = 0.5\mu_s + 0.5\mu_m = 0.5(9.00) + 0.5(4.50) = 6.75$$

The expected value of the sum of random variables is equal to the sum of the expected values, adjusted for any proportional shares, which in this case is 50 percent in each stock.

In general, the expected value of any sum of random variables formed by a multiple β_1 of a random variable x plus a multiple β_2 of a random variable y plus a multiple β_3 of a random variable z plus . . . can be represented as

Expected value of a weighted sum of random variables

$$E(\beta_1 x + \beta_2 y + \beta_3 z + \ldots) = \beta_1 E(x) + \beta_2 E(y) + \beta_3 E(z) + \ldots \tag{4.5}$$

Where the $x, y, z, \ldots$ are the random variables and the β's are fixed coefficients.

Notice that Formula (4.5) holds regardless of the relationship among the random variables. No assumption of independence is required to calculate the expected value of a sum of random variables. In terms of an investment strategy, forming a portfolio of different investments simply yields an expected value that is a weighted sum of the expected returns of the investments, where the weights are the proportion of funds invested.

The advantage of diversification shows up in the dispersion to be expected. If the prices of the two pharmaceutical stocks that form the above portfolio are independent, then the variance of the return to the portfolio is

$$\text{Var}(0.5m + 0.5s) = 0.25\text{Var}(m) + 0.25\text{Var}(s) =$$

$$= 0.25(92.25) + 0.25(729) = 205.3125,$$

where the 0.5 is squared because the dollar values in the random variables m and s are squared. But therein lies the advantage of diversification. The standard deviation is a measure of risk; it is the square root of the variance. Because the square root is based on a multiplicative process while the variance is calculated as an additive process, gains through diversification are possible. The standard deviation of this portfolio is $\$14.33 = \sqrt{205.3125}$, which is less than half-way between the standard deviation of the startup (\$27) and the mature stock (\$9.61), even though 50 percent of the total investment was in each.

Another way to see the advantage of diversification for risk reduction is to consider the coefficients of variation for a \$100 investment in the startup, the mature corporation, and a portfolio consisting of \$50 in each.

Startup: $\sigma_s/\mu_s = 27/9.00 = 3$

Mature: $\sigma_m/\mu_m = 9.605/4.50 = 2.134$

Diversified: $\sigma_d/\mu_d = 14.3287/6.75 = 2.123$

The diversified portfolio (with 50 percent of the total investment in each stock) has an expected return half-way between a portfolio that consists of only the startup and another that has only the mature corporation, but the coefficient of variation (2.123) for the diversified portfolio is even smaller than that of the mature stock (2.134).

In general, the variance and standard deviation of any sum of independent random variables that is formed by a multiple β_1 of a random variable x plus a multiple β_2 of a random variable y plus a multiple β_3 of a random variable z plus . . . can be represented as

Variance of a weighted sum of independent random variables

$$\text{Var}(\beta_1 x + \beta_2 y + \beta_3 z + \ldots) = \beta_1^2\sigma_x^2 + \beta_2^2\sigma_y^2 + \beta_3^2\sigma_z^2 + \ldots \quad (4.6)$$

Where the σ's are standard deviations of the x, y, z . . . variables and the β's are fixed coefficients.

Standard deviation of a weighted sum of independent random variables

$$\text{St. Dev.}\left(\beta_1 x + \beta_2 y + \beta_3 z + \ldots\right) = \sqrt{\beta_1^2\sigma_x^2 + \beta_2^2\sigma_y^2 + \beta_3^2\sigma_z^2 + \ldots} \quad (4.7)$$

4.12 Covariance and Dependent Random Variables

As already hinted in Query 4.7, the prices of two stocks in the same industry are likely to be related. As the demand for products within an industry increases, all companies can expect to benefit to some degree. Similarly, as the demand for the industry's products falls, all companies within it can expect to suffer. As the industry expands or contracts, however, competition within the industry may favor one company to the detriment of another. The assumption of independence between the stock prices of a startup and a mature corporation within the pharmaceutical industry is questionable.

Without the assumption of independence, the probability that the price of the startup rises when the price of the mature corporation falls cannot be obtained, unless the joint probability distribution for the two random variables is known. In the real world, joint probabilities are seldom known. At best, we know marginal probabilities and conditional probabilities from which we can infer joint probabilities. For multiple variables, however, it is unlikely that we would have sufficient information to infer all the joint probabilities that go into forming the entire multivariate probability distribution. Later chapters will address the estimation of these missing joint probabilities. For now, it is important to recognize these implications for the calculation of the variance of two random variables.

If two random variables x and y tend to move in the same direction, then many of the products of x deviations $(x - \mu_x)$ and y deviations $(y - \mu_y)$ should be positive. When x is above its mean, for example, y would usually be above its mean. More specifically, consider a bivariate distribution in which x_i is the ith value of variable x and y_j is the jth value of variable y, and the joint probability $P(x_i, y_j)$ is relatively large whenever the product $(x_i - \mu_x)(y_j - \mu_y)$ is positive. Likewise, the joint probability $P(x_i, y_j)$ is relatively small whenever the product $(x_i - \mu_x)(x_j - \mu_y)$ is negative. For such a bivariate distribution, the probability weighted sum of (i,j) cross products should be positive:

$$\sum_i \sum_j (x_i - \mu_x)(y_j - \mu_y) P(x_i, y_j) > 0$$

Alternatively, if x and y tend to move in opposite directions, then the products of deviations in x and deviations in y times their respective probabilities should tend to be negative:

$$\sum_i \sum_j (x_i - \mu_x)(y_j - \mu_y) P(x_i, y_j) < 0$$

When there is no relationship (independence) between x and y, positive and negative deviations will tend to cancel so

$$\sum_i \sum_j (x_i - \mu_x)(y_j - \mu_y) P(x_i, y_j) = 0$$

Covariance of x and y
A measure of the joint or "co" variability of two variables x and y.

This sum of deviation cross products weighted by probabilities is called the **covariance of x and y,** abbreviated Cov (x,y). It shows how, on the average, deviations of x are related to deviations of y. In the case of the pharmaceutical companies, a positive covariance indicates that as the price of the startup rises (or falls), the price of the mature corporation tends to rise (or fall). A negative covariance says that as the price of the startup rises (or falls), the price of the mature corporation stock falls (or rises). If the two are independent, then the covariance is zero and there is no relationship between changes in the price of the two companies. Unfortunately, we seldom know a covariance with certainty; as discussed in later chapters, it typically must be estimated.

Covariance for random variables x and y

$$\sum_i \sum_j (x_i - \mu_x)(y_j - \mu_y) P(x_i, y_j) \tag{4.8}$$

When the covariance between two random variables x and y is known to be nonzero, the variance for the sum of the two variables must take account of this. If the two variables are positively related, then the positive covariance will add to the variability in the sum. If the two variables are negatively related, then the negative covariance will reduce variability.[8]

In general, the variance and standard deviation of any sum of random variables that is formed by a multiple β_1 of a random variable x plus a multiple β_2 of a random variable y plus a multiple β_3 of a random variable z plus . . . is represented as

Variance of a weighted sum of any random variables

$$\begin{aligned} \mathrm{Var}(\beta_1 x + \beta_2 y + \beta_3 z + \ldots) &= \beta_1^2\sigma_x^2 + \beta_2^2\sigma_y^2 + \beta_3^2\sigma_z^2 + \ldots \\ &+ 2\beta_1\beta_2\mathrm{Cov}(xy) + 2\beta_1\beta_3\mathrm{Cov}(xz) + 2\beta_2\beta_3\mathrm{Cov}(yz) + \ldots \end{aligned} \tag{4.9}$$

Where the σ's are standard deviations of the x, y, z...variables and the β's are fixed coefficients.

Again the standard deviation of the sum of the random variables is the square root of the variance.

Standard deviation of any weighted sum of random variables

$$\text{St. Dev.}\left(\beta_1 x + \beta_2 y + \beta_3 z + \ldots\right) = \sqrt{\mathrm{Var}\left(\beta_1 x + \beta_2 y + \beta_3 z + \ldots\right)} \tag{4.10}$$

Notice in Formula (4.9) that if the covariances are zero, as is the case for independent variables, then Formula (4.6) and Formula (4.9) are the same. To the extent that covariance is positive, with β's > 0, the variance of the sum of random variables is increased. To the extent that covariance is negative, the variance of the sum of random variables is decreased. It is for this reason that financial managers advise investors to put offsetting investments in their portfolios to reduce risk while attempting to maintain expected returns. "The idea is to own a variety of funds that tend to do well at different times, so that the overall value of your portfolio doesn't jump around too much," as stated in a *Wall Street Journal* article on "Putting Together Right Mix of Funds in Your Portfolio."

EXERCISES

4.22 For the three investments listed below, what is the expected net return for a portfolio that consists of \$4,000 in each of the three investments (for a total portfolio investment of \$12,000)?

Investments:	*A*	*B*	*C*
Expected net returns	\$ 1,000	\$ 1,500	\$ 2,000
Standard deviation	\$ 500	\$ 700	\$ 1,150

4.23 In Exercise 4.22, would your answer be affected if you learned that investments *A*, *B*, and *C* are independent? Explain.

4.24 What is the standard deviation of the return in Exercise 4.23, assuming the returns are independent? What is the significance of the assumption of independence?

4.25 The following investments are available at a price of \$100,000 each:

Investments:	*A*	*B* (in thousands of dollars)
Expected net returns	11	16
Standard deviation	4	5

A third investment may be formed by placing \$50,000 in investment *A* and \$50,000 in investment *B*. What is the standard deviation of this third investment, assuming *A* and *B* are independent? What is the significance of the assumption of independence? If an investor ignores risk, which investment would he or she select [*A*, *B*, or the third option (.5*A* + .5*B*)]? Why?

4.26 Let x and y be two *independent discrete random variables.* The probability distributions of x and y are given below:

x	1	2	3	4
$P(x)$	.4	.1	.3	.2

y	4	3	2	1
$P(y)$	.2	.3	.1	.4

a. What is $E(x)$?
b. What is $E(y)$?
c. What is $E(x - y)$?

4.27 From the x and y distributions described in Exercise 4.26, form the bivariate probability distribution. What is the probability that $x = 2$ and $y = 3$?

4.28 Use the data in Exercise 4.26 and a computer spreadsheet package to calculate the
a. variance of x
b. variance of y
c. covariance of x and y

4.29 Let x be the annual return on a share of GM's stock and y be the annual return on a share of Chrysler's stock. $E(x) = \$20$, $\text{Var}(x) = 10$ square dollars, $E(y) = \$15$, $\text{Var}(y) = 5$ square dollars, $\text{Cov}(x,y) = 2$ square dollars.
a. What is the expected return for a portfolio that contains one unit of each type of stock?
b. What is the variance of return for the portfolio?

4.13 Concluding Comments

You are now sufficiently versed in the notion of probability and its application to business and economics problems involving random variables. The importance of knowing whether variables are independent should be clear. Using the basic rules of probability, you should be able to make probability calculations for everyday business and economic decisions involving joint probabilities. Finally, you should be able to calculate and interpret the expected value and variance of sets of random variables and relate these measures to the notion of risk.

Chapter Exercises

4.30 A carnival game involves placing money on one of six colored squares. The spinning of a wheel determines the winning color. If you place a \$10 bet on blue (for which you either lose your \$10 if blue is not spun or win \$10 if blue is spun), what is your expected win?

4.31 The probability distribution for the number of sales calls (x) made by a salesperson is given in the following table.

x	0	1	2	3	4 Calls per day
$P(x)$	.10	.40	.25	.15	.10

a. What is the expected value for the random variable x?
b. What is the standard deviation of x?
c. What is the approximate shape of the above distribution?

4.32 An article in the *Sunday Herald Times* (June 28, 1992) quoted John Gordon, chief financial officer of Domino's Pizza, in Dayton, Ohio, as saying that he did not understand the hassles pizza delivery drivers may get from insurance companies. He cited "a company study that found drivers who deliver fast food have fewer accidents per mile driven than the national average." Why is this an irrelevant fact to the insurance company when it is considering expected loss and the risk associated with a policy?

4.33 In a malpractice case following the death of a man during a cardiac operation, a medical doctor stated that even if the cardiac procedure had been a complete success, the deceased could not have lifted more than 25 pounds and there would have been a 30- to 40-percent likelihood that the arteries would have narrowed again, leaving little or no lifting ability after six months. The plaintiff's attorney argued that had the operation been a success, the deceased could have worked in retail sales. Professor Becker wrote for the defense that since two gallons of milk or two gallons of paint or two gallons of most anything else weighs in excess of 17.5 pounds, and since the *Occupational Handbook* stated that most retail sales workers are required to bag and package purchases and stock shelves and racks, prior to the operation the deceased could not realistically have expected to work in retail sales even if the operation had been a success. On what basis was Becker basing his opinion?

4.34 "Pepsi has said it expects to grab more than 2% of the \$48 billion soft-drink market with Crystal Pepsi in its first year as a national product," according to *The Wall Street Journal* (December 15, 1992). In statistical terms, what does the word "expects" mean here?

4.35 A note in *The Wall Street Journal* (December 30, 1987) reported that, "Last year, 52 percent of all calls (to the Internal Revenue Service) were put on hold for an average of 55 seconds." What is the expected wait time for someone calling in to the IRS?

4.36 At a dinner party, an economist was heard saying that "the state lottery is a tax on stupid people." What did he mean by this?

4.37 If the economist's statement in Exercise 4.36 is true, would you expect the state lottery to be a progressive or regressive tax with respect to personal income?

4.38 When state lotteries became popular in the 1970s, proponents argued that the revenue could go to education, roads, and other infrastructure needs. Some pointed to the University of Delaware's use of state lottery money to build College Hall in 1834 as the earliest example of higher education's involvement with lotteries. As argued by Duke University economics professor Charles Clotfelter in his book on lotteries, however, the cost of administering lotteries is extremely high (e.g., in 1991, $151 million was turned over to the state of Indiana at a cost of $68 million) and revenues are erratic (e.g., between the first quarter of 1990 and the last of 1991, the Indiana state lottery has seen its profits cut in half); thus, lotteries have not delivered what was expected.

a. As more and more states introduced lotteries, why did they fail to deliver the expected profits?

b. Had expected profits been realized and placed into more effective education, why might this have led to future reductions in lottery revenues?

4.39 Suppose you make a $2000 investment. The gross payoffs (x) from the investment have the following probability distribution.

x	$P(x)$
5000	0.50
2000	0.20
0	0.30

a. What is the expected value of the gross payoffs from your investment of $2000?

b. What is the expected value of the net payoffs from your investment of $2000?

c. What is the standard deviation of the gross payoffs?

d. What is the standard deviation of the net payoffs?

e. How do a and b relate to each other and how do c and d relate to each other?

4.40 Two experimental corporate aircraft are flying on the same approximate route over the ocean: one has a single engine, the other has two engines. The reliability of each engine is the same, with a chance of failure being 0.001. Neither plane can maintain flight if an engine quits. Although the two-engine plane has a longer glide path, if only one engine goes out, the glide path of neither plane is sufficient to make it to land. The planes are equally fast and alike on all other physical factors. The single engine plane has a value of $1M and the two engine plane has a value of $2M. If either plane goes down in the ocean it is a total loss.

a. Which plane has a greater chance of going down in the ocean because of engine failure?

b. In part a what was the critical assumption you had to make to do your calculation?

c. Given your answers in parts a and b, what is the break even point for an insurance policy written to cover the expected loss?

4.41 As part of the annual performance review, employees are given merit ratings. The question is how do these merit ratings relate to annual salary increases? Below is a joint probability table of ratings and salary increases

	Merit Rating	0	1	2	3
Annual	$ 0	0.08	0.10	0.05	0.00
Salary	$2,000	0.06	0.20	0.20	0.02
Increase	$4,500	0.01	0.10	0.10	0.08

a. Without doing any calculations, can you tell if salary and merit rating are independent and have a zero covariance? Explain.
b. What is the expected merit rating?
c. What is the expected salary increase?
d. Are your calculations in parts b and c influenced by the magnitude of the covariance?

4.42 Investments *A* and *B* are available at a price of $100,000 each, and have the following payback characteristics:

Investments:	*A*	*B*
Expected net returns	$10,000	$15,000
Standard deviation	$ 3,000	$ 4,000

An investor is only interested in returns over a long period of time and does not care about a gain or loss on any single purchase and sale of a security.

a. If the investor could purchase one or the other security but not both, which investment would he or she buy?
b. If a new investment was available that was formed by placing $50,000 in investment *A* and $50,000 in investment *B*, what would the standard deviation of this new investment be, assuming the returns on the two investments were independent?

4.43 In large national lotteries, in which the pots accumulate or roll over when the selected series of numbers does not yield a winning ticket holder, can a ticket purchaser's expected net return be positive on a ticket purchased in a subsequent running of the lottery? Explain.

4.44 After 28-year-old Nicholas William Leeson incurred billion dollar losses at the Singapore branch of the Baring Bank of England, and forced the bank into bankruptcy hearings, a Hong Kong security trader was quoted in *Newsweek* (March 13, 1995) saying that Lesson's investment strategy (in which his bets on the long side of the market doubled between his big loss on January 23, 1995, and his disastrous loss on the 27th) was like the classic roulette strategy in which a player doubles his or her bet following a loss. For example, starting with a $5 bet on red, if the wheel is spun and the ball does not land in the red slot you lose. On the next play, however, if you bet $10, your expected win is approximately the $5 lost on the previous play. If you lose again, put $20 on red in the next play and your expected win will be about $10. The idea is that sooner or later you will win back the money you lost. In what sense could this strategy be considered logically consistent? But why does it not ensure that the gambler (and security trader) will never lose in the end? (In the U.S., roulette wheels typically have 18 black, 18 red, and 2 green slots but in Europe, where roulette originated and then spread to Hong Kong, there is only one green on a wheel with a total of 37 slots.)

4.45 The prospectus for Putnam Voyager Fund (November 30, 1996) reported a mean return of 16.67 percent and standard deviation of 14.72 percent.

a. What was the expected return for Putnam Voyager Fund?

b. What was the coefficient of variation for Putnam Voyager Fund?

c. Could the returns to Putnam Voyager Fund behave in accordance with the empirical rule for bell-shaped distributions? Explain.

4.46 A farmer is considering the option of taking out an insurance policy to cover possible losses from crop damage. If there is a major crop failure, the farmer feels that a loss of $80,000 will be incurred. If there is a moderate failure, a loss of $20,000 would be incurred. Insurance actuaries have determined that the probabilities of major failure and moderate failure are .01 and .05, respectively. Ignoring all other possible losses, and assuming risk neutrality, what is the break even insurance policy premium for these prospects?

4.47 A manufacturing representative is considering taking out an insurance policy to cover possible losses from a new product. If the product is a complete failure, the representative feels that a loss of $90,000 will be incurred. If it is only moderately successful, a loss of $20,000 would be incurred. Insurance actuaries have determined from market surveys and other available information that the probabilities the product will be a failure or only moderately successful are .01 and .05, respectively. Assuming no other possible losses, and risk neutrality, what is the break even insurance policy premium for these prospects?

4.48 A *Wall Street Journal* (March 17, 1997) article advised "Jittery Fund Investors Should Diversify...The idea behind diversification is that -- not always, but often enough to help-- when one type of security zigs, another type may zag, helping balance out an overall portfolio." Show the advantage of diversification in moving from a one to a two stock portfolio.

ACADEMIC REFERENCES

Ayers, Ian. "Fair Driving: Gender and Race Discrimination in Retail Car Negotiations." *Harvard Law Review*, February, 1991.

Chernoff, H. "How to Beat the Massachusetts Number Game." *Mathematical Intelligencer*, 1981, pp. 166–172.

ENDNOTES

1. As described in the previous chapter, the Indiana state lottery has six window tickets that are scratched open by contestants. Three matching windows win the holder $1 to $5,000 in instant cash. Alternatively, the holder may lose or have three matching windows that enable him or her to mail in an entry to an ongoing and more involved TV contest. Only about 75 out of 75 million tickets will place holders in a pool from which six go onto a weekly TV show, where they pick from unmarked doors for $3,000 to $30,000 prizes. Each week, the big prize winner on this TV show gets to try for $1 million. (*HT*, October 8, 1989) The variant proposed here allows holders of each of the 75 million tickets to be one of those selected for a chance at the $1 million prize, regardless of the outcome in the instant cash game. There

need be no TV show for awarding the \$1 million; three of the six windows match for \$1 million along with a match (or no match) on the other three windows.

2. This expected value of \$0.475 is close to that suggested by published estimates. "If all 75 million tickets are sold, there will be more than 10 million cash prize winners who will pocket more than \$35 million." This quote implies an expected value of \$0.467 per ticket (= 35000000/75000000). An alternative estimate of the mean return can be obtained from actual payouts. In 1991, 54 percent of total revenue was paid in prize money, implying an average return to a \$1 ticket of 54 cents, which is slightly higher than the expected return.
3. In the case of big, ongoing lotteries, as with horse racing, a caveat must be added to the interpretation of the expected value of a winning entry. Unlike fixed payoff games of chance involving dice (for example, craps), cards (for example, blackjack), the Indiana instant cash game, or even the stock market, horse racing and some lotteries offer a parimutuel betting system, in which the payoff is really not fixed. If you place \$10 on number 15 in roulette and the wheel stops with the marker resting on 15, you receive the same amount (\$380) no matter how many other players bet on number 15, assuming the house has the funds. In most big, ongoing lotteries, the payoff to the winning ticket is shared equally by all holders of tickets with the winning six numbers. We will not go into the calculation of the expected value for these types of random variables. The interested reader is referred to H. Chernoff (1981, pp. 166–172), who describes the calculation of expected returns in these lotto games and uses basic probability concepts to analyze alleged strategies to beat the Massachusetts lotto.
4. As an alternative computation formula, some textbooks emphasize the use of the variance formula $\sigma^2 = \sum_x x^2P(x) - \mu^2$, which is algebraically equivalent to Formula (4.2).

$$\sigma^2 = E[x - E(x)]^2 = E(x - \mu)^2 = \Sigma\,(x - \mu)^2P(x)$$
$$= \Sigma\,(x^2 - 2x\mu + \mu^2)P(x) = \Sigma x^2P(x) - 2\mu\,\Sigma xP(x) + \mu^2\Sigma P(x)$$
$$= \Sigma x^2P(x) - 2\mu^2 + \mu^2 = \Sigma x^2P(x) - \mu^2$$

5. In our discussion of a random variables, we have made a distinction between the variable and the occurrence of one of its numerical values. There is no universally accepted notation for making this distinction in algebraic form, although many textbooks use an upper case letter (A) when introducing the concept of a random variable, and a lower case (a) for its realizations, only to abandon this usage later in the book. Similarly, in some scholarly journals, an italic letter (*a*) is to be used for the random variable and a bold letter (**a**) for its realizations, only to have this rule violated by the type setter. More confusion than enlightenment is introduced by these different standards and failure to maintain the consistency throughout the text. Thus, we are not making a distinction between the algebraic notation for the random variable and its realization. We will use upper and lower case letters to represent random variables and make their realizations obvious in the discussion.
6. If two occurances are mutually exclusive, then they must be dependent. For example, if the marginal probability of each is 0.5, but the probability of their intersection is 0, then

$$P(A|B) = \frac{P(A \text{ and } B)}{P(B)} = \frac{0}{0.5} = 0 \neq 0.5 = P(A)$$

7. This result follows from the following proof:

$$E(y) = \sum_y yP(y)$$

$$E(y) = \sum_x (a + bx)P(x)$$

$$E(y) = \sum_x \left[aP(x) + (bx)P(x)\right]$$

$$E(y) = a\sum_x P(x) + b\sum_x xP(x)$$

$$= a + bE(x)$$

since $\Sigma P(x) = 1$ and $\Sigma xP(x)$ is the mean of x.

8. Let x and y be two random variables, and let A and B be two constants; then,

$$\text{var}(Ax + By) = E\left[(Ax + By) - E(Ax + By)\right]^2$$

$$= E\left[A(x - \mu_x) + B(y - \mu_y)\right]^2$$

$$= E\left[A^2(x - \mu_x)^2 + B^2(y - \mu_y)^2 + 2AB(x - \mu_x)(y - \mu_y)\right]$$

$$= A^2\text{Var}(x) + B^2\text{Var}(y) + 2AB\text{Cov}(xy)$$

FORMULAS

- Expected value of x

  $$E(x) = \mu = \sum_x xP(x)$$

  where $P(x)$ is the probability of x,

  $\sum_x xP(x)$ is the sum of x and $P(x)$ products, for all the values of x,

  $E(x)$ is the expected value of x, and μ is the mean of x.

- Variance of random variable x

  $$\sigma^2 = E\left[x - E(x)\right]^2 = E(x - \mu)^2 = \sum_x (x - \mu)^2 P(x)$$

  where $P(x)$ is the probability of x,

  $\sum_x (x - \mu)^2 P(x)$ is the sum of products of squared deviations multiplied by respective probabilities, for all the values of x, $E(x)$ is the expected value of x, and μ is the mean of x.

- Standard deviation of random variable x

$$\sigma = \sqrt{E[x - E(x)]^2} = \sqrt{E(x-\mu)^2} = \sqrt{\sum_x (x-\mu)^2 P(x)}$$

The standard deviation of random variable x is the positive square root of the variance.

- Coefficient of variation

The coefficient of variation is a ratio of the standard deviation to the expected value or mean of a variable.

$$C = \frac{\sqrt{E[x - E(x)]^2}}{E(x)} = \frac{\sqrt{E(x-\mu)^2}}{\mu} = \frac{\sigma}{\mu}$$

- Expected value of a weighted sum of random variables

$$E(\beta_1 x + \beta_2 y + \beta_3 z + \ldots) = \beta_1 E(x) + \beta_2 E(y) + \beta_3 E(z) + \ldots$$

where the x, y, z, . . . are the random variables and the β's are fixed coefficients.

- Variance of a weighted sum of independent random variables

$$\text{Var}(\beta_1 x + \beta_2 y + \beta_3 z + \ldots) = \beta_1^2\sigma_x^2 + \beta_2^2\sigma_y^2 + \beta_3^2\sigma_z^2 + \ldots$$

where the σ's are standard deviations of the x, y, z . . . variables and the β's are fixed coefficients.

- Standard deviation of a weighted sum of independent random variables

$$\text{St. Dev.}(\beta_1 x + \beta_2 y + \beta_3 z + \ldots) = \sqrt{\beta_1^2\sigma_x^2 + \beta_2^2\sigma_y^2 + \beta_3^2\sigma_z^2 + \ldots}$$

- Covariance for random variables x and y

$$\sum_i \sum_j (x_i - \mu_x)(y_j - \mu_y) P(x_i, y_j)$$

- Variance of a weighted sum of any random variables

$$\begin{aligned}\text{Var}(\beta_1 x + \beta_2 y + \beta_3 z + \ldots) &= \beta_1^2\sigma_x^2 + \beta_2^2\sigma_y^2 + \beta_3^2\sigma_z^2 + \ldots \\ &+ 2\beta_1\beta_2\text{Cov}(xy) + 2\beta_1\beta_3\text{Cov}(xz) + 2\beta_2\beta_3\text{Cov}(yz) + \ldots\end{aligned}$$

where the σ's are standard deviations of the x, y, z. . .
variables and the β's are fixed coefficients.

- Standard deviation of any weighted sum of random variables

$$\text{St. Dev.}\ (\beta_1 x + \beta_2 y + \beta_3 z + \ldots) = \sqrt{\text{Var}(\beta_1 x + \beta_2 y + \beta_3 z + \ldots)}$$

CHAPTER 5

THE BINOMIAL DISTRIBUTION

If thou must choose
Between the chances,
choose the odd;
Read the New Yorker;
trust in God;
And take short views.

Wystan Hugh Auden
1907–1973

5.1 Introduction

The following four problems share in common a probability calculation of a discrete random variable involving a count.

- The defense for boxer Mike Tyson in his 1992 trial for rape in Indianapolis claimed that the pool of 50 persons from which a jury of 12 members was selected was not representative of the community at large. With 22 percent of the community black, what is the probability of randomly selecting a pool of 50 with seven or fewer blacks?
- A *Wall Street Journal* (April 20, 1992) article reported on a study by University of Delaware Professor Valerie P. Hans of jurors' attitudes toward business in wrongful death and injury cases. "Of the 18 cases, 14 were decided in favor of plaintiffs, higher than the national norm of about 50%." The question is: How likely was a sample with 14 out of 18 decisions for the plaintiff, if the expected outcome was nine out of 18 by the national norm?
- A *Wall Street Journal* (August 29, 1991) article reported on the problems that General Motors is having at its plant in Orion Township, Michigan. According to the article, "On some days, the cars have more than three times the company goal of two defects per car." For 20 key checkpoints, what is the probability that a randomly selected car from the Orion Township plant will have six or more defects, if the plant is producing cars that average only two defects per car?

- In "Why Investors Shouldn't Listen to Economists," (*WSJ*, January 22, 1993), statistics compiled by Robert Beckwitt, a portfolio manager at Fidelity Investment, showed "only five of 34 economists who participated in 10 or more surveys managed to guess correctly which way long-term bond yields were going more than half of the time." The conclusion drawn was that economists cannot forecast as well as flipping a coin. But what is the probability of five of 34 individuals predicting correctly six or more yield movements in 10 tries? What are the implications of this probability for the accuracy of economists' forecasts?

The number of blacks, number of favorable decisions, number of defects, and number of accurate forecasts are the outcomes of processes that can result only in a whole number count, where the count is determined by a series of independent trials that result in either "success" or "failure." This chapter provides the skills needed to use the binomial distribution in probability calculations involving such counts. By the end of this chapter, you will be able to state when the binomial distribution is an appropriate representation of the process underlying a discrete random variable. You will be able to make probability calculations with this distribution using either a formula or a computer program.

5.2 The Binomial Distribution

Each of the 20 checkpoints on a car produced at the Orion Township plant represents a quality characteristic, factor, or attribute that either is conforming to a standard set by GM or is not. At each of these checkpoints, a random variable can be defined that is equal to one if the check conforms to the standard or that is equal to zero if it does not. The sum of these individual random variables then forms a random variable that is the number of checkpoints that conform to the standard. Similarly, in the jury selection case, each selection of a juror can be viewed as an experiment in which the random variable is equal to one if a black is selected and to zero if not. The sum of these individual random variables is the number of blacks in the preselection pool. The composite random variable x in either of these two cases assumes only the values 0, 1, 2, 3, . . . , n, where n is the sample size ($n = 20$, for the car and $n = 50$, in the jury preselection pool).

Binomial Probability Distribution
A discrete probability distribution for the sum of a series of n independent and identical trials, where each trial results in one of the two possible outcomes, (0 or 1) that occur with fixed probabilities.

The **binomial probability distribution** is formed by a probability mass function that may be used when the random variable x can only take on values $x = 0$, $x = 1$, $x = 2$, $x = 3$, and so on. The unique feature of the binomial process, however, is that these nonnegative whole number values are obtained as the sum of n identical and independent trials in which each trial yields either a one or zero as an outcome. That is, each trial itself is a random experiment yielding either a one or zero as its outcome. In the car example, each checkpoint can be viewed as a trial, with the outcome either defect or no defect. If we are interested in the total number of defects (x), then on each of the 20 trials (checkpoints), a one is recorded ($x_i = 1$) if the checkpoint does not conform to the standard and a zero is recorded if it does ($x_i = 0$). The total number of defects is then the sum of the outcomes on the 20 trials.

$$x = x_1 + x_2 + \ldots + x_{20} = \sum_{i=1}^{20} x_i$$

Similarly, each person selected for the preselection pool can be thought of as the outcome of a trial in which the outcome is either black or nonblack, with the total number of blacks determined by the outcome ($x_i = 1$ if black or $x_i = 0$ if nonblack) on each of the 50 trials.

$$x = x_1 + x_2 + \ldots + x_{50} = \sum_{i=1}^{50} x_i$$

For the binomial distribution, one trial cannot influence or be associated with the outcome of another; the outcome of each of the n trials must be independent of one another; the probability of each outcome cannot change from trial to trial. Each trial must be an exact replication of the others. For example, on the first trial in the hiring of 10 workers from an applicant pool of eight women and 12 men applicants, the probability that a woman is hired is 0.40 = 8/20. If a woman is hired, then the probability that a woman is hired on the second trial falls to 0.368 = 7/19. The probability of hiring a woman does not remain fixed from trial to trial, and the binomial distribution cannot be used to calculate probability because the trials are not independent.

In laboratory experiments or drawing balls from an urn, the probability of "success" or "failure" on each trial can be held fixed by replacement. That is, we can draw a ball from an urn, record the color, place the ball back in the urn, and on the next draw the probability of getting that color ball is the same as on the first draw, regardless of the number of balls in the urn.

In real-world problems in business and economics, seldom will the probability of an event remain fixed from trial to trial. In the case of jury selection, for example, when the first of 50 people is selected, there is one fewer person remaining in the pool, thus the probability of selecting a black on the second trial must be different than on the first, but the change is trivial. In the Indianapolis area, where the Tyson trial took place, there are more than 400,000 registered voters. Selecting one, two, or 49 blacks from this base is not going to greatly influence the probability that the next person selected is black. Without replacement, the probability of selecting a black cannot remain exactly fixed from trial to trial, but any change in probability is minuscule because the sample size (n = 50) is extremely small relative to the population size (N = 428,318). Unlike the hiring example in which 10 applicants are to be selected from 20, selecting only 50 potential jurors from a population that exceeds 400,000 allows us to use the binomial in probability calculations.

In the car example, we do not know for sure from the quote if the probability of a defect is fixed at 0.10 for each checkpoint, which represents the average of two defects over 20 checkpoints. The likelihood of a defect at each checkpoint could be different. Each checkpoint could constitute a totally different trial. If such is the case, then the binomial could not be used. In addition, the consequence (dissatisfied customer, expense of repair, lost sale, etc.) could differ depending on the defect—in which case, the likelihood of a defect might be weighted by its cost. Here we will assume that the likelihood of a defect at any one of 20 checkpoints is fixed at 0.10 and that each checkpoint involves an identical visual inspection. We will also assume that the consequence of the defect is identical across defects.

In summary, the binomial distribution is applicable only if

1. the random variable of interest takes on the values of 0, 1, 2, 3, . . . *n*, where this value is the event formed by the sum of *n* random variables;
2. there are *n* trials that give rise to the *n* random variables;
3. only one of two outcomes (0 or 1) is possible for each trial;
4. the probability of either outcome on each trial remains fixed (or at least approximately fixed) from trial to trial. That is, the trials are independent and identically distributed.

5.3 The Binomial Probability Mass Function

The probability of one of the two outcomes on each of the *n* trials is a parameter of the binomial distribution. There is no universally agreed on symbol for this binomial parameter, but in this book it will be designated by the letter π. In the car example, if the goal of only two defects at 20 checkpoints is achieved, then the probability of finding a defect at any one of the 20 checkpoints might be $\pi = 0.10$. In the case of jury selection, 22 percent of the Indianapolis population is black, so the probability of a black on each of the 50 selections is $\pi = 0.22$, assuming draws are random selections from the population.

From the discussion of independence in Chapter 4, the probability that all 20 checkpoints on a car are not conforming to the standard is the product of the probability of a defect at each checkpoint, if the checkpoints are independent. That is, the probability of 20 defects in 20 trials, with the probability of a defect on any trial fixed at $\pi = 0.10$, is $(0.10)^{20}$.

$$\begin{aligned} P(20 \text{ defects}) &= P(\text{defect at 1st checkpoint}) \text{ times} \\ &\quad P(\text{defect at 2nd checkpoint}) \text{ times} \\ &\quad P(\text{defect at 3rd checkpoint}) \text{ times} \\ &\quad \ldots \\ &\quad P(\text{defect at 19th checkpoint}) \text{ times} \\ &\quad P(\text{defect at 20th checkpoint}) \\ &= (\pi)(\pi)\ldots(\pi)(\pi) \\ &= (0.10)(0.10)\ldots(0.10)(0.10) = (0.1)^{20} \\ &= 0.00000000000000000001 = 1.0(10)^{-20} \end{aligned}$$

The probability of 20 perfect checkpoints is likewise determined to be the probability of zero defects, which is 0.121577.

$$\begin{aligned} P(0 \text{ defects}) &= P(\text{1st no defect}) \times P(\text{2nd no defect}) \times \ldots \\ &\quad \ldots \times P(\text{19th no defect}) \times P(\text{20th no defect}) \\ &= (1-\pi)(1-\pi)\ldots(1-\pi)(1-\pi) \\ &= (0.90)(0.90)\ldots(0.90)(0.90) = 0.1215766546 \end{aligned}$$

These are extreme possibilities. Joint probabilities of the different combinations of defects can be calculated, but attention must be given to the different ways in which the defects can occur over the 20 checkpoints. One defect, for example, can occur separately at each checkpoint, so the probability of one defect over the 20 checkpoints is

$$\begin{aligned} P(1 \text{ defect}) &= 20 \times P(\text{one defect}) \times P(\text{no defects at 19 points}) \\ &= 20(\pi)(1-\pi)^{19} \\ &= 20(0.10)(0.90)^{19} = 0.270170 \end{aligned}$$

Two defects can occur over the 20 checkpoints in 190 different ways. As presented in Chapter 3, this is calculated by the combination

$$20!/2!18! = (20)(19)/(2)(1) = 190$$

Factorial
The product of all positive integers from 1 up to and including a given integer; as in $5! = 5 \times 4 \times 3 \times 2 \times 1 = 120$, where $1! = 0! = 1$.

where again 20!,18!, and 2! are **factorials** standing for the products

$$20! = 20 \times 19 \times 18 \times \ldots \times 3 \times 2 \times 1,\ 18! = 18 \times 17 \times \ldots 3 \times 2 \times 1, \text{ and } 2! = 2 \times 1$$

Thus, the probability of two defects is

$$\begin{aligned} P(2 \text{ defects}) &= 190 \times P(\text{two defects}) \times P(\text{no defects at 18 points}) \\ &= 190(\pi)^2(1-\pi)^{18} \\ &= 190(0.10)^2(0.90)^{18} = 0.285180 \end{aligned}$$

Three defects can occur over the 20 checkpoints in 1,140 different ways [20!/3!17! = (20)(19)(18)/(3)(2)(1) = 1140]; thus, the probability of three defects is

$$\begin{aligned} P(3 \text{ defects}) &= 1140 \times P(3 \text{ defects}) \times P(\text{no defects at 17 points}) \\ &= 1140(\pi)^3(1-\pi)^{17} \\ &= 1140(0.10)^3(0.90)^{17} = 0.190120 \end{aligned}$$

In general, the binomial probability of x "ones" and $(n-x)$ "zeros," in n trials, where π is the probability of a "one" on any of n trials, is given by the following formula.

Binomial Probability Mass Function

$$P(x) = \frac{n!}{x!(n-x)!}\pi^x(1-\pi)^{n-x} \qquad (5.1)$$

The GM executive stated "On some days, the cars have more than three times the company goal of two defects per car." Although it is not clear from this quote how many cars had six or more defects in a day, if the production process is "in control" and producing a mean of only two defects per car, the probability of randomly drawing a car with exactly six defects is calculated with Formula 5.1 to be 0.008867.

$$\begin{aligned} P(6 \text{ defects}) &= (20!/6!14!)(.1)^6(.9)^{14} \\ &= 38760(0.1)^6(0.9)^{14} = 0.008867 \end{aligned}$$

The probability of exactly seven defects is

$$\begin{aligned} P(7 \text{ defects}) &= (20!/7!13!)(.1)^7(.9)^{13} \\ &= 77520(0.1)^7(0.9)^{13} = 0.001970 \end{aligned}$$

These are rare events and might be taken as evidence that something is wrong with the production process. That is, if the production process was operating with a mean of only 2 defects at 20 checkpoints it is unlikely (0.008867 probability) that we would randomly select a car with six defects. It is more unlikely that we would select one with seven defects (0.00197) and even more unlikely that we would get one with eight defects (0.000356 probability, which the reader should verify).

As discussed in Chapter 3, if events are mutually exclusive, then the probability of a union of the events can be obtained as the sum of the probabilities. For one car, if six defects are found then no other count is possible. If seven defects are found then no other count is possible, and so on. Thus, the probability of six or more defects is the sum of the probability of six defects plus the probability of seven defects . . . plus the probability of 20 defects, which is

$$\begin{aligned} P(x \geq 6) &= P(6) + P(7) + \ldots + P(20) \\ &= 0.008867 + 0.001970 + 0.000356 + \ldots \\ &= 0.0112 \end{aligned}$$

Only about 112 in 10,000 cars (or approximately one in a hundred cars) should have six or more defects if the production process is operating with an average of only 2 defects at 20 checkpoints per car. Thus if we observe 6, 7, 8 or more defects we have evidence that the cars are not being produced at the company goal of two defects per car.

QUERY 5.1:
A multiple-choice test has four unrelated questions. Each question has five possible choices but only one is correct. Thus, a person who guesses randomly has a probability of 0.2 of guessing correctly. Draw a tree diagram showing the ways in which a test taker could get 0, 1, 2, 3, and 4 correct. What is the probability of guessing two correct? What is the probability of guessing more correct?

ANSWER:
Let x be the number of correct answers, where the probability of a correct answer on each question is 0.2. The probability tree diagram shows the branches that must be followed to calculate the binomial mass function for $n = 4$ and $\pi = 0.2$. For example, the tree diagram shows the six different branch systems that yield two correct answers (which corresponds to $4!/2!2! = 6$). The probability of two correct answers is thus

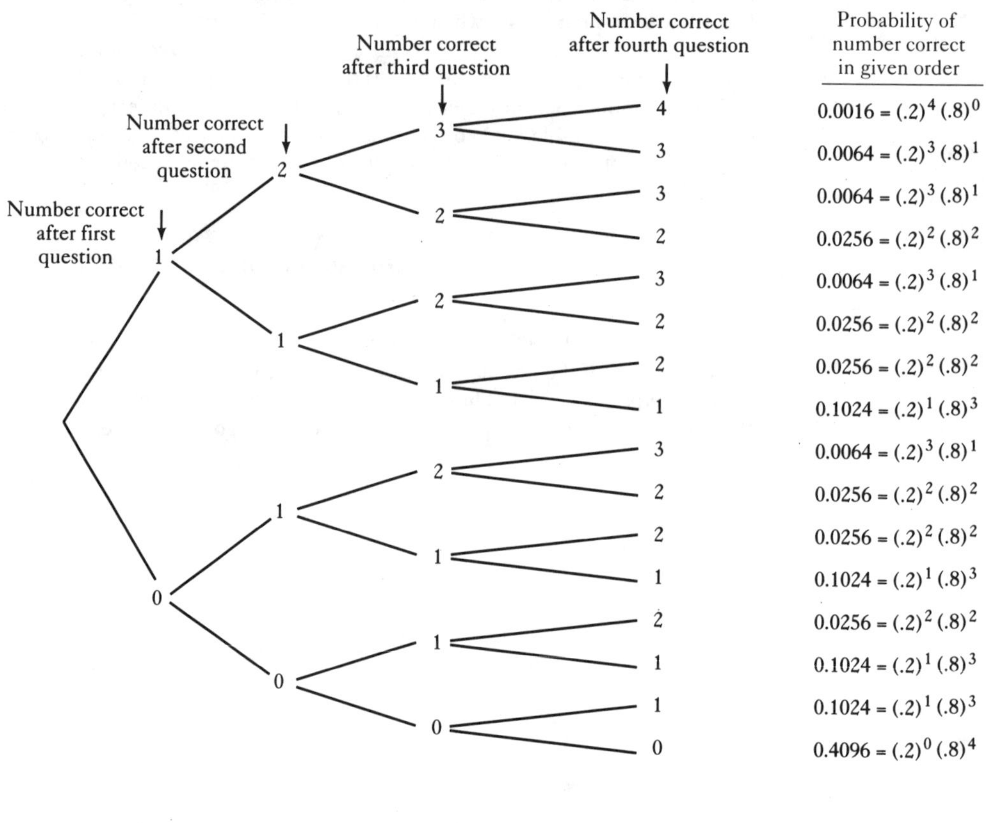

As an alternative to hand calculations, the "Function Wizard" in the EXCEL spreadsheet can be used to determine binomial probabilities. The following steps lead to the $P(x = 2 | n = 4, \pi = 0.2) = 0.1536$.

1. After opening EXCEL click on cell A1 to select it for output. Clicking on the "Insert" menu and then clicking on "Function..." leads to the "Paste Function" screen.
2. In the Paste Function, click once on "Statistical" from the function category, in the left-hand column. To the right, under "Function name," several statistics functions will appear. Click on "BINOMDIST." Now clicking on "OK," in the lower right-hand corner of the screen, yields the Chart 5.1 screen without the values.
3. The first value to enter is "number_s," which is the number of successes: 2. After entering 2 for the number of successes move to the next position with the Tab key. The second entry is "trials," which is $n = 4$. Again move between positions with the Tab key. The third entry is "probability_s," which is $\pi = 0.2$. The fourth entry is "cumulative," which requires an entry of 0 or False to indicate that a probability of one x value is desired and not the cumulative probabilities associated with $x \leq 2$. Once these four entries are made, the probability mass at $x = 2$ will appear (= 0.1536), as seen in Chart 5.1. Clicking on "OK" will place this probability in cell A1. (Notice in Chart 5.1 that the actual command EXCEL used for this binomial probability calculation was "=BINOMDIST(2,4,.2,0)" The direct use of this command is demonstrated in Query 5.2.)

CHART 5.1 Binomial Probability Calculation with the Function Wizard in EXCEL

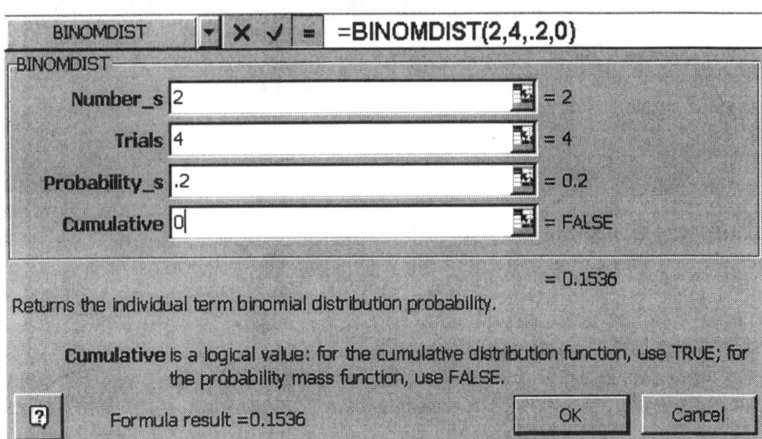

Similar entries into the "Function Wizard" of EXCEL can be used to check the following hand calculations for $x = 3$ and $x = 4$:

The probability of three correct answers is

$$P(x = 3 \mid n = 4, \pi = 0.2) = 4(.2)^3(.8) = 4(0.0064) = 0.0256 = P(3)$$

The probability of four correct answers is

$$P(x = 4 \mid n = 4, \pi = 0.2) = (.2)^4 = 0.0016 = P(4)$$

Thus, the probability of two or more correct answers by guessing is

$$\begin{aligned} P(x \geq 2 \mid n = 4, \pi = 0.2) &= P(2) + P(3) + P(4) \\ &= 0.1536 + 0.0256 + 0.0016 \\ &= 0.1808 \end{aligned}$$

QUERY 5.2:

Following the development of the nationally normed *Test of Economic Literacy* (TEL), authors William Walstad and John Soper reported that the typical student in their selected sample of 2,483 students averaged about 20 out of 46 questions correct, in a midschool year administration of the TEL. Later, in a session at the 1988 annual meeting of the American Economic Association, Walstad stated that guessing would, on average, yield 11.5 questions correct, because each question had four choices. In *Vital Speeches of the Day* (March 25, 1989), Walstad stated:

> So typical high school students score only 15 percentage points above a chance score on this test. Clearly 40 percent correct represents a failing grade under even the most liberal grading standards. This level of economic knowledge among most high school students is shocking!

Are these results really shocking? How likely is a score of 20 questions correct if a student is just guessing, assuming questions are independent? Assuming questions are independent, calculate the probability of 20 correct if students are just guessing, and state whether you think they are just guessing or actually know some economics. State why you would question the assumption of independence and its implications.

ANSWER:

The probability of 20 correct out of 46 independent multiple-choice questions, with four choices, is

$$P(x = 20 \mid n = 46, \pi = 0.25) = \frac{46!}{20!26!}(0.25)^{20}(0.75)^{26} = 0.003$$

which is most easily determined with a statistics computer program. As an alternative to "Function Wizard" in EXCEL, as used in Query 5.1, the "BINOMDIST" command can be employed. To get $P(x = 20 \mid n = 46$ and $\pi = 0.25) = 0.003$, type the command "=BINOMDIST(20,46,0.25,0)" into any cell and push the enter key. EXCEL will then place the value 0.002879 in the cell as the exact probability of getting 20 correct answers by random guessing on 46 questions, with a 0.25 chance of success on each.

Any binomial probability can be obtained with EXCEL by entering a

0, for a single probability mass, as in $P(S{=}s \mid n, \pi)$ =BINOMDIST(s,n,π,0), or

1, for a cumulative probability, as in $P(S \leq s \mid n, \pi)$ =BINOMDIST(s,n,π,1),

where S is the random variable, s is a specific value, and π is the probability of success on each trial.

Notice that the probability 0.003 says that only three in 1,000 times, over a large (infinite) number of tests, will a student get exactly 20 correct answers by random guessing. Binomial probabilities approach zero for guesses of more than 20 correct answers. That is, there is little chance of a student guessing 20 questions correctly. The fact that students averaged around 20 questions correct suggests that something other than chance is at work here.

Before concluding that students know economics, however, we should call attention to the manner in which the TEL was constructed. Each question was put on the test because it tended to identify students who know economics and those who do not. Reliability was built into the test by using questions that differentiate the same students in the same way—students with higher scores on the test should get any question correct with higher probability than those with lower scores. As concluded by Becker, Greene, and Rosen,"This rule for inclusion makes questions dependent, and the probability of successful guessing on each question is not fixed at 0.25."(1990, p. 14) In addition, it is likely that some questions made use of information in others, making them related and thus dependent.

Binomial Probability Mass Function for 46 Test Questions and $\pi = 0.25$

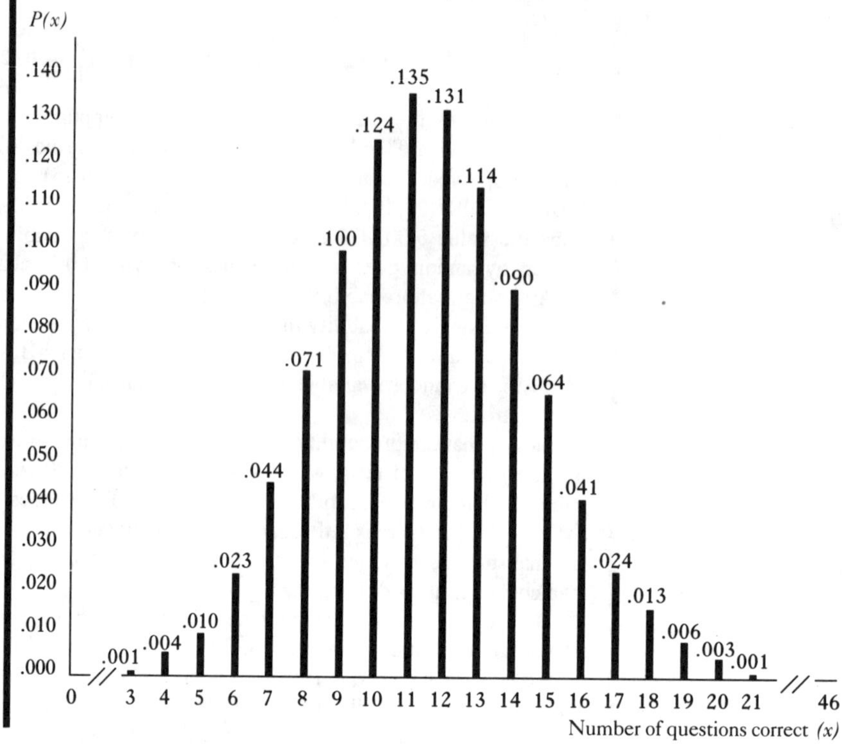

QUERY 5.3:

The defense for boxer Mike Tyson in his 1992 trial for rape claimed that the pool of 50 persons from which a jury of 12 members was to be selected was not representative of the community at large. With 22 percent of the community black, what is the probability of randomly selecting a pool of 50 with seven or fewer blacks?

ANSWER:

Entering the EXCEL command "=BINOMDIST(7,50,0.22,1)" into any cell places the value 0.112594 in that cell as the probability of getting 7 or fewer blacks in a jury pool of 50. Alternatively, we could use the "Function Wizard," which is accessed through the "Insert" menu, as in Query 5.1. The resulting "Paste function" screen display is shown in Chart 5.2.

CHART 5.2 Cumulative Binomial Probability Calculation Using the Function Wizard in EXCEL

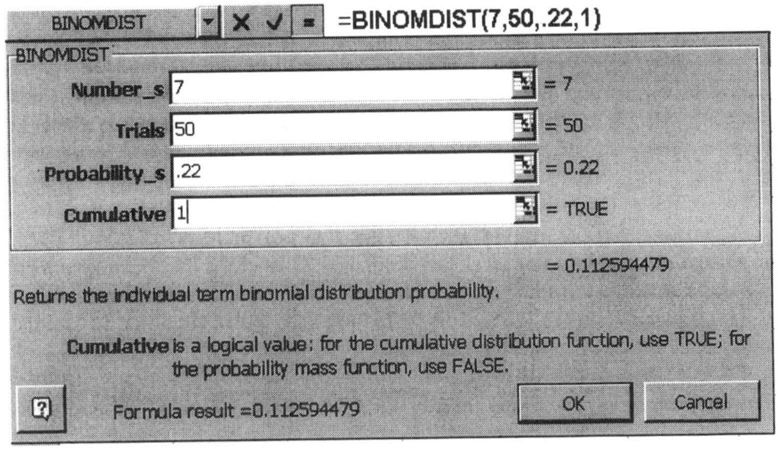

Hand calculations yield:

$$P(x \leq 7|n = 50, \pi = .22) = .0000 + .0001 + .0004 + .0018 + .0059 + .0152 + .0322 + .0571 = .1127$$

which is not an unusual occurrence. That is, observing seven or fewer blacks in a 50-person group selected at random from a population with 22 percent blacks would occur by chance approximately 11 out of 100 times over many (infinite) draws of samples of 50.

EXERCISES

5.1 Find the following binomial probabilities
   a. $P(X \leq 7|n = 20, \pi = 0.3)$
   b. $P(Y = 3|n = 10, \pi = 0.7)$
   c. $P(2 < W \leq 9|n = 30, \pi = 0.2)$
   d. $P(U > 10|n = 12, \pi = 0.75)$

5.2 Eric von Hippel, an MIT professor, and Cornelius Herstatt, of the Swiss Federal Institute of Technology, in their monograph "An Implementation of the Lead User Market Research Method In a 'Low-Tech' Product Area: Pipe Hangers" (Alfred P. Sloan School of Management, MIT, 1992), describe their work with Hilti AG, a leading European manufacturer of fastening, hanging, and shelving related products. To test whether designers were designing what customers wanted, the authors presented 12 regular customers with the designers' new products: 10 preferred the new product. If the probability of each customer preferring the new product is akin to flipping a coin ($\pi = 0.5$), what is the probability of getting a sample of 12 in which 10 or more say they prefer it?

5.3 A headline in the *Wall Street Journal* (June 12, 1992) reported: "Sears Is Accused of Billing Fraud at Auto Centers." The article reports on a year-long study by the California Department of Consumer Affairs in which undercover agents established that 89.5 percent of the owners of cars with worn brakes but no other major mechanical defects were told that additional and more expensive repairs were needed. "In a second phase, the department informed Sears of the investigation in December, 1991, and then conducted 10 more tests in January, of which seven resulted in unnecessary repairs." What is the probability of seven or fewer unnecessary repairs if, in the population of all Sears repairs, 89.5 percent of the cars were still getting unnecessary repairs?

5.4 *Business Week* (June 29, 1992) reported in an article about Cadillac production at its Detroit-Hamtramck plant that, "Today paint jobs are right on 82% of the cars after the first pass, a 90% improvement and that has all but eliminated costly end-of-the-line paint repairs." (p. 89) If this is a true statement, what is the probability of randomly selecting 10 Cadillacs coming off the line and finding fewer than four defective paint jobs?

5.5 In an attempt to curb excessive executive pay, a *Wall Street Journal* (July 15, 1992) article reported that institutional investors are getting more assertive. Of the 56 institutions surveyed, 66 percent (37 of 56) said they favored the creation of compensation committees to review or even set executive pay. If this sample was representative of the population, what is the probability of drawing another random sample of 56 institutions for which 50 percent or less of the institutions would favor the creation of compensation committees?

5.6 A *Wall Street Journal* article (August 11, 1992) reported that "Most American men—eight out of 10—use a hair dryer, according to industry estimates." If you ask five of your male friends whether they use a hair dryer, what is the probability that four will say they do? What did you assume to reach your answer?

5.7 A fire detection device utilizes three temperature-sensitive cells acting independently of each other in such a manner that any one or more may activate an alarm. Each has a probability of 0.8 of activating the alarm when the temperature reaches 100 degrees. What is the probability that the alarm will function if the temperature reaches 100 degrees?

5.8 If the nine-member United States Supreme Court is hearing a case for which a verdict is upheld or overturned, what is the probability that five or more jurists will uphold a guilty verdict if there is a 95 percent chance that any one of them will do so? What do you have to assume to make this probability calculation? Why might this assumption be unreasonable?

5.9 The "American Journal" (February 25, 1995) television show reported that the probability of a restaurant substituting pork for veal is approximately 0.667. (Pork is cheaper than veal and after browning the difference is hard to spot.) Assuming this probability is correct and fixed, what is the probability of visiting 10 restaurants at random and finding more than half substituting pork for veal?

5.10 An article in *The Wall Street Journal* (Friday, January 13, 1995) on "Ten Ways (Some) Lawyers (Sometimes) Fudge Bills" reported that 40 percent of senior partners are not in their law offices on Friday afternoons. Thus, Paul McMenaman of Litisci, Inc., says "if your bill shows a senior partner working every Friday it is suspicious." What is the probability of observing a senior partner working three of the next four Fridays if $\pi = 0.40$?

5.11 Dollar Rent A Car System has a catchy phrase for its ads: "Right on the airport. Right on the money." A *Wall Street Journal* (June 4, 1993) feature reported, however, "Dollar isn't in 15 of the top 100 airport markets. Instead, it operates off airport or not at all in those other locations." If the *WSJ* is correct, what is the probability of finding a random sample of 20 top airport markets for which at least 17 have on-site Dollar operations?

5.4 Location and Dispersion

Random variables have means (that measure central location), variances (that measure dispersion), and probability distributions that may be symmetric or skewed. For the binomial π and n determine central location, dispersion, and skewness.

Chapter 4 showed the mean or expected value for any random variable x to be calculated by the formula

$$\mu = E(x) = \Sigma\, xP(x)$$

This formula can now be used to determine the average value for a specific random variable that conforms to the binomial distribution. For example, the expected number of questions guessed correctly on a four-question, multiple-choice test, where each independent question has five choices, is

$$\mu = 0(0.4096) + 1(0.4096) + 2(0.1536) + 3(0.0256) + 4(0.0016) = 0.80$$

Guessing on this test will yield an average of 0.8 questions correct, over a large (infinite) number of tests where each test has four independent questions with five alternatives. Notice that this mean value could have been obtained by simply multiplying the sample size n by the probability of success, π;

$$\mu = (4)(0.2) = 0.8$$

Thus, the mean or expected value of a binomial random variable can be obtained by the shortcut Formula (5.2).[1]

Mean of a Binomial Random Variable

$$\mu = E(x) = n\pi \tag{5.2}$$

The variance, or expected squared deviation, was given in Chapter 4 by the formula

$$\sigma^2 = E(x - \mu)^2 = \Sigma(x - \mu)^2 P(x)$$

For the four-question multiple-choice test, where the expected number correct is 0.80, the variance is

$$\sigma^2 = (0 - 0.8)^2(0.4096) + (1 - 0.8)^2(0.4096) + (2 - 0.8)^2(0.1536) + (3 - 0.8)^2(0.0256) + (4 - 0.8)^2(0.0016) = 0.64$$

But this variance value could have been calculated by multiplying the sample size n by the probability of success π times the probability of failure $(1 - \pi)$;

$$\sigma^2 = (4)(0.2)(0.8) = 0.64$$

The variance of a binomial random variable can be obtained by the shortcut Formula (5.3).[2]

Variance of a Binomial Random Variable

$$\sigma^2 = E(x - \mu)^2 = n\pi(1 - \pi) \tag{5.3}$$

Notice that if $\pi = 0.5$, the variance of a binomial random variable is at its maximum. With $\pi = 0.5$, the binomial distribution is also symmetric. If $\pi < 0.5$, then the binomial distribution is right skewed. If $\pi > 0.5$, then the binomial distribution is left skewed. As n gets larger, however, the skewness in the binomial distribution vanishes; even with $\pi \neq 0.5$ it will appear symmetric.

Figure 5.1 shows four different binomial distributions for $n = 4$, 8, 16, and 32, and $\pi = 0.2$. In panel a, where $n = 4$, the right skewness is apparent. In panel d, where $n = 32$, the distribution looks more symmetrical than skewed. Additional increases in n would blur the skewness further, to the point that the binomial mass function would appear to be a bell-shaped curve. In fact, as described in the next chapter, it was this observation that gave rise to the normal distribution.

QUERY 5.4:

When an experimental munitions production process is first set up, it is thought to have promise for future refinement if 70 percent of the bullets in a magazine fire properly. Samples of $n = 50$ are to be tested. What is the expected number of bullets that should fire properly if the process has promise? What is the likelihood of getting a sample of bullets one or two standard deviations from either side of this mean? To what use can you put this information in deciding when the production process does or does not have promise?

ANSWER:

The expected number of bullets that should fire properly if the production process has promise is 35, assuming the firing of each of the 50 bullets is an independent and identical trial where the probability of success on each trial is 0.7. That is,

$$\mu = \pi n = (0.7)(50) = 35$$

This, of course, is the average number of properly firing bullets over a large (infinite) number of samples of size 50. For any given sample of 50, the observed number of properly firing bullets may be somewhat higher or lower, even if the production process has promise. Below is the binomial mass function that shows the probabilities of getting a sample of 50 bullets with 29 through 42 good bullets.

FIGURE 5.1 Vanishing Skewness as the Sample Size is Increased

Panel a: $\pi = 0.2$, and $n = 4$

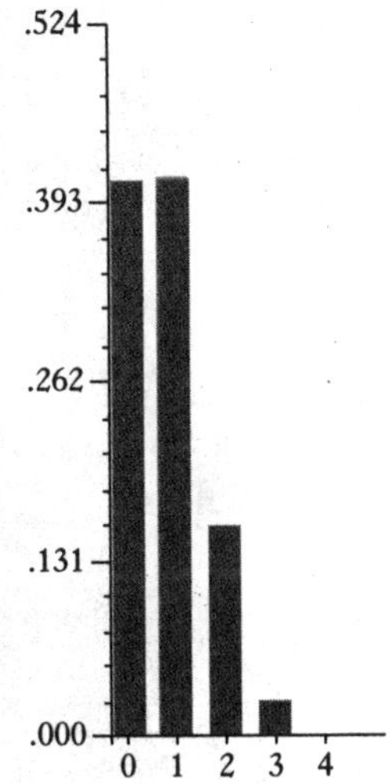

Panel b: $\pi = 0.2$, and $n = 8$

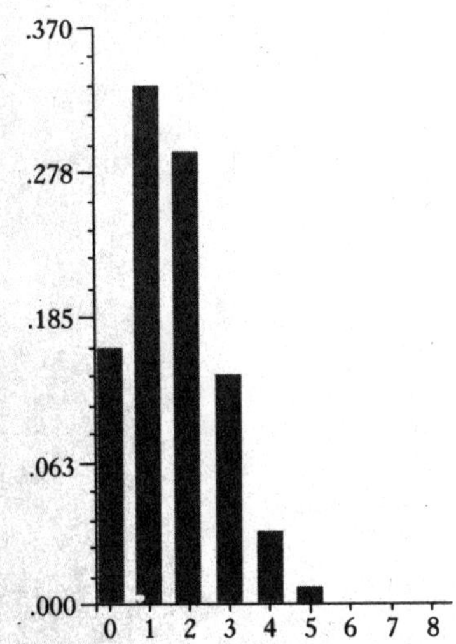

(continued)

FIGURE 5.1 Vanishing Skewness as the Sample Size is Increased (*continued*)

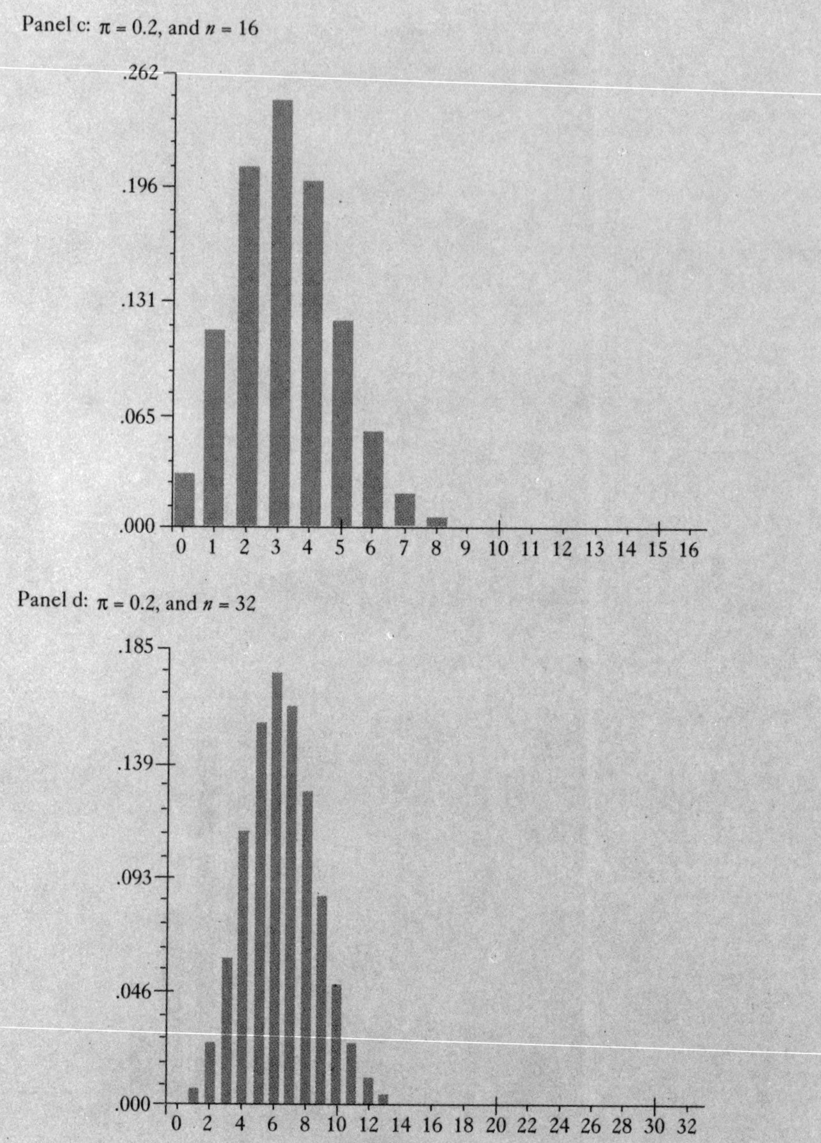

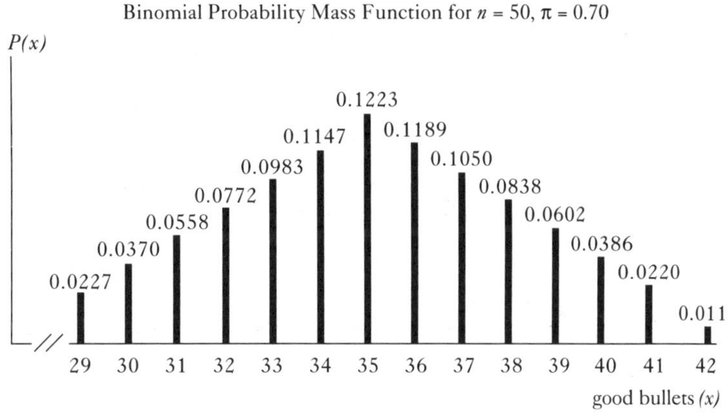

The variance and standard deviation for this binomial are

$$\sigma^2 = n(\pi)(1 - \pi) = 50(.70)(.30) = 10.5 \text{ bullets squared}$$

$$\sigma = \sqrt{10.5} = 3.24 \text{ bullets}$$

If the distribution of bullets was perfectly bell shaped, then by the rule of thumb for bell-shaped distributions presented in Chapters 3 and 4, approximately 68 percent of the distribution should be within one standard deviation of the mean, which is

$$\mu \pm \sigma = 35 \pm 3.24, \text{ or } 31.76 \text{ to } 38.24$$

From the above probability mass function, the sum of the probabilities for x values between 31.76 and 38.24 is 0.7202.

$$P(x = 32) + P(x = 33) + \ldots + P(x = 37) + P(x = 38)$$

$$= 0.0772 + 0.0983 + 0.1147 + 0.1223 + 0.1189 + 0.1050 + 0.0838$$

$$= 0.7202$$

The difference between the exact binomial probability of 0.7202 and the bell-curve approximation of 0.68 reflects the fact that this binomial is not perfectly symmetric and it is not continuous.

By the rule of thumb for bell-shaped distributions, approximately 95 percent of the observations should be within two standard deviations of the mean. That is, 95 percent of the observations should be between 28.52 and 41.48 [$\mu \pm 2\sigma = 35 \pm 2(3.24)$]. The exact sum of the probabilities of values in this interval is 0.9565, which again is close to that suggested by the rule of thumb.

Since only about 5 percent of the time will a sample of 50 bullets yield less than 28.5 or more than 41.5 firing properly, when these extremes are realized the production process should be reviewed to see what is wrong (when $x < 28.5$) or what has changed to cause the improvement (when $x > 41.5$).

QUERY 5.5:
A *Wall Street Journal* (April 20, 1992) article reported on a study by University of Delaware Professor Valerie P. Hans of jurors' attitudes toward business in wrongful death and injury cases. "Of the 18 cases, 14 were decided in favor of plaintiffs, higher than the national norm of about 50%." How many standard deviations are there between 14 and the expected number of cases favoring the plaintiffs based on the national norm? What is the probability of 14 or more cases decided for the plaintiffs, given this expected number?

ANSWER:
The expected number of cases to be decided in favor of the plaintiffs based on the national norm is nine [$= \pi n = (0.50)(18)$]. The standard deviation is

$$2.12132\left[= \sqrt{\pi(1-\pi)n} = \sqrt{(0.5)(0.5)(18)}\right]$$

Thus, the observed number of 14 cases is 2.357 standard deviations higher than the expected number of nine cases. The probability of observing 14 or more out of 18, when the expected number is nine, is calculated as follows:

$$\begin{aligned}
P(x = 14 \mid \pi = 0.5, n = 18) &= 0.01167\\
P(x = 15 \mid \pi = 0.5, n = 18) &= 0.00311\\
P(x = 16 \mid \pi = 0.5, n = 18) &= 0.00058\\
P(x = 17 \mid \pi = 0.5, n = 18) &= \underline{0.00007}\\
P(x \geq 14 \mid \pi = 0.5, n = 18) &= 0.01543
\end{aligned}$$

With $\pi = 0.50$ the binomial distribution is symmetric and is close to being a smooth bell-shaped distribution with just 18 cases. By the rule of thumb for bell-shaped distributions, the probability of being two standard deviations above the expected number is approximately 0.025, which in this case is

$$P(x > \mu + 2\sigma) = P(x > 9 + 4.24264) = P(x > 13.24264) \cong 0.025$$

which is not far from

$$P(x \geq 14 \mid \pi = 0.5, n = 18) = 0.01543$$

QUERY 5.6:
The introduction to this chapter included a report that "only five of 34 economists who participated in 10 or more surveys managed to guess correctly which way long-term bond yields were going more than half of the time." It asked: Are these results as likely if done by 34 people each flipping a coin 10 times to predict yields? It also asked about the implications of this probability for the accuracy of economists' forecasts.

ANSWER:
The probability of five of 34 individuals predicting six or more yield movements in 10 tries by flipping a coin is obtained by first using the binomial distribution to find

the probability of a coin tossed 10 times giving six or more heads (corresponding to six or more correct yield predictions, $x \geq 6$). Using a statistics package

$$P(x \geq 6 \mid n = 10, \pi = 0.5) = 0.377$$

Next, assuming the 34 individuals operate independently, the probability of five individuals, $y = 5$, predicting six or more yield movements correctly by each flipping a coin 10 times is 0.0023:

$$P(y = 5 \mid n = 34, \pi = 0.377) = 0.0023$$

That is, only about 23 out of 10,000 times would we expect to see five individuals predict six or more yield movements correctly if they were predicting by 50-50 guessing, as in flipping a coin. Observing five of 34 economists predicting correctly more than half of the long-term bond yields in 10 tries is an extremely rare occurrence if based on 50-50 coin-toss-type guessing. Contrary to the implications of the *WSJ* article, economists appear to predict long-term bond yields better than what would be expected if they were just guessing.

Exercises

5.12 Find the mean and standard deviation of the number of successes in the binomial distribution as specified by
  a. $\pi = 0.2, n = 10$
  b. $\pi = 0.5, n = 17$
  c. $\pi = 0.75, n = 30$

5.13 In Exercise 5.11, what is the expected number and standard deviation of the number of airports in a sample of 20 of the 100 top airports for which Dollar has on-site operations?

5.14 In May 1992, NordicTrack was advertising that its exerciser was still being used on a regular basis (at least three hours per week) by seven out of 10 buyers five years after purchase. If this claim is true:
  a. What is the expected number still using the exerciser five years later in a random sample of three purchasers? What does this number mean?
  b. What is the probability of drawing a random sample of three with no regular users five years later?

5.15 For the data and conditions in Exercise 5.14, if you select a sample of three buyers and find no regular users, what could you conclude (and why) about the correctness of NordicTrack's ad?

5.16 If only 50 percent of the buyers of the NordicTrack exerciser are regular users five years later, and you select a sample of 10 buyers, what is the probability of selecting a sample that seven or more are regular users five years later? What can you conclude from this and your answer in Exercise 5.15?

5.17 According to *Newsweek* (June 8, 1992), "American drug companies are justly famous for their largesse . . . they spend \$550 million a year on advertising in medical journals . . . (but) of the 109 ads reviewed (by UCLA researchers), 100 contained 'deficiencies in areas for which the FDA has established explicit standards for quality.'" If the expected number of deficiencies was 55 ads, what is the probability of finding 100 or more deficiencies? What did you have to assume to calculate this probability with the binomial distribution?

5.18 During the Persian Gulf operation in 1991, 53 of the 291 Americans who lost their lives were black. About a quarter of those who took part in Desert Storm were black.
   a. Did fewer or more blacks die than would be expected by chance during Desert Storm?
   b. What was the probability of getting 53 or fewer blacks losing their lives if proximity to risk was random?

HISTORICAL PERSPECTIVE

The Bernoulli family produced no fewer than five scholars who contributed to the study of probability and statistics, and several other academics whose contributions to other areas of science are noteworthy. Jacob Bernoulli (1654–1705) advanced the study of combinatorial probabilities, as found in the binomial and hypergeometric distributions of today. His primary objects of analysis were the fabled urn (from which white or black pebbles were drawn), coins (flipped for a desired side), and dice (rolled for a specific face value).

Bernoulli was a testy and discontented person who spent more time competing with and denigrating his academic brother John than collaborating with him. After his death, John wanted nothing to do with Jacob's yet-unpublished papers. It wasn't until eight years later, when nephew Nicholas edited them in *Ars Conjectandi*, that the papers became a seminal work on the mathematics of probability and introduced the first law of large numbers and the "Bernoulli numbers." In this work, the vocabulary of "fertile cases" or "sterile cases" was used for successful and unsuccessful trials that could actually be enumerated in the context of urns, coins, and dice. Bernoulli argued that simple extensions to the study of disease, weather, or games of skill "would be a sign of insanity," because the underlying processes in real-world applications were hidden, making the enumeration of cases impossible. For such situations, he recognized the common-sense idea that the more observations there were on the unknown proportion of "cases," the closer the calculated proportion would be to the true proportion, but he could not formalize this notion mathematically.

Mathematician Siméon Denis Poisson (1781–1840) derived his distribution in its cumulative form as a limit to Bernoulli's binomial distribution when the number of trials is large but the chance of success is small. Poisson, a fun-loving and socially minded Frenchman, was an innovator in applying algebra and probability to analyses of guilty verdicts and juror errors. When it came to deriving the distribution that would later bear his name, however, he was not concerned with real-world applications; as were the Bernoullis before him, he was intrigued with its mathematical properties.

5.5 CONCLUDING COMMENTS

Within almost all areas of business practices, legal proceedings, and the science of economics generally, discrete distributions such as the binomial distribution have become key tools of statistical analysis. As concluded by Donald Roberts, 275 years after Jacob Bernoulli's death, applied statisticians were able to show that while the simple urn, coin, and dice models of the early years of probability were viewed as insufficient to support the needs of business and economic applications, they did provide the focus for debate on the mathematics of probability theory. Nearly three centuries later, desk-top computers put the power of these distributions at the fingertips of analysts for everyday use in problems never envisioned by the mathematicians who invented them.

In the next chapter, we will see how further extensions of the binomial probability distribution gave rise to the most famous of all distributions: the normal distribution. Curiously, the normal distribution was first proposed as a way to approximate the cumulative binomial probabilities. It was not until well into the eighteenth century that applications of the normal distribution came into their own.

CHAPTER EXERCISES

5.19 An article titled "Four Pros Took the $100,000 Challenge. Two Passed" (*Business Week* June 9, 1995) describes how four acclaimed financial managers picked stocks but only two of the four portfolios yielded a return higher than what could be earned from an "indexed portfolio" consisting of stocks picked randomly from the S&P 500. What is the number of pros' portfolios that could be expected to beat the indexed portfolio if each of the four pros claims he or she is able to beat the index 9 out of 10 times?

5.20 In Exercise 5.19, what is the probability of only two of four portfolios yielding a return higher than the indexed portfolio if each pro claims he or she is able to beat the index 9 out of 10 times? What is the probability of only two of four portfolios yielding a return higher than the indexed portfolio if each pro's predictions are equivalent to flipping a coin with a 50-50 chance of beating the index? Which do you believe better describes what the pros are able to do – predict in such a way that they beat the index 9 of 10 times or with only a 50-50 chance?

5.21 A feature on the "Insider" TV show (Feb. 15, 1995) quoted a New York city official saying that no more than one percent of the cars that are towed off city streets and impounded have objects inside stolen. The TV show put 4 cars on streets where they would get towed; one had stuff inside taken by the tow truck operator. If the city official is correct, what is the maximum expected number of cars to have something taken from their inside in this TV show experiment?

5.22 In Exercise 5.21, assuming the probability of theft is 0.01 for each car, what is the probability that a) none of the four cars is burglarized? b) one of the four cars is burglarized? c) two of the four cars are burglarized? d) three of the four cars are burglarized? e) four of the four cars are burglarized?

5.23 Using the information in Exercises 5.21 and 5.22, is the claim of the city official reasonable? Explain.

5.24 *The Wall Street Journal* (November 15, 1996) article titled "The Business Cycle Is Tamed, Many Say, Alarming Some Others" reported that "the latest Blue Chip newsletter survey found 51 of 53 top economists predicting the economy will grow at least 1.53% next year." If the 53 top economists predicting the economy for next year are each making the prediction of "continued expansion" versus "no continued expansion" by independently tossing a coin, then what is the probability of observing 51 or more of these economists predicting continued expansion?

5.25 On CNN's "Headline NEWS" (December 30, 1996), a psychologist was interviewed about people's ability to keep New Year's promises. He stated that instead of promising oneself to exercise everyday, the promise should be to exercise three days a week because "that way there are seven ways to succeed (in exercising)." Was this psychologist correct regarding the number of ways of achieving success in exercising? If the probability of exercising on any day is 0.5, assuming independence, what is the probability of exercising 3 in 7 days? Is this assumption of independence reasonable?

5.26 Assume a quality control expert randomly selects three items from the end of an assembly line, for which it is claimed that there is a 0.8 probability, π, that an item is totally error free. If the number of items that are error free is a binomial random variable x, then

a. the expected number of error-free items is calculated by the shorthand formula $E(x) = n\pi$, which yields a numerical value of_________ .

b. by summing over the two values and their probabilities for each of the three trials, show how the resulting six terms form the above expected value.

c. explain what your numerical expected value means.

d. the variance is calculated by the shorthand formula $E(x - \mu)^2 = n\pi(1 - \pi)$, which yields a numerical value of__________ .

e. by summing over the numerical values and their probabilities for each of the three trials, show how the six resulting terms form the above value of the variance.

5.27 In testing the items in Exercise 5.26, the items are destroyed and cannot be replaced. Thus, for this process to be treated as a binomial, what do you have to assume?

5.28 In testing the three items in Exercise 5.26, if you find one totally error-free item, are you willing to conclude that the assembly line is running in a way that the probability of any given item being error free is 0.8? Explain and justify your answer in terms of probabilities.

5.29 In a survey of 105 female judges, 54 percent said sexual bias was widespread in California state courts, according to the *Wall Street Journal* (August 20, 1992). How likely was this sample result if, in fact, the majority of female judges (50 percent) do not think that sexual bias was widespread?

5.30 On CBS's TV program "Shame On You" (June 2, 1993), the announcers described their experiment in which five VCR repair centers were randomly selected and brought new VCR units that had a blown fuse inserted. Three of the five repair centers said major repairs were needed, with the cost of repair exceeding \$90; two of the centers correctly diagnosed the \$1 blown fuse. What is the probability of getting these results if the majority (50 percent) of all VCR repair centers are honest and good at diagnostics?

5.31 A *Wall Street Journal* (August 14, 1987) article reported that, "IBM samples 50 circuit boards out of every 270-board lot; if one is defective, every board in the lot is rejected." (p. 12) Why is this a demanding standard?

5.32 As reported in the *American Economic Review* (May 1992), a sample of 600 economists was surveyed by mail to assess their reactions to certain economic policies. One proposition was "Wage-Price Controls are a useful policy option in the control of inflation." (p. 204) Out of the 464 responding economists, 73.9 percent said they disagreed. What is the probability of getting this response if three quarters of economists did not favor wage-price controls?

5.33 An Associated Press release (*HT*, June 22, 1992) reported on research by psychologist Marsha Kaitz of the Hebrew University in Jerusalem in which "seventy-two blindfolded people in the study tried to distinguish their romantic partner from two decoys of similar age, weight and height . . .the blindfolded people were correct 58 percent of the time in the forehead test."

a. What is the expected number of correct identifications if only guessing is involved?
b. What is the probability of correct identification of 42 or more persons if participants were just guessing?
c. Do you think they were just guessing?

5.34 In the research reported in Exercise 5.33 about the blindfolded identification of partners, "women identified their man's hand 69 percent of the time." What is the probability that 72 women will correctly identify 50 or more men if the women were just guessing? Do you think the women were just guessing?

Academic Reference

Becker, William, William Greene, and Sherwin Rosen. "Research on Economic Education." *American Economic Review*, May 1990, pp. 14–22.

Endnotes

1. $\mu = \Sigma\, xP(x)$, which for the binomial yields

$$\mu = \underbrace{[(1)(\pi) + (0)(1-\pi)]}_{\text{1st trial}} + \underbrace{[(1)(\pi) + (0)(1-\pi)]}_{\text{2nd trial}} + \ldots + \underbrace{[(1)(\pi) + (0)(1-\pi)]}_{n\text{th trial}}$$

$$\mu = \pi + \pi + \ldots + \pi$$

$$\mu = n\pi$$

2. For the binomial random variable $x = x_1 + x_2 + \ldots + x_3$, the variance of x is

$$\sigma^2 = \text{Var}(x_1 + x_2 + \ldots + x_3) = \text{Var}(x_1) + \text{Var}(x_2) + \ldots + \text{Var}(x_3)$$

because the trials are independent $\text{Cov}(x_i x_j) = 0$

Thus, for the binomial random variable x,

$$\sigma^2 = \underbrace{[(1-\pi)^2\pi + (0-\pi)^2(1-\pi)]}_{\text{1st trial}} + \underbrace{[(1-\pi)^2\pi + (0-\pi)^2(1-\pi)]}_{\text{2nd trial}} + \ldots$$

$$= [\pi - 2\pi^2 + \pi^3 + \pi^2 - \pi^3] + [\pi - 2\pi^2 + \pi^3 + \pi^2 - \pi^3] + \ldots$$

$$= \pi(1-\pi) + \pi(1-\pi) + \ldots$$

$$= n\pi(1-\pi)$$

FORMULAS

- Binomial Probability Mass Function

$$P(x) = \frac{n!}{x!(n-x)!}\pi^x(1-\pi)^{n-x}$$

where

$$x = x_1 + x_2 + \ldots + x_n = \sum_{i=1}^{n} x_i$$

$$x_i = 0 \text{ or } 1$$

$$P(x_i = 1) = \pi \text{ and } P(x_i = 0) = 1 - \pi$$

- Mean of a Binomial Random Variable

$$\mu = E(x) = n\pi$$

- Variance of a Binomial Random Variable

$$\sigma^2 = E(x-\mu)^2 = n\pi(1-\pi)$$

Chapter 6

Distributions of Continuous Random Variables

A single death is a tragedy;
a million deaths is a statistic.

Joseph Stalin
1879–1953

6.1 INTRODUCTION

The height of men and women, length of ears of corn, and many other variables involving measures of time and weight have been shown to be approximately normally distributed. The bell-shaped curve commonly identified as the normal distribution in the popular press has even played a key role in Michael Crichton's suspense novel *Jurassic Park*:

> Arnold was pushing buttons. Another screen came up.
>
> Height Distribution: Procompsognathids
>
> 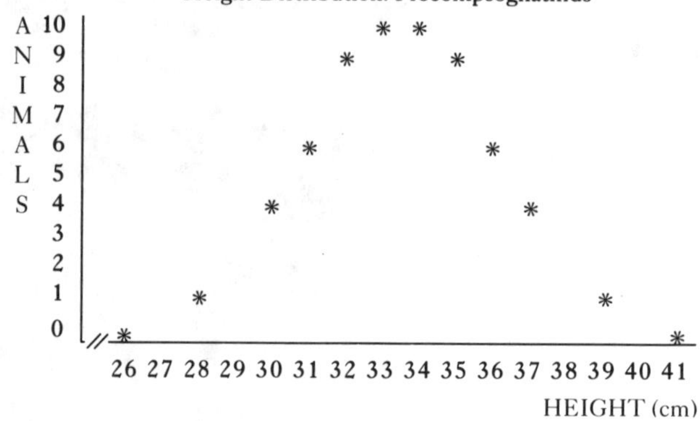
>
>
> . . . You see here we have a normal . . . . It shows that most of the animals (Procompsognathids) cluster around an average central value, and a few are either larger or smaller than the average, at the tails of the curve. (p. 132)

Although this bell-shaped curve is possibly the most well-known shape within and outside of academe, its origin and properties are often misrepresented. For instance, the historical perspective in this chapter presents Abraham De Moivre as the 1733 originator of the normal distribution, which he advanced as a way to approximate the binomial distribution. In addition, as you will learn in this chapter, because the normal distribution is continuous (with an infinite number of possible outcome values), the probability of any one value occurring is zero. Thus, the vertical axis in Arnold's diagram does not represent the frequency (or relative frequency) of values appearing on the horizontal axis. These are typical errors made in the popular use of the normal distribution.

This chapter presents the normal distribution as a continuous distribution for use in problems of the following type.

- *The Wall Street Journal* (February 28, 1997) reported that "stock volatility has declined, as measured by the standard deviation in long-term returns." In the past 40 years the standard deviation dropped 9 percentage points to 16 percent. If the expected return on stock purchases in the mid-1990s was 23 percent and returns were normally distributed, what was the probability of losing equity in the mid-1990s?

- *The Wall Street Journal* (February 26, 1992) reported that the average tenure of marketing directors employed by law firms in 1987 was about six months. By 1990 it had increased to 2.1 years, but almost one-third of the marketing directors had been on the job for a year or less. The question: Could tenure be normally distributed?
- *The Economist* (May 13, 1995) reported that in Britain "around three-quarters of beer is drunk in pubs - many of them owned by brewers." Not surprising, therefore, the brewers fought, and in 1994 won the repeal of a Weights and Measurement Act that required bigger beer glasses to accommodate a full 20-ounce British pint. An earlier Associated Press release (December 21, 1991), cited an Institute of Trading Standards Administration report that 80 percent of the "pints" were short before the Act. The questions: how short was (and will be) the average fill in the absence of the Act? How large do glasses have to be to insure that fills are at least 20-ounces?

By the end of this chapter, you will be able to answer these and similar questions involving continuous random variables. You will be able to specify the conditions required to use the normal distribution in probability calculations. You will be able to make probability calculations using the normal distribution. You will know the characteristics of the normal distribution that distinguish it from other distributions. You will know when to use the normal versus these other probability distributions and the general procedure of determining probabilities for any continuous distribution.

6.2 Continuous Random Variables and Probability Distributions

Continuous Random Variable
A random variable that may take on any value along an uninterrupted interval of a number line.

Within the limits of the glass, the volume of beer in the glass is a **continuous random variable**: the amount of beer can be any value between zero and the maximum volume of the glass. Time to complete a test is likewise continuous, as is the height and weight of animals and numerous other variables that can be expressed as decimals (e.g., 19.135 ounces, 1.25 hours, or 5.6 feet).

Economic and financial variables such as interest payments and wages may also be continuous, even though transactions are typically reported only to a cent. Folklore has a dishonest bank computer programmer in Minneapolis capitalizing on the one-cent reporting limit in calculating interest payments. He programmed the bank's computer to place the truncated fractions of cents in his own bank account when interest calculations were made for thousands of bank customers. A senior citizen doing cumulative calculation on a hand-held calculator caught the discrepancy in her account. Her repeated inquiries finally got the bank management's attention.

For a discrete random variable, the probability that the variable equals one of its limited number of values is given by the mass of the associated bar in a histogram. We have already seen in the case of the binomial distribution that if the population proportion of successes is $\pi = 0.50$, then the probability that x equals 0, 1, 2, 3, or 4 is the mass (= height times the one unit width) of the identified bar in Figure 6.1, panel a. For $n = 8$, the probability of $x = 0, 1, 2, \ldots 7$ or 8 is the mass of the associated bar in panel b, and so on for $n = 16$ in panel c, and $n = 32$ in panel d. Because each bar associated with

$x = 1, 2, 3, \ldots$ in a binomial distribution is of equal unit width, with $\Sigma_x P(x) = 1$, the probability of any discrete x is simply its bar's height.

Notice as n increases from $n = 4$ to $n = 32$ in Figure 6.1, the binomial probability mass function looks more and more like a smooth bell-shaped curve. As the number of bars increase, they appear to get narrower, because the total sum of their masses must continue to be unity, $\Sigma_x P(x) = 1$. In the limit, for the truly smooth bell-shaped curve, the mass associated with each value on the horizontal axis would be infinitesimal (zero). That is, the probability of realizing a specific x value would be zero.

FIGURE 6.1 Binomial Probability Mass Functions: as n Increases the Binomal Approaches the Normal Probability Density Function

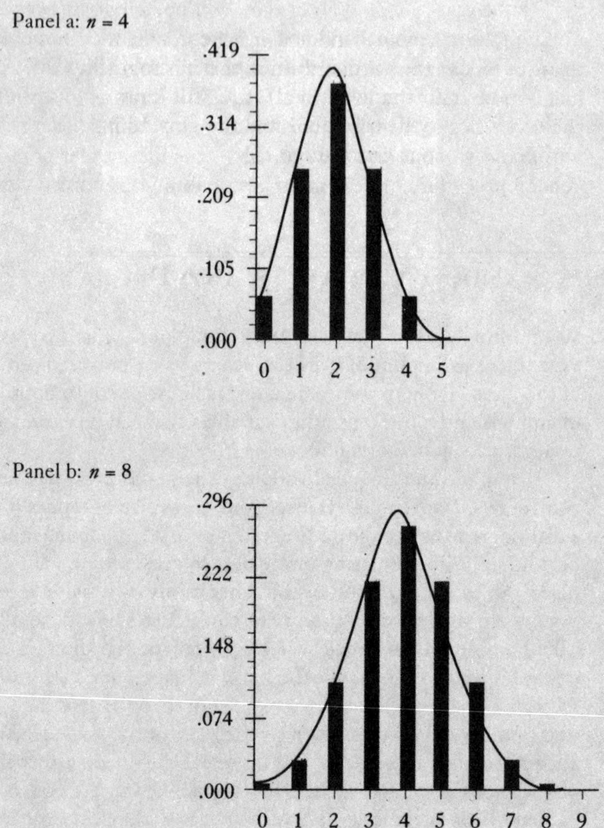

(continued)

FIGURE 6.1 Binomial Probability Mass Functions: as n Increases the Binomial Approaches the Normal Probability Density Function *(continued)*

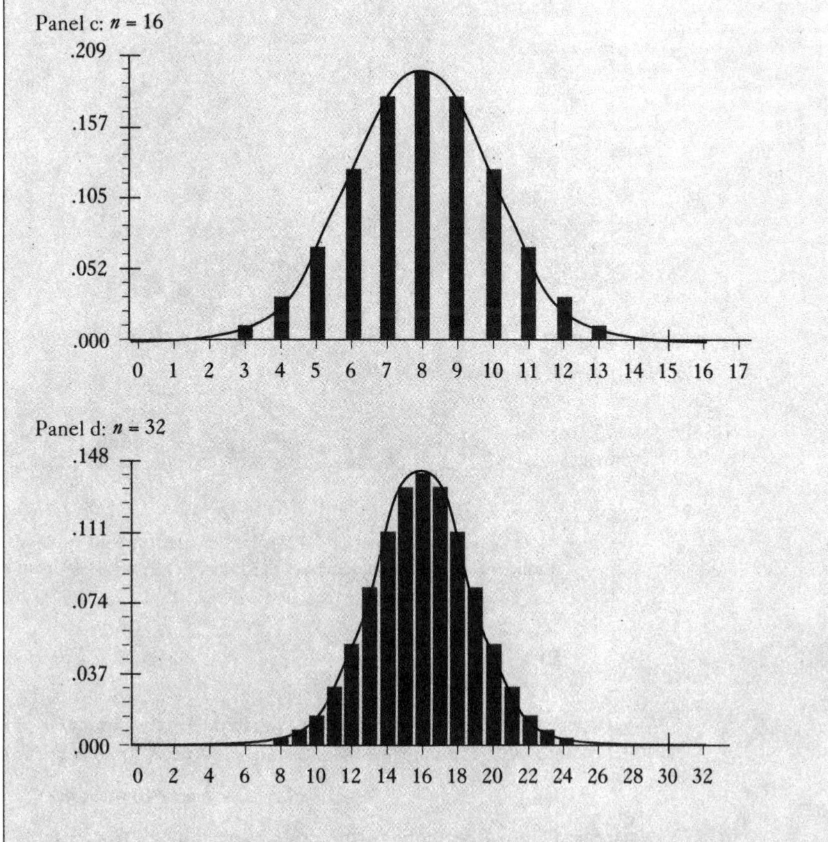

Probability Density Function (pdf)
A function that, for any interval of values, gives the probability that the associated random variable, x, takes a value in the interval.

A random variable x is continuous if it can take any value along a number line but the probability of any one of these infinite values is zero. Because the probability mass at any one value is zero, only a range of x values have a meaningful non-zero probability. The curve showing the area or density of this range of x values is called the **probability density function (pdf)** of x. The probability that x takes a value in a range between a and b is $P(a < x < b)$, which is the area under the probability density function between a and b. For a normal probability density function, Figure 6.2 shows such an area.

The normal probability density function is not the only continuous distribution used in statistics. All continuous distributions have probability density functions—examples include the rectangular (panel a) and the right-skewed (panel b) distributions in Figure 6.3. In each of these cases, the probability that a continuous random variable

FIGURE 6.2 Normal Probability Density Function

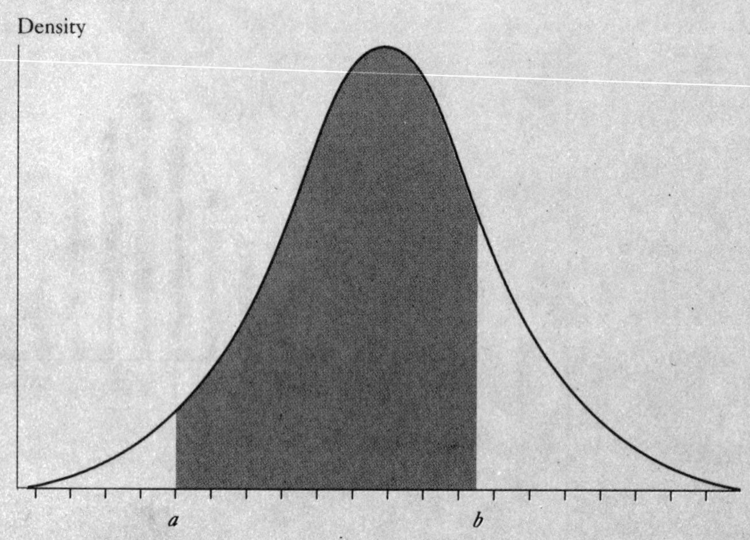

Note: The shaded area under the bell-shaped normal density function is the probability that the continuous random variable x takes a value between a and b.

takes a value between $\boldsymbol{a}$ and $\boldsymbol{b}$ is the shaded area under the pdf. Because there is a zero probability that a continuous random variable x equals the single value $\boldsymbol{a}$ (or $\boldsymbol{b}$),

$$P(\boldsymbol{a} < x < \boldsymbol{b}) = P(\boldsymbol{a} \leq x \leq \boldsymbol{b})$$

regardless of the shape of the probability density function.

If $\boldsymbol{a}$ is the smallest value for which a continuous random variable is defined and $\boldsymbol{b}$ is any larger value, then the curve or function giving the area under the density function between $\boldsymbol{a}$ and $\boldsymbol{b}$ is called the cumulative distribution function or simply the distribution function. For instance, the density function for the uniform distribution in Figure 6.3, panel a, is

$$\text{Density of } u = f(u) = 1/h, \text{ for } 0 < u < h$$

and the distribution function is

$$P(u < \boldsymbol{b}) = \boldsymbol{b}/h,$$

which is shown in Figure 6.4, panel a, as the continuous straight line.

FIGURE 6.3 Some Continuous Nonnormal Probability Density Functions

Panel a: Density Function for a Uniform or Rectangular Distribution, where the continuous random variable u can take any value from 0 to h (called the support of u) and the hatched area is the probability of u taking a value between a and b. The total area under this density function is one.

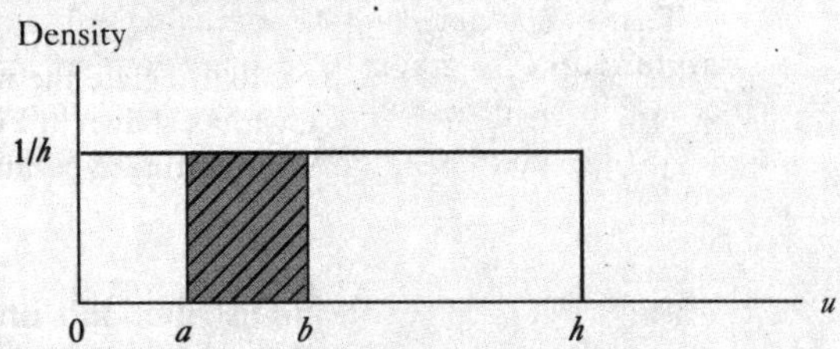

Panel b: Density function for a Right-Skewed Distribution, where the continuous random variable v can take any value and the hatched area is the probability of v taking a value between a and b. The total area under this density function is one.

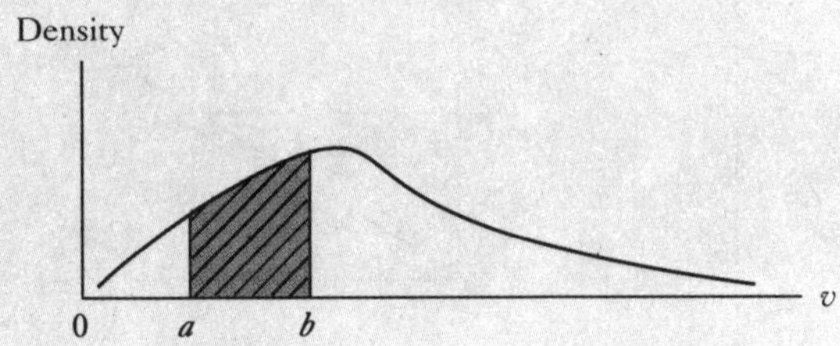

The density function for a normal random variable x is

$$f(x) = \frac{1}{\sigma\sqrt{2\pi}} e^{-(x-\mu)^2/2\sigma^2}$$

where $-\infty < x < +\infty$

μ is the mean of x

σ is the standard deviation of x

π is 3.14159

e is 2.71828

The probability of normal random variable *x* yielding a value between *a* and *b* is

$$P(a < x < b) = \int_a^b \frac{1}{\sigma\sqrt{2\pi}} e^{-(x-\mu)^2/2\sigma^2}\,dx$$

Probability Distribution Function
A function giving the probability that a random variable takes on values less than a specific upper limit.

which is the area under the density function between *a* and *b*. Notice that this probability is not defined at a point for the normal distribution, as ***a*** goes to ***b*** in the above integral, $P(a < x < b)$ goes to 0.

The integral for $P(-\infty < x < b)$ is typically referred to as the **probability distribution function**. We never have to integrate the normal probability distribution function because its shape is well known. As shown in Figure 6.4, panel b, the normal probability distribution function is a serpentine-type line that rises ever faster from negative

FIGURE 6.4 Density and Distribution Functions

Panel a: The distribution function for a uniform distribution is a straight line whose uniform rise shows an accumulation of probability as *u* increases from 0 to its maximum value of *h* in the density function.

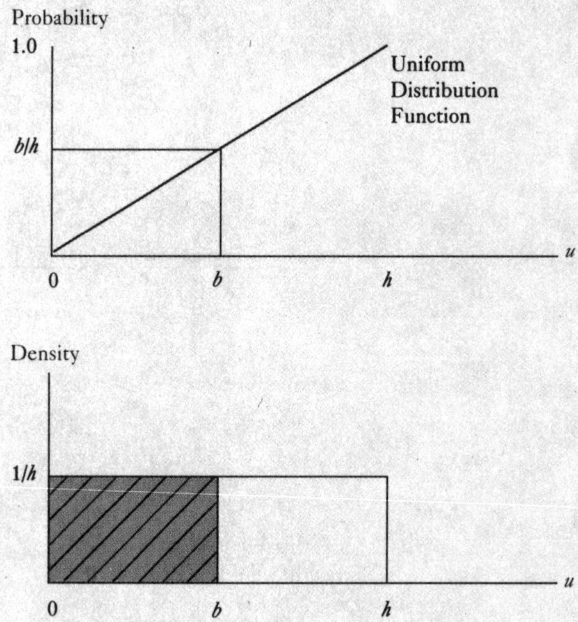

(continued)

infinity to the mean, where 50 percent of the distribution has accumulated. It then rises ever slower to a 100 percent cumulative probability as x approaches a positive infinity. Probability is read from the vertical axis. For example, approximately 16 percent of the distribution is in the lower tail of the normal density function below $\mu - \sigma$. This is the probability that is shown on the vertical axis of the normal probability distribution function for the area under the density function between $-\infty$ and $\mu - \sigma$.

$$P(-\infty < x < \mu - \sigma) = 0.16$$

Other probabilities can be obtained from the vertical axis of the normal distribution function in a similar fashion. As we will see, tables and computer programs make reading of this vertical axis easy and more precise than what can be accomplished by visual inspection.

FIGURE 6.4 Density and Distribution Functions *(continued)*

Panel b: The distribution function for the normal distribution is a "serpentine type" line that rises ever faster from negative infinity to the mean, where 50 percent of the distribution has accumulated. It then rises ever slower to a 100 percent cumulative probability as x approaches a positive infinity.

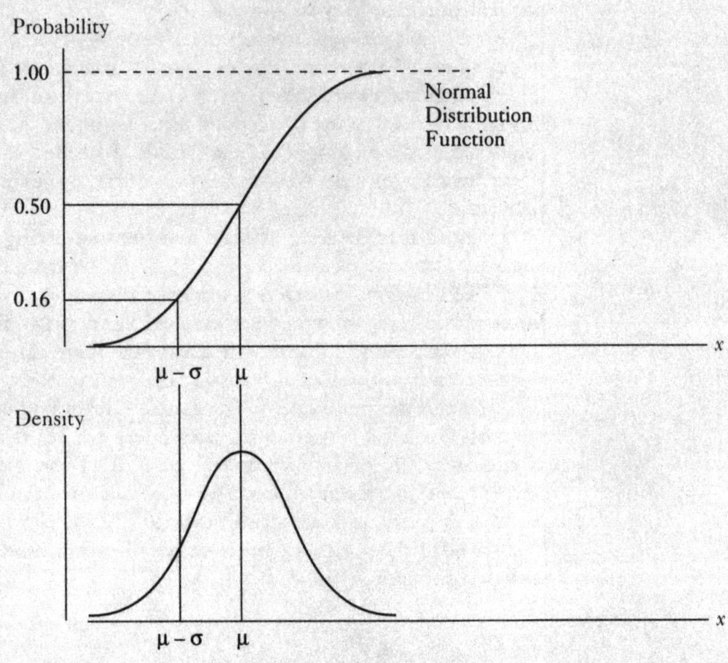

6.3 Normal Distributions

The distribution of any normal random variable requires the specification of two parameters: the mean μ and the standard deviation σ (or variance σ^2). The mean or expected value gives the central location of the variable, and the standard deviation is a measure of its variability. Because normal random variables can have different means and standard deviations, there is a family of normal distributions where each member is identified by its mean and standard deviation.

The mean of the normal distribution simply centers the distribution on the horizontal axis; the higher the mean, the farther to the right the center of the distribution. Differences in the size of a standard deviation, however, do not affect the probability of being within one standard deviation of the mean. Figure 6.5 shows three normal density functions with different means and different standard deviations. The area within one standard deviation of the mean remains the same, regardless of the magnitude of the standard deviation and position of the mean. That is, distribution *s* is less variable than distribution *w* ($\sigma_s = 2.1 < \sigma_w = 4.9$), but the area under the respective density functions within one standard deviation of the mean is fixed. It is for this reason that the rules of bell-shaped distributions, as presented in Chapter 2, hold regardless of the variability in a normal random variable. As a bell-shaped distribution, regardless of the size of μ or σ, a normal random variable has **approximately 68 percent of the values within $\mu \pm \sigma$, about 95 percent of the values within $\mu \pm 2\sigma$, and almost 100 percent of the values within $\mu \pm 3\sigma$.**

Notice that this rule implies that about 84 percent of the distribution is less than $\mu + \sigma$, about 97.5 percent is below $\mu + 2\sigma$, and almost 100 percent is beneath $\mu + 3\sigma$. These percentages are shown on the vertical axis of the normal distribution function in Figure 6.6 and as the corresponding areas under the density function. As an example of their use, consider the beer glass size needed to ensure that nearly all the fills are at least 20 ounces. We must assume first, however, that "fills" are normally distributed.

It seems reasonable to assume that the underlying distribution of glass fills (x) is normal. The amount of liquid in a glass can be treated as a continuous random variable. The fill is not restricted to integer values, and any decimal is possible within the limits of the glass volume. Furthermore, the errors in filling a glass should vary symmetrically around the mean, with most fills being close to the center value. (Look at the difference in fluid levels in soda bottles in an eight-pack, for example.)

Although the press release cited at the beginning of this chapter did not give the standard deviation, experienced bartenders can set σ at 0.15 ounces. From the rule of normality, if approximately 100 percent of the glasses are to have 20 or more ounces, then the mean fill must be three standard deviations higher, at 20.45 ounces [= 20 + 3(0.15)], and the glass must be able to accommodate at least 20.9 ounces [= 20 + 6(0.15)]. For this normal density function, the relevant values and areas are shown in Figure 6.7.

FIGURE 6.5 Different Variability in Normal Densities

Normal random variables z, s, and w with different standard deviations σ_z, σ_s, and σ_w, and different means μ_z, μ_s, and μ_w

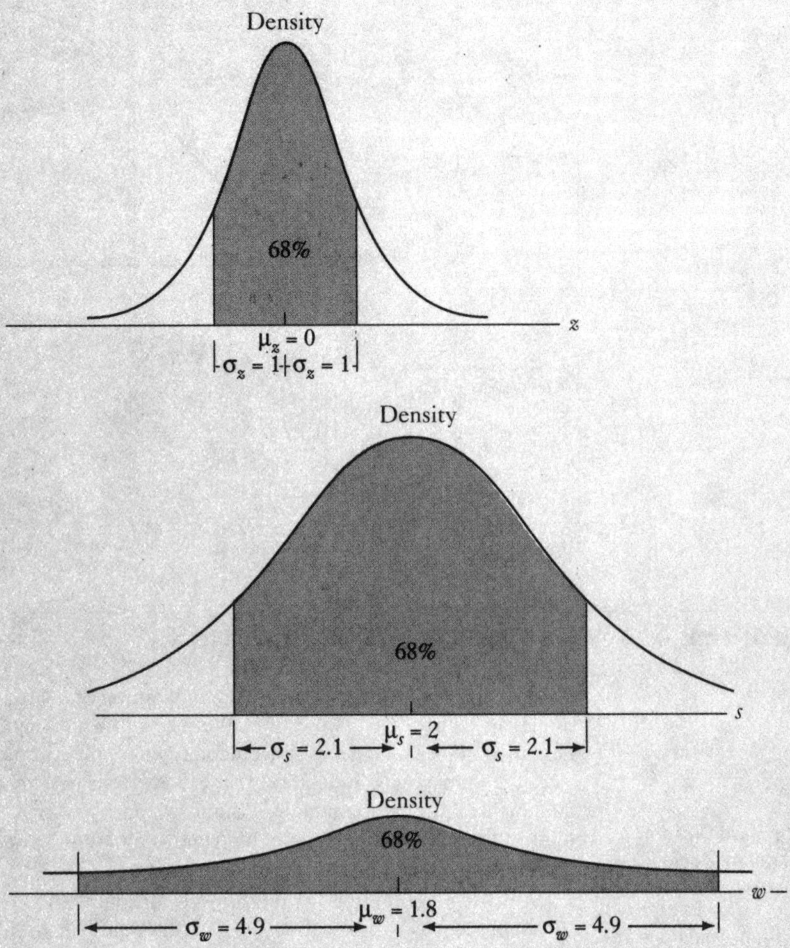

FIGURE 6.6 **The Rule for Bell-Shaped Distributions as Related to the Normal Density and Distribution Function**

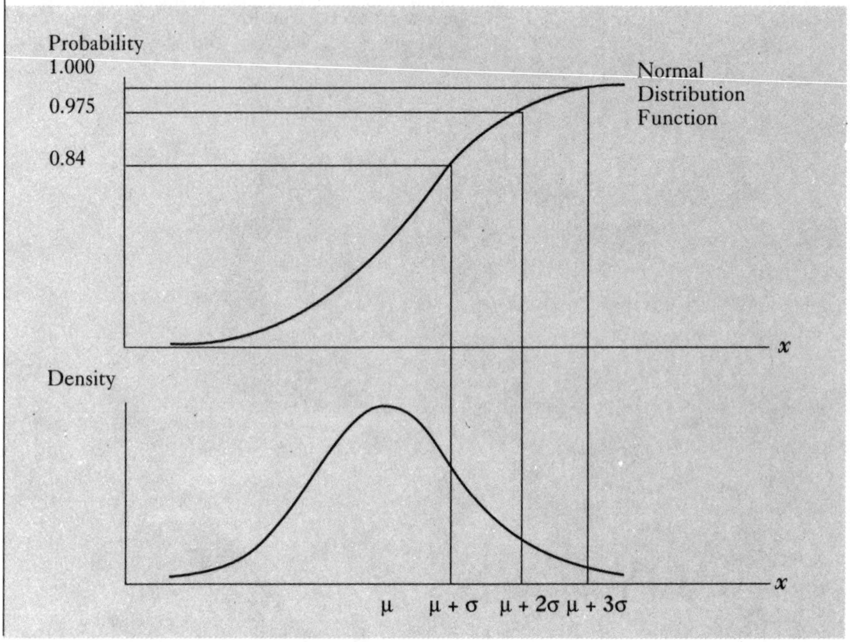

6.4 THE STANDARD NORMAL DISTRIBUTION

Standard Normal Random Variable
A normal random variable, z, that has a mean of 0 and standard deviation of 1.

According to Great Britain's Institute of Trading Standards Administration, 80 percent of glasses of beer were short of a 20-ounce fill in the past. To answer the question of how short the average fill was, we need to know the number of standard deviations between 20 ounces and a mean fill that is consistent with 80 percent of the fills less than 20 ounces. This can be done by "standardizing" or "transforming" fills to form a random variable that has a mean of zero and standard deviation of one—a **standard normal random variable.**

The standard normal distribution is a special member of the family of normal distributions. It is the distribution for a normal random variable that has a mean of zero and the standard deviation of one, which is designated by the letter z. That is, z is the standard normal random variable that is distributed normally with mean zero and standard deviation of one. In mathematical notation, this is written

$$z \sim N(\mu = 0, \sigma = 1), \text{ or simply } z \sim N(0, 1)$$

As shown in Figure 6.5, changing the mean of a normal random variable only changes the position of the distribution without changing the probabilities assigned to

FIGURE 6.7 The Normal Density for Desired Ounces of Beer in a Glass

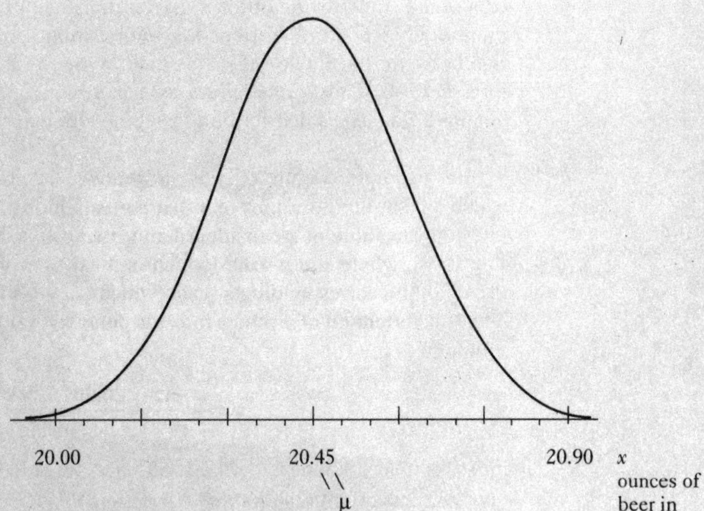

If glasses are designed to hold 21 ounces of beer, then nearly all fills can be in excess of 20 ounces (one British pint).

being a certain number of standard deviations from the mean, panel a. In addition, changing the size of a standard deviation does not affect the probability of being within a given number of standard deviations of the mean, panel b. These observations are captured in an important theorem: **any linear transformation of a normal random variable is also a normal random variable.** Any normal random variable x can be transformed into a standard normal random variable z by Formula (6.1).

Standard normal random variable: $z = \dfrac{x - \mu}{\sigma}$ (6.1)

where x is a normal random variable with mean μ and standard deviation of σ so z has a mean of zero and standard deviation of one. That is, if $x \sim N(\mu, \sigma)$, then $z \sim N(0, 1)$.

Although it may not be obvious in Formula (6.1), z is a linear transformation of the random variable x because it can be written as a straight line function of x:

$$z = (1/\sigma)x - (1/\sigma)\mu$$

If x is distributed normally, with $E(x) = \mu$ and standard deviation σ, then z is distributed normally with $E(z) = 0$ and standard deviation of one.

In essence, the standard normal random variable z gives the number of standard deviations a particular value x is above (or below) the mean of x. The standard normal distribution is a redrawing of the x distribution such that the vertical axis for z shows the number of standard deviations between x and μ, and the area under the density function between these two values is equal to the probability of getting a value of z in the interval $z - 0$. Thus, probabilities associated with any normal random variable x can be obtained from the z distribution by simply "transforming" or "standardizing" x to form a z.

For example, Figure 6.7 can be redrawn in terms of "standardized" values of x, which are simply the values of z that correspond to the number of standard deviations between the value of x considered and its mean. These transformations are shown in Figure 6.8, where the x scale (which is measured in ounces, in panel a) has been replaced by the corresponding z scale (which counts standard deviations in x, in panel b). The transformation of x values into z is done via Formula (6.1). For example, the transformation

$$z = \frac{x - \mu}{\sigma} = \frac{20.00 - 20.45}{0.15} = -3.00$$

indicates that 20 ounces is three standard deviations below a mean glass fill of 20.45 ounces. Thus, the probability of x less than 20, *if* $\mu = 20.45$ and $\sigma = 0.15$, is the same as the probability of z less than −3, which is known to be approximately 0. Similarly,

$$z = \frac{x - \mu}{\sigma} = \frac{20.15 - 20.45}{0.15} = -2.00$$

shows that 20.15 ounces is two standard deviations below the mean of 20.45 ounces and the probability of x less than 20.15 is the same as the probability of z less than −2, which is known to be approximately 0.025. The reader is left to show that 20.30 is one standard deviation below an assumed mean of 20.45 ounces. The probability of x being less than 20.30 is the same as the probability of z being less than −1, which is approximately 0.16.

But we do not know the old mean fill of beer glasses. We want to find the old mean fill for which 80 percent of the glasses had less than 20 ounces. In essence, this is done by sliding the normal distributions in Figure 6.5 to the left until 80 percent of the glasses have less than 20 ounces of beer. Figure 6.9 shows this point as a "standardized" z value of 0.84, which is discussed in more detail in the next section. Here it is only necessary to recognize that the probability of z less than 0.84 is 0.80 and this probability is all of the area under the standard normal density function to the left of a z of 0.84; this is also the area under the density function to the left of x at 20 ounces. We needed z to obtain the probabilities associated with x:

$$P(z < 0.84) = P(x < 20) = 0.80$$

FIGURE 6.8 Normal Density for Beer Glasses and the Corresponding Standard Normal z

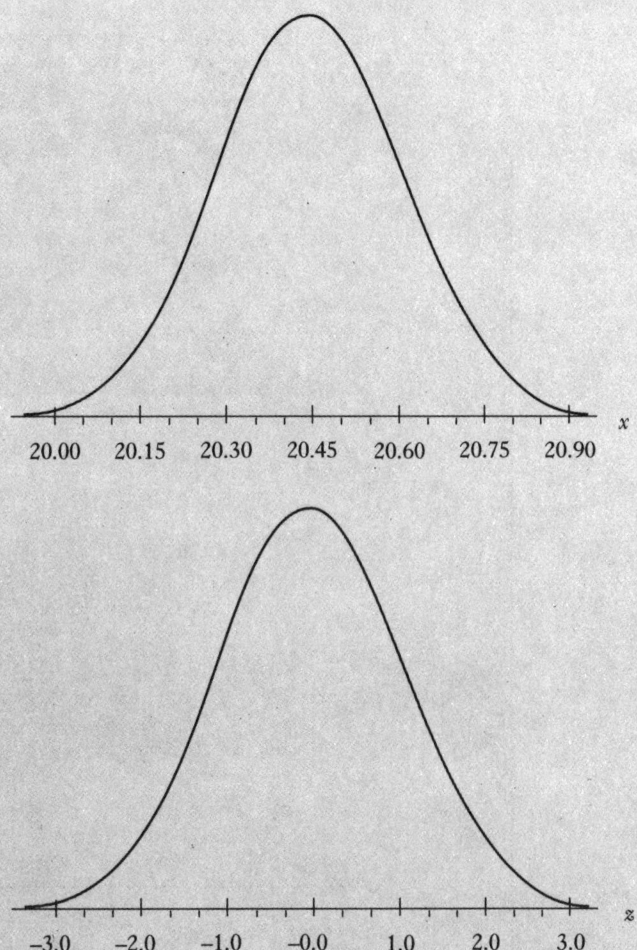

Notice that $z = 3.0$ indicates that 20.90 ounces is 3 standard deviations above the mean of 20.45. Similarly $z = -3.0$ states that 20 ounces is 3 standard deviations below the mean of 20.45. A z of 2.0 shows that 20.75 is 2 standard deviations above the mean of 20.45 and a z of -2.0 shows that 20.15 is 2 standard deviations below the mean of 20.45, and so on.

FIGURE 6.9 Normal Density for Fills of the Old Beer Glasses

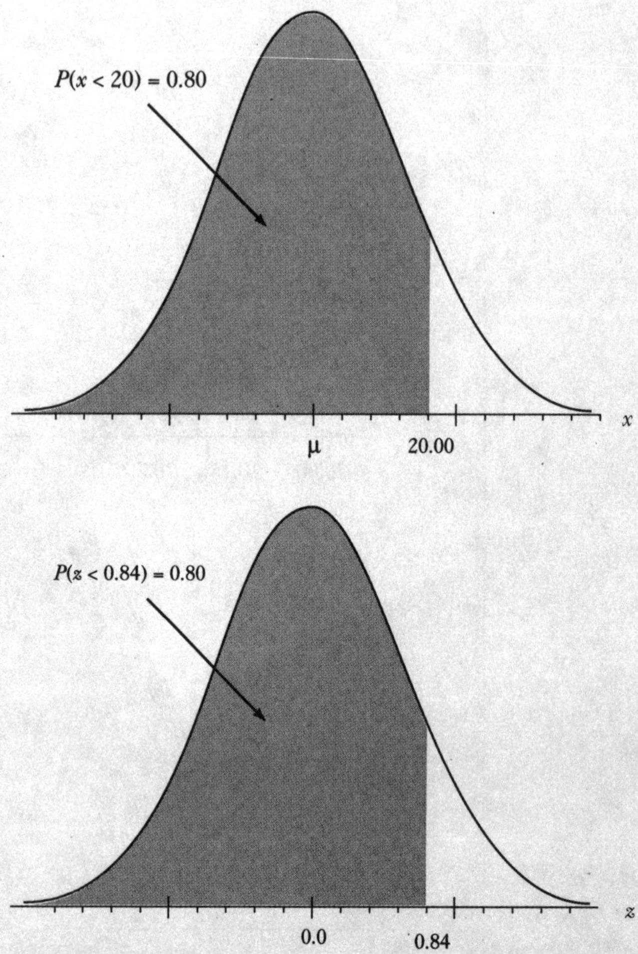

If the old mean glass fill μ was 19.874 ounces, which is 0.84 standard deviations below a fill of 20 ounces, then 80 percent of the glasses will contain less than 20 ounces of beer.

The old mean fill now can be found, because 20 ounces must be 0.84 standard deviations above the mean glass fill; otherwise 80 percent of the fills could not be less than 20 ounces. Thus, the old mean glass fill was 19.87 ounces, which is found by Formula (6.1):

$$z = \frac{x - \mu}{\sigma}$$

$$0.84 = \frac{20.00 - \mu}{0.15}$$

$$19.874 = \mu$$

6.5 Calculations with the Standard Normal Table

Appendix Table A.3 is a cumulative probability table for the standard normal distribution. The body of this table provides the probabilities of z less than the indicated positive z value $\boldsymbol{b}$, that is, $P(-\infty < z < b)$. The use of this table can be illustrated by first finding a probability we already know, such as $P(-\infty < z < b) = P(z < 1.00) \cong 0.84$.

For bell-shaped density functions, about 68 percent of the distribution is within one standard deviation on either side of the mean. Thus, about 16 percent is above one standard deviation of the mean and about 84 percent is between $-\infty$ and $\mu + \sigma$, as shown in the distribution function in Figure 6.6. This is a probability that can be obtained exactly from the standard normal tabulations in Appendix Table A.3, a part of which is reproduced in Table 6.1. Look down the left-hand margin of this standard normal table until 1.0 is reached, and then move one column to the right (to the column headed .00): the number in the corresponding cell is .8413. This is the cumulative probability $P(z < 1.00) = 0.8413$, which we already knew to be approximately 84 percent from the rule of bell-shaped densities.

From Appendix Table A.3, and as reproduced in Table 6.1, the area corresponding to other z values can be obtained. For example, the probability of $z < 0.84$ can be seen to be 0.7995, which is approximately the 0.80 area shown in Figure 6.9. Notice, however, that the distribution for a normal random variable is still not exhausted completely, even at three standard deviations above the mean; for example, $P(z < 3.49) = 0.9998 \neq 1.00000$. The normal distribution has a range that extends from a negative infinity to a positive infinity. Nevertheless, most of its mass is within three standard deviations of the mean, as suggested by the rule for bell-shaped distributions.

Cumulative probabilities for negative z values are not provided in Appendix Table A.3. Because the normal distribution is symmetric, however, they can be determined indirectly from the information provided. To illustrate, consider $P(z < -1.08)$. The reader should be able to identify this probability in Appendix Table A.3; it is graphed in panel a, Figure 6.10. Panel b shows that the area below -1.08 is the same as the area above $+1.08$; i.e., $P(z < -1.08) = P(z > 1.08)$. The area above 1.08 is one minus the area below 1.08, $P(z > 1.08) = 1 - P(z < 1.08)$. From Appendix Table A.3, the cumulative

TABLE 6.1
Reading the Standard Normal Table

To find the cumulative probability associated with any z value, accurate to the tenths position as in $z = 1.0$, go down the left margin until the corresponding tenths are found, then read probability in the column titled .00. Thus $P(z < 1.0)$ is 0.8413. To find the probability for z values accurate at the hundredths position, say $P(z < 0.84)$, go down the first column to the row .8 and then go across this row to the column headed .04 to find $P(z < 0.84) = 0.7995$. Notice that 50 percent of the distribution is below $z = 0$ and the distribution is still not exhausted completely, even at $z = 3.49$.

z	.00	.01	.02	.03	.04	.05	.06	.07	.08	.09
.0	.5000	.5040	.5080	.5120	.5160	.5199	.5239	.5279	.5319	.5359
.1	\\									
.	$P(z < 0.00)$									
.										
.					$P(z < 0.84)$					
.7					//					
.8	.7881	.7910	.7039	.7967	.7995	.8023	.8051	.8078	.8106	.8133
.9										
1.0	.8413	.8438	.8461	.8485	.8508	.8531	.8554	.8577	.8599	.8621
1.1	\\									
.	$P(z < 1.00)$									
.										
.									$P(z < 3.49)$	
3.3										\\
3.4	.9997	.9997	.9997	.9997	.9997	.9997	.9997	.9997	.9997	.9998

value $P(z < 1.08)$ is 0.8599, panel c, which upon subtraction from one gives the area under the density function above 1.08.

$$P(z > 1.08) = 1 - P(z < 1.08)$$
$$= 1 - 0.8599$$
$$= 0.1401$$

Because the normal distribution is symmetric, 0.1401 is also the area under the density function below −1.08.

$$P(z < -1.08) = P(z > 1.08) = 0.1401$$

QUERY 6.1:
If the time required to complete an examination by those with a certain learning disability is believed to be distributed normally, with a mean of 65 minutes and a standard deviation of 15 minutes, then when can the exam be terminated so that 99 percent of those with the disability can finish?

ANSWER:
Because the average and standard deviation are known, what needs to be established is the amount of time, above the mean time, such that 99 percent of the distribution is lower. This is a distance that is measured in standard deviations, as given

FIGURE 6.10 Cumulative Probabilities for Negative z Values

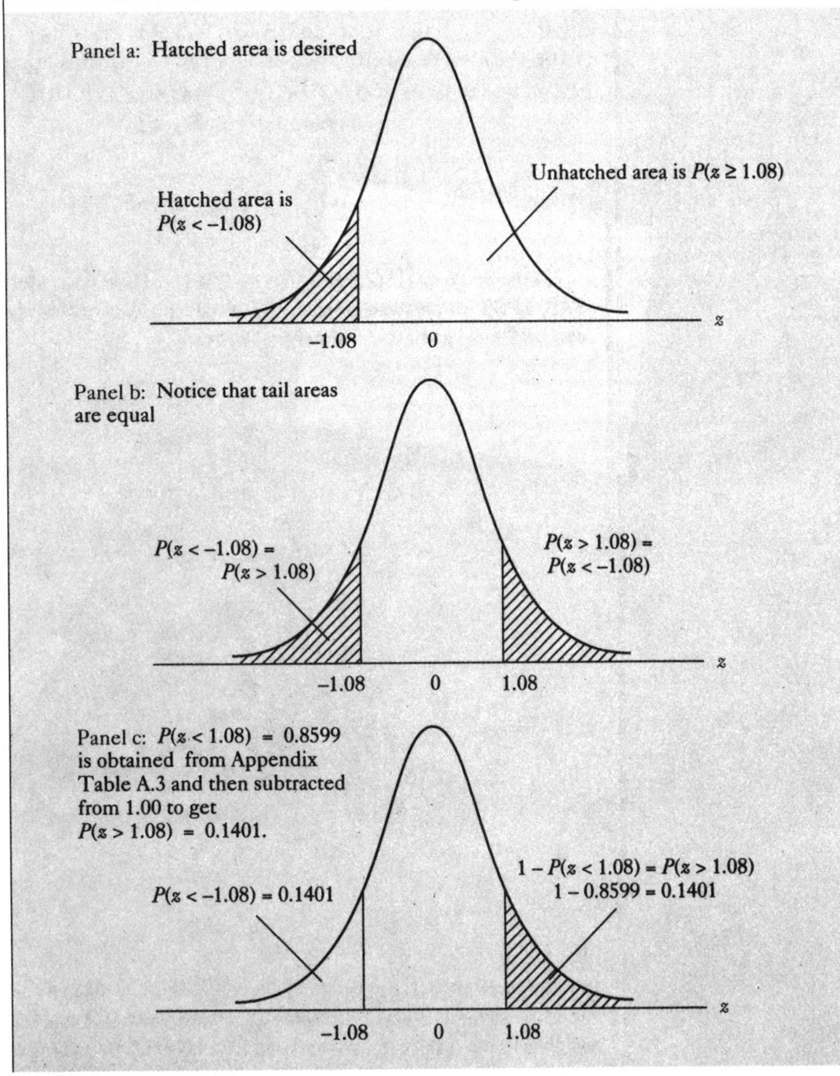

by the z value corresponding to the 0.99 probability found in the body of Appendix Table A.3. The closest cumulative probability that can be found is .9901, in the row labeled 2.3 and column headed by .03, $z = 2.33$. The time needed so that 99 percent of the learning disabled can complete the test is thus approximately 100 minutes, which can be derived by solving for x, in Formula (6.1).

$$z = \frac{x - \mu}{\sigma}$$

$$2.33 = \frac{x - 65}{15}$$

Thus, $x = 65 + 15(2.33) = 99.95$ minutes. Using a computer program such as the SAS, SPSS, or any one of the other programs now available, the relevant quantities can be found as in the following diagram.

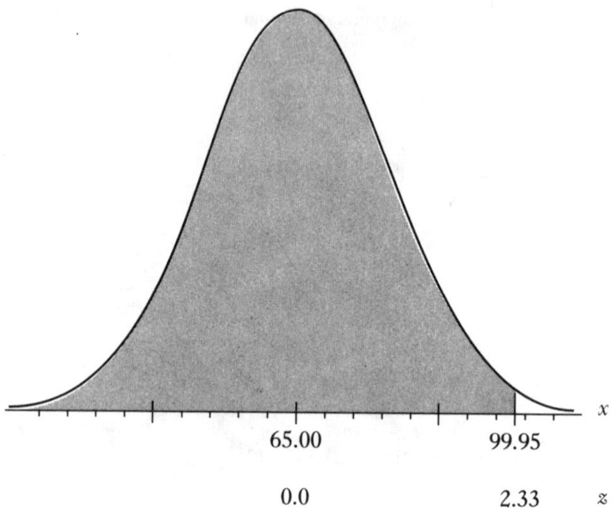

QUERY 6.2:

In the early 1980s, the Toro Company of Minneapolis, Minnesota, advertised that it would refund the purchase price of a snowblower if the following winter's snowfall was less than 21 percent of the local average. If the average snowfall is 45.25 inches, with a standard deviation of 12.2 inches, what is the likelihood that Toro will have to make refunds?

ANSWER:

Within limits, snowfall is a continuous random variable that can be expected to vary symmetrically around its mean, with values closer to the mean occurring most often. Thus, it seems reasonable to assume that snowfall (x) is approximately normally distributed with a mean of 45.25 inches and standard deviation of 12.2 inches. Nine and a half inches is 21 percent of the mean snowfall of 45.25 inches and, with a standard deviation of 12.2 inches, the number of standard deviations between 45.25 inches and 9.5 inches is z:

$$z = \frac{x - \mu}{\sigma} = \frac{9.50 - 45.25}{12.2} = -2.93$$

Now $P(x < 9.50) = P(z < -2.93)$, where the hatched area below is the area of interest

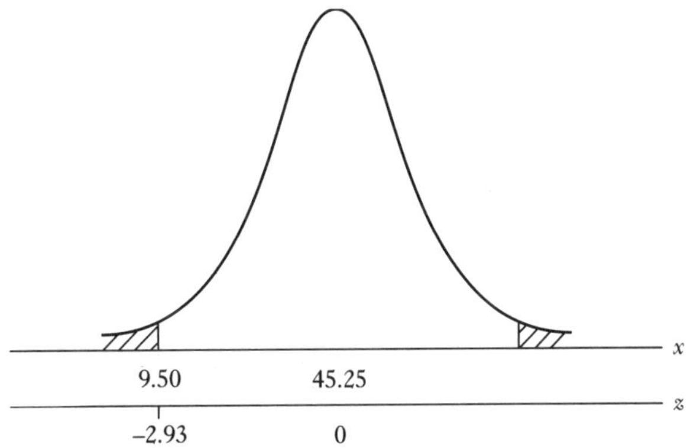

Using Appendix Table A.3, $P(z > 2.93) = 1 - P(z < 2.93)$ $= 1 - 0.9983 = 0.0017$, which is also $P(z < -2.93)$

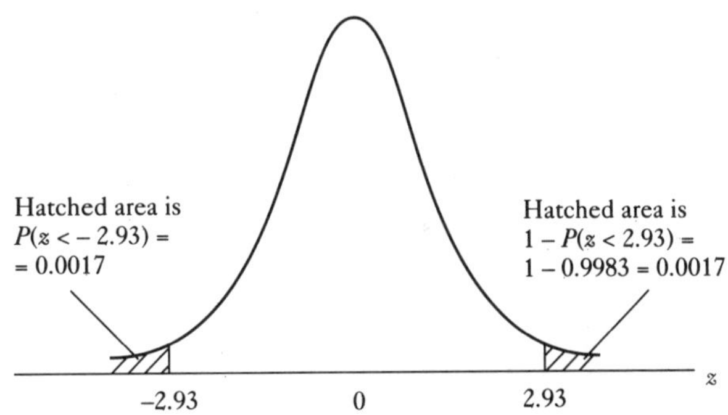

Thus, there is a 0.17 percent chance that the snowfall next winter will be less than 9.5 inches and that Toro will have to make refunds.

QUERY 6.3:
When workers are paid by the piece, the average time required to complete the task is usually well publicized by the employer. Suppose that a time study shows that a task takes 2.4 minutes to complete, on the average, with a standard deviation of 0.6 minute. If time of task is normally distributed, how often is the task completed in one to three minutes?

Answer:

At the lower limit, where $x = 1.0$,

$$z = \frac{x - \mu}{\sigma} = \frac{1.0 - 2.4}{0.6} = -2.33$$

At the upper limit, where $x = 3.0$,

$$z = \frac{x - \mu}{\sigma} = \frac{3.0 - 2.4}{0.6} = 1.00$$

Thus, the desired area is

$$P(1.0 < x < 3.0) = P(-2.33 < z < 1.00)$$

From Appendix Table A.3, we get

$$P(z < 1.00) = 0.8413$$

which graphically is the undotted area below

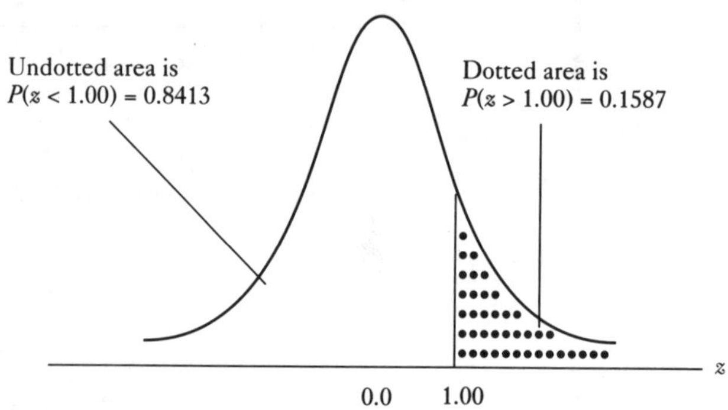

Using the symmetry property of the normal distribution and Appendix Table A.3, we can determine

$P(z < -2.33) = 1 - P(z < 2.33) = 1 - 0.9901 = 0.0099$, which graphically is

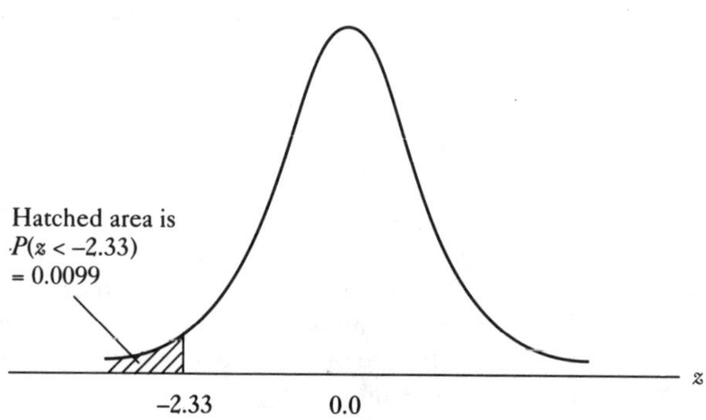

Subtracting the hatched area from the undotted area above gives

$$P(-2.33 < z < 1.00) = P(z < 1.00) - P(z < -2.33)$$
$$= 0.8413 - 0.0099 = 0.8314$$

Thus, 83.14 percent of the time, the task is completed between one and three minutes.

As an alternative to Appendix Table A.3, EXCEL provides several ways to determine probabilities with the normal distribution. For the standard normal distribution, typing the "=NORMSDIST (*z*)" function command into any EXCEL cell yields the probability of *z* being less than the number entered for *z*. For example, entering "=NORMSDIST(-2.33)" in cell A1 yields $P(z < -2.33) = 0.009903$. Entering "=NORMSDIST(1.00)" in cell A2 yields $P(z < 1.00) = 0.841345$. Subtracting the two cells, by entering "=A2-A1" in cell A3, then yields 0.8314 as shown by the unshaded area in the below graph.

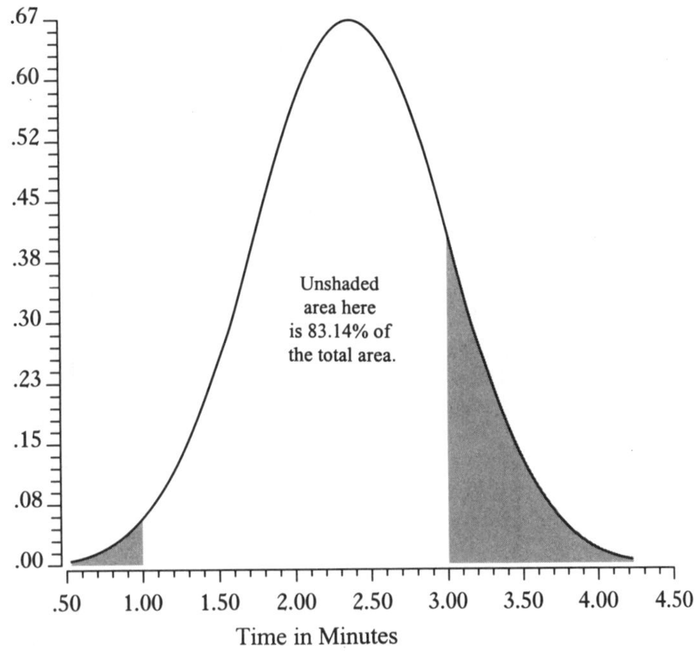

QUERY 6.4:
The Wall Street Journal (February 26, 1992) reported that in 1990 the job tenure of marketing directors at law firms was 2.1 years but that one-third had been on the job for a year or less. The question: Could marketing director tenure be approximately normally distributed?

ANSWER:
What we know in this problem is reflected in the following diagram, where *x* is job tenure, which we tentatively assume is normally distributed.

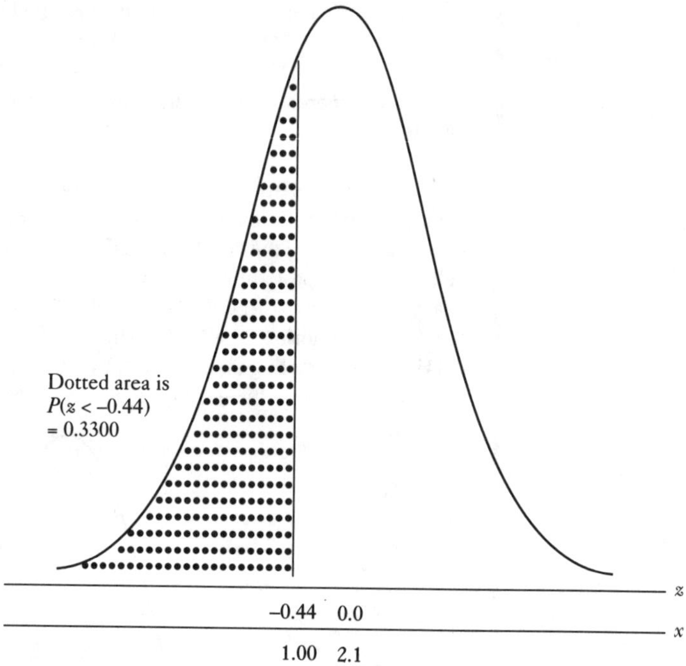

What we do not know is the standard deviation of x, but this can be solved for in the Formula (6.1), assuming x is normally distributed. Substituting for x, μ, and z and solving for σ gives

$$z = \frac{x - \mu}{\sigma}$$

$$-0.44 = \frac{1.0 - 2.1}{\sigma}$$

$$\sigma = 2.5$$

If the distribution of tenure is normally distributed, then the standard deviation is 2.5 years. But, with a mean of 2.1 years, $\mu - \sigma$ would be a negative 0.4 years, which is impossible. Thus, it would not be appropriate to assume that job tenure of marketing directors is approximately normally distributed.

EXCEL provides alternatives for determining the value of a normal random variable that puts a given percentage of the distribution below it. For the standard normal distribution, typing the "=NORMSINV(alpha)" function command into any EXCEL cell yields the value of z that puts alpha percent below it. For example, entering "=NORMSINV(0.33)" into cell A1 yields $P(z < -0.43991) = 0.33$, which is the dotted area and z value in the above graph obtained from Appendix Table A.3.

HISTORICAL PERSPECTIVE

Many students think that scholarship and the development of scientific ideas has always been harmonious and civilized. The historical development of the normal distribution, however, is filled with controversy and turbulence. Germans, for example, credit the great scientist Carl Friedrich Gauss (1777–1855) for deriving the normal distribution; the French cite the equally renowned Pierre Simon Laplace (1749–1827). But Abraham De Moivre (1667–1754), a French expatriate living in London, invented the normal distribution, and Englishman Thomas Simpson (1710–1761) popularized it.

In 1733, De Moivre proposed what is now called the normal density function as an equation that, when integrated, would approximate Bernoulli's binomial distribution for large sample sizes. He calculated the probability of the value of a variable falling within one, two, and three standard deviations of its mean. The precision of his equation and method of calculation, and his emphasis on measuring distance from the mean in terms of standardized units, met with indifference from his contemporaries, possibly because of the absence of applications in De Moivre's work and his highbrow style. Empirical scientists were not interested in mathematical nuances; they wanted techniques or methods that would lead to generalizations from observable data, and De Moivre failed to provide any.

In 1740, Thomas Simpson published two books that presented ideas and concepts similar to those of De Moivre but in a manner that was readable by a wider audience. Simpson's early interest in astrology led him to the study of astronomy and then mathematics, which he learned on his own. At the age of 19, he married a 50-year-old widow with two children. He supported his family by weaving and teaching mathematics. It may have been his need for money that led him to write books that appealed to a readership beyond the highbrows for whom De Moivre wrote.

Simpson cited De Moivre appropriately, but De Moivre was envious of Simpson's success. De Moivre may have felt that the sale of his earlier books would suffer, because in 1743 he came out with a second edition to compete with Simpson's. In the preface, De Moivre blasted Simpson for writing on the same subject and mutilating his work. More to the point, however, is De Moivre's condemnation of Simpson for selling his book at a very moderate price. Needless to say, a war of words between Simpson and De Moivre followed.

Stephen Stigler (1986, pp. 88–94) asserts that, unlike De Moivre, Simpson opened the door to practical applications of the normal distribution for assessing uncertainty by making it the distribution of errors in measurement, as introduced in the next chapter. Lagrange, Laplace, Bayes, and then Gauss slipped through this door and advanced the normal distribution as the most important error distribution in statistics (as discussed in the next chapter and applied throughout the remainder of this book).

QUERY 6.5:
An article in *The Wall Street Journal* (February 28, 1997) reported that "stock volatility has declined, as measured by the standard deviation in long term returns ... making stocks less risky." The accompanying diagram showed the standard deviation dropping from about 25 to 16 percent between 1955 and 1996. The article cited a Dean Witter strategist saying that during the 1995 to 1996 period stocks yielded a 15 percent-plus return over the safe bond yield, which a J.P Morgan strategist placed at 7 percent. If the expected return on stock in 1996 was 22 percent, with a standard deviation of 16 percent, and returns are normally distributed, what is the probability of losing equity?

ANSWER:

Equity loss occurs if the rate of return is below zero; thus, we are looking for $P(x < 0)$, where x is the rate of return. If x is normally distributed, with mean 22 and standard deviation 16, then we can use the "NORMDIST" command in EXCEL for this probability calculation:

1. Select the cell in which you would like the answer to appear.
2. Click once on "Insert" pull down menu.
3. Click once on "Function..." A box with several options will then appear.
4. Click once on "Statistical" from the function category.
5. To the right, under "Function Name," several statistics functions appear. Scroll down to find "NORMDIST," which you highlight by clicking on it.
6. Click the mouse on the "OK" in the bottom lower-right hand corner. Another box will appear into which the first entry is the x value of 0, the second is the mean 22, and the third is standard deviation 16. The fourth entry is cumulative (1 for true), which gives the area under the density curve to the left of $x = 0$. (An entry of 0 for false for cumulative returns the height of the density function at $x = 0$.) Your screen now looks like that in Chart 6.1.

CHART 6.1 The NORMDIST command for $P[x < 0| x \sim N(\mu=22, \sigma = 16)]$

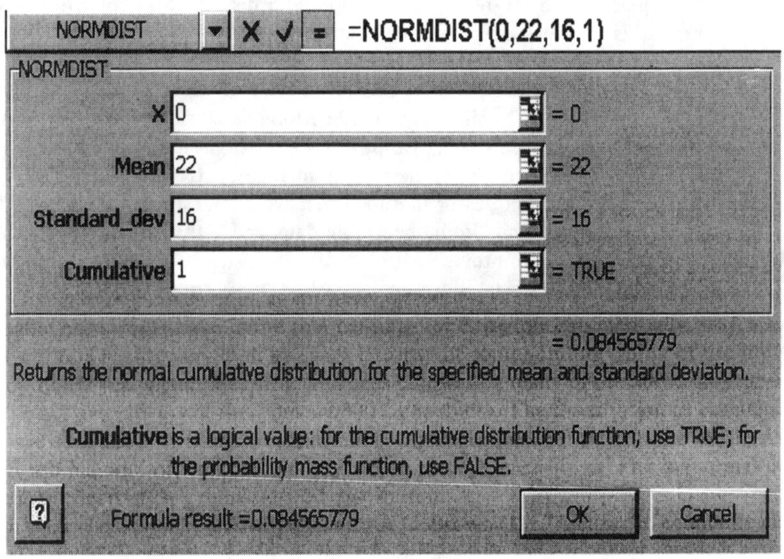

7. Click once on "OK" to obtain the answer of $P(x<0) = 0.08457$.

That is, the probability of losing equity is about 8.5 percent, given normally distributed returns, an expected return of 22, and a standard deviation of 16.

QUERY 6.6

Using *The Wall Street Journal* (February 28, 1997) information in Query 6.5 on stock volatility, if the safe bond yield in 1955 was 3 percent, what would the expected premium on stocks need to be for the same probability of equity loss calculated in Query 6.5? Does this seem to be a reasonable risk premium for the stock market of that period? Comment on what has happened to stock volatility versus the risk premium between 1955 and 1996.

ANSWER:

Again, we are working with the probability $P(x < 0)$. Now, however, this probability has been set at 0.084565779. We have to find the value of μ that would produce this probability for a normal random variable with a standard deviation of 25 (as stated in Query 6.5, for 1955). That is, we need to find the expected return that gives an approximate 8.46 percent chance of losing equity. EXCEL does not have a normal distribution function that directly solves for the mean. We can find the value of z that puts 0.084565779 in the lower tail of the standard normal distribution from which we can calculate the value of μ for the distribution of x via the formula

$$z = (x - \mu)/\sigma = (0 - \mu)/25$$

Within the EXCEL spreadsheet

1. Select the cell in which you would like the answer to appear.
2. Click on the "Insert" pull down menu.
3. Click on "Function..." A box with several options will then appear.
4. Click on "Statistical" from the function category.
5. To the right, under "Function Name,"several statistics functions will appear. Scroll down to "NORMINV," and highlight it with a click.
6. Click "OK" in the bottom lower-right hand corner and the NORMINV screen appears, which requires three entries to return the desired value of z. Enter the left-hand tail probability of 0.084565779, a mean of 0 and standard deviation of 1. Your screen looks like Chart 6.2.

CHART 6.2 The NORMINV command for 0.084565779 = $P[x < 0 | x \sim N(\mu=??, \sigma = 25)]$

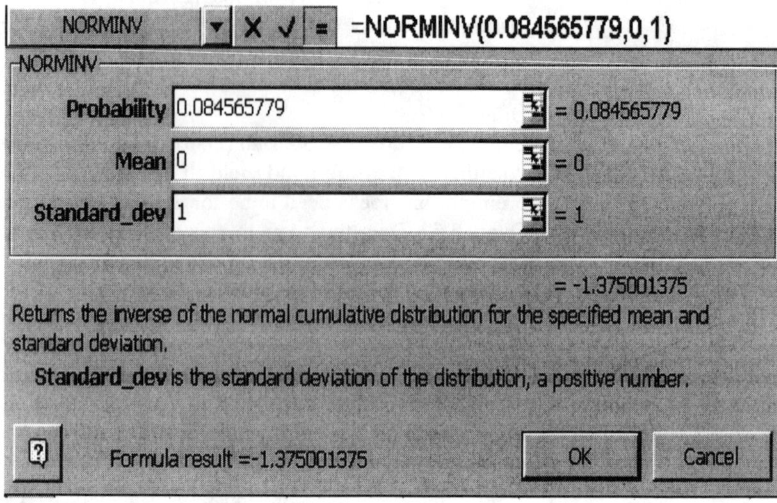

7. Clicking "OK" gives the desired value of z = -1.375.
8. Next solving for μ in the equation -1.375= (0 - μ)/25 gives μ = 34.375.

An expected return of 34.375 percent in 1955 implies an equity loss 8.457 percent of the time. Subtracting the 3 percent safe bond yield for 1955 gives a risk premium for stocks equal to 31.375 percent, which a trip to the library would confirm is not an unreasonable guess for the actual risk premium (as reported in publications by Roger Ibbotson of Ibbotson Associates). The risk premium for stocks decreased marginally from 1955 to 1995 while volatility decreased substantially from 25 to 16 percent.

6.6 CONCLUDING COMMENTS

The bell-shaped density of the normal distribution is the most widely used curve in statistics. Many variables have been shown or assumed to behave as a normal random variable. This chapter presents the properties of the normal distribution for use in a wide range of problems.

The normal distribution can be used as a way of describing the behavior of data. Although helpful in many types of problems, it does not address the central role of the normal distribution in statistical inference. It does not address how the normal distribution is used to make inferences about an unknown population based on sample observations. That is the focus of the next chapter.

CHAPTER EXERCISES

6.1 Classify the following variables as continuous or discrete:
   a. the gender of a chief executive officer
   b. the time it takes to be serviced at Sears
   c. the number of new housing starts in Tucson in June
   d. the age at which a person purchases his or her first car

6.2 State the differences and similarities between a standard normal distribution and any other normal distribution.

6.3 The random variable z is normally distributed with zero mean and variance of one. Find the following probabilities:
   a. $P(z < 2.01) =$ _____
   b. $P(z > 2.95) =$ _____
   c. $P(z > -2.05) =$ _____
   d. $P(z < -1.45) =$ _____
   e. $P(-2.03 < z < 1.06) =$ _____
   f. $P(1.04 < z < 1.99) =$ _____

6.4 The random variable z is normally distributed with zero mean and variance of one. Find the following values of b:
   a. $P(z > b) = 0.9946$
   b. $P(z < b) = 0.8186$
   c. $P(z > b) = 0.0003$
   d. $P(-b < z < b) = 0.673$
   e. $P(z < b) = 0.0228$
   f. $P(0 < z < b) = 0.1664$

6.5 The random variable x is normally distributed with mean 5.00 and standard deviation 2.00. Determine the following.
   a. $P(x < 2.00) =$ _____
   b. $P(2.00 < x < 6.4) =$ _____
   c. $P(-1.00 < x < 0) =$ _____
   d. $P(x < 6.40) =$ _____
   e. $P(x > -2.00) =$ _____
   f. $P(x > 6.23) =$ _____

6.6 The random variable Y is normally distributed with mean of 25.00 and standard deviation of 9.0. Find the following values of b:
   a. $P(y > b) = 0.0007$
   b. $P(y > b) = 0.0550$
   c. $P(y < b) = 0.9948$
   d. $P(b > y > 25) = 0.032$
   e. $P(b < y < 25) = 0.5429$
   f. $P(y < b) = 0.2123$

6.7 As director of a local welfare agency, you are responsible for the allocation of food stamps. You are to provide food stamps only to those households in the lowest 12 percent of the income distribution in your area. Although most income distributions are skewed right, your area's income distribution is approximately normal, with mean income of \$21,340 and standard deviation of 4,980. Below what income level should food stamps be provided?

6.8 From time studies, it is determined that a task should take an average of 2.05 minutes to complete, with a standard deviation of 0.4 minutes. What is the probability that a randomly selected employee will take between 1.45 minutes and 2.95 minutes? (Sketch and calculate the area, assuming completion time is normally distributed.)

6.9 A recruiting firm states that it is only interested in students from the top 5 percent of a graduating class. The average grade of the graduating class is well known to be 2.65, with a standard deviation of 0.45. Nevertheless, a student with a grade point of 3.61 applies for an interview and is turned down because the cutoff is set at 3.6265 based on the following calculation:

$$2.17 = z = (b - \mu)/\sigma = (b - 2.65)/0.45 => b = 3.6265$$

Is this calculation justified? That is, is it appropriate to assume the normal distribution? Explain.

6.10 According to a *Wall Street Journal* (April 1, 1983) article, Americans have voluntarily contributed to reducing the \$1.2 trillion public debt with checks totaling \$135,575.15. "'Nearly half of the contributions are for less than \$10,' says IRS spokeswoman Ellen Murphy, 'but a very generous soul' forwarded \$25,000." Is it reasonable to assume that the distribution of contributions to reduce the debt is normal? Why or why not?

6.11 What are the properties of normal versus binomial random variables?

6.12 "Sears Is Accused of Billing Fraud at Auto Centers" was a headline in *The Wall Street Journal* (June 12, 1992). The article reported on a year-long study by the California Department of Consumer Affairs in which "its agents were overcharged nearly 90% of the time, by an average of \$223." If the other 10% average \$25 in under charges, and if the distribution of the amount of over, under, and correct charges is normally distributed, what is the standard deviation of those charges?

6.13 Using your standard deviation estimated in Exercise 6.12, what proportion of overcharges were above \$585?

6.14 In *The Wall Street Journal* article about Sears billing fraud, "The worst example was in the San Francisco suburb of Concord, where an agent was overcharged \$585 to have the front brake pads, front and rear springs, and control arm bushings replaced." Is this consistent with the assumption of normality in Exercise 6.12 and the probability calculated in Exercise 6.13? Explain.

6.15 A soft-drink machine can be regulated so that it discharges an average of μ ounces per cup. If the ounces of fill are normally distributed with standard deviation equal to 0.3 ounces, what is the setting of μ so that 8-ounce cups will overflow only 1 percent of the time?

6.16 The achievement scores for a college entrance examination are normally distributed with a mean of 75 and a standard deviation of 10. What fraction of the scores would you expect to lie between 70 and 90?

6.17 The random variable y is normally distributed with a mean of 90 and a standard deviation of 18. How are the areas between 72 and 90 and between 90 and 108 related?

6.18 A radio manufacturer knows the length of time until a set needs servicing is normally distributed with a mean of 36 months and standard deviation of eight months. The probability that a randomly selected radio will require servicing within the first six months after purchase is approximately ________.

6.19 An article in *The Wall Street Journal* (September 2, 1992) reported on the ability and willingness of insurance companies to pay customer claims following disasters. The article stated: "Customers receive an average of 87 cents for every dollar they claim in losses." If the standard deviation is 13 cents, why is it unreasonable to assume that the amount received per dollar claimed is normally distributed?

6.20 A *Wall Street Journal* (November 11, 1992) article on the clothing sizes that retailers carry stated, "In good times retailers use a sort of bell curve of sizes, with the greatest number of items in the midrange. For an estimated 35% to 40% of women, that means sizes 6, 8, and 10." Assuming sizes are normally distributed, with a mean size of 8, what values for the standard deviation would give 35 percent to 40 percent of the distribution in the size 6 to 10 interval?

6.21 The article on clothing sizes in Exercise 6.20 continued: "For men, it's waist sizes 30–36 inches" which constitute the midrange of 35 percent to 40 percent. If men's waist sizes are normally distributed with a mean of 33, what must the magnitude of the standard deviation be so that 35 percent to 40 percent of the distribution is in the 30 to 36 interval?

6.22 A note in *The Wall Street Journal* (December 9, 1992) stated "the average American worked 81 days this year just to pay federal taxes." Assume the distribution of days worked to pay taxes is normally distributed, with a mean of 81 days and standard deviation of 10 days. What is the probability of selecting a taxpayer who worked more than 100 days to pay taxes?

6.23 According to *The Chronicle of Higher Education* (December 2, 1992), the average time in office of university presidents was seven years; 14 percent of the presidents left office within the first year of appointment. If presidential job tenure is normally distributed, what is the standard deviation of this distribution?

6.24 Using the standard deviation you calculated in Exercise 6.23 and the other information provided, what is the probability that a president stays in office more than 10 years?

6.25 A section of the *DEMOS Tutorial: An Introduction to DEMOS*, Version 3.0b2 (June 1992), which is a computer program for use in decision making states:

> Probability Density. The height of the curve at a given value along the horizontal axis denotes the relative probability that the variable has that value. (p. 15)

What is wrong with this definition of probability density?

6.26 In response to reports of needles being found in Pepsi-Cola soda cans in June 1993, Pepsi reported that tampering with cans in plants was unlikely. Pepsi officials stated that the lines run at a rate that fills 11,000 to 12,000 cans per minute, with each fill and seal taking less than eight seconds. If, on average, the line fills and seals 11,500 cans per minute, with a standard deviation of 142 cans per minute, what is the probability of randomly checking the speed of the line and finding an average line speed of 11,250 to 11,750 cans per minute? What do you have to be able to assume to calculate this probability? Is this assumption reasonable?

6.27 Members of a large church congregation are known to have yearly salaries between \$20,000 and \$330,000, with an average of \$81,240. Why would it be inappropriate to use the normal distribution to calculate the proportion who have salaries within one standard deviation of the mean?

6.28 On January 2, 1995, "TV News 8" (WISH-TV in Indianapolis) reported that a Detroit jewelry store advertised that it would give a 100 percent refund on items purchased New Years day if the January 1 snowfall was 3 inches or more, which had an approximate 0.03 probability based on historical record. If the historical record suggests an expected snowfall of 2 inches, and if snowfall is normally distributed, what is the standard deviation for Detroit snowfall on New Years day?

6.29 Based on the population parameters and probabilities in Exercise 6.28, what is the probability of getting little if any noticeable snowfall on New Years day? Using this probability calculation, explain why the assumption of a normally distributed snowfall is or is not reasonable.

6.30 In "Testing the Science of Intelligence" in *Newsweek* (October 24, 1994), Geoffrey Cowley reported that "IQ's for a whole population can be arrayed on a single graph. Roughly two-thirds of all Americans fall between 85 and 115, in the fat midsection of the bell-shaped curve, and 95 percent score between 70 and 130."

a. The author is asserting that IQ is distributed like a ________.

b. The author is asserting that IQ has a mean of ________.

c. If the author is correct, then the standard deviation of IQ is __________.

d. If a person is randomly selected from this population, what is the approximate probability that his or her IQ will be greater than 115?

6.31 The *Putnam Voyager Fund Prospectus* (November 30, 1996) reported a historic mean return of 16.67 percent, and standard deviation of 14.72 percent. If returns to this fund are normally distributed, what is the probability of getting a negative return?

ACADEMIC REFERENCE

Stigler, Stephen. *The History of Statistics: The Measurement of Uncertainty before 1900.* Cambridge: Harvard University Press, 1986.

FORMULA

- Standard normal random variable: $z = \dfrac{x - \mu}{\sigma}$

where x is a normal random variable with mean μ and the standard deviation of σ so z has a mean of zero and standard deviation of one. That is, if $x \sim N(\mu, \sigma)$, then $z \sim N(0, 1)$.

Chapter 7

Sampling and Sampling Distributions

Statistical figures referring to economic events are historical data. They tell us what happened in a nonrepeatable historical case.

Ludwig Edler von Mises
1881–1973

7.1 Introduction

The previous chapter was devoted to situations in which only one item was drawn from a population. Rewriting the introductory problems makes the single draw explicit.

- If there is an 80 percent probability that *one* randomly selected glass will have less than 20 ounces of beer, and fills are normally distributed, what is the mean fill?

- If the average job tenure of a marketing director at a law firm is 2.1 years and the probability of randomly selecting *one* director who has been in the job for a year or less is one-third, could tenure be normally distributed?

This chapter is concerned with the drawing of more than one item from a population. It is devoted to probability calculations based on the average of items in a sample. In contrast to the previous chapter, problems of the following type are considered.

- During the 1994 debate in Great Britain over legislation requiring beer glasses to accommodate a 20 ounce British pint, a government agent checked on compliance by visiting a pub at nine random times ($n = 9$), ordering a draft on each visit with the following results: 19.77, 20.10, 19.95, 19.89, 20.09, 20.08, 19.89, 19.67, and 20.01 ounces. What is the probability of a mean as low as that calculated from this sample if the pub is serving glasses of beer averaging 20 ounces?

- If the average job tenure of a marketing director at a law firm is 2.1 years, how many directors ($n = ?$) would have to be sampled for the sample mean tenure to be approximately normally distributed? Why would we want the sample mean to be normally distributed?

This chapter first describes how sampling is done and then addresses the calculation of probabilities based on multiple-item samples. By the end of this chapter, you will be able to describe simple random sampling, systematic sampling, stratified sampling, and cluster sampling. You will be able to use a random number table and a computer program to generate simple random samples. You will be able to describe and work with the sampling distribution of the sample mean and sample proportion and to use the z distribution in probability calculations.

7.2 Probability Samples

The idea of drawing samples of one or more items to make statements about the population has been used throughout this book. For example, in Chapter 5, we asked how likely was a sample with 14 out of 18 decisions for the plaintiff, if the expected count was nine out of 18 by the national norm? In calculating this probability, we acknowledged that each sample of 18 decisions could give a different count for the plaintiff. Similarly, not new to this chapter are the notions that any two randomly selected numbers need not be the same and that no two collections of randomly selected sets of numbers need have the same distribution. The fact that no single sample can be expected to be a perfect representation of its population is likewise not new.

What is introduced in this chapter is the manner in which probability is assigned to the chance of getting any given sample. The probability or likelihood of getting a sample result is introduced as the measure of "how close" the sample result is to the result expected in the population. Before attempting to calculate this probability, consideration must be given to the different ways in which sampling might give rise to mathematically defensible probabilities.

7.3 Simple Random Samples

Simple Random Sampling
A procedure in which items are drawn or selected from a population in such a way that each item (and every subset of items) in the population is equally likely to be chosen.

Simple random sampling techniques are designed to ensure that each element (and, in turn, each subgroup of elements) in a population has an equal probability of being included in the sample. With simple random sampling, if a population consists of N elements, then each and every sample of n elements (where n may equal 1, 2, 3, . . . $N - 1$) should have a probability $1/N^n$ of being selected.

From Chapters 3, 4, and 5, we know that the size of the sample n relative to the size of the population N and whether sampling is done with or without replacement are critical pieces of information if every possible subset of n items is to be assumed to have an equal probability of being selected. For a finite population of size N, the probability of selecting the first sample of size n, without replacement, is $n!(N - n)!/N!$; the probability of the second sample is $n!(N - 2n)!/(N - n)!$. Only with replacement of the items after each draw would the probability of getting n items from sample to sample remain fixed at $1/N^n$.

In the laboratory, replacement might seem possible; in actual business and economics practices, replacement is seldom possible. If, however, the population is extremely large relative to the sample size, then even though the probability of each sample in repeated sampling does not remain fixed, the changes in probability could be trivial. For instance, if $n = 30$ and $N = 30{,}000$, then for the first sample the probability of drawing 30 items is

$$n!(N - n)!/N! = 0.1307 \times 10^{-101}$$

On the second sampling,

$$n!(N - 2n)!/(N - n)! = 0.1347 \times 10^{-101}$$

using the computer program MAPLE V for calculations.

As long as N is large relative to n, whether there is or is not replacement will not be critical in the drawing of simple random samples. In practice, randomization based on the notion of fixed sampling probabilities is more a matter of degree than an absolute. As a crude rule of thumb, if the population size is at least 10 times greater than the sample size, then sampling with or without replacement should be of little consequence.

The most frequently used methods of simple random sampling are blind draws, random number tables, and random number generators within statistics programs.

Blind Draw

In cases where the elements or items in a population may be numbered easily, a blind draw may be used as a way of selecting a simple random sample. A blind draw may entail selecting cards from a shuffled deck, choosing names out of a hat, picking Bingo numbers from a revolving drum, or letting numbered ping-pong balls float or fall into a bin, as is common in many state lotteries.

In the blind-draw approach, the analyst might place the names of each of the 400 customers who entered a store contest on separate but identical cards, and then thoroughly shuffle the cards in a revolving drum. Then 10 customer cards might be blindly drawn, so that there is no reference to the information on the cards. The cards would not be replaced, since the same customer might be selected more than once, but again, since the sample is small relative to the population, this is of little concern. We do not know, however, whether this procedure will result in a sample of customers that is truly representative of the customers who shop in the store or only the customers who enter the contest.

Putting name cards, numbered ping-pong balls, or the like in a revolving drum may give the appearance of good mixing or randomizing, but the results of selection need not produce a sample that is a perfect representation of the desired population. In 1970 during the Vietnam War, the order in which birthdays were selected from a drum was used to determine the order of being taken in the military draft into the U.S. armed service. A total of 366 capsules were placed in a drum, each representing a birthday. The Selective Service director and delegates selected capsules "at random," after the drum was rotated several times.

Although the above method looked impressive on television, as pointed out by S. Fienberg (1971), the results did not produce a good representation of birthdays. Randomization suggests that among the first 183 birthdays selected, about 30 days should have been from November and December. Of the first 183 days selected, however,

November and December birthdays were overrepresented with 46 capsules. Thus, Fienberg questioned the randomness of the process.

If the capsules were put in the drum in monthly order and then not thoroughly mixed, the days from the sequential months would have tended to come up together. This would be an example of **nonsampling error** because it was a mistake that could have been avoided by spinning the drum more times to more fully mix the capsules. On the other hand, it is possible that the drum was turned enough to adequately mix the capsules but that the noncontrollable random error inherent in the sampling process produced these results. Because a nonsampling error is identifiable, however, the pure sampling error of a randomization process is in doubt.

Nonsampling Error A discrepancy between a sample value and a population parameter that might result from such things as sampling from the wrong population, improperly worded questions, or adding a column of numbers incorrectly.

The job of the analyst is to avoid nonsampling errors. Intrinsic in randomization, however, is sampling error that makes it impossible to know for sure whether a particular sample result is representative of an unknown population. Reviewing the method of sampling, and reviewing the results themselves to see if they are consistent with what would be expected from a random process, may shed light on the adequacy of the process used for randomizing. This exploration, however, will never tell you whether the sample is or is not representative of an unknown population.

Random Number Table

Because of the possibility of nonsampling error in the blind draw approach (caused by inadequate mixing, clerical errors, or even fraud), the better method for simple random sampling is to use a table of random numbers. Appendix Table C.1 (partly reproduced in Table 7.1) consists of rows and columns of five-digit random numbers. Each of the digits in the five-digit number, as well as the five-digit number itself, are random numbers because they appear with no identifiable order or pattern. Random number tables were first produced by the Rand Corporation in 1955. As discussed in the next section, random numbers can be generated by most statistical software programs for microcomputers .

To use the random number table, each item or element in the population is first given a number. To illustrate, the 1992 special bonus issue of *Business Week* lists 1,000 of "America's Most Valuable Companies," ranked and identified by the numbers one through 1,000. These 1,000 companies and their market values are reproduced in Appendix Table B.1.

To minimize the occurrence of superfluous numbers, the number of digits in the *BW* list of 1,000 companies must be renumbered 0 to 999. To select a simple random sample of 10 companies, an arbitrary starting point is now selected in the random number table by dropping a pencil on the page and taking the closest three-digit number hit by the tip (or by dropping a coin and taking the number under the coin or any like procedure).

Assume the pencil tip hits in the seventh column of grouped numbers, on the 12th five-digit number from the top. This number is 93551. Because a three-digit number (0 to 999) is desired, the first three digits of 93551 are all that is needed as a starting point. The number 935 indicates that the first company selected for the sample is actually numbered 936 on the *BW* list.

TABLE 7.1
Random Numbers and Sample of *Business Week's* Most Valuable Companies

Random Number 0–999	*Business Week* Rank 1–1,000	Company Name	Market Value $Mil.
935	936	Weingarten Realty	522
588	589	Kelly Services	1069
345	346	Blockbuster Entertainment	2215
075	76	Scecorp	8963
859	860	Cypress Semiconductor	610
896	897	Teradyne	572
771	772	Banponce	722
008	9	Bristol-Myers Squibb	41431
632	633	Hartford Steam Boiler Inspection	959
601	602	Hannaford Brothers	1029
			Sum = 58092.0
			Average = 5809.2

Any systematic plan for selecting the next nine three-digit numbers may be used as long as the plan was determined without first looking at the table. The easiest planned sequence is to read down the nine five-digit numbers. The next three-digit number is 588, indicating that the second company in the sample is 589 in the *BW* list. The remaining eight numbers are 345, 075, 859, 896, 771, 008, 632, and 601, which identify the *BW* companies numbered 346, 76, 860, 897, 772, 9, 633, and 602, as shown in Table 7.1.

If a selected sample number occurs more than once in the random number table sequence, the repeat numbers are skipped, unless sampling is with replacement. If sampling is with replacement, then each number is used in the order selected, even if it appears more than once. In the selection of the 10 companies from *BW*, sampling is without replacement because 10 separate companies are desired. In most real-world situations, it may make no sense to include the same company twice, or to repeat an interview with the same person, or test the same part more than once. Again, if the sample size is small relative to the population size, the question of whether sampling is with or without replacement should be of minor importance.

If a population size is between 100 and 999, say $N = 400$, then three-digit numbers are needed, but it is possible to get three-digit numbers from the random number table that exceed the population size. In such cases, these values are simply skipped. For instance, if $N = 400$ and the random number table calls for observation 567 to be included, then this overly large number is ignored and the next number in the random number systematic sequence is selected.

Computerized Random Number Generator

Random numbers are generated by programs that are keyed to a computer's internal clock. Typical microcomputer programs require the user to enter the sample size (10) and population size (1,000); the random generator then gives a screen display of the random numbers. For example, Table 7.2, panel a, shows the commands that are

TABLE 7.2 Random Number Generation in RESAMPLING STATS

Panel a: RESAMPLING STATS commands that generate 10 random numbers, from 1 to 1,000, and place them in a file A, which is then printed on screen.

```
GENERATE 10 1,1000 A [enter]
PRINT A [enter]
F5
```

Panel b: RESAMPLING STATS screen display of the 10 numbers generated in panel a.

```
Start execution

A = 460  90  445  735  30  578
    705   4  239  102

Successful compilation (0.2 seconds)
```

Panel c: The market values of the 10 *Business Week* companies identified in panel b.

Random Number and *Business Week* Rank 1–1,000	Company Name	Market Value $Mil.
460	Premark International	1523
90	Apple Computer	7583
445	Parker Hannifin	1592
735	Equitable Resources	772
30	Southwestern Bell	17449
578	Penn Central	1092
705	Commerce Clearing House	819
4	Wal-Mart Stores	60954
239	Ingersoll-Rand	3183
102	Allied-Signal	6769

Sum = 101736
Average = 10173.6

needed in the computer program RESAMPLING STATS to generate 10 random numbers out of 1,000; the resulting 10 observation numbers then appear as the screen printout shown in Table 7.2, panel b. The market values of the corresponding companies from *Business Week* are shown in panel c.

7.4 SYSTEMATIC SAMPLING

Systematic random sampling involves the selection of every kth element from a list of elements, starting with any randomly selected element before the kth element. Systematic sampling is a popular way of generating samples in accounting. It is typically less expensive to select every kth element than to search for the n randomly

Systematic Random Sampling
Selection of every kth element on a list of all elements in the population, starting with any randomly selected element before the kth element.

determined items. In systematic sampling, however, only the first of n items can be considered as randomly determined.

Systematic sampling is not the same as simple random sampling. With systematic sampling every element and, in turn, each subgroup of elements in the population does not have the same opportunity of being included in the sample after the first element is selected—only the starting point is randomly determined. For example, if every 100th item is selected from the *Business Week* list of 1,000 most valuable companies, then consecutively numbered companies will never be included after the first company is randomly selected. If a phone book is the source of a list, systematic sampling could be used to minimize the likelihood that relatives would be included in a sample—after the first name is selected, systematic sampling leads to a name down the alphabetized list.

Systematic sampling is convenient for populations formed by lists, stacks, or series. For example, a sample of 10 companies from the *Business Week* list is quickly obtained by selecting every 100th company (after randomly starting within the first 100 names). Table 7.3 shows this systematic sample for a random starting point of the 35th company, followed by companies 135 to 935.

Quality control analysts regularly use systematic sampling for periodic monitoring of production processes. Accountants also employ systematic sampling to check for fraudulent shipping statements, billing statements, and other financial records that follow an orderly posting. When the quantity of interest is in a continuous series or is in a rank order (as with the *Business Week* data on market value), a systematic sample gives a good estimate of the true population average.

There are situations, however, in which systematic sampling should be avoided. If the data have cyclical components, then systematic sampling may be an inappropriate method of sampling. For instance, an article in *The Wall Street Journal* (May 18, 1992) said that people are most likely to move in August. If every 12th month was selected, then the result would not give a good representation of average revenue of a moving

TABLE 7.3
Systematic Sample of *Business Week*'s Most Valuable Companies

Business Week Rank Order Number	Company Name	Market Value $Mil.
35	Boeing	15828
135	Chemical Banking	5679
235	Dow Jones	3223
335	Florida Progress	2336
435	Marriott	1630
535	National Service Industries	1257
635	Amsouth Bancorporation	958
735	Equitable Resources	772
835	Hon Industries	638
935	Delta Woodside Industries	514

Sum = 32835.0
Average = 3283.5

company for the years under study. Either revenue would be overestimated, if August was selected, or underestimated, if August was not selected as the starting month. As another example, consider the Chapter 5 Query 5.7 that presented the case of *Ultramares Corp. v. Touche.* In that case, accountants used systematic sampling, but the sample failed to turn up the pattern in the fraudulent invoices.

Many variations on systematic sampling have been designed to overcome the periodicity in data. For instance, instead of selecting only one element at a fixed interval, a group of elements may be selected at a fixed interval. This is known as block sequence sampling. Block sequence selection requires taking a group of observations that are next to each other in a series. This is systematic sampling because the group, or "blocks," are at fixed intervals in the series. As with systematic sampling, block sequence sampling gives a probability sample as long as the starting point is random. This process is not equivalent to simple random sampling, because, once the starting point is selected, the remaining elements do not have an equal chance of getting into the sample.

7.5 Stratified Sampling

When important characteristics of the population are known prior to sampling, the sampling process can be made more efficient if the population is divided into subgroups of those with common characteristics. For example, in a study of starting salaries at a college, graduates might be grouped, or stratified, by their majors. In a study of higher education costs, schools might be placed in one of two subgroups: public or private. Heterogeneous populations can always be divided into subgroups that are more homogeneous if those in the population can be identified by the characteristic. These more homogeneous subgroups are referred to as **strata.**

Strata
Subgroups of a population that share a given characteristic or are homogeneous with respect to some attribute.

The Gallup and Harris polls and other national surveys use stratification techniques to get a better representation of the population than what would be possible by simple random sampling for a given same size. For a given amount of time and money invested in sampling, more information is gleaned from using stratified samples than simple random samples. Stratified sampling is efficient. That is, the added information about characteristics of the population reduces the sample error found in simple random sampling because we have more information. This, of course, assumes that easily identifiable and correct information about population strata are available.

Proportional Stratified Sampling
A form of sampling in which items are randomly drawn from known subgroups of the population (called *strata*), where items in each subgroup have at least one shared characteristic.

If an analyst can identify strata, and knows the proportion of the population contained in these strata, then small, but highly representative, samples can be chosen by randomly drawing from each strata in accordance with the population proportions. Such sampling is sometimes called **proportional stratified random sampling.** For example, suppose the list of graduates mentioned above is classified by four majors in which 1,500 are liberal arts majors, 1,000 are business majors, 850 are education majors, and 150 are natural science majors. A proportional stratified random sample of 100 graduates would reflect these same proportions, with 43 liberal arts majors, 29 business majors, 24 education majors, and four natural science majors.

7.6 Cluster Sampling

There are many combinations of sampling and groupings that can give rise to random samples. For instance, in a marketing survey, if face-to-face communication is required for sampling and the members of a population are at distant locations, then it would be very costly to visit randomly selected persons. Instead, the sampling design might be restricted to a few randomly selected cities. Within these cities, a surveyor visits specific neighborhoods, which might be randomly selected, where they then might interview an adult from every fourth house on every sixth street. Such sampling is called **cluster sampling,** because groups or clusters of elements are first selected and then elements within a cluster are chosen.

Cluster Sampling
A form of sampling in which the population is divided into groups or clusters. These clusters are randomly selected, and elements within the selected clusters are then chosen randomly.

In cluster sampling, the idea is to form groups of diverse subjects; whereas, in stratified sampling, a group's members are supposed to be similar. In cluster sampling there is little difference between groups, while in stratified sampling differences between the groups are desired.

In addition to distance between possible subjects being an impetus for cluster sampling, it is also useful when all the members of a population cannot be individually identified. For instance, we might want to survey students at certain types of colleges on their attitudes about free enterprise. There is no single list identifying and classifying the more than 12 million students currently in U.S. higher education institutions. As discussed in Becker and Lewis (1992, pp. 3–4), however, the Carnegie Foundation for the Advancement of Teaching has classified the 3,400 accredited institutions in American Higher Education under 20 major categorical types. Colleges within a major categorical type are supposedly alike, but students within each college are different. Thus, each college within a major category is a cluster of students for which a student list could be obtained. Colleges to be sampled within a major category could be selected randomly, and then students within the selected colleges could be selected randomly to form a cluster sample for surveying attitudes.

The disadvantage of cluster sampling is that the sampling error is larger than in simple or stratified random sampling. Each step in the cluster sampling process increases sampling error. As we will learn in the next sections, however, sampling error can always be decreased by increasing the sample size.

Exercises

7.1 What alternative methods of sampling (simple random, systematic, block sequence, etc.) may be used in the following situations:
   a. to check the daily attendance record of students?
   b. to audit weekly average accounts receivable?
   c. to monitor error rates in computer chips?

7.2 How does stratification cut the cost of national surveys and increase the precision of predictions?

7.3 A graduate student is heard to say that "a good random sample is one that is a perfect representation of the population, and a bad one is one that does not." Comment on the appropriateness of this student's understanding of sampling.

7.4 In March 1991, J. D. Power & Associates mailed a six-page questionnaire to 73,000 owners of 1990 model cars. Recipients received $1 for responding. According to *Business Week* (June 10, 1991), about 23,000 of the questionnaire recipients responded. Why wouldn't these 23,000 respondents be a simple random sample of 1990 car owners?

7.5 For the hospital data set provided in the file "EX7-5.PRN," use a computer random number generator or table of random numbers to select a simple random sample of size $n = 10$, with replacement, from the 235 patients. Calculate the average wait in the emergency room for your sample.

7.6 From the data in Exercise 2.54, select a systematic sample of 10 states and calculate the mean number of farms. Now use a random number generator to select 10 states without replacement and calculate the sample mean number of farms. Which sample yielded a mean closer to the mean of all the states in Exercise 2.54?

7.7 Sampling Distribution of the Sum of Random Variables

Classical statistics is based on simple random sampling. We have seen in Figures 5.1 and 6.1 that when the size of the simple random sample is large, the distribution of the binomial random variable x, which is formed as the number of "successes" in n trials, can be approximated by the normal distribution. That is,

$$\text{if } x = x_1 + x_2 + \ldots + x_n$$

$$\text{where } x_i = 1 \text{ or } 0, \text{ with } P(x_i = 1) = \pi$$

$$\text{and } p(x_i = 0) = 1 - \pi, \text{ then}$$

$$x \to N\left[\mu = n\pi,\ \sigma = \sqrt{n\pi(1-\pi)}\right] \text{ as } n \to \infty$$

Although not emphasized in Chapters 5 and 6, this result can be explained by constructing the distribution of x from repeated sampling, where each sample is of size n. For instance, Figure 7.1 shows the code written to generate 13 samples in the computer program RESAMPLING STATS. Each of the 13 samples shown represents 32 independent and identical trials. The outcome of each trial is either a one or a zero, $x_i = 1$ or 0, where the probability of a one is 0.20 and the probability of a zero is 0.80, $P(x_i = 1) = 0.2$ and $P(x_i = 0) = 0.8$. The sum of the 32 outcomes, for each of the 13 samples, yields one of the values for x, where $x = \sum_{i=1}^{32} x_i$. As seen in the histogram for x, the distribution of x has a pattern that is bell shaped.

Increasing the number of samples from 13 to 130 and then to 1,000, as shown in Figures 7.1, 7.2, and 7.3, simply makes the bell shape more defined as an approximately symmetric and smooth curve that approximates the normal distribution. It is

FIGURE 7.1 Printout from RESAMPLING STATS for 13 Samples, Each of Size n = 32, and the Probability of Success on Each Trial is π = 0.2

```
PROGRAM: 1: REPEAT 13              (produce 13 samples)
         2: GENERATE 32 1,5 x      (sample is x, where there is a 1 in 5 chance of success on
                                   on each of 32 trials)
         3: PRINT x                (print x)
         4: COUNT x = 1 J          (sum l's in x and place count in J)
         5: SCORE J Z              (keep track of successes in each sample and place in Z)
         6: END                    (end the loop)
         7: HISTOGRAM Z            (graph histogram of number of successes per sample of
                                   size 4)
```

13 SIMPLE RANDOM SAMPLES, EACH OF SIZE n = 32, WITH CHANCE OF SUCCESS π = 0.2

```
x: 0 1 0 0 0 0 0 0 1 0 0 0 0 1 0 0 0 0 1 0 1 0 0 1 1 0 0 0 1 0 0 0    8 = x
x: 0 0 0 0 0 1 0 0 0 0 1 1 0 0 1 0 0 1 0 0 1 0 0 0 0 0 0 0 0 0 0 1    7 = x
x: 1 0 0 0 0 0 1 0 0 0 0 0 0 0 0 0 1 1 0 0 0 0 0 0 0 0 0 0 1 0 0 0    5 = x
x: 0 0 1 0 0 0 0 1 0 0 0 1 0 0 0 1 0 0 0 0 0 0 1 0 0 0 0 0 0 0 0 0    5 = x
x: 0 1 0 0 0 1 1 0 0 1 0 0 0 1 0 0 0 0 1 0 0 0 0 0 0 0 0 0 0 0 0 0    6 = x
x: 1 0 0 1 0 0 0 0 0 0 0 0 1 0 0 1 0 1 0 0 0 0 0 1 0 0 0 0 0 0 0 0    6 = x
x: 0 0 1 0 1 0 0 1 0 0 0 0 0 0 1 0 0 0 0 0 0 0 1 1 0 0 0 0 0 0 0 0    6 = x
x: 0 0 0 1 0 0 0 1 1 1 0 0 0 0 0 1 1 0 0 0 0 1 0 0 0 1 0 0 0 0 0 0    8 = x
x: 0 0 0 0 0 0 0 0 0 0 0 1 1 0 1 0 1 1 0 1 0 1 1 0 0 0 1 0 0 0 1 0   10 = x
x: 0 0 0 0 0 0 0 0 1 0 0 0 0 1 0 0 1 0 0 0 0 0 0 0 0 1 0 0 0 0 0 0    4 = x
x: 0 0 0 0 1 1 0 0 1 0 0 0 0 0 0 0 0 0 0 0 1 0 1 0 0 1 0 0 0 0 0 1    7 = x
x: 1 0 0 0 0 0 0 0 0 0 0 0 0 0 0 0 0 0 0 0 1 0 1 0 0 0 0 0 0 0 0 0    3 = x
x: 0 1 1 1 1 0 0 0 1 0 0 0 0 0 0 0 1 0 0 0 1 0 0 1 0 0 1 0 0 0 0 0    9 = x
```

```
Frequency

4 |
  |                *
2 |          *     *     *     *
  |    *     *     *     *     *     *     *     *
0 L_____________________________________________
       3     4     5     6     7     8     9    10
```

Bin Center	Freq	Pct	Cum Pct
3	1	7.7	7.7
4	1	7.7	15.4
5	2	15.4	30.8
6	3	23.1	53.8
7	2	15.4	69.2
8	2	15.4	84.6
9	1	7.7	92.3
10	1	7.7	100.0

FIGURE 7.2 Printout from RESAMPLING STATS for 130 Samples, Each of Size $n = 32$, and the Probability of Success on Each Trial is $\pi = 0.2$

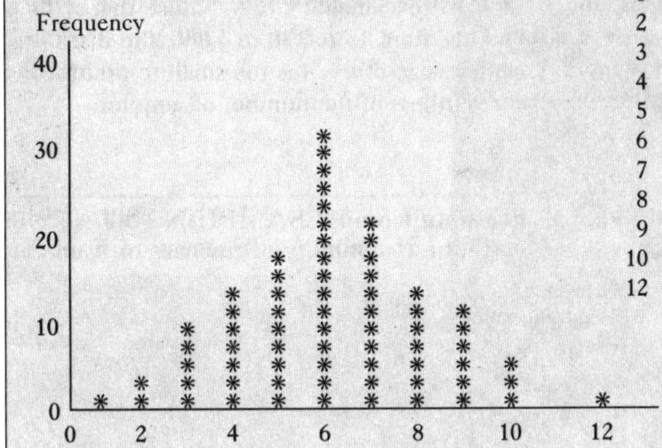

Bin Center	Freq	Pct	Cum Pct
1	1	0.8	0.8
2	3	2.3	3.1
3	10	7.7	10.8
4	14	10.8	21.5
5	17	13.1	34.6
6	32	24.6	59.2
7	22	16.9	76.2
8	13	10.0	86.2
9	11	8.5	94.6
10	5	3.8	98.5
12	2	1.5	100.0

FIGURE 7.3 Printout from RESAMPLING STATS for 1000 Samples, Each of Size $n = 32$, and the Probability of Success on Each Trial is $\pi = 0.2$

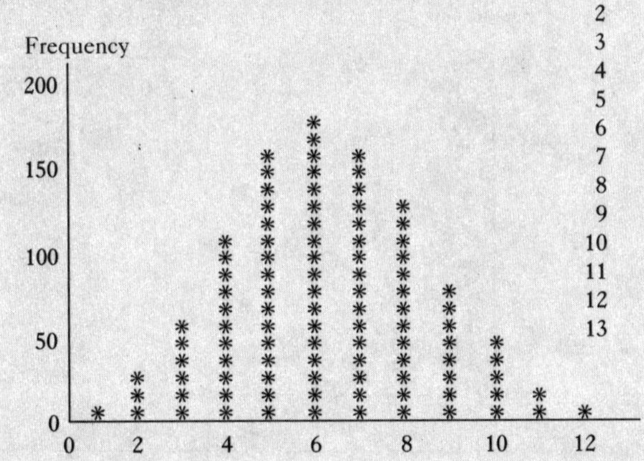

Bin Center	Freq	Pct	Cum Pct
0	1	0.1	0.1
1	5	0.5	0.6
2	27	2.7	3.3
3	62	6.2	9.5
4	108	10.8	20.3
5	163	16.3	36.6
6	180	18.0	54.6
7	160	16.0	70.6
8	127	12.7	83.3
9	83	8.3	91.6
10	48	4.8	96.4
11	22	2.2	98.6
12	10	1.0	99.6
13	4	0.4	100.0

important to recognize that it is the relatively large sample size of $n = 32$ that is producing the bell-shaped distribution for x and not the number of samples (13, 130, and 1,000). Increasing the number of simple random samples simply smooths the pattern.

To fully appreciate that the large n is producing the bell-shaped distribution of x, consider a relatively small sample of $n = 4$. Figures 7.4, 7.5, and 7.6 show the distributions generated by the RESAMPLING STATS program that correspond to Figures 7.1, 7.2, and 7.3, but with a smaller n of 4. Notice that as the number of samples, each of size $n = 4$, increases from 13 to 130 to 1,000, the distribution of x does not become bell shaped. A sample size of $n = 4$ is too small to produce the symmetric bell-shaped distribution of x, regardless of the number of samples.

FIGURE 7.4 Printout from RESAMPLING STATS for 13 Samples, Each of Size $n = 4$, and the Probability of Success on Each Trial is $\pi = 0.2$

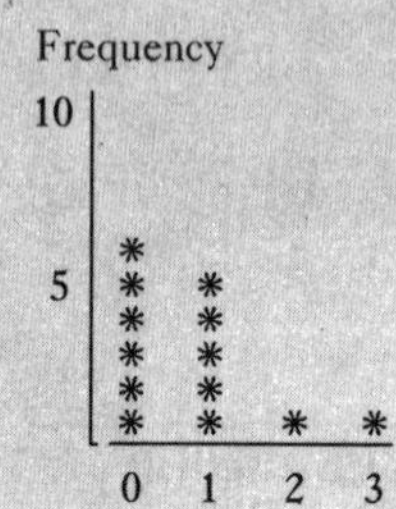

Bin Center	Freq	Pct	Cum Pct
0	6	46.2	46.2
1	5	38.5	84.6
2	1	7.7	92.3
3	1	7.7	100.0

FIGURE 7.5 Printout from RESAMPLING STATS for 130 Samples, Each of Size $n = 4$, and the Probability of Success on Each Trial is $\pi = 0.2$

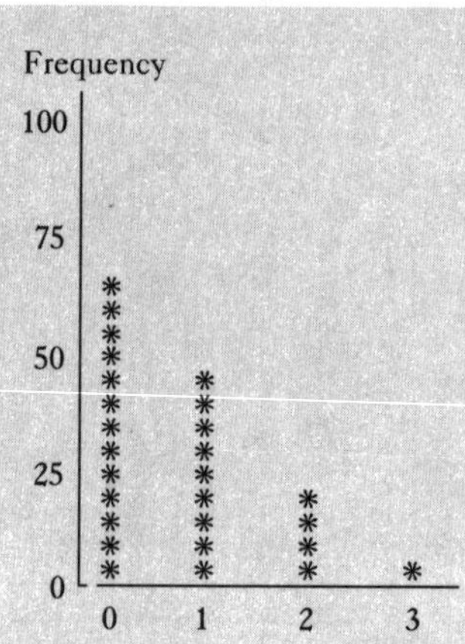

Bin Center	Freq	Pct	Cum Pct
0	64	49.2	49.2
1	43	33.1	82.3
2	20	15.4	97.7
3	3	2.3	100.0

FIGURE 7.6 Printout from RESAMPLING STATS for 1000 Samples, Each of Size n = 4, and the Probability of Success on Each Trial is π = 0.2

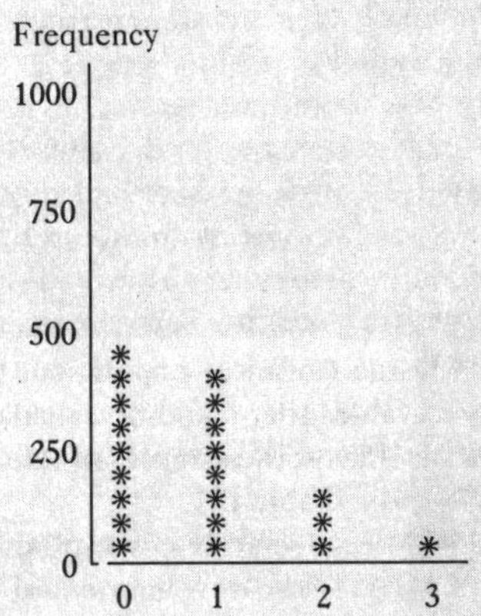

Bin Center	Freq	Pct	Cum Pct
0	428	42.8	42.8
1	392	39.2	82.0
2	152	15.2	97.2
3	28	2.8	100.0

The distributions of x, as portrayed by the patterns in the histograms in Figures 7.1 through 7.6, are called sampling distributions of x. When the shape of the sampling distribution is known, it is used as the probability density function for probability calculations associated with specific sums. As in the case of the binomial random variable, if the sample size is large, then the sampling distribution of x can be approximated by the normal distribution. As demonstrated in the next sections of this chapter, any sampling distribution representing the sum of random variables can be approximated by the normal distribution if the sample size is sufficiently large. The normality of the sampling distribution forms the basis of estimation and hypothesis testing in all the remaining chapters of this book. It is thus a most important concept.

7.8 SAMPLING DISTRIBUTION OF THE SAMPLE MEAN

Sampling Distribution of the Sample Mean, $\bar{x}$ The probability distribution of the means of all possible samples of fixed size randomly drawn from a given parent population.

In the case of sampling from populations in which the mean is of interest, the random error intrinsic to sampling causes the mean calculated from any one sample to differ from the population mean. It also causes the mean of one sample to differ from that of another. Unlike the population mean (μ), which has a specific fixed value, the mean of a sample ($\bar{x}$) is a random variable that takes on different values from sample to sample. The random variable $\bar{x}$ has a probability distribution that is called the **sampling distribution of the sample mean,** or, in its short-hand form, the distribution of $\bar{x}$.

The conceptualization of the distribution of $\bar{x}$ is the most important notion in statistics. It provides the logical foundation for estimation and hypothesis testing, as discussed in the following chapters. If you can learn to visualize the theoretical construction of the sampling distribution of the sample mean, then the statistical estimation and testing procedures introduced in the next three chapters will make sense. If you cannot grasp the difference between obtaining a specific value for $\bar{x}$, as calculated from a single simple random sample of size n, and the distribution of all the values of $\bar{x}$ that could be calculated from a large number of such samples, each of size n, then estimation and hypothesis testing may never seem reasonable.

In most real-world applications, only one sample of size n is drawn from which a sample mean is calculated—a single value of $\bar{x}$. If another sample could be drawn, however, then a different value of $\bar{x}$ most likely would be obtained. If yet another sample of size n could be selected, still another value of this sample mean might be realized. Because there are a large (infinite) number of possible samples, each of size n, that could be drawn from a large (infinite) population, theoretically there are an infinite number of sample mean values that could be calculated. To begin to visualize the resulting distribution, let us draw some samples of size $n = 20$ from the *Business Week* data on market value in Appendix Table B.1.

Samples of $n = 20$ will be selected by a sampling plan tailored to the random number table of Appendix C.1. As in the development of Table 7.1, a random starting point is selected, with the next 10 three-digit numbers taken but then a random skip is enacted, with the next 10 three-digit numbers taken to make a total of 20 random numbers. For example, building on the 10 random numbers in Table 7.1 (as reproduced in the first three lines of Table 7.4), a random skip to a new part in the random number table gives the next 10 three-digit numbers, shown in the second three lines of Table 7.4, where the associated information on firm rank and market value is taken from the *Business Week* data in Appendix B.1. The next 12 samples of size $n = 20$ were constructed in a like manner. Notice that, although the individual companies in a sample of 20 were selected without replacement, once a sample of 20 is drawn and the mean market value calculated, all 20 companies are returned to the population, so that the probability of drawing any sample of $n = 20$ remained fixed from sample to sample. This process of repeated sampling is called resampling.

The 13 sample means in Table 7.4 are summarized in a frequency distribution and represented in a histogram in Figure 7.7. Although not shown here, the population of 1,000 companies had a mean market value of 3375 million dollars and a median of 1390 million dollars. This population is highly right skewed. On the other hand, the overall mean of sample means is 3045.426 and the median of the sample means is 2958.65; this distribution of sample means is almost symmetric.

Notice also that the mean of the sample means ($\Sigma\bar{x}/13 = 3045.426$) is close to the population mean ($\mu = 3375$), with six of the 13 sample means within \$1,000 of the population mean. In addition, approximately 68 percent of the 13 observations are within plus or minus one standard deviation of the overall mean of the sample means; that is, nine means are within 3045.426 ± 1447.673, which is consistent with 8.84 (or 68 percent of 13) to be expected from the rule of normality. In summary, the mean of sample means appears to be close to the mean of the population from which samples are drawn, and the distribution of the means around the mean of sample means appears to be almost symmetric, bell shaped, and approximately normal.

Table 7.4 Thirteen Samples of Size $n = 20$ of *Business Week's* Most Valuable Companies (Market Value in Millions of Dollars)

											Mean ($\bar{x}$)
First simple random sample of size $n = 20$											
BW Rank	936	589	346	76	860	897	772	9	633	602	
Sample x	522	1069	2215	8963	610	572	722	41431	959	1029	
BW Rank	870	273	400	492	930	964	4	690	988	883	
Sample x	601	2804	1830	1425	529	498	60954	850	476	587	6432.30
Second simple random sample of size $n = 20$											
BW Rank	68	423	379	986	55	660	933	737	624	845	
Sample x	9808	1681	1965	476	10964	908	525	771	977	627	
BW Rank	462	546	26	532	933	583	811	473	964	375	
Sample x	1516	1197	20229	1261	525	1081	677	1492	498	1995	2958.65
Third simple random sample of size $n = 20$											
BW Rank	286	553	844	676	543	304	721	814	297	379	
Sample x	2680	1157	628	876	1210	2519	786	671	2573	1965	
BW Rank	968	454	790	775	594	938	300	279	187	421	
Sample x	494	1542	702	717	1046	519	2564	2763	4204	1685	1565.05
Fourth simple random sample of size $n = 20$											
BW Rank	26	428	100	549	958	303	467	88	996	294	
Sample x	20229	1664	7091	1182	505	2520	1504	8007	469	2620	
BW Rank	958	303	567	88	996	294	50	24	789	513	
Sample x	505	2520	1123	8007	469	2620	12423	21039	704	1340	4827.05
Fifth simple random sample of size $n = 20$											
BW Rank	516	536	288	950	629	627	476	152	298	969	
Sample x	1318	1248	2666	512	968	974	1482	5160	2570	493	
BW Rank	417	216	358	496	870	579	166	707	827	531	
Sample x	1715	3463	2104	1412	601	1089	4801	817	654	1266	1765.65
Sixth simple random sample of size $n = 20$											
BW Rank	531	681	849	64	898	946	345	610	330	131	
Sample x	1266	863	619	9877	570	514	2218	1012	2359	5739	
BW Rank	605	95	284	729	259	566	999	727	66	705	
Sample x	1023	7237	2701	779	2943	1126	466	783	9843	819	2637.85
Seventh simple random sample of size $n = 20$											
BW Rank	578	964	334	235	544	507	172	808	316	968	
Sample x	1092	498	2337	3223	1208	1361	4737	681	2458	494	
BW Rank	536	413	74	777	433	908	882	723	518	631	
Sample x	1248	1742	9309	715	1636	562	587	785	1314	962	1847.45

(continued)

Table 7.4 Thirteen Samples of Size $n = 20$ of *Business Week's* Most Valuable Companies (Market Value in Millions of Dollars) *(continued)*

											Mean ($\bar{x}$)
Eighth simple random sample of size $n = 20$											
BW Rank	720	270	746	561	93	337	142	564	64	486	
Sample x	789	2821	752	1132	7307	2321	5535	1130	9877	1439	
BW Rank	61	820	418	416	921	507	725	781	46	419	
Sample x	10088	665	1708	1723	543	1361	784	710	13835	1706	3311.30
Ninth simple random sample of size $n = 20$											
BW Rank	301	259	101	380	922	462	546	26	532	933	
Sample x	2547	2943	7009	1963	542	1516	1197	20229	1261	525	
BW Rank	729	259	566	990	727	66	705	20	591	302	
Sample x	779	2943	1126	474	783	9843	819	21962	1063	2540	4103.20
Tenth simple random sample of size $n = 20$											
BW Rank	862	676	510	544	213	214	531	422	596	39	
Sample x	608	876	1351	1208	3547	3530	1266	1682	1043	15619	
BW Rank	80	150	551	249	118	461	290	359	791	591	
Sample x	8715	5253	1169	3008	6043	1516	2653	2097	699	1063	3147.30
Eleventh simple random sample of size $n = 20$											
BW Rank	968	917	604	405	591	562	374	290	889	642	
Sample x	494	554	1024	1789	1063	1132	2001	2653	580	944	
BW Rank	369	713	302	592	596	520	619	919	588	258	
Sample x	2027	805	2540	1058	1043	1303	984	549	1073	2950	1328.30
Twelfth simple random sample of size $n = 20$											
BW Rank	326	679	883	669	777	664	96	451	164	675	
Sample x	2405	866	587	894	715	900	7225	1563	4809	878	
BW Rank	608	842	696	222	859	257	226	134	200	849	
Sample x	1018	629	832	3366	611	2958	3345	5701	3881	619	2190.10
Thirteenth simple random sample of size $n = 20$											
BW Rank	781	699	850	43	153	227	678	206	417	216	
Sample x	710	829	618	14308	5157	3345	868	3709	1715	3463	
BW Rank	254	207	86	54	369	713	302	592	596	520	
Sample x	2969	3688	8155	11217	2027	805	2540	1058	1043	1303	3476.35

Median of the 13 sample means = 2958.65 Mean of the 13 sample means = 3045.426

FIGURE 7.7 Frequency Distribution and Histogram for Means of 13 Samples, Each of Size $n = 20$, of *Business Week's* Most Valuable Companies (Market Value in Millions of Dollars)

Summary measures of the 13 sample means
Median = 2958.650 Mean = 3045.426 Standard Deviation = 1447.673

Frequency distribution of the 13 sample means

Sample means of market values		Frequency		Cumulative	
Lower Limit	Upper Limit	Total	Relative	Total	Relative
8.000	1600.000	2	.153846	2	.1538
1600.000	2400.000	3	.230769	5	.3846
2400.000	3200.000	3	.230769	8	.6154
3200.000	4000.000	2	.153846	10	.7692
4000.000	4800.000	1	.076923	11	.8461
4800.000	5600.000	1	.076923	12	.9231
5600.000	6433.000	1	.076923	13	1.0000

Histogram of the frequency distribution of the 13 sample means

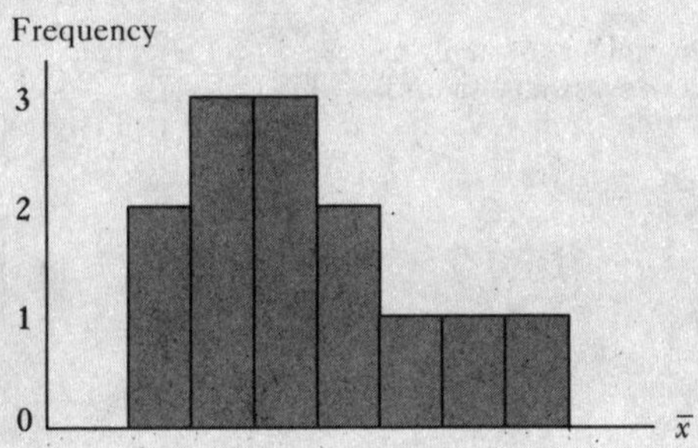

If we increased the sample size from $n = 20$ to $n = 40$, the distribution of $\bar{x}$ would become even more bell shaped and symmetric than that shown in Figure 7.7. This can be seen in the change in shape from panel a to panel b in Figure 7.8. The critical recognition here is that increasing the sample size n makes the distribution of the sample mean more bell shaped and symmetric.

If we now increase the number of samples from 13 to a larger number, where each continues to be of size $n = 40$, the distribution of $\bar{x}$ would become smoother and appear more continuous, but it would continue to appear bell shaped and symmetric. The smoothing of the distribution of $\bar{x}$ is shown by the movement from panels b to d in Figure 7.8. Remember, it was the increase in the sample size from $n = 20$ to $n = 40$ that made the distribution of $\bar{x}$ more symmetric and bell shaped. Increasing the number of

Figure 7.8 Sampling Distribution of the Sample Mean

Panel a: Histogram for 13 sample means, where each sample size is $n = 20$

Panel b: Histogram for 13 sample means, where each sample size is $n = 40$

Panel c: Histogram for 96 sample means, where each sample size is $n = 40$

Panel d: Approximate normal density for a large (infinite) number of sample means, where each sample size is $n = 40$

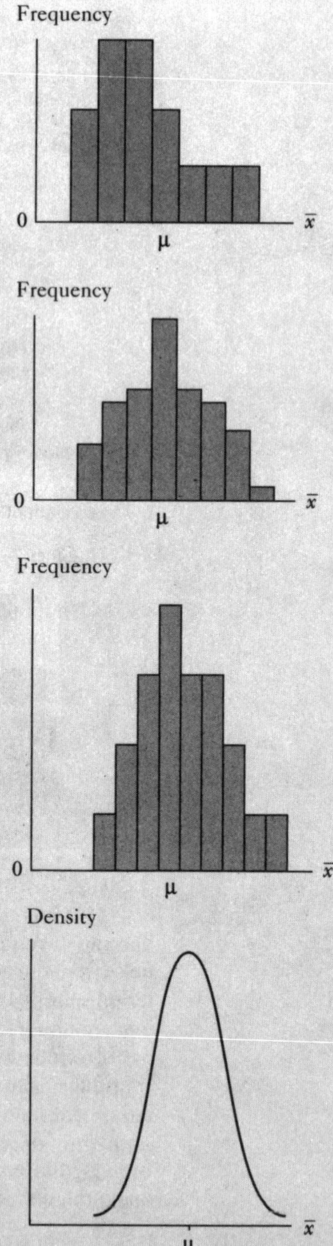

samples only smoothed the distribution of the sample mean. In what follows, we will always assume that, at least theoretically, an infinite number of sample means can be calculated from an infinite number of samples where each sample is of size n.

Possibly the most important theorem in statistics is the Central Limit Theorem. In the case of the sample mean, it says that as the sample size n increases (as from $n = 20$ to $n = 40$) the distribution of the infinite $\bar{x}$ values that theoretically could be calculated with resampling will take on the symmetric and bell shape of the normal distribution. More precisely,

Central Limit Theorem (for sample mean $\bar{x}$)

If $x_1, x_2, x_3, \ldots x_n$ is a simple random sample of n elements from a large (infinite) population, with mean μ and standard deviation σ, then the distribution of $\bar{x}$ takes on the bell-shaped distribution of a normal random variable as n increases and the distribution of the ratio

$$\frac{\bar{x} - \mu}{\sigma/\sqrt{n}}$$

approaches the standard normal distribution as n goes to infinity.

The precise statement of the Central Limit Theorem is based on an infinite number of simple random samples, each of size n, so that the expected value of the sample mean, $E(\bar{x})$ is equal to the population mean μ. This *does not* say that any one sample mean is the population mean. It says that the overall average of an extremely large (infinite) number of $\bar{x}$'s is equal to the population mean. That is, if we could continue to resample as in Table 7.4 and Figure 7.7, and calculate the overall mean of all the $\bar{x}$'s from these samples, then that overall mean would eventually equal the population mean.

Notice in Table 7.4 and Figure 7.7, that with only 13 samples, each of size $n = 20$, we are already close to the population mean as reported in *Business Week*. The sampling distribution of $\bar{x}$ is based on an infinite number of samples, each of which is of size n. As a rule of thumb, n should be at least 30 to invoke the Central Limit Theorem to establish the shape of the distribution of $\bar{x}$. That is, each of an infinite number of samples must be at least of size $n = 30$ to assert that the sampling distribution of their means is approximately normal.

Finally, the Central Limit Theorem requires that the population variable x has a fixed standard deviation σ so that the sampling distribution of the sample mean $\bar{x}$ can have a standard deviation of $\sigma_{\bar{x}} = \sigma/\sqrt{n}$.[1] Other names statisticians give to this standard deviation of the sample mean are the **standard error of the mean** or **standard deviation of $\bar{x}$,** which is calculated by dividing the standard deviation of the population σ by the square root of the sample size $\sqrt{n}$; i.e., $\sigma_{\bar{x}} = \sigma/\sqrt{n}$. The ratio $\sigma/\sqrt{n}$ is a measure of the sampling error. It is a measure of dispersion of the sample means around their expected value $E(\bar{x})$. As the sample size n increases, the distribution of $\bar{x}$ collapses on the point at which $E(\bar{x}) = \mu$, because $\sigma/\sqrt{n}$ decreases as n increases. This is portrayed in Figure 7.9 as a movement from a sample size of $n = 30$, in panel a, to $n = 120$, in panel d.

FIGURE 7.9 The Effect of Increasing the Sample Size on the Distribution of the Sample Mean

Panel a: Approximate normal density for a large (infinite) number of sample means, where each sample size is $n = 30$

Panel b: Approximate normal density for a large (infinite) number of sample means, where each sample size is $n = 60$

Panel c: Approximate normal density for a large (infinite) number of sample means, where each sample size is $n = 90$

Panel d: Approximate normal density for a large (infinite) number of sample means, where each sample size is $n = 120$

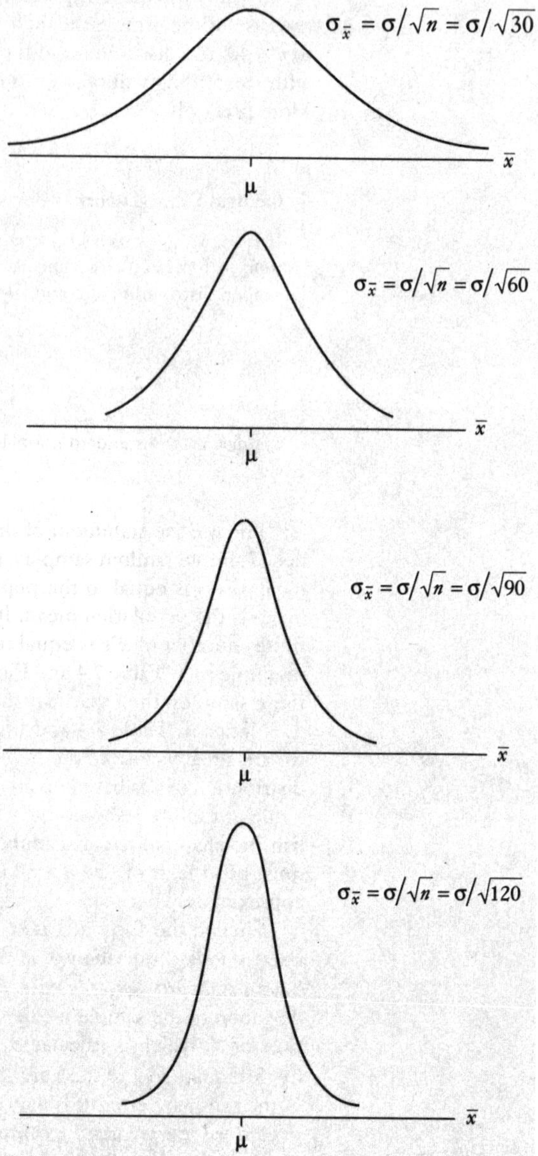

Historical Perspective

In statistics, as in all walks of life, credit is not always given to the right person. That is, even in the history of statistical thought, errors have not been eliminated.

Abraham De Moivre (1667–1754) invented the normal distribution, and Thomas Simpson (1710–1761) opened the door for its use in practice problems. The great German scientist Carl Friedrich Gauss (1777–1855), however, gets credit for its development in the context of the Central Limit Theorem and its role as the most important error distribution in statistics. But Gauss was not the originator of the Central Limit Theorem. (As discussed in later chapters of this book, Gauss's contribution was the application of the normal distribution to least-squares.)

Pierre Simon Laplace (1749–1827) formulated the Central Limit Theorem in 1810. Laplace extended the work of De Moivre and Simpson to a major generalization: Most any random variable formed by a sum (such as a mean) will be approximately normally distributed, if the number of terms in the sum is large. From the early formulation of the Central Limit Theorem, there was confusion about the sum to which it applies and the use to which it might be put.

To this day, it is common to hear students say: "As the sample size gets large, *its* distribution becomes normal." But to what does the pronoun "its" refer? The distribution of a sample obviously will approach that of the population from which it is drawn as the sample size increases. If the population is normal, then the sample will approach the normal distribution as the sample size increases. If the population is not normal, then the sample will not approach the normal distribution as the sample size increases. The Central Limit Theorem, however, does not apply to the distribution of the sample; it pertains to the distribution of all the sample means that could be calculated from an infinite number of samples where each sample is of size n.

In the nineteenth century, "curve fitting" and the finding of "normality in nature" and the characteristic of the "average man" were popular, but this had little to do with the implications of the Central Limit Theorem. As discussed in Chapter 2, for example, Adolphe Quetelet (1797–1874) made his early reputation by applying a form of cluster sampling in a failed attempt to make probabilistic statements about the population. He never made the connection between the mean of one simple random sample and the distribution of means from all such samples.

Quetelet had not been educated in statistics, but he finally learned the errors in his ways and then discarded all notions of sampling and probability analysis in favor of a complete census. Although he was an extremely productive scholar, he never fully grasped the difference between (1) simple random sampling and the use of the Central Limit Theorem and (2) his nonrandom sampling techniques and his inability to make mathematically defensible probabilistic statements from such samples. Gauss and Laplace made the Central Limit Theorem operational as a mathematical concept for assessing uncertainty through probability and making an inference about a parameter of a large population from a single simple random sample.

Exercises

7.7 If the population standard deviation is $25 and the sample size is 25, then the standard error of the mean is __________.

7.8 If the sample size increases by a multiple of four, then the standard error of the mean ________ by a multiple of ________.

7.9 The average yearly salary of retail store managers in a particular city is known to be \$22,000, with a standard deviation of \$120. A random sample of 100 store managers reveals a sample average salary of \$23,000 and sample standard deviation of \$122. From this information, what is the distribution of the sample mean and what is its mean and standard deviation?

7.10 Writing in the *British Medical Journal* (March 15, 1986), Martin Gardner and Douglas Altman state:

> The distinction between two widely quoted statistics—the standard deviation and the standard error—is, however, often misunderstood. The standard deviation is a measure of the variability between individuals in the level of the factor being investigated, such as blood alcohol concentrated in a sample of car drivers, and is thus a descriptive index. By contrast, the standard error is a measure of the uncertainty in a sample statistic. For example, the standard error of the mean indicates the uncertainty of the mean blood alcohol concentration among the sample of drivers as an estimate of the mean value among the population of all car drivers (p. 748).

Comment on the correctness of this quote.

7.11 A court case, *Cuomo et al. v. Baldrige: 2629,* was brought by New York State and others to require the U.S. Census Bureau to adjust the 1980 Census numbers for alleged undercounting. In 1987, Judge Sprizzo ruled against New York. At one point in the trial, J Sprizzo said, "I take it your standard error should be a fixed statistical number which you then subtract from your results and you get what is left, basically which is supposed to measure the accuracy of what you are measuring?" The witness (David Freedman), responded, "I hate to argue with you, but it isn't quite like that." Explain the problem with the judge's understanding of the standard error and its relationship to accuracy.

7.12 An article in *Newsweek* on "The Science of Polling" (September 28, 1992) implied that the standard error of estimation varies inversely with the sample size, but increasing the sample size does not result in proportional reductions in the standard error. Is this correct? Explain.

7.13 Sherlock Holmes, in A.C. Doyle's *The Sign of the Four* (1890), said: "You can, for example, never foretell what any one man or woman will do, but you can say with precision what an average number will be up to." How does this quote relate to the notion of precision in statistics and the sampling distribution of the mean?

7.9 Sampling Distribution of the Sample Mean for Large Samples

By the Central Limit Theorem, the distribution of $\bar{x}$ is approximately normal and the ratio

$$z = \frac{\bar{x} - \mu}{\sigma/\sqrt{n}}$$

is an approximate standard normal random variable, where

1. the population variable x can have most any distribution provided it has a fixed mean, $E(x) = \mu$, and variance σ^2
2. the sample size n is large ($n \geq 30$), and
3. the distribution of $\bar{x}$ has $E(\bar{x}) = \mu$ and $Var(\bar{x}) = \sigma^2/n$

The development of the Central Limit Theorem from Table 7.4 and Figure 7.7 was unusual because the population mean was known and we were able to resample with replacement. Typically the value of the population mean is something under study, and only one simple random sample of size n is available. As long as n is sufficiently large, however, the Central Limit Theorem tells us that the sampling distribution of the mean will be approximately normally distributed. Only one sample is needed to make probability calculations.

The Central Limit Theorem enables us to calculate probabilities associated with the sample mean. For instance, an article (*HT* May 26, 1992) on the use of hot rod Ford Mustangs and Chevrolet Camaros by Indiana State Police quoted an officer as saying, "It is not uncommon for the average daily speed of people stopped to be 83 miles an hour." If a sample of 36 vehicles stopped on a given day shows a mean speed of 83 miles per hour, what is the probability of observing this or a higher sample mean speed if the overall mean speed of vehicles stopped is 65 miles per hour, assuming a population standard deviation of 12 mph?

Because the sample size is large ($n = 36$), and assuming it was based on simple random sampling techniques, the $\bar{x}$ distribution is approximately normal and the z ratio is close to the standard normal. Thus, from the information provided we have

$$z = \frac{\bar{x} - \mu}{\sigma/\sqrt{n}} = \frac{83 - 65}{12/\sqrt{36}} = 9.0$$

The mean of the $\bar{x}$ distribution is the same as the mean of the population. If the population mean is 65 miles per hour, then the mean of all possible sample means must also equal 65; that is, $E(\bar{x}) = \mu = 65$. The standard deviation of the sampling distribution of all the possible $\bar{x}$ values is $\sigma_{\bar{x}} = \sigma/\sqrt{n} = 12/\sqrt{36} = 2.0$. Thus, $z = 9.0$ indicates that the sample mean of 83 miles per hour is nine standard deviations above the expected sample mean of 65 miles per hour, as shown in Figure 7.10.

The highest z value given in Appendix Table A.3 is for 3.49, for which only 0.0002 of the values are higher. To be practical, we treat the probability of observing values nine standard deviations above the mean as zero because the probability is minute. If vehicles stopped by the state police were averaging 65 mph, it is next to impossible that a simple random sample of 36 vehicles would be observed averaging 83 miles per hour. Observing this 83 mile per hour average is thus extremely strong evidence that vehicles stopped by the state police are not averaging 65 miles per hour, Figure 7.10. (More tests of this type are done with the sampling distribution of $\bar{x}$ in Chapter 9.)

FIGURE 7.10 Probabilities of Vehicle Speed

Step 1: The desired probability

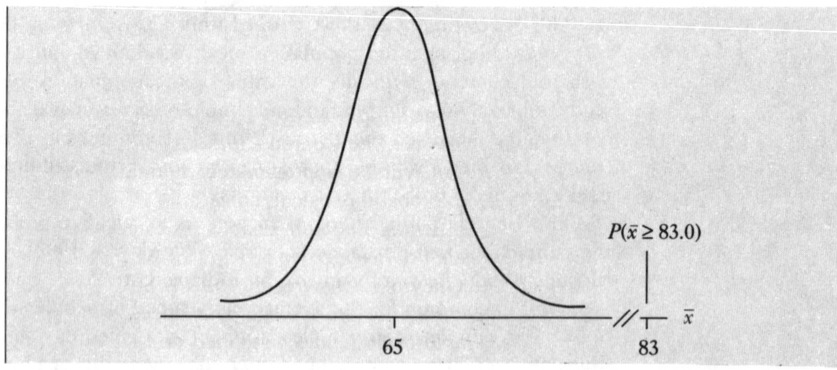

Step 2: Areas obtained using Appendix Table A.3 or EXCEL command "=NORMSDIST (3.49)"
Unhatched area is $P(z < 3.49) = 0.9998$

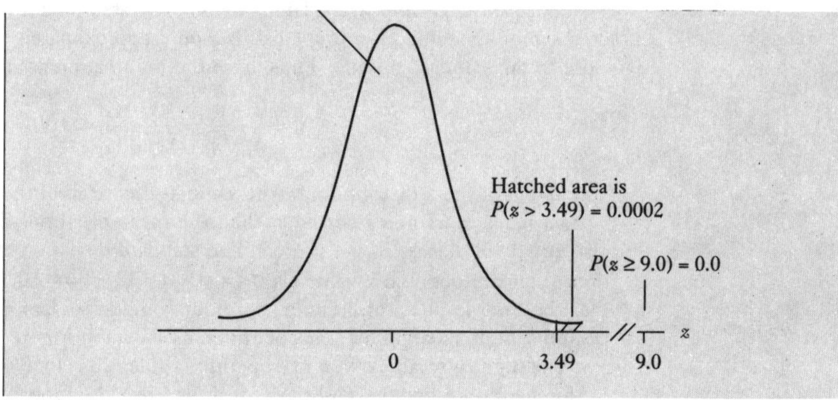

QUERY 7.1:
If the length of time required to complete an examination is normally distributed, with a mean of 65 minutes and a standard deviation of 15 minutes, then what is the sample mean time for which 99 percent of the samples of 60 test takers would have a smaller mean completion time?

ANSWER:
The population mean is 65 minutes, so the mean of all possible sample means must also equal 65 minutes; that is, $E(\bar{x}) = \mu = 65$. The standard deviation of the sampling distribution of all the possible $\bar{x}$ values is $\sigma_{\bar{x}} = \sigma/\sqrt{n} = 15/\sqrt{60} = 1.9365$. We also

know that the $\bar{x}$ value for which we are looking puts 99 percent of the distribution below it. As shown in the diagram below, the z value that puts 99 percent of the distribution below it is 2.33. Thus, we know that $\bar{x}$ value we want is 2.33 standard deviation above the mean, or

$$z = \frac{\bar{x} - \mu}{\sigma/\sqrt{n}} = \frac{\bar{x} - 65}{1.9365} = 2.33$$

from which we can solve for $\bar{x}$ as

$$\bar{x} - 65 = (1.9365)(2.33) = 4.512$$

$$\bar{x} = 65 + 4.512 = 69.512$$

The 99 percent of the samples of 60 test takers will yield a mean of 69.512 minutes or less to complete the test.

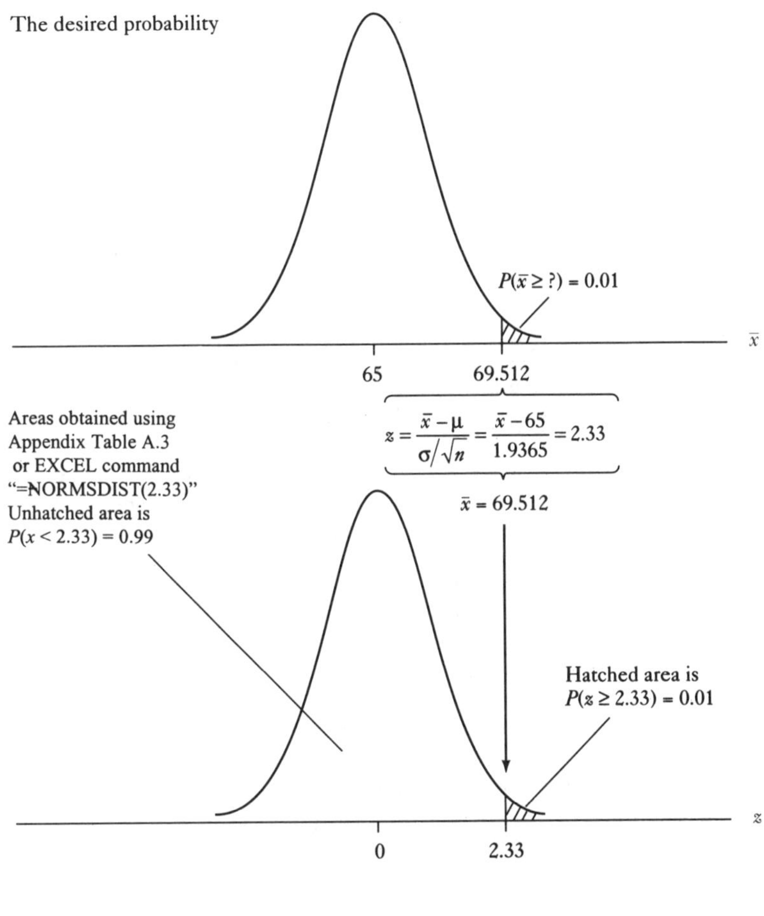

7.10 Sampling Distribution of the Sample Mean for Small Samples

The question to be asked here is what is the shape of the sampling distribution of the sample mean if the sample size n is relatively small ($n < 30$)? To answer this question, notice that the z formula used to standardize x in the previous chapter is a special case of the more general z formula for standardizing $\bar{x}$. This can be seen by setting $n = 1$

$$z = \frac{\bar{x} - \mu}{\sigma_{\bar{x}}} = \frac{\bar{x} - \mu}{\sigma/\sqrt{n}} = \frac{\bar{x} - \mu}{\sigma/\sqrt{1}} = \frac{x - \mu}{\sigma}$$

For $n = 1$, the mean of the sample is the value of the single element selected, so $\bar{x} = x$.

To make probability calculations with z in Chapter 6, where $n = 1$, we had to first establish that the population x was normally distributed. The same is true here when $n = 1$ because $x = \bar{x}$. Clearly, for $n = 1$, if x is normally distributed, then $\bar{x}$ is normally distributed. If x is normally distributed, then $\bar{x}$ must also be normally distributed for $n = 2, 3, 4$, and so on, since increasing the sample size does not make the sampling distribution of the sample mean "less normal." As long as x is normally distributed, $\bar{x}$ will be normally distributed, regardless of the sample size.[2]

Query 7.2:
If the average job tenure of a marketing director at a law firm is 2.1 years, how many directors would have to be sampled for the sample average tenure to be approximately normally distributed?

Answer:
Query 6.4 in the previous chapter addressed a question about the normality of job tenure of marketing directors and concluded that job tenure could not be normally distributed and that it was right skewed. Thus, the only way that samples drawn from this population distribution could give rise to a sampling distribution of sample means that is approximately normally distributed would be if the samples were large enough to involve the Central Limit Theorem. As a rule of thumb, the Central Limit Theorem should become operational if the sample size n is at least 30. This general rule of thumb, however, holds only if the population is not extremely skewed. If the population of job tenure is highly skewed right, then a sample larger than 30 may be needed for the sampling distribution of the sample mean to be approximately normal.

Query 7.3:
A press release (December 21, 1991) reported on a new regulation in Great Britain that requires bigger beer glasses that can accommodate a full 20-ounce British pint and a creamy head; brewers and pub landlords are to be fined for selling less. To test

for compliance, an agent visits a pub at nine random times, ordering a draft on each visit with these results:

19.77, 20.10, 19.95, 19.89, 20.09, 20.08, 19.89, 19.67, and 20.01 ounces.

What is the probability of a mean as small as that calculated from this sample if the pub is serving glasses of beer with a mean of 20 ounces?

ANSWER:
Although this query did not provide information on the dispersion in the population, from Chapter 6 we know that experienced bartenders would produce the population fill that is normal, with a standard deviation σ of 0.15 ounces. The sample average is calculated as

$$\bar{x} = \sum_{i=1}^{9} x_i / 9 = \begin{pmatrix} 19.77 + 20.10 + 19.95 + 19.89 + 20.09 \\ +20.08 + 19.89 + 19.67 + 20.01 \end{pmatrix} / 9 = 19.9389$$

Thus the z ratio is

$$z = \frac{\bar{x} - \mu}{\sigma_{\bar{x}}} = \frac{\bar{x} - \mu}{\sigma/\sqrt{n}} = \frac{19.9389 - 20}{0.15/\sqrt{9}} = -1.22$$

The sample average fill of 19.9389 ounces is 1.22 standard deviations less than the expected average fill of 20 ounces, as portrayed in the diagram below. The probability of observing a sample of $n = 9$ with a mean of 19.9389 or less if the actual population average fill is 20 ounces is determined using

$$P(\bar{x} < 19.9389 | \mu = 20, \sigma = 0.15) = P(z < -1.22)$$
$$= P(z > 1.22) = 1 - P(z < 1.22)$$
$$= 1 - 0.8888 = 0.1112$$

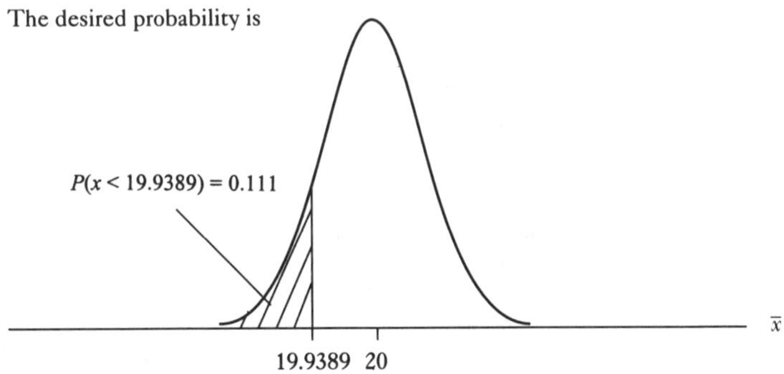

which may be obtained directly with the EXCEL function command "NORMDIST (19.9389, 20, 0.05, 1)" or with the standard normal as

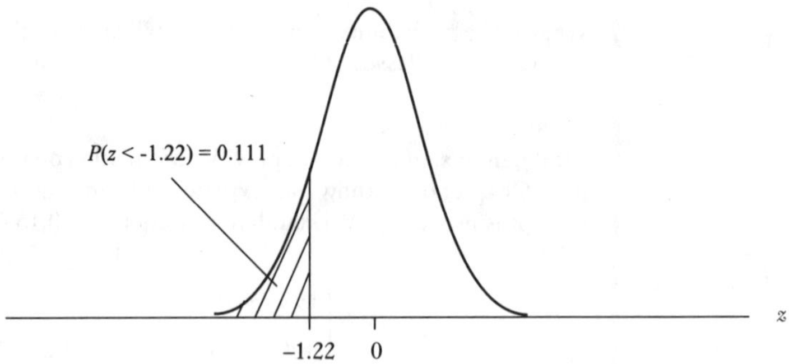

where "=NORMSDIST(-1.22)" is entered, into EXCEL.

Something that occurs with a probability of 11.1 percent is not that unusual. So even though this sample gave an average fill of less than 20 ounces, it is possible that in the population the average fill is 20 ounces. The difference could result from the random error inherent in sampling.

EXERCISES

7.14 What is required to assert that the sampling distribution of the sample mean is approximately normally distributed?

7.15 Are the following statements true or false? Why?

a. The population mean is equal to a sample mean.

b. The population mean is equal to the sample mean if and only if the sample size exceeds 30.

c. The population mean is equal to the mean of all sample means, if sampling is random.

d. The variance of the mean is the same as the variance of x.

e. The variance of the distribution of the mean is s^2.

f. The variance of the distribution of the mean is σ_x^2/n.

7.16 A bakery sells an average of 24 loaves of bread per day. Sales (x) are normally distributed with a standard deviation of four.

a. If a random sample of size $n = 1$ (day) is selected, what is the probability this x value will exceed 28?

b. If a random sample of size $n = 4$ (days) is selected, what is the probability that $\bar{x}$ will exceed 28?

c. Why does the answer in part a differ from that in part b?

7.17 The state police believe that the average speed of trucks exceeds the 55 mph speed limit. A random sample of 100 trucks shows a mean speed of 61.8 mph. What is the probability of observing a sample average speed of 61.8 mph or more if the population average speed is 55 mph, assuming a population standard deviation is six mph?

7.18 Kathryn Walker and William Gauger, in "Time and Its Dollar Value in Household Work" (*Family Economic Review*, Fall 1973), report that "time spent on household work by husbands averages about 1.5 hours per day . . . ." A small sample of four families showed an average of 1.25 hours per day spent by the husband in household work. The question is: What is the probability of observing a sample average of 1.25 hours or less if the true population average is 1.5 hours, with a standard deviation of 0.4 hours? In your answer to this question, what did you assume about the population of time in household work and the distribution of the mean time? What did you have to assume about the sample of four families?

7.19 A given type of TV set can be expected to be service free for 36 months, with a standard deviation of six months. The distribution of required service is also known to be normally distributed. If four televisions of this type are purchased, the probability that the average service-free period will exceed two years for this random sample of four sets is approximately ________.

7.20 It is known that students graduating from a certain large university have a mean grade point average of 2.80, with a standard deviation of 0.80, and that all complete the same number of credits for graduation. Furthermore, it is known that these grade-point averages are not normally distributed. If a sample of 36 students is selected, what is the approximate probability that the mean grade point average is at least 2.60?

7.11 Sampling Distribution of the Sample Proportion

The sample proportion $p = x/n$ is a type of sample mean; it is the average number of "successes" in a sample of size n, where $x = \Sigma x_i$ and $P(x_i = 1) = \pi$ and $P(x_i = 0) = 1 - \pi$. Like $\bar{x}$, the sample proportion p varies from sample to sample. The shape of the sampling distribution of p can be determined by the Central Limit Theorem.

Central Limit Theorem (for sample proportion p)
If $x_1, x_2, x_3, \ldots x_n$ is a simple random sample of n elements from a binomial population, with a proportion of success π, then the distribution of $p = \Sigma x_i/n$ takes on the bell-shaped distribution of a normal random variable as n increases and the distribution of the ratio

$$\frac{p - \pi}{\sqrt{\pi(1-\pi)/n}}$$

approaches the standard normal distribution as n goes to infinity.

Because p is just a sample mean, its expected value in simple random sample is π, the population proportion.[3] The standard error of p (standard deviation of p) likewise can be shown to be $\sqrt{\pi(1-\pi)/n}$.

Although the sample proportion $p = x/n$ can be treated as a mean in applying the Central Limit Theorem, there is no accurate way of getting normality on p for small samples, since p's numerator x is a binomial random variable. As first shown in Figure 5.1, and recast here as a sampling distribution in Figures 7.4, 7.5, and 7.6, when the sample size n is small, the binomial random variable x does not approach the normal; it only approaches the normal for large sample sizes. When n is small, probability calculations are best done with x and the binomial distribution itself.

QUERY 7.4:

During the Indianapolis 500 time trials, TV Channel 13 in Indianapolis telecast a show called "Speed Quest." (May 23, 1993) The show was devoted to the new role of microcomputers in auto racing. The announcer stated that IBM supplied computers to all but a few of the competitors because it believed that 60 percent of racing fans are prospective computer purchasers. For a simple random sample of 30 racing fans, what is the probability that 15 or fewer would be prospective computer purchasers if IBM is correct in its belief that the true proportion is 60 percent?

ANSWER:

This sample is sufficiently large to invoke the Central Limit Theorem and assume that the sampling distribution of the sample proportion (p) of fans who are prospective computer purchasers is approximately normal. The mean of the sampling distribution of p is $E(p) = \pi = 0.60$, if IBM is correct, and the standard error of p is

$$\sigma_p = \sqrt{\pi(1-\pi)/n} = \sqrt{(.6)(.4)/30} = 0.0894427$$

The probability of p less than or equal to 0.50 ($p = x/n = 15/30$) is now calculated as

$$P(p < .5 \mid \pi = .6,\ n = 30) = P\left(z < \frac{0.5 - 0.6}{0.0894427}\right) = P\left(z < -1.12\right) = 0.1314$$

This probability calculation is shown graphically as the hatched area in the sampling distribution of p.

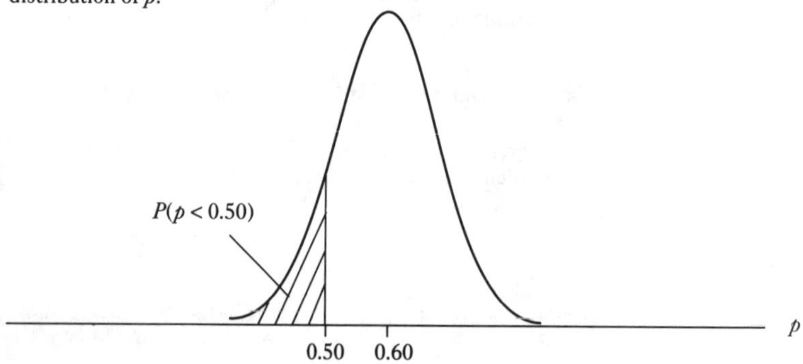

In the standard normal distribution this area is

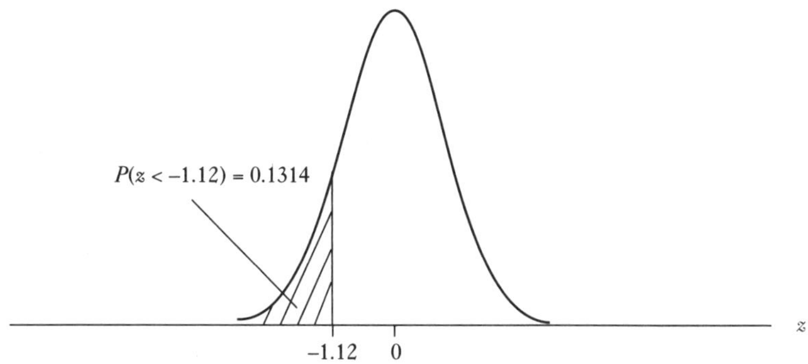

This probability of 0.1314 is obtained from EXCEL by entering the function command "=NORMSDIST(-1.12)" into any cell.

EXERCISES

7.21 What is required to assert that the sampling distribution of the sample proportion is approximately normally distributed?

7.22 Are the following statements true or false? Why?

a. The population proportion is equal to a sample proportion.
b. The population proportion is equal to the sample proportion if and only if the sample size exceeds 30.
c. The population proportion is equal to the mean of all sample proportions, if sampling is random.
d. The variance of the sample proportion is the same as the variance x.
e. The variance of the distribution of the proportion is s^2/n.
f. The variance of the distribution of the proportion is $\pi(1 - \pi)/n$.

7.23 According to a survey of 111 CPA firms, conducted by Professor David Doran of Pennsylvania State University, 18 percent wrongly thought they were shielded from disclosure to the IRS, as clients' talks with lawyers are privileged. (*Wall Street Journal,* May 26, 1993) If most (50 percent) CPA firms think they have such privileges, when they do not, what is the probability of getting 18 percent or fewer in a simple random sample of 111 CPA firms saying they do? Draw the sampling distribution of the sample proportion and label all points of interest.

7.24 In her nationally syndicated column, Ann Landers stated, "Your story (on poor nursing care) is a chilling one . . . (however) I would say at least 90 percent of the nurses are compassionate and caring. Too bad you ran into a few who were not." (*HT,* May 28, 1993) If the true proportion of compassionate and caring nurses is 90 percent, for 40 randomly selected nurses what is the probability that 34 or fewer will be compassionate and caring?

a. using the binomial distribution?
b. using the standard normal approximation?

7.25 A note in *The Wall Street Journal* (December 9, 1992) stated, "One year ago, 37 of 42 economists surveyed by *The Wall Street Journal* predicted a tax cut in 1992—and 36 of 42 predicted President Bush would be re-elected." Of course, neither of these events took place. Is this evidence that the distribution of the sample proportion was not normally distributed? Discuss.

7.12 Concluding Comments

The idea of a sampling distribution for the sample mean is possibly the most important concept in classical statistics. The sample mean is approximately normally distributed if the sample size is large (regardless of the shape of the population from which samples are drawn). This distribution will also be normal (regardless of the sample size) if the population is normally distributed.

The normality of the sampling distribution of the sample mean must first be established before the standard normal distribution can be used to calculate the probabilities involving the sample mean. In addition, these probability calculations will require that the population mean, standard deviation, and sample size are known. When these parameters of the population are not known, estimation techniques must be employed. Estimation is the subject of the next chapter in this book.

Chapter Exercises

7.26 In Chapter 9, reference is made to the attempts of Bloomington (Indiana) Hospital to assess employee satisfaction. In 1991, Bloomington Hospital hired a consulting firm to survey 35 of 1,700 employees. The 35 employees were hand picked by division managers to determine whether or not employees were satisfied (and would or would not want to unionize). Why can't these 35 employees be considered a simple random sample of the 1,700 employees?

7.27 Why won't increasing the sample size necessarily reduce nonsampling error while it will reduce sampling error?

7.28 A random sample of size n people has been drawn from a population distributed around a mean weight of 320 pounds with a population standard deviation of 60 pounds.

a. If $n = 144$, the sample average will be distributed with a mean and a standard deviation of approximately what?

b. With what approximate probability will the average weight for the 144 people lie beyond 335 pounds?

c. If the sample size had been 36 rather than 144, what would have been the standard deviation for the sampling distribution of the average weight?

7.29 In the early days of microcomputers, hard disk drives had a mean time between failures (MTBF) of 5,000 to 20,000 hours. Today, drives should last 20,000 to 40,000 hours, making disk drive failure rare in the first several years of service. If the average time between failures for a new type of drive is 40,000 hours, with standard deviation of 5,000 hours, what is the probability that a sample of 10 drives will have a mean time between failures of less than 35,000 hours? less than 30,000 hours? less than 25,000 hours? less than 20,000 hours? Why don't these probabilities fall off in the same proportion as the hours?

7.30 A production process turns out washers with an inside average diameter of 0.25 inches and a standard deviation of 0.00001 inches. Every half hour, a lot of 16 washers is checked. The latest sample had a mean of 0.25007 inches. Approximately how likely is it to observe this sample mean or one larger if the population average diameter is in control producing washers that average 0.25? In order to calculate this probability, what needs to be assumed?

7.31 Sheet steel is produced to automobile company specifications that call for an average thickness of 0.20 inches, with a standard deviation of 0.021 inches. A random sample of 25 different locations on a roll of steel showed a mean width of 0.191 inches. Past steel shipments have had normally distributed thicknesses. If the entire roll actually averages 0.20 inches, how likely is a sample average of 0.191, or less?

7.32 The amount of beer in a bottle is normally distributed with a mean of 11.7 ounces, and a standard deviation of 0.40 ounces. An independent research firm takes a sample of 16 bottles and finds the value of the sample mean, which it fails to report. If the probability of getting a sample mean $\bar{x}$ less than the unreported sample mean is 0.025, what is the value of the unreported sample mean?

7.33 Chuck Stone, in his Newspaper Enterprise Association syndicated column (*HT*, September 5, 1992) wrote: "Increases of one or two points are monumentally insignificant because the SAT's standard error of measurement is 18 points." If this standard error is correct, what is the probability of the average SAT score rising by one or more points from its previous mean?

7.34 An article in *The Wall Street Journal* (August 31, 1989) reported on the release of U.S. government statistics that later have to be revised substantially. The article mentioned that one widely reported series of statistics that measures the monthly change in sales of new homes showed a huge 5.5 percent increase, but a footnote stated that two standard errors were equal to approximately nine percentage points. What does this imply about the likelihood that sales decreased?

7.35 A *Wall Street Journal* (November 11, 1992) article on the clothing sizes that retailers carry stated, "In good times retailers use a sort of bell curve of sizes, with the greatest number of items in the midrange. For an estimated 35% to 40% of women, that means sizes 6, 8 and 10." If the average population size is 8, what are the limits on the implied standard error of the mean for a sample of size 4, if in the population 35 to 40 percent of the distribution is in the size 6 to 10 interval? Why is it reasonable to assume that the sampling distribution of the mean is normally distributed?

7.36 *The Wall Street Journal* (November 11, 1992) article on the clothing sizes referenced in Exercise 7.35 also stated that "For men, it's waist sizes 30–36 inches," which constitutes the midrange of 35 percent to 40 percent. If the population average men's waist size is 33, what are the limits on the implied standard error of the mean for a sample of size 4, if 35 to 40 percent of the population distribution is in the 30 to 36 interval?

7.37 A *Wall Street Journal* (August 14, 1987) article reported that "IBM samples 50 circuit boards out of every 270-board lot; if one is defective, every board in the lot is rejected." Why is this a demanding standard?

7.38 A Lanier TV advertisement on CNN (April 20, 1993) stated, "Lanier copiers are up and running 98 percent of the time." On thirty randomly selected days, the operating status of a Lanier copier is checked; it is found to be "up and running" 29 times. Why wouldn't it be appropriate to calculate the probability of getting a sample of 30, containing 96.67 percent or less "successes," by assuming that $p = x/n$ is normally distributed, with mean of 98 percent? How should this probability be calculated?

7.39 Chapter 5 investigated the correctness of the article "Why Investors Shouldn't Listen to Economists." *WSJ* (January 22, 1993) The article reported that "only five of 34 economists who participated in 10 or more surveys managed to guess correctly which way long-term bond yields were going more than half of the time." We found that the probability of five individuals each predicting six or more yield movements correctly, where each flipped a coin 10 times, was 0.0023. Now use the normal approximation, where appropriate, to find the probability of 14.7059 percent or fewer of the 34 individuals predicting six or more yield movements correctly by each flipping a coin 10 times.

7.40 Below are data on the differences between claimed and actual miles of New England ski areas from "Resort Ads Caught Snowing the Ski Set" (*Wall Street Journal*, December 22, 1992). Calculate the mean difference between claimed and actual miles. What is the probability of at least this mean difference if the true population mean difference is zero, assuming the population is normally distributed with standard deviation of two miles?

Ski Area	Actual Miles of Trails	Miles Claimed by Resort	Claimed Less Actual
Killington	70	77	7
Sugarbush	46	53	7
Sunday River	29	36	7
Sugarloaf	36	45	9
Okemo	25	32	7
Smuggler's Notch	22	32	10

7.41 In Exercise 7.40, if an area owner questioned whether this was a representative sample and a legitimate test, how would you respond?

7.42 In June 1993, there were reports of needles in Pepsi-Cola soda cans. Pepsi reported that tampering with cans in plants was unlikely, because the lines run at a rate that fills 11,000 to 12,000 cans per minute, with each fill and seal taking less than eight seconds. If, on average, the line fills and seals 11,500 cans per minute, with a standard deviation of 142 cans per minute, what is the probability of randomly checking the speed of the line

a. once and finding a line speed of 11,250 or fewer cans per minute? What do you have to assume to calculate this probability? Is this assumption reasonable?

b. on 36 different occasions and finding a mean line speed of 11,250 or fewer cans per minute? What do you have to assume to calculate this probability?

7.43 During World War II many economists, mathematicians, and statisticians were members of Columbia University's Statistics Research Group, which did high-level consulting work for the armed services. As part of this group's work, statistician Abraham Wald was asked where to place armor on planes. It seemed obvious to the aircraft engineers that armor was needed at the places most frequently hit, as found in a large sample of battle-proven airplanes. After studying the bullet holds of a sample of returning planes, Wald's conclusion was to place the armor where bullet holds were least frequently found in these planes. What was wrong with the aircraft engineers' sampling design? What did they overlook?

Academic References

Becker, W., and D. Lewis. (eds.) *The Economics of American Higher Education.* Boston: Kluwer Academic Publishers, 1992.

Fienberg, S. "Randomization and Social Affairs: The 1970 Draft Lottery." *Science,* January 22, 1971.

Endnotes

1. For the variance of $\bar{x}$, we need to determine $E[\bar{x} - E(\bar{x})]^2$
For simple random samples we know that $E(\bar{x}) = \mu$. Thus, $E[\bar{x} - E(\bar{x})]^2 = E(\bar{x} - \mu)^2$, which can be expanded as

$$E(\bar{x}-\mu)^2 = E\left[n^{-1}\sum_{i=1}^{n}(x_i-\mu)\right]^2 = n^{-2}E\left[\sum_{i=1}^{n}(x_i-\mu)\right]^2$$

$$= n^{-2}E\left[\sum_{i=1}^{n}(x_i-\mu)^2 + \sum_{\substack{i=1\\ i\neq j}}^{n}\sum_{j=1}^{n}(x_i-\mu)(x_j-\mu)\right]$$

$$= n^{-2}\left[\sum_{i=1}^{n}E(x_i-\mu)^2 + \sum_{i=1}^{n}\sum_{j=1}^{n}E(x_i-\mu)(x_j-\mu)\right]$$

$$= n^{-2}\left(n\sigma^2\right)$$

$$= \sigma^2/n$$

(The variance of x: $E(x_i-\mu)^2$. As long as x's are independent, the expected value of a crossproduct is zero.)

We now know that $E(\bar{x} - \mu)^2$ is σ^2/n. That is, the variance of the sampling distribution of the sample mean is the population variance divided by n.

2. The normal density function for the sample mean with $n = 2$, for example, is

$$f(\bar{x}) = \frac{e^{-\left[(x_1+x_2)/2-\mu\right]^2/\sigma^2}}{\sigma\sqrt{2\pi}}$$

where $x \sim N(\mu, \sigma)$, and x_1 and x_2 are random variables formed by independent and identical draws from x. The expected value of the sum of the two random variables,

$(x_1/2) + (x_2/2)$, is $E[(x_1/2) + (x_2/2)] = (\mu/2) + (\mu/2) = \mu$

For the variance of $\bar{x}$, we need to determine the variance of the sum of the two random variables $(x_1/2)$ and $(x_2/2)$. From Chapter 4,

$$\text{Var}[(x_1/2) + (x_2/2)] = (1/2)^2\text{Var}(x_1) + (1/2)^2\text{Var}(x_2) + 2(1/2)(1/2)\text{Cov}(x_1x_2)$$

If values of x_1 and x_2 are drawn independently from the same distribution (simple random sampling), then $\text{Cov}(x_1x_2) = 0$

$$\text{and } \text{Var}[(x_1/2) + (x_2/2)] = (1/4)\text{Var}(x_1) + (1/4)\text{Var}(x_2)$$
$$= (1/4)\sigma^2 + (1/4)\sigma^2 = \sigma^2/2$$

Thus, $\bar{x} \sim N(\mu, \sigma/\sqrt{2})$, for $n = 2$, and similarly for $n = 3, 4 \ldots$ to the most general large sample case, as shown in the first endnote of this chapter.

3. The expected value of a binomial random variable x is

$$E(x) = n\pi$$

which upon dividing through by n yields

$$E(x/n) = n\pi/n = \pi$$

Thus, $E(p) = \pi$

The variance of a binomial random variable x is

$$E[x - E(x)]^2 = n\pi(1 - \pi)$$

which upon dividing through by n^2 yields

$$E[(x/n) - E(x/n)]^2 = n\pi(1 - \pi)/n^2 = \pi(1 - \pi)/n$$

Thus, $E(p - \pi)^2 = \pi(1 - \pi)/n$

FORMULAS

- Formula for transforming the normal random variable $\bar{x}$ to a standard normal random variable z

$$z = \frac{\bar{x} - \mu}{\sigma/\sqrt{n}} = \frac{\bar{x} - \mu}{\sigma_{\bar{x}}}$$

where the population random variable x has a mean of μ and a standard deviation of σ, and the sample mean $\bar{x}$ has a mean of μ and a standard deviation of $\sigma_{\bar{x}} = \sigma/\sqrt{n}$.

- Formula for transforming the normal random variable p to a standard normal random variable z

$$z = \frac{p - \pi}{\sqrt{\pi(1 - \pi)/n}}$$

where $x_1, x_2, x_3, \ldots x_n$ is a simple random sample of n elements from a binomial population, with a proportion of success π, and $p = \sum x_i/n$

Appendix 7 Avoiding Errors in Sampling

Sampling Error
The discrepancy between a sample value and the population parameter resulting from the drawing of only a subset from the population.

The essence of statistics is making inferences about a population using a sample. A statistical analysis must be concerned with error, because even if a perfect experiment could be conducted, some samples will not perfectly represent the population from which they are drawn. The chance element inherent in simple random sampling is called experimental error or **sampling error** or random error.

Although sampling error cannot be avoided, increasing the sample size will reduce its magnitude, as shown in this chapter. There are errors, however, that are not affected by sample size. These systematic and persistent errors are known as nonsampling errors or bias. The Chapter 1 discussion of Griliches's argument that diminishing returns may not exist in inventiveness, even though the sample data of Figure 1.2 suggest otherwise, is an analysis of nonsampling error that was caused by the exclusion of less profitable small firms from the sampling process. Other nonsampling errors may result from invalid and unreliable measurement instruments, measurement errors, and errors due to omitted or missing observations.

Validity

Validity
The degree to which a survey instrument measures what it purports to measure.

In surveys, errors caused by lack of **validity** are a form of nonsampling error that may result because a respondent does not understand the question. For example, the U.S. Bureau of Labor Statistics has found that poorly defined questions aimed at establishing a person's work status might be misunderstood. Retired persons might classify themselves as "unemployed" in a survey.

Another error of validity may occur if the respondent does not know the information with certainty. In completing a dental questionnaire, for example, a respondent might not remember the exact date of the last check-up and thus record the wrong date. David Mingay, a cognitive psychologist at the National Center for Health Statistics warns in *Business Week* (February 17, 1987) that, "Most of us just don't have a good internal calendar for dating events."

Problems of validity make it difficult or impossible to interpret results. For example, from personal correspondence with *Business Week*, the author learned that the respondent percentages in Appendix Table 7.1 were to a questionnaire given to participants at a conference of executives of smaller enterprises. They were asked for yearly compensation to the approximate values indicated; the respondents only had the option of choosing among the seven alternatives provided.

But how did an executive who makes $950,000.01 respond when confronted with compensation options "$900,000" or "$1,000,000 or more"? If he/she thinks "$1,000,000 or more," then would he or she have expected the class bound in a frequency distribution to have been "$950,000 or more" and not "$1,000,000 or more." Alternatively, he/she may think that $900,000 is closer to his/her $950,000.01 compensation than is the "or more" portion of the "$1,000,000 or more" option and thus select the $900,000 option. Similarly, at the lower end, an executive making $149,999.99 may say that the "$200,000" option is closer to his/her compensation than the midpoint ($50,000) or the lower limit (zero) in the "$100,000 or less" option.

APPENDIX TABLE 7.1 What the Boss Makes at the Up-and-Comers

A new survey of 235 small and midsize companies, most with annual sales of $2 million to $50 million, sheds some light on the boss's paycheck.

Approximate Annual Compensation (salary and bonus)	Respondents (percent)
$ 100,000 or less	40 %
200,000	39
300,000	9
400,000	6
500,000	3
900,000	1
1,000,000 or more	1
No Answer	1

Source: *Business Week,* June 27, 1992, p. 76.

The possible confusion regarding the interpretation of responses at the extremes makes this survey invalid. Given that 79 percent of the responses were in the two lowest options, the issue of validity is not trivial.

Reliability

Closely tied to the need for valid data collection instruments is the need for reliable instruments. Reliable surveys are ones that give stable results.

Reliability
The degree to which a survey instrument yields stable results.

There are generally two types of **reliability** that researchers consider. Reliability over time implies that the respondents would respond the same if asked the same questions at another time. For example, a response that is preferred on one day is still preferred on another. Internal reliability pertains to the degree of similarity between the manner in which each question on a survey characterizes responders and the way in which the entire survey does. For example, one multiple-choice question on a 20-question exam is said to be reliable if those who received high scores on the exam also tended to get that one question correct. Internal reliability also implies that if on one question a respondent says A is preferred to B which in turn is preferred to C, then on another like question the respondent does not reverse this order.

Chapter 8

Estimation

What good are analytical skills if the information you're analyzing is skimpy or misleading?

Tom Peters
September 14, 1994

8.1 INTRODUCTION

We have already learned that random variables have probability distributions from which data are assumed to be generated. As will be seen, both the observed sample data and the assumed probability distribution enable us to 1) estimate population parameters, 2) test specific parameter values, and 3) make predictions. Estimation is discussed in this chapter; later chapters address testing and prediction. Here we consider problems of the following types.

- An Associated Press release (*HT*, February 5, 1992) stated that "A majority of adults surveyed in Japan complained of fatigue and emotional stress . . . 53 percent said they felt somewhat tired . . . and stressed. . . ." According to the news release, the survey was based on a random sample of 3,000 people over the age of 20, but "the poll did not give a margin of error." Of what value is this estimate?
- In the survey of Japanese workers, it was also found that "the average Japanese employee worked 2,044 hours, including 185 hours of overtime, in fiscal 1990, which ended March 31, 1991, the equivalent of 51 40-hour weeks a year." Again the article stated that no margin of error was given for inferences about the total Japanese population.
- A recruiting firm's survey of 64 "highly mobile" executives shows that the average raise received by these executives was \$25,320, with a standard deviation of \$5,429. From this, the recruiting firm concluded that a 95 percent interval estimate for the mean raise received by all such executives ranges from \$23,990 to \$26,650.
- An article in *PCWEEK* (February 11, 1991) reports on a study of the number of PCs shipped that failed in the first year after installation. In a sample of 47 Compaq computers, 17 percent failed in the first year. The question: With 95 percent confidence, what proportion of all Compaq computers would you expect to fail within the first year?
- An article in *The Wall Street Journal* (June 20, 1991) stated: "According to Wall Street lore, a headquarters move tends to be an ominous sign. If a company is 'spending a lot of money on a trophy headquarters, it's a negative indicator' for the stock, says Charles Biderman, editor of the newsletter *Market Trim Tabs.*" The *WSJ* did a "minisurvey" of the stock prices of 10 companies that moved between 1986 and the end of 1988: five stocks beat the market and five underperformed. To do a better job of estimating the effect of moving, what size sample is needed?

Sample Statistic
A function of the observations in a sample that does not depend upon any unknown parameter.

Statistical inference in examples such as these requires the construction of mathematical models that represent the populations from which the observed data are thought to originate. Chapters 5 and 6 dealt with some common population distributions from which data are often generated. Estimation of the parameters of these probability distributions as incorporated in statistical models requires the calculation of sample statistics. A **sample statistic** is a formula or rule by which a value is obtained as a descriptive measure of the sample. If the sample statistic is then used as a predictor of a population parameter, it is called an estimator of the parameter.

For a specific sample, a statistic has one value. Across all possible samples, however, the statistic may take an infinite number of values; the likelihood of any given value is determined by a probability distribution. That is, a statistic is a random variable. From the Central Limit Theorem (Chapter 7), we know that statistic $\bar{x}$ (which is determined by the rule $\bar{x} = \Sigma x_i/n$, where x_i is the ith observed value in a sample of size n) is approximately normally distributed for large sample sizes. Similarly, the statistic p (which is the sample proportion $p = x/n$, where x is the number of successes in a sample of size n) is approximately normally distributed for large sample sizes.

Point Estimate
The single value, calculated from sample data, used to infer a parameter (characteristic) of the population from which the sample data are assumed to be generated.

In the case involving the survey of Japanese workers, the sample proportion (p = 0.53) is used to estimate the population proportion (π) of the Japanese workers feeling tired or stressed. In the second case involving Japanese workers, the sample mean ($\bar{x}$= 2,044) is the statistic used to estimate the population mean (μ) hours worked per year. The specific numerical values p = 0.53 and $\bar{x}$ = 2,044 are called the **point estimates** of the respective parameters π and μ. A point estimate is the single value, calculated from a specific sample statistic (the estimator) that is used to predict the population parameter of interest.

Interval Estimate
A range or set of values, calculated from sample data, that is used to infer a parameter (characteristic) of the population from which the sample data are drawn.

The chance factor inherent in sampling makes it unlikely that a point estimate for any given sample will exactly equal the parameter value being estimated. It is unlikely, for example, that 53 percent of Japanese workers feel tired or stressed. To capture this uncertainty, a range of values may be calculated as the estimate of a population parameter. A specific range of values is called an **interval estimate.** For example, the recruiting firm's prediction that highly mobile executives are getting raises between \$23,990 and \$26,650 is an interval estimate of the true population average raise. When interval estimates are associated with specific confidence levels, they are called **confidence intervals.**

Confidence Interval
An interval that, with stated probability, includes a parameter value.

By the end of this chapter, you will be able to calculate and use the point and interval estimates for the population parameters μ and π. You also will be able to approximate an interval estimate for the population median, if you complete the optional sections at the end of this chapter. You will be able to use the idea of an interval estimator to determine the sample size needed for statistical inferences involving either a population mean or a population proportion.

8.2 Point Estimation

A point estimate is a single numerical value that is calculated from a sample and used to make an inference about a population parameter. In the example of pay raises for mobile executives, the sample average of \$25,320 is a point estimate of the population mean raise. Similarly, 53 percent is a point estimate of the population proportion of Japanese workers who feel tired and stressed. In both examples, however, had different samples been drawn, different values of $\bar{x}$ and p would likely have resulted and, thus, different estimates of μ and π would have been obtained.

The actual value that is calculated from sample data as an estimate of a population parameter is the outcome of the sampling process. This value is the realization of a

Point Estimator
A formula applied to sample data and used to infer the value of a population parameter.

statistic (or random variable) that represents all the estimated values that could be calculated from a large number of samples, each of size n. This statistic is called the **point estimator,** and the observed value is called the point estimate. The following five point estimators are considered in this chapter:

1. the sample mean ($\bar{x}$), which is a point estimator of the population mean (μ)
2. the sample proportion (p), which is a point estimator of the population proportion (π)
3. the sample variance (s^2), which is a point estimator of the population variance (σ^2)
4. the sample standard deviation (s), which is a point estimator of the population standard deviation (σ)
5. the sample median, which is a point estimator of the population median.

Remember that a point estimator is a statistic and that every statistic is a random variable having its own probability distribution. The point estimate is the realization of the point estimator.

8.3 Properties of Estimators

Although we would like an estimator that always yields the exact value of the population parameter of interest, the chance factors in sampling make this impossible. At a minimum, it seems reasonable that an estimator should have an expected value equal to the population parameter estimated and have minimal dispersion around that mean value. Estimators with these two properties are said to be "unbiased" and "efficient."

Unbiasedness
The property of any estimator whose expected value equals the population parameter being estimated.

Unbiasedness says that the mean of the estimator is the value of the population parameter being estimated. Unbiasedness does not say that any one estimate will equal the population parameter. The sample mean ($\bar{x}$) is an unbiased estimator of the population mean μ, if simple random samples are drawn, where each sample is of size n. Another way to say this is that the expected value of $\bar{x}$ equals μ or simply $E(\bar{x}) = \mu$.[1] Recognize that unbiasedness says nothing about the outcome of one sample of size n. For an infinitely large population, an infinite number of samples of size n can be drawn and an infinite number of $\bar{x}$ values can be calculated. It is the mean of all these $\bar{x}$ values that equals the population mean.

In the case of the mobile executive pay raises, $\bar{x}$ is the estimator of the population mean (μ) raise for all such executives; the point estimate is $\bar{x} = \$25,320$ for our one sample. If many (infinite) samples of size $n = 64$ could be selected, then the average of all these sample means would equal the population mean. The point estimate \$25,320, however, need not equal the population mean. It is but one value that $\bar{x}$ may realize; only the expected value or mean of $\bar{x}$ is equal to μ.

The sample mean is an unbiased estimator of the population mean. The sample median is an unbiased estimator of the population median. The sample proportion is an unbiased estimator of the population proportion. But not all sample statistics are unbiased estimators of their population counterparts. For example, the population variance is

$$\sigma^2 = (1/N)\Sigma(x - \mu)^2$$

which suggests the formula $(1/n)\Sigma(x - \bar{x})^2$ as its estimator. The formula $(1/n)\Sigma(x - \bar{x})^2$, however, is a biased estimator of σ^2. (Recall that once a value for a sample mean is determined, only $n - 1$ of the observations can be treated as free to vary.) For this reason, the sample variance is calculated by the formula[2]

$$s^2 = [1/(n - 1)]\Sigma(x - \bar{x})^2$$

The sample variance s^2 is an **unbiased** estimator of the population variance σ^2; the average of all possible values of s^2 equals σ^2. The sample variance for the mobile manager pay raises is $s^2 = (\$5{,}429)^2$, but notice that since the variance is in squared units of measurement, the sample standard deviation ($s = \$5{,}429$) is reported. Again $5,429 is not necessarily equal to the population's standard deviation; it is only an estimate. Different samples would give different estimates. Only the expected value (mean) of s^2 is equal to the population variance σ^2.

If the value of the population mean is known, then bias could be measured as the difference between the expected value of the estimator and the population mean. But if the population mean is known, we would not need to estimate it. Typically, we have no way of measuring biasedness; it is a theoretical concept.

Every estimator has some dispersion around its expected value. The "best" estimators will not only be unbiased but will also have minimal variability. To appreciate this idea, consider the analogy of two guns used during the American Revolution. Englishmen equipped with smooth bored muskets were able to shoot 100 yards, but with a three-foot side error (six-foot range) for five out of 10 shot accuracy. Colonials with Pennsylvania flintlock 58-inch grooved barrel rifles could sharp shoot (with little side error for nine out of 10 shot accuracy) at well over 100 yards. A soldier equipped with either of these guns can be viewed as an estimator or finder of a target. Both sets of armed soldiers were accurate (unbiased), in the sense that on average they could hit a target at 100 yards. The colonials armed with Pennsylvania rifles were more "precise" or **efficient**, in the sense that their average shots had less dispersion. In statistics, one estimator is said to be more efficient (or more precise) than another if its variance is smaller than the other.

Efficiency
The property of an estimator whose variance is smaller than that of any other estimator using the same sample size.

As introduced and discussed in the previous chapter, the sample mean $\bar{x}$, has a variance of σ^2/n, where σ^2 is the variance of the population from which samples of size n are drawn.[3] The standard deviation of the estimator is obtained by taking the square root of the variance, $\sigma/\sqrt{n}$. The standard deviation of the estimator is called the **standard error.** The standard deviation of the estimator $\bar{x}$ should not be confused with the standard deviation of the sample. The standard deviation of the sample is

Standard Error of an Estimator
The standard deviation of the estimator.

$$s = \sqrt{\left[1/(n-1)\right]\Sigma\left(x - \bar{x}\right)^2}$$

which reflects variability in a sample around the sample's mean $\bar{x}$. The standard deviation or standard error of $\bar{x}$ is

$$\sigma_{\bar{x}} = \sigma/\sqrt{n}$$

FIGURE 8.1 The Population and Sampling Distribution of $\bar{x}$

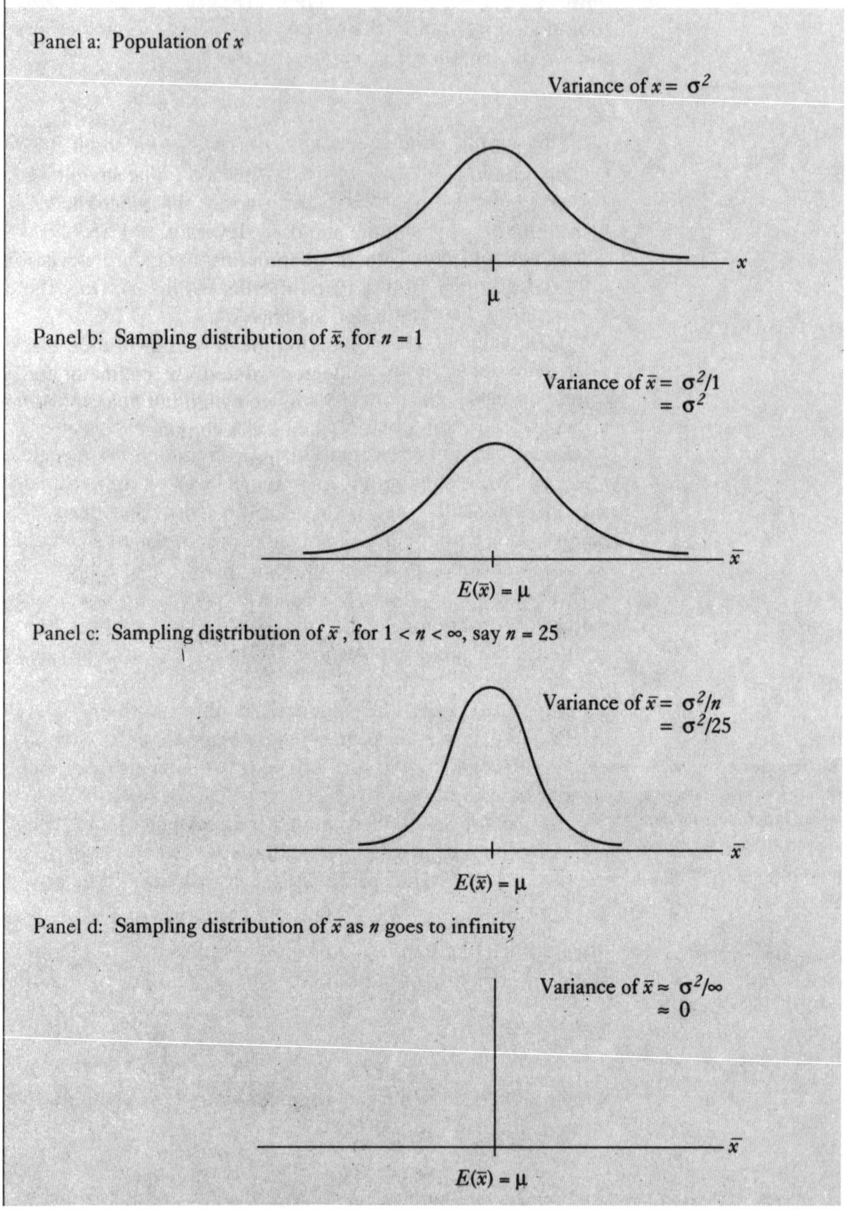

The standard error of $\bar{x}$ measures variability in the $\bar{x}$'s around their expected value $E(\bar{x})$. Although s is an estimator of σ, and thus can be used in the estimation of the standard error of $\bar{x}$ (as $s/\sqrt{n}$), it should not be confused with σ or $\sigma/\sqrt{n}$.

Along with its mean and standard error, every estimator has a probability distribution that determines its values. This distribution, which is called the sampling distribution of the estimator, is determined by the model. For instance, if the population of x is normal, with mean μ and variance σ^2, then the sampling distribution of $\bar{x}$ is also normal but its variance is σ^2/n, where again n is the sample size. Under these assumptions, the model for $\bar{x}$ is

$$\bar{x} \sim N\left(\mu, \sigma/\sqrt{n}\right)$$

which says that $\bar{x}$ is distributed normally with mean μ and standard deviation (standard error) of $\sigma/\sqrt{n}$. Alternatively, and as discussed in the previous chapter, if each random sample is large ($n > 30$), then from the Central Limit Theorem we know that the sampling distribution of the estimator is approximately normally distributed, regardless of the population distribution.

Critical in our understanding of the sampling distribution is the recognition that the variance of the sampling distribution is not the same as the variance of population from which samples are drawn. In fact, $\bar{x}$ will have a variance equal to the population variance only in the extreme case of $n = 1$. If $n = 1$, then $\bar{x}$ is the one value in the sample. At the other extreme, if each sample is extremely large (infinite), then the variance of $\bar{x}$ approaches zero; that is, the sampling distribution of the sample mean is a spike at its mean. These extremes are shown in Figure 8.1, where for simplicity the population is pictured as being normal, which implies that the sampling distributions of $\bar{x}$ are likewise normal, regardless of the sample size. Notice in Figure 8.1 that as n increases (from panel a to panel d), the deviations from the expected value of $\bar{x}$ (that is, μ) decrease to the point of no noticeable dispersion when n is extremely large.

Consistency
The property of an estimator by which the probability that its value is near the parameter's value approaches unity as the sample size increases.

The property of an estimator that reflects the influence of sample size on precision is **consistency**. An estimator is consistent if the probability that its value is near the population parameter's value increasingly approaches unity as the sample size increases. As seen in Figure 8.1, because the sampling distribution of $\bar{x}$ collapses on μ as n increases (movement from panel b to d), $\bar{x}$ is a consistent estimator of μ.

8.4 Confidence Intervals

A point estimate is a single number; it provides no idea of the error associated with the estimator. For this reason, estimates are often reported with a "margin of error." Unfortunately, it is not always clear what this expression means. For example, what does a reporter on the six o'clock news mean when he or she talks about the outcome of a poll and its margin of error? The implication is that there is a point estimate to which one may add or subtract some measure for chance events. Such interval estimates that provide information on variability in sampling may be preferred to point estimates.

The interpretation of the error in sampling, however, requires knowledge of the probability distribution underlying the sampling distribution of the estimator, which the newscaster seldom provides.

Because it is only one number, a point estimate is sharp or more precise than an interval estimate, but it is also more often wrong. An interval estimate, on the other hand, provides a range of values. Its center value is typically the point estimate of the population parameter being estimated, and its upper and lower end values are determined by the margin of error. The margin of error is based on probability considerations.

For a random variable L less than a certain number θ, we write $Prob(L < \theta)$; similarly, we know that $Prob(\theta < U)$ is the probability that the random variable U is greater than the number θ. Thus, the

$$Prob(L < \theta < U) \tag{8.1}$$

is the probability that a population parameter θ is between a lower limit L and an upper limit U, where L and U are still the random variables and the parameter θ is still the certain number. The range L to U is an interval estimate of the parameter θ.

The interval $L < \theta < U$ is called a confidence interval, where the random values L and U are defined by the probability of the interval containing the population parameter. The population parameter θ to be estimated might be either the population mean μ or population proportion π.

8.5 Confidence Interval for the Population Mean

The confidence interval for the population mean is written $L < \mu < U$. If, prior to sampling, there is a 95 percent chance that this L–U interval will contain the true μ, then after sampling the resulting interval is called a 95 percent confidence interval for μ. This means that if 100 samples are randomly selected, and for each sample a value of L and a value of U are determined, then the population mean will be between the L and U values for 95 of the 100 intervals, on the average.

L and U are random variables that yield different values from sample to sample, but the population mean μ is a certain number. Thus, the probability statement

$$P(L < \mu < U) = 0.95 \tag{8.2}$$

does not say that there is a 95 percent probability that μ is between specific values of L and U. The interpretation is rather that for a large (infinite) number of samples, each sample would yield different values of L and U, but 95 percent of these L–U intervals will contain μ and 5 percent of the L–U intervals will not contain μ. This interpretation says nothing about any specific interval.

Consider the case in which $\bar{x}$ is normally distributed, with mean μ and variance σ^2/n. From the previous chapter, we know that there is a 0.95 probability that an $\bar{x}$ value is obtained between $\mu - 1.96\sigma/\sqrt{n}$ and $\mu + 1.96\sigma/\sqrt{n}$. That is,

$$Prob\left(\mu - 1.96\sigma/\sqrt{n} < \bar{x} < \mu + 1.96\sigma/\sqrt{n}\right) = 0.95 \quad (8.3)$$

Notice the difference between Equations (8.3) and (8.2). To express (8.3) as written in (8.2), both μ and $\bar{x}$ must be subtracted from each side of the inequalities in Equation (8.3), yielding

$$Prob\left(-\bar{x} - 1.96\sigma/\sqrt{n} < -\mu < -\bar{x} + 1.96\sigma/\sqrt{n}\right) = 0.95 \quad (8.4)$$

which upon multiplying through by a negative one gives

$$Prob\left(\bar{x} + 1.96\sigma/\sqrt{n} > \mu > \bar{x} - 1.96\sigma/\sqrt{n}\right) = 0.95$$

or

$$Prob\left(\bar{x} - 1.96\sigma/\sqrt{n} < \mu < \bar{x} + 1.96\sigma/\sqrt{n}\right) = 0.95 \quad (8.5)$$

Equation (8.5) can be seen to be identical to (8.2), where

$$L = \bar{x} - 1.96\sigma/\sqrt{n} \text{ and } U = \bar{x} + 1.96\sigma/\sqrt{n}$$

As in the interpretation of Equation (8.2), (8.5) says that before sampling, when $\bar{x}$ has not yet been calculated, there is a 95 percent chance that the interval between $L = \bar{x} - 1.96\sigma/\sqrt{n}$ and $U = \bar{x} + 1.96\sigma/\sqrt{n}$ will include the population mean. Here $\bar{x}$ and thus L and U are still random variables whose values have not yet been determined. Now if samples are drawn one after another, each of size n, then 95 out of 100 L–U intervals constructed will contain μ, on the average.

A confidence interval is based on a probability statement about $\bar{x}$ and not μ. As shown in Figure 8.2, the value of $\bar{x}$ will differ from sample to sample, but it will always be the middle of the confidence interval. The 20 theoretical intervals in the lower part of Figure 8.2 show only one interval that does not cover μ, which is what should be expected over a large (infinite) number of samples, on the average. Unfortunately, once an actual value of $\bar{x}$ is calculated from a sample, we do not know whether the resulting interval does or does not include μ. After all, μ is the parameter being estimated; if it were known, there would be no need for its estimation.[4]

The assignment of 95 percent probability is not relevant after a sample is actually drawn and after an $\bar{x}$ value is substituted into the formula $\bar{x} \pm 1.96\sigma/\sqrt{n}$. After the 64 "highly mobile" executives were sampled and a 95 percent confidence interval for the mean raise was calculated to be \$23,990 to \$26,650, it is not correct to say that there is a probability that μ is between \$23,990 and \$26,650. Either the interval \$23,990 to \$26,650 includes the population mean raise or it does not. Because there is no random variable in the interval

$$\$23{,}990 < \mu < \$26{,}650$$

there is no probability. We can say only that under repeated sampling, 95 percent of similarly constructed intervals would contain the true population mean, and the interval \$23,990 < μ < \$26,650 may (or may not) be one of those correct intervals.

FIGURE 8.2 Interpreting a 95 Percent Confidence Interval

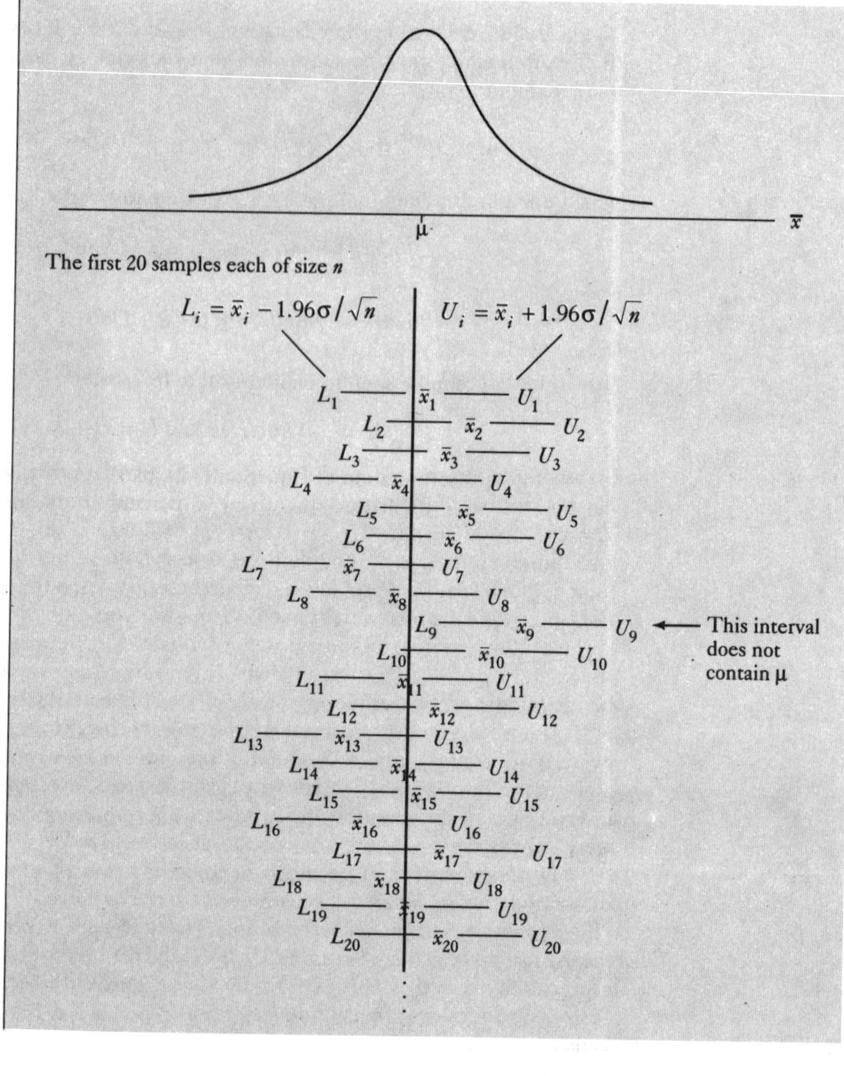

8.6 Level of Confidence

Typically 90, 95, or 99 percent confidence intervals are constructed. For these three levels of confidence, the probability that the *L–U* interval does not contain μ is thus 0.10, 0.05, or 0.01. The probability of the *L–U* interval not containing μ is designated by the Greek letter alpha (α), where for the typical three confidence intervals, α is either the decimal 0.10, 0.05, or 0.01, and the level of confidence is then given by $(1 - \alpha)100\%$. If $\alpha = 0.01$, for example, then the confidence interval is 99 percent: $(1 - \alpha)100\% = (1 - 0.01)100\% = 99\%$. In the general case, a $(1 - \alpha)100\%$ confidence interval for μ is

$(1 - \alpha)100\%$ confidence interval for μ

$$\bar{x} - z_{\alpha/2}\left(\sigma/\sqrt{n}\right) < \mu < \bar{x} + z_{\alpha/2}\left(\sigma/\sqrt{n}\right) \quad (8.6)$$

where $z_{\alpha/2}$ is the value of the standard normal variable z that puts $\alpha/2$ percent in each tail of the distribution.

As an application of Equation (8.6), consider the mobile executive pay raise example of a 95 percent confidence interval for the mean raise where $\alpha = 0.05$ and $z_{.025} = 1.96$. For a 90 percent confidence interval, $\alpha = .10$ and $z_{.05} = 1.645$. For $\alpha = .01$, $z_{.005} = 2.575$.

Alpha typically is set by considering the tradeoff between the desired level of confidence and the required accuracy. If alpha is low ($\alpha = 0.01$), then the width of the interval will be wide and 99 out of 100 of the *L–U* intervals will, on the average, contain the population parameter being estimated. Such an interval, however, may not be highly informative because of its width. In the mobile executive pay raise example, a 99 percent confidence interval for μ is

$$\bar{x} - z_{\alpha/2}\left(\sigma/\sqrt{n}\right) < \mu < \bar{x} + z_{\alpha/2}\left(\sigma/\sqrt{n}\right)$$

$$25320 - (2.575)\left(5428.57/\sqrt{64}\right) < \mu < 25320 + (2.575)\left(5428.57/\sqrt{64}\right)$$

$$\$23{,}572.68 < \mu < \$27{,}067.32$$

The width of this 99 percent confidence interval is \$3,494.64, versus the \$2,660 width for the 95 percent confidence interval. That may be too wide for some purposes. Increasing the confidence level further, by decreasing alpha, would simply widen the interval still further.

At a fixed level of confidence, and for a given population variance, the width of the confidence interval can be narrowed by increasing the sample size. As the sample size is increased, the standard deviation of the sampling distribution of the estimator is reduced and the margin of error $\pm z_{\alpha/2}\left(\sigma/\sqrt{n}\right)$ is likewise decreased. It is for this reason that larger samples are preferred to smaller samples in the construction of confidence intervals.

EXERCISES

8.1 Are the following statements true or false, and why?

a. The sample mean is an unbiased estimator of the population mean because they are equal for large samples.

b. The expected value of the sample standard deviation is equal to the population standard deviation; therefore, it is an unbiased estimator of the population standard deviation.

c. The sample variance is equal to the population variance for large samples; therefore, it is an unbiased estimator of the population variance.

8.2 At what stage in the construction of a confidence interval are the words "confidence" and "probability" interchangeable? At what stage are they not?

8.3 After surveying 100 new Cadillac owners, a marketing analyst at General Motors has established a 99 percent confidence interval for the mean income of all new Cadillac owners: $\$65{,}345 < \mu < \$123{,}145$.

a. What was the alpha for this interval?

b. What value of $z_{\alpha/2}$ was used in this interval?

c. What was the point estimate of the mean income?

d. What was the value of the standard deviation used in this interval?

8.4 Suppose two demographers independently take random samples of size $n = 64$ to estimate the mean age in a geographical region and then construct a 95 percent confidence interval based on their separate samples.

a. Would the two demographers necessarily have the same point estimate for μ?

b. Would you expect the margin of error for the two demographers to be the same? Explain.

8.5 If the sample size is increased fourfold, what happens to the width (or length) of the confidence interval, assuming σ is known?

8.6 A simple random sample of size 16 is drawn from a normal population of prices, with $\sigma =$ \$12. A confidence interval for the mean price is constructed and found to have a width from lower to upper end of \$18.60. What was the level of confidence?

8.7 A *Wall Street Journal* survey just prior to the launching of the Desert Storm action in 1991 reported that the majority of Americans were hawkish on Iraq and that "chances are 19 to 20 that if all registered voters in the U.S. had been surveyed . . . the findings would differ from these poll results by no more than 3.2 percentage points in either direction." Comment on this interpretation of the margin of error.

8.8 In a Gallup telephone poll of 767 adults, as reported in *Newsweek* (March 2, 1992), 73 percent said George Bush was not doing enough for the economy, with a margin of error of plus or minus 4.13 percent. What value of z would give this margin of error?

8.9 For the Gallup/*Newsweek* survey reported in Exercise 8.8, what is the implied level of confidence and the confidence interval for the population proportion that would say Bush was not doing enough on the economy?

8.10 The Gallup/*Newsweek* survey reported in Exercise 8.8 involved many questions. Would the margin of error be the same for each question, as suggested by the reporting of a single 4.13 percent margin? Explain.

8.7 When σ Is Unknown

The formula for the upper or lower limits of a confidence interval, $\mu = \bar{x} \pm z_{\alpha/2}(\sigma/\sqrt{n})$, requires that the population standard deviation σ be known. In most situations, this is not the case. In the mobile executive pay raise case, for example, σ is unknown; only the sample standard deviation s = \$5,428.57 is actually known. We used s^2 as our estimator of σ^2 . . . and simply substituted s for σ. But this substitution introduces more variability into the confidence interval than what is assumed in z. In particular, the standard normal transformation z of the sampling distribution of the mean involves only one statistic $\bar{x}$:

$$z = \frac{(\bar{x} - \mu)}{\sigma/\sqrt{n}}$$

Substituting s for σ results in a ratio involving two statistics $\bar{x}$ and s:

$$\frac{(\bar{x} - \mu)}{s/\sqrt{n}}$$

At the turn of the century, William Gosset developed the distribution for this ratio. He called his ratio the t statistic and used it to calculate confidence intervals for μ.

To standardize $\bar{x}$, when σ is unknown:	$t = \dfrac{\bar{x} - \mu}{s/\sqrt{n}}$	(8.7)
For small samples, the population x must be normal for $\bar{x}$ to be normal.		
The confidence limits for μ, when σ is unknown:	$\mu = \bar{x} \pm t_{\alpha/2}\, s/\sqrt{n}$	
where $t_{\alpha/2}$ is the value of t that puts α/2 in each tail, and	$s = \sqrt{\dfrac{\Sigma(x - \bar{x})^2}{n-1}}$ and $\bar{x} = \dfrac{1}{n}\Sigma x_i$	
The t distribution has $n - 1$ degrees of freedom.		

t Distribution
A probability distribution formed by the ratio of a normal random variable to the square root of an independently distributed Chi-square random variable divided by its degrees of freedom.

The ***t* distribution** in Equation (8.7) depends on randomness in both $\bar{x}$ and s.[5] The sample standard deviation s depends on the number of observations in a sample of size n that are free to vary around the sample mean $\bar{x}$. If the sample size is n = 1, for example, then there is no variability around the mean—the value of this single observation is also the mean of the sample. If the sample size is n = 2, then one of the values is free to vary. Once either of the two values is selected, the other value is determined by the mean and the first value. To illustrate, let a be the first value and b be the second. For any $\bar{x}[= (a + b)/2]$, b depends on the value of a and, hence, is not free to vary. For example, if $\bar{x} = 12$ and a is 15, then b must be 9. Similarly, when $n = 3$, any two values are free to vary, but once two are selected, then the third is fixed. In general, for any $\bar{x}$ value and sample size of n, once $n - 1$ values are determined, the remaining value is no longer free to vary. Thus, "the degrees of freedom" are said to be $n - 1$.

Degrees of Freedom for the Mean (df) The number of observations that are "free to vary" around the mean of a sample.

The **degrees of freedom** (abbreviated df) represent the number of observations in a sample that are "free to vary" around the mean of the sample. For the sample mean, the degrees of freedom for use in the t distribution are df $= n - 1$.

With the notable exception of the degrees of freedom adjustment, the t distribution is similar to the standard normal distribution. Both z and t are continuous, unimodal, bell-shaped distributions, with means of zero. They both require that the sample mean $\bar{x}$ be normally distributed. The t distribution differs from the z in that the sample standard deviation s is used as an estimator for the population standard

FIGURE 8.3 Examples of the Family of t Distributions

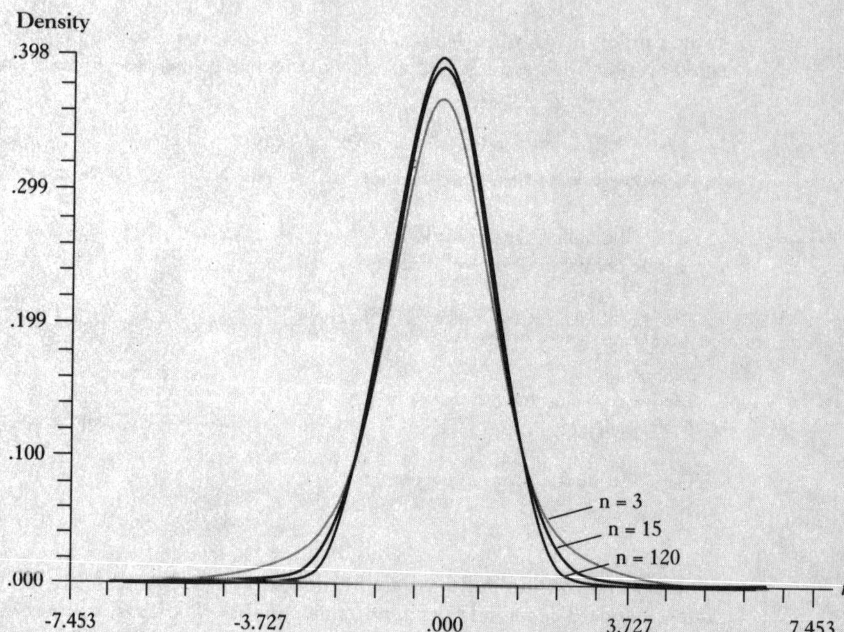

For these three t distributions, the flattest and most spread out density is for a sample size of $n = 3$. The middle density is for a sample of size $n = 15$. The most peaked density is for a sample of size $n = 120$, which appears no different from the standard normal density function.

deviation σ. Unlike σ, values of s vary from sample to sample, which tends to make the t more spread out than the z, with heavier or larger areas in the tails of the t.

Although the expected value of s^2 is σ^2, the probability that any individual s value is close to σ depends on the sample size n—the larger the sample size, the more likely it is that an individual s value will be close to σ. For large samples, little difference between s and σ should be expected. Thus, for relatively large samples, it should be of minor importance whether the t or z ratio is used to "standardize" $\bar{x}$, or whether t or z is used in a confidence interval.

Because the variability in t depends on the degrees of freedom, the t distribution can be thought of as a family of distributions—a separate member for each degree of freedom. Three of these member distributions are shown in Figure 8.3. With 120 degrees of freedom, the t distribution is indistinguishable from the z. Even with only 15 degrees of freedom, the t distribution does not appear greatly different from the z. At three degrees of freedom, a difference is easily discernible. Use of the t distribution for small samples is critically important.

HISTORICAL PERSPECTIVE

Few people think of the beer industry as employing path-breaking scientists. Yet, William S. Gosset (1877–1937) invented the t distribution while working for Guinness brewery in Ireland.

Gosset recognized that in most applications involving the estimation of the population mean, the value of the population variance is unknown. In 1908, he published "The Probable Error of a Mean" under the pseudonym "Student." Gosset's introduction of the t distribution eventually revolutionized statistical work with small samples. At first, however, the wide applicability of Student's t was not recognized. It was not until 1925, when Sir Ronald A. Fisher called attention to them in his textbook, that applications became popular in scientific inquiry.

Gosset was a student of both chemistry and mathematics. He learned statistics from Karl Pearson (1857–1936), one of a few distinguished English statisticians at the turn of the century. Unlike most scientists of his time, however, Gosset did not pursue a life in academe.

Gosset made his major scholarly contribution while working for private industry. His employer, Guinness, employed many university educated scientists but did not encourage scholastic publishing. So, Gosset published under his pseudonym.

In the United States, Chemical Rubber Co., a private firm in Cleveland, Ohio, assumed a key role in the preparation, maintenance, and dissemination of probability tables for statistical research. Not all contributions in statistics have come from academic institutions and think tanks.

Although Gosset discovered the t distribution and Fisher perfected and popularized it, it was Edward Paulson (1942) who provided a convenient algorithm for approximating probabilities based on Student's t. Paulson showed that the area more extreme than the absolute value of t, with $n-1$ degrees of freedom, could be approximated with the area in the upper tail of the standard normal distribution. Provided that the degrees of freedom are greater than three ($n-1>3$), the approximate relationship between $|t|$ and the value of z is

$$z^* = \frac{\left[1-\frac{2}{9(n-1)}\right]t^{2/3}-\frac{7}{9}}{\sqrt{\frac{2}{9(n-1)}t^{4/3}+\frac{2}{9}}}$$

The accuracy of this algorithm can be assessed in the following table. The exact absolute value of *t* that put 0.10 and 0.025 in *each of the tails* of the *t* distribution was used to calculate the associated z^* values that put approximately 20 and 5 percent in the upper tail of the standard normal distribution. These approximate z^* values compare favorably with the exact *z* values of 0.843 and 1.646.

n-1	*t*	z^*	Exact *z*
5	1.476	0.845962	0.843
5	2.571	1.650117	1.646
10	1.372	0.848719	0.843
10	2.228	1.661954	1.646
20	1.325	0.840333	0.843
20	2.086	1.667223	1.646

Today, inexpensive computer programs can calculate probabilities associated with the *t* distribution. W.I. Kennedy and J.E. Gentile (1980) review some of the alternative algorithms used by programmers. Calculations with the *t* distribution can be made in spreadsheets. In EXCEL, the command for probability calculations is "=TDIST (value,df,tails)," where "value" is the *t* value of interest, "df" are the degrees of freedom, and "tails" equals 1 or 2, for one or two tail areas. The absolute *t* value that puts an equal area in both tails is given by the command "TINV(area in both tails,df)." For example, "=TDIST(1.476,5,1)" gives the $P(t>1.476|df=5) = 0.099985$, and "TINV(.10,4)" gives the absolute *t* value of 2.13185 for $P(|t|>2.13185|df=4) = 0.10$.

8.8 Confidence Interval for the Mean, σ Unknown (and *n* small)

Whether the standard normal distribution or the *t* distribution is used in the construction of a confidence interval only affects the calculation of the margin of error. Let's consider that calculation now for the *t* distribution.

From Equations (8.6) and (8.7), the $(1-\alpha)100\%$ confidence interval for μ when σ is unknown is

$$Prob\left(\bar{x} - t_{\alpha/2}s/\sqrt{n} < \mu < \bar{x} + t_{\alpha/2}s/\sqrt{n}\right) = 1 - \alpha \tag{8.8}$$

where $t_{\alpha/2}$ is the value of t that puts α/2 percent of the *t* distribution in the upper tail and $-t_{\alpha/2}$ puts α/2 percent of the distribution in the lower tail, with $n-1$ degrees of freedom. These values of *t* can be obtained in several different ways, including computer programs. Appendix Table A.4 also presents some key cumulative probabilities for a limited number of members of the *t* distribution, which are identified by the degrees of freedom in the left-hand column. Only 34 different t distributions are presented for df = 1 through 30 and for df = 40, 60, 120, and infinity.

To appreciate the influence of the degrees of freedom, consider the value of *t* that puts 2.5 percent in the upper tail. If the degrees of freedom are infinite, then this *t* value is 1.96, which is the last value in the column headed by the cumulative probability 0.975. The *t* for df = ∞ is the same as the *z* value that puts 2.5 percent above it and 97.5 percent below. If the degrees of freedom fall to 120, in the second to the last row, the *t* value that puts 2.5 percent in the upper tail rises to 1.98. With df = 60, the critical *t* that puts 2.5 percent above it is 2.00; with df = 40, this *t* rises to 2.021. Notice that even with only 30 degrees of freedom, the *t* that puts 2.5 percent in the upper tail is 2.042, which is still close to the *z* of 1.96.

For a 95 percent confidence interval, the critical *t* values for df = ∞, 120, 60, 40, and 30 are ±1.96, ±1.98, ±2.00, ±2.021, and ±2.042. Clearly the width of a confidence interval is not going to be greatly affected if the *z* value of ±1.96 is used instead of the more appropriate *t* value. For extremely small samples, however, use of the appropriate *t* is essential. With only one degree of freedom, for example, the critical *t* that puts 2.5 percent in the upper tail is 12.706, which is not close to the 1.96 value for *z*.

Critical *t* values for different confidence levels are determined in Appendix Table A.4 by looking across the row specified by the degrees of freedom. Suppose, for example, that we have a sample of $n = 23$ observations and $n - 1 = 22$ degrees of freedom; row 22 from Appendix Table A.4 is reproduced in the top part of Figure 8.4. The

FIGURE 8.4 Cumulative Probabilities for the *t* Distribution, df = 22

From Appendix Table A.4, for 22 degrees of freedom,

df	0.75	0.90	0.95	0.975	0.99	0.995	0.9995
•							
•							
•							
22	0.686	1.321	1.717	2.074	2.508	2.819	3.792
•							
•							
•							

the cumulative probabilities given across the top of the table are associated with the *t* values within the table in the following way

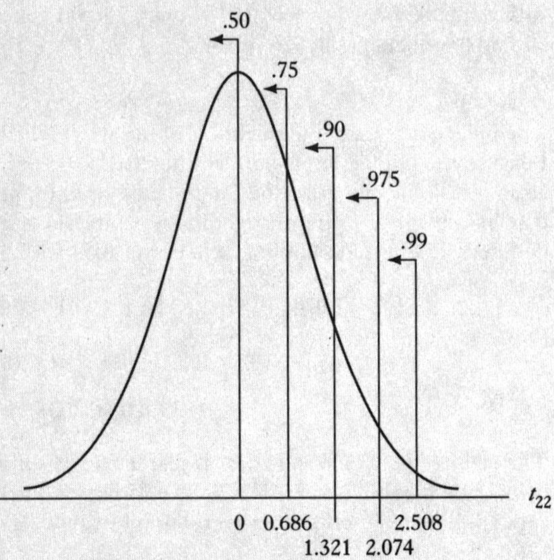

relationship between the cumulative probability, given as the column headers, and the t value in the body of the table is shown in the lower part of Figure 8.4.

The first cumulative probability in Figure 8.4 is 0.75, and its corresponding t value is 0.686. As indicated in the lower part of Figure 8.4, 75 percent of the distribution is below $t = 0.686$, with 22 degrees of freedom. A 50 percent confidence interval for μ, with 22 df, is now given by

$$Prob\left(\bar{x} - 0.686s/\sqrt{23} < \mu < \bar{x} + 0.686s/\sqrt{23}\right) = 0.50 \tag{8.9}$$

The second cumulative probability in Figure 8.4 is 0.90, and the corresponding t value is 1.321. This indicates that with 22 degrees of freedom, 90 percent of the distribution will be below t = 1.321; thus, –1.321 and +1.321 are the t values for an 80 percent confidence interval:

$$Prob\left(\bar{x} - 1.321s/\sqrt{23} < \mu < \bar{x} + 1.321s/\sqrt{23}\right) = 0.80 \tag{8.10}$$

And since 95 percent of the distribution is less than 1.717, a 90 percent confidence interval is

$$Prob\left(\bar{x} - 1.717s/\sqrt{23} < \mu < \bar{x} + 1.717s/\sqrt{23}\right) = 0.90 \tag{8.11}$$

and so on.

QUERY 8.1:

A mill produces sheet metal that it says will average 0.20 inch in thickness, with deviations determined by the normal distribution. A truckload is received for which a sample of 23 different locational measurements yields a mean width of 0.192 inch, with a standard deviation of 0.0187 inch. Should you accept the shipment as having an average thickness of 0.20 inch?

ANSWER:

The point estimate of the thickness of the sheet metal in the shipment is 0.192 inch. Because the population is normal, the distribution of sample average thickness $\bar{x}$ is also normal, but the t distribution must be used for probability calculations because σ is unknown. A 95 percent confidence interval is constructed to reflect the randomness inherent in sampling, where $t = 2.074$ with 22 degrees of freedom.

$$.192 - 2.074\left(.0187/\sqrt{23}\right) < \mu < .192 + 2.074\left(.0187/\sqrt{23}\right)$$

$$.192 - .0081 < \mu < .192 + .0081$$

$$.1839 < \mu < .2001$$

The claimed 0.20 inch thickness is just inside this interval, suggesting that the true μ could be that high, as estimated by a 95 percent confidence interval. For a 90 percent confidence interval, however, the interval is

$$.192 - 1.717\left(.0187/\sqrt{23}\right) < \mu < .192 + 1.717\left(.0187/\sqrt{23}\right)$$

$$.192 - .0067 < \mu < .192 + .0067$$

$$.1853 < \mu < .1987$$

which does not include the claimed 0.20 thickness. If it is critical that the steel average thickness be 0.20, then this shipment should be rejected. On the other hand, if the exact thickness is not that critical, it can be accepted.

QUERY 8.2:
It is common for business travelers not to submit receipts for the cost of a taxi ride from airports to city centers; they "estimate the fare to have been . . . ." The accounting department of a large firm wants to know when to question these "estimates."

ANSWER:
An interval estimate of the mean cost of taxi service for a given city can be estimated from a random sample of taxi costs from the airport to the city center. Below is such a sample reported by eight travelers:

Traveler 1	\$28.00	Traveler 5	\$22.00
Traveler 2	\$27.00	Traveler 6	\$15.00
Traveler 3	\$24.50	Traveler 7	\$14.00
Traveler 4	\$24.00	Traveler 8	\$ 7.00

By typing the following four command lines into the MINITAB computer program, a 99 percent confidence interval for the mean taxi fair will be calculated.

```
MTB  > set into c4
DATA > 28 27.0 24.5 24 22 15 14 7
DATA > end
MTB  > tinterval 99 percent c4
```

MINITAB provides the following printout:

	N	MEAN	STDEV	SE MEAN	99.0 PERCENT C.I.
C4	8	20.19	7.40	2.62	(11.03, 29.34)

MINITAB did the calculations for this 99 percent confidence interval with the t distribution. This computer program did not know if the sample mean was or was not normally distributed; it simply followed the commands. Here we justify the normality of $\bar{x}$ based on the assumed normality of the population.

Because all values are rounded to the nearest cent, it is worthwhile to see the calculations MINITAB did:

$$20.188 - 3.499(2.615) < \mu < 20.188 + 3.499(2.615)$$

where the estimated standard error of the mean is

$$s/\sqrt{n} = 7.397/\sqrt{8} = 2.615$$

Thus, our interval estimate of the average cost of a taxi ride between the airport and the city center is $11.03 to $29.34. The accounting department might be wise to question any "estimated" charges outside this interval—a reported cost higher than $29.34 might indicate exaggerated costs, and a reported cost less than $11.03 might indicate that a taxi was never taken.

QUERY 8.3:
Business Week (July 24, 1995) reported on the Toyota Motor Corporation's rethinking of the market for Camry. The competition was not to be the luxury car market but the Ford Taurus, Chevrolet Lumina, Dodge Intrepid, and Honda Accord. Camry chief engineer Kosaku Yamada said that "Affordability is the No. 1 priority...The Camry is not a luxury car." A sample of customer negotiated prices on "fully loaded" 1995 Camry competitors yields the following, in $1,000: 23.9, 24.8, 20.7, 21.5, 20.6, 25.3, 25.8, 23.0. At a fully-loaded Camry price of $25,700, are Camrys priced outside a 95 percent confidence interval for the mean price of the competition?

ANSWER:
A 95 percent confidence interval for the population mean negotiated price of Camry competitors is $18,306.77 to $28,118.23, in Chart 8.1, panel a. The entries for these commands are shown in panel b, with the data in cells A1 through A8. The Camry price of $25,700 is well within this 95 percent confidence interval.

CHART 8.1 Calculating a Confidence Interval with EXCEL Commands

Panel a

	A	B	C	D	E	F	
1	23.9		n	8			
2	24.8		mean	23.2125			
3	20.7		st. dev.	2.0746342			
4	21.5		t	2.3646226			
5	20.6						
6	25.3		Limits				
7	25.8		Upper	28.118227			
8	23.1		Lower	18.306773			

Panel b

	A	B	C	D	E	F	G
1	23.9		n	=COUNT(A1:A8)			
2	24.8		mean	=AVERAGE(A1:A8)			
3	20.7		st. dev.	=STDEV(A1:A8)			
4	21.5		t	=TINV(0.05,7)			
5	20.6						
6	25.3		Limits				
7	25.8		Upper	=D2+D3*D4			
8	23.1		Lower	=D13-D3*D4			

QUERY 8.4:

Data from a *Wall Street Journal* (November 15, 1996) article on the duration of economic expansions that began and ended between WW II and November 1996 are provided in Query 2.11. Treating these data as a random sample of all possible expansions, obtain a 95 percent confidence interval for the expected duration of an economic expansion.

Beginning to End of U.S. Expansion	Duration (in months)	Beginning to End of U.S. Expansion	Duration (in months)
Oct-45 to Nov-48	37	Nov-70 to Nov-73	36
Oct-49 to Jul-53	45	Mar-75 to Jan-80	58
May-54 to Aug-57	39	Jul-80 to Jul-81	12
Apr-58 to Apr-60	24	Nov-82 to Jul-90	92
Feb-61 to Dec-69	106		

ANSWER:

After entering these 9 durations into cells A1 through A9 of an EXCEL spreadsheet, the "Descriptive Statistics" routine, which is accessed through the "Tools" menu described in Query 2.11, can be used to find the summary measures and confidence interval for the input range "A1:A9." This requires that the boxes be checked for the "Summary Statistics" and "Confidence Level for Mean." With the output range set to "C1," the results appear as Chart 8.2.

CHART 8.2 EXCEL Summary Statistics and Margin of Error for Duration of Expansion

A	B	C	D
37		Column1	
45		---------------------	-----------------
39		Mean	49.88888889
24		Standard Error	10.27056804
106		Median	39
36		Mode	#N/A
58		Standard Deviation	30.81170413
12		Sample Variance	949.3611111
92		Kurtosis	0.080068248
		Skewness	0.955462191
		Range	94
		Minimum	12
		Maximum	106
		Sum	449
		Count	9
		Confidence Level(95.0%)	23.68398769

The last line in Chart 8.2, "Confidence Level (95.0%) 23.68398769" is the margin of error, which was automatically calculated in this EXCEL routine as 2.306(10.270568), where 2.306 is the t value that put 0.025 in the upper tail, as determined with the "=TINV(0.05,8)" EXCEL command, and 10.270568 is the standard error from Chart 8.2. The 95 percent confidence interval for the mean duration is 49.889 ± 23.684 or 26.2 weeks to 73.6 weeks: $26.2 \leq \mu \leq 73.6$

EXERCISES

8.11 In what ways do the z distribution and the t distribution differ? In what ways are they the same?

8.12 Find the probabilities for Student's t distribution and the values of b.

a. $P(|t| > 2.1|\text{df} = 21) =$ ____
b. $P(t > -2.6|\text{df} = 15) =$ ____
c. $P(t < b|\text{df} = 17) = 0.025, b =$ ____
d. $P(t > b|\text{df} = 25) = 0.05, b =$ ____

8.13 Find the probabilities for Student's t distribution and the values of b.

a. $P(t < 1.721|\text{df} = 21) =$ ____
b. $P(t > 3.707|\text{df} = 6) =$ ____
c. $P(t > -2.306|\text{df} = 8) =$ ____
d. $P(t > b|\text{df} = 13) = 0.995, b =$ ____
e. $P(t < b|\text{df} = 3) = 0.9995, b =$ ____
f. $P(t > b|\text{df} = 23) = 0.005, b =$ ____

8.14 What is the consequence of using the t distribution versus the z distribution in the construction of a confidence interval?

8.15 What assumptions are involved in the use of the t distribution to form a confidence interval for μ?

8.16 When is the z distribution more appropriate than the t distribution for constructing a confidence interval? When is the distinction irrelevant?

8.17 An audit of a retailer's inventory was conducted by randomly selecting the purchase invoices from $n = 100$ unsold units in stock. The average purchase price per unit was found to be \$17.50, with a standard deviation of \$6.75.

a. Find a 95 percent confidence interval for the mean purchase price of all units of inventory held by the retailer.

b. Audit results are interpreted in terms of the stated precision and the materiality of the derived estimate. The precision of the estimate is the level of confidence in the confidence interval, while materiality is synonymous with accuracy—the absolute difference between population and sample mean. How does changing σ, n, and α change the level of confidence and width of the interval?

8.18 In the 1992 "Red Book" that most banks and credit unions use to assess car loans, the average retail price of 1989 Corvette convertibles was \$21,750. A sample of attempted purchases of these cars, as advertised in the local "Wheels & Deals" periodical, resulted in the following sampling of "firm and final prices":

\$19,500, \$25,550, \$21,995, \$22,500, \$23,500, and \$21,000

What is the probability of getting the mean for this sample of size 6, or one with a higher mean, if the average retail purchase price is \$21,750, with a population standard deviation approximately equal to that of this sample? What assumptions did you make in your analysis?

8.19 In the early 1980s, a Baltimore directory-assistance operator was suspended because she averaged three seconds more than the 30-second standard. If this suspension was based on the random sample of the length of 12 different calls given below, would a 99 percent confidence interval suggest that this operator had exceeded the 30-second standard?

Call	Time (seconds)	Call	Time (seconds)
1	29	7	37
2	28	8	28
3	26	9	35
4	39	10	30
5	44	11	32
6	40	12	26

8.20 Below is a computer output of descriptive statistics on profits (in cents) per dollar of sales. (The numbers under the minimum and maximum headings are the lowest and highest profits in the sample.)

NAME	n	MEAN	STD. DEV.	MINIMUM	MAXIMUM
profit	23	6.28	1.34	2.96	11.21

a. What is the point estimate of average profit per dollar of sales?
b. What is the estimated standard error of average profit per dollar of sales?
c. Construct a 95 percent confidence interval for average profits per unit of sales.

8.9 Estimating the Population Proportion π

Recall from the discussion of the binomial distribution in Chapter 5 that if π is the proportion of computers that do not fail in the first year, then $n\pi$ is the expected number of failure-free machines in a sample of n computers.

$$E(x) = n\pi \tag{8.12}$$

When π is not known, it is estimated by $p = x/n$, where p is the proportion of successes x in a sample of size n. From Equation (8.12), we can see that

$$E(x/n) = \pi \tag{8.13}$$

Thus, as shown in Chapter 7, the expected value of p is π.

Equation (8.13) states that the sample proportion of successes is an unbiased estimator of the population proportion of successes. Within any one sample, p need not equal π; only over a large number of samples will the average p equal π. The values of p will vary around its expected value π in accordance with a variance given by[6]

$$\sigma_p^2 = E(p - \pi)^2 = \pi(1 - \pi)/n \tag{8.14}$$

Thus the distribution of p has a mean of π and standard deviation of $\sqrt{\pi(1-\pi)/n}$. From the Central Limit Theorem, we know that the distribution of p will be approximately normal if n is sufficiently large. Thus, for large sample sizes, we have the model

$$p \sim N\left(\pi, \sqrt{\pi(1-\pi)/n}\right) \tag{8.15}$$

which enables us to define the $(1 - \alpha)100\%$ confidence interval for π as

$$p - z_{\alpha/2}\sqrt{\pi(1-\pi)/n} < \pi < p + z_{\alpha/2}\sqrt{\pi(1-\pi)/n} \tag{8.16}$$

where $z_{\alpha/2}$ is the value of the standard normal variable z that puts $\alpha/2$ percent in the tail of the distribution. Since π must be between 0 and 1, if a confidence interval for π includes values outside this range, then the sample size was clearly not sufficiently large to invoke the Central Limit Theorem.

Equation (8.15) cannot be used directly to calculate a confidence interval for π, because it requires knowledge of π. The estimator p is substituted for π, which is legitimate as long as the sample size n is large. Regardless of how large the sample is, however, this substitution results in only an approximate $(1 - \alpha)100\%$ confidence interval of π. Thus, the approximate computational formula for the confidence interval is

$(1 - \alpha)100\%$ confidence interval for π:

$$p - z_{\alpha/2}\sqrt{p(1-p)/n} < \pi < p + z_{\alpha/2}\sqrt{p(1-p)/n} \tag{8.17}$$

where $z_{\alpha/2}$ is the value of the standard normal variable z that puts $\alpha/2$ percent in each tail of the distribution.

QUERY 8.5:
In a sample of 47 Compaq computers, 83 percent did not fail in the first year. The question: With 95 percent confidence, what proportion of all Compaq computers would you expect not to fail within the first year?

ANSWER:
The point estimate of the population proportion of Compaq computers that did not fail in the first year is 83 percent. A 95 percent confidence interval estimate of this proportion is

$$.83 - 1.96\sqrt{.83(.17)/47} < \pi < .83 + 1.96\sqrt{.83(.17)/47}$$

$$.7226 < \pi < .9374$$

which means that our interval estimate of the percentage of Compaq computers that will not fail in the first year is 72.26 percent to 93.74 percent.

QUERY 8.6:
"Statisticians Occupy Front Lines in Battle Over Passive Smoking" (*Wall Street Journal*, July 28, 1993), reports that Kenneth Brown, a statistical consultant on whom the U.S. Environmental Protection Agency has relied, "produced the controversial 90% confidence interval, or 90% probability that the lung-cancer-risk range is between 4% and 35% higher for passive smokers than those who aren't so exposed." Gio Gori, a medical doctor and frequent expert witness for the tobacco industry, was cited as stating "that the standard in such studies is to calculate the range within

which it is 95% certain that the true answer lies . . . (but) it would be so wide it might even hint that passive smoking actually reduced the risk of lung cancer." Comment on the correctness of these comments and on the use of a 95 versus a 90 percent confidence interval.

ANSWER:
First, the interpretations of the 90 percent confidence intervals as having a "90% probability that the lung-cancer-risk range is between 4% and 35%" and the 95 percent interval as "the range within which it is 95% certain that the true answer lies" are both wrong. Probability for a confidence interval is only defined before the sample is drawn; after the calculations are made, there is no longer a random variable on which probability is defined. Second, there is nothing sacred about a 90 percent or a 95 percent confidence interval; selection of either depends on the intended use. Finally, going from a 90 to a 95 percent confidence interval will lead to a wider confidence interval. If a resulting lower limit yields a percentage less than zero and such is viewed as meaningless, then this is evidence of the incorrectness of the assumptions and model upon which both the 90 and 95 percent confidence intervals were constructed.

EXERCISES

8.21 An article in the *Herald Telephone* (May 2, 1985) provided survey results showing that 75 percent of the 811 adult Indiana residents polled said they supported a state-controlled lottery. The margin of error for this survey was reported to be plus or minus 4 percent at the 95 percent confidence level. The article quoted Jon Masland as saying, "This means we are 95 percent confident that we would have gotten results within 4 percent either way of these results (0.75 ± 0.04) if we had interviewed every adult Indiana resident who has a telephone." Does this statement provide a correct interpretation of a confidence interval? Explain.

8.22 Indianapolis TV Channel 8 reported on February 24, 1992, that it had selected a random sample of 100 school bus drivers and found 32 had "blemished" driving records within the past five years. Construct a 95 percent confidence interval for the population proportion of Indiana school bus drivers with blemished driving records.

8.23 According to an article in *The Wall Street Journal* (February 24, 1992), 75 percent of the 134 current first-year M.B.A. students at the University of Pennsylvania's Wharton School said they expected to be running businesses 10 years hence. Construct a 90 percent confidence interval for the population proportion of students who expect to be running businesses ten years from now. To whom does your confidence interval apply?

8.24 A note in *The Wall Street Journal* (February 24, 1992) stated that 86 percent of the 120 women executives polled by Exec-U-Net, a western Connecticut networking group, said they once had a boss who was a "significant helper." Construct a 95 percent confidence interval for the population proportion of bosses who are significant helpers to women who become executives.

8.25 In car-buying situations, a common notion is that dealers steer customers to certain types of salespersons. This phenomenon was studied by Ian Ayers in "Fair Driving: Gender and Race Discrimination in Retail Car Negotiations," *Harvard Law Review* (February 1991).

He found, in a sample of 119 encounters, that black salesmen were paired with black male buyers 11.1 percent of the time. What is the 90 percent confidence interval for the proportion of times this pairing can be expected in the population?

8.26 Effective in 1991, interstate truck drivers were required to maintain national driver licenses. Unaddressed, however, was the state of the equipment they were using. A random sampling of 114 trucks showed 69 with faulty brakes. Construct a 95 percent confidence interval for the population proportion with faulty brakes.

8.10 Selecting the Sample Size

To this point in the analysis, we have assumed that a sample has already been drawn and n is known. At the beginning of any analysis, however, the sample size is unknown and must be determined before any statistical analysis can be undertaken. To determine the "best" sample size prior to actually drawing the sample, three factors must be considered:

1. The purpose of the sample. If it is for estimation purposes, then the reliability or confidence level must be set; that is, α must be specified. (The next chapter presents hypothesis testing as an alternative purpose for drawing a sample. Hypothesis testing provides a different set of considerations for sample selection.)
2. The "margin of error" to be tolerated in estimation. In confidence interval estimation, this margin is called M.
3. The cost of sampling. Typically the more expensive the sampling, the smaller the sample and the larger the margin of error. (In Chapters 1 and 7, alternative methods and problems of sampling were considered.)

Here we will consider two estimation situations: sample selection for estimation of either a population mean μ or a population proportion π. A researcher might want to estimate many other parameters, but the associated sample selection procedures are just variations on the two procedures demonstrated below. (As an alternative to procedures based on the confidence interval, the careful reader will want to consider the appendices to the next chapter, where sample selection criteria are based on tradeoffs in hypothesis testing.)

Selecting a Sample Size to Estimate μ

The margin of error, M, in estimating μ when the population variance is known, is $\pm z_{\alpha/2}\left(\sigma/\sqrt{n}\right)$; it is expressed as:

$$M = \pm z_{\alpha/2}\left(\sigma/\sqrt{n}\right)$$

After specifying M and α, this equation can be solved for n, which yields

Sample size for estimating μ, σ known

$$n = \left[\frac{z_{\alpha/2}\sigma}{M} \right]^2 \tag{8.18}$$

In most situations, the population standard deviation σ is unknown. After all, if we do not know μ and need to select a sample to estimate it, how could we know σ?

In some situations, a guess about the value of σ is possible. For instance, if it is reasonable to assume that the population is normally distributed, then there should be at least four to six standard deviations between the highest and lowest observable values. A reasonable guess for the standard deviation in Equation (8.18) thus might be the highest observed value minus the lowest divided by 4, 5, or 6. In the absence of any better prior information, we will arbitrarily use a divisor of 5.

Rule of thumb for guessing σ value prior to sampling

$$\sigma^* = \frac{\text{highest minus lowest observed value}}{5} \tag{8.19}$$

This rule of thumb estimate of σ can be substituted into the formula for n so that

$$n = \left[\frac{z_{\alpha/2}\sigma^*}{M} \right]^2$$

From this formula for n, it should be apparent that decreasing the desired margin of error will increase the needed sample size. Similarly, increasing the level of confidence (by lowering α and increasing z) will increase the required sample size. Finally, the more variability in the population, the larger the sample size that will be required.

QUERY 8.7:

An accountant wants to estimate the average time between the issuing of the first billing statement and the receipt of payment, for those bills paid before a second billing statement is sent the following month. How large a sample should be drawn from the records of a large retailer? Assume the accountant wants to be 99 percent confident that her estimate of the mean is within plus or minus two days of the true mean time.

ANSWER:

The accountant can quickly check to see that some bills are paid immediately, within a day of billing, and a like number are paid just before the next billing statements are sent (31 days). Thus, a rule of thumb guess at the population standard deviation, as given in Equation (8.19), is

$$\sigma^* = \frac{\text{highest} - \text{lowest}}{5} = \frac{31 - 1}{5} = 6 \text{ days}$$

The desired sample size, using Equation (8.18), is thus calculated to be

$$n = \left[\frac{z_{\alpha/2}\sigma}{M}\right]^2 = \left[\frac{2.575(6)}{2}\right]^2 = 59.7$$

The best guess of the approximate sample size is now found by rounding up to the next highest integer. As a guess at the appropriate sample size, the accountant should sample 60 accounts receivable.

Selecting a Sample Size to Estimate π

In Equation (8.17), the margin of error in a confidence interval for the population proportion π was

$$M = \pm z_{\alpha/2}\sqrt{p(1-p)/n}$$

This equation cannot be solved for n, because the sample proportion of successes $p = x/n$ has not yet been determined—remember no sample has been drawn, so x is unknown. If we can make a reasonable guess about the value of p, we can substitute this guess (denoted p^*) for p. Thus for estimating the population proportion, we can approximate the sample size using Equation (8.20).

Sample size for estimating π:

$$n = \left[\frac{z_{\alpha/2}}{M}\right]^2 p^*(1-p^*) \quad (8.20)$$

where p^* denotes a guess for p and M is the margin of error

From past experience, we might have an intuitive idea or hunch about a possible value for p; this value can serve as p^* in Equation (8.20). If we have no idea about p, then set $p^* = 1/2$ in Equation (8.20). A value of $p^* = 1/2$ results in the highest value of n at any given confidence level and is thus a good starting point. The required sample size will also be increased if we lower the margin of error (M) or increase the level of confidence and reliability (which lowers α and increases z).

QUERY 8.8:

As stated in the introduction to this chapter, Wall Street lore suggests that a headquarters move tends to be an ominous sign. A *WSJ* survey of 10 companies that moved between 1986 and the end of 1988 found that the price of stocks for five companies beat the market and the other five underperformed. What size sample would we have to draw to estimate the proportion of companies whose stock fell after the move to within plus or minus 0.06 of the true proportion, with 90 percent reliability?

ANSWER:
From the *WSJ*'s minisurvey, our best guess of p prior to sampling is 0.5. The margin of error is ±0.06 and α is 10 percent. Thus

$$n = \left[\frac{z_{\alpha/2}}{M}\right]^2 p^*\left(1-p^*\right) = \left[\frac{1.645}{0.060}\right]^2 (.5)(.5) = 187.9$$

We must therefore consider the stock prices of a random sample of 188 firms that moved headquarters if we are to be 90 percent confident that our estimate is within 0.06 of the true proportion whose stock price fell after the move.

Almost every statistics textbook discusses formulas similar to Equations (8.18) and (8.20) for determining sample size. Yet, Lawrence Kupper and Kerry Hafner (1989) have questioned these formulas in small-sample situations. Kupper and Hafner conclude that these confidence-interval-based formulas for determining sample size "behave so poorly in all instances that their future use should be strongly discouraged." (*Am Stat,* May 1989 p. 101) Unfortunately, without more information about the population, these formulas may be the only available indication of minimum sample requirements.

EXERCISES

8.27 A computer chip manufacturer produces large quantities of ROM chips to control engine emission. The production process has been running with a 30 percent defect rate. To check if a new method of production is generating fewer defects, the manufacturer plans to draw a random sample of chips. The company wants to be 95 percent confident that the estimated defect rate is within 0.05 of the true rate. How large a sample should be drawn?

8.28 A student in statistics determines that an adequate sample size to estimate a population mean dollar earnings is 100.

a. If she had set $\alpha = 0.05$, but now decides that $\alpha = 0.01$ is required, how is the sample size affected?

b. If she learns that the population standard deviation is twice as large as what she assumed originally, what happens to the desired sample size? (Ignore the changes in part a.)

c. If she originally was working with a margin of error of $125 but now decides that a margin of error of $200 is sufficient, how is the desired sample size influenced? (Again, ignore the changes in parts a and b.)

8.29 According to a *Wall Street Journal* (April 1, 1983) article, Americans have voluntarily contributed to reducing the $1.2 trillion public debt with checks totaling $135,575.15. "'Nearly half of the contributions are for less than $10,' says IRS spokeswoman Ellen Murphy, but 'a very generous soul' forwarded $25,000."

a. How large a sample size would be required to re-estimate the proportion of those who gave less than \$10, with 90 percent confidence that you are within 3 percent of the true proportion giving less than \$10?

b. Specify the assumptions you must make in part a.

8.30 The owner of a large auto repair service claims that 80 to 90 percent of customers believe his mechanics do an excellent job. You wish to estimate the proportion of customers who actually hold this belief to within 0.05, with 90 percent confidence. How large a sample is needed?

8.31 The average daily withdrawals from new savings accounts are to be estimated. You know that the maximum withdrawal from these accounts is \$2,400. You want to be 90 percent confident that your estimate is accurate to within \$55. How many accounts should you sample?

8.11 MARGIN OF ERROR IN LARGE SURVEYS

As reported at the beginning of this chapter, no margin of error was given for the survey in which "the majority of adults surveyed in Japan complained of fatigue and emotional stress." These results, as well as others pertaining to worker preferences in Japan, were reportedly based on a sample of 3,000 people.

For a large, multiple-question survey pollsters have accepted a rule of thumb for determining the margin of error. With little regard for the method of sampling, and little concern about the normality of the estimator, pollsters typically assume that the margin of error is plus or minus two standard errors of an estimator. This standard error is determined by assuming that prior to sampling there is a 50 percent chance that the respondent will select one alternative versus another on each of the questions in the survey. The margin of error, *M*, is then just a modification of Formula 8.20, where *z* is set equal to 2 and p^* is 0.50. That is,

$$M = \pm 2\sqrt{\pi(1-\pi)/n} = \pm 2\sqrt{.5(.5)/n} = \pm 1/\sqrt{n}$$

For a sample of 3,000 people, the so called "survey margin of error" is then 1.8 percentage points, or approximately 2 percentage points.

QUERY 8.9:

Business Week (March 13, 1995) reported on a multi-question Louis Harris & Associates survey on whom the U.S. government represents, the expected well-being of the next generation, faith in institutions, and like issues for which respondents suggested that "most think the American Dream is slipping out of their grasp -- and they know whom they blame." The sample consisted of 1,250 adults, with "results accurate to within 3 percentage points." If only half of the respondents answered a subset of questions, for those questions what would have been the survey margin of error?

ANSWER:

For the full sample of 1,250, the survey margin of error was calculated as $\pm 1/\sqrt{1250}$ = 2.83 percentage points. For the subset of questions on which only 625 responded the survey margin of error would have been $\pm 1/\sqrt{625}$ = 4.00 percentage points.

8.12 CONCLUDING COMMENTS

This chapter introduced the notion of a model for the estimation of the population mean, proportion, and median. In essence, it was the first step in inferring population parameters with sample values. The next two chapters deal with testing specific parameter values based on these sample measures. Later chapters will return to the idea of prediction when regression analysis is considered. Unlike armchair predictions based on hunches, all our work with estimation and hypothesis testing relies on probability theory and sample data.

CHAPTER EXERCISES

8.32 Is the t or z distribution more appropriate for calculating probabilities associated with the sample mean under the following conditions?

a. A small sample from a skewed population with known standard deviation
b. A small sample from a normal population with known standard deviation
c. A small sample from a skewed population with an unknown standard deviation
d. A small sample from a normal population with an unknown standard deviation

e. A large sample from a skewed population with an unknown standard deviation

f. A large sample from a skewed population with known standard deviation

8.33 Individual A constructed a 90 percent confidence interval for the proportion of graduates who do not get jobs within a year of graduation and reported the interval to be $0.15 < \pi < 0.19$. Using the same data, individual B constructed a 95 percent confidence interval and reported the interval to be $0.16 < \pi < 0.18$. Could both individual A and individual B be right? Explain.

8.34 A study in *Parade* (June 10, 1984) magazine reported that the median pay in the United States was $18,700. Why might this be a better point estimate of central location than the mean pay level?

8.35 A *Wall Street Journal* (February 4, 1992) article reported on a survey of 466 corporate-benefit managers by consultant Towers Perrin. The survey showed "77% support tax credits for people who buy their own health insurance." What is the margin of error associated with a 95 percent confidence interval of the true proportion who favor such tax credits? How wide would the 95 percent confidence interval be?

8.36 An article in *The Chronicle of Higher Education* (December 1984) reported on a survey of faculty members showing that their average yearly salary was $29,700. The article stated "the 'confidence interval' for that figure is $410, meaning that there is a 95 percent probability that the estimated average varies from the true average of the sample population by no more than plus or minus $410." Does this statement provide a correct interpretation of a confidence interval? Explain.

8.37 A Scripps Howard News Service (*HT*, February 9, 1992) release reported on a test carried out by the Insurance Institute for Highway Safety. The test showed that at five miles per hour, crashes of 24 cars resulted in repair bills ranging from $769 to $3,864. To be 95 percent confident that your estimated mean is within $200 of the true average cost of repair, how large a sample need be drawn?

8.38 An Associated Press (*HT*, February 11, 1992) release stated, "A leading test critic accused the makers of the Scholastic Aptitude Test in January of 'covering up' evidence that coaching can improve scores by an average of 100 points or more." The article went on to say that coaching is big business since "at least 100,000 students pay $500 or more each year to commercial coaching firms." (Each section of the two-part test is scored on a scale of 200 to 800.) To be 95 percent confident that your estimate of the mean improvement is within 15 points of the true mean, how large a sample is needed to estimate the improvement in test scores?

8.39 A note in *The Wall Street Journal* (February 18, 1992) describes a National Car Rental system that allows customers to rent and return cars with a machine similar to an automatic teller. But the system does not provide travelers with information on mileage. To estimate the mileage on National cars, you walk through one of its large lots and record the following mileage on a random sample of nine cars.

9,876	11,346	12,321
8,564	12,590	3,210
7,487	8,886	9,389

a. What is your point estimate of the average mileage on National cars?

b. What is a 95 percent confidence interval estimate of the average mileage on National cars?

c. What does your answer in part b tell you?

8.40 In economic recessions, small businesses tend to suffer because accounts receivable rise as the time between billing and payment increases. For a small plumbing and heating supply firm, the number of days since billing for 25 sample accounts receivable is:

42, 59, 30, 35, 40, 39, 101, 55, 92, 55, 81, 37, 73, 87, 12, 55, 63, 23, 72, 66, 71, 41, 20, 31, and 82.

a. What is the point estimate of the average days to payment?

b. What is the 90 percent interval for the average days to payment?

c. How are your estimators in parts a and b "biased" because of bills that are never paid?

8.41 Below is a MINITAB computer printout of descriptive statistics for a sample of the starting salaries of 31 graduating seniors. What is the margin of error? What is the value of the t statistic?

	N	MEAN	STDEV	SE MEAN	95.0 PERCENT C.I.
C4	31	24342.0	3246.0	583.0	(23151.5, 25532.5)

8.42 An article in *The Wall Street Journal* (February 24, 1992) stated that "for Biotech (companies), pure genius isn't enough." It said that companies had to be adequately capitalized. Below are stock market capitalizations (in millions of dollars) for a sample of biotech companies. Use a computer program to calculate a 95 percent confidence interval for the average capitalization of all biotech firms.

Amgen	$8,309.7
Genentech	3,080.2
Chiron	1,509.6
Centocor	1,296.8
Synergen	1,205.4
Genzyme	935.9
Biogen	879.8
Gensia	860.1
Immunex	791.8
Alliance	644.0
US Bioscience	570.8
Zoma	489.5
Medimmune	448.8
Affymax	409.6
Immune Response	395.2
Genetics Institute	379.6
Molecular Biosystems	373.8
Cytogen	352.3
Immunomedics	337.1
Liposome Co.	334.9

8.43 An article in *The Wall Street Journal* (February 3, 1992), titled "Depressed Job Market Prompts Paradox: Upsurge of Interest in M.B.A. Programs," reported on the number of applications to 10 programs: Dartmouth, Harvard, Stanford, U. of Pennsylvania, MIT, Columbia, Northwestern, U. of Virginia, U. of Chicago, and UCLA, for the past 11 years.

Year	Applications for fall of identified school year, in thousands
1981	32.578
1982	30.498
1983	28.916
1984	25.701
1985	28.365
1986	27.686

1987	31.569
1988	33.522
1989	33.357
1990	35.944
1991	36.531

a. What is the average number of applications for these 11 years at these 10 schools?

b. Why, in this case, is the average a biased estimator of the average number of applications to MBA programs?

8.44 The average price of Canadian fir, the lumber industry pricing benchmark, is to be estimated to within \$10 with 95 percent confidence. From *The Wall Street Journal* (February 27, 1992), you learn that this fir has "fetched from \$164 to \$206 per 1,000 board feet." How many contracts should you sample to estimate this mean with the desired accuracy?

8.45 Writing on "Confidence Intervals Rather Than P Values: Estimation Rather Than Hypothesis Test," *British Medical Journal* (March 15, 1986), Martin Gardner and Douglas Altman provided the following interpretation of a 95 percent confidence interval for the difference in means:

> Put simply, this means that there is a 95% chance that the indicated range includes the 'population' difference in mean blood pressure levels—that is, the value which would be obtained by including the total population of diabetics and non-diabetics at which the study is aimed. (p. 747)

Comment on the correctness of this interpretation.

8.46 An article in *The Wall Street Journal* (April 14, 1992) reported, "a study of 515 companies acquired in recent years found that 65% of their CEOs had departed, mostly in the first year after the transaction." Form a 95 percent confidence interval for the mean proportion of CEOs who depart after a takeover.

8.47 An article in *Business Week* (May 11, 1992) on mail-order computers, quoted Michael S. Dell, CEO of Dell Computer, saying "Our people handle an average of 40 to 60 calls a day." How large a sample is needed to estimate the mean number of calls Dell's people are handling to within plus or minus two calls, with 99 percent confidence?

8.48 Eric von Hippel, an MIT professor, and Cornelius Herstatt, of the Swiss Federal Institute of Technology, in their monograph "An Implementation of the Lead User Market Research Method In a 'Low-Tech' Product Area: Pipe Hangers" (Alfred P. Sloan School of Management, MIT, 1992), describe their work with Hilti AG, a leading European manufacturer of fastening, hanging, and shelving related products. To test whether designers were too far ahead of what customers wanted, the authors tested the designers' ideas on a sample of 12 regular customers: 10 preferred the new product and said they would pay up to 20 percent more for it.

a. Using Formula (8.17), construct a 95 percent confidence interval for the population proportion π of customers that would prefer the new product and be willing to pay up to 20 percent more for it.

b. What is wrong with this interval estimate in part a, and why did you get these strange results?

8.49 A *Business Week*/Harris Poll (June 15, 1992) of 400 female executives at companies with \$100 million or more in sales found that 27 percent had been harassed. Give a 95 percent confidence interval for the proportion of female executives who have been harassed.

8.50 According to the U.S. Bureau of Labor Statistics, *Occupational Outlook Handbook* (April 1990), "When listing property for sale, agents and brokers make comparisons with similar property being sold to determine its fair market value . . . parties to the transaction usually seek the advice of real estate appraisers, objective experts who do not have a vested interest in the property. . . . An appraisal is an unbiased estimate of the quality, value, and best use of specific property."(p. 234) Compare and contrast the meaning of the word "unbiased" as used in this quote versus its use in statistical estimation.

8.51 A headline in *The Wall Street Journal* (June 12, 1992) read "Sears Is Accused of Billing Fraud At Auto Centers." The article reports on a year-long study by the California Department of Consumer Affairs in which "Undercover agents took 38 cars with worn brakes but no other mechanical defects to 27 Sears automotive centers throughout California. . . . In 34 instances . . . agents were told of other defects. . . ." Construct a 95 percent confidence interval for the true proportion of cars for which nonexistent defects could be expected.

8.52 According to a *WSJ* (July 14, 1992) article, "Only 7% of 434 companies surveyed by the International Foundation of Employee Benefit Plans have a 'very complete' understanding of the new Americans With Disabilities Act." What is a point estimate of the population proportion of companies that have a very complete understanding of this act and a point estimate of the standard deviation of the distribution of the sample proportion of companies that have a very complete understanding of this act?

8.53 A *WSJ* (August 11, 1992) article reported that "of 104 personnel managers surveyed by Bureau of National Affairs, a newsletter firm, 76% worry about possible lawsuits under the new disability law." What is a point estimate of the population proportion (and its standard deviation) of personnel managers who are worried about lawsuits under this law?

8.54 An IRS agent questions the daily receipts reported by Healthy House Foods. Healthy claims receipts averaging \$517.40 per day. A random sample of receipts for five days yielded totals of \$558, \$501, \$478, \$490, and \$579.

a. What is the probability of getting this sample average, or larger value, if Healthy's claim is true?
b. What assumption is needed to do the probability calculation in part a?
c. Should the IRS continue to pursue Healthy House Foods based on this sample information? (Give reasons.)

8.55 A machine that is set to produce two-inch bolts is known to turn them out with deviations in length that appear to follow the normal distribution. The process is monitored with a sample of 10 bolts selected at random every 10 minutes. The last lot showed the following lengths:

Sample	Length	Sample	Length
1	1.99992	6	2.00021
2	2.00014	7	2.00007
3	2.00001	8	2.00014
4	2.00010	9	1.99996
5	1.99995	10	2.00042

a. What are the mean and standard deviation of this sample?
b. What is the probability of getting a mean as large or larger than the one calculated in part a, if the process is in control?
c. Based on your answer to part a, does it appear the machine is working properly?

8.56 A simple random sample of size 25 is drawn from a normal population of weights, with $\sigma = 15$ pounds. A confidence interval for the mean weight is constructed and found to have a width from end to end of 11.76 pounds. What was the level of confidence?

8.57 A simple random sample of size 9 is drawn from a population of hourly wages, with an unknown variance. A 98 percent confidence interval for the mean is constructed and found to have a margin of error of ±\$9.67/hr.

a. What was the standard error of the mean?
b. What was the sample's standard deviation?

8.58 In a survey of 105 female judges, 54 percent said sexual bias was widespread in California state courts, according to *The Wall Street Journal* (August 20, 1992). Construct a 90 percent confidence interval for the true proportion of female judges who think sexual bias is widespread in California state courts. Does this interval include the majority of judges?

8.59 *Newsweek* (September 28, 1992), in an article on polling, said:

> To be fair, polls that at first blush look contradictory may not be. A *Miami Herald* poll last week had George Bush ahead of Bill Clinton by 7 points (48–41) in Florida; in a *New York Times*/CBS News poll, Bush trailed (42–48). But since the polls had margins of error of about 4 points, they overlapped (add and subtract 4 from each number to get the possible range). The margin of error, calculated according to a textbook statistical formula, varies inversely with the sample size. In general, about 500 responses gives a possible error of 5 percent either way, 2,500 responses decreases it to 1 percent. (p. 38)

Comment on the correctness of this quote.

8.60 Exercise 7.38 describes a Lanier TV advertisement on CNN (April 20, 1993) that stated "Lanier copiers are up and running 98 percent of the time," and the results of a status check of a Lanier copier on thirty randomly selected days in which the copier was "up and running" 29 times. Why wouldn't it be appropriate to calculate a 99 percent confidence interval (based on the z distribution) for the true population proportion of up time in this problem?

8.61 A *Wall Street Journal*/NBC News poll (January 29, 1993) of the views of 1,009 adults toward President Clinton included a statement that "Chances are 19 of 20 that if all adults with telephones in the U.S. had been surveyed, the findings would differ from these poll results by no more than 3.1 percentage points in either direction." Is this wording a correct representation of the implications of the margin of error? Explain.

8.62 The statement accompanying a *Wall Street Journal* (February 19, 1993) report on a Roper Organization survey of 500 black business owners said: "According to Roper, the odds are 19 to 20 that if the survey of entrepreneurs had been expanded to include the entire SBA list of black-owned businesses, with annual revenue of at least $100,000, the findings would differ from these poll results by no more than five percentage points in either direction." Comment on the correctness of this interpretation of the margin of error.

8.63 (Requires Endnotes) In the March 1991 issue of the *Journal of the American Statistical Association*, there was an article on "Bayesian and Frequentist Predictive Inference for the Patterns of Care Studies." A year earlier, in the March 1990 issue, there was an article on "Approaches to Bayesian Confidence Intervals." What distinction between classical (frequentist) and Bayesian estimation is called to your attention by these article titles?

8.64 An article in *The Wall Street Journal* (June 29, 1995) reported on profits per partner in the top U.S. law firms. These profits (in millions of dollars) were: 1.400, 1.225, 1.200, 1.185, 0.940, 0.930, 0.885, 0.820, 0.805, 0.800, 0.740, 0.700, 0.655, 0.645, 0.625. Construct a 95 percent confidence interval for the population mean profit per partner in top U.S. law firms. What is the margin of error?

8.65 In the discussion of cluster sampling in the previous chapter, a *Wall Street Journal*/NBC News Poll of 1006 adults was conducted by the polling organization of Peter Hart and Robert Teeter. The article stated that "Chances are 19 of 20 that if all adults with telephones in the U.S. had been surveyed, the findings would differ from these poll results by no more than 3.1 percentage points in either direction. A limited number of questions were asked of half the sample; for these, the margin of error was 4.5 percentage points." (*WSJ*, September 16, 1993).

a. How were the two margins of error calculated?

b. Comment on the correctness of the 19 of 20 interpretation of the implied confidence interval. In your answer do not overlook the importance of simple random sampling.

8.66 A March 1997 survey of 400 senior executives at large corporations, with the complete results available from *Business Week* (March 31, 1997) and on the World Wide Web at www.businessweek.com, showed "68% favor ending unlimited soft-money contributions". What is the margin of error for this survey?

ACADEMIC REFERENCES

Fisher, Ronald A. *Statistical Methods for Research Workers*, first edition. New York: Hafner Publishing Company, Inc., 1925.

Gosset, William (under pseudonym Student). "The Probable Error of a Mean." *Biometrica* VI, 1908, pp. 1–25.

Kennedy, W.I., and J.E. Gentile. *Statistical Computing*. New York: Marcel Dekker, 1980.

Kupper, Lawrence, and Kerry Hafner. "How Appropriate are Population Sample Size Formulas?" *American Statistician*. May 1989, pp. 101–105.

Paulson, Edward. "An Approximate Normalization of the Analysis of Variance Distribution." *Annals of Mathematical Statistics* 13, 1942, pp. 233–235.

Zehna, Peter. "On Proving That $\bar{x}$ and s^2 Are Independent." *American Statistician*, May 1991, pp. 121–122.

ENDNOTES

1. To demonstrate that the expected value of the sample mean $\bar{x}$ is μ we have

$$E(\bar{x}) = En^{-1}\sum_{i=1}^{n} x_i = n^{-1}\sum_{i=1}^{n} Ex_i = n^{-1}n\mu = \mu$$

2. A natural estimator of σ^2 to consider is

$$s_*^2 = n^{-1}\sum_{i=1}^{n}\left(x_i - \bar{x}\right)^2$$

But this is a biased estimator of σ^2. The bias can be demonstrated by deriving the expected value s_*^2.

$$s_*^2 = n^{-1}\sum_{i=1}^{n}\left(x_i - \mu\right)^2 - \left(\bar{x} - \mu\right)^2$$

Since s_*^2 is $n^{-1}\sum_{i=1}^{n}\left(x-\bar{x}\right)^2$, an unbiased estimator of σ^2 is

$$s^2=\left(n-1\right)^{-1}\sum_{i=1}^{n}\left(x_i-\bar{x}\right)^2$$

3. For this derivation, see the latter part of endnote 2.
4. In contrast with the classical view in which the population parameter is fixed and its estimator is a random variable, Bayesians treat the population parameter as if it is the random variable and the estimator is fixed. Bayesians argue that since the calculated sample statistic is known with certainty, a distribution should be assumed for what is unknown—the population parameter. Thus, Bayesians can calculate the probability that the population parameter is within a specific numerical interval.
5. "Student's *t*" is defined by the ratio of a normal random variable to the square root of an independently distributed chi-square random variable divided by its degrees of freedom. For this statistic, $= \bar{x} = \Sigma x/n$ and $s^2 = \Sigma(x-\bar{x})^2/(n-1)$ must be independent and $(n-1)s^2/\sigma^2$ must have a chi-square distribution with $n-1$ degrees of freedom. This relationship is demonstrated by Peter Zehna (1991).
6. For a binomial random variable x, the variance was given by

$$E(x-\pi n)^2=\pi(1-\pi)n$$

which can be rewritten as

$$n^2E[(x/n)-\pi]^2=\pi(1-\pi)n$$

Dividing both sides by n^2 yields the variance of p:

$$E[(x/n)-\pi]^2=\pi(1-\pi)/n$$

FORMULAS

- $(1-\alpha)100\%$ confidence interval for μ, where σ is known:

$$\bar{x}-z_{\alpha/2}\left(\sigma/\sqrt{n}\right)<\mu<\bar{x}+z_{\alpha/2}\left(\sigma/\sqrt{n}\right)$$

where $z_{\alpha/2}$ is the value of the standard normal variable z that puts $\alpha/2$ percent in each tail of the distribution.

- $(1-\alpha)100\%$ confidence interval for μ, where σ is unknown:

$$\bar{x}-t_{\alpha/2}\left(s/\sqrt{n}\right)<\mu<\bar{x}+t_{\alpha/2}\left(s/\sqrt{n}\right)$$

where $t_{\alpha/2}$ is the value of t that puts $\alpha/2$ in each tail, and

$$s=\sqrt{\frac{\Sigma\left(x-\bar{x}\right)^2}{n-1}}\text{ and }\bar{x}=\frac{1}{n}\Sigma x_i$$

and the t distribution has $n-1$ degrees of freedom. For small samples, the population x must be normally distributed so $\bar{x}$ can be normally distributed.

- The t statistic

$$t = \frac{\bar{x} - \mu}{s/\sqrt{n}}$$

where

$$s = \sqrt{\frac{\sum\left(x - \bar{x}\right)^2}{n - 1}}$$

and

$$\bar{x} = \frac{1}{n}\sum x_i$$

For small samples, the population x must be normally distributed so $\bar{x}$ can be normally distributed.

- $(1 - \alpha)100\%$ approximate confidence interval for π:

$$p - z_{\alpha/2}\sqrt{p\left(1 - p\right)/n} < \pi < p + z_{\alpha/2}\sqrt{p\left(1 - p\right)/n}$$

where $z_{\alpha/2}$ is the value of the standard normal variable z that puts $\alpha/2$ percent in each tail of the distribution.

- Sample size for estimating μ, σ known

$$n = \left[\frac{z_{\alpha/2}\sigma}{M}\right]^2$$

where M is the margin of error.

- Sample size for estimating μ, σ unknown

$$n = \left[\frac{z_{\alpha/2}\sigma^*}{M}\right]^2$$

where M is the margin of error, and σ^* is an educated guess for σ, which might be given by

$$\sigma^* = \frac{\text{highest minus lowest observed value}}{5}$$

- Sample size for estimating π:

$$n = \left[\frac{z_{\alpha/2}}{M}\right]^2 p^*\left(1 - p^*\right)$$

where M is the margin of error, and p^* denotes an educated guess for p.

Now to determine the expected values of the right-hand terms, we have

$$E\left(s_*^2\right) = n^{-1}\sum_{i=1}^{n} E\left(x_i - \mu\right)^2 - E\left(\bar{x} - \mu\right)^2$$

$$= n^{-1}n\sigma^2 - E\left(\bar{x} - \mu\right)^2 = \sigma^2 - E\left(\bar{x} - \mu\right)^2 \neq \sigma$$

To get an unbiased estimator, we need to determine $E(\bar{x} - \mu)^2$, which is the variance of the sampling distribution of $\bar{x}$.

$$E\left(\bar{x} - \mu\right)^2 = E\left[n^{-1}\sum_{i=1}^{n} x_i - \mu\right]^2 = n^{-2}E\left[\sum_{i=1}^{n}\left(x_i - \mu\right)\right]^2$$

$$= n^{-2}E\left[\sum_{i=1}^{n}\left(x_i - \mu\right)^2 + \sum_{i=1_{i\neq j}}^{n}\sum_{j=1}^{n}\left(x_i - \mu\right)\left(x_j - \mu\right)\right]$$

$$= n^{-2}\left[\underbrace{\sum_{i=1}^{n} E\left(x_i - \mu\right)^2}_{\text{The variance of } x} + \underbrace{\sum_{i=1}^{n}\sum_{j=1}^{n} E\left(x_i - \mu\right)\left(x_j - \mu\right)}_{\text{As long as } x\text{'s are independent, the expected value of a crossproduct is zero}}\right]$$

$$= n^{-2}\left(n\sigma^2\right)$$

$$= \sigma^2/n$$

We now know that $E\left(\bar{x} - \mu\right)^2$ is σ^2/n. Thus,

$$E\left(s_*^2\right) = n^{-1}n\sigma^2 - E\left(\bar{x} - \mu\right)^2 = \sigma^2 - E\left(\bar{x} - \mu\right)^2 = \sigma^2 - \sigma^2/n$$

Therefore,

$$E\left[ns_*^2/\left(n-1\right)\right] = \sigma^2$$

CHAPTER 9

SINGLE SAMPLE HYPOTHESIS TESTING

Who can refute a sneer?

William Paley
1743–1805

9.1 Introduction

In addition to parameter estimation, we want to test for specific parameter values in a model. We have already seen how a confidence interval can suggest a range of values that a parameter might assume, but what about the correctness of any one value? That is the question for this and the next two chapters.

Hypothesis
A claim or assumption about the value of a population parameter.

Hypothesis Testing
The process of judging which of two contradictory statements is correct.

A claim or an assumption about the value of a population parameter is called a **hypothesis.** Making a decision about the correctness of one hypothesis versus another is called **hypothesis testing.** For example,

- The task of filing a 1040 tax form is supposed to take a person, on average, a mere nine hours and five minutes, according to the Internal Revenue Service. Several professional tax preparers cited anecdotal evidence and personal experiences, in a *Wall Street Journal* article, that implies an average time much longer. A hypothesis test might shed light on this apparent contradiction.
- An article in *Popular Mechanics* reported that a major rubber company had found that the mean (alternator, fan, power steering, or air conditioning) accessory-drive belt lasts at least four years and 11 months, while mechanics typically use a rule of thumb based on an expected belt life failure before that point. A test could determine the reasonableness of the rubber company's claim versus that of the mechanics.
- An Associated Press release (January 3, 1991) stated that for the 14 states participating in Lotto America as of January 1991, Wisconsin residents had won the most jackpots (14 out of 51), but they also had bought the most tickets (31 percent of tickets purchased). Lottery spokesperson Bret Vorhees was quoted as emphasizing that "a person's residence has nothing to do with the chance of winning." A hypothesis test could be used to see if the proportion of Wisconsin winnings is significantly different from the 31 percent expected based on ticket sales.
- Andy Rooney on "60 Minutes" (May 2, 1993) asked: "How do manufacturers decide on how much to put in a package?" In the case of paper toweling, a marketing expert says 60 feet, "because that's the average amount used by a family of four between pay checks." A hypothesis test could assess whether or not the mean amount of paper toweling used by such families is 60 feet per two-week pay period.

A decision about the correctness of one hypothesis versus another alternative hypothesis could be based on a hunch, an anecdote, the flip of a coin, or even the positions of the stars. Unlike decisions that are based on isolated incidents, the statistical hypothesis testing procedures demonstrated in this chapter require the use of sample information and decision rules founded in probability models that fit the situation.

This chapter considers business and economic decision-making situations in which, at least conceptually, repeat simple random sampling is possible, as in an experiment. The rules for choosing among alternatives will take into account the uncertainty inherent in such sampling. Decision rules that identify, control, and minimize the chance of errors in reaching a conclusion will be emphasized.

By the end of this chapter, you should be able to identify hypothesis testing situations, specify the hypotheses to be tested, use a probability based decision rule for rejecting or accepting a hypothesis based on observed sample data, and reach a conclusion. You will be able to test statements about means and proportions.

9.2 HYPOTHESES: AN ILLUSTRATION

Null Hypothesis
A statement about a population parameter that is assumed true until sufficient contrary sample evidence is presented.

Alternative Hypothesis
A statement about a population parameter that is being tested; it is true if the null hypothesis is false.

To assess the correctness of the rubber company's claim that the mean life of accessory-drive belts is at least four years and 11 months requires the specification of an alternative statement, which is supplied by the mechanics. Statistical hypothesis testing requires a pair of hypotheses: one which is initially assumed true, called the **null hypothesis,** and the other representing a challenging view, called the **alternative hypothesis.** If the rubber company is wrong, then the mechanics' experience would suggest that the average belt life is less than 59 months (4 years and 11 months).

The null and alternative hypotheses typically are written as mutually exclusive and exhaustive statements about the value of a parameter of a population model. As in Chapter 4, mutually exclusive means that both the null and alternative hypotheses cannot be accepted as true; exhaustive means that there are no other options. For the drive belts, any one of four outcomes is thus possible.

1. The mean time to failure is actually at least 59 months, and we conclude that this is so by not rejecting the null hypothesis. That is, we draw the correct inference.
2. The mean time to failure is actually at least 59 months, but we conclude that this is not the case by rejecting the null hypothesis. That is, we draw the wrong inference.
3. The mean time to failure is actually less than 59 months, and we reject the null hypothesis. That is, we draw the correct inference.
4. The mean time to failure is actually less than 59 months, but we do not reject the null hypothesis. That is, we draw the wrong inference.

Similarly, there are four possible outcomes in any other hypothesis testing situation.

Because the null and alternative hypotheses form a mutually exclusive and exhaustive set of options, a choice between them is either correct (options 1 or 3 above) or one of two errors is made (options 2 or 4 above). The null hypothesis may be rejected when it is true, as in case 2, or the null hypothesis may not be rejected when it is false, as in case 4.

Types and Cost of Errors

The chance factors in sampling can lead to the wrong conclusion in hypothesis testing. When this occurs, an error of inference is said to occur. As depicted in Table 9.1, the

TABLE 9.1
The Four Outcomes in Hypothesis Testing

		Population Situation	
		Null hypothesis is actually true	Null hypothesis is actually false
Conclusion reached based on sample data	Null hypothesis is rejected	Type I error	correct conclusion
	Null hypothesis is not rejected	correct conclusion	Type II error

Type I error is
rejecting the null hypothesis when it is true.

Type II error is
not rejecting the null hypothesis when it is false.

Type I Error
Rejecting the null hypothesis when it is true.

Type II Error
Not rejecting the null hypothesis when it is false.

Maintained Assumptions
A model and its related assumptions that are taken to be true during a hypothesis test.

Specification Error
A situation in which the maintained assumptions in a hypothesis test are, in fact, wrong.

first type of error of inference (rejecting the null when it is true) is called a **Type I error.** The second type of error (not rejecting the null when it is false) is called a **Type II error.** Later in this chapter, we will assign probabilities to these errors; for now, we need only keep in mind these two types of errors of inference that could occur whenever a decision is made.

Because hypothesis testing is based on sample information, an inference about the population requires a model of the population and the sampling distribution of the statistic used to estimate the population parameter of interest. The model and its related assumptions are called **maintained assumptions** because they are assumed true during the test. If these maintained hypotheses are wrong and lead to incorrect inferences about the population, then a **specification error** is said to have occurred.

We never want to make an error. The only way the possibility of an error could be eliminated, however, would be if we knew the population and its parameters with certainty, but then there would be no need for the test. Typically we have to assume a model of the population and estimate the parameters of the model. As long as sample information is used to make an inference about the population, errors are possible. It is the researcher's obligation to set up the test to minimize the likelihood of errors, given the budget available and the cost of the errors.

The costs or the seriousness of the two different types of errors of inference are not equal. If we conclude, for example, that the average life of a drive belt is at least four years and 11 months (and do not replace the belt earlier), when in fact the average life is much less, then an error could be costly. Relative to the cost of replacing a belt, a belt that breaks 50 miles from the nearest service station right before an important business meeting could be extremely costly. As discussed later in this chapter, ideally the probability of incurring such costs is minimized by the criterion or decision rule for choosing between the null and alternative hypotheses.

Stating the Hypotheses

The null hypothesis is typically denoted by the symbol H_0 and the alternative hypothesis by H_A. In the case of the drive belt illustration, the null hypothesis is

$$H_0: \mu \geq 59$$

where μ is the population mean belt life (time before breakage) measured in months. This null hypothesis says that the population mean is greater than or equal to 59 months (four years and 11 months). Often along with the null hypothesis, there are other maintained assumptions that are not tested. For instance, if a spokesperson for the rubber company was quoted saying that "the average belt goes for four years and 11 months (or more), with a standard deviation of 3.333 months and almost all of the distribution ranging from just over four years to just under six," then the null hypothesis H_0: $\mu \geq 59$ says nothing about the observable range being from about 49 months to 69 months or the standard deviation being 3.333 months. This information about the dispersion of belt life is given or maintained during the test of the mean. These maintained assumptions are considered to be true during the test of the mean. Of course, if they are false, then the test of the mean may not be valid.

The alternative hypothesis, as suggested by the mechanics' statements, is that consumers should expect a belt life of less than 59 months:

$$H_A: \mu < 59$$

This alternative hypothesis says that the population mean is less than 59 months. It allows for the population mean to differ from the value in the null hypothesis in only one direction and is thus called a one-tailed alternative. The null and alternative hypotheses are mutually exclusive and exhaustive because the null hypothesis is consistent with any value that *is* at least 59 months and the alternative includes any value that *is not* at least 59 months.

The null hypothesis is assumed correct until sufficient sample information is obtained to refute it. Thus, the null hypothesis is the statement that is tested for possible rejection in favor of the alternative. By implication, the alternative hypothesis is accepted when the null is rejected. Because the truth of either hypothesis is never known with certainty, some statisticians prefer to say only that "H_0 can (or cannot) be rejected" instead of saying that "H_A is (or is not) accepted."

In the belt life example, $\mu \geq 59$ is not rejected until sample information suggests that it can be rejected in favor of $\mu < 59$. If that sample information is not forthcoming, technically we should not say that $\mu \geq 59$ is accepted. It is more correct to say that $\mu \geq 59$ cannot be rejected. This subtle distinction between not rejecting the null hypothesis and accepting it is often overlooked in the statement of the conclusion.

The subtlety in wording in the statistical hypothesis testing procedure is similar to the legal process in the United States, where the defendant is assumed to be innocent until the evidence indicates guilt beyond a reasonable doubt. If the jury determines that the weight of the evidence is not sufficient to conclude guilt, the defendant is not proven innocent; he or she is said to be "not guilty" and "not convicted" or simply "freed."[1]

9.3 Decision Rule: An Illustration

A statistical hypothesis test requires sample information. In the case of the test of drive belts, time until failure might be obtained from a local taxicab company, a limousine service, or any other company that maintains fleets of motor vehicles. The National Association of Fleet Administrators also may be contacted for data, assuming there is no difference in belt life between vehicles used in fleets and those in individual use.

The sample we are going to use here consists of 36 drive belts that averaged 57.8 months before failure. This sample evidence ($\bar{x} = 57.8$) is used to decide whether H_O: $\mu \geq 59$ should be rejected in favor of H_A: $\mu < 59$. That is, we will try to establish if the sample result $\bar{x} = 57.8$ is sufficiently below $\mu = 59$ to be reasonably sure that the null hypothesis should be rejected.

p-Value

The difference between the observed $\bar{x}$ value of 57.8 and the smallest value of $\mu = 59$ in the null hypothesis H_O: $\mu \geq 59$ is associated with a probability; namely, the probability that a sample of size $n = 36$ results in a $\bar{x}$ value between 57.8 and 59, Figure 9.1, panel a. The bigger the probability of a $\bar{x}$ value between 57.8 and 59, the smaller the probability of one at or below 57.8. These probability calculations are the same type of probability determinations we did in Chapters 7 and 8. Now, however, the probability of obtaining a sample $\bar{x}$ value at or below 57.8, if $\mu = 59$, is called a **"*p*-value."** That is, the *p*-value is $P(\bar{x} \leq 57.8 \mid \mu = 59)$. As can be seen in Figure 9.1, panel a, the *p*-value is the area under the density function and below $\bar{x} = 57.8$. It is all in one tail because this is a one-tailed test.

_p_-Value
The probability that a test statistic assumes a value more extreme than the observed value, assuming the null hypothesis is true.

The *p*-value requires the calculation of probabilities for values of the estimator in the tail (or tails) of the sampling distribution.[2] In the drive belt example, the sampling distribution is centered at $\mu = 59$, which is called the "limiting value" in the null hypothesis because it represents the lower limit of the values $\mu \geq 59$. If the observed $\bar{x}$ value is below the limiting value in this null hypothesis, then the probability of values less than the observed $\bar{x}$ value (e.g., $\bar{x} < 57.8$) is the *p*-value. The *p*-value is the probability of values "beyond" or "more extreme than" the observed $\bar{x}$ value. If the observed $\bar{x}$ value is above the limiting value in H_O, then values "beyond" or "more extreme than" the observed $\bar{x}$ value are those values that are greater than the observed $\bar{x}$ value, and it is the probability of these values that is reflected in a *p*-value. (In Section 9.6, a *p*-value based on areas in both tails of the sampling distribution is introduced when "two-tailed tests" are considered. For now, we are dealing with *p*-values defined only for a one-tailed test.)

To calculate a *p*-value, the probability density function for the estimator must be known. If the population distribution of belt life is normal, with mean μ and variance

σ^2, then the sampling distribution of $\bar{x}$ will be normal and our model for $\bar{x}$ is

$$\bar{x} \sim N\left(\mu, \sigma / \sqrt{n}\right)$$

Alternatively, if the sample size is large, then from the Central Limit Theorem, $\bar{x}$ is known to be approximately normally distributed for simple random sampling.

Because H_0 is assumed true until contrary information is obtained, for the limiting value ($\mu = 59$) for which the null hypothesis is true, the expected value of $\bar{x}$ is 59, as shown in Figure 9.1. Assuming the population standard deviation is $\sigma = 3.333$, the standard deviation of the $\bar{x}$ distribution (also called the standard error of the mean, $\sigma_{\bar{x}}$) is

$$\sigma_{\bar{x}} = \sigma/\sqrt{n} = 3.333/\sqrt{36} = 0.5555$$

To calculate $P(\bar{x} \leq 57.8 \mid \mu = 59)$, $\bar{x}$ can be standardized as in Chapter 7. Now, however, the calculated value of z is denoted z_c.

$$z_c = \frac{\bar{x} - \mu}{\sigma_{\bar{x}}} = \frac{\bar{x} - \mu}{\sigma/\sqrt{n}} = \frac{57.8 - 59.0}{3.333/\sqrt{36}} = -2.16$$

From Appendix Table A.3 or a computer program such as EXCEL,

$$P(z \leq -2.16) = 1 - 0.9846 = 0.0154$$

Thus, the p-value is 0.0154. There is a 1.54 percent chance of observing a mean of 57.8 or less, in a sample of 36 belts, when the expected mean is 59.0 and $\bar{x}$ is normally distributed with mean of 59 and standard error of 0.5555. That is, if the population model is true, as assumed, then in only 154 out of every 10,000 randomly selected samples, on the average, will the sample mean be less or equal to 57.8.

The p-value is a conditional probability that can be used to show how far the sample result is from that assumed in the null hypothesis. An unlikely sample result (an $\bar{x}$ value far away from the μ value in H_0) is signified by a small p-value. The observation of sample data that is highly unlikely casts doubt on the correctness of the null hypothesis. On the other hand, a large p-value is the result of the sample mean being "close to" the limiting value of μ in H_0 and thus does not cast doubt on the correctness of the null hypothesis.

Decision Rule

Determining what constitutes a small or large p-value requires reference to the probability of a Type I error, which will be discussed further in the next section. Clearly, though, extremely small p-values indicate a sample result far away from that expected from the null hypothesis. An extremely small p-value is strong evidence against the null hypothesis. A large p-value indicates that the sample results are close to that expected when the null hypothesis is true.

FIGURE 9.1 Calculating the p-value in the Drive Belt Life Illustration

Panel a: Hatched area is the p-value for testing $\mu = 59$ versus $\mu < 59$.

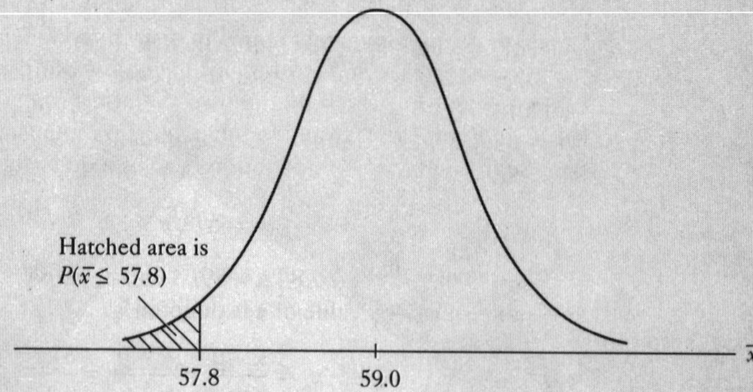

Panel b: Standardizing $\bar{x}$ gives the desired hatched area in the z distribution.

$$z_c = \frac{\bar{x} - \mu}{\sigma/\sqrt{n}} = \frac{57.8 - 59.0}{3.333/\sqrt{36}} = -2.16$$

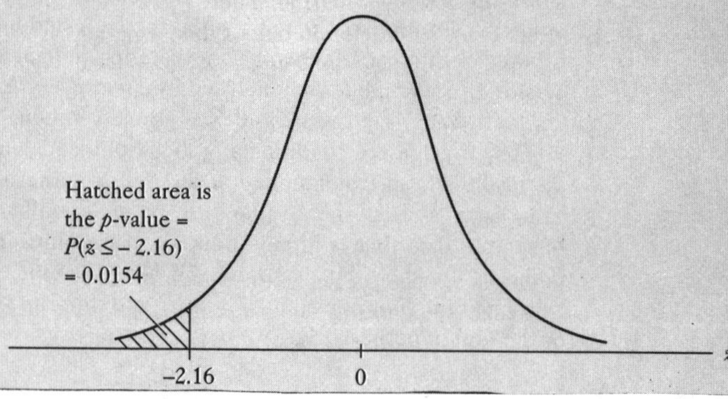

Recall from Chapter 7 that $P(x \leq 57.8) = 0.0154$ can be determined directly with the EXCEL command "=NORMDIST(57.8,59,0.5555)." Alternatively, $P(z \leq -2.16) = 0.0154$ can be determined with the EXCEL command "=NORMSDIST(-2.16)."

Decision Rule for selecting between H_0 and H_A:
Reject the null hypothesis (H_0) if the p-value is small.
Do not reject the null hypothesis if the p-value is large.

As in a legal proceeding, where the defendant is assumed innocent unless sufficient evidence is presented for a guilty verdict, H_0 is assumed true unless there is sufficient sample evidence (as reflected in a small p-value) to reject H_0. In a court of law, sometimes a defendant that seems guilty is not convicted because of lack of evidence. If the defendant is guilty but incorrectly acquitted, then in statistical language a Type II error is made. A Type II error occurs in statistical testing when the p-value is too big to reject H_0 even though H_0 is false, although unknowingly so by the researcher. On the other hand, an innocent person may be found guilty—in hypothesis testing, there is always the possibility of incorrectly rejecting H_0 when it is true, and the Type I error is made. As with the law, in a statistical decision there is always a tradeoff between the cost and probability of making a Type II versus a Type I error.

The p-value of 0.0154 in the drive belt illustration would be a small probability in the eyes of most any jurist. Something that occurs with such a low probability (0.0154) is so unlikely that when it does occur, there is good reason to suspect that the null hypothesis is wrong. Replacing alternator, fan, power steering, and air conditioning drive belts more frequently than every four years and 11 months seems advisable since the average life of these belts may be less than 59 months. In reaching this conclusion, however, we must acknowledge that there is a chance we might be wrong. The population standard deviation might not be 3.333; the sampling process might be biased toward an understatement of the mean because it was drawn from fleet vehicles[3] or, because of the chance factors inherent in a random sample, the sampling error could have brought about an unlikely sample. The cost of being wrong, however, seems trivial compared to an error on the other side.

HISTORICAL PERSPECTIVE

Ronald A. Fisher (1890–1962), Jerzy Neyman (1894–1981), and Egon S. Pearson (1895–1980) are credited with codifying and advancing the objective science of statistical testing. This development was not accomplished in a spirit of cooperation or appreciation for alternative views; even to this day heated debate about the merits of classical hypothesis testing continues.

Sir Ronald Fisher was a determined, feisty, and combative scholar. He overcame his handicap of poor eyesight, developing the almost microscopic handwriting that was a mark of distinction in pre-word-processing scholarship. He was schooled in mathematics and physics, and made major contributions to genetics and eugenics. Yet, he denigrated theoretical mathematicians and stressed the need to avoid contact with those in the natural sciences who did not know statistics. Possibly because of his interest in applying statistics to the biological sciences, he was unable to appreciate developments of a statistical methodology within economics and the other social sciences.

Being human, Fisher was known for making some major errors in practical empirical matters. In the service of the tobacco industry, for example, Fisher erred greatly in assessing the evidence against cigarette smoking. Based in part on faulty calculations, Fisher ascribed the harmful effects of smoking exclusively to genetic disposition.

Fisher's approach to statistical testing emphasized observed phenomena and not explicit theoretical constructs; his arguments were developed through examples. To Fisher, the observation of highly unlikely sample evidence was sufficient to reject a null hypothesis, but observed likely sample evidence had no informational value. That is, sample evidence could lead only to the rejection of the null hypothesis. Researchers had to be concerned only about the probability of a Type I error, because the speculative nature of a Type II error made it irrelevant.

In contrast to Fisher's emphasis on the Type I error, statisticians Jerzy Neyman and Egon Pearson viewed testing as a contest in which either the null or alternative hypothesis was rejected at the expense of the other: If the null was rejected, then by implication the alternative was not rejected and vice versa. The Neyman-Pearson theory of hypothesis testing emphasized both the probabilities and costs of Type I and Type II errors. They sought tests that had the "power" to differentiate between the null and alternative hypotheses. To them, unlikely sample information supported the alternative hypothesis and likely sample information supported the null hypothesis. Fisher tried to dismiss Neyman and Pearson as mere mathematicians without experience in the natural sciences and without real scientific problem-solving skills.

The distinction between the approaches of Fisher and Neyman–Pearson are lost in most modern-day studies. The logic and efficacy of hypothesis testing in general, however, continues to be debated, as reflected in the exchange of Spielman (1974), Carlson (1976), and Spielman (1978) on "The Logic of Tests of Significance." Of particular interest is the philosophical importance of Spielman's assertion that the rejection of the null hypothesis is only justified, when a rare event has been observed, if it is also reasonable to believe that the significant outcomes are not rare when the null hypothesis is false. According to Spielman, for classical hypothesis testing to be logically consistent, it also must be true that prior to sampling and testing "it is not incredible that the (null) hypothesis is false." (For instance, if one was convinced that the null hypothesis was true—from past experience or divine intervention—how could one rare occurrence justify its rejection?) This prior subjective judgment, however, is viewed as contrary to the objective nature of the classical methods popularized by Fisher, his followers, and his critics.

EXERCISES

9.1 What is the meaning of a p-value in a hypothesis test in which the alternative hypothesis calls for a lower-tailed null hypothesis rejection region?

9.2 Why does a small p-value imply that the sample does not represent the population assumed in the null hypothesis?

9.3 The "Transportation Notes" section of the *Chicago Tribune* (February 11, 1996) reported on a new all-season radial replacement tire called Infinitred. According to the article, "Goodyear says it expects the Infinitred to last more than 80,000 miles." This claim is to be tested.

a. Specify H_O and H_A, and state the consequences of a wrong conclusion.

b. If you work for *Consumer Reports*, how would you prefer to specify H_O and H_A? If you were a salesperson for the tire company, how might you prefer to specify the null and alternative hypotheses? Could the way the hypotheses are specified make a difference in the conclusion reached on the basis of sample information? Explain.

c. Let H_O: $\mu \leq 80{,}000$ and H_A: $\mu > 80{,}000$, and assume a sample of size $n = 36$ yields a mean of 86,380. Calculate the z test statistic and a p-value, assuming the population standard deviation is 5,234.

d. What conclusion can you draw in part c at $\alpha = 0.01$?

9.4 If the statement on the side of a light bulb package is as follows:

Watts	Light Output (Lumens)	Expected Life (Hours)	Stand. Dev.
60	855	1000	50

How could the correctness of the expected life claim be tested?

9.5 A *Wall Street Journal* (July 1, 1991) on P&G development of a low-calorie fat for candy bars quoted Joan Steuer, president of Chocolate Marketing, Inc., a Los Angeles consulting firm, saying, "It's one of the last indulgences people have. The average U.S. chocolate consumption is 11 pounds per person a year." State the null and alternative hypotheses implied by this quote, and describe the nature of the Type I and Type II errors for a test of these hypotheses.

9.4 General Procedures for Hypothesis Testing

Statistical testing can involve many different types of hypotheses and different test statistics. The procedure for conducting statistical tests of hypotheses, however, follows roughly the same steps, regardless of what is tested. Although not explicitly identified in the drive belt example, the steps are as follows.

1. Specify the model and the null and alternative hypotheses.
2. Formulate a decision rule to reject or not reject the null hypothesis based on tolerable error levels.
3. Select a test statistic.
4. Collect the sample data.
5. Calculate the value(s) of the test statistic and the associated *p*-value.
6. Reach a conclusion (reject or do not reject H_O).

The next sections will provide a discussion of these steps in more detail than was provided in the introductory drive belt illustration. The drive belt illustration, however, provides an ideal example of this testing procedure in which the reader does not have to get bogged down in technical matters. What follows is a more general, yet more technical, discussion of the hypothesis testing procedure.

9.5 The Null and Alternative Hypotheses (Step 1)

The determination of the null and alternative hypotheses and the model in which the test will be performed is not always easy, for there may be several different ways of formulating the problem. In tests of the population mean μ based on the sample mean $\bar{x}$, the model typically will be

$$\bar{x} \sim \text{Normal}\left(\mu, \sigma_{\bar{x}}\right), \text{ for } \sigma_{\bar{x}} = \sigma/\sqrt{n}$$

where σ is the population standard deviation.

Justification for assuming that $\bar{x}$ is approximately normally distributed is based either on the Central Limit Theorem or information that the population is normally distributed. Other models and hypotheses also can be specified. As will be discussed later in this chapter, for example, a test of the population proportion π based on the sample proportion $p = x/n$ can be based on the model[4]

$$p \sim \text{Approximately Normal } (\pi, \sigma_p), \text{ for } \sigma_p = \sqrt{\pi(1-\pi)/n}$$

where now only the Central Limit Theorem can be used to justify this model since x is a binomial random variable. That is, the sample must be large ($n > 30$).

Even when such models are not explicitly identified with the null and alternative hypotheses, they are implicit, since a test of a population parameter cannot be done without an assumption about the distribution of the estimator. Models contain all of the assumptions that are maintained throughout the test. The appropriateness of these maintained assumptions will receive more attention in later chapters; our primary concern here is to acknowledge that there are implicit assumptions about the model that are required to test the null and alternative hypotheses.

Rules of thumb for specifying the null and alternative hypotheses are often based on the Fisherian idea that a new theory is required to dispute an older one. In accordance with this notion of testing, the null hypothesis will reflect the old theory and the new theory will be captured in the alternative. More generally, the alternative hypothesis contains the statement being tested.

For example, when Barbara A. Metz, a researcher at Battelle Memorial Institute in Columbus, Ohio, claimed to "have an antidote that could make tires last longer" (*Business Week*, September 28, 1992), the average life of the old tires goes in the null hypothesis and the alternative is that the average life of new tires exceeds the old. Unfortunately, not all testing situations are as clear-cut.

In claiming that they were underpaid, the female employees who brought suit against a large midwestern bank for sex discrimination in the 1980s would have found it advantageous to have the null hypothesis be that the average salary of women is less than that of men, since the null is assumed true until contrary evidence is provided. The bank, on the other hand, would want the null to be the reverse (average salary of women is greater than or equal to that of men).[5] As will be shown, and as discussed in the 1991 deposition of the author as an expert witness in this case, a statistical test of discrimination is possible if the latter is used but is not possible if the former is used.[6]

As another example, consider the debate over the use of Retin-A as a wrinkle-prevention ointment. (*Wall Street Journal*, June 12, 1991) Johnson & Johnson (the producer of Retin-A) was alleged to be promoting Retin-A for removing wrinkles (the null hypothesis). The U.S. Food and Drug Administration was not convinced and asked the U.S. Justice Department for a decision on whether to proceed with a civil lawsuit against the giant pharmaceutical company. FDA Commissioner David Kessler was quoted by the *WSJ* as saying, "We do not have data to assess the long-term safety of Retin-A for chronic use in wrinkles." The FDA wanted the null hypothesis to be that Retin-A does not work and the alternative hypothesis to be that it does. Although a pharmaceutical company might like the FDA to assume that a new treatment works until proved otherwise, the FDA insists that the null hypothesis be that it does not work with the alternative accepted only when sufficient sample data supports such a conclusion.

As an alternative to the rules of putting that which is new and challenging in the alternative, a Neyman-Pearson approach suggests that the null hypothesis should contain the statement that implies the highest cost if it is rejected wrongly. This is a good rule of thumb, and it may help shed light on the appropriate statement of the null and the alternative hypotheses in some situations. In the case of Retin-A, however, whose costs should be considered? The person with wrinkles? Johnson & Johnson's? The FDA's? Or society's? In the case of the women's suit against the bank for sex discrimination in salary determination, whose cost should be used to determine the null hypothesis? The women's? The bank's? Or society's? Specifying the null and alternative hypotheses on the basis of the cost of making an error clearly depends on whose costs are considered.

There are exceptions to the rules of thumb commonly used to determine the null and alternative hypotheses. The null hypothesis, however, can never be that the population parameter is not equal to a specific value. In tests of the population mean or population proportion, the null must contain an equal sign, a less than or equal to sign, or a greater than or equal to sign. To perform a statistical hypothesis test of the type considered here, the sampling distribution must be centered at a specific value; thus, the null hypothesis must always include equality with that value.

Formulating the Null Hypothesis

To test a population mean or a population proportion, the null hypothesis must contain an equal sign, a less than or equal to sign, or a greater than or equal to sign.

The null hypothesis can never be that the population parameter is not equal to a specific value, is only less than a specific value, or is only greater than a specific value.

One-Tailed Tests

The tax preparers cited in *The Wall Street Journal* article at the beginning of this chapter claimed the average time required to complete a tax form is higher than that claimed by the IRS. They argued that the Internal Revenue Service had understated the time required to find and check documents required to complete a tax form and that the average time for completion was greater than the IRS's nine hours and five minutes. Thus the null and alternative hypotheses are

$$H_O\text{: } \mu \leq 9.0833 \text{ and } H_A\text{: } \mu > 9.0833$$

Unlike the drive belt illustration, the alternative hypothesis in this tax illustration allows for the population average to be greater than that in the null hypothesis. The alternative hypothesis for belt life illustration was "one tailed," but it stated that the population average would be less than that given in the null hypothesis.

$$H_O\text{: } \mu \geq 59 \text{ and } H_A\text{: } \mu < 59$$

But like the belt life illustration, the test of the time to complete a tax form is a unidirectional test. Thus, they are both said to be "one-tailed" tests.

One-Tailed Hypothesis Test A test in which the alternative hypothesis allows for departure from the value given by H_O in only one direction.

A **one-tailed hypothesis test** is appropriate whenever direction is indicated by the use of words such as "greater than," "less than," "inferior to," "superior to," "at least," or "at most." The alternative hypothesis in a one-tailed test will always contain either a < or > sign. The implied null hypothesis will then contain either a ≥ sign or a ≤. For example, if H_A: $\mu > 9.0833$ is the alternative hypothesis, then the implied null hypothesis is the reverse statement H_O: $\mu \leq 9.0833$.

Although the null hypothesis H_O: $\mu \leq 9.0833$ includes all the values at or below 9.0833, only $\mu = 9.0833$ need be used in a one-tailed test against the alternative $\mu > 9.0833$. If $\mu = 9.0833$ is rejected in favor of the alternative $\mu > 9.0833$, then any value of $\mu < 9.0833$ likewise would be rejected, regardless of its actual magnitude. Thus, the null and alternative in a one-tailed test are often written as H_O: $\mu = 9.0833$ versus H_A: $\mu > 9.0833$, where the equal sign in the null is understood to imply equal to or less than. It is the alternative hypothesis that establishes the test as one-tail.

Two-Tailed Tests

Two-Tailed Hypothesis Test A test in which the alternative hypothesis allows for departure from the values given by H_O in either direction.

In contrast to one-tailed tests, in a **two-tailed hypothesis test** the alternative hypothesis allows for values on either side of a value for which equality is claimed in the null hypothesis. For example, in deciding on the amount of paper toweling to place on a roll, the marketing expert said 60 feet. This expert could be wrong if μ is greater than 60 or less than 60, $\mu \neq 60$. In the absence of any other information, however, we would have to assume he is correct, $\mu = 60$. Putting the assumed equality in the null hypothesis now gives

$$H_O\text{: } \mu = 60 \text{ and } H_A\text{: } \mu \neq 60$$

In addition to means, we will be testing statements about the population proportion, π. As an example, consider the Lotto America situation in which the official claimed that a person's residence has nothing to do with the chances of winning. If this is true, then 31 percent of the jackpots can be expected to go to Wisconsin residents since that is the proportion of tickets they purchased. Any deviation in either direction from this percentage might be used to cast doubt on its validity. Thus, if π is the population proportion expected by chance, the null and alternative hypotheses are

$$H_O\text{: } \pi = 0.31 \text{ and } H_A\text{: } \pi \neq 0.31$$

If no direction is suggested, and departure from the value in the null hypothesis can go in either direction, then a two-tailed test is required. Often, in questions words such as "equal to," "similar to," and "no different from" are indications that a two-tailed test may be needed. For a two-tailed test, the null hypothesis will contain an equal sign and the alternative hypothesis will have a not-equal-to sign.

9.6 The Probabilities of Type I and II Errors (Step 2)

As already presented in Table 9.1, there are four outcomes associated with a choice between the null and alternative hypotheses; two lead to mistakes. A Type I error occurs if the null hypothesis (H_O) is rejected when it is true. A Type I error may also be stated as accepting the alternative hypothesis (H_A) when it is false. A Type II error occurs if the null hypothesis (H_O) is not rejected when it is false. A Type II error may also be stated as rejecting the alternative (H_A) when it is true. Unfortunately, since the true value of a population parameter is typically unknown, we never know for sure whether a conclusion based on sample information is correct or incorrect.

Before sampling, a decision rule should be established for determining when H_O is to be rejected and when it is not rejected. This decision rule is based on the probability of a Type I error versus the probability of a Type II error. The Greek letter **alpha,** (α) is used to represent the probability of making a Type I error and the letter **beta,** (β) represents the probability of a Type II error.

Alpha, α
The probability of making a Type I error.

Beta, β
The probability of making a Type II error.

Ideally both the probabilities of a Type I error and a Type II error would be made as small as possible in a hypothesis test. Values of α can be specified easily, but, as shown in two appendices to this chapter, determining β is an involved process. Because a decision rule for rejecting (or not rejecting) the null hypothesis can be formulated with only knowledge of the probability of a Type I error, many analysts rely on the fact that there is an inverse relationship between α and β and never attempt to actually determine β. This **α–β tradeoff** and related issues are also discussed in the appendices to this chapter.

α–β Tradeoff
Decreasing the probability of a Type I error (α) increases the probability of a Type II error (β), holding the sample size constant.

The researcher sets α in accordance with the cost of making a Type I error. If rejecting the null hypothesis when it is true would result in an extremely costly error, then α is set relatively small, at $\alpha = 0.01$, for example. (The α–β tradeoff implies, however, that β is then relatively large.) If rejecting the null hypothesis when it is true would result in little cost, then α is set relatively large, at $\alpha = 0.10$, for example. (The α–β tradeoff implies, however, that β is then relatively small.) The α–β tradeoff prevents the analyst from setting $\alpha = 0$: if α is decreased to zero, then β is increased to its maximum. Recall from our earlier discussions, however, that assignment of cost to Type I and Type II errors is not an easy task.

In the drive belt illustration, suppose that the probability of a Type I error had been preset at $\alpha = 0.05$. This **level of statistical significance** means that 5 percent of the time we are willing to be wrong when the null hypothesis H_O: $\mu \geq 59$ is rejected and the alternative H_A: $\mu < 59$ is accepted. This probability of a Type I error is shown in Figure 9.2. The shaded area that is 5% of the area under the density function is associated with the $\bar{x}$ values for which H_O will be rejected. The H_O rejection region is in the lower tail because the alternative hypothesis is true only if the population mean is less than 59.

Level of Statistical Significance
The (lowest) level of α for which the null hypothesis can be rejected.

In Figure 9.2, the value of $\bar{x}$ for which 5 percent of the $\bar{x}$ values are lower is $\bar{x}$ = 58.09, which is called the critical value. The critical $\bar{x}$ value is identified by the letter *b*

FIGURE 9.2 Probability of a Type I Error and the Critical $\bar{x}$ Value in the Drive Belt Illustration

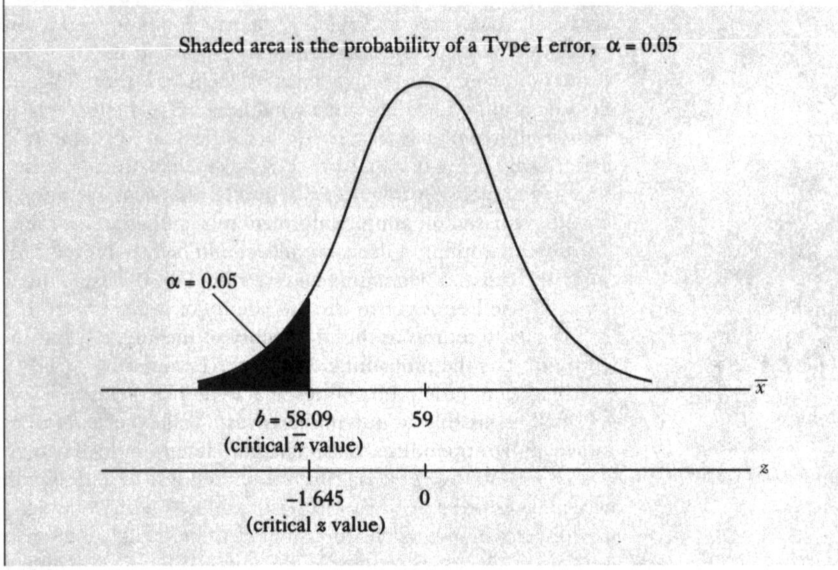

in Figure 9.2. The critical $\bar{x}$ value, $b = 58.09$, is found by substituting b for $\bar{x}$ in the z formula in Chapter 7, which gives Formula (9.1).

Critical $\bar{x}$ value is b, which is standardized as z_b

$$z_b = \frac{b - \mu_0}{\sigma/\sqrt{n}} \tag{9.1}$$

Corresponding to the critical $\bar{x}$ value, b, is its corresponding standardized value; this critical value of z is z_b. From Appendix Table A.3 or a computer program, the critical value of z that puts 5 percent of the distribution in the lower tail of the z distribution is −1.645.

$$P(z \leq -1.645) = 0.05$$

$z_b = -1.645$ is called the critical z value; its relationship to the critical $\bar{x}$ value b is shown in Figure 9.2. This b value is determined directly from EXCEL with the command

=NORMINV(0.05,59,0.5555).

Alternatively, substituting $z = -1.645$, $\mu_0 = 59$, $\sigma = 3.333$, and $n = 36$ into Formula (9.1) yields:

$$-1.645 = \frac{b - 59}{3.333/\sqrt{36}} = \frac{b - 59}{0.5555}$$

and $b = 58.09$

This critical value of b is shown in Figure 9.2, along with the corresponding critical z value of -1.645. As shown, 58.09 months is 1.645 standard errors ($1.645\sigma/\sqrt{n}$) below 59 months in the $\bar{x}$ distribution.

Calculated Test Statistic
The value of the statistic that is calculated from observed sample data and then used to test a hypothesis about the parent population.

Figure 9.1 and Figure 9.2 provide all the ingredients for a statistical decision between rejecting or not rejecting the null hypothesis. We already had decided that the observed sample mean of 57.8 months, the **calculated test statistic** value, was significantly below the null hypothesis value of 59 because 57.8 was 2.16 standard errors below 59, Figure 9.1, which was reflected in a small p-value of 0.0154. Now in Figure 9.2, the critical $\bar{x}$ value of 58.09 and critical z of -1.645 and α-risk of 0.05 can be used to define what constitutes "significantly below" and "a small p-value." Since the observed sample values ($\bar{x} = 57.8$ and $z = -2.16$) are beyond or more extreme than their critical values (58.09 and -1.645), the null hypothesis should be rejected because the observed sample values are "significantly far away." Another way to say this is that since the p-value of 0.0154 is smaller than the α-level of 0.05, the null hypothesis should be rejected. Our earlier decision rule for choosing between the null and alternative hypotheses now can be restated with more rigor.

Decision rule for selecting between H_0 and H_A:

Reject the null hypothesis (H_0) if the p-value is smaller than α.

Do not reject the null hypothesis if the p-value is larger than α.

One-Tailed Hypothesis Tests

For one-tailed tests, the decision rule based on an α-risk and a p-value comparison has already been illustrated in the drive belt example. The general principle is summarized in Figure 9.3 and Figure 9.4. In both graphs, H_0 is not rejected if the p-value $\geq \alpha$ and H_0 is rejected if the p-value $< \alpha$. These are the same conclusions that would be reached by comparing the observed $\bar{x}$ value (and its calculated z) with the critical $\bar{x}$ value (and critical z).

Two-Tailed Hypothesis Tests

For a two-tailed hypothesis test, the decision rule continues to be the same: reject H_0 if the p-value is less than α. Now, however, account must be taken of the fact that the

FIGURE 9.3 Decision Rules for Lower One-Tailed Hypothesis Tests

Panel a: In a lower-tailed alternative hypothesis test where the population mean μ is being tested as

$H_O: \mu \geq \mu_0$

$H_A: \mu < \mu_0$

the decision is to "not reject H_O" if the p-value $\geq \alpha$ as shown below

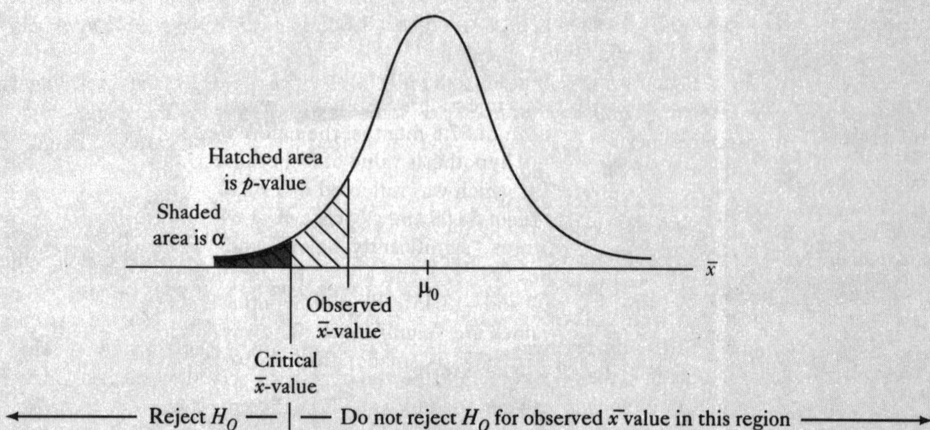

Panel b: In a lower-tailed alternative hypothesis test where the population mean μ is being tested as

$H_O: \mu \geq \mu_0$

$H_A: \mu < \mu_0$

the decision is to "reject H_O" if the p-value $\leq \alpha$ as shown below

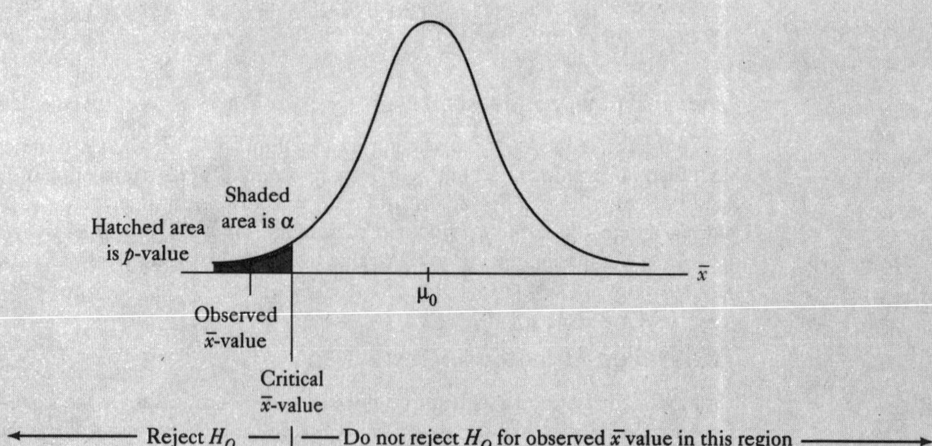

FIGURE 9.4 Decision Rules for Upper One-Tailed Hypothesis Tests

Panel a: In an upper-tailed alternative hypothesis test where the population mean μ is being tested as

H_O: $\mu \leq \mu_0$

H_A: $\mu > \mu_0$

the decision is to "not reject H_O" if the p-value $\geq \alpha$ as shown below

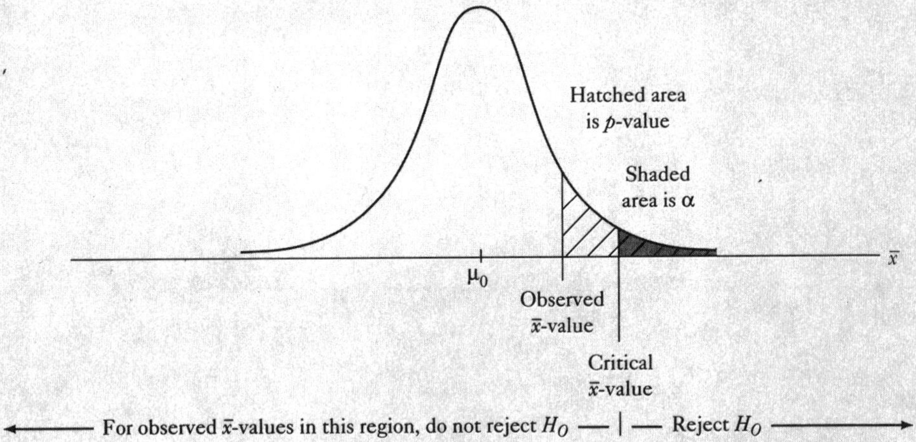

Panel b: In an upper-tailed alternative hypothesis test where the population mean μ is being tested as

H_O: $\mu \leq \mu_0$

H_A: $\mu > \mu_0$

the decision is to "reject H_O" if the p-value $\leq \alpha$ as shown below

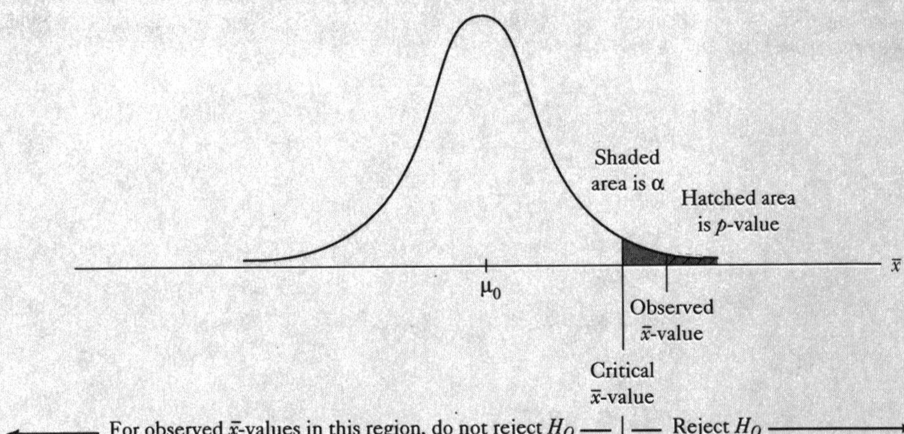

FIGURE 9.5 Decision Rules for Two-Tailed Hypothesis Tests Where $H_O: \mu = \mu_0$ and $H_A: \mu \neq \mu_0$

Panel a: When H_O cannot be rejected.

Because the alternative hypothesis allows for μ to differ from μ_0 in either direction, this graph shows shaded areas in both tails as α so that one tail contains only half of α. The hatched area beyond the observed $\bar{x}$-value is now only half of the *p*-value; thus, the hatched area must be doubled to obtain the *p*-value. Since half the *p*-value is greater than $\alpha/2$, the *p*-value is greater than α, and H_O is not rejected.

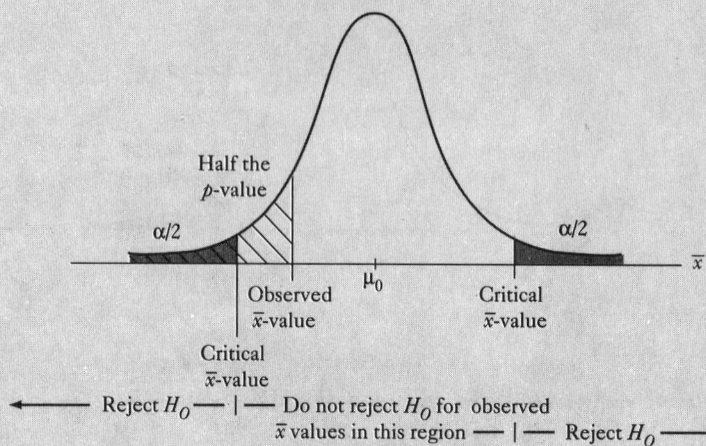

Panel b: When H_O can be rejected.

Because the alternative hypothesis allows for μ to differ from μ_0 in either direction, this graph shows shaded areas in both tails as α so that one tail contains only half of α. The hatched area beyond the observed $\bar{x}$-value is now only half of the *p*-value; thus, the hatched area must be doubled to obtain the *p*-value. Since half the *p*-value is less than $\alpha/2$, the *p*-value is less than α, and H_O is rejected.

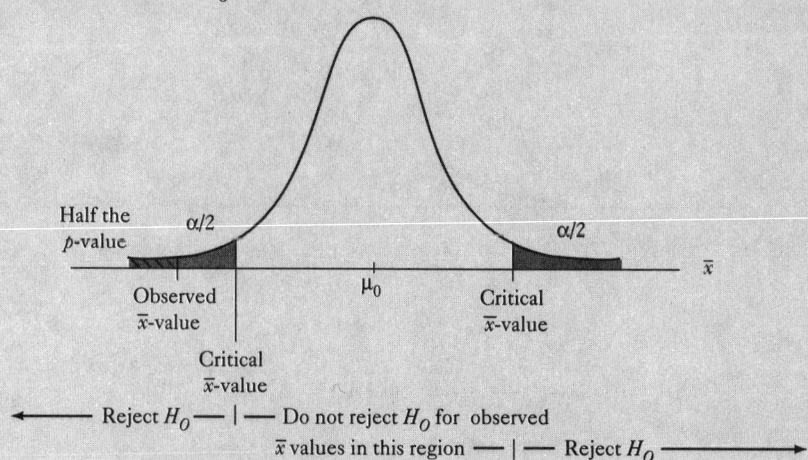

alternative hypothesis permits values on either side of the single value specified in the null hypothesis. The probability of a Type I error is not put in one tail of the distribution, but rather it is split equally between the two tails. That is, $\alpha/2$ is put in each tail beyond the critical test statistic value, as shown in Figure 9.5.

Students often have difficulty distinguishing between the determination of the critical test statistic value for a given α-level in a two-tailed test and the calculation of the p-value based on the observed $\bar{x}$ value. Unlike dividing α in two to determine the critical test statistic value, as shown in Figure 9.5, the calculation of the p-value in a two-tailed test requires a doubling of the area under the density function for $\bar{x}$ values more extreme than the observed $\bar{x}$. Thus, for a two-tailed test, only half of α is the probability of $\bar{x}$ values more extreme than the critical test statistic value on just one side of the mean. For a two-tailed test, only half of the p-value is the probability of $\bar{x}$ values more extreme than the observed $\bar{x}$ value.

EXERCISES

9.6 State the null and alternative hypotheses for each of the following, using the notation given in this chapter.

a. The mean number of applicants for a training program in sales for the past five years has been 87.4. Has this average changed?

b. An econometric analysis was obtained to determine if the rate of inflation in the area had changed from last year, when the mean rate was 5 percent.

c. The personnel director believes that sick leaves have decreased since a policing program was implemented. In the past, employees averaged three sickdays per month.

d. A machine stamps parts at a defect rate of 10 percent, when it is operating correctly. When is the defective rate much too high (out of control)?

e. A sailboat racer believes that on average a new line stretches no more than his old line. The old line stretched 1.8 percent of its length at 15 percent of its working load.

f. A management study was to determine if the mean cost of piece work had changed since last year, when the cost was \$378 per piece.

g. An engineer thinks a new composite has a mean breaking strength greater than the old composite. The old breaking strength averaged 1,000 pounds per square inch.

h. The claim is made that at most 7 percent of the population will be unemployed in the next recession.

i. An accounting study is to assess if there has been a decrease in the percentage of overdue accounts receivable. At the last audit, 6 percent of these accounts were overdue.

9.7 An article in *The Wall Street Journal* (March 25, 1997) discusses the merits of "actively managed vs. index funds."

a. If π is the probability of an active manager picking a winner, state the hypotheses to test whether active managers' picks are better than flipping a coin.

b. If μ is the mean rate of return to active managers' portfolios, and if the stock market in general has averaged a return of 20 percent, state the hypotheses to test whether the active managers' mean return differs from the market in general.

9.8 Find the critical z or t value for each of the following.

a. For a two-tailed test, where H_O: $\mu = \mu_0$, $\alpha = 0.02$, $n = 36$, and the population variance is known.

b. For a one-tailed test, where H_A: $\mu > \mu_0$, $\alpha = 0.05$, $n = 16$, and the population variance is unknown but the population is normal.

c. For a two-tailed test, where H_O: $\pi = \pi_0$, $\alpha = 0.05$, and $n = 40$, and π_0 or its estimate is not close to 0 or 1.

9.9 What are the different rules of thumb for deciding whether a hypothesis test is one- or two-tailed? What are the rules for determining which statement is to go into the null versus the alternative hypothesis?

9.10 Why doesn't the probability of a Type II error equal one minus the probability of a Type I error?

9.11 A *Wall Street Journal* article (January 18, 1985) on computer product design systems quoted Henry Eichfield, an official at Computervision Corp., as saying, "Thirty percent down time isn't atypical for the world of data processing." Design an experiment to test this claim based on sample information. What are the costs you need to consider?

9.12 *A Business Week* (January 30, 1995) article tells of Peter Chevalier's inability to have the most advanced pacemaker made by Medtronic installed when he needed his heart rate regulated electronically. As a researcher and development chief at Medtronic, Chevalier was convinced from tests in Europe that the new model was superior to the older one, but the U.S. Food & Drug Administrations hadn't reached that conclusion. Chevalier complained that "In an attempt to eliminate all risk, the FDA is delaying the entry of new technology." Was the FDA using a larger or a smaller alpha than that desired by Chevalier?

9.7 Selecting a Test Statistic (Step 3)

The values of a test statistic behave according to a known probability distribution. In this chapter, we use two familiar test statistics introduced in Chapters 7 and 8—the z and the t statistics. In the case of the sample mean, both of these test statistics are based on the model

$$\bar{x} \sim \text{Normal}\left(\mu, \sigma_{\bar{x}}\right), \text{ for } \sigma_{\bar{x}} = \sigma/\sqrt{n}$$

In this model, and as discussed in Chapter 8, if the population standard deviation σ is known, then the z test statistic can be used to calculate probabilities for the $\bar{x}$ distribution, assuming the expected value of $\bar{x}$ is μ_0, as given in the null hypothesis, and either the parent population is normal or the sample size is large ($n > 30$) so that $\bar{x}$ is approximately normal. This formula for this z statistic is[7]

z test statistic for $\mu = \mu_0$

$$z = \frac{\bar{x} - \mu_0}{\sigma/\sqrt{n}} \tag{9.2}$$

Formula (9.2) gives the standardized value of $\bar{x}$ around its expected value of $\bar{x}$ as given in H_O. This formula was used in the drive belt illustration, where the z was calculated as

$$z_c = \frac{\bar{x} - \mu}{\sigma/\sqrt{n}} = \frac{57.8 - 59.0}{3.333/\sqrt{36}} = -2.16$$

Usually the population standard deviation is unknown. When the population standard deviation is unknown, as discussed in Chapter 8, the Student's t test statistic is used to standardize $\bar{x}$ around its expected value μ_0, as given in the null hypothesis.

t test statistic for $\mu = \mu_0$

$$t = \frac{\bar{x} - \mu_0}{s/\sqrt{n}} \quad \text{where } s = \sqrt{\Sigma(x_i - \bar{x})^2/(n-1)} \tag{9.3}$$

Formula (9.3) requires that $\bar{x}$ is normally distributed, which for small samples is assured if the population x is normal. Unlike Formula (9.2), in (9.3) the population standard deviation σ is not used, since it is unknown. σ is estimated by the sample standard deviation. The denominator of Formula (9.2), $\sigma/\sqrt{n}$, is the standard deviation of the distribution (also called the standard error of the mean). The denominator of the Formula (9.3), $s/\sqrt{n}$, is called the **estimated standard error of the mean;** it is the estimator for the standard deviation of all the $\bar{x}$'s that could be obtained under repeated sampling.

Estimated Standard Error of the Mean The estimated value of the standard deviation of $\bar{x}$; computed as s divided by the square root of the sample size, n.

To illustrate the use of the t test statistic, consider the claim of the marketing expert who said the mean amount of paper toweling used by a family of four is 60 feet per pay period. The null and alternative hypotheses were given as

$$H_O\text{: } \mu = 60 \text{ and } H_A\text{: } \mu \neq 60$$

For this test, suppose a simple random sample of 31 families was selected; each family was paid to have its paper towel use monitored. The sample mean amount of toweling used was 64.1 feet, and the sample standard deviation was 13.452 feet. The population standard deviation is unknown, so the appropriate test statistic is t, and its calculated value is

$$t_c = \frac{\bar{x} - \mu_0}{s/\sqrt{n}} = \frac{64.1 - 60}{13.452/\sqrt{31}} = 1.697$$

Even if the population was not normally distributed in this case, approximate normality of $\bar{x}$ can be justified in this case by the Central Limit Theorem, since n is relatively large. The calculated t statistic can be used to determine the p-value, as done in the section following our discussion of the sample.

9.8 THE SAMPLE (STEP 4)

Throughout this book we assume that simple random sampling is possible. Recall that this does not imply that samples are "representative" of the population; after all, if a sample was representative, there would be no need for hypothesis testing, since the sample mean would be the population mean. Classical hypothesis testing requires simple random sampling, as discussed in Chapter 7.

Typically, data collected by simple random sampling are not available. For example, in March 1991, J.D. Power & Associates mailed a six-page questionnaire to 73,000 owners of 1990 model cars. Recipients received $1 for responding, and, according to *Business Week* (June 10, 1991), about 23,000 did. Whether these 23,000 represent a simple random sample of 1990 car owners is debatable. Are the less wealthy more likely to respond? Are those who are pleased (or upset) with their cars more likely to respond? Are those who bought a certain make or model more likely to respond? Were owners more likely to respond to different types of problems?

As another example of problems caused by nonrandom sampling, consider the case of Bloomington (Indiana) Hospital and its attempts to assess employee satisfaction. In 1991, Bloomington Hospital hired the consulting firm Alpha Company (of Minneapolis) for $12,000 to survey 35 of 1,700 employees. The 35 employees were picked by division managers, and the Alpha Group provided probability estimates as to whether or not employees were satisfied (and would or would not want to unionize). Because the 35 employees were hand picked and not selected by simple random sampling, the use of classical statistics to make inferences is dubious.

If we have reason to believe that simple random sampling was not employed, then the validity of the testing procedure must be called into question. Discussions of biases that are introduced through sample selection were presented in Chapters 1 and 7 and the Chapter 7 appendix. Sample selection problems and the absence of a plausible probability model, however, do not necessarily imply that probability-based testing is worthless. University of Chicago Professor of Statistics Paul Meier (1986) argues that

> such testing serves a useful purpose as a benchmark: if the observed association would not be counted statistically significant had it arisen from a randomized study, it could not be counted as persuasive, when even that foundation is lacking. If the observed association is highly statistically significant, however, the extent of its persuasiveness depends on many uncertain judgments about background factors, and its persuasive value is not at all reflected in the significance level itself. (p. 271)

What one can learn from nonrandom samples clearly depends on the situation and the conclusion suggested by the data.

9.9 DETERMINING *p*-VALUES (STEP 5)

We have already calculated the *p*-value for one-tailed tests involving the z test statistic. Those *p*-values involved one of the following probability calculations: $P(z \geq z_c)$ or $P(z \leq z_c)$. Determining *p*-values using the t test statistic for a one-tailed test is the same as for the z except that the t distribution is used. As shown in Figure 9.5, calculating the p-value in a two-tailed test is not as straightforward because the alternative hypothesis allows for a difference from the value in the null hypothesis in either direction.

In a two-tailed test, the absolute difference between the observed $\bar{x}$ value and the value in the null hypothesis is the measure of interest; the direction (– or +) of the difference is irrelevant. Because the absolute value of the test statistic is of interest, the area under the density function for values of $\bar{x}$ beyond or more extreme than the observed $\bar{x}$ value in the one tail is only half of the p-value (as the area beyond a critical test statistic is only half of the α-level). Doubling the area under the density function for $\bar{x}$ values beyond the observed $\bar{x}$ value gives the p-value in a two-tailed test. Thus we have the following rules for p-values.

Rules for determining *p*-values

If H_A is $\mu > \mu_0$, then

$$p\text{-value} = P(z \geq z_c)$$

If H_A is $\mu < \mu_0$, then

$$p\text{-value} = P(z \leq z_c)$$

If H_A is $\mu \neq \mu_0$, then

$$p\text{-value} = P(z \geq |z_c|)$$
$$= 2P(z \geq z_c), \text{ if } z_c > 0$$

or

$$= 2P(z \leq z_c), \text{ if } z_c < 0$$

Determining the *p*-value for a One-Tailed *t* Test

A p-value for a one-tailed t test follows the same steps as used in a z test, except probabilities are calculated from the t distribution in a computer package or as contained in Appendix Table A.4. As an example, consider a test to determine whether or not a computer disk drive has an average access time of no more than nine milliseconds versus an alternative that the average access time is greater than nine milliseconds; that is,

$$H_O\text{: } \mu \leq 9 \text{ and } H_A\text{: } \mu > 9$$

Assume the model is

$$\bar{x} \sim \text{Normal}\left(\mu, \sigma_{\bar{x}}\right), \text{ for } \sigma_{\bar{x}} = \sigma/\sqrt{n}$$

but that the population standard deviation σ is unknown. A sample of 16 disk drives yields a sample mean of $\bar{x} = 11.21$ and a sample standard deviation of $s = 3.40$. Assuming that population distribution of computer disk access time is normally distributed (to justify the assumption that $\bar{x}$ is approximately normal), the t test statistic is appropriate and its calculated value is 2.60.

$$t_c = \frac{\bar{x} - \mu_0}{s/\sqrt{n}} = \frac{11.21 - 9.00}{3.40/\sqrt{16}} = 2.60$$

FIGURE 9.6 The *p*-value for an Upper-Tailed *t* Test

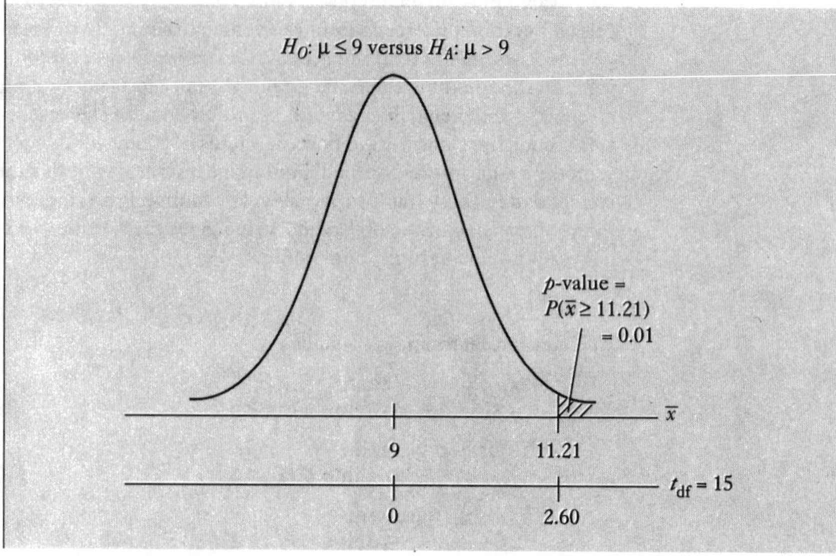

Because this is an upper-tail test, the *p*-value is $P(t \geq 2.60|\text{df}=15)$. This probability is determined most easily with a computer program such as EXCEL. Entering "=TDIST(2.60,15,1)" into any EXCEL cell yields 0.01005, which is the *p*-value shown in Figure 9.6. Recall from Chapter 8, that the general EXCEL command for probability calculations with the *t* distribution is "=TDIST(value,df,tails)," where "value" is the *t* value of interest, "df" are the degrees of freedom, and "tails" equals 1 or 2, for one or two tail areas.

QUERY 9.1:

A *Wall Street Journal* (April 1, 1991) article reported that because of price wars, the average retail price for a gallon of self-serve regular unleaded gasoline was only $1.04, with some places charging less than 90 cents per gallon, even though market analysts say prices should be higher. As additional information on gasoline prices, the article reported prices in ten cities:

Atlanta	$ 0.94
Los Angeles	0.94
Dallas	0.98
Miami	1.03
San Francisco	1.05
Philadelphia	1.08
Las Vegas	1.12

Long Island	1.15
Boston	1.15
Chicago	1.19

But this sample has an average of \$1.063, suggesting that it is not representative of the population or that the national average might be higher than \$1.04 or that sampling error caused the difference. Do these data refute or support the idea that the national average is greater than \$1.04?

ANSWER:
The null and alternative hypotheses are

$$H_O: \mu \leq 1.04 \text{ and } H_A: \mu > 1.04$$

The t test statistic is calculated using a spreadsheet as

x	$(x - \bar{x})$	$(x - \bar{x})^2$
0.94	–0.123	0.015129
0.94	–0.123	0.015129
0.98	–0.083	0.006889
1.03	–0.033	0.001089
1.05	–0.013	0.000169
1.08	0.017	0.000289
1.12	0.057	0.003249
1.15	0.087	0.007569
1.15	0.087	0.007569
1.19	0.127	0.016129

$$\sum x = 10.63 \qquad 0.07321 = \sum(x - \bar{x})^2$$

$$\bar{x} = 1.063 \qquad s^2 = 0.00813 = \sum(x - \bar{x})^2 / (n - 1)$$

$$s = 0.09019$$

$$s/\sqrt{n} = 0.02852$$

$$t = 0.8064 = (\bar{x} - \mu)/s/\sqrt{n}$$

We are using t here because σ is unknown and the sample is small. Furthermore, assuming that the population is normally distributed does not seem unreasonable. At any of the typical α-levels, the null hypothesis cannot be rejected because the calculated $t = 0.8064$ is so small. (For example, at $\alpha = .10$ the critical t is 1.383, with nine degrees of freedom.) Similarly, using a computer program such as EXCEL, the p-value can be determined to be 0.22:

$$P(\bar{x} > 1.063 \mid \mu = 1.04) = P(t > 0.8064 \mid \text{df} = 9) = 0.22$$

This p-value is relatively large, suggesting that \$1.063 is "close to" \$1.04, given the variability in sampling. Thus, these ten sample observations on the price of gasoline are not inconsistent with the claim that the national average is \$1.04, and they do not support the claim that the national average is greater than \$1.04. The *p*-value and the related statistics are shown in the diagram below.

(Note that without a computer program, exact *p*-values cannot be obtained. From the *t* table in Appendix A.4, for example, there is no information for $t = 0.8064$, with nine degrees of freedom. In this table, however, 25 percent of the distribution can be seen to be beyond $t = 0.703$, df = 9. In the absence of accurate *p*-values, we are restricted to comparing calculated and critical test statistics values to complete a statistical hypothesis test.)

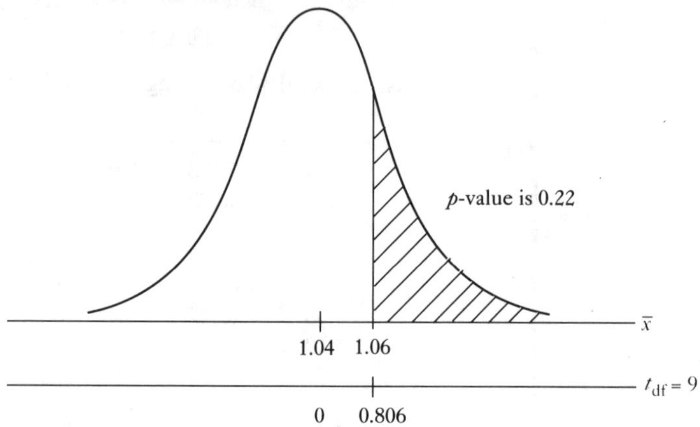

Determining a *p*-value for a Two-Tailed Test

Determining the *p*-value for a two-tailed alternative hypothesis requires attention because the sample value can fall on either side of the value in the null hypothesis. The absolute value of the difference between the value in the null hypothesis and the observed $\bar{x}$ value is of interest. Thus, the area beyond the observed $\bar{x}$ value (as given by the corresponding area beyond the calculated test statistic value) is only half of the *p*-value. For comparisons with α, the area beyond the observed $\bar{x}$ value (when it is in either tail) must be doubled to obtain the absolute value of being beyond this value. That is, the *p*-value in a two-tailed test of μ is either

$$P(z \geq | z_c |) \text{ or } P(t \geq | t_c |)$$

In the paper towel example, the null and alternative hypotheses were $\mu = 60$ and $\mu \neq 60$. For a sample of size 31, the mean was 64.1, the estimated standard error was 2.416, and the calculated *t* test was 1.697. The area beyond 1.697 can be obtained from the 30th row in Appendix Table A.4, because the degrees of freedom are 30. The area beyond 1.697 is 0.05—that is, $P(t \geq 1.697) = 1 - 0.95 = 0.05$. But this is only the *p*-value for an upper-tailed test. A two-tailed test accommodates $\bar{x}$ values on both sides of

FIGURE 9.7 The p-value in the Two-Tailed Test of Paper Towel Use

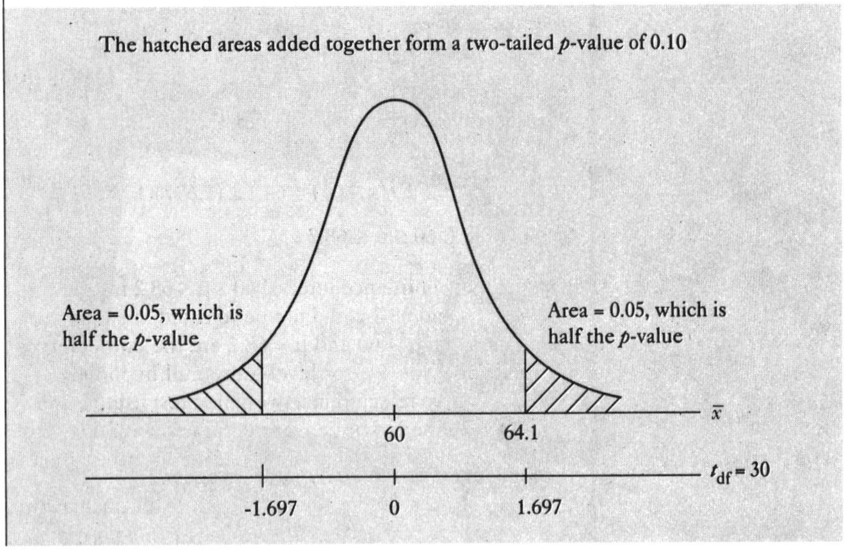

the value in the null hypothesis. Thus, the p-value for this two-tailed test is twice as large as the one-tailed p-value. In Figure 9.7, the p-value is 0.10.

9.10 REACHING A CONCLUSION (STEP 6)

As we have seen, the observation that a sample mean (or sample proportion) differs from the expected value contained in the null hypothesis does not necessarily imply that this expected value is wrong. The chance factors inherent in simple random sampling could account for the difference. What matters is the probability of observing sample values at or beyond this distance by chance (the p-value). If this probability is small, then the null hypothesis is rejected because the sample mean is "not close" to that expected. When the null hypothesis is rejected, the sample information is said to be "statistically significantly different" from that expected. When it is not rejected, the sample mean is said to be "not significantly different" from that expected from the null hypothesis.

Whether sample data is judged to be statistically significant or not can be sensitive to the α-risk at which the test is conducted. In the paper towel illustration, for example, the p-value was 0.10, which implies that H_0 is rejected if $\alpha = 0.15$, but is not rejected if $\alpha = 0.05$; it is "statistically significant" at exactly the 0.10 level.

QUERY 9.2:

After reading "Four Pros Took the $100,000 Challenge. Two Passed" (*Business Week,* June 9, 1995) -- about how four acclaimed financial managers picked stocks -- Professor Mark Weber, Rockefeller University, raised the question: "Do money managers have useful information for picking stocks that will provide an advantage over just investing in a portfolio that approximates a stock index?"(*Business Week,* July 10, 1995). Weber stated that even though a sample of four is small, the managers' returns (21.2, 16.9, 14.6, and 6.9 percent) are consistent with draws from a normal distribution. He concluded that these four returns are no different from what could be expected by chance, as "the average return of these four managers, 14.9%, with a standard error of 3.0%, is not significantly different from the S&P 500-stock index gain of +16.6%." What were Weber's null and alternative hypotheses? Why did he emphasize that the sample was consistent with draws from a normal distribution? What was he using as a test statistic? What was the magnitude of the *p*-value?

ANSWER:

The null and alternative hypotheses are

H_0: $\mu = 16.6$; the mean gain of all financial managers is the same as the market index of 16.6 percent

H_A: $\mu \neq 16.6$; the mean gain of all financial managers differs from the market index of 16.6 percent

Because the sample mean is an average of percentages, the base upon which each sample percentage is calculated must be the same, which is the case here as long as the initial portfolios are each $100,000. Next, because the sample size is small, the population from which these returns are drawn must be normally distributed so that the distribution of the sample mean can be assumed to be normal, with a mean of 16.6 percent as given in the null hypothesis. The calculated *t* statistic is -0.567. For a two-tail test, with 3 degrees of freedom, the *p*-value is then the sum of the area below $t = -0.567$ and the area above $t = +0.567$, which is 0.610, as shown in the following spreadsheet printout:

return						
21.2		n	4			
16.9		mean	14.9			
14.6		st dev	5.993886			
6.9		st error	2.996943			
		null	16.6			
		calc t	-0.56724			
		p-value	0.61022			

where the four returns are entered in cells A2 to A5, and the computations are made by entering the following commands into EXCEL 5.0 for WINDOWS:

return					
21.2		n	=COUNT(A2:A5)		
16.9		mean	=AVERAGE(A2:A5)		
14.6		st dev	=STDEV(A2:A5)		
6.9		st error	=(D4)/SQRT(D2)		
		null	16.6		
		calc t	=(D3-D6)/D5		
		p-value	=TDIST(ABS(D7),3,2)		

QUERY 9.3:
According to a TV news special, on the Indianapolis Channel 13 (August 18, 1994), the mean time to complete an operator assisted calls is not to exceed 25 seconds. To test for compliance, 16 randomly spaced operator assisted calls are made. For this sample, the mean time to complete calls was 26.753 seconds, with a standard deviation of 4.0 seconds. It is assumed that the population of time is normally distributed. State the null and alternative hypotheses to test for compliance. What is the value of the calculated test statistic? What is the approximate *p*-value? What conclusion can be drawn?

ANSWER:
The null and alternative hypotheses to test the TV station's statement are

H_O: $\mu \le 25$ Population mean (μ) does not exceed 25 sec.

H_A: $\mu > 25$ Population mean is greater than 25 sec.

The value of the calculated test statistic is 1.753.

$t = (26.753 - 25)/(4/\sqrt{16}) = 1.753$

The p-value, as obtained from EXCEL, is approximately 0.05.

$\text{Prob}(t > 1.753 | \text{df} = 15) = \text{TDIST}(1.753,15,1) = 0.050004$

The conclusion depends on the alpha risk. For instance, if the probability of a Type I error is set at 0.01, then the *p*-value of 0.05 implies that the null hypothesis is not rejected. On the other hand, if the probability of a Type I error is 0.10, then the null hypothesis is rejected. The limiting case for rejecting the null hypothesis is approximately 0.05, which is given by the *p*-value. The point at which the null hypothesis can be rejected is often called "the level of statistical significance."

EXERCISES

9.13 Test the following null and alternative hypothesis, at the 5 percent Type I error level.

H_O: $\mu_x \geq 29$ versus H_A: $\mu_x < 29$ and the population standard deviation is 16.

a. for a random sample of 64 observations, with a mean of 26

b. for a random sample of 64 observations, with a mean of 23

9.14 How does the interpretation of a confidence interval compare to a two-tailed test?

9.15 D.A.S. Fraser, writing in the *Journal of the American Statistical Association* (June 1991), tells of Ronald A. Fisher's (*Statistical Methods for Research Workers*, 1925) use of data that had been previously analyzed by Student (William Gosset) to test for an improvement in health associated with a new drug therapy. The ten observations of improvement were 1.2, 2.4, 1.3, 1.3, 0.0, 1.0, 1.8, 0.8, 4.6, 1.4.

Fraser assumed the population variance was known to be 1.5.

a. Why is it critical to know if the population variance is known or unknown?

b. Do you think Fisher knew that the population variance was 1.5? Why or why not?

c. Does the assumption of a known population variance affect the conclusion?

9.16 A note in *The Wall Street Journal* (February 18, 1992) describes a National Car Rental system that allows customers to rent cars with a machine similar to an automatic teller used by banks. But the system does not provide information on mileage, which customers want to ensure that their rental car has low mileage. The note quotes a company representative saying that this is not a problem because ". . . on average its cars have fewer than 10,000 miles . . . ."

a. State the null and alternative hypotheses to test the company representative's claim.

b. Based on the random sample of the mileage on nine rental cars (9,876, 11,346, 12,321, 8,564, 12,590, 3,210, 7,487, 8,886, 9,389), can the company's claim be accepted as true? At what level of significance?

9.17 *The Wall Street Journal* (October 27, 1992) reported that of the 94 patients treated for skin cancer (melanoma lesions), "the average time from their surgery and injection to the recurrence of melanoma was 30 months." In the past, the population average for other groups of melanoma patients receiving alternative types of treatment had been 17.5 months.

a. State the null and alternative hypotheses to test whether the new treatment results in a greater average time before the recurrence of the melanoma. (Define all notation.)

b. Draw a diagram showing the null hypothesis rejection region for a test at a 5 percent Type I error level. (Make sure to label all points of interest.)

c. If the *p*-value for this test was 0.0002, what was the population standard deviation?

d. Given your answer in part c, why can't the population of time before melanoma recurrence be normally distributed?

9.18 Prior to the introduction of a new process, the piece rate per worker was 80 units per hour. For a sample of 47 workers, the mean piece rate was 96 units per hour, with a standard deviation of 21. Is the new process better? (Test at the 5 percent Type I error level.)

9.19 In 1994 in Great Britain there was hot debate over a regulation that required bigger beer glasses to accommodate a full 20-ounce British pint and a creamy head; brewers and pub landlords would be fined for selling less. As a test, an agent visited a pub at nine random times, ordering a draft on each visit with the following results: 19.77, 20.10, 19.95, 19.89, 20.09, 20.08, 19.89, 19.67, and 20.01 oz. Would you conclude that on average this pub was serving glasses of beer with less than 20 ounces? (Test at the 5 percent level.)

9.11 Testing a Population Proportion

As already stated, hypothesis testing is not restricted to tests of means. The proportion of items possessing a given attribute or characteristic can be tested in exactly the same way as a mean; only a different model and statistics are required. The population proportion π might represent the proportion of females in a workforce, the percentage of executives flying commercial airlines during a year, the anticipated ratio of defective items to total monthly production, Coca-Cola's market share next year, or the fraction of lottery jackpots that Wisconsin residents can expect to win.

Consider the Lotto America situation in which 31 percent of the tickets were purchased by Wisconsin residents and 27.45 percent (14 of 51) of the jackpots were won by Wisconsin residents. We wanted to test whether a person's residence had anything to do with the chances of winning. The null and alternative hypotheses are

$$H_O\!: \pi = 0.31 \text{ and } H_A\!: \pi \neq 0.31$$

where π is the population proportion of Wisconsin winners expected by chance and the model of its sample estimator is

$$p \sim \text{Normal}\left(\pi, \sigma_p\right), \text{ for } p = \left(x/n\right) \text{ and } \sigma_p = \sqrt{\pi\left(1-\pi\right)/n}$$

Although x is the number of winners from Wisconsin, which is a discrete count distributed as a binomial, the sample proportion p can be approximately normal because the sample size n is relatively large.[8] For this model, the z test statistic is

z Test Statistic for a Population Proportion π

$$z = \frac{p - \pi_0}{\sqrt{\pi_0\left(1-\pi_0\right)/n}} \tag{9.4}$$

where π_0 is the limiting proportion in the null hypothesis, and there are x successes in a large sample of size n, and the estimator of π is $p = x/n$

A calculated value for this test statistic is determined by inserting the proportion of successes in the sample ($p = x/n = 14/51$) and setting π equal to its expected value ($\pi_0 = 0.31$) from the null hypothesis.

$$z = \frac{\left(x/n\right) - \pi_0}{\sqrt{\pi_0\left(1-\pi_0\right)/n}} = \frac{0.2745 - 0.31}{\sqrt{0.31\left(0.69\right)/51}} = \frac{-0.0355}{0.06476} = -0.548$$

FIGURE 9.8 Test of Wisconsin Residency and Winning the Lotto America Jackpots

H_0: $\pi = 0.31$ versus H_A: $\pi \neq 0.31$

The hatched areas added together form a two-tailed p-value of 0.5824, which is greater than typical α-risks so the null hypothesis is not rejected.

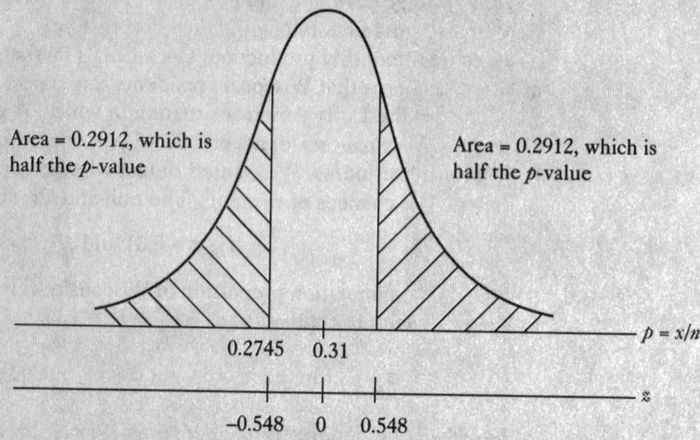

The use of the z test statistic is justified here by the Central Limit Theorem, because n is large, the distribution of p is approximately normal. As before, a p-value is the area in the tails of the distribution. Because it is a two-tailed test, the p-value in this case is $2P(z \leq -0.55) = 2(0.2912) = 0.5824$, which is very large. Thus, for typical α-levels, the null hypothesis cannot be rejected and the lottery spokesman may be correct—Wisconsin residency is not related to winning. This testing process is summarized in Figure 9.8. Remember, however, that in our failure to reject the null hypothesis, we have not proven it. There are many other values that one could assume for π that could not be rejected with this sample data.

If the sample size is small, then the z-statistic cannot be used to test a proportion. As demonstrated in the next section for a test of the median (the value of x that puts 50 percent of the values below it), small sample tests of proportions must be done with the binomial distribution. The definition of the p-value for the binomial distribution is the same as when the normal approximation is employed. Because the binomial distribution is discrete, however, care must be taken to include the probability of the observed value of x plus the probability of any more extreme values in the calculation of the one-tailed p-value.

QUERY 9.3:
According to Fancorp Inc. (a consulting firm), "more than 42 percent of franchises are purchased by husband-and-wife teams." (*Business Week*, May 6, 1991, p. 70.) If

this is true, a house maintenance service aimed at these couples may be profitable. In your area, are more than 42 percent of the franchises owned by husband-wife teams?

ANSWER:
The null hypothesis is $\pi \le 0.42$, and the alternative is $\pi > 0.42$. A simple random sample of 36 franchise owners shows that 19 are owned by husband-wife teams. The calculated z statistic for this relatively large sample is

$$z = (0.5278 - 0.42) / \sqrt{(0.42)(0.58)/36} = 1.31$$

The p-value is 0.0951, as determined with the EXCEL command "=1-NORMSDIST(1.31)." At the 5 percent Type I error level the null hypothesis is not rejected, but at the 10 percent Type I error level it is. That is, the conclusion is sensitive to the α-level. The cost of making a Type I versus a Type II error is practically important here.

QUERY 9.4:
In "Statisticians Occupy Front Lines in Battle Over Passive Smoking" (*Wall Street Journal,* July 28, 1993), statistical consultant Kenneth Brown was cited for the calculation "that there were only two chances in 100—a probability of 0.02—that the 19% figure was a matter of happenstance. That more than meets the standard of 0.05 (five chances out of 100) at which most scientific studies are considered statistically significant." Brown also produced a 90 percent confidence interval for the increased risk of cancer as being approximately 4 percent to 35 percent higher for passive smokers than those who aren't so exposed. Are Brown's hypothesis test and confidence interval consistent?

ANSWER:
Brown appears to be reporting a one-tailed hypothesis test with a p-value of 0.02 and α-level of 0.05. He also calculated a two-tailed confidence interval with $\alpha = 0.10$, which is not comparable to his one-tailed hypothesis test. Had he done a two-tailed hypothesis test, then estimation with a corresponding two-tailed hypothesis test would be appropriate.

EXERCISES

9.20 A *Business Week* (June 29, 1992) article had a headline that read: "It's Not All That Easy Having a Hit. Just Ask Caddy." The article was about the success General Motors is having with the Cadillac Seville made at its Detroit–Hamtramck plant. According to the article, "Still, an internal quality audit in early June found 5.1 defects per car vs. a target of 1.0." What would you need to know to assess whether this was a statistically significant difference?

9.21 A *Wall Street Journal* (July 26, 1984) article reported that a survey of 1,200 hourly workers found "only 45% of hourly workers think their firm is a good place to work." At the 5 percent significance level, can you conclude that less than 50 percent of all hourly workers think their firm is a good place to work?

9.22 A *Wall Street Journal* (October 27, 1992) article stated that the "past is no guarantee of (Money) manager's future." It cited a study by Frank Russell Co., a pension-consulting firm, that "tested whether an investor could predict future performance from the track records of 106 hand-picked managers monitored by the firm. It found that the winners' chances of repeating their success were 'statistically indistinguishable (in either direction) from a proportion of 50% (the coin flipping chance of success).'"

a. State the null and alternative hypotheses for this test. (Make sure to define all notation.)

b. Draw a diagram showing the null hypothesis rejection region, assuming the test was done at a 5 percent Type I error level. (Make sure to label all points of interest.)

c. If the null hypothesis is assumed true, what is the value of the standard error of the estimator?

d. In the limiting case, how high (or low) could the estimate have been?

9.23 As stated in Exercise 7.24, Ann Landers, in her nationally syndicated column, wrote: "Your story (on poor nursing care) is a chilling one . . . (however) I would say at least 90 percent of the nurses are compassionate and caring. Too bad you ran into a few who were not . . . ."(*HT*, May 28, 1993).

a. For a test of Ann's claims, what are the null and alternative hypotheses?

b. If a random sample of 40 nurses yields 34 compassionate and caring, what conclusion would you draw at the 5 percent Type I error level?

9.24 A soft drink bottler is considering introducing one of three new plastic bottles. The bottler believes that if customers could select among the three types, more than one-third would pick bottle A. As a check, the bottler surveys 100 consumers and finds that 36 percent prefer bottle A, 29 percent prefer bottle B, and 35 percent prefer bottle C. Do more than one-third of the customers prefer bottle A over bottles B and C? (Test at the 0.1 Type I error level.)

9.25 As a mandate for change, a union leader wants to get more than 60 percent of the membership vote. She surveys 64 of the voting members and finds that 40 intend to vote for her and her platform of change. At the 1 percent significance level, should she expect to get her victory with the mandate for change?

9.12 Concluding Comments

University of Chicago Business School Professor Harry Roberts (1990) argues that "in business the major emphasis is in solving immediate problems, while in science the major emphasis is on broad empirical generalizations." (p. 372) In business, he asserts, "the most serious misunderstanding is interpreting tests of sharp null hypotheses as business decision procedures. It is very difficult to find a realistic business decision that is clarified by formulation as a statistical test . . . significance levels are irrelevant to the manager who must make the business decision." (p. 382)

There are many illustrations one can cite to document the misuse of concepts from statistical hypothesis testing, especially in the case of legal proceedings where "the 5 percent level of significance" has been treated as something magical and unquestionable, as discussed by Paul Meier (1986). Numerous books and articles have been written on the use of statistical hypothesis testing in legal proceedings aimed at settling disagreements over business decisions. For an example, see Michael Finkelstein and Bruce Levin (1990). The use of statistical hypothesis testing in legal matters involving personnel matters (salary determination, hiring, firing, and promotion decisions), acquisitions and corporate takeover attempts, antitrust, safety, production and quality control, promotion and marketing, and numerous other areas cannot be ignored by managers who may be held liable for their actions in court. In this day and age of litigation, no top-level manager can be ignorant of the concepts underlying classical statistical hypothesis testing. An understanding of statistical significance is relevant to the manager who must make decisions with personal, social, political, and economic consequences.

Even in day-to-day decision making, a knowledge of hypothesis testing is needed. The idea of Type I and II errors and the cost of making one or the other certainly should influence what is assumed true until contrary information is obtained. In quality control, samples of output are periodically taken to assess whether production is in control. In modern-day accounting, sampling is used to determine whether or not fraud has occurred. It is very easy to find realistic business decisions that are clarified by the ideas of a statistical test. It may be true that a manager may never have to base his or her decision on the outcome of a single statistical test. However, no good manager is going to ignore the accumulation of evidence against one hypothesis, in favor of the other, when there are profits to be made.

CHAPTER EXERCISES

9.26 A *Business Week* (July 8, 1991) note reported that steelmakers test each batch of high-quality alloys by drawing a sample of molten metal. This sample is then heated in a vacuum and the vapors tested. If the composition of the vapors does not deviate too greatly from the norm, the batch is accepted as being satisfactory (the process is in control).

Describe the null and alternative hypotheses in this test and the nature of the Type I and Type II errors.

9.27 The U.S. Supreme Court in *International Brotherhood of Teamsters v. United States* (1977) stated, "It is ordinarily to be expected that nondiscriminatory hiring practices will in time result in a work force more or less representative of the racial and ethnic composition of the population in the community from which employees are hired." In one area, 25 percent of the accountants available for new accounting jobs are black. Thus, a company that has not discriminated against black applicants should hire a proportion of blacks that is not significantly different from 0.25. A company in this area hired 80 new accountants over the past several years, 16 of whom were black. Does this indicate discriminatory hiring at the 5 percent significance level?

9.28 A *Wall Street Journal* (August 29, 1991) article reported on the problems that General Motors is having at its plant in Orion Township, Michigan. According to the article, "On some days, the cars have more than three times the company goal of two defects per car."

a. To test whether the average is more than six defects per car, 16 cars are selected at random with the following results:

3, 6, 8, 9, 5, 7, 10, 4, 5, 12, 8, 4, 6, 9, 1, and 7 defects.

What distribution can be used for this test?

b. What conclusion can you draw from this data? (Test at the 5 percent Type I error level.)

9.29 In a *Wall Street Journal* (August 17, 1987) article on selling machine tools to U.S. firms, Toyoda representatives claimed that "Toyoda machines would operate 95% of the time." In 47 randomly selected eight-hour shifts, it was found that the Toyoda machines were down because of breakage an average of a half hour per shift, with a standard deviation of ten minutes. Can you reject the Toyoda claim?

9.30 A *Wall Street Journal* (June 20, 1991) article reported that there was no clear pattern to whether corporate relocation influenced stock prices. In some cases, the corporate moves were associated with spending a lot of money on a trophy headquarters, which tended to lower the company's stock price, but in other cases the move was to a less expensive place. A sample of 30 companies that recently moved showed the stock price of 17 falling after the move. Does this contradict the *WSJ* hypothesis?

9.31 An article by John Cunniff (Associated Press, January 21, 1992) reported on a survey of American workers, which was conducted by Towers Perrin, a human resource consultant. It was conducted for the National Association of Manufacturers and included its 4,000 member companies. Cunniff states:

> While the response rate was only 10 percent, the findings were significant. The survey revealed, for example, that the average manufacturer rejected five out of every six candidates for a job . . . more than half the companies reported major employee skill deficiencies . . . . American companies are crippled in applying technological advances and in otherwise improving productivity.

Comment on the "significance" of these findings.

9.32 As a result of the deregulation of U.S. airlines, regulators claimed that many airlines would go bankrupt, even if the industry expanded. They predicted that following deregulation, the airline industry would be represented by average revenue-generating passenger miles of 42 billion. The 1990 revenue passenger miles, shown on the following page from the *Philadelphia Inquirer*, are from the Air Transportation Association, in billions of miles. Has the regulators' claim been realized?

Airline	Miles
American	76.9
United	76.0
Delta	59.0
Northwest	51.5
Continental	41.2
USAir	35.6
Trans World	34.2
America West	11.1
Southwest	10.0
Alaska	4.5

9.33 The defense for boxer Mike Tyson in his 1992 trial on a rape charge claimed that the pool of 50 persons from which a jury of 12 members was to be selected was not representative of the community at large. Twenty-two percent of the community was black, while only 14 percent of the pool was black. At the 5 percent Type I error level, is it reasonable to assume that the jury was selected randomly from the community at large?

9.34 Procter & Gamble wants to know if Folgers' market share has increased since it cut the price of Folgers coffee "an average of 10% to 15% since 1991" (*Business Week*, July 19, 1993). P&G knows that its market share last year was 0.19 (19 percent of the market) in test areas. In 10 randomly selected market test sites, P&G now has the following shares of the market:

.20 .19 .17 .21 .15 .20 .25 .24 .22 .18

a. Specify a model that can be used for testing here.

b. Test whether P&G market share can be expected to exceed 19 percent this year.

9.35 Mothers Against Drunk Driving claims that the majority of crimes committed in the United States involve alcohol. This view is challenged by an Orange County beer distributor who noted that of the 621 crimes recorded in Orange County last year, only 306 involved drunken driving, public intoxication, or charges against minors for illegal use or possession of alcohol. Comment on the distributor's challenge, and provide statistical evidence to support your position.

9.36 A consumer protection group interprets the claim on the side of the General Electric light bulb package to imply that more than 50 percent of GE's 60-watt Soft-White light bulbs should last longer than 1,000 hours. A sample of 36 bulbs is tested, and 23 are found to last longer than 1,000 hours. Is this sufficient evidence to conclude that 50 percent of all GE 60-watt bulbs will last more than 1,000 hours? (Test at the 5 percent Type I error level.)

9.37 In the week prior to Super Bowl XXVI in Minneapolis in 1992, the "Super Bowl Theory of Stock Prices" was circulating. It stated that if the Washington Redskins (of the NFC conference) won, then a bull market (prices up) would characterize 1992. If the Buffalo Bills (of the AFC) won, then a bear market (prices down) would prevail in 1992. Empirical support for this theory was that for 22 of the previous 25 Super Bowls, conference affiliation of the winner predicted the stock market correctly. Pure randomness suggests that the relationship should have been 50 percent. Thus, a finance analyst calculated the test statistic

$$z = \left(0.88 - 0.50\right) \Big/ \sqrt{\left(0.5\right)\left(0.5\right)/25} = 3.80$$

and concluded that the Super Bowl Theory of Stock Prices is correct. Comment on this test and conclusion.

9.38 The Super Bowl was won by the Washington Redskins (NFC) in 1992, the San Francisco 49ers (NFC) in 1995, and the Dallas Cowboys (NFC) in 1993, 1994, and 1996. The stock market finished with higher prices in each of these five years. Articles in *The Wall Street Journal* called the Super Bowl a "quirky indicator"(December 31, 1996) of stock prices and warned with a play on names that "If the Packers Win, the Bears Lose"(January 24, 1997). How would this information affect the financial analyst's calculations of the *z* statistic and your comments on the conclusion to be drawn from this test in Exercise 9.37?

9.39 In a study of the way individuals are treated by car dealers, "testers" were sent into dealerships as would-be buyers. Author Ian Ayers, in "Fair Driving: Gender and Race Discrimination in Retail Car Negotiations" (*Harvard Law Review*, February 1991), stated, "When the seller did reveal his cost, the represented cost was substantially higher than independent estimates of seller cost for the same model, as seen (below) . . . they systematically overstate their costs. The greatest misrepresentation was made to white female testers."

Seller Misrepresentation of Cost Data

	Average Misrepresentation
White Male Testers	$ 849
White Female Testers	1046
Black Male Testers	752
Black Females	–

a. Comment on the statistical significance of the white male and female difference in misrepresentation.

b. Comment on the statistical significance of the white and black male difference in misrepresentation.

9.40 An article titled "The Bloodbath In Market Research" in *Business Week* (February 11, 1991) stated that "the validity of surveys is being jeopardized by the growing refusal of Americans to participate. Annoyed by the intrusiveness, 36 percent of consumers declined to answer a phone query in 1990."

a. How does refusal to participate jeopardize validity of surveys?

b. How could you test the correctness of the claim that 36 percent of Americans called would not respond to questions?

9.41 A *Wall Street Journal* (January 4, 1991) article reported that "The average American consults with a doctor 5.4 times a year. Most contacts are at the doctor's office, an average of 3.2 visits a person each year." To test whether the average is 3.2 visits at the doctor's office, a local group of physicians pooled data on the average number of visits for those who actually came to their offices and concluded that their sample average was 6.5 visits a person each year, well above the claimed average of 3.2 visits. Comment on their sample design and the validity of their conclusion.

9.42 A *Business Week* (May 28, 1990) article claimed that "In the past two years, Grano (head of retail sales at Paine-Webber) has hired 150 brokers, each of whom had gross commissions of at least $500,000." To test the accuracy of this statement, a competitor interviewed a sample of 25 of these brokers as potential candidates for a fictitious position. The average reported by these brokers was $450,000, which was close to *Business Week's* average, with a standard deviation of $50,000.

a. What conclusion would you draw regarding the correctness of the *Business Week* statement about gross commissions?

b. What might you question about the sampling technique employed by the competitor? What are the implications of this for your test in part a?

9.43 Writing for the *Washington Post* (*HT*, February 9, 1992) Frank Swoboda reported on the sixth annual health-care benefits survey by Foster Higgins & Co. Foster claimed that "the average cost to employers for health care rose 12.1 percent per employee in 1991—to \$3,605—as more and more companies shifted costs of medical coverage to their employees." This cost seemed high, so a personnel manager sampled 10 of his counterparts at other companies and found the following costs:

\$4,145	\$2,950	\$3,320	\$2,978	\$3,576
\$3,423	\$3,398	\$3,975	\$3,552	\$3,502

At the 5 percent Type I error level, does this sample data support a population average cost of \$3,605 or is the population average less?

9.44 Foster, Higgins & Co. also claimed, following its survey of health-care benefits, that health-care costs average 12 percent of total payroll cost. For the ten similar companies contacted in Exercise 9.43, the following health-care costs as a percentage of payroll were recorded:

14.1%	10.2%	12.1%	10.3%	11.8%
11.6%	12.1%	13.7%	11.5%	11.9%

At the 5 percent Type I error level, does this sample data support a population average of 12 percent?

9.45 A headline in *The Wall Street Journal* (February 25, 1992) stated, "The Temporary Help Business is Likely to Rebound This Year." Yet, the article cited a survey of 600 companies by TempForce, Inc., a temporary personnel firm, as showing "37% plan staff increases for 1992, and 48% don't see any change, while 15% expect cuts." Comment on the correctness of this headline based on the reported data.

9.46 Although law firms are now free to advertise, it is generally believed that the majority of firms do not employ marketing specialists. A *Wall Street Journal* (February 26, 1992) article reported that a survey of 400 firms "found that 48% had marketing directors." Is there a significant difference here between the observed 48 percent and the hypothesized 50 percent?

9.47 There is a claim of sex discrimination in hiring. In the relevant period, the employer has hired 64 workers, only eight of whom were women. In the preselection pool of equally qualified applicants, 20 percent were women. An expert witness for the employer states that the probability of observing the eight or fewer women in a random sample of 64 when drawn from this pool was 6.68 percent, implying that the employer could have been randomly sampling from this pool with no consideration to the sex of the applicants.

a. State the null and alternative hypotheses the expert was testing.
b. Conduct the statistical test performed by the expert. Is the conclusion of no sex discrimination supported? At what level of significance?

9.48 A *Wall Street Journal* (April 20, 1992) article reported on a study by University of Delaware Professor Valerie P. Hans of jurors' attitudes toward business in wrongful death and injury cases. "Of the 18 cases, 14 were decided in favor of plaintiffs, higher than the national norm of about 50%." Is there a significant difference between Hans' sample and the national norm?

9.49 In the mail-order computer business, a 30 percent failure rate for systems is considered average. An article in *Business Week* (May 11, 1992) reported on an order of 50 Gateways placed by Thomas Walsh, executive director for Houston law firm Mayor, Day, Caldwell

& Keaton: "3 wouldn't work out of the box, and 14 monitors and 10 more computers soon failed." Do these 27 failures from this sample of 50 support the result that Gateway's average defect rate is 30 percent?

9.50 A report by the U.S. Centers for Disease Control (*HT*, May 15, 1992) examined the blood-alcohol content of 13 people killed in North Carolina by falling or being thrown from a horse between 1979 and 1989. Five, or 39 percent, had been drinking, prompting a government warning against drinking and riding. Dr. Thomas Cole stated, "It makes as little sense to drink and ride as it does to drink and drive." Comment on the correctness of the conclusion that drinking alcohol prior to riding increases the risk of falling or being thrown from the horse and dying.

9.51 An expert witness in a labor dispute concluded that there was no significant difference between the wage paid at the firm ($13.45/hour) and the national average ($14.78/hour). The sample standard deviation was $3.99 for a sample of 36. What was the maximum Type I error level at which this expert could have been testing?

9.52 "A Nation of Speed Demons," ***Business Week*** (February 10, 1997) reported on a study by the Insurance Institute for Highway Safety that found "on California urban interstates (now 65 mph), the average driver goes about 67." If the speeds of 49 cars were randomly checked and found to average 67 mph, yielding a *p*-value of 0.04 in a one-tailed *t* test, then what was the sample standard deviation?

9.53 *The Wall Street Journal* article titled "The Business Cycle Is Tamed, Many Say, Alarming Some Others" (November 15, 1996) reported that "the latest Blue Chip newsletter survey found 51 of 53 top economists predicting the economy will grow at least 1.53% next year." If these 53 economists predicting the economy for next year were each making the prediction of "continued expansion" versus "no continued expansion" by independently tossing a coin (with 0.5 probability of heads and 0.5 probability of tails), then

a. the expected number saying the economy will continue to expand is _____?
b. the probability of observing 51 or more of these economists predicting continued expansion is _____?
c. Is it reasonable to conclude that the 53 economists are making their individual predictions for 1997 in a manner similar to flipping a coin?

9.54 "Foggy Crystal Balls," ***Business Week*** (April 17, 1995) reported on a study of the asset allocation recommendations of some 236 investment letters. University of Utah economist John Gram and Duke University economist Campbell Harvey found that "75% of the letters underperformed buy and hold portfolios based on the Standard & Poor's 500 stock index." If the probability is 0.5 for each one of these newsletters making recommendations that result in performance poorer than the S&P 500 stock index, what is the probability that at least 177 of the 236 letters will underperform this S&P index? Are investment newsletters making recommendations that are poorer than what could be expected by chance?

9.55 (Endnote 4 Required) Exercises 5.21 and 5.22 describes a feature on the "Insider" TV show (Feb. 15, 1995) quoting a New York city official saying that no more than one percent of the cars that are towed off city streets and impounded have objects inside stolen. Test this claim at the 0.01 Type I error level using the data provided in Exercises 5.21 and 5.22.

9.56 An article in ***The Wall Street Journal*** (April 25, 1997) reported that a survey of 55 McDonald's restaurants showed 14 had raised prices on large fries and medium-sized Cokes from two cents to as much as 14 cents, for an average of just over 6 cents (6.1 cents) in the six weeks prior to the announced 75 percent discounting of the Big Mac. The article concluded that "While that's pocket change, on a percentage basis the increase can be significant." But was there a significant increase in the price of these fries and Cokes across all McDonald's restaurants? Specify your assumptions.

Academic References

Carlson, Roger. "The Logic of Tests of Significance." *Philosophy of Science*, 43, 1976, pp. 116–128.

Finkelstein, Michael, and Bruce Levin. *Statistics for Lawyers*. New York: Springer Verlag, 1990.

Fisher, Franklin. "Statisticians, Econometricians, and Adversary Proceedings." *Journal of the American Statistical Association* 81, June 1986: pp. 277–286.

Kiefer, Nicholas. "Economic Duration Data and Hazard Functions." *Journal of Economic Literature* 26, June 1988, pp. 646–679.

Meier, Paul. "Damned Liars and Expert Witnesses." *Journal of the American Statistical Association* 81, June 1986, pp. 269–276.

Roberts, Harry V. "Business and Economic Statistics." *Statistical Science*, November 1990, pp. 372–390.

Spielman, Stephen. "The Logic of Tests of Significance." *Philosophy of Science* 41, 1974, pp. 211–226.

Spielman, Stephen. "The Logic of Tests of Significance," *Philosophy of Science* 45, 1978, pp. 120–135.

Endnotes

1. Kirk Bloodsworth, after two trials and almost nine years in prison for raping and murdering a 9-year-old girl in Maryland, "walked out of prison a free man thanks to DNA testing." (Associated Press, *HT:* June 29, 1993) County State's Attorney Sandra O'Connor was quoted saying: "I am not prepared to say that he is innocent . . . but we do not have enough evidence to convict him beyond a reasonable doubt." Notice the newspaper story simply said Bloodsworth was a "free man," and attorney O'Connor would not say that he was innocent beyond a reasonable doubt. Innocence is assumed, not proved. Innocence is rejected by the evidence, and errors are sometimes made.
2. Recall from Chapter 7 that $P(\bar{x} \leq 57.8) = P(\bar{x} < 57.8)$ because probability at a single value is defined to be zero for a continuous probability density function. The area in the tail of the sampling distribution $P(57.8 < \bar{x} < 59 \mid \mu = 59)$ is of interest because $P(57.8 = \bar{x})$ is zero, regardless of the population mean assumed. The occurrence of any specific value, even when drawn from a discrete distribution, can be viewed as rare or unusual, regardless of its distance from the mean. Calculating the area beyond or more extreme than the observed value eliminates this problem.
3. Any assessment of the life of an item (be it a light bulb, tire, or human life) may involve a truncation of the period of observation before all items have ceased working. If these long-life items are ignored (deleted from the sample), then the mean will be understated. If the time for these long-life items is recorded for only the span of the period of observation, the mean again will be understated but not as badly as when the observations are deleted. Guessing at the remaining life of these long-life items may result in still less understatement, but it might also lead to an overstatement—we can never know what goes on outside the observation period. These and other "censoring problems" in "duration data" are discussed by Nicholas Kiefer (1988).

4. Instead of testing for a value of π, based on a value of p, the expected value of x, given by πn, could be tested with the number of successes in the sample, pn. The model would then be

$$x \sim \text{Binomial}\left(\pi n, \sigma_x\right), \text{ for } \sigma_x = \sqrt{\pi\left(1-\pi\right)n}$$

As long as n is large, and π is not too close to 0 or 1, the normal and the binomial models will give similar results. If n is small, however, the binomial model must be used.

5. On May 1, 1989, the U.S. Supreme Court made it easier for plaintiffs to prevail in a major category of lawsuits involving sex, race, and age discrimination in personnel matters. In *Hopkins v. Price Waterhouse,* the Court rejected the accounting firm's argument that Ann Hopkins should be required to prove that it was sex discrimination rather than legitimate judgment that led to her lack of a promotion to partner. When Hopkins brought the charges, the firm was assumed innocent (the null hypothesis), but the Court said the derogatory comments made by firm partners were enough to establish the existence of illegal discrimination (the alternative hypothesis). The Court said that once this prima facia case was made, it was then the firm's obligation to show it was innocent (the null hypothesis becomes guilt and the alternative innocence). But the Court ruled that the firm had to show only by "a preponderance of the evidence" that the firm's reasons for denying promotion were legitimate. This standard of proof is the least onerous. It is equivalent to a large probability of a Type I error level in which the firm's reasons were "more likely than not" legitimate ones. A lower court had required "clear and convincing" evidence, which is equivalent to a small probability of a Type I error level.
6. For a discussion of how courts have viewed statistical hypothesis testing, see Franklin Fisher (1986) and Paul Meier (1986).
7. We have been and will continue to assume that samples are drawn from large (infinite) populations. If the population is not large relative to the sample, then the standard error of $\bar{x}$ is

$$\frac{\sigma}{\sqrt{n}}\left(1-\frac{n}{N}\right)$$

where the factor $(1-\frac{n}{N})$ is called the finite population correction factor, and n/N is the fraction of the population included in the sample. If n is small relative to N, then the finite population correction factor is approximately 1. If the n is large relative to N, however, then the z test statistic is

$$z = \frac{\bar{x}-\mu_0}{\frac{\sigma}{\sqrt{n}}\left(1-\frac{n}{N}\right)}$$

As a rule of thumb, as long as $n < 0.10N$, the finite population correction factor is ignored.

8. For p to be approximately normal, the expected value of p $[E(p) = \pi]$ as well as its realization $(p = x/n)$ cannot be overly close to the extreme values of 0 or 1, and n must be sufficiently large to ensure that the interval $p \pm 3.5\sigma_p$ does not include 0 or 1. If these conditions are not met, then the binomial distribution must be used to calculate probabilities for x based on the sample of size n.

Chapter 10

Two-Sample Hypothesis Testing

Moreover, it sometimes appears that statistics are less likely to be relied upon if they challenge one's own interest.

Mary W. Gray
(*Statistical Science*, 1993)

10.1 INTRODUCTION

So far our estimation and testing has involved a single random variable. This chapter extends those ideas to tests involving two variables. Later chapters will continue this extension to estimation and predictions involving multiple variables.

Tests of the difference between two means, are presented in this chapter in the following type situation.

> Women managers brought suit against a large midwestern bank for salary discrimination. At a deposition, an expert witness presented data in which the average annual salary of 219 women managers was \$34,593, while that of 392 male managers was \$43,331. The question: Are women managers receiving significantly less than men?

The hypothesis testing procedure described in Chapter 9 can be used in many personal and business situations. Because many different statements of hypotheses are possible, however, care must be taken to correctly specify the null and alternative hypotheses to test for specific numerical values of the parameters (Step 1). This chapter introduces new test statistics that must be employed when testing for differences between two values (Step 3). The t and z statistics are used to test differences in means. In testing for differences between two measures of central tendency, potential differences in measures of dispersion must also be considered, because sampling may now be from two different populations (Step 4).

The specification of Type I error probabilities (Step 2), the determination of a p-value (Step 5), and the process of reaching a conclusion (Step 6) typically vary little from one problem to another. These steps were discussed in detail in Chapter 9, and little need be added in this chapter. By the end of this chapter, you should fully recognize why only Steps 1, 3, and 4 in the hypothesis testing procedures need to be changed to fit the context of the situation, while Steps 2, 5, and 6 generally remain the same from situation to situation.

10.2 Difference Between Means

Possibly the most common tests in statistics are those involving differences between means. For example, we might want to compare revenues from sales in two different cities, or the average number of units sold in two different months, or two factory shifts might be compared on the basis of defective items produced. These situations may involve hypotheses tests of the difference between two population means based on samples that share no common elements. The samples may be completely independent of each other and may be of unequal size. The objective is to determine if there is a significant difference between the two populations based on the two sets of independent randomly selected samples. The test statistic may be a z or a t test, with the familiar form

$$\text{Test statistic} = \frac{\text{Estimator} - \text{Expected value of estimator}}{\text{Standard deviation of estimator}}$$

where the expected value of estimator is again given by the null hypothesis, and the estimator's standard deviation is called the standard error. Now, however, the estimator and its standard error will be based on the difference between two random variables.

Let the mean of the first of two possibly different populations be μ_1, and that of the second population be μ_2. If the theory is that there is no difference between these two means, then the null and alternative hypotheses are

H_O: $\mu_2 - \mu_1 = 0$

H_A: $\mu_2 - \mu_1 \neq 0$, if μ_1 is suspected to be different than μ_2.

If the theory suggests that one population mean is less than the other, the null and alternative hypothesis for a one-sided, two-sample test may be specified as

H_O: $\mu_2 - \mu_1 \geq 0$

H_A: $\mu_2 - \mu_1 < 0$, if μ_1 is suspected to be greater than μ_2;

or H_O: $\mu_2 - \mu_1 \leq 0$

H_A: $\mu_2 - \mu_1 > 0$, if μ_1 is suspected to be less than μ_2.

Conceptually, in a test of means using two samples, any numerical difference between the population means may be tested, but usually the value in the null hypothesis is zero.

The point estimator of the population difference in means $(\mu_2 - \mu_1)$ is the difference in sample means $(\bar{x}_2 - \bar{x}_1)$. This is an unbiased estimator, since on average it will equal the population difference in means. To use either the t or z statistics, the distribution of the estimator $(\bar{x}_2 - \bar{x}_1)$ must be normally distributed, which it will be if each sample mean is itself normally distributed or if the sample sizes are large. Whether the t or z statistic is appropriate will once again depend on knowledge of the variances and sample sizes.

When Variances Are Known (or Samples Are Large)

If the population variances are known, then the standard error of the estimator will be related positively to these two individual population variances, σ_1^2 and σ_2^2, and negatively to the two sample sizes, where

$$\sigma_{(\bar{x}_2 - \bar{x}_1)} = \sqrt{\frac{\sigma_1^2}{n_1} + \frac{\sigma_2^2}{n_2}}$$

Because s_2^2 and s_1^2 are unbiased estimators of σ_2^2 and σ_1^2 and because $s/\sqrt{n}$ approaches $\sigma/\sqrt{n}$ quickly as n is increased, the sample variances provide good approximations for the population variances for large sample sizes. Thus, if the sample sizes are large, tests of differences in means can be conducted using the z statistic, even if the population variances are unknown.

z test statistic for two independent samples

$$z = \frac{(\bar{x}_2 - \bar{x}_1) - D_O}{\sqrt{\frac{\sigma_1^2}{n_1} + \frac{\sigma_2^2}{n_2}}} \qquad (10.1)$$

where D_O is the difference specified by the right-hand side of H_O. D_O is typically zero.

FOR USE WHEN:

1. The two parent population variances are known, the random samples are independent of each other, and
   a) each is at least of size $n = 30$, or
   b) each is drawn from a normal parent population.

OR 2. Each independent sample is sufficiently large ($n > 30$) that the sample variances are good approximations of their respective population variances.

Although population variances are seldom known, Formula (10.1) is extremely useful for the initial check of mean differences. For instance, Table 10.1 provides the sample data presented by the econometrician in the suit brought by the women managers at the midwestern bank for discrimination in the salary determination process. Data are provided for the beginning and end of the liability period, which was predetermined by the court. In the beginning of the liability period, for example, the sample of 219 women averaged \$34,593, with a standard deviation of \$6,229; the highest salary paid a woman was \$66,800, and the lowest was \$21,240. A sample of 392 men in the same time period averaged \$43,331, with a standard deviation of \$15,842; the highest salary paid a man was \$195,900, and the lowest was \$25,500. The question: Do women receive significantly less than men?

For this question, the null and alternative hypotheses are

H_O: $\mu_m - \mu_w \leq 0$
H_A: $\mu_m - \mu_w > 0$

where the subscripts designate men (m) or women (w). Although the population variances are unknown, the sample sizes are large, so the z in Formula (10.1) can be used. At the beginning and end of the liability period, the calculated values of the test statistics are:

Beginning of liability period

$$z = \frac{(\bar{x}_2 - \bar{x}_1) - 0}{\sqrt{\frac{\sigma_1^2}{n_1} + \frac{\sigma_2^2}{n_2}}} \approx \frac{(43331 - 34593) - 0}{\sqrt{\frac{(15842)^2}{392} + \frac{(6229)^2}{219}}} = 9.665$$

End of liability period

$$z = \frac{(\bar{x}_2 - \bar{x}_1) - 0}{\sqrt{\frac{\sigma_1^2}{n_1} + \frac{\sigma_2^2}{n_2}}} \approx \frac{(45809 - 36840) - 0}{\sqrt{\frac{(17601)^2}{376} + \frac{(6998)^2}{199}}} = 8.671$$

Each of the two calculated values of the z test statistic ($z = 9.665$ and 8.671) is well above the critical values associated with the typical Type I error levels (at $\alpha = 0.05$ in a one-tailed test, the critical z is 1.645). Thus, the null hypothesis is rejected, and the conclusion is that women are paid significantly less than men. To jump from this "statistical significance" to the practical conclusion that women are discriminated against on the basis of their sex is not justified, however.

Recall that classical hypothesis testing requires simple random samples. These samples of salaries are not simple random samples; there are many factors involved here besides just sampling error. Notice, for instance, that the standard deviations for male salaries are over two and a half times larger than those of females, and that at the high end of the salary ranges, males are receiving over three times what the highest paid females are receiving. The source of this additional variability in male salaries must be assessed before any firm conclusions are advanced. Consideration of the sources and consequences of this additional variability will have to wait until later chapters, when multivariate analysis is introduced.

TABLE 10.1
Salaries at Midwestern Bank

LIABILITY PERIOD	SIZE	AVERAGE	ST. DEV.	LOW	HIGH
Beginning of liability period					
MEN	392	43331	15842	25500	195900
WOMEN	219	34593	6229	21240	66800
MEN – WOMEN	173	8738		4260	129100
End of liability period					
MEN	376	45809	17601	26700	211000
WOMEN	199	36840	6998	24000	71400
MEN – WOMEN	177	8969		2700	139600

Query 10.1:

During a period in the late 1980s, automobile ads claimed that "Leasing a New Car Is Now Smarter and More Advantageous Than Buying," as stated, for example, in a Bay Leasing ad in the *Chicago Tribune* (March 8, 1988). In particular, a sample of domestic vehicles was presented as substantially less expensive to lease than imports. Based on the Bay Leasing data given in its ad (as reproduced in the table below), are domestic vehicles less expensive to lease than imports?

Domestics	Amount
Buick Electra	$237.00
Buick Reatta	$357.00
Buick Regal	$177.00
Cadillac Brougham	$327.00
Cadillac Deville	$317.00
Cadillac Eldorado	$337.00
Cadillac Seville	$357.00
Chevy Astrovan	$147.00
Chevy Blazer	$157.00
Chevy Beretta	$147.00
Chevy Celebrity	$157.00
Chevy Corsica	$147.00
Chevy Corvette	$387.00
Chevy Corvette Conv	$447.00
Chrysler Lebaron Coupe	$177.00
Chrysler Fifth Avenue	$257.00
Dodge Caravan	$167.00
Eagle Premier	$217.00
Ford Aerostar	$167.00
Ford F-250	$187.00
Ford Mustang	$127.00
Ford Thunderbird	$167.00
Ford Taurus	$157.00
Jeep	$177.00
Lincoln Town Car	$337.00
Lincoln Continental	$347.00
Mercury Sable	$157.00
Olds Ciera	$157.00
Olds Delta 88	$217.00
Olds Regency 98	$247.00
Pontiac Bonneville	$207.00
Pontiac Grand Am	$147.00
Pontiac Grand Prix	$187.00
Pontiac Trans Am	$207.00

Imports	Amount
Acura Integra	$147.00
Acura Legend	$247.00
Audi 80	$267.00
BMW 325	$277.00
BMW 528	$327.00
BMW 735	$677.00
Honda Accord Coupe	$157.00
Honda Accord	$147.00
Honda Civic	$117.00
Honda CRX	$127.00
Honda Prelude	$167.00
Isuzu Trooper	$177.00
Jaguar XJ-S	$657.00
Jaguar XJ6	$577.00
Mazda MX6 or 626	$147.00
Mazda 929	$257.00
Mazda RX-7	$167.00
Mercedes 190E	$357.00
Mercedes 300E	$537.00
Mercedes 420SEL	$587.00
Mercedes 560	$747.00
Nissan 300ZX	$287.00
Nissan Maxima	$227.00
Porsche 911	$517.00
Porsche 928	$887.00
Porsche 944	$397.00
Saab 900	$207.00
Saab 9000	$317.00
Saab Convt	$387.00
Sterling 825S	$277.00
Toyota Camry	$177.00
Toyota Celica	$137.00
Toyota Cressida	$237.00
Toyota Supra	$287.00
Volvo 240DL	$207.00
Volvo 740	$277.00
Volvo 760	$357.00

ANSWER:

The average monthly cost of leasing is \$226.71 for domestic vehicles and \$325.65 for imports. Within the sample, domestic cars are \$98.94 less expensive than imports to lease, on average. If these data are viewed as simple random samples of all such leasing expenses, then from a hand calculation or a computer printout the following can be obtained:

SAMPLE	IMPORTS	DOMESTIC
Mean	325.65	226.71
Variance	37695.35	7530.21
St. Dev.	194.15	86.78

Because the samples are relatively large, the z statistic can be used for testing; its calculated value for a test of $\mu_2 - \mu_1 \le 0$ versus $\mu_2 - \mu_1 > 0$ is

$$z = \frac{(\bar{x}_2 - \bar{x}_1) - 0}{\sqrt{\dfrac{\sigma_1^2}{n_1} + \dfrac{\sigma_2^2}{n_2}}} \approx \frac{(325.65 - 226.71) - 0}{\sqrt{\dfrac{37695.35}{37} + \dfrac{7530.21}{34}}} = \frac{98.94}{35.22} = 2.81$$

The p-value is 0.0025, which is small. It implies that the null hypothesis ($\mu_2 - \mu_1 \le 0$) can be rejected, and the conclusion is that domestic cars are significantly less expensive than imports to lease.

When Variances Are Unknown but Assumed Equal

The two-sample z test in the last section typically is used only when the samples are large, because population variances are seldom known. Here we consider a two-sample test that may be appropriate when the samples are small and the population variances are *unknown*. This two-sample t test requires the following assumptions:

1. The population variances are unknown but reasonably assumed to be equal.
2. The samples are independent of each other and are drawn from normal parent populations.

These assumptions are maintained through the testing procedure. In essence, they imply that the two populations are identical except for their means, the difference of which is being tested.

Unlike a z statistic, the t statistic is based on an estimate of the standard error of the estimator $(\bar{x}_2 - \bar{x}_1)$. As discussed in Chapters 8 and 9, when the standard error of one mean is estimated, the degrees of freedom are $n - 1$. For two samples of identical size, the degrees of freedom would be $2(n - 1)$. If the samples are of different sizes n_1 and n_2, then the degrees of freedom are $n_1 + n_2 - 2$.

The test statistic for this two-sample test is:

***t* test statistic for difference between means,** with equal population variances and independent samples

$$t = \frac{(\bar{x}_2 - \bar{x}_1) - 0}{s_{\bar{x}_2 - \bar{x}_1}} \tag{10.2}$$

where

$$s_{\bar{x}_2 - \bar{x}_1} = \sqrt{\left(\frac{s_1^2(n_1 - 1) + s_2^2(n_2 - 1)}{n_1 + n_2 - 2}\right)\left(\frac{n_1 + n_2}{n_1(n_2)}\right)}$$

with $n_1 + n_2 - 2$ degrees of freedom and 0 is the value on the right-hand side of H_O.

FOR USE WHEN:

1. The two parent population variances are unknown but equal, and
2. Both independent samples are small but drawn from populations that are normally distributed.

As an illustration of this two-sample test, consider a quality control problem in which there are two shifts of workers at a large restaurant. Patrons are provided with questionnaires that ask them to assess service on a scale from 0 (bad) to 100 (great). Suppose that the following ratings are obtained:

Day shift scores:
91.0 55.0 62.0 64.0 41.0 63.0 35.0 57.0 94.0 68.0 48.0 72.0

Night shift scores:
81.0 86.0 73.0 77.0 90.0 91.0 75.0 48.0 97.0 74.0

The question is whether there is a statistically significant difference in ratings between the two shifts. That is, the null and alternative hypotheses are

$$H_O: \mu_2 - \mu_1 = 0$$

$$H_A: \mu_2 - \mu_1 \neq 0$$

where μ_2 is the average night shift service rating, and μ_1 is the average day shift service rating.

Using a spreadsheet computer program (such as EXCEL, LOTUS 1-2-3, or QUATTRO), the calculations in Table 10.2 can be made easily. Substituting into Formula (10.2), we obtain the calculated test statistic value of $t = 2.44$, where we assume the day shift and night shift populations of ratings are normally distributed.

Table 10.2 Calculated Values for a Pooled, Two-Sample t Test with Equal but Unknown Variances

DAY SHIFT (x_1)

Scores

91.0	55.0	62.0	64.0	41.0	63.0	35.0	57.0	94.0	68.0	48.0	72.0

$\bar{x}_1 = 62.50$

Squared Deviations

812.25	56.25	0.25	2.25	462.25	0.25	756.25	30.25	992.25	30.25	210.25	90.25

$s^2_1 = 313.00$

$s_1 = 17.69$

NIGHT SHIFT (x_2)

Scores

81.0	86.0	73.0	77.0	90.0	91.0	75.0	48.0	97.0	74.0

$\bar{x}_2 = 79.20$

Squared Deviations

3.24	46.24	38.44	4.84	116.64	139.24	17.64	973.44	316.84	27.04

$s_2^2 = 187.07$

$s_2 = 13.68$

Estimated Standard Error = 6.86

$t = 2.44$

$$t = \frac{(\bar{x}_2 - \bar{x}_1) - 0}{\sqrt{\left(\frac{s_1^2(n_1 - 1) + s_2^2(n_2 - 1)}{n_1 + n_2 - 2}\right)\left(\frac{n_1 + n_2}{n_1(n_2)}\right)}} = \frac{(79.2 - 62.5) - 0}{\sqrt{\left(\frac{(313)(11) + (187.07)(9)}{12 + 10 - 2}\right)\left(\frac{12 + 10}{12(10)}\right)}}$$

$$t = \frac{16.7}{6.86} = 2.44$$

The p-value for this calculated statistic is obtained as in the past with a computer program, where again the area beyond 2.44 is doubled because this is a two-tailed test.

$$p\text{-value} = 2P(t > 2.44, \text{ with df} = 20) = 0.024$$

This p-value indicates that the null hypothesis can be rejected for a Type I error probability as low as 0.024; that is, the level of significance is 0.024. If the probability of a Type I error is preset at the 5 percent level (critical t of 2.086), then the null hypothesis is rejected, but at the 2 percent Type I error level (critical t of 2.528), the null hypothesis is not rejected. The sensitivity of the conclusion to these critical values is depicted in Figure 10.1.

As an alternative to calculating from scratch on a spreadsheet program, most statistical packages do a two-sample t test on command once the data have been entered.

FIGURE 10.1 Decision Rules for a Two-Tailed, Pooled Two-Sample t Test

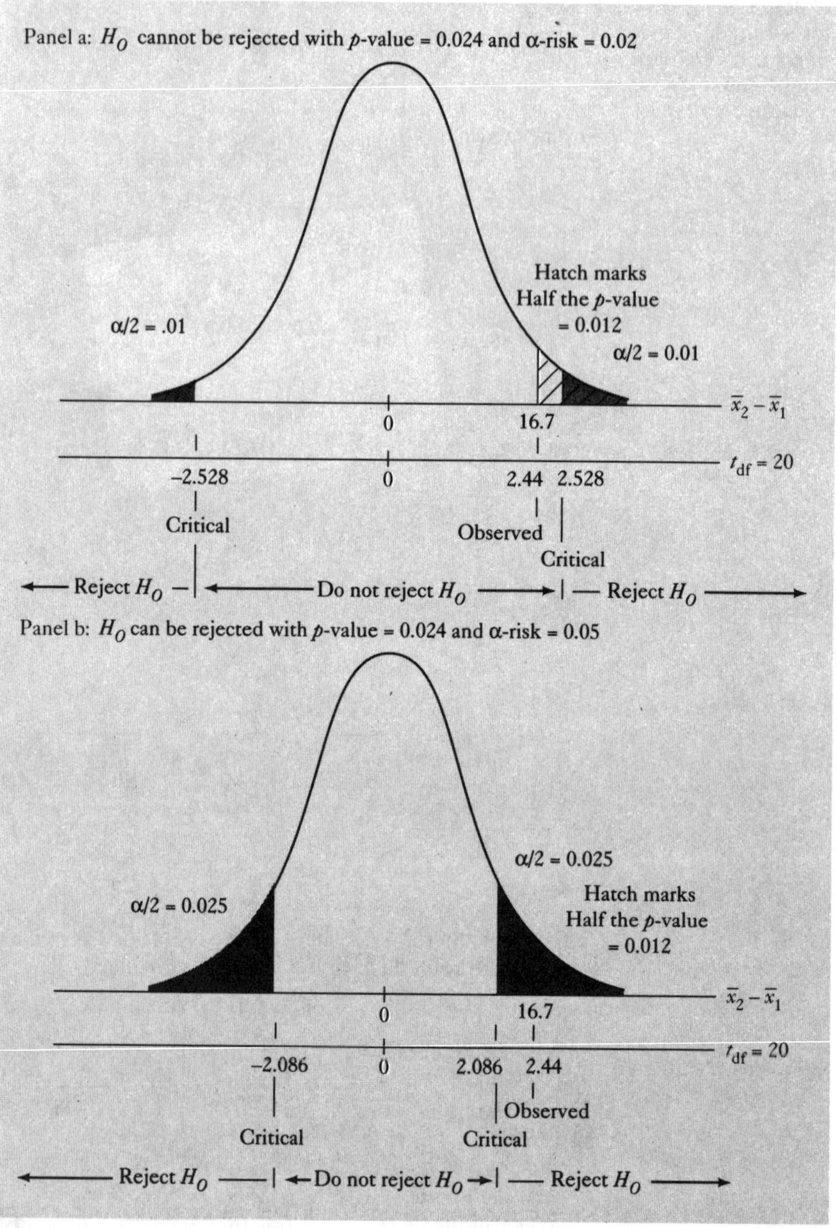

TABLE 10.3
MINITAB Output for Restaurant Service Ratings

MINITAB commands for data are columns named "DAY" and "NIGHT" in a file named "REST":

```
MTB > RETRIEVE "REST"
MTB > TWOSAMPLE 'DAY' 'NIGHT'
SUBC > ALTERNATIVE = 0
```

MINITAB output:

TWOSAMPLE T FOR NIGHT VS DAY

	N	MEAN	STDEV	SE MEAN
DAY	12	62.50	17.69	5.11
NIGHT	10	79.20	13.68	4.33

TEST MU DAY = MU NIGHT (VS NE): T = 2.44 P = 0.024 DF = 20

For instance, using MINITAB or EXCEL one can easily obtain the output in Table 10.3 after entering the data and the appropriate commands. These prepackaged computer routines are easy to use, highly accurate, and thus worth using. Make sure, however, that you know what the program is doing and that you have checked its accuracy. To check the accuracy of a program, take a small data set (such as one found here) and work through a test procedure with a hand calculator or spreadsheet program and then have the package do the same routine. In addition, if you have access to more than one program, you can check one against the other.

EXERCISES

10.1 An article in *The Wall Street Journal* (March 27, 1992) reported that tests show U.S. students have only a basic understanding of science. "Moreover, students at parochial and other private schools scored better than public school students at all grades, though test officials said that for twelfth-graders the gap wasn't statistically significant."

a. What are the null and alternative hypotheses to which the "statistical significance" refers?

b. What is the meaning of "statistical significance" in this context?

10.2 A study by the EPA compared the highway fuel economy of domestic and imported passenger cars. In the 3,000-pound weight class, 18 domestic cars showed an average of 34.3 mpg (miles per gallon) and 14 imported cars yielded an average of 34.8 mpg. The population gas mileage is known to be normally distributed in both cases and the variances are known to be $\sigma_1^2 = 2.1$ (domestic) and $\sigma_2^2 = 1.9$ (imported). At the the 5 percent Type I error level, are the means the same?

10.3 An article in *The Wall Street Journal* (January 29, 1991) reported on Domino's plans to introduce a new pizza that will have 45 percent more cheese than the company's old pizza and a thicker crust. "The average pizza will cost about 7 percent more as a result of the extra ingredients. That will lift the price of the average Domino's pizza, currently $7.84 including discounts, by about 50 cents." On the next page are old and new pizza prices from a sample obtained at 10 outlets. Was Domino's projection that the average price would rise by 50 cents reasonable?

Outlet	1	2	3	4	5	6	7	8	9	10
Old($)	8.00	9.00	7.50	6.75	8.50	7.20	6.50	7.77	8.00	9.20
New($)	8.25	10.00	8.00	7.50	8.25	7.90	7.00	8.88	8.50	9.75

10.4 A software house is experimenting with a new font size that is expected to increase the reading speed of older people. After testing thousands of people with the original font, it was established that a certain passage took older people an average of $\mu_1 = 0.16$ minutes and younger readers an average of $\mu_2 = 0.12$ minutes, with standard deviations of $\sigma_1 = 0.015$ minutes for older folks, and $\sigma_2 = 0.011$ minutes for the younger. For a sample of 16 older people, the average time to read the passage printed in the new font is now 0.12 minutes. For the sample of 12 younger readers, it is 0.11 minutes.

a. Is there now a difference in the reading times, assuming no change in measures of dispersion? (Test at the 5 percent Type I error level.)

b. Are the assumptions (the model) you had to assume to do your test reasonable?

10.5 An article in *The Wall Street Journal* (November 25, 1992) suggested women doctors in private practice have incomes that average 34 percent less than male colleagues. Below are descriptive statistics for analysis of this issue, where the mean earnings are reported in thousands of dollars for females and males.

Variable	Mean	Standard Deviation	S.E.Mean	Cases
FEMALE	117.180	89.17444	.89174	100
MALE	185.730	143.3742	.71687	200

a. What is the approximate value of the standard error of the differences in means? Explain why you used the formula you did.

b. At the 0.01 Type I error level, do women doctors, on the average, earn less than male doctors? State the assumptions you had to make to conduct this test.

10.6 A recent study suggests that licensed engineers serving as tenured university faculty members have higher incomes (university salary plus earnings from consulting) than their industry counterparts. Use the following information to test this claim at the 5 percent level. Specify the assumptions you needed to make to do this test.

Academic Engineers	Industry Engineers
$\bar{x}_1 = \$95,000$	$\bar{x}_2 = \$84,000$
$s_1 = \$9,000$	$s_2 = \$7,000$
$n_1 = 12$	$n_2 = 13$

CHAPTER 11

CHI-SQUARE TEST OF INDEPENDENCE

That's not an experiment
you have there,
that's an experience.

Sir Ronald A. Fisher
1890–1962

Tests of differences in the proportion of observations possessing a given attribute versus the proportion possessing the attribute in a second sample can be generalized to multiple attributes that might be defined for two different variables. The chi-square test of independence is designed to test whether two variables are related on the basis of the different attributes they have. For example, in the case of the midwestern bank introduced in Chapter 10, we might expect that as the liability period progresses, the bank might attempt to change the gender mix in its workforce. Thus, one variable is the gender of managers and the other variable is the time in the liability period. The question is whether the gender mix of managers is independent of the beginning, middle and end of the liability period? The hypotheses for this test are

H_O: gender and time are independent
H_A: gender and time are dependent

The Chi-Square Statistic

Contingency Table A table showing the frequency of joint occurrences of two variables.

Development of the statistic for the chi-square test requires the introduction of a new conceptual framework. First, the test for these hypotheses is said to determine the "goodness-of-fit" between an observed joint occurrence of these two variables and a set of expected joint occurrences. The observed frequencies of these joint occurrences are presented in a **contingency table.** Table 11.1 is the contingency table for the midwestern bank data on gender and time period.

Let the symbol O_{ij} represent the observed frequency in the *i*th row and the *j*th column of the contingency table. Table 11.1 then gives $O_{11} = 392$, indicating that at the beginning of the liability period there were 392 men employed; $O_{21} = 219$ indicates that 219 women were employed at the beginning of the liability period. In the next column, $O_{12} = 394$ indicates that 394 men were at the bank in the middle of the period, and so on until the last cell in the second row and third column, $O_{23} = 199$.

The expected frequency of the *i*th row and *j*th column (E_{ij}) is calculated by assuming that the two variables are independent; that is, H_O is true. As discussed in

Table 11.1 Women and Men Employed at the Beginning, Middle and End of the Liability Period

Number	Begin	Middle	End	
Men	392	394	376	1162
Women	219	223	199	641
	611	617	575	1803

Relative Frequency	Begin	Middle	End	
Men	0.217415	0.218524	0.208541	0.644481
Women	0.121464	0.123682	0.110371	0.355518
	0.338879	0.342207	0.318912	1.00000

Chapters 3 and 4, when two events are independent, the product of their marginal probabilities equals the probability of their intersection. If H_0 is true, the probability of randomly drawing a man *and* selecting the beginning of the liability period is the product of the probability of a man *times* the probability of being at the beginning of the liability period. These two marginal probabilities are estimated by the observed first row relative frequency (1162/1803) and the first column relative frequency (611/1803). Thus, the estimated joint probability of drawing a man *and* the beginning of the liability period is 0.217868 = (1162/1803)(611/1803). The expected frequency of men in the first period is then this estimated joint probability times the total number of executives. That is,

$$E_{11} = \frac{1162}{1803} \times \frac{611}{1803} \times 1803 = 0.218401 \times 1803 = 393.7781$$

In formula form, the expected frequency of any one of the cells in the *i*th row and *j*th column can be written as

$$E_{ij} = \hat{p}_i \hat{p}_j n \qquad (11.\ 1)$$

where $\hat{p}_i$ is the estimated marginal probability of the *i*th row (as calculated from the relative frequency data in the *i*th row of the contingency table);

$\hat{p}_j$ is the estimated marginal probability of the *j*th column (as calculated from the relative frequency data in the *j*th column of the contingency table); and n is the number of observations in the contingency table.

Expected frequencies (the E_{ij}'s) are easily calculated with a spreadsheet program such as LOTUS 1-2-3. Table 11. 2 gives the joint probabilities for each of the six cells (i.e., $\hat{p}_i\hat{p}_j$), and Table 11. 3 gives the expected frequencies. Movement from Table 11. 2 to Table 11. 3 shows the multiplication of each cell in Table 11. 2 by n = 1803. As a rule of thumb, each E_{ij} must be at least five for the chi-square distribution to be appropriate. Next, the chi-square goodness-of-fit test requires a numerical comparison of the observed frequencies (as in Table 11. 1) with the expected frequencies (as in Table 11. 3). If the "fit is good" (meaning the frequencies in the two tables are fairly close), then the null hypothesis of independence is not rejected. If the fit is not good, then the null hypothesis is rejected in favor of the alternative hypothesis of dependence. The

TABLE 11. 2 Estimated Joint Probabilities of Women and Men Employed at the Beginning, Middle, and End of the Liability Period, Assuming Independence

	Beginning	Middle	End	$\hat{p}_i$
Men	0.218401	0.220546	0.205533	0.644481
Women	0.120478	0.121661	0.113379	0.355518
$\hat{p}_j$	0.338879	0.342207	0.318912	1.000000

TABLE 11. 3
Expected Number of Women and Men Employed at the Beginning, Middle and End of the Liability Period, Assuming Independence

	Beginning	Middle	End	
Men	393.7781	397.6450	370.5768	1162
Women	217.2218	219.3549	204.4231	641
	611	617	575	1803

numerical measure for making this decision is the chi-square (the Greek letter χ, squared) test statistic, which is determined by the following formula:

Chi-Square Statistic

$$\chi^2 = \sum_{i=1}^{r}\sum_{j=1}^{c}\frac{\left(O_{ij} - E_{ij}\right)^2}{E_{ij}} \qquad (11.2)$$

where O_{ij} is the observed frequency in *ij*th cell; E_{ij} is the expected frequency in *ij*th cell ($E_{ij} \geq 5$); and the degrees of freedom are df = $(r - 1)(c - 1)$, for a contingency table with r rows and c columns.

Using the information in Tables 11.1 and 11. 3, the chi-square test statistic is calculated using Formula (11.2) as follows:

$$\chi^2_{\text{calc}} = \sum_{i=1}^{2}\sum_{j=1}^{3}\frac{\left(O_{ij} - E_{ij}\right)^2}{E_{ij}} = 0.3398 \qquad (11.\ 3)$$

$$= \frac{(392 - 393.7781)^2}{393.7781} + \frac{(394 - 397.6450)^2}{397.6450} + \frac{(376 - 370.5768)^2}{370.5768}$$

$$+ \frac{(219 - 217.2218)^2}{217.2218} + \frac{(223 - 219.3549)^2}{219.3549} + \frac{(199 - 204.4231)^2}{204.4231}$$

We will learn that this calculated chi-square value of $\chi^2_{\text{calc}} = 0.3398$ is relatively small, indicating that there is not much difference between the observed and expected values from the contingency table. As with other hypothesis tests, small calculated test statistic values indicate that the null hypothesis should not be rejected. That is, the calculated $\chi^2_{\text{calc}} = 0.3398$ is small, so we conclude that there is a "good fit" between the observed and expected relative frequencies—gender and the time within the liability period appear to be independent.

The p-value

What constitutes a small chi-square value can be determined by getting the p-value that is associated with the calculated chi-square test statistic. This requires knowledge of the degrees of freedom and the shape of the chi-square distribution. The degrees of freedom for the chi-square are

$$\text{df} = (r-1)(c-1) \tag{11. 4}$$

where r is the number of rows in the contingency table, and

c is the number of columns in the contingency table.

In the case under consideration, there are two rows and three columns so

$$\text{df} = (2-1)(3-1) \tag{11. 5}$$

The p-value in a chi-square test is the probability

$$P(\chi^2 > \chi^2_{\text{calc}}) \tag{11. 6}$$

which in the bank employment case is the probability of a chi-square value larger than $\chi^2_{\text{calc}} = 0.3398$, with 2 degrees of freedom. As with other test statistics, if the calculated test statistic is large, then its p-value will be small. If the p-value is less than a preset probability of a Type I error (α), then H_0 is rejected. On the other hand, if the calculated test statistic is small, then its p-value will be large. If the p-value is greater than α, then H_0 is not rejected.

The p-values are easily determined using a computer program. A chi-square computer routine gives the probability of obtaining a chi-square value of 0.3398 or larger [i.e., $P(\chi^2 \geq 0.3398)$, with 2 degrees of freedom] equal to 0.844. Because this p-value is extremely large, for any typical probability of a Type I error (say $\alpha = 0.10$), the null hypothesis of independence is not rejected, and the conclusion is that gender and the time of observation during the liability period may be independent.

11.2 Critical Values and the Chi-Square Distribution

An alternative to finding the p-values with a computer program is to determine the chi-square critical value for $(r-1)(c-1)$ degrees of freedom. Critical values for the chi-square distribution are displayed in Appendix Table A.2. Like other tests, if the calculated χ^2_{calc} value is less than the critical value in Appendix Table A.2, for $(r-1)(c-1)$ degrees of freedom, then H_0 is not rejected. If χ^2_{calc} is greater than the critical value, then H_0 is rejected.

The chi-square distribution is a continuous distribution. Its shape depends on the degrees of freedom, df = $(r-1)(c-1)$. It is thus a family of distributions, one for each degree of freedom. A few of these distributions are shown in Figure 11.5, for df = 2, df = 16, and df = 30. For df = 2, the chi-square density function appears to be decreasing

FIGURE 11.1 Chi-Square Distribution

Family of chi-square distributions, for df = 2, 16, and 30

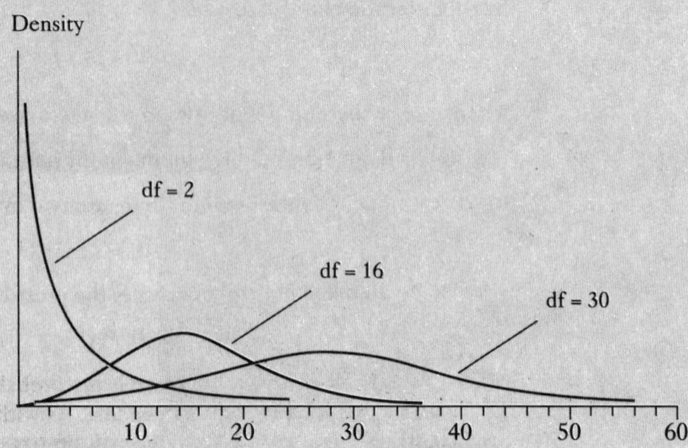

(which is also the case for df = 1, although not shown here). If df increases, as seen in Figure 11.1 for df = 16, the chi-square distribution is at first noticeably right skewed. It becomes more symmetrical, however, as the degrees of freedom increase further. For df = 30, the chi-square distribution is very close to the normal distribution. As degrees of freedom increase and approach infinity, the chi-square distribution becomes indistinguishable from the normal distribution.

If the probability of a Type I error is α = 0.10, the critical chi-square value, with 2 degrees of freedom (as shown in Figure 11.2 with values obtained from Appendix Table A.2) is 4.61. In the midwestern bank case, the calculated chi-square value (χ^2_{calc} = 0.335415) is less than this critical value (4.61), as shown in Figure 11.2. Thus, H_0 is not rejected; the conclusion is that the gender and time within the liability period are independent.

Most of the large computer programs such as SAS and SPSS have routines for doing chi-square tests of independence. They may be listed as "goodness-of-fit tests," "test of homogeneity," or "cross-tab tests." Regardless of the name given, the procedures described here for the chi-square test of independence are appropriate for an analysis of the relationship between the rows and columns of a contingency table.

FIGURE 11.2 Chi-Square Test for Bank Employment

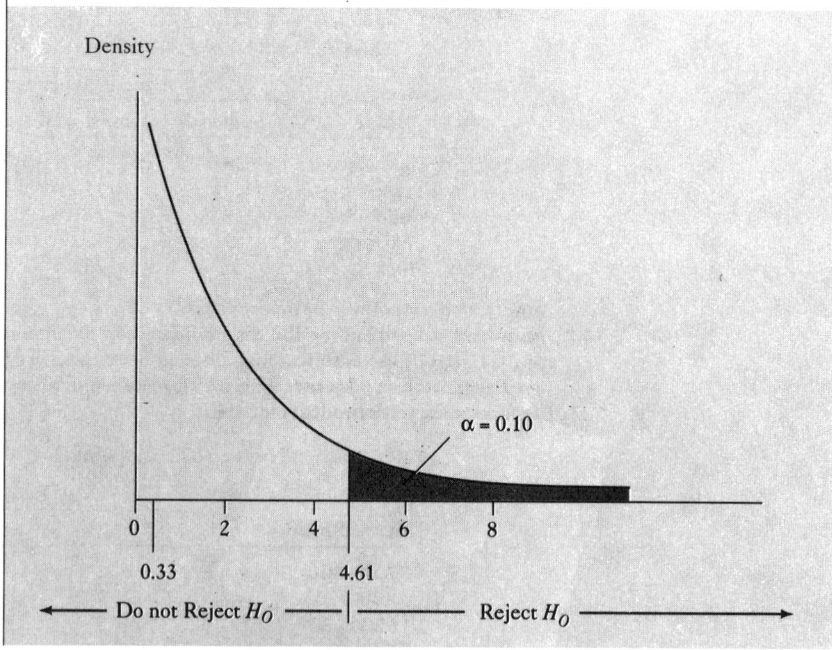

EXERCISES

11.1 If two events X and Y are not related and the probability of event X is 0.30 and the probability of Y is 0.25, then for a sample of 200 what is the expected frequency of X and Y?

11.2 What is the null hypothesis rejection region in the chi-square test of independence for the following contingency table sizes and Type I error levels?

a. Contingency table is $r = 3$ by $c = 4$ and $\alpha = 0.05$.

b. Contingency table is 3 by 3 and $\alpha = 0.10$.

c. Contingency table has 5 rows and 7 columns and the probability of a Type I error is 0.01.

11.3 Absenteeism among assembly line workers is of concern. In particular, there may be a relationship between the day of the week on which absences occur and the type of job performed by the worker. Workers are classified as skilled, semiskilled, and laborer. A random sample of days absent was selected from records kept over the past several years; workers were never included more than once in the following results:

Days Absent Among Assembly Line Workers

	Type of Worker		
Days	Skilled	Semiskilled	Laborer
Mondays	18	23	21
Tuesdays	10	16	17
Wednesdays	12	11	9
Thursdays	17	16	16
Fridays	22	26	20

Are days and type of worker independent?

11.4 A manager wants to know if there is a difference in the number of trucks unloaded during the three different shifts, at four different dock sites. The following sample information is collected on dock sites. At the 0.05 level of significance, are trucks unloaded at the four dock sites independent of the shifts?

Number of Trucks Unloaded

	Dock Site			
Time of Shift	1	2	3	4
7:30– 3:30	8	12	7	10
3:30–11:30	11	9	8	9
11:30– 7:30	10	12	10	9

11.5 *The Business Failure Record,* compiled by Dun and Bradstreet, reports business failures by industry type and period of observation. For the four periods below, is the type of business related to the period of observation in which failures occurred? (Use a spreadsheet program.)

	Number of Failures in Period			
Industry	1st	2nd	3rd	4th
Mining and Manufacturing	2,455	2,074	2,612	2,035
Wholesale Trade	1,316	1,016	1,473	984
Retail Trade	8,495	4,429	7,386	4,650
Construction	760	912	2,607	1,687
Commercial Service	593	731	1,367	1,392

11.6 An article in *The Wall Street Journal* (December 23, 1993) reported that although President Clinton had only 27 confirmed appointments to the U.S. District and Appeals Courts, only 72.3 percent (20 of 27) were white compared to Bush's 89.2 percent (165 of 185) and Reagan's 93.5 percent (344 of 368). Is the race of the judicial appointments independent of the president in power? (Test at the 0.05 Type I error level.)

CHAPTER 12

CORRELATION AND REGRESSION ANALYSIS WITHIN A SAMPLE

Too many use statistics as a drunk man uses a lamp post—for support and not illumination.

Keely v. Westinghouse
Elec. Comp.
(E.D. Mo. 1975)

12.1 INTRODUCTION

Knowing the algebraic relationship between two variables enables predictions for one of the variables based on values of the other. For example:

- How do highway deaths change when the speed limit is changed? A letter to the editor of *The New York Times* (November 29, 1986) by an official of the Sports Car Club of America suggests that there is no relationship.
- *Business Week* (March 30, 1992) asks if more school days are a "remedy for the mediocrity that characterizes American education, a mediocrity that hampers America's ability to compete in a global economy." International comparisons of days spent in school and scores on a standardized math exam suggest that a longer school year boosts performance.
- A *Business Week* (June 22, 1987) article argued that as the percentage of women among those holding Master in Business Administration (MBA) degrees has increased, the percentage of women in management and administration jobs has also increased. Is this relationship supported by the data? Can future changes be predicted from this relationship?
- *Newsweek* (April 4, 1994) reported on the U.S. Congress's desire to encourage "thought over memorization." It provided an excerpt from a problem on the National Achievement Test involving the relationship between shoe lace length and the number of eyelets and the answer. Does the "top-rated" answer provide the best estimate of the relationship?
- An *American Economic Review* (June, 1994) article asked what would be the effect on cigarette consumption if the cigarette tax were increased by 10 percent? The regression analysis of Nobel Laureate economist Gary Becker and fellow economists Michael Grossman and Kevin Murphy suggests that current consumption will fall by 4 percent in the short run and 7.5 percent in the long run.

This chapter is devoted to statistical techniques for describing the association between paired sample observations. It presents covariance, correlation, and regression for this purpose. The principle of least squares is developed and demonstrated. By the end of this chapter, you will be able to calculate and interpret all these descriptive measures of the sample relationship between two variables. The next chapter introduces the ideas of population modeling and parameter estimation and testing based on the descriptive statistics presented in this chapter.

12.2 SPEED AND DEATH: AN ILLUSTRATION

Questions and issues involving the relationship between variables appear regularly in the popular press, business and trade publications, and scholarly journals. For example, in a letter to the editor of *The New York Times* (November 29, 1986, p. 26), David Rivkin provided data on two variables: highway deaths per 100 million vehicle miles and highway speed limits for 10 countries, Table 12.1. He states:

> From this we can see that five countries with the same speed limit have very different positions on the safety list. Britain . . . with a speed limit of 70 is demonstrably safer than Japan, at 55. Clearly, speed has little to do with safety.

Table 12.1
Death Rates and Speed Limits

	Deaths Per 100 Million Vehicle Miles	Speed Limit (mph)
1. Norway	3.0	55
2. United States	3.3	55
3. Finland	3.4	55
4. Britain	3.5	70
5. Denmark	4.1	55
6. Canada	4.3	60
7. Japan	4.7	55
8. Australia	4.9	60
9. Netherlands	5.1	60
10. Italy	6.1	75

Although Rivkin argues that there is no sample relationship between speed and death, his argument is susceptible to statistical analysis. Better measures are needed of the sample relationship between Rivkin's notion of highway safety and the speed limit. Those measures must describe both central tendencies and dispersion.

12.3 Conditional Means and Deviations

Rivkin does not define exactly what he means by "a safety list." He does state that the five countries with 55 mph speed limits have very different positions on this list. In other words, there is considerable variability in the rate of deaths at 55 mph. The conditional mean death rate at a speed limit of 55 mph is 3.7 deaths per 100 million vehicle miles.

$$\text{Mean death rate, at 55 mph speed limit} = \frac{3.0 + 3.3 + 3.4 + 4.1 + 4.7}{5} = 3.7$$

Deviations from this mean or average are calculated by subtracting the conditional average from each of the five death rates. The deviations in death rates at a 55 mph speed limit are 3.0 – 3.7 = –0.7 for Norway, and, similarly, –0.4 for the United States, –0.3 for Finland, +0.4 for Denmark, and +1.0 for Japan.

We now have a quantitative safety list for the sample of five countries with 55 mph speed limits. As suggested by Rivkin, countries on this safety list have very different positions. Three are below this speed-specific average death rate of 3.7, and two are above. Death rates vary from 0.7 deaths below the average to one death above the average, per 100 million vehicle miles.

A similar listing for deaths at 60 mph can be obtained, where the conditional mean death rate is 4.767. For the three sample observations at a speed limit of 60 mph, deviations from this conditional mean death rate are –0.467 for Canada, +0.133 for Australia, and +0.333 for the Netherlands. Now only one country is below the 60 mph conditional mean death rate of 4.767, and the death rate only varies from 0.467 deaths below this mean to 0.333 deaths above the mean, per 100 million vehicle miles.

At each of the speed limits of 70 mph and 75 mph, there is no variability in deaths within the sample, because only one country is listed at each speed. The importance of these single observations at 70 mph and 75 mph versus the multiple observations at the slower speed limits can be seen by constructing a scatterplot and connecting the conditional means to form a **regression** line. A regression line shows the central tendency (in our example the mean) of y at each value of x in the sample.

Regression of y on x The relationship between a measure of central tendency of one variable, y, across values of another variable, x. Because y is said to depend on x, y is called the dependent variable and x is the independent variable.

Sample regression lines can be obtained in many different ways. One way is to connect the conditional means of the dependent variable at each value of the independent variable in a scatterplot or scatter diagram. As introduced in Chapters 10 and 11, a scatterplot measures one variable along the vertical axis and the other variable along the horizontal axis. It is conventional to place the variable to be explained, called the dependent variable (y), on the vertical axis. The variable used to do the explaining, called the independent variable (x), is placed on the horizontal axis. In Figure 12.1, death rate is the dependent variable; it is measured along the vertical axis. The speed limit is the independent variable; it is measured along the horizontal axis.

Using the data in Table 12.1, point I in Figure 12.1 gives the x and y values for Italy. It is plotted at the intersection of a vertical line drawn from 75 mph and a horizontal line drawn from 6.1 deaths per 100 vehicle miles. Point B is for Britain and is the intersection of a vertical line from 70 and a horizontal line from 3.5. The remaining eight countries are identified and plotted in a similar manner. (Note that this is the same type of two-dimensional scatterplot drawn for the pretest, x, and posttest, y, in Chapter 10.)

Each point in Figure 12.1 is marked with a letter that identifies the country. Point I, for example, gives the x and y values for Italy: 75 mph and 6.1 deaths per 100 vehicle miles. Figure 12.1 also shows a line that connects the conditional mean death rates for the different speed limits for which there are data. This is a regression line. It shows how the central tendency (conditional mean) of y changes between x values. It does not show a uniformly positive or negative slope.

The single observations at 70 and 75 miles per hour are more influential in determining the slope of the regression line than any one of the observations at 55 or 60 miles per hour because there are multiple observations at 55 and 60 mph. For instance, if the single death rate at 70 mph were higher, then the slope of the line might be positive throughout its range. If one of the observations at 55 mph were higher (or lower), however, the slope of the line need not change because this observation enters the conditional mean with only a one-fifth weight.

Comparing one country's death rate at 55 mph with another at 70, as Rivkin does, overlooks the variability in death rates at 55 mph. Comparing the conditional mean death rate at 55 mph with the mean deaths at 60 mph or the death rates at 70 mph or 75 mph overlooks how variability in deaths changes across speed limits. What is needed is a single equation or regression line that can be used to assess how deaths deviate from their overall sample mean as the speed limit deviates from its overall sample mean.

FIGURE 12.1 Scatterplot of Death Rates and Speed Limits

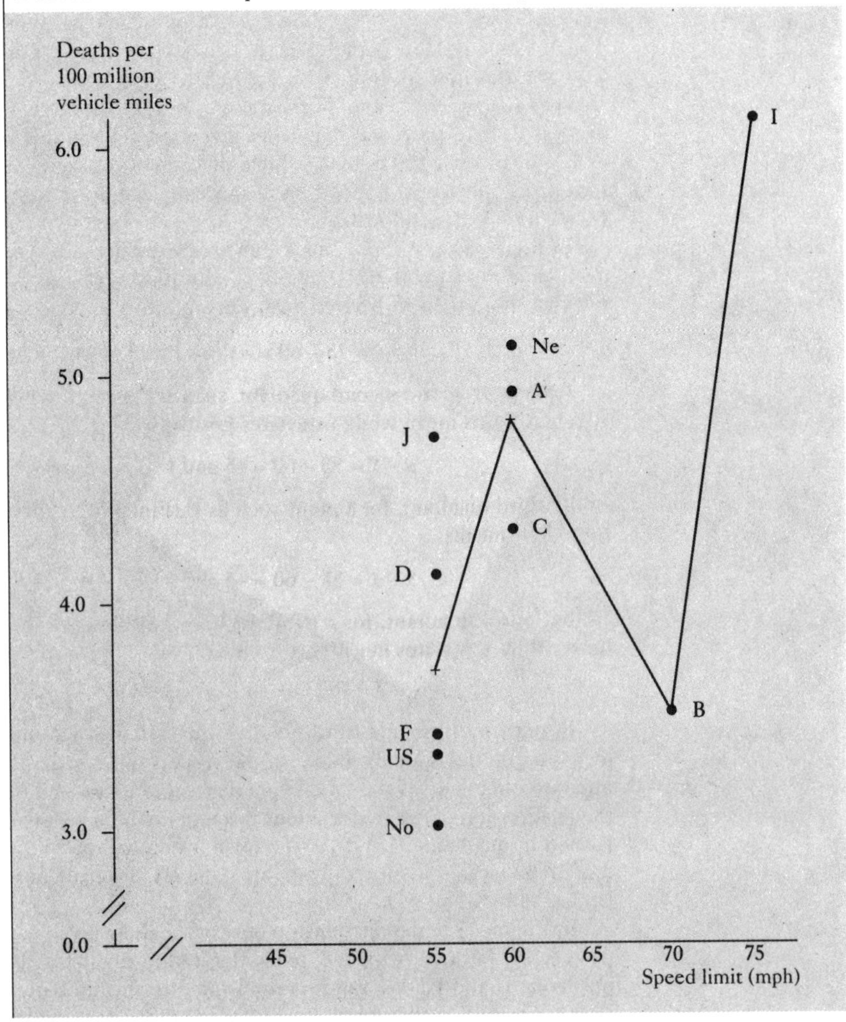

12.4 Deviations from the Means

The question is: How does the death rate deviate from its sample average as the speed limit deviates from its sample average? Letting the letter y represent the death rate, the mean or average death rate for the 10 sample observations is $\bar{y} = 4.24$. Unlike the mean death rates that were conditional on a given speed limit, this sample average death rate of 4.24 deaths per 100 million vehicle miles involves no reference to the speed limits. Letting x represent the speed limit, the sample average speed limit for all 10 cases is $\bar{x} = 60$; its calculation involves no reference to deaths.

In Figure 12.2, $\bar{y} = 4.24$ and $\bar{x} = 60$ divide the death and speed scatterplot into four quadrants. For a point in the first quadrant, such as that representing Italy, both x and y deviate from their respective means in a positive direction; that is,

$$x - \bar{x} = 75 - 60 = +15 \text{ and } y - \bar{y} = 6.1 - 4.24 = +1.86$$

For a point in the second quadrant, such as that representing Japan, x deviates negatively from its mean while y deviates positively:

$$x - \bar{x} = 55 - 60 = -5 \text{ and } y - \bar{y} = 4.7 - 4.24 = +0.46$$

In the third quadrant, for a point such as F (Finland), both x and y deviate negatively from their means:

$$x - \bar{x} = 55 - 60 = -5 \text{ and } y - \bar{y} = 3.4 - 4.24 = -0.84$$

In the fourth quadrant, for a point such as B (Britain), x deviates positively from its mean while y deviates negatively from its mean:

$$x - \bar{x} = 70 - 60 = +10 \text{ and } y - \bar{y} = 3.5 - 4.24 = -0.74$$

In both the first and third quadrant, deviations in x and y from their respective means are in the same direction. In the second and fourth, deviations in x and y are in opposite directions. If the sample points tend to be located in the quadrants I and III, the relationship between deviations in x and y will be positive. If the points tend to be located in quadrants II and IV, the relationship will be negative. If the points do not tend to be located in either quadrants I and III, or quadrants II and IV, there is no relationship between x and y.

In Figure 12.2, the relationship between x and y is not negative. If anything, it appears to be positive, with five points located in quadrants I and III and only two in quadrants II and IV. We can represent the relationship between x and y by drawing a single straight line through the point for the mean of x and the mean of y and into the quadrants with the most points. This single straight line regression would be the one that appears to "fit the data best." For the data in Figure 12.2, this line would pass through $\bar{y} = 4.24$ and $\bar{x} = 60$ and into quadrants I and III. It would have a positive slope, as drawn in Figure 12.3.

The positive relationship between x and y in Figure 12.3 is not strong, since three sample points show y deviating from its mean when x did not deviate from its mean, and two points are in quadrants II and IV. Curiously, Rivkin only emphasized these

FIGURE 12.2 Deviations in Death Rates and Speed Limits

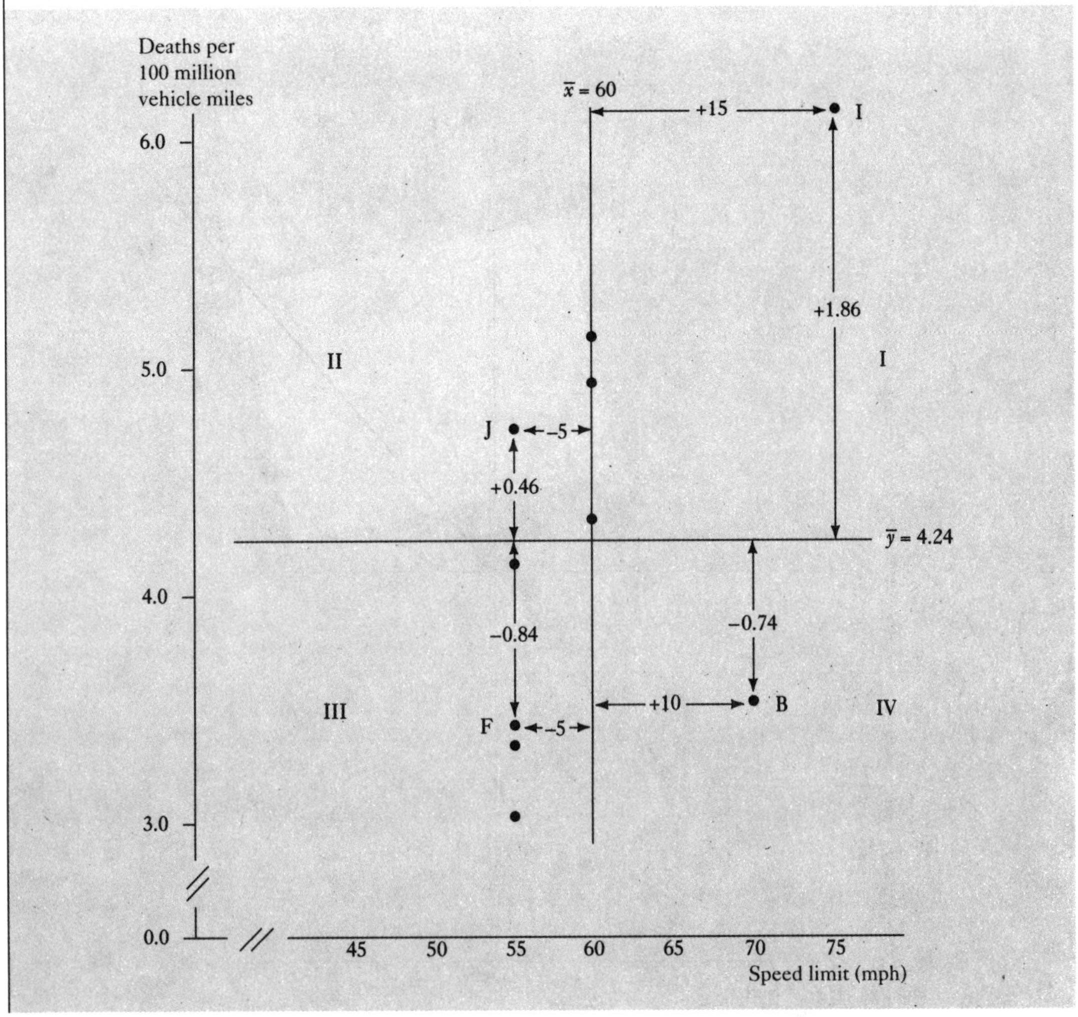

FIGURE 12.3 Scatterplot of Death Rates and Speed Limits With Continuous, Straight Regression Line

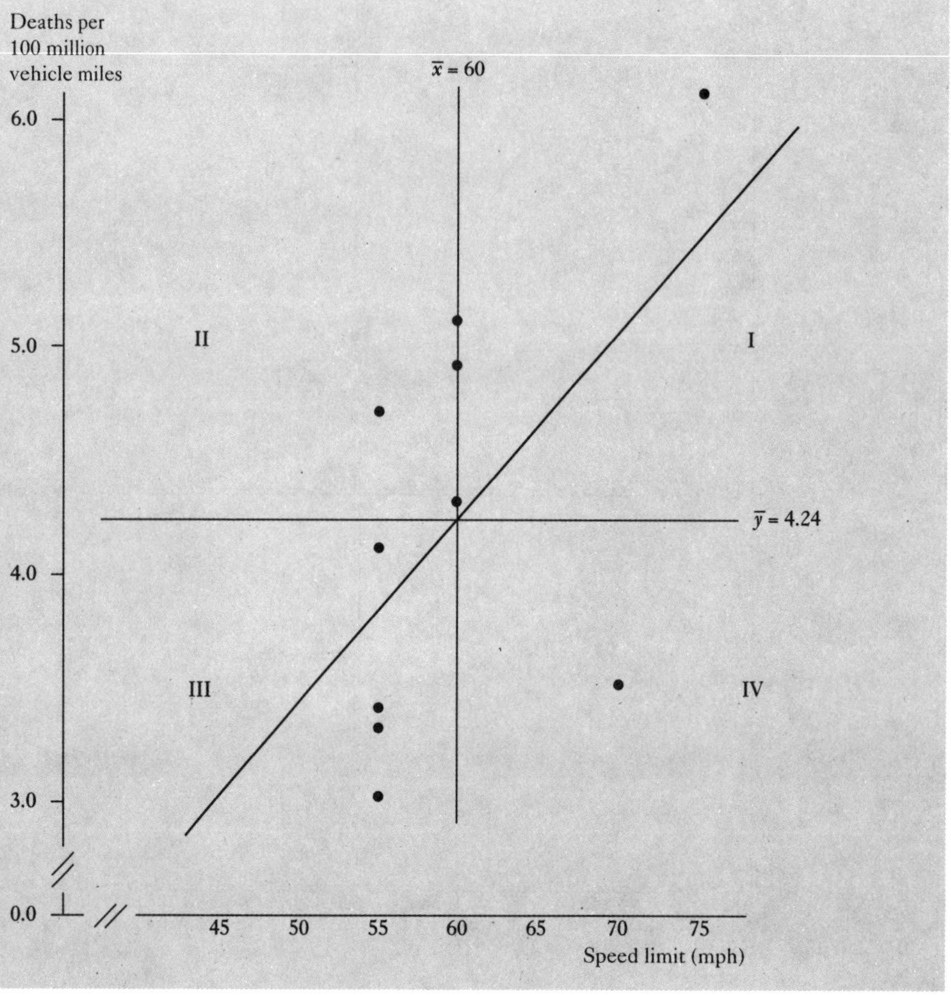

two points (Japan and Britain) in quadrants II and IV; he never mentioned that five death and speed limit pairs show a positive relationship in accordance with our positively sloped, single, and continuous straight regression line.

QUERY 12.1:

Business Week (March 30, 1992) featured a commentary that questioned whether more school days were a "remedy for the mediocrity." The following data on days spent in school and average scores on a standardized math achievement exam of 13 year olds, by country, were provided to answer the question "Does a longer school year boost academic performance?"

Country	School Days	Exam Scores
China	251	80
South Korea	222	73
Switzerland	207	71
Former USSR	210	70
France	174	64
Israel	215	63
Canada	188	62
Britain	192	61
United States	180	55
Jordan	191	40

Calculate the deviations from the mean school days and exam scores and draw a scatterplot to determine how deviations from the mean days are related to deviations from the mean score. Draw a single straight regression line. Finally, use all of these pieces to answer the question of how these countries' school days are related to their exam scores.

ANSWER:

Let x be the length of the school and let y be the associated exam score for each country. The mean days of school, mean test score, deviations from the means, and the scatterplot are then

$\bar{x} = 203$ and $\bar{y} = 63.9$

Country	$x - \bar{x}$	$y - \bar{y}$
China	48	16.1
South Korea	19	9.1
Switzerland	4	7.1
Former USSR	7	6.1
France	-29	0.1
Israel	12	-0.9
Canada	-15	-1.9
Britain	-11	-2.9
United States	-23	-8.9
Jordan	-12	-23.9

The scatterplot with the regression line drawn in follows

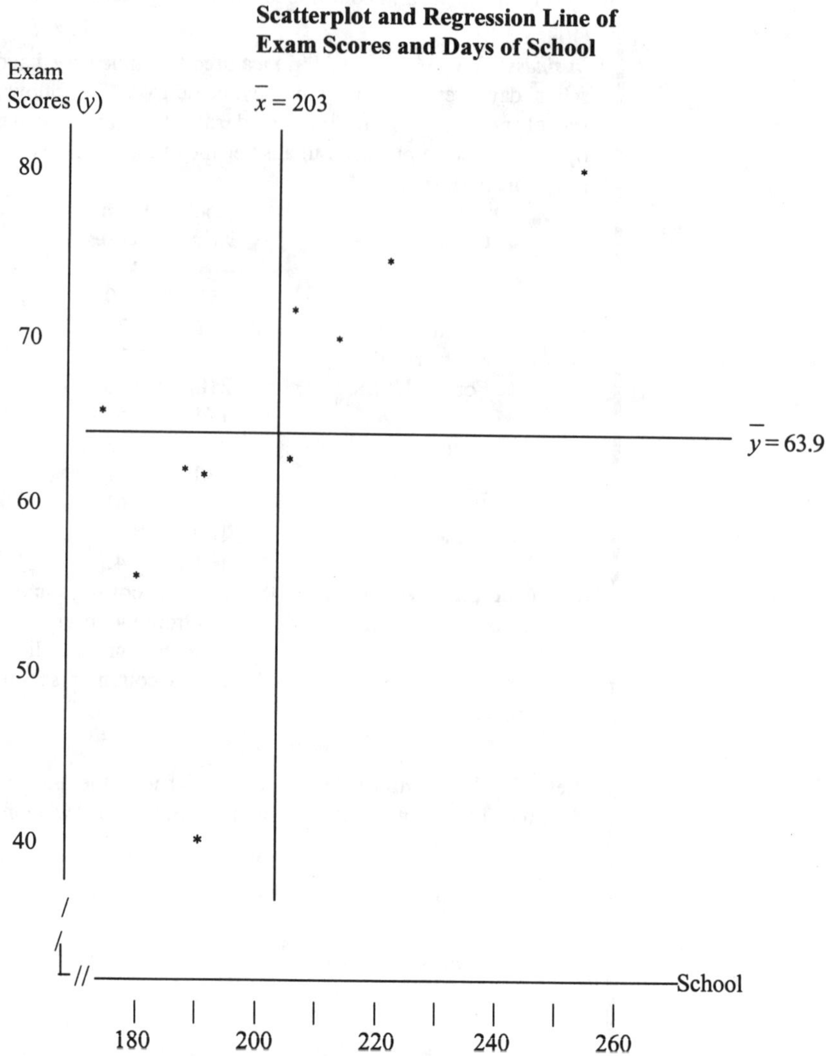

There appears to be a strong positive relationship between exam scores and days in school, because eight of the ten points lie in quadrants I and III. For these eight points, deviations from the exam-score mean are in the same direction as deviations from the mean of school days. This relationship is far from perfect, with two points (France and Israel) falling in quadrants II and IV, where deviations are in the opposite directions.

12.5 Measures of Covariance

Covariance is a measure of the strength of the linear relationship between two variables. It provides a quantitative answer to the question, "As the values observed for one variable rise (or fall), what tends to happen to the values observed on another variable?"

Reconsider Figure 12.2, where $\bar{y} = 4.24$ and $\bar{x} = 60$ divide the death and speed scatterplot into four quadrants. For a point in the first quadrant, both x and y deviate from their respective means in a positive direction, so the products of $(x_i - \bar{x})$ deviations and $(y_i - \bar{y})$ deviations will be positive. For a point in the second quadrant, x deviates negatively from its mean, while y deviates positively, and the product of deviations is negative. In the third quadrant, both x and y deviate negatively from their means, so the product of deviations is positive. In the fourth quadrant, x deviates positively from its mean, while y deviates negatively from its mean, and the product of deviations is negative.

If x and y tend to move in the same direction, then most products of deviations in x and deviations in y will be positive, and the sum of all such cross products should be positive; that is,

$$\sum_{i=1}^{n}\left(x_i - \bar{x}\right)\left(y_i - \bar{y}\right) > 0$$

Alternatively, if x and y tend to move in opposite directions, then the products of deviations in x and deviations in y will tend to be negative and

$$\sum_{i=1}^{n}\left(x_i - \bar{x}\right)\left(y_i - \bar{y}\right) < 0$$

When there is no relationship between x and y, with the observations appearing evenly in all four quadrants, positive and negative deviations from means will tend to cancel, and

$$\sum_{i=1}^{n}\left(x_i - \bar{x}\right)\left(y_i - \bar{y}\right) \approx 0$$

The quantity $\Sigma(x_i - \bar{x})(y_i - \bar{y})$ is a measure of variability between x and y. In the case of death rates and speed limits, Table 12.2 shows that $\Sigma(x_i - \bar{x})(y_i - \bar{y}) = 34$, which is consistent with our earlier assessment that death rates and speed limits were positively related in Rivkin's sample.

As with the calculation of the sum of squared deviations in x, $\Sigma(x_i - \bar{x})^2$ or sum of squared deviations in y, $\Sigma(y_i - \bar{y})^2$, the magnitude of the sum of x and y deviation

TABLE 12.2
Sum of Death Rate and Speed Limit Deviation Cross Products

i	y_i	x_i	$y_i - \bar{y}$	$x_i - \bar{x}$	$(y_i - \bar{y})(x_i - \bar{x})$
1	3.0	55	−1.24	−5	6.2
2	3.3	55	−0.94	−5	4.7
3	3.4	55	−0.84	−5	4.2
4	3.5	70	−0.74	10	−7.4
5	4.1	55	−0.14	−5	0.7
6	4.3	60	0.06	0	0.0
7	4.7	55	0.46	−5	−2.3
8	4.9	60	0.66	0	0.0
9	5.1	60	0.86	0	0.0
10	6.1	75	1.86	15	27.9
Sum =	42.4	600	0.00	00	34.0

products, $\Sigma(x_i - \bar{x})(y_i - \bar{y})$, depends on the sample size. Like the variance, a measure of variability between x and y based on the sum of deviation cross products must involve an adjustment for the degrees of freedom $n - 1$. The **covariance of x and y** is defined as the average variability between x and y; it is represented by the symbol s_{xy} and calculated by the formula

Covariance of x and y
A measure of average cross variability between x and y.

$$s_{xy} = \frac{\sum_{i=1}^{n}\left(x_i - \bar{x}\right)\left(y_i - \bar{y}\right)}{n-1} \tag{12.1}$$

For death rates and speed limits, the covariance is $s_{xy} = 34/9 = 3.78$.

Together with the individual variances of x and y, the concept of the covariance between x and y forms the basis for correlation and regression analysis. As already discussed, a regression line is used to visualize changes in the central tendency of y as x changes. It can be defined by the line that connects the conditional means of y at each value of x in a scatterplot. The idea of covariance (and correlation), however, is based on deviations from $\bar{x}$ and $\bar{y}$. The calculation of covariance implicitly assumes that one continuous straight line is drawn through the intersection of $\bar{x}$ and $\bar{y}$ and into the two opposing quadrants containing the bulk of data.

12.6 CORRELATION

The sign of the covariance gives the direction of the relationship between two variables; its size gives some idea of the strength of that relationship. The actual magnitude of the covariance, however, depends on the units in which x and y are measured. (Suppose death rates had been given in one million vehicle miles instead of 100 million vehicle miles; y values would have been 100 times smaller and hence s_{xy} would have been 100 times smaller.) This problem is removed by dividing each deviation from the variable's mean by the standard deviation of the variable; that is,

$$\frac{(x_i - \bar{x})}{s_x} \text{ and } \frac{(y_i - \bar{y})}{s_y} \qquad (12.2)$$

where

$$s_y = \sqrt{\frac{\sum_{i=1}^{n}(y_i - \bar{y})^2}{n-1}} \qquad s_x = \sqrt{\frac{\sum_{i=1}^{n}(x_i - \bar{x})^2}{n-1}}$$

The covariance based on these standardized variables is now written

$$\left[\frac{1}{n-1}\right]\sum_{i=1}^{n}\left[\frac{x_i - \bar{x}}{s_x}\right]\left[\frac{y_i - \bar{y}}{s_y}\right] = \frac{\sum_{i=1}^{n}(y - \bar{y})(x - \bar{x})}{(n-1)s_x s_y}$$

This standardized covariance is called the sample correlation and is typically denoted by the symbol r. Both s_x and s_y have the square root of $n - 1$ in their denominators, which will cancel with the $n - 1$ multiplicative factor in the denominator of r. Thus, the **coefficient of correlation** can now be written

Coefficient of Correlation
A standardized measure of the strength of the linear relationship between two variables.

$$r = \frac{\sum_{i=1}^{n}(x_i - \bar{x})(y_i - \bar{y})}{\sqrt{\sum_{i=1}^{n}(x_i - \bar{x})^2 \sum_{i=1}^{n}(y_i - \bar{y})^2}} \qquad (12.3)$$

Table 12.2 provides the value for the numerator of r, for the speed limit and death data. Table 12.3 has the appropriate sum of squared deviations for the denominator. Substituting these quantities into 12.3 gives

$$r = \frac{34}{\sqrt{(450)(8.544)}} = \frac{34}{\sqrt{3844.8}} = \frac{34}{62} = 0.548$$

An appreciation of the sign and magnitude of the correlation coefficient can be gained from Figure 12.4. In panel a, where there is a perfect positive relationship, the sum of products of x and y deviations from their respective means is always positive. In addition, $\Sigma(x - \bar{x})(y - \bar{y})$ is at its maximum and, hence, r is at its maximum. In panel b, the products of x and y deviations are always negative and r is at its minimum. As will be shown in the next section, the maximum value of r is +1 and its minimum is –1.

An r value of 0 indicates no straight line relationship between x and y, because the sum of positive products of x and y deviations are offset by the sum of negative products, panel c. Notice in panel d, however, that an r of 0 need not imply a lack of a relationship between x and y; an $r = 0$ only indicates no straight line association.

Correlation of x and y
A standardized measure of the average cross variability between x and y.

For r values between 0 and +1, and for r values between –1 and 0, some **correlation between x and y** is indicated, panels e and f. The closer an r value is to +1, the stronger the positive relationship between x and y; the closer to –1, the stronger the negative relationship. An r value of +0.548 indicates some positive correlation between x and y.

FIGURE 12.4 Scatterplots of Different Correlation Values

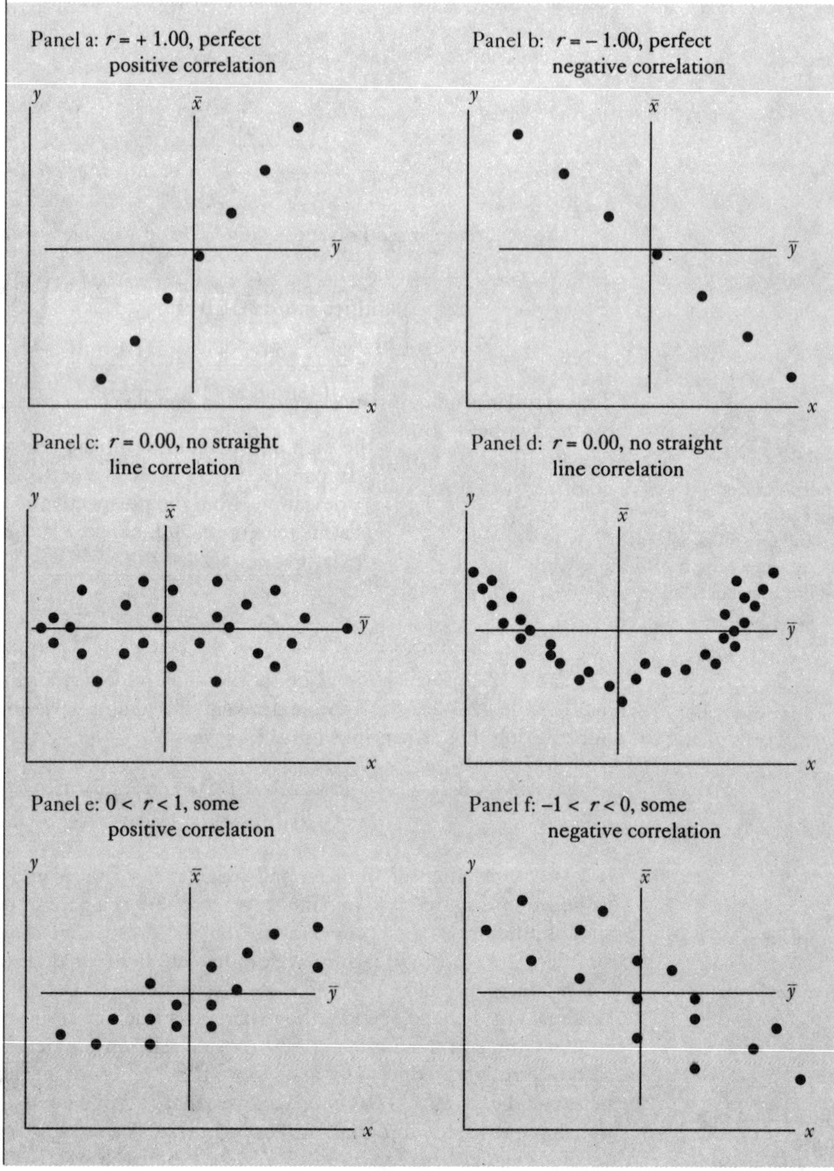

TABLE 12.3 Sum of Squared Deviations in Death Rates and Speed Limits

i	y_i	x_i	$y_i - \bar{y}$	$x_i - \bar{x}$	$(y_i - \bar{y})^2$	$(x_i - \bar{x})^2$
1	3.0	55	−1.24	−5	1.5376	25
2	3.3	55	−0.94	−5	0.8836	25
3	3.4	55	−0.84	−5	0.7056	25
4	3.5	70	−0.74	10	0.5476	100
5	4.1	55	−0.14	−5	0.0196	25
6	4.3	60	0.06	0	0.0036	0
7	4.7	55	0.46	−5	0.2116	25
8	4.9	60	0.66	0	0.4356	0
9	5.1	60	0.86	0	0.7396	0
10	6.1	75	1.86	15	3.4596	225
Sum =	42.4	600	0.00	00	8.5440	450

Although this correlation between deaths and speed is not perfect, it is not negative, as suggested by Rivkin in his *NYT* letter to the editor.

In closing this discussion of correlation, note that correlation does not imply causality. Although we call y (death rate) the dependent variable and x (speed limit) the independent variable, and conclude that in the sample of 10 observations there is a positive relationship between y and x, we did not prove that x causes y. First, we are working only with sample data, and we have not provided any means to assess what could happen in other samples. Second, we have not ruled out the possibility that y causes changes in x. It is possible that as highway death rates fall (or rise) countries increase (or decrease) their speed limits. Interestingly, later in his letter to the editor, Rivkin asserted that in Britain the Chiefs of Police Association petitioned the government to raise the speed limit from 70 mph to 80 mph, because highway death rates were relatively low. If other countries behaved in a similar manner, then it could be argued that lower highway death rates would lead to higher speed limits. Issues of correlation and causality will be addressed in later chapters.

QUERY 12.2:
For the *Business Week* data on school days and exam scores in Query 12.1, what is the sample variance for each variable, the covariance between the variables, and the correlation coefficient? (In your answer relate this correlation to the scatterplot in Query 12.1.)

ANSWER:
We will need the following sums

Days x	Scores y	$x-\bar{x}$	$y-\bar{y}$	$(x-\bar{x})^2$	$(y-\bar{y})^2$	$(x-\bar{x})(y-\bar{y})$
251	80	48	16.1	2304	259.21	772.8
222	73	19	9.1	361	82.81	172.9
207	71	4	7.1	16	50.41	28.4
210	70	7	6.1	49	37.21	42.7
174	64	-29	0.1	841	0.01	-2.9
215	63	12	-0.9	144	0.81	-10.8
188	62	-15	-1.9	225	3.61	28.5
192	61	-11	-2.9	121	8.41	31.9
180	55	-23	-8.9	529	79.21	204.7
191	40	-12	-23.9	144	571.21	286.8
----	------			-------	----------	---------
$\bar{x} = 203$	$63.9 = \bar{y}$			4734	1092.90	1555.0

The variances are

$$s_y^2 = \frac{\sum_{i=1}^{n}(y_i - \bar{y})^2}{n-1} = \frac{1092.9}{9} = 121.4$$

$$s_x^2 = \frac{\sum_{i=1}^{n}(x_i - \bar{x})^2}{n-1} = \frac{4734}{9} = 526$$

The covariance is

$$s_{xy} = \frac{\sum_{i=1}^{n}(x_i - \bar{x})(y_i - \bar{y})}{n-1} = \frac{1555}{9} = 172.8$$

The coefficient of correlation is

$$r = \frac{\sum_{i=1}^{n}(x_i - \bar{x})(y_i - \bar{y})}{\sqrt{\sum_{i=1}^{n}(x_i - \bar{x})^2 \sum_{i=1}^{n}(y_i - \bar{y})^2}} = \frac{1555}{\sqrt{(4734)(1092.9)}} = 0.68$$

As an alternative to hand calculations, EXCEL can be used to produce the correlation coefficient. This requires that the data be placed in abutting columns. With x(days) in cells A1 through A10, and y(scores) in cells B1 through B10, the EXCEL function command is

"=CORREL(A1:A10,B1:B10)"

which yields $r = 0.6836$.

This correlation coefficient of +0.68 indicates a positive relationship between x and y. This is consistent with the observation that eight of the ten points lie in quadrants I and III in the scatterplot of Query 12.1. For these eight points, deviations from the exam score mean are in the same direction as deviations from the mean of school days. The sum of these eight positive products is larger than the sum of the two negative products associated with the two points in quadrants II and IV.

Exercises

12.1 Answer true or false; if false, state why.

a. The sum of deviations around the mean is always zero.

b. The calculation of the sample variance involves a division by $n - 1$, instead of n, because there are only $n - 1$ deviations.

c. The variance is a measure of the average squared deviation of values around their mean.

d. If the x and y covariance is negative, then the standard deviation of either x or y must be negative.

e. If the correlation coefficient is negative, then the covariance is negative.

f. The bigger the coefficient of correlation, the stronger the relationship between two variables. Thus, $r = +0.75$ shows a stronger relationship than $r = -0.85$.

g. A positive correlation coefficient indicates that as values of one variable rise, values of the other tend to rise, and as values of the one variable fall, values of the other tend to fall.

h. A variable is "standardized" by dividing deviations from its mean by the standard deviation.

i. A negative covariance indicates that for negative deviations from the mean of one variable there tend to be negative deviations from the mean of the other variable.

j. If the covariance is zero, then we know that the coefficient of correlation is zero and that there is no relationship between the variables.

k. If the variance of one variable is zero, then the correlation coefficient is infinite because its denominator is zero.

l. If the correlation coefficient is zero, then all the y values must be equal to $\bar{y}$.

12.2 What is the value of the covariance if $r = +1$, if $r = -1$, and if $r = 0$?

12.3 Does the magnitude of r^2 or r give any information about the number or percentage of sample points lying on a line drawn through the scatterplot?

12.4 In an experimental executive training program, 60 trainees were chosen at random and given a test before the program began (pre) and were then given the test at the middle of the program (mid). The scatterplot of their scores is as follows:

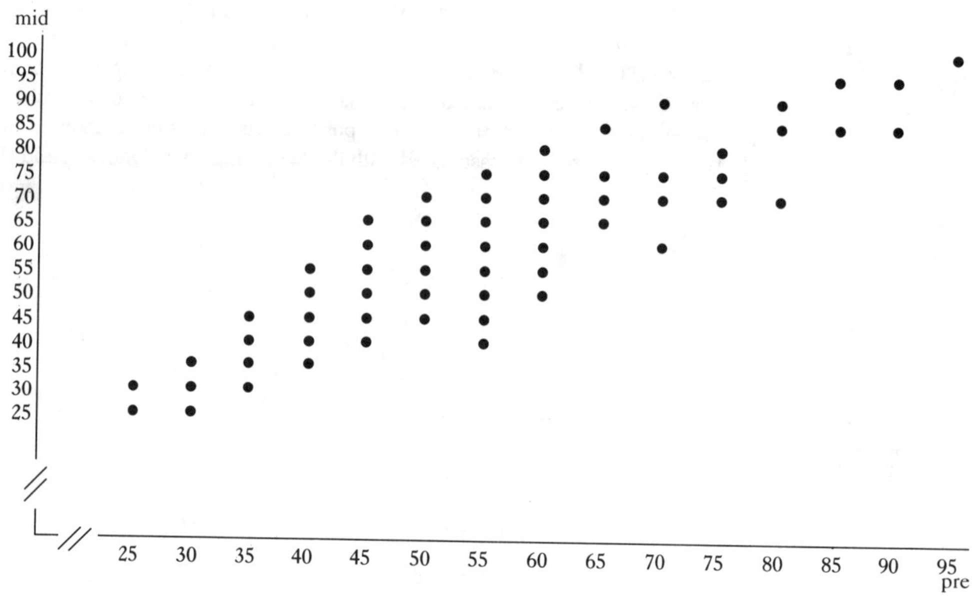

a. On the pretest and midtest frequency distributions on the next page, those who scored a 95, 90, and 85 on the pretest are matched with their midtest score, as obtained from the scatterplot. Complete this matching for the remaining 55 trainees.

b. Calculate the mean of the pretest score.

c. Calculate the change in score (change score equals midtest score minus pretest score) for each of the 60 trainees.

d. Calculate the average change score for those who scored below the average on the pretest.

e. Calculate the average change score for those who scored above the average on the pretest.

Pretest Score	Frequency	Percent	Cumulative Frequency	Cumulative Percent
25	2	3.33	2	3.33
30	3	5.00	5	8.33
35	4	6.67	9	15.00
40	5	8.33	14	23.33
45	6	10.00	20	33.33
50	6	10.00	26	43.33
55	8	13.33	34	56.67
60	7	11.67	41	68.33
65	4	6.67	45	75.00
70	4	6.67	49	81.67
75	3	5.00	52	86.67
80	3	5.00	55	91.67
85	2	3.33	57	95.00
90	2	3.33	59	98.33
95	1	1.67	60	100.00

Midtest Score	Frequency	Percent	Cumulative Frequency	Cumulative Percent
25	2	3.33	2	3.33
30	3	5.00	5	8.33
35	3	5.00	8	13.33
40	4	6.67	12	20.00
45	5	8.33	17	28.33
50	5	8.33	22	36.67
55	5	8.33	27	45.00
60	5	8.33	32	53.33
65	5	8.33	37	61.67
70	7	11.67	44	73.33
75	5	8.33	49	81.67
80	2	3.33	51	85.00
85	4	6.67	55	91.67
90	2	3.33	57	95.00
95	2	3.33	59	98.33
100	1	1.67	60	100.00

12.5 For the following data set, construct a scatterplot, show the lines representing the x and y means, and calculate the 10 deviations from these means. Without doing any other calculations, do x and y appear to be related? Why or why not?

y: 2 −3 7 8 −2 −5 −7 4 −6 2

x: 0 4 −5 −7 8 9 9 −3 5 −1

12.6 Draw in the lines representing the average pretest and midtest scores in the scatterplot given in Exercise 12.4. How do deviations from the means of the pretest and midtests tend to be related?

12.7 The following summary statistics were calculated from the data in Exercise 12.4, where y is the midtest score and x is the pretest score:

$$\Sigma(x_i - \bar{x})^2 = 17490 \quad \Sigma(\bar{y}_i^2 - y) = 21471.25 \quad r = 0.8881$$

a. What is the standard deviation of x?

b. What is the standard deviation of y?

c. What is the value of the covariance of x and y?

12.8 An article in the business section of *The Saint Paul Pioneer Press* (May 28, 1995) featured the Eau Claire, Wisconsin based household gadgetry company, National Presto Industries. The article provided data on Presto's earnings (measured in thousands of dollars) and sales (measured in thousands of dollars). What is the relationship between Presto's sales (x) and earnings (y)? That is, what is the r^2 and what does it tell you about the relationship between sales and earnings at Presto?

Year	Earnings	Sales
1994	21,455	128,070
1993	18,655	118,580
1992	25,882	128,263
1991	36,703	161,522
1990	29,120	127,008

12.9 For the following data set, calculate the coefficient of correlation and draw the scatterplot.

i	y	x
1	2	−2
2	5	0
3	4	−1
4	7	2
5	5	1

12.10 For the following data set, calculate the coefficient of correlation and draw the scatterplot.

i	y	x
1	−1	5
2	2	0
3	0	3
4	3	−2
5	6	−6

12.11 Without doing any calculations, determine the covariance and coefficient of correlation for the following two scatterplots.

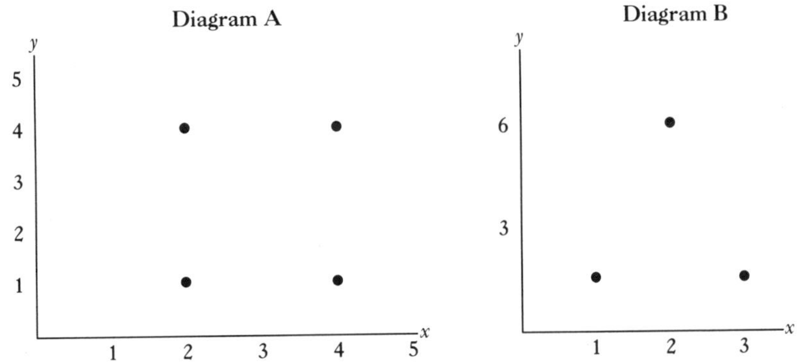

12.12 Based on the pretest and midtest scores in 12.4, suppose that only the trainees with pretest scores exceeding the average were selected for executive positions (unknown to the trainees until after the program was completed). Calculate the coefficient of correlation between the pretest and midtest scores for those selected for executive positions and those not selected. Also calculate the coefficient of correlation for the total group of 60 trainees. Are the two correlation coefficients for the subsamples greater or less than the correlation for the entire sample? If so, why; if not, why not?

12.13 Below is a bivariate frequency distribution that shows the number of times each x and y pair of observations occurred. For example, the first entry indicates that $x = 11$ and $y = 18$ occurred five times.

a. Graph the scatterplot represented by these data.
b. Calculate the variance of both x and y.
c. Calculate the covariance of x and y.
d. Calculate the coefficient of correlation.

	y									
x	18	19	20	21	22	23	24	25	26	Total
11	5	2	1	1	1	1	0	0	0	11
13	1	3	2	1	0	2	1	0	0	10
15	1	1	2	3	0	1	1	0	0	9
17	0	2	3	1	1	0	1	0	0	8
19	0	0	3	2	1	1	0	0	0	7
21	0	0	0	0	2	1	0	1	1	5

12.14 On the following page are the results of a city council race in a small town in Indiana. Is there a relationship between the number of votes obtained by candidates in the primary and the general election?

Candidate	Number of Votes in Primary	General
A	1,346	1,509
B	979	1,125
C	1,378	1,278
D	1,125	1,978
E	874	378
F	1,002	1,200

12.15 From the time of Irving Fisher, economists have been doing empirical studies of the relationship between the nominal rate of interest (i) and the expected rate of change in the general price (p_e), where the difference between these two rates is called the real rate of interest ($r_e = i - p_e$). If investors form price expectations "rationally," then they should be correct, on average, and according to a discussion by Santoni and Stone, "The Fed and the Real Rate of Interest" (Federal Reserve Bank of St. Louis, December 1982), the observed nominal rate of interest at time t should be positively related to observed rate of price inflation at time $t + 1$. While there may be a positive relationship between nominal rate at time t and inflation rate at time $t + 1$, comparing a nominal rate at time t with an inflation rate at time t may be misleading since they need not be related. Use the following Santoni and Stone data to calculate the two coefficients of correlation for the

a. relationship between the nominal rate of interest at time t, and rate of inflation at time $t + 1$.
b. nominal rate of interest at time t and the rate of inflation at time t.
(Note, for comparison purposes, the maximum number of observations is 22, after associating each nominal interest rate at time t with the inflation rate at time $t + 1$.)

Year	90-day T-Bill Rate	Inflation Rate	Year	90-day T-Bill Rate	Inflation Rate
1960	3.2	1.6	1972	4.4	4.2
1961	2.0	0.9	1973	8.7	5.8
1962	2.7	1.8	1974	10.5	8.8
1963	3.2	1.5	1975	5.8	9.3
1964	3.5	1.5	1976	5.0	5.2
1965	4.1	2.2	1977	5.5	5.8
1966	5.1	3.2	1978	7.9	7.4
1967	4.2	3.0	1979	11.2	8.6
1968	5.6	4.4	1980	13.4	9.3
1969	8.2	5.1	1981	16.4	9.4
1970	7.2	5.4	1982	13.3	4.8
1971	4.7	5.0			

12.7 The Regression Line

Knowing the coefficient of correlation does not enable us to predict values of the dependent variable from values of the independent variable. The single straight line that appears to describe the relationship between two variables in a scatterplot, however, could be used for such predictions. The discussion of Figures 12.2 and 12.3, for example, suggests that the line that best describes the relationship between the speed limits and average death rates at each speed goes through the $\bar{y}$ and $\bar{x}$ intersection and into quadrants I and III, illustrating a positive relationship between death rates and the speed limit.

The equation of the straight line drawn in the speed limit and death scatterplot in Figure 12.3 and extended down to the *y* axis in Figure 12.5 is of the form

$$\hat{y} = a + bx \tag{12.4}$$

where $\hat{y}$ is the predicted dependent variable (death rate) at a specific value of *x*,
x is the independent variable (speed limit),
a is the *y*-axis intercept, and
b is the slope.

Once the values of the slope *b* and intercept *a* are determined, this line can be used to describe the relationship between deaths and speed and to predict death rates at various speed limits. These values could be determined by visual inspection using a ruler or preferably by an algebraic method.

Predicted Dependent Variable
The value of the variable being explained in a regression.

Interpreting the slope *b* and *y*-axis intercept *a* requires recognition of the subtle difference between the actual death rates observed and those predicted. The symbol *y* represents the actual value of the dependent variable. The **predicted dependent variable** values are represented by the symbol $\hat{y}$; these values are calculated from Equation (12.4) for the line that "best fits" the scatterplot. Calculation of a $\hat{y}$ is conditional on the *x* value specified. In Figure 12.5, for example, beginning on the horizontal axis at a speed limit of 70 mph, a vertical line may be drawn to the positively sloped $\hat{y}$ line. Next, a horizontal line may be drawn to the *y* axis to obtain predicted deaths, which with a highly accurate ruler and a magnifying glass could be read as 4.996 per 100 million vehicle miles at 70 mph.

Slope
For a regression equation, the change in the predicted dependent variable resulting from a one unit change in the independent variable.

The **slope** *b* is measured as the change in predicted death rate divided by the change in speed limit. For example, at a speed limit of 70 mph, predicted deaths are 4.996 per 100 million vehicle miles. At 75 mph, predicted deaths are approximately 5.374 per 100 million vehicle miles. Thus, the slope is

$$b = \frac{5.374 - 4.996}{75 - 70} = 0.0756$$

Similar calculations between any other points on the line would yield a slope of 0.0756, because the line is straight. This slope indicates that for a one mile per hour increase in the speed limit, predicted deaths rise by 0.0756 deaths per 100 million vehicle miles. For a five mile per hour increase, predicted deaths rise by 0.378 (= 0.0756 times 5) per 100 million vehicle miles. Contrary to Rivkin's claim about the data in Table 12.1, the speed limit appears to have something to do with safety; as the speed limit increases, predicted deaths rise.

The *y*-axis intercept (which is also called the "constant term") is the point where the line crosses the vertical axis; that is,

$$a = -0.293$$

This point corresponds to a speed limit of zero miles per hour and a predicted death rate of negative 0.293 deaths per 100 million vehicle miles. A negative death rate is im-

FIGURE 12.5 Death Rates and Speed Limit Relationship

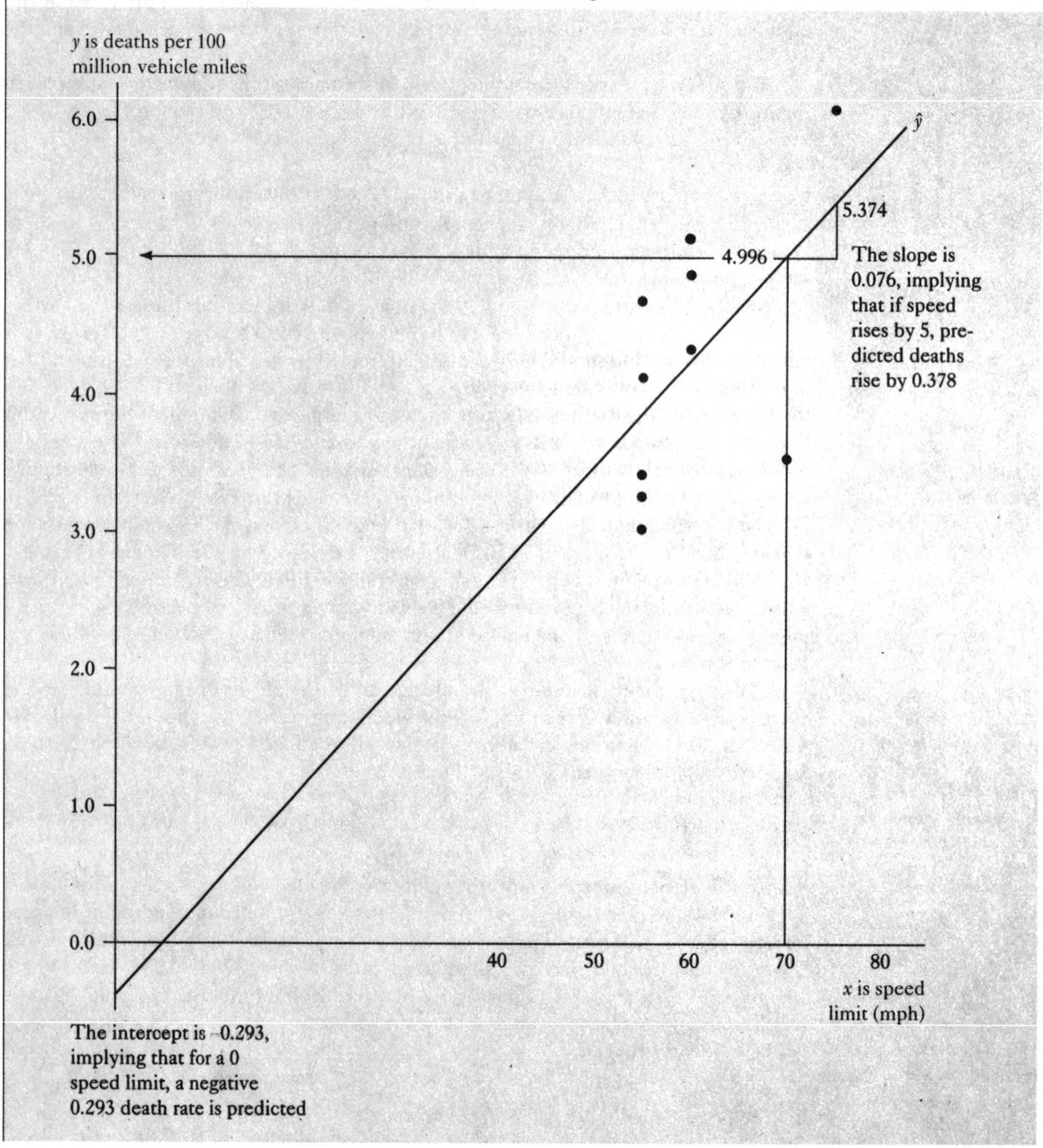

possible; here the y intercept is an artifact of fitting a straight line to a sample with only relatively high values. As will be discussed later, the y intercept may have little practical meaning if it is a value well outside the range of values found in the sample.

The equation for the straight line relating speed limits to deaths is a regression of y on x. But, unlike the line formed by connecting the conditional means of y, at each x, the regression line $\hat{y} = a + bx$ has a fixed intercept and slope. In the case of death rates and speed limits, our visual inspection and ruler measurements in Figure 12.5 yield a regression line given by the equation

$$\hat{y} = -0.293 + 0.076x \qquad (12.5)$$

With this equation, we can predict the deaths for any speed limit within the range of our sample values. For example, the predicted death rate for a speed limit of 55 mph is

$$\hat{y} = -0.293 + 0.076(55) = 3.862$$

which is 3.86 deaths per 100 million vehicle miles.

Although the entire equation of the regression line is important and predictions with the line are useful, attention typically focuses on the slope. For instance, a *Business Week* (June 18, 1990) article on cigarette smokers' desire to quit never reported the form of the entire regression line fit by economists Gary Becker, Kevin Murphy, and Michael Grossman to annual per capita cigarette consumption from 1955 to 1985. It simply reported that "the economists found that a 10% increase in cigarette prices reduces current consumption by 4% in the short term and 7.5% in the long term . . . a 16¢ a pack tax hike would therefore cut consumption significantly. Americans puffed about 100 packs per capita in 1989—but that number would fall to 96 packs in the first year of the tax hike . . . at the end of four or five years, consumption would fall to about 92 packs per capita."(p. 20) From this quote we know that the implied short-term slope of a regression line of packs per capita on cigarette price, at a 160-cents-per-pack price in 1989, is $-4/16 = -0.25$. The original short-term regression, where both variables were measured in percentage terms, however, implied a slope of $-4/10 = -0.40$. The apparent difference in slopes does not reflect an error, however. The difference simply reflects the differences in units of measurement. The original regression was defined in terms of percentages, while the implied regression is in terms of cents per pack. The magnitude of the slope is defined in terms of the units in which the independent and dependent variables are measured.

12.8 Errors in Predictions

Prediction Error The difference between the observed value of the dependent variable and the value predicted by the regression line.

Returning to the speed limit example, the observed death rates are not predicted perfectly with our straight line regression at the different speed limits in the sample. At a speed limit of 55 mph, for example, the predicted death rate is 3.862 deaths per 100 million vehicle miles while the observed deaths are 4.7, 4.1, 3.4, 3.3, and 3.0 deaths per 100 million vehicle miles. The **prediction errors** for these five observations are the differences between the observed death rates and the predicted death rate. They are calculated by subtracting the predicted death rate from the observed death rates.

for Japan, the error is 4.7 – 3.862 = 0.838

for Denmark, the error is 4.1 – 3.862 = 0.238

for Finland, the error is 3.4 – 3.862 = –0.462

for the United States, the error is 3.3 – 3.862 = –0.562

for Norway, the error is 3.0 – 3.862 = –0.862

At a speed of 60 mph, the predicted death rate is 4.24 deaths per 100 million vehicle miles. That is,

$$\hat{y} = -0.293 + 0.076(60) = 4.24$$

Again, there is variability in observed death rates around this predicted value. The three errors made in predicting death rates at 60 mph are

for the Netherlands, the error is 5.1 – 4.24 = 0.860

for Australia, the error is 4.9 – 4.24 = 0.660

for Canada, the error is 4.3 – 4.24 = 0.060

Similarly, the remaining two errors in predicting death rates at 70 and 75 mph can be calculated:

for Britain, the error is 3.5 – 4.996 = –1.496

for Italy, the error is 6.1 – 5.37 = 0.727

Although there is only one reported death rate at both 70 mph and 75 mph, our straight line regression suggests variability even at these speed limits as reflected in the difference between the actual and predicted death rates.

Residual
A prediction error measured as the vertical difference between the observed value of the dependent variable and the value predicted with the regression equation.

The errors made in predicting the sample values of the dependent variable reflect variability in observed values across all the values of the independent variable. These errors reflect the amount of y that is "left over" or "left unexplained" by the regression line; they are thus also called **residuals**. Each error or residual value is represented graphically as the vertical distance between the observed sample point and the y value predicted by the regression line at the specified x value. The 10 residuals for the straight line death rate regression are depicted in Figure 12.6.

12.9 The Method of Least Squares

The graphical method of fitting a straight line to a scatterplot is not very precise because it relies on the researcher's ability to eyeball the data and accurately read a rule. For a large data set, it would be extremely difficult, if not impossible, to use. A more reliable method of fitting a line is to use formulas that minimize the sum of the squares of the errors (or residuals). To derive these formulas, it is first necessary to introduce some notation.

FIGURE 12.6 Residuals for Straight Line Death Rate Regression as Drawn in Figure 12.5

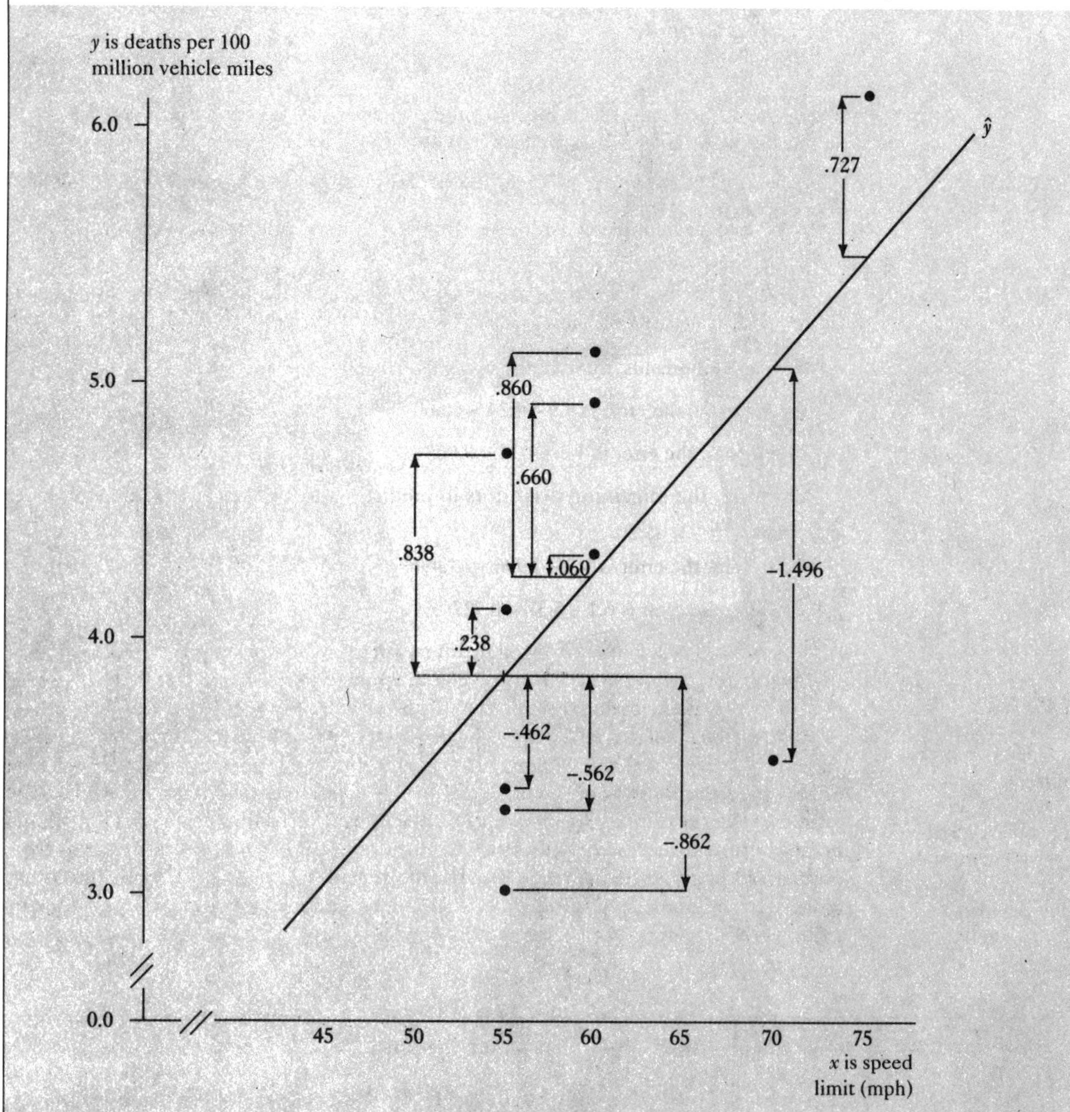

Let the residuals or prediction errors associated with the regression line be denoted by the letter e. The subscript i is used to identify a residual associated with a given point; e_i is the error for the ith observation on y.

$$e_i = y_i - \hat{y} \tag{12.6}$$

For example, in Table 12.1, Norway is the first country listed in the sample; the residual for Norway was previously calculated as

$$e_1 = y_1 - \hat{y}_1 = -0.862$$

Italy is the tenth country listed in the sample; its error was previously calculated as

$$e_{10} = y_{10} - \hat{y}_{10} = 0.727$$

and similarly for the other eight countries. The 10 residuals calculated in this way will always sum to approximately zero. Substituting the values from the speed limit case gives

$$\sum_{i=1}^{10} e_i = -0.862 - 0.562 - 0.462 - 1.496 + 0.238$$

$$+ 0.060 + 0.838 + 0.660 + 0.860 + 0.727 \approx 0$$

If we could read values from a graph with great precision, then an equation that is accurate to many decimal places could be obtained. With such accuracy, the sum of negative residuals would exactly cancel the sum of positive residuals, and the sum of residuals would be exactly zero. All properly drawn regression lines have the property that *the residuals sum to approximately zero.*

$$\sum_{i=1}^{n} e_i = e_1 + e_2 + e_3 + \ldots + e_{n-1} + e_n = 0 \tag{12.7}$$

$$= y_1 - \hat{y}_1 + y_2 - \hat{y}_2 + \ldots + y_{n-1} - \hat{y}_{n-1} + y_n - \hat{y}_n = 0$$

Because there are other lines about which deviations from the actual observed value of y sum to zero, this is not a unique property of the regression line. **The unique property of the regression line is that it minimizes the sum of the squares of the errors (or residuals) with respect to the slope and intercept.** To see this, the residuals must be expressed as a function of the intercept and slope, which can be done by writing $\hat{y}$ in its general slope-intercept form; that is,

$$e_i = y_i - \hat{y}_i = y_i - (a + bx_i) = y_i - a - bx_i \tag{12.8}$$

where the i subscript has been added to x, y, and $\hat{y}$ to identify the ith paired observations and calculated value. The sum of the squares of the residuals is now written

$$\sum_{i=1}^{n} e_i^2 = \sum_{i=1}^{n} \left(y_i - \hat{y}_i\right)^2 = \sum_{i=1}^{n} \left(y_i - a - bx_i\right)^2 \tag{12.9}$$

The necessary mathematical condition for minimizing the sum of the squared errors is that the partial derivatives of Σe_i^2, with respect to b and a, are both zero. The equations for b and a derived from this calculus are:[1]

$$b = \frac{\sum_{i=1}^{n}(x_i - \bar{x})(y_i - \bar{y})}{\sum_{i=1}^{n}(x_i - \bar{x})^2} \tag{12.10}$$

$$a = \bar{y} - b\bar{x} \tag{12.11}$$

As with the numerator of the coefficient of correlation, the numerator of b reflects how y deviates from its mean as x deviates from its mean. It captures the quadrant position of points in Figure 12.2. For example, for the first x and y pair of values in Table 12.1 (Norway),

$$x_1 - \bar{x} = -5 \text{ and } y_1 - \bar{y} = -1.24$$

Since both x and y deviate in the same direction from their respective means, the relationship between x and y for this pair of values is positive (i.e., –5 times –1.24 = + 6.2). For the fourth x and y pair (Britain, also shown in quadrant IV, Figure 12.2),

$$x_4 - \bar{x} = +10, \text{ and } y_4 - \bar{y} = -0.74$$

indicating a negative relationship between x and y (i.e., +10 times –0.74 = –7.4). In Figure 12.2, all x and y pairs in quadrants I and III are positive, while all x and y pairs in quadrants II and IV are negative.

The sum of the products of x and y deviation determines the sign and the magnitude of the numerator of b. As shown in column six of Table 12.4, the sum of the 10 $(x_i - \bar{x})$ and $(y_i - \bar{y})$ products is positive.

$$\sum_{i=1}^{n}(x_i - \bar{x})(y_i - \bar{y}) = 6.2 + \ldots + 27.9 = 34$$

The denominator of b reflects the variability in x around its mean. It is always positive because each $x - \bar{x}$ deviation is squared and is simply the sum of squared deviations used in the calculation of the variance of x introduced in Chapter 2. As shown in column seven of Table 12.4, the sum of the 10 $(x_i - \bar{x})^2$ values is 450.

$$\sum_{i=1}^{n}(x_i - \bar{x})^2 = (-5)^2 + \ldots + (15)^2 = 450$$

The slope of the least squares death rate regression line is

$$b = \frac{\sum_{i=1}^{n}(x_i - \bar{x})(y_i - \bar{y})}{\sum_{i=1}^{n}(x_i - \bar{x})^2} = \frac{34}{450} = 0.075556$$

The y intercept is

$$a = \bar{y} - b\bar{x} = 4.24 - (0.075556)(60) = -0.29333$$

The least squares regression line is $\hat{y}_i = -0.2933 + 0.0756x_i$, which is a more exact version of the equation we found by visual inspection of the scatterplot and ruler measurements. It is the straight line that best fits the sample data, after rounding coefficient estimates to the nearest ten thousands.

Table 12.4 Calculation of the Regression Slope and Intercept

i	x_i	y_i	$x_i - \bar{x}$	$y_i - \bar{y}$	$(x_i - \bar{x})(y_i - \bar{y})$	$(x_i - \bar{x})^2$
1	55	3.0	–5	–1.24	6.2	25
2	55	3.3	–5	–0.94	4.7	25
3	55	3.4	–5	–0.84	4.2	25
4	70	3.5	10	–0.74	–7.4	100
5	55	4.1	–5	–0.14	0.7	25
6	60	4.3	0	0.06	0.0	0
7	55	4.7	–5	0.46	–2.3	25
8	60	4.9	0	0.66	0.0	0
9	60	5.1	0	0.86	0.0	0
10	75	6.1	15	1.86	27.9	225
	600	42.4			34.0	450

Means: $\bar{y} = 42.4/10 = 4.24$ and $\bar{x} = 600/10 = 60$

Slope: $$b = \frac{\sum_{i=1}^{n}(x_i - \bar{x})(y_i - \bar{y})}{\sum_{i=1}^{n}(x_i - \bar{x})^2} = \frac{34}{450} = 0.07556$$

Intercept: $a = \bar{y} - b\bar{x} = 4.24 - (0.07556)(60) = -0.2933$

The least squares regression equation is

$$\hat{y}_i = -0.2933 + 0.0756x_i$$

QUERY 12.3:
In Query 12.1, a *Business Week* article was cited for questioning whether days spent in school led to better student exam scores. What is the least squares regression that is implied by this statement, using the data from the ten countries given in Query 12.1? In your answer interpret the slope in terms of a regression line drawn correctly in the scatterplot constructed in the answer to Query 12.1. Finally, what would the predicted exam scores be if the "average country's school year" was increased from 203 days to 223 days?

ANSWER:
The column sums calculated already in the answer to Query 12.2 enable the determination of the slope and intercept:

The slope is $$b = \frac{\sum_{i=1}^{10}\left(x_i - \bar{x}\right)\left(y_i - \bar{y}\right)}{\sum_{i=1}^{10}\left(x_i - \bar{x}\right)^2} = \frac{1555}{4734} = 0.328$$

The intercept is $a = \bar{y} - b\bar{x} = 63.9 - 0.328(203) = 2.78$

The least squares regression equation is

$$\hat{y}_i = 2.78 + 0.328x_i$$

Because time in school is measured in days and exam scores are measured as percentage points, the slope of the regression line indicates that for a one day increase in the school year exam scores are predicted to rise by 0.328 of a percentage point. Thus, for a 10 day increase in the school year, exam scores are predicted to rise by 3.28 percentage points, which is accurately portrayed by a movement anywhere along the regression line drawn in the scatterplot in the answer to Query 12.1. Because a least squares regression line always passes through the mean x and y values, an increase from the mean of 203 school days to 223 days will be associated with a predicted increase in exam scores from 63.9 to 70.46.

QUERY 12.4:

A *Business Week* (June 22, 1987) article argued that as the percentage of women among those holding Master in Business Administration (MBA) degrees has increased, the percentage of women in management and administration jobs has also increased. To support this thesis, *BW* presented the following data from U.S. Education Department and Bureau of Labor Statistics.

AS MORE WOMEN GET MBAs... percentage of women among graduating MBAs	**...THEIR ROLE AS MANAGERS INCREASES** percentage of women in management and administrative jobs
1972 : 4%	**1972 : 20%**
1976 : 12%	**1976 : 24%**
1987 : 33%	**1987 : 37%**

Are these data consistent with the idea that both the percentage of women among graduating MBAs and the percentage of women in management and administrative jobs move together? Find the least squares regression that describes the relationship between the percentage of women among graduating MBAs and the percentage of women in management and administrative jobs for these data. If the percentage of women among graduating MBAs rises to 35 percent, what is the predicted percentage of women in management and administrative jobs?

ANSWER:

Let y be the proportion of women in management and administrative jobs and x be the proportion of women among graduating MBAs. The following sums are needed to obtain the regression line.

Proportion of Women					
MBAs x	Managers y	$x-\bar{x}$	$y-\bar{y}$	$(x-\bar{x})^2$	$(x-\bar{x})(y-\bar{y})$
0.04	0.20	–0.123	–0.070	0.015129	0.00861
0.12	0.24	–0.043	–0.030	0.001849	0.00129
0.33	0.37	0.167	0.100	0.027889	0.01670
0.49	0.81			0.044867	0.02660

The slope b and intercept a are

$$b = \frac{\sum_{i=1}^{3}(x_i-\bar{x})(y_i-\bar{y})}{\sum_{i=1}^{3}(x_i-\bar{x})^2} = \frac{0.02660}{0.044867} = 0.592868$$

$$a = \bar{y} - b\bar{x} = 0.27 - 0.592868(0.1633) = 0.173165$$

The least squares regression equation is

$$\hat{y}_i = 0.1732 + 0.5929x_i$$

If the percentage of women among graduating MBAs rises to 35 percent, the predicted percentage of women in management and administrative jobs rises to approximately 38 percent, because

$$\hat{y}_i = 0.1732 + 0.5929(0.35) = 0.3807$$

QUERY 12.5:

In finance, the "historical beta" is the slope of a regression line between a single stock's return and the return from all stocks. This beta (slope) is a measure of the riskiness of the single stock relative to the rest of the stock market. The higher the beta, the more volatile and risky the stock in question. Below is a scatter diagram of returns for American Telephone and Telegraph stock and for the S&P 500 (the proxy for the stock market) assembled by Burton Malkiel (1990, p. 250) before the divestiture of AT&T. What is the beta for this data and what does it mean?

ANSWER:
The slope of this regression line can be seen to be about 0.5. If the return to all S&P 500 stocks rises (or falls) by 1 percent, the predicted return to AT&T stock will rise (or fall) by half a percent; thus, the AT&T return is less prone to change than the overall market return. If we assume that the future is like the past, then this relationship could be expected to continue. But the breakup of AT&T in 1983 and the deregulation of the communication industry have made predictions about AT&T outside of this sample period meaningless. (More will be said about predicting in later chapters.)

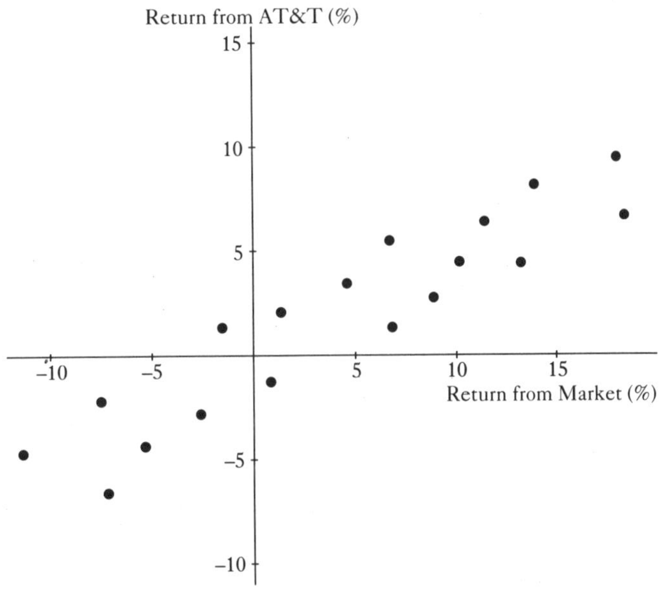

12.10 GOODNESS-OF-FIT AND CORRELATION

Total Sum of Squares (TSS)
The sum of squared differences between observed values of the dependent variable and their mean. It is the variability to be explained

Earlier in this chapter, the coefficient of correlation was introduced as a descriptive measure of the degree of association or covariance between two variables. Here the correlation coefficient is reexamined in the context of least squares regression and the analysis of variance breakdown we considered in Chapter 11.

In an analysis of variance, the measure of total or overall variability in the dependent variable is the sum of squared deviations in observed y_i values around their mean $\bar{y}$ value. This quantity is called the **total sum of squares,** abbreviated TotalSS or just TSS.

$$\text{TSS} = \sum_{i=1}^{n}\left(y_i - \bar{y}\right)^2 \tag{12.12}$$

This quantity is the numerator of the variance of y. In the case of death rates, it was calculated to be 8.544, in Table 12.3. It represents the total sum of squared errors we would make if we used $\bar{y}$ to predict each y_i value in the sample.

Our regression line should do a better job than $\bar{y}$ in predicting the values of y_i. If it does, there will be less variability in the y_i values around the regression line $\bar{y}_i$ than there is in the y_i values around the mean line $\bar{y}$. How much less depends on how well the regression line fits the sample data.

To measure the fit of the regression line, the total sum of squares is separated into two parts. The first part represents the variability in y_i that is "unexplained" by the regression; that is, the variability in y reflected in the error when $\hat{y}_i$ is used to predict y_i. This unexplained variability is called the **error (or residual) sum of squares, ErrorSS.** ErrorSS (or just ESS) is the expression given earlier in Equation (12.9); it is the quantity that is minimized by the method of least squares.

Error (or residual) Sum of Squares (ESS)
In regression, the sum of squared prediction errors. It reflects the unexplained variability in the dependent variable.

$$\text{ErrorSS} = \sum_{i=1}^{n}\left(y_i - \hat{y}_i\right)^2 \qquad (12.13)$$

The second part of the total sum of squares represents the variability in y_i that is "explained" by the regression line. It is what we called the factor sum of squares in Chapter 11. It is the difference between TSS and ESS and is now called the **regression sum of squares, RegSS (or just RSS).**

Regression Sum of Squares (RSS)
The sum of the squared differences between the predicted values of the dependent variable and their mean; also, the difference between TSS and ESS.

$$\text{RegSS} = \text{TSS} - \text{ErrorSS} = \sum_{i=1}^{n}\left(\hat{y}_i - \bar{y}\right)^2 \qquad (12.14)$$

The method of least squares minimizes ErrorSS and thus maximizes RegSS. It cannot force ErrorSS to zero, since the regression line typically does not predict all y_i values perfectly.[2]

We have already seen that ErrorSS is calculated by first predicting y for each of the x values in the sample. Errors in prediction are then calculated by subtracting these predicted y values from the observed y values. Squaring the errors and summing gives ErrorSS. In column five of Table 12.5, the variability in death rates unexplained by the speed limit is calculated to be ErrorSS = 5.9751.

TABLE 12.5
Calculation of the Error or Residual Sum of Squares

i	y_i	$\hat{y}_i$	e_i $y_i - \hat{y}_i$	ErrorSS $(y_i - \hat{y}_i)^2$
1	3.0	3.862	–0.862	.7433
2	3.3	3.862	–0.562	.3160
3	3.4	3.862	–0.462	.2136
4	3.5	4.996	–1.496	2.2365
5	4.1	3.862	0.238	.0565
6	4.3	4.240	0.060	.0036
7	4.7	3.862	0.838	.7019
8	4.9	4.240	0.660	.4356
9	5.1	4.240	0.860	.7396
10	6.1	5.373	0.727	.5281
				5.9751

The regression sum of squares is calculated after TSS and ESS have been obtained. In particular, the regression sum of squares is

$$\text{RegSS} = \text{TSS} - \text{ErrorSS} = 8.544 - 5.975 = 2.569$$

which is the explained variance.

How well the regression line fits the data is measured by the portion of the variability in the dependent variable that is "associated with" or "explained by" the independent variable. For example, in the speed limit case, the proportion of total variability in deaths explained by the regression is

$$\frac{\text{RegSS}}{\text{TSS}} = \frac{2.569}{8.544} = 0.301$$

This indicates that 30.1 percent of the variability in deaths is explained by the speed limit in Rivkin's sample and 69.9 percent is unexplained. Denoted by r^2, the coefficient of determination measures the goodness-of-fit of the regression line.

$$r^2 = \frac{\text{RegSS}}{\text{TSS}} \qquad (12.15)$$

Coefficient of Determination r^2
A number between 0 and 1 that indicates the proportion of variability in the dependent variable explained by the independent variable. It is the square of the coefficient of correlation.

Ranging from 0 to 1, the **coefficient of determination, r^2**, indicates the proportion of variability in the dependent variable that is explained by the independent variable. If $r^2 = 1.00$, then 100 percent of the variability in y is explained by the regression equation and ErrorSS must be zero; all the y values are predicted perfectly. If $r^2 = 0$, then none of the variability in y is explained by x and ErrorSS = TSS; the $\hat{y}$ regression line and $\bar{y}$ line are one and the same. Since less than 50 percent of the varability in death rates is explained by speed limits, we can conclude that even the best fitting regression equation $\hat{y}_i = -0.2933 + 0.0756x_i$ does not fit the sample data very well and that there is not a good straight line relationship between death rates and speed limits.

Research reports often present the coefficient of correlation along with the regression equation. Symbolized by r, the coefficient of correlation is calculated by taking the square root of the coefficient of determination.

$$r = \sqrt{\frac{\text{RegSS}}{\text{TSS}}} \qquad (12.16)$$

As discussed when the correlation coefficient was introduced in Equation (12.3), r is a measure of standardized covariance between y and x; it also measures the correlation between y and $\hat{y}$. The sign of r is positive when the regression line's slope is positive, and the sign of r is negative when the slope is negative. When ErrorSS = 0, the correlation coefficient has a maximum value of +1.00, and minimum of –1.00. It is zero if ErrorSS = TSS.[3] Our earlier discussion of Equation (12.3) continues to hold for Equation (12.16), only now the correlation coefficient is linked to the least squares regression equation.

QUERY 12.6:
From the information in Query 12.4 concerning MBA women and jobs, and Equation (12.16), what is the correlation coefficient? Comment on the appropriateness of this regression and predictions from it.

Answer:

For the correlation coefficient, we need the following sums.

y	$\hat{y}$	$y-\hat{y}$	$y-\bar{y}$	$(y-\hat{y})^2$	$(y-\bar{y})^2$
.200	.19688	.00312	–.07	9.74 (10^{-6})	.0049
.240	.24431	–.00431	–.03	18.56 (10^{-6})	.0009
.370	.36881	.00119	.10	1.42 (10^{-6})	.0100
.810	.81000	.00000	.00	29.72 (10^{-6})	.0158

The residual sum of squares is ESS = 2.972 $(10)^{-5}$, which is scientific notation for 2.972 times 1/100000, so ESS = 0.00002972. The total sum of squares is TSS = 0.0158. Thus, the regression sum of squares is RSS = TSS – ESS = 0.01577028, the coefficient of determination is r^2 = RSS/TSS = 0.9981, and the correlation coefficient is r = 0.9991, which is extremely high, especially for only three paired observations. Although this correlation coefficient is high, predictions from this regression equation are suspect because there are so few observations.

Linear Extrapolation Predicting values of y based on the slope of the line connecting the two known points and the x axis distance from the closest of these points to the x value for which the prediction is to be made.

Three paired observations on y and x are the smallest number of observations for which a regression can be estimated. Some computer programs give an error message for $n = 3$, but as long as there is at least one degree of freedom ($n - 2 \geq 1$), least squares calculations are feasible. If there were only two paired observations on y and x, however, then the best fitting line would be the one drawn between the two points. A prediction from this line would be done by linear extrapolation. **Linear extrapolation** only requires knowledge of the slope of the line connecting the two known points and the x axis distance from the closest of these to point to the x value for which the prediction is to be made. For instance, if one known point is at $x = 2$ and $y = 2$ and the other known point is at $x = 4$ and $y = 3$, then the linear extrapolation for $x = 5$ is $\hat{y} = 3.5$.

Historical Perspective

The widespread application of regression and correlation analysis attests to their usefulness. The origins of these techniques are traceable to French mathematician Adrien Marie Legendre (1752–1833) and German mathematician Carl Friedrich Gauss (1777–1855), who each claimed the method of least squares as his own invention. The introduction of these techniques to the social sciences, however, is associated with Sir Francis Galton (1822–1911).

Galton was trained as a physician, but he quickly became bored with the practice of medicine and turned to the study of anthropology for intellectual excitement. In *Natural Inheritance*, (London: Macmillan and Company, 1889), Galton advanced the idea of regression. His "law of universal regression" held that, "Each peculiarity of man is shared by his kinsman, but on the average in a less degree." Below is one of his famous scatter diagrams of average sibling height and mid-parent height. (Mid-parent height is the average of the father's and the mother's heights, where the latter is scaled by 1.08.) For ease in calculation and for intuitive appeal, Galton used many simple approximations: for the average, he employed the median; for dispersion, he used the median deviation from the median rather than the mean squared deviation from the mean; his regression coefficient estimates came directly from graphs, as evidenced by the following diagram, in which he calculated the slope of the regression line to be 2/3.

The single straight line that goes through the paired points in the diagram rises less steeply than the line for which the average height of children equals mid-parent height. This is the regression effect: taller (shorter) parents beget shorter (taller) children, on average. Galton called this phenomenon "regression" or "reversion" to "mediocrity," reflecting his noble upbringing and training as a physician. Galton recognized that knowing how much regression toward the mean there is for a pair of variables enabled prediction—a little regression gave good predictions, and a lot of regression gave poor predictions.

Although initially shunned by mathematicians, Galton's 100-year-old use of the word "regression," as in *y* regressed on *x*, has been accepted as an alternative to the word "function," as used in mathematics to express *y* as a function of *x*. Galton's spelling and use of the word "co-relation," however, has not survived the test of time. Generations of econometricians, biometricians, and statisticians (such as Francis Ysidro Edgeworth, 1845–1926, and Karl Pearson, 1857–1936, and Pearson's student George Yule, 1871–1951) have advanced regression and correlation analyses as alternative, but related, ways of describing the association between variables. In fact, the "*r*" used to symbolize Pearson's correlation coefficient was originally used to stand for regression.

What stands out in tracing the development of the least squares method, regression, and correlation is that the early work was driven more by observation and geometric demonstrations than by theory and algebraic presentations. Galton and his associates collected thousands of empirical examples of the regression effect in nature. Today, as discussed in the next chapter, many researchers, in their use of regression analysis, emphasize theory, and its algebraic representation in a model, as the engine of inquiry.

Galton's 1889 Scatter Diagram and Regression of Average (median) Height of Children on Mid (average)-Parent Height

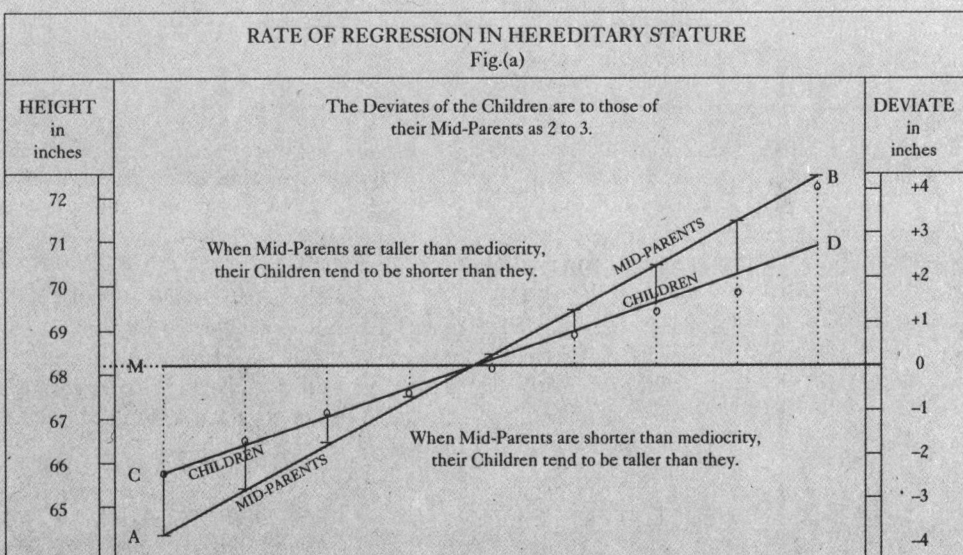

Source: Stephen Stigler (1986, p. 295).

QUERY 12.7:

A *Newsweek* (April 4, 1994) article reported on the desire of the U.S. Congress to encourage "thought over memorization." The article provided the following excerpt from a sample problem on the National Achievement Test and "a top-rated" solution. Can you top this top-rated solution with a better rule, table, and statement of justification?

EXCERPT FROM ACHIEVEMENT TEST PROBLEM:

> Dear Problem Solver,
>
> We have decided to sell laces ... We will sell different lengths for shoes with different numbers of eyelets (4 to 18) ... You have to figure out what lengths to make and which lengths go with which shoes, based on the number of eyelets... We collected some data from store customers ... It is confusing because there haven't been very many lengths available. That means that sometimes the customers have had to use lengths that are too short or too long... We want a unique length for each number of eyelets. Write your decisions about lace length so the advertising people can understand it. They want a table... They also want a rule... You better explain how your decisions make sense ... Thanks, Your Boss, Angela

DATA FROM STORE CUSTOMERS WITH SPORTS SHOES

Lace Length (inches)	Eyelets (numbers)	Lace Length (inches)	Eyelets (numbers)
45	8	54	24
54	10	24	4
26	4	72	14
63	14	54	12
63	12	72	16
36	8	72	18

TOP-RATED SOLUTION:

> The rule is $L = 3(E - 1) + 20$, where E is number of eyelets and L is length of lace. Thus, the length of each lace allows enough for 3 inches between each eyelet, plus 20 inches for the bow. Of course, many people use more than 20 inches for their bow, but most don't use a whole 3 inches for each eyelet, so there should be plenty. My table also pretty much corresponds with the data from the customers... Sincerely, The Problem Solver

Eyelets	4	6	8	10	12	14	16	18	
Lace Length	29	35	41	47	53	59	65	71	inches

ANSWER:

This student's rule, $L = 3(E-1)+ 20$, correctly has L as the dependent variable and E as the independent variable but the principle by which this student obtained the slope, 3, and intercept, 17, was not specified. Thus, the sense in which this rule is "desirable" is unknown. Its negative properties, however, can be demonstrated. First, the within sample prediction errors do not sum to zero; they sum to 35, as seen in the "$L - R$" column in the table below. This implies that on average the predicted lace lengths are too short (by 2.92 inches). Second, the error sum of squares for this rule [461, in the ($L - R$)^2 column] is not as small as that achievable by fitting an ordinary least squares (OLS) regression to the 12 records. The equation of the ordinary least squares regression is

$$\text{Predicted } L = 11.7704 + 3.74057E$$

as calculated by hand with Formulas (12.10) and (12.11) or in a computer program as in Query 12.8). The table below (column "Error$L$-OLS") shows that the prediction errors for this OLS regression sum to zero. The sum of squared prediction errors for this OLS regression is only 242.648, which is far less than the 461 for the rule found in the "top-rated" solution.

Lace --L--	Eyes --E--	Predicted by Top-Rated Rule -----R-----	Error $L-R$ -----	Error Square $(L-R)$^2 -----------	Predicted by Least Square Regression ---OLS------	Error L-OLS ----------	Error Square (L-OLS)^2 -----------
45	8	41	4	16	41.6950	3.3050	10.923
54	10	47	7	49	49.1761	4.8239	23.270
26	4	29	-3	9	26.7327	-0.7327	0.537
63	14	59	4	16	64.1384	-1.1384	1.296
63	12	53	10	100	56.6572	6.3428	40.231
36	8	41	-5	25	41.6950	-5.6950	32.433
54	12	53	1	1	56.6572	-2.6572	7.061
24	4	29	-5	25	26.7327	-2.7327	7.468
72	14	59	13	169	64.1384	7.8616	61.805
54	12	53	1	1	56.6572	-2.6572	7.061
72	16	65	7	49	71.6195	0.3805	0.145
72	18	71	1	1	79.1007	-7.1007	50.419
			---	----		----------	----------
			35	461		0.0000	242.648

Thus, the preferred eyelet and lace length table, based on the least squares principle, is

Eyelets	4	6	8	10	12	14	16	18
Lace Length	27	34	42	49	57	64	72	79 inches

EXERCISES

12.16 Answer true or false; if false, state why.

a. If the means of x and y are zero, then the y intercept is zero.
b. The slope of the sample regression line indicates how the actual value of y changes as x changes.
c. At the mean of x, the predicted value of y is the same value as the sample mean of y.
d. The residuals from a least squares regression are all zero.
e. The method of least squares minimizes the residuals.
f. If the covariance is zero between x and y, then the slope of the least squares regression line is zero.
g. If the total sum of squares is equal to the residual sum of squares, then the slope of the regression line is zero.
h. The coefficient of determination indicates the proportion of the total sum of squares "explained" by the regression line.
i. If the residuals sum to zero, then the y intercept is zero.

12.17 For the data in Exercise 12.5,

a. calculate the total sum of squares.
b. calculate the slope and intercept of the regression line.
c. calculate the 10 residuals.
d. calculate the residual sum of squares.
e. why does the total sum of squares exceed the residual sum of squares? Is this a general characteristic of least squares or specific to this data set?

12.18 For the following data set,

y:	7	–5	4	–2	1	–5
x:	–4	6	–2	–1	–3	4

a. calculate the slope and intercept of the least squares regression line, and write the equation in slope intercept form.
b. what is unique about this data set and your intercept value?
c. what does the slope value indicate?

12.19 For the data sets in Exercises 12.9 and 12.10, calculate the respective least squares slopes. How do the slopes relate to the coefficients of correlation that you calculated in Exercises 12.9 and 12.10?

12.20 Use the following information to calculate the slope and intercept of the regression line.

$$\Sigma(x_i - \bar{x})(y_i - \bar{y}) = 655 \qquad \Sigma(x_i - \bar{x})^2 = 1305 \qquad \Sigma(y_i - \bar{y})^2 = 510$$

$$\Sigma x_i = 475 \qquad \Sigma y_i = 405 \qquad n = 8$$

a. What is the equation of the regression line in slope intercept form?
b. If $x = 40$, what is the predicted value of y?

12.21 Without doing any calculations, try to determine the slope and intercept for the two diagrams in Exercise 12.11. What problems did you encounter? How does the slope relate to the covariance and coefficient of correlation for these two diagrams?

12.22 Use the following information to determine the slope and intercept of the regression line.

$$\Sigma(y_i - \bar{y})(x_i - \bar{x}) = 1710 \qquad \Sigma(x_i - \bar{x})^2 = 3640$$

$$\Sigma x_i = 1350 \qquad \Sigma y_i = 720 \qquad n = 20$$

12.23 Using the information on variances and covariance calculated in Exercise 12.13, determine the slope of the least squares regression line for the x and y pairs.

12.24 In Exercise 12.14, for each additional vote a candidate receives in the primary, how many additional votes would you predict that he or she will receive in the general election?

12.25 According to the discussion in Exercise 12.15, we should be able to use the interest rate to predict the inflation rate in the next year. Using the data on T-bill rates and price inflation in Exercise 12.15, and a computer package, estimate the least squares regression equation between these two rates. What is your predicted inflation rate in the next year, if the T-bill rate in this year is 7 percent?

12.26 Franklin Fisher (*JASA*, June 1986, p. 278) reports on a regression he estimated in which TV station advertising revenue was the dependent variable and audience size was the independent variable. "The regression passed very close to the origin and had a slope of about \$27 per year for each additional household viewing in the average half-hour of prime evening time." He reports that his estimate was attacked as incorrect until an economist at the Federal Communications Commission "took all television revenues in the United States and divided them by the number of television households multiplied by 60 percent, the fraction of prime time that the average household was found in surveys to watch television . . . (and) came up with approximately \$27 per household." Demonstrate why it is not surprising that these two estimates are the same.

12.11 Linear Regression and Correlation Via Computers

Computers are typically used to do the computations required to find the slope and intercept of a least squares regression. Most programs will also calculate the residuals and provide myriad other computations. For problems involving large data sets, computers provide the only practical way to do the tedious calculations.

Software programs that perform least squares regression analysis can be found at any computer center. All of the spreadsheet programs now have least squares regression routines.

Part of the EXCEL regression menus and resulting output are shown in Table 12.6. After the ten paired y and x data are typed into cells A2 to A11 and B2 to B11, with the "death" rate label in A1 and "speed" limits label in B1, the following steps produce the regression output.

1. Choose "Regression" from "Data Analysis" in the "Tools" menu. The Regression dialog box shown in Table 12.6 will appear.

Note: Use the mouse to move between the boxes and buttons. Click on the desired box or button. The large rectangular boxes require a range from the worksheet. A range may be typed in or selected by highlighting the cells with the mouse after clicking on the box. If the dialog box blocks the data, it can be moved on the screen by clicking on the title bar and dragging.

2. For the "Input Y Range," enter A1 to A11, and for the "Input X Range" enter B1 to B11.
3. Because the Y and X ranges include the "Death" and "Speed" labels in A1 and B1, select the "Labels" box with a click.
4. Click the "Output Range" button and type reference cell, which in this demonstration is A13.
5. To get the predicted values of Y (Death rates) and residuals select the "Residuals" box with a click.

Your screen display should now look like that in Table 12.6. Clicking "OK" will give the "SUMMARY OUTPUT," "ANOVA" and "RESIDUAL OUTPUT" also shown in Table 12.6.

The first section of the EXCEL printout gives "SUMMARY OUTPUT." The "Multiple R" is the square root of the "R Square;" the computation and interpretation of which we have already discussed. The "Standard Error" of estimate (which will be discussed in the next chapter) is $s = 0.86423$; it is the square root of "Residual SS" = 5.97511 divided by its degrees of freedom, df = 8, as given in the "ANOVA" section. The "Adjusted R square" of 0.21325 has meaning only for multiple regression, Chapter 14.

Under the "ANOVA" section are the estimated regression coefficients and related statistics that will be discussed in detail in the next chapter. For now it is sufficient to recognize that the calculated coefficient values for the slope and y intercept are provided ($b = 0.07556$ and $a = -0.29333$). Next to these coefficient estimates is information on the variability in the distribution of the least-squares estimators from which these specific estimates were drawn: the column titled "Std. Error" contains the standard deviations (standard errors) of the intercept and slope distributions; the "t-ratio" and "p" columns give the calculated values of the t statistics and associated p-values. As we will see in the next chapter, the t statistic of 1.85458 and p-value of 0.10077, for example, will be used to test whether the sample slope value of 0.07556 is sufficiently different from zero to conclude that there is a population relationship between deaths and speed limits. That conclusion would be contrary to Rivkin's assertion that "speed has little to do with safety."

QUERY 12.8:

Data on lace length and the number of shoe eyelets, as obtained from a National Achievement Test question appearing in *Newsweek* (April 4, 1994), were provided in Query 12.7. The regression equation used to predict lace length based on the number of eyelets was

$$\text{Predicted } L = 11.7704 + 3.74057E$$

where E is number of eyelets and L is length of lace. Now use a computer program to check the correctness of this equation and the predicted lace lengths provided in the answer. What is the coefficient of determination and its meaning?

ANSWER:

After bringing up EXCEL, we type the 12 pairs of lace lengths and number of eyelets into a worksheet, putting the lace length in cells A1 to A12 and the associated number

TABLE 12.6 Computer Printout for Regression of Death on Speed Limit

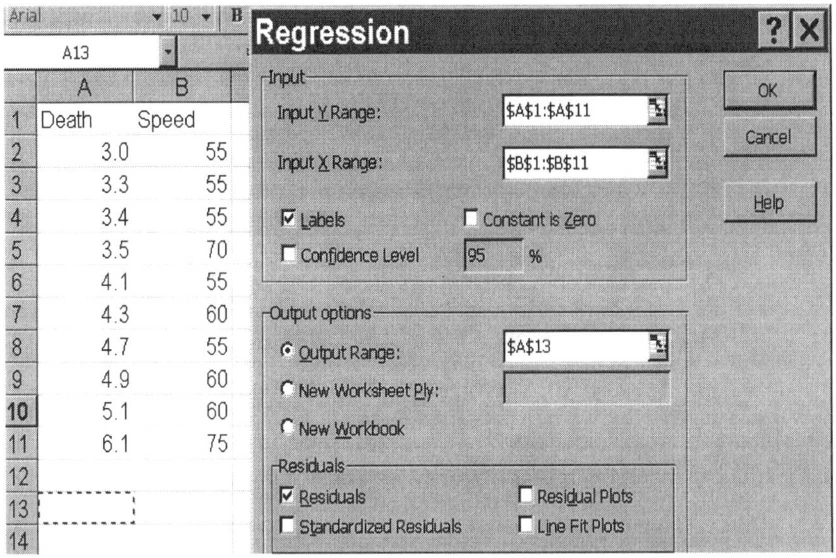

SUMMARY OUTPUT

Regression Statistics	
Multiple R	0.54833
R Square	0.30067
Adjusted R Square	0.21325
Standard Error	0.86423
Observations	10

ANOVA	df	SS	MS	F	Significance F
Regression	1	2.56889	2.56889	3.43945	0.10077
Residual	8	5.97511	0.74689		
Total	9	8.54400			

	Coefficients	Std.Error	t Stat	P-value	Lower 95%	Upper 95%
Intercept	-0.29333	2.45963	-0.11926	0.90801	-5.96526	5.37860
Speed	0.07556	0.04074	1.85458	0.10077	-0.01839	0.16950

RESIDUAL OUTPUT

Observation	Predicted Death	Residuals
1	3.86222	-0.86222
2	3.86222	-0.56222
3	3.86222	-0.46222
4	4.99556	-1.49556
5	3.86222	0.23778
6	4.24000	0.06000
7	3.86222	0.83778
8	4.24000	0.66000
9	4.24000	0.86000
10	5.37333	0.72667

of eyelets in cells B1 to B12, without labels. The path "Tools" to "Data Analysis" to "Regression" leads to the Regression dialog screen shown in Table 12.6 with no entries in the boxes. Entering A1:A12 as the "Input Y Range" and B1:B12 as the "Input X Range," and clicking on the "Residual" box, gives the following output, which was specified to appear in cells A14.

Under the "Coefficient" column, this EXCEL printout shows that the intercept is 11.77044 and the slope is 3.74057, as used in Query 12.7. (Notice in this printout the independent variable "eyelets" appears as "X Var 1" because no labels were inserted as EXCEL column headers.) Other than rounding differences, the column of "Predicted Y" values is the same as in Query 12.7. Finally, the coefficient of determination is the *R* square value 0.924, given in the top section under title the "Regression Statistics;" $R^2 = 0.924$ indicates that 92.4 percent of the variability in shoe lace length is associated with or explained by the number of eyelets.

SUMMARY OUTPUT

Regression Statistics	
Multiple R	0.961448525
R Square	0.924383266
Adjusted R Square	0.916821592
Standard Error	4.925929341
Observations	12

ANOVA

	df	SS	MS	F	Signif. F
Regression	1	2966.2689	2966.2689	122.2459	6.286E-07
Residual	10	242.6478	24.2648		
Total	11	3208.9167			

	Coefficient	St.Error	t Stat	P-value	Lower 95%	Upper 95%
Intercept	11.77044	3.98388	2.95	0.0144	2.8938	20.6471
X Var 1	3.74057	0.33831	11.06	6.3E-07	2.9868	4.4944

RESIDUAL OUTPUT

Observation	Predicted Y	Residuals
1	41.6949686	3.30503145
2	49.1761006	4.82389937
3	26.7327044	-0.73270440
4	64.1383648	-1.13836478
5	56.6572327	6.34276730
6	41.6949686	-5.69496855
7	56.6572327	-2.65723270
8	26.7327044	-2.73270440
9	64.1383648	7.86163522
10	56.6572327	-2.65723270
11	71.6194969	0.38050315
12	79.1006289	-7.10062893

EXERCISES

12.27 Below are the 60 pretest and midtest scores for the scatterplot in Exercise 12.4.

a. Use a computer program to calculate the slope, intercept, and coefficient of determination of the regression of midtest on pretest.

b. Plot the least squares regression line on the scatterplot.

c. How do the slope, intercept, and r^2 relate to the fit of your regression line?

Record	pre	mid	Record	pre	mid
1	25	25	31	55	70
2	25	30	32	55	75
3	30	30	33	55	65
4	30	25	34	55	45
5	30	35	35	55	40
6	35	30	36	60	50
7	35	35	37	60	55
8	35	40	38	60	70
9	35	45	39	60	65
10	40	35	40	60	80
11	40	40	41	60	75
12	40	50	42	65	75
13	40	55	43	65	65
14	40	45	44	65	85
15	45	45	45	65	70
16	45	50	46	70	70
17	45	40	47	70	60
18	45	65	48	70	90
19	45	55	49	70	75
20	45	60	50	75	70
21	50	65	51	75	75
22	50	50	52	75	80
23	50	45	53	80	70
24	50	55	54	80	85
25	50	70	55	80	90
26	50	60	56	85	95
27	55	60	57	85	85
28	55	55	58	90	85
29	55	50	59	90	95
30	60	60	60	95	100

12.28 From the following computer printout for variables x and y, and $n = 10$,

a. determine the slope and intercept of the fitted regression line.

b. what is the value of the total sum of squares and the residual sum of squares?

NAME	MEAN	STD.DEV.	R-SQUARE
x	9.700	5.3135	0.6968
y	12.9000	6.5056	

12.29 Given the following computer printout,

a. determine the coefficient of determination.

b. determine the slope and intercept of the regression line.

NAME	MEAN	STD.DEV.
x	6.3333	2.1602
y	7.8333	2.3166

OBSERVED y	CALCULATED y	RESIDUAL
8.000	5.700	2.3000
10.000	8.900	1.1000
6.000	7.300	–1.3000
5.000	6.500	–1.5000
11.000	10.500	.5000
7.000	8.100	–1.1000

12.30 The manager of a utilities-included rental complex (of 200 units) is curious as to how good a predictor October heating bills are of heating bills for that winter. Having kept records for the last 15 years, she regressed winter heating bills (in thousands of dollars) on respective October heating bills (in thousands of dollars) with the following results.

Ordinary Least Squares

Dependent Variable	Y	Number of Observations	15
Mean of Dep. Variable	104.8034	Std. Dev. of Dep. Var.	34.733122
Std. Error of Regr.	29.8509	Sum of Squared Residuals	11584.0
R-squared	.31413	Adjusted R-squared	.26137
F(1, 13)	5.9540	Prob. Value for F	.02976

Variable	Coefficient	Std. Error	t-ratio	Prob|t| > x	Mean of X	Std.Dev.of X
Constant	15.9374	37.23	.428	.67557		
X	17.5466	7.191	2.440	.02976	5.06456	1.10944

a. The best point estimate of the increase in the winter heating bill if the October heating bill increases by $1,000 is ____________.

b. If next October's heating bill is $5,000, the predicted heating bill for that winter is.

c. The sample correlation coefficient is ____________.

d. In the above regression, the minimum sum of the squared vertical deviations of the points in the scatter diagram from the sample regression line is ____________.

(NOTE: "Constant" as used in this printout is the "Intercept.")

CHAPTER EXERCISES

12.31 Below are data on the objective and subjective probability of a horse winning a race, as calculated by Peter Asch and Richard Quandt, *Racetrack Betting: The Professors' Guide to Strategies* (New York: Praeger 1991). Construct a scatter diagram for the data, where the objective probability is the dependent variable and the subjective probability is the independent variable. Calculate the least squares estimates of the intercept and slope of the "best" straight line to describe these paired observations. Predict the objective probability of a horse winning if the subjective probability is 0.22.

Groups	Objective Probability	Subjective Probability
Favorites	0.361	0.325
Second-lowest odds	0.218	0.205
Third-lowest odds	0.170	0.145
Fourth-lowest odds	0.115	0.104
Fifth-lowest odds	0.071	0.072
Sixth-lowest odds	0.050	0.048
Seventh-lowest odds	0.030	0.034
Eighth-lowest odds	0.017	0.025
Ninth-lowest odds	0.006	0.018

12.32 Calculate the R-square for the objective probability regression in Exercise 12.31. What does this value tell you about the quality of your predictions?

12.33 For the regression of objective and subjective probability in Exercise 12.31, predict the objective probability of a horse that has $4,000 bet on it, where the total wagered on all the horses in the race is $20,000 (which is called the pool). Why is this subjective probability of 0.2 less than the objective probability you predicted?

12.34 Peter Asch and Richard Quandt, *Racetrack Betting: The Professors' Guide to Strategies* (New York: Praeger 1991, p. 95), provide the following data on the speed of the horse for jockeys of differing years of experience.

Jockey's Experience	Horse Speed (mph)
5	37.0
2	34.8
8	39.0
6	38.0
4	37.2
1	34.5
7	39.5

a. Draw the scatter diagram for horse speed as a function of jockey experience.
b. Calculate the "best" straight line regression equation for predicting horse speed. Write the equation and give the R-square.
c. For a jockey with three years of experience, what is the predicted horse speed?

12.35 Below are data on populations for the biggest 25 cities in 1986 and 1988. Regress the 1988 populations for the 25 cities on their 1986 populations. Is there a negative relationship between the 1986 and 1988 populations for this sample of 25 cities?

	1988	1986
New York	7353000	7263000
Los Angeles	3353000	3259000
Chicago	2978000	3010000
Houston	1698000	1729000
Philadelphia	1647000	1643000
San Diego	1070000	1015000
Detroit	1036000	1086000
Dallas	987000	1004000
San Antonio	941000	914000
Phoenix	924000	894000
Baltimore	751000	753000
San Jose	738000	712000
San Francisco	732000	749000
Indianapolis	727000	720000
Memphis	645000	653000
Jacksonville	635000	610000
Washington	617000	626000
Milwaukee	599000	605000
Boston	578000	574000
Columbus	570000	566000
New Orleans	532000	554000
Cleveland	521000	536000
El Paso	511000	492000
Seattle	502000	486000
Denver	492000	505000

12.36 A *Wall Street Journal* (June 28, 1990) article reported on the "Giant Pension Funds' Explosive Growth." Below are the data used to support this headline. Use regression analysis to determine the average rate of growth between 1985 and 1989 for these funds.

Top 20 Pension Funds in millions of dollars

	1985	1989
TIAA/CREF	40000	81000
Calif. Public Employees	29166	54000
General Motors	26300	40900
N.Y. State/Local	25997	44238
N.Y. City Employees	25063	45422
AT&T	24887	42700
General Electric	15812	28912
N.Y. State Teachers	15303	28130
California Teachers	15100	30335
IBM	13939	25775
N.J. Investment Div.	12494	24526
Texas Teachers	11188	23500
Ford Motor	11000	22800
Wisconsin Investment	10800	20033
Ohio Public Employees	10760	19305
Mich. Public Employees	10516	17948
Ohio Teachers	10178	18059
DuPont	9665	18681
Nynex	9447	16062
Florida State Board	8911	18700

12.37 An article in *The Wall Street Journal* (February 27, 1992) suggested that there is a relationship between "sensitivity" and the "market value" of lumber stocks. What is this correlation?

Company	x Market Value Canadian $ in Millions	y Sensitivity*
Siocan Forest Products	$ 103	61.6
Doman Industries	115	53.9
Intl. Forest Products	300	30.3
West Fraser Timber	400	24.8
Canfor	698	20.5
Crestbrook Forest Inds.	173	17.9
Weldwood of Canada	495	16.8
Noranda Forest	1,071	16.5
Donohue	434	13.2
Domtar	603	5.8
Canadian Pacific For. Prod.	1,115	3.9
MacMillan Bloedel	2,119	3.8
Abitibi Price	1,056	0.5

*Thousands of board feet of lumber per C$10,000 in stock-market value

12.38 Use the data on Presto sales and earnings in Exercise 12.8 to answer parts a and b.

a. What is the linear regression relationship between sales (x) and earnings (y)?

b. If sales are increased from $120,000,000 to $125,000,000 by how much and in which direction will predicted earnings change?

12.39 An article in *The Economist* (November 16, 1996) on the "capital-asset pricing model" presented two investments. "Project A has a beta of ½: when the market rises or falls by 10% its return tends to rise or fall by 5%. So its risk premium is only half that of the market. Project B's risk premium is twice that of the market, so it must earn a higher return to justify the expenditure." What is the beta coefficient of Project B? Draw the two regression equations for these two projects.

12.40 The article in *The Economist* (November 16, 1996) on the "capital-asset pricing model" reported that some financial economists say that there is little to be learned from beta coefficients and advocate the use of "the ratio of a firm's book value (value of its assets at the time they entered the balance sheet) to its market value" to predict returns: "companies that have high book-to-market ratios tend to earn excess returns." What is the nature of this relationship for the following six companies? What are the predicted excess returns for a company with a book-to-market ratio of 0.55?

Excess returns:	Book-to-market ratio:
7%	0.3
10%	0.4
8%	0.5
11%	0.6
13%	0.7
12%	0.8

12.41 A *Washington Post* (January 29, 1995) article stated "The Beta for an average fund is 1.0; a fund with a Beta of 1.5 will be 50 percent more volatile than the market while a Beta of 0.28 (the rating of a less risky fund like Valley Forge) means that the fund is 72 percent less volatile." What is the beta coefficient for the following paired portfolio and market returns? What does this beta tell you?

Portfolio Returns (y)	S&P Market Returns (x):
14%	12%
13%	14%
16%	21%
19%	19%
17%	15%
15%	16%

12.42 An article in *The Wall Street Journal* (October 12, 1992) reported the average compensation of CEOs in seven countries. On September 24, 1992, the *WSJ* reported information, including the home country of origin, of the world's 100 largest public companies. Below are summary data on CEO compensation and number of headquartered companies in the identified countries.

	CEO Compensation	Number of headquartered companies in country
United States	\$717,237	49
France	\$479,772	2
Italy	\$463,009	1
Britain	\$439,441	16
Canada	\$416,066	0
Germany	\$390,933	4
Japan	\$390,723	23
Other	not avail	5

What is the correlation coefficient for CEO compensation and number of headquartered companies in each country?

12.43 For the data in Exercise 12.42, what is the least squares regression of CEO compensation on number of headquartered companies in each country? What does this regression tell you?

12.44 For each of the following scatterplots, draw in the approximate least squares regression line. (No calculations are required.)

Diagram A

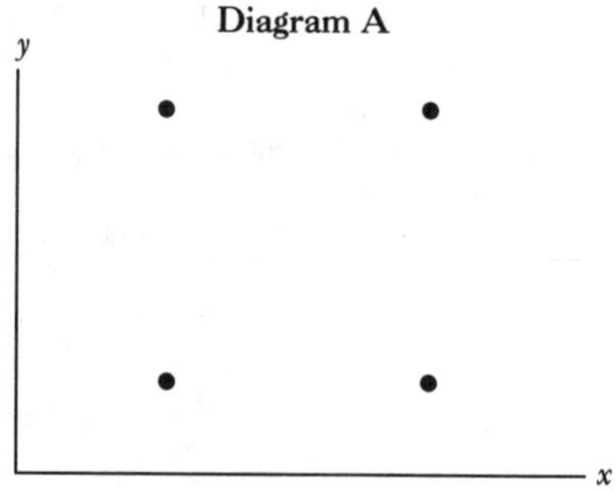

Diagram B

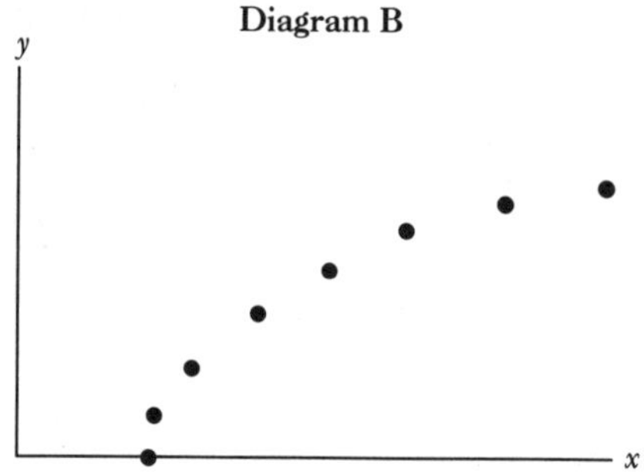

Diagram C

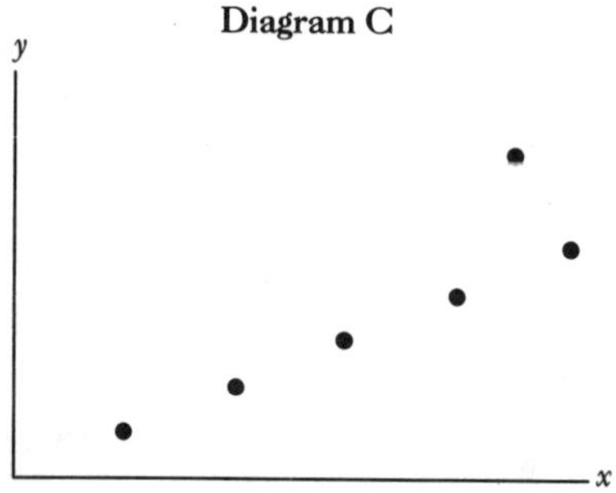

Diagram D

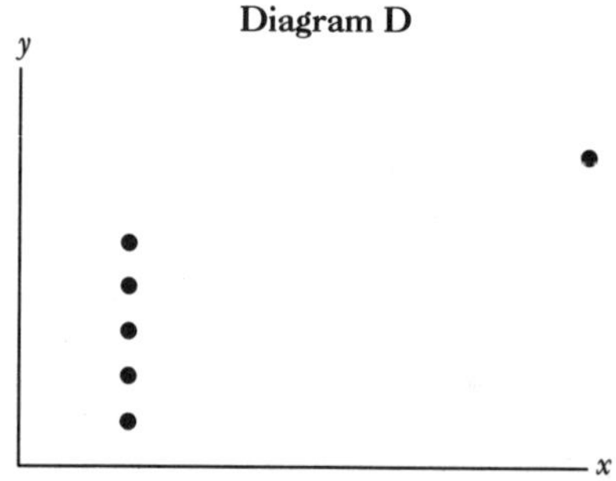

12.45 "KPMG Peat Marwich reported that cash compensation for CEOs last year rose 11.6% at 20 high-performing companies, but was up just 5% for 20 poor performers."(*WSJ*, May 11, 1993) What is the sign of the regression line slope implied by this quote?

12.46 For the data below on car weight and mileage, find the "best" fitting straight line relationship. For a car of 2,910 pounds, what is the predicted gas mileage from your equation? Why is your prediction from the least squares regression better than just taking an average of the gas mileage of the two cars that weigh 2,910 pounds?

Car	Weight	mpg	Car	Weight	mpg
1	2429	41.7	7	2700	39.1
2	2600	39.9	8	2800	39.2
3	2626	41.3	9	2731	39.9
4	2589	39.6	10	2910	37.4
5	2568	39.8	11	2875	38.9
6	2910	36.5	12	2493	42.1

12.47 Research Institute of America, New York, figures that the IRS can determine adjusted gross income for U.S. taxes on the basis of other tax deductions taken. Below is the RIA's sample data for adjusted-gross income and tax deductions calculated from preliminary 1991 data, as published in *The Wall Street Journal* (June 16, 1993).

Adjusted gross-income	Deducted taxes
\$ 27500	\$ 2115
35000	2540
45000	3141
62500	4161
87500	6012
150000	9616
350000	21374
750000	48289

a. What is the sample relationship betweeen income and tax deductions?

b. If someone reports adjusted-gross income of \$100,000 and deducts \$20,000 for other taxes paid, would you suspect the person is underreporting income or overreporting tax deductions? Explain?

12.48 According to Carnegie-Mellon University Professor M. Granger Morgan, "A simple linear relation, for instance, accurately describes the average cancer risk incurred by smokers: 10 cigarettes a day generally increase the chance of contracting lung cancer by a factor of 25; 20 cigarettes a day increase it by a factor of 50."(*Scientific American*, July 1993) Write the regression equation that Morgan has described.

12.49 The data in the computer ASCII file "EX12-49.PRN" is from *Car and Driver* (April 1993). The first column identifies the car tested and issue of *Car and Driver* in which the test appeared. The second column is the estimated price of the car tested. The third and fourth columns are 0 to 60 mph and 1/4 mile time in seconds. The fifth column is top speed. The sixth column is 70 to 0 braking distance in feet. EPA estimated fuel economy is in the seventh column. Finally, in column eight, road holding ability (measured as *g* force) is provided as obtained from a 300-foot skidpad. Which of the six variables (which you might name TO60, quarter, top, braking, fuel, hold) has the highest r^2 with car price?

12.50 Song Won Sohn, chief economist at Norwest Corp. in Minneapolis, asked: "Is there a reason to believe stocks and bonds move in different directions? I don't think so . . . The bond market is an excellent leading indicator of the stock market."(*Wall Street Journal,* September 13, 1993) According to the article, Sohn has studied the relative performance of the U.S. Treasury's 30-year bond and the Dow Jones Industrial Average since 1989; he predicted that the bond yield would fall from just less than 6 percent to 5.5 percent and the DOW would rise 50 to 100 points. From monthly data reported in the *Economic Report of the President,* estimate the relationship between the Dow and bond yield. Is there a strong negative correlation? Is Sohn's predicted relationship correct?

12.51 Suppose the salaries (y) of salespersons and revenue generated through sales (x) have a correlation coefficient of $r = 0.92$. What can you conclude from this value?

12.52 An article in *The New York Times* (April 11, 1994) reported on how Federal District Court Judge Clarence Newconner turned to Princeton University economics professor Orley Ashenfelter to help him decide whether to order a new election in Pennsylvania's Second State Senatorial District in Philadelphia or declare the losing candidate Bruce Marks, a Republican, the winner in the November 1993 election. In this special election to fill a Senate vacancy, Marks received 19,691 votes on voting machines and his Democrat opponent, William Stinson, received 19,127. But in absentee ballots, Stinson received 1,396 to Marks' 371. The Republicans charged that many of the absentee ballots were falsified by the Democrat-controlled County Board of Election. Professor Ashenfelter provided the author of this book with the following data used in his analysis:

		Absentee Votes			Machine Votes		
Year	District	Democrat	Republican	Difference	Democrat	Republican	Difference
82	2	551	205	346	47767	21340	26427
82	4	594	312	282	44437	28533	15904
82	8	338	115	223	55662	13214	42448
84	1	1357	764	593	58327	38883	19444
84	3	716	144	572	78270	6473	71797
84	5	1207	1436	–229	54812	55829	–1017
84	7	929	258	671	77136	13730	63406
86	2	609	316	293	39034	23363	15671
86	4	666	306	360	52817	16541	36276
86	8	477	171	306	48315	11605	36710
88	1	1101	700	401	56362	34514	21848
88	3	448	70	378	69801	3939	65862
88	5	781	1610	–829	43527	56721	–13194
88	7	644	250	394	68702	12602	56100
90	2	660	509	151	27543	26843	700
90	4	482	831	–349	39193	27664	11529
90	8	308	148	160	34598	8551	26047
92	1	1923	594	1329	65943	21518	44425
92	3	695	327	368	58480	12968	45512
92	5	841	1275	–434	41267	46967	–5700
92	7	814	423	391	65516	14310	51206
93	2	1396	371	1025	19127	19691	–564

a. Fit a regression of the difference between Democrat and Republican absentee ballots (y) to the difference between Democrat and Republican machine ballots (x) in the 21 election points between 1982 and 1992, excluding the twenty-second contested election in 1993. Write the equation for the regression. Interpret the slope intercept.

b. Show your regression line in a scatterplot. Make sure to identify the slope and intercept of the regression and to label the axis. Identify where the point would be for the contested election in 1993. Why didn't Ashenfelter include this point in the estimation of his regression?

c. What is the correlation coefficient for your regression in part a? What does it tell you?

d. Using your regression in part a, what is the predicted Democrat and Republican difference in absentee ballots in the contested election in 1993? By how many votes does this differ from the actual results? (Note: Questions for analysis of the voting issue in Exercise 12.52 are continued in Exercises 13.50 and 14.49.)

12.53 A *Business Week* (April 1, 1996) article reports on a sex discrimination case in which: "The central charge is that Publix hires women into dead-end, low-wage jobs and blocks them from the stock and clerk positions that would put them on a management track." As supporting evidence a plaintiff provided the following table of management positions held by women at Publix Supermarkets and maximum weekly pay for the positions. What is the relationship between the percentage of females in managerial positions (x) and maximum weekly pay (y)?

Managerial position	Percent female	Maximum weekly pay
Store Manager	2%	$820
Meat Department	1%	640
Produce Dept.	2%	590
Bakery	20%	630
Deli	90%	600

12.54 After reviewing the shoe lace problem in Query 12.7, a student in Professor Becker's class argued that the "high-low method" of equation fitting, as described in Ray Garrison and Eric Noreen's textbook *Managerial Accounting* (Irwin 1997, pp. 253-255), was better than the least squares line. This method requires the fitting of a line through the high and low points in the scatter diagram. This student 1) calculated the slope as (72-24)/(18-14) = 3.429, and 2) calculated the intercept as 72 - 3.429(18) = 10.28. Is this line "better" than the least squares line obtained in Query 12.7? Explain the criteria used for comparisons.

ACADEMIC REFERENCES

Malkiel, Burton. *A Random Walk Down Wall Street.* (New York: Norton, 5th edition, 1990).

Stigler, Stephen M. *The History of Statistics: The Measurement of Uncertainty before 1900.* (Cambridge: Belknap Press of Harvard University Press, 1986).

ENDNOTES

1. Ignoring the subscript i, the sum of the squared errors is

$$\Sigma e^2 = \Sigma(y - a - bx)^2$$

Differentiating with respect to a and b gives

$$\frac{\partial\left(\Sigma e^2\right)}{\partial a} = -2\Sigma\left(y - a - bx\right) = 2\Sigma y - 2na - 2b\Sigma x$$

$$\frac{\partial\left(\Sigma e^2\right)}{\partial b} = -2\Sigma x\left(y - a - bx\right) = 2\Sigma xy - 2a\Sigma x - 2b\Sigma x^2$$

These two derivatives must equal zero for the sum of squared errors to be at a minimum. The equations that result from this necessary condition are called normal equations, so named by Carl Gauss in 1809. Because there will be one equation for each unknown, they can be solved by "ordinary methods," as shown by Adrien Legendre in 1805. That is,

$$\Sigma y = na + b\Sigma x$$

$$\Sigma xy = a\Sigma x + b\Sigma x^2$$

Solving for a in the first equation gives

$$a = (\Sigma y/n) - b(\Sigma x/n),$$

which, upon rearranging, shows that the regression line must pass through the mean of x and mean of y. Substituting for a in the second normal equation gives

$$\Sigma xy = [(\Sigma y/n) - b(\Sigma x/n)]\Sigma x + b\Sigma x^2$$

$$\Sigma xy = (\Sigma y\Sigma x/n) - b[(\Sigma x)^2/n] + b\Sigma x^2$$

$$\Sigma xy - \Sigma x\Sigma y/n = b[\Sigma x^2 - (\Sigma x)^2/n]$$

$$\Sigma xy - 2(\Sigma x\Sigma y/n) + \Sigma x\Sigma y/n = b\{\Sigma x^2 - 2[(\Sigma x)^2/n] + (\Sigma x)^2/n\}$$

$$\Sigma xy - \bar{y}\Sigma x - \bar{x}\Sigma y + \Sigma\bar{x}\bar{y} = b(\Sigma x^2 - \bar{x}\Sigma x - \bar{x}\Sigma x + \Sigma\bar{x}^2)$$

$$\Sigma(xy - \bar{y}x - \bar{x}y + \bar{x}\bar{y}) = b\Sigma(x^2 - \bar{x}x - \bar{x}x + \Sigma\bar{x}^2)$$

$$\Sigma(x - \bar{x})(y - \bar{x}) = b\Sigma(x - \bar{x})^2$$

$$b = \frac{\Sigma\left(x - \bar{x}\right)\left(y - \bar{y}\right)}{\Sigma\left(x - \bar{x}\right)^2}$$

2. The use of the RSS and ESS notation is unfortunate because it is not standardized across books or computer programs. You should be aware that some use RSS to represent the residual sum of squares and ESS the explained sum of squares. We follow the convention of using RSS for the regression sum of squares and ESS for the error sum of squares. Readers should take care to check the definition of this notation in using computer programs and text material.

FORMULAS

- Covariance of x and y

$$s_{xy} = \frac{\sum_{i=1}^{n}(y_i - \bar{y})(x_i - \bar{x})}{n-1}$$

- Standardized deviation of x

$$\frac{x_i - \bar{x}}{s_x}$$

- Coefficient of correlation

$$r = \frac{\sum_{i=1}^{n}(x_i - \bar{x})(y_i - \bar{y})}{\sqrt{\sum_{i=1}^{n}(x_i - \bar{x})^2 \sum_{i=1}^{n}(y_i - \bar{y})^2}}$$

- General equation of a (regression) line
  $\hat{y} = a + bx$
  where $\hat{y}$ is the predicted dependent variable,
  x is the independent variable,
  a is the y axis intercept, and
  b is the slope.
- Specific example of a regression line

$$\hat{y} = -0.293 + 0.076x$$

where a one-unit increase in x is associated with a 0.076-unit increase in $\hat{y}$ and for $x = 0$, $\hat{y} = -0.293$.

- Residual

$$e_i = y_i - \hat{y}_i$$

- Sum of residuals

$$\sum_{i=1}^{n} e_i = e_1 + e_2 + e_3 + \ldots + e_{n-1} + e_n = 0$$

$$= y_1 - \hat{y}_1 + y_2 - \hat{y}_2 + \ldots + y_{n-1} - \hat{y}_{n-1} + y_n - \hat{y}_n = 0$$

- Residuals as a function of a and b

$$e_i = y_i - \hat{y}_i = y_i - (a + bx_i) = y_i - a - bx_i$$

- Sum of squared residuals as a function of a and b

$$\sum_{i=1}^{n} e_i^2 = \sum_{i=1}^{n}(y_i - \hat{y}_i)^2 = \sum_{i=1}^{n}(y_i - a - bx_i)^2$$

- Slope of the regression equation

$$b = \frac{\sum_{i=1}^{n}\left(x_i - \bar{x}\right)\left(y_i - \bar{y}\right)}{\sum_{i=1}^{n}\left(x_i - \bar{x}\right)^2}$$

- *y* intercept of the regression equation

$$a = \bar{y} - b\bar{x}$$

- Total sum of squares

$$\text{TSS} = \sum_{i=1}^{n}\left(y_i - \bar{y}\right)^2$$

- Residual or error sum of squares

$$\text{ErrorSS} = \sum_{i=1}^{n} e_i^2 = \sum_{i=1}^{n}\left(y_i - \hat{y}_i\right)^2$$

- Regression sum of squares

$$\text{RegSS} = \text{TSS} - \text{ErrorSS}$$

- Coefficient of determination

$$r^2 = \text{RegSS/TSS}$$

- Coefficient of correlation

$$r = \sqrt{\text{RegSS}/\text{TSS}}$$

CHAPTER 13

THE TWO-VARIABLE POPULATION MODEL

If you can't generalize
from data
there's nothing else you can do
with it either.

Robert M. Pirsig
(Lila 1991, p.55)

13.1 Introduction

Chapter 12 described the sample relationships between observations on two variables: speed limits and death rates, days of school and test scores, number of shoe eyelets and lace length, percentage of women MBAs and percentage of women managers, and so on. Here, least squares regression analysis is extended to inferences about the more general population relationship that might exist between two variables. This chapter shows how to:

- Construct a mathematical model of the population relationship between two variables.
- Use the sample least squares regression line to estimate the parameters of the population model.
- Employ the least squares estimates to test for a population relationship between the variables.
- Use the least squares regression line to estimate the expected values of the dependent variable at a certain value of the independent variable.
- Use the least squares regression line to predict a value of the dependent variable for a given value of the independent variable.

Whether a researcher should first look at the data and then construct a theoretical model of the population or specify the model and then confront it with the data is hotly debated in statistics. For classical regression analysis, the latter approach has been the dominant view, and it will receive more attention in this and the following chapters. This chapter focuses on the population relationship between just two variables. The parameters of bivariate population models will be estimated and tested using the least squares regression. The next chapter will extend this model to multiple explanatory variables.

To begin our extension of least squares regression line fitting to population inferences, consider the so-called Phillips curve relationship between inflation and unemployment.

13.2 The Phillips Curve

A negative relationship between the rate of inflation (in wages and prices) and the rate of unemployment in the United Kingdom was discovered by Alban Phillips in the 1950s. Phillips, an unassuming and relatively obscure New Zealand economist, never claimed any fixed and general relationship. He never made a statistical inference from his sample data to a population relationship. Yet, policymakers in the United States accepted the existence of such a relationship and used a "Phillips curve" to assess the relationship between inflation and unemployment in the 1960s. For example, S. Fischer and R. Dornbusch, in *Introduction to Macroeconomics* (1983, p. 292), write:

FIGURE 13.1 The Theoretical Phillips Curve

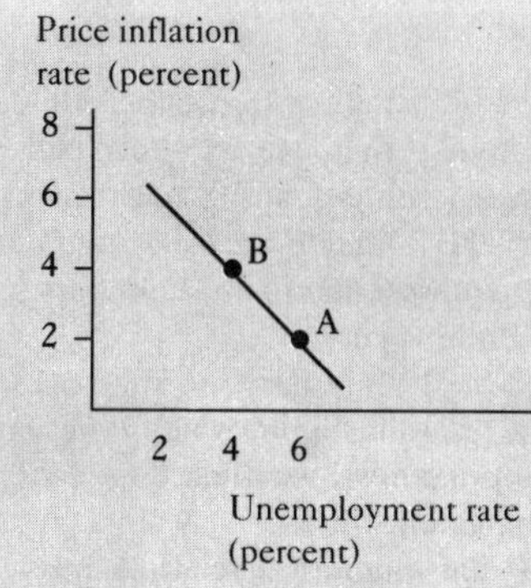

> The Phillips curve represents a trade-off between inflation and unemployment... If aggregate demand is expanded... output can be increased and the unemployment rate can be reduced. But with lower unemployment and less slack in the economy, there is more pressure on wages, costs, and prices. Therefore, prices will be rising at a more rapid rate the lower the rate of unemployment. . . . In the 1960s policymakers thought that a Phillips curve in the general shape of [Figure 13.1] in fact represented their policy trade-off. And they used it.

As evidenced by economist Alan Blinder's article in *Business Week* (November 27, 1989), in which he said the Phillips curve returned in the 1980s, Paul Craig Roberts' *Business Week* (September 27, 1993) article, in which he claimed it had vanished, and politician Jack Kemp's *Wall Street Journal* (April 2, 1997) accusation that the Humphrey-Hawkins Act of 1978 "codifies the Phillips curve into federal law," interest in the Phillips curve tradeoff continues. After four decades, the question persists: How is a two percentage point increase in the unemployment rate associated with a two percentage point decrease in the inflation rate?

13.3 Deterministic Versus Stochastic Relationships

The theoretical Phillips curve in Figure 13.1 represents a **deterministic relationship,** because each value of the independent variable (unemployment rate) is paired with only one value of the dependent variable (inflation rate). At point A, the unemployment rate is 6 percent and the inflation rate is 2 percent. From point A to point B, the unemployment rate drops to 4 percent and the inflation rate rises to 4 percent. Thus, the slope of this theoretical relationship between points A and B is –1.00.

Deterministic Relationship
An association in which each value of the independent variable is paired with only one definite value of the dependent variable.

Letting y^* represent the inflation rate associated with the unemployment rate x, a deterministic linear relationship between these two rates can be written as

$$y^* = \alpha + \beta x \tag{13.1}$$

The Phillips curve in Figure 13.1 shows a straight line drawn through points A and B; the slope is the parameter (or fixed) value $\beta = -1.00$. Extending the straight line drawn between points A and B to the y axis implies that the intercept is the parameter value $\alpha = 8.00$. (Outside the AB range, in Figure 13.1, a straight line may not be an appropriate representation of the theory. For the moment, we will ignore this nonlinearity in the Phillips curve.)

The Phillips curve in Figure 13.1 may or may not be a good representation of the actual relationship between inflation and unemployment in the 1960s. To establish its appropriateness, we must first estimate it and then compare the estimated slope with its expected value.

If the theoretical relationship were exactly true, we would only need to get two sample points, use a ruler to join them, and then calculate the slope. Additional sample points would convey no information since they would also lie on this line. We saw in the previous chapters, however, that all the points in a scatterplot typically do not lie on a straight line. There is variability in values of the dependent variable that is not associated with the independent variable. Some of this variability is due to variables that affect inflation (e.g., the money stock, government spending, taxes, technological bottlenecks) but are not included in the study, because they are unknown or unmeasured. Some is due to purely chance occurrences beyond the control of anyone. Let all these other unknown, unmeasured, and chance factors be represented by a single random variable ε. The variable ε is called the **disturbance term.**

Disturbance Term, ε
The difference between y and its expected value at each x value in a population model.

The specification of the theoretical relationship between the observed rate of inflation and the rate of unemployment is now expanded to

$$y = \alpha + \beta x + \varepsilon \tag{13.2}$$

where y is the observed inflation rate and ε is a random variable that causes y to deviate from y^*. (Note that $\varepsilon = y - y^*$.)

The relationship between the inflation rate y and the unemployment rate x in Equation (13.2) is no longer deterministic. It is said to be **stochastic,** because for each value of x there are random disturbances that also affect y. Thus, for any given value of x, the variable y may take any one of many different values.

Stochastic Relationship
An association in which more than one value of y may be assigned to a value of x by a random process.

The distribution of ε typically is unknown, so we must infer its characteristics. In particular, ε may take negative or positive values since the net effect of any omitted and unmeasured variables may cause y to be above or below that predicted by the theory. But if the theory is correct, then there is no reason to expect a bias. Such will be the case if the mean or expected value of ε is zero at each value of x, which we will assume. This assumption about the disturbance term is written

$$E(\varepsilon \mid x) = 0 \tag{13.3}$$

where $E(\varepsilon \mid x)$ designates the expected value of the random disturbance term ε. $E(\varepsilon \mid x) = 0$ says that if we selected a large (infinite) number of ε values, the average value would be zero.

It seems reasonable that negative and positive values of ε close to zero will occur more frequently than values far from zero and that negative and positive values are equally likely to occur. That is, most values of y will be close to the deterministic component $\alpha + \beta x$ with values of ε adding little to y. In addition, in the absence of any other information, it seems reasonable to assume that the occurrence of any given value of ε is not affected by the occurrence of any other value of ε, or the value of x considered. Adding the assumption that ε has a constant variance then implies that the distribution of ε at each x value is the same. Finally, if ε is normally distributed, then the distribution of ε, and in turn y, around the deterministic line $y^* = \alpha + \beta x$ would be as shown in Figure 13.2. Notice in Figure 13.2 that only two of the ε density functions are shown. At each value of x there is an identical ε density.

Figure 13.2 shows y^* to be the conditional mean or expected value of y, at each value of x. This expected value of y, conditional on an x value, is written $E(y \mid x)$; thus,

$$E(y \mid x) = y^* = \alpha + \beta x \tag{13.4}$$

Equation (13.4) shows that $E(y \mid x)$ and y^* are the same quantity.[1] In Figure 13.2 (where $\alpha = 8.00$ and $\beta = -1.00$), $y^* = E(y \mid x) = 8 - x$ says that the expected rate of inflation is

FIGURE 13.2 Population Model of the Phillips Curve Relationship $y = \alpha + \beta x + \varepsilon$

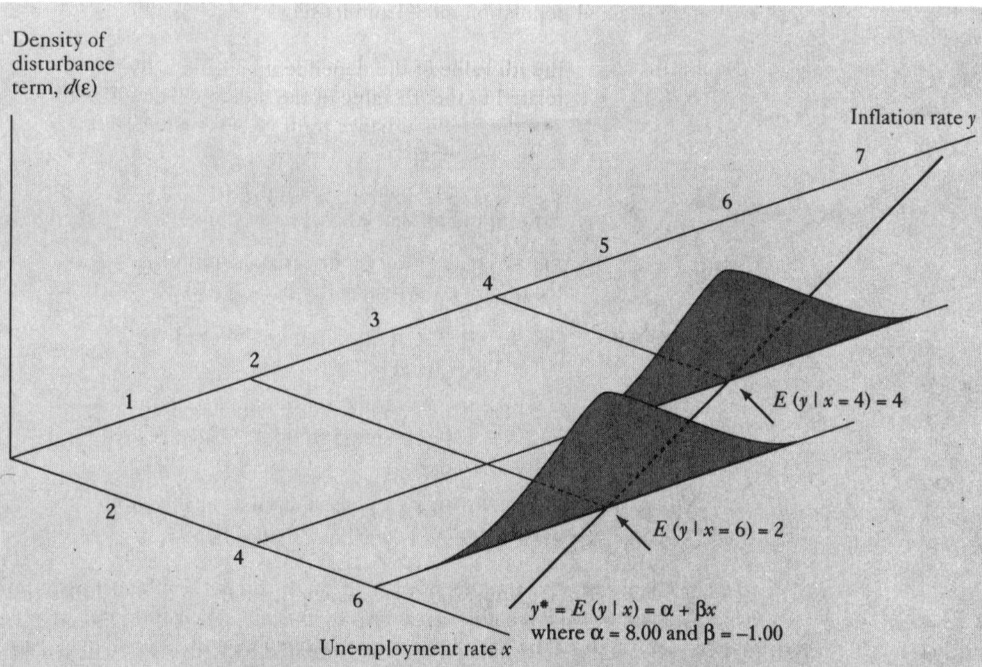

Shown here are two of the ε densities. At each value of x, there is an ε density identical to the two shown here.

4 percent when the unemployment rate is 4 percent, and the expected inflation rate is 2 percent when the unemployment rate is 6 percent. Figure 13.2 represents a redrawing of the relevant section of the Phillips curve in Figure 13.1. Here, however, the deterministic line of the Phillips curve relationship is shown on the *x-y* plane that is now positioned horizontally. The new idea shown in Figure 13.2 is that for each level of unemployment *x*, the inflation rate *y* can take on values other than $E(y|x)$. These random values are determined by the density function $d(\varepsilon)$. The two bell-shaped curves that rise vertically from the *x–y* plane show density functions for ε that are normal.

When values of ε are assumed to be generated by the normal probability distribution, the probability that *y* is a value within some interval of its expected value at each *x* is known. For instance, as drawn in Figure 13.2, at an unemployment rate of 4 percent, there is almost a 100 percent probability that the observed inflation rate will be between 2.5 percent and 5.5 percent. At an unemployment rate of 6 percent, there is almost a 100 percent likelihood that the observed inflation rate will be between 0.5 percent and 3.5 percent. Observed values of *y* outside these extremes should be rare if this graphical representation of the Phillips curve model is correct.

The specification of a population model of the Phillips curve is now complete. In general, the theory, the equational form used to represent it, and the assumptions about the disturbance term make up the **population model.** In the two variable case, where now the paired *y* and *x* values and the ε values are made explicit by adding the *i* subscript, the general population model and its six assumptions are:

Population Model
An equation used to represent a theoretical relationship among variables.

$y_i = \alpha + \beta x_i + \varepsilon_i$, the *i*th value of the dependent variable is linearly related to the *i*th value of the independent variable and the *i*th disturbance term value, where α and β are parameters; (13.5)

$E(\varepsilon_i) = 0$, the expected value of the *i*th disturbance term is zero [implying that $E(y|x) = \alpha + \beta x$]; (13.6)

$\text{Var}(\varepsilon_i) = \sigma_\varepsilon^2$, the variance of the *i*th disturbance term is a parameter σ_ε^2, which is the same for all *i*; (13.7)

$\text{Cov}(\varepsilon_i, \varepsilon_j) = 0$, the disturbance terms are unrelated so their covariances are zero; (13.8)

$\text{Cov}(\varepsilon_i, x_i) = 0$, the disturbance terms and the independent variable *x* are unrelated so their covariances are zero; and (13.9)

$\varepsilon_i \sim N(0, \sigma_\varepsilon^2)$, the disturbances are distributed normally with zero means and constant variance σ_ε^2. (13.10)

In what follows, the parameters of a model (α, β and σ_ε) will be estimated. Based on these parameter estimates, the expected value of *y*, at a specific value of *x*, will be estimated. Next, tests of the parameter values implied by a theory will be constructed and demonstrated. In the case of the Phillips curve, for example, both $\alpha = 8.00$ and

$\beta = -1.00$ will be tested against their separate alternative hypotheses that $\alpha \neq 8.00$ and $\beta \neq -1.00$. Consideration also will be given to the ways in which the assumptions of a model may be violated.

13.4 Estimation of Coefficients

Because of the chance factors inherent in sampling, the sampling error associated with different samples give rise to different paired observations on the two variables. In turn, different intercept and slope coefficients for the regression lines that best fit each scatterplot are obtained. If the samples are randomly generated, and if the population model believed to be generating the samples is correct, then across a large (infinite) number of samples, the mean of the intercepts and the mean of the slopes will equal the respective population parameters α and β. In terms of expected values, this is written as

$E(a) = \alpha$, mean of the least squares intercepts equals the population parameter α; and (13.11)

$E(b) = \beta$, mean of the least squares slopes equals the population parameter β, where again for brevity (ignoring the i subscript): (13.12)

$y = \alpha + \beta x + \varepsilon$, $\hat{y} = a + bx$, and
y is observed and $\hat{y}$ is predicted, and a
and b values are obtained by least squares.[2]

Because $E(a) = \alpha$ and $E(b) = \beta$, a and b are said to be unbiased estimators of the respective parameters α and β. It is essential to recognize that unbiasedness *does not* imply that, for any one sample, the value of the intercept a and the slope b equal the population intercept α and slope β. Equations (13.11) and (13.12) say that if a large (infinite) number of samples could be drawn, each with n matched x-y pairs, and if for each sample a least squares regression is fit, then the mean of all the intercept values would equal α. Similarly, the mean of all the slope values would equal β, if the population model is correct.

Table 13.1 contains yearly data on the unemployment and inflation rates for the United States in the 1960s. A random sample interpretation of these data is required to show that the least squares coefficient b is an unbiased estimator of β, and a is an unbiased estimator of α.[3] As discussed in Chapter 12, drawing a line through these data, as portrayed in Figure 13.3, and hand calculations with the least squares formulas (12.10) and (12.11), yield

$$b = \frac{\sum_{i=1}^{n}(x_i - \bar{x})(y_i - \bar{y})}{\sum_{i=1}^{n}(x_i - \bar{x})^2} = \frac{-12.226}{10.776} = -1.1346$$

$$a = \bar{y} - b\bar{x} = 2.52 - (-1.1346)(4.78) = 7.9432$$

TABLE 13.1
Rates of Unemployment and Inflation in the United States, 1960-1969

Year	Inflation Rate (%)	Unemployment Rate (%)
1960	1.6000	5.5000
1961	0.9000	6.7000
1962	1.8000	5.5000
1963	1.5000	5.7000
1964	1.5000	5.2000
1965	2.2000	4.5000
1966	3.2000	3.8000
1967	3.0000	3.8000
1968	4.4000	3.6000
1969	5.1000	3.5000

Source: *Economic Report of the President;* inflation rate is GNP implicit price deflator (1972 base = 100, percentage change from previous period) and unemployment rate is for civilian work force.

FIGURE 13.3 Scatterplot of Inflation and Unemployment Rates, 1960–1969

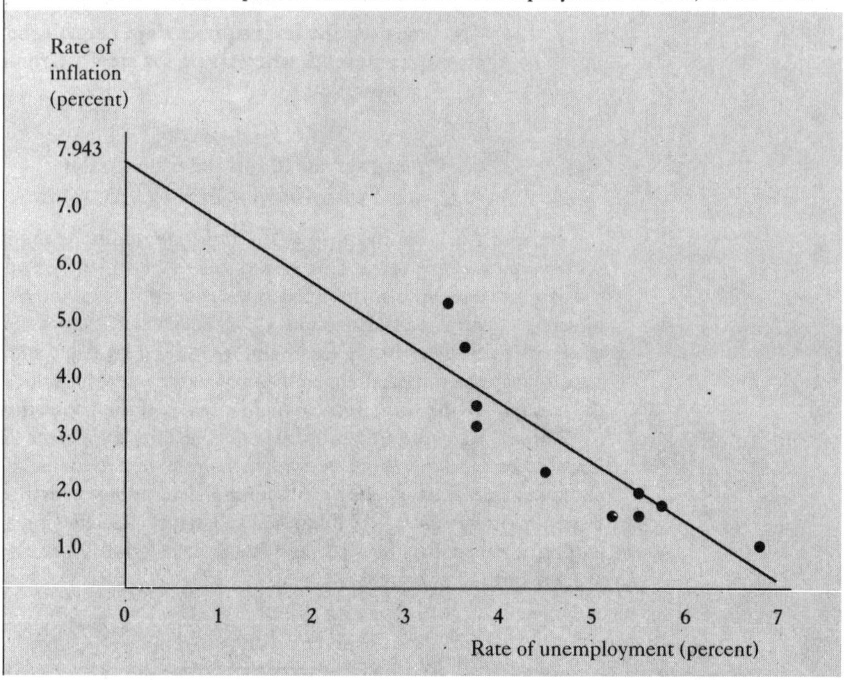

TABLE 13.2 Computer Output for the Least Squares Regression of the Unemployment Rate on the Inflation Rate in the 1960s

Regression Statistics	
Multiple R	0.901814
R Square	0.813269
Adjusted R Square	0.789927
Standard Error	0.630961
Observations	10

ANOVA	df	SS	MS	F	Significance F
Regression	1	13.871110	13.871110	34.842289	0.000361
Residual	8	3.184890	0.398111		
Total	9	17.056000			

	Coefficients	Std. Error	t Stat	P-value	Lower 95%	Upper 95%
Intercept	7.943189	0.940175	8.448631	0.000029	5.775141	10.111236
Unemploy	-1.134558	0.192209	-5.902736	0.000361	-1.577793	-0.691323

These values of b and a are also shown in the computer printout in Table 13.2 in the column headed "Coefficients."

The values $b = -1.1346$ and $a = 7.9432$ are called point estimates of the respective parameters β and α. Because of the randomness in sampling, the point estimate -1.1346 does not necessarily equal the true value of β, but it should be close. Similarly, the point estimate 7.9432 should be close to the true value of α.

We should anticipate that if the assumptions of the model are correct, then most of the x-y pairs in the sample should fall close to the deterministic part of the population model ($y^* = \alpha + \beta x$, in Figure 13.2). The best fitting least squares regression line should, in turn, give values of a and b that are close to the population α and β parameters. So until we have information to the contrary, we proceed as if the model and its assumptions are correct. That is, in the absence of any other facts, we anticipate that our calculated values of a and b will be close to the parameter values we are estimating.

"Closeness" can be defined in many different ways. For instance, the sample regression line

$$\hat{y} = 7.9432 - 1.1346x \tag{13.13}$$

can be drawn on the graph of the population model, Figure 13.4. If the sample regression line lies within the main bodies of the bell-shaped curves, as is the case in Figure 13.4, then the estimated line is consistent with the theory and the sample regression supports the Phillips curve theory that $y^* = 8.00 - x$.

The graphical demonstration of closeness in Figure 13.4 requires that the dispersion of the density function $d(\varepsilon)$ be known. But the variance of ε, σ_ε^2, is not even mentioned in Fischer and Dornbusch's discussion of the Phillips curve theory. It is a parameter to be estimated. It is estimated by s_e^2,

$$s_e^2 = \frac{\text{ErrorSS}}{n-2} \tag{13.14}$$

where ErrorSS was defined in the previous chapter by $\sum_{i=1}^{n}(y_i - \hat{y}_i)^2$

FIGURE 13.4 Population Model and Sample Regression of the Phillips Curve Relationship

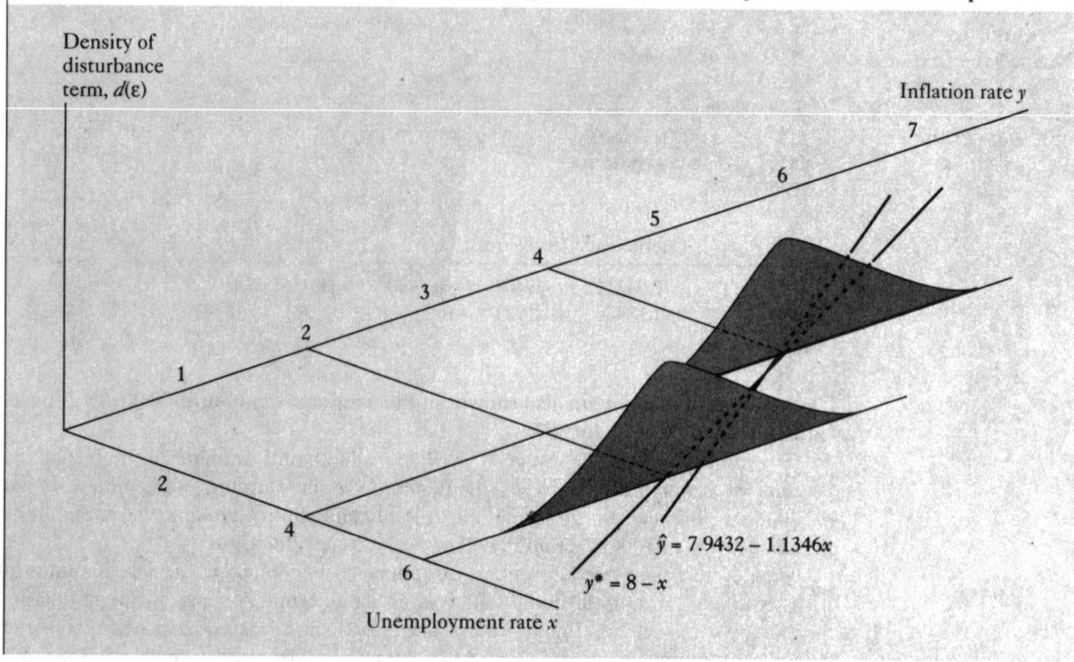

You should remember from Chapter 12 that the prediction error $e = y - \hat{y}$ and ErrorSS are calculated from values in one sample. In estimating the variance of ε using the ErrorSS, the degrees of freedom are $n - 2$, because two of the paired observations on y and x must be treated as predetermined when we use our sample specific a and b values in the calculation of $\hat{y}$. That is, two degrees of freedom are lost because the sample data is used to estimate two regressor coefficients.

If the assumed population model is correct, it is the division by $n - 2$ that makes s_e^2 an unbiased estimator of σ_ε^2. The expected value of s_e^2 is σ_ε^2, the variance of the disturbance term.[4] Remember that this does not say that for any given sample, s_e^2 equals σ_ε^2; it says that the mean of all the s_e^2 values that could be calculated will equal σ_ε^2.

The value of $s_e^2 = \text{ErrorSS}/(n - 2)$ can be calculated by hand. But as demonstrated in Chapter 12, it is typically obtained with a computer program. In Table 13.2, it is found on the line titled "Std. Error of Regression." The value of s_e^2 can also be calculated with the "sum of squared residuals,"

Standard Error of Regression
An estimator of the standard deviation of the population disturbance term in a regression.

$$s_e^2 = \frac{\text{ErrorSS}}{n-2} = \frac{3.1849}{8} = 0.39811 = (0.63096)^2 \tag{13.15}$$

The square root of 0.39811 is called the standard error of the regression, 0.63096. The **standard error of regression,** s_e, is the estimator of the standard deviation of the population disturbance term σ_ε.

13.5 The Confidence Interval for the Expected Value of Y

If the expected value of ε is zero, the expected value of y at any given x value, $E(y \mid x)$, is given by the deterministic equation $y^* = \alpha + \beta x$. As stated earlier, $E(y \mid x)$ and y^* are two different ways of saying the same thing.

The least squares regression line $\hat{y} = a + bx$ gives the point estimate of the expected value of y, at an x value. For any given sample there is no reason to believe that $\hat{y}$ will be the same as y^*, at each value of x. If the population model is correct, the expected value of $\hat{y}$ over a large (infinite) number of samples will equal y^*, for a given value of x. That is, $E(\hat{y} \mid x) = E(y \mid x) = y^*$, but randomness in sampling causes variability in $\hat{y}$, so $\hat{y}$ need not equal $E(\hat{y} \mid x)$.

To reflect variability in estimation, a confidence interval estimate of $E(y \mid x)$ can be defined. For instance, a 99 percent confidence interval for the expected value of y, at the specific x value designated by x^*, is

$$\hat{y} \pm t_{0.005} s_e \sqrt{\frac{1}{n} + \frac{\left(x^* - \bar{x}\right)^2}{\sum_{i=1}^{n}\left(x_i - \bar{x}\right)^2}} \qquad (13.16)$$

where $+t_{0.005}$ is the value of t for which 0.5 percent of the area is in the upper tail and $-t_{0.005}$ is the t value for which 0.5 percent of the area is in the lower tail. As with all confidence intervals, the amount added to and subtracted from the point estimator is called the **margin of error**.

Margin of Error
A measure of the precision of an estimator.

Confidence intervals for $E(y|x)$ are not easily calculated with EXCEL, although as demonstrated in Table 13.3 they can be done with specialized statistical programs such as MINITAB. We will not emphasize these calculation routines here. Notice, however, that the margin of error for $E(y|x)$ is not constant at a fixed level of confidence. At the mean of x, the margin of error for $E(y|x)$ is smallest, and the farther from the mean of x the larger this margin of error becomes. For a 99 percent confidence interval for $E(y|x)$, at the mean unemployment rate of 4.78, the margin of error is ± 0.6695, and the confidence interval is $1.85 \le E(y|x = 4.78) \le 3.19$. For an unemployment rate of 6.00 percent, the margin of error is ± 1.033 for a 99 percent confidence interval of $0.103 \le E(y|x = 4.78) \le 2.169$. On the other side of the mean, for example, by the time x falls to an unemployment rate of 0 percent, the margin of error for $E(y|x)$ is ± 3.15 percent. The effect on the confidence interval as the margin of error increases for values of x away from its mean can be seen in Figure 13.5. Because the margin of error is relatively large for extreme values of x, we cannot place much faith in predictions made outside the sample domain of x.

FIGURE 13.5 Confidence Interval for Rate of Inflation, 1960–1969

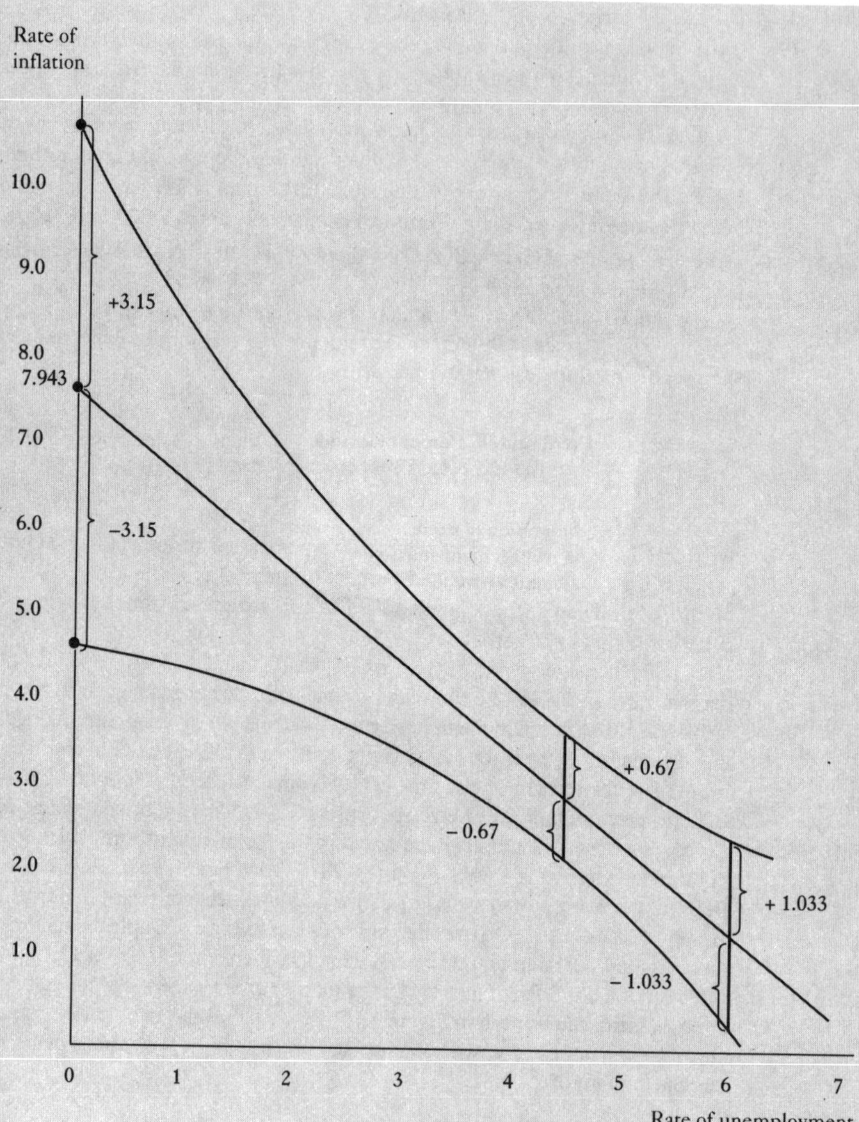

13.6 THE PREDICTION INTERVAL FOR AN INDIVIDUAL VALUE OF Y

In addition to estimating the expected value of y at given x values, $\hat{y}$ can be interpreted as providing a prediction of an individual value of y. If so, then additional variability must be recognized. The confidence interval for $E(y \mid x)$ only involves variability of $\hat{y}$ around $E(y \mid x)$, as reflected in the difference $\hat{y} - E(y \mid x)$. Any individual value of y that might occur with an x value, however, would involve the variability reflected in the difference $\hat{y} - E(y \mid x)$ plus the difference between $E(y \mid x)$ and the individual value of y that might be observed. This added variability can be seen in a comparison of Formula (13.16) and the $(1 - \alpha)$ prediction interval in Formula (13.17):

$$\hat{y} \pm t_{\alpha/2} s_e \sqrt{\frac{1}{n} + \frac{\left(x^* - \bar{x}\right)^2}{\sum_{i=1}^{n}\left(x_i - \bar{x}\right)^2} + 1} \tag{13.17}$$

The only difference between the confidence interval for $E(y|x)$, Formula (13.16), and the prediction interval for y, Formula (13.17), is that the latter is wider than the former for all values of x. They both reflect more imprecision the farther x is from it mean. Neither is easily calculated with EXCEL, but as demonstrated in Table 13.3 both can be calculated in a dedicated statistics program such as MINITAB.

QUERY 13.1:
A real estate report in *The Wall Street Journal* (February 28, 1997) gave "the top 10 condominium sales (in millions) in New York City, January and February 1997:"

Address	Square Feet	Price
353 Central Park West	2,733	1.6
22 W. 66th St.	2,241	1.5
160 W. 66th St	1,775	1.3
111 W. 67th St.	3,177	2.2
101 W. 67th St.	2,731	2.2
101 W. 67th St.	1,793	1.4
721 Fifth Ave.	3,000	3.6
308 E. 72nd St	2,575	1.4
30 E. 76th St.	2,480	1.4
255 E. 49th St.	3,256	2.9

What is the relationship between price(y) and condominium square footage(x)? Predict the price of the mean square footage condominium and each of the quartiles. Which predicted prices have the smallest standard errors?

ANSWER:

Queries in Chapter 12 show how to obtain the least squares regression line and related statistics using the EXCEL Data Analysis dialog boxes. An alternative method can provide the intercept and slope coefficients directly through the function commands "=INTERCEPT(y data, x data)" and "=SLOPE(y data, x data)" as shown in column E of Chart 13.1. The resulting relationship between price (x) and square footage (y) is

$$\hat{y} = -0.84557 + 0.00109x$$

CHART 13.1 Regression of Price on Square Footage

	A	B	C	D	E	F	G	H	I
1	sqfeet	price			Coefficients				
2	2,733	1.6				Function entered into column E			
3	2,241	1.5			-0.8455688	=INTERCEPT(B2:B11,A2:A11)			
4	1,775	1.3			0.0010852	=SLOPE(B2:B11,A2:A11)			
5	3,177	2.2							
6	2,731	2.2			Predictions				
7	1,793	1.4				Function entered into column E			
8	3,000	3.6			1.95	=$E$3+$E$4*A13			
9	2,575	1.4			1.6511918	=$E$3+$E$4*A14			
10	2,480	1.4			2.0334514	=$E$3+$E$4*A15			
11	3,256	2.9			2.3375771	=$E$3+$E$4*A16			
12		Function entered into column A				Function entered into column E			
13	2576	=AVERAGE(A2:A11)			1.95	=FORECAST(A13,$B$2:$B$11,$A$2:$A$11)			
14	2301	=QUARTILE(A2:A11,1)			1.6511918	=FORECAST(A14,$B$2:$B$11,$A$2:$A$11)			
15	2653	=QUARTILE(A2:A11,2)			2.0334514	=FORECAST(A15,$B$2:$B$11,$A$2:$A$11)			
16	2933	=QUARTILE(A2:A11,3)			2.3375771	=FORECAST(A16,$B$2:$B$11,$A$2:$A$11)			

The mean and quartile square footages are obtain in column A using the "=AVERAGE(x data)" and "=QUARTILE(x data,q)" function commands. The predicted prices for the mean and for the three quartiles (in square footage) for the condominiums are shown in column E using two different function commands. The first method makes use of the regression equation and cell arithmetic, where the $ signs around letters indicate the identified cell values were fixed during copying. The second method makes use of the "=FORECAST(x value,y data,x data)" command function. For the mean-sized condominium, the predicted price is $1.95 million, which is also the sample mean condominium price. The three quartile sized condominiums are priced at $1.65 million, $2.03 million, and $2.34 million. The prediction for the mean-sized condominium has the smallest standard error of prediction. The standard error in predicting the price of the third quartile-sized unit is the largest of the three quartile predictions because it is made for a condominium size farthest from the mean size.

QUERY 13.2:
Did those who bought the 2,241 square foot condominium at 22 W. 66th St. and 2,731 square foot condominium at 101 W. 67th St., pay too little or too much for the respective properties according to your regression in Query 13.1? Explain.

ANSWER:
The predicted price of the 22 W. 66th St. condominium is \$1,586,351 and its actual price is \$1.5 million; thus, the buyer paid \$86,351 less than what is predicted by the relationship between price and size found in the sample of 10 New York City condominiums described in the *WSJ*.

$$\hat{y} = -0.84557 + 0.00109x = -0.84557 + 0.00109(2241) = 1.586351$$

The predicted price of the 101 W. 67th St. condominium is \$2,118,097 and its actual price is \$2.2 million; thus, the buyer paid \$81,903 more than what is predicted by the relationship between price and size found in the sample of 10 New York City condominiums described in the *WSJ*.

$$\hat{y} = -0.84557 + 0.00109x = -0.84557 + 0.00109(2731) = 2.118097$$

QUERY 13.3:
The MINITAB printout in Table 13.3 provides both 95 percent confidence intervals for $E(y|x)$ and the prediction interval for y. What was the critical value of the t statistic used in these calculations? For an unemployment rate of 4 percent, use the quantities provided to show how the 95 percent confidence interval for $E(y|x)$ was calculated.

ANSWER:
The critical t for a 95 percent confidence interval, with 8 degrees of freedom, is determined with the EXCEL function command "=TINV(0.05, 8)" to be 2.306. Thus, the 95 percent confidence interval for $E(y|x = 4)$ is calculated as $3.405 \pm 2.306(0.250) = 3.405 \pm 0.5765$, giving

$$2.829 \leq E(y|x = 4) \leq 3.981$$

EXERCISES

13.1 Using a computer program and the 60 matched pre- and midtest scores in Exercise 12.4:

a. For a pretest score of 55, what is the predicted value of y?

b. For a pretest score of 55, what is the estimate of $E(y|x = 55)$?

c. Why are your answers in parts a and b the same?

13.2 Why is a lot of variability in the independent variable desirable? (Hint: consider the formula for the confidence interval for $E(y|x)$.)

13.3 If a 95 percent prediction interval for starting salaries is from $45,500 to $51,300, what is the point estimate of those salaries? What is the margin for error?

13.4 Using your information on variances and covariance calculated with the data set in Exercise 12.13, determine the point estimate of the expected value of y at $x = 5$.

13.5 A study of six piece workers yields the following sample data, where x = number of years worked, and y = number of returned clothing items.

y	x
13	1
7	2
5	3
3	3
3	5
6	4

a. For a worker with three years of experience, what is the predicted y?

b. For a worker with three years of experience, what is the estimate of $E(y|x = 3)$?

c. What is the sample mean of y?

d. What is the difference between parts a, b and c?

13.6 How is the confidence interval for the expected value of y at an x influenced by the size of the x value?

13.7 THE SAMPLING DISTRIBUTION OF b

Sampling Distribution of b
The probability density function that assigns values to the least squares estimator, b.

The "closeness" of a specific value of b to the hypothesized value β is assessed by introducing the sampling distribution of b. The **sampling distribution of b,** or, simply, the distribution of b, represents the probabilities of alternative values of b that could be obtained from repeated sampling. If the expected value of ε is zero, and if x and ε are not related, then the expected value of b is β. In addition, if the population disturbance term ε is distributed normally, then the distribution of b will also be normal.

If b is distributed normally, as shown in Figure 13.6, there is approximately 68 percent of the distribution within one standard deviation of the mean of b, $\beta \pm \sigma_b$. That is, the probability of obtaining a b value within the range $\beta \pm \sigma_b$ is approximately 0.68. Within two standard deviations, $\beta \pm 2\sigma_b$, there is approximately 95 percent of the distribution. Almost the entire distribution lies within three standard deviations of the mean.

Typically the magnitude of the standard deviation of the distribution of b, σ_b, is unknown. It is estimated by the standard error of b, s_b, which is calculated by[6]

$$s_b = \sqrt{\frac{s_e^2}{\sum_{i=1}^{n}\left(x_i - \bar{x}\right)^2}} \tag{13.18}$$

FIGURE 13.6 The Sampling Distribution of b

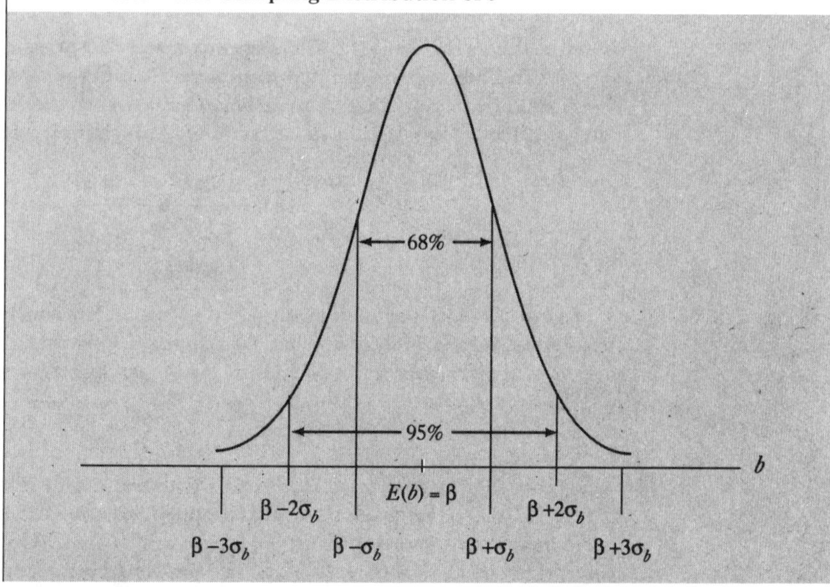

The estimated standard error of a coefficient estimator is typically calculated by computer programs. For example, in Table 13.2 the standard errors of the coefficient estimates are given in the column headed "Std. Error." For the unemployment coefficient, b, the standard error is $s_b = 0.1922$, which is calculated by

$$s_b = \sqrt{\frac{\text{ErrorSS}/(n-2)}{\sum_{i=1}^{n}(x_i - \bar{x})^2}} = \sqrt{\frac{3.1849/8}{10.776}} = 0.1922$$

When s_b is used as an estimator of σ_b, to assess how far a coefficient estimate (e.g., $b = -1.1346$) is from its hypothesized expected value ($\beta = -1.00$), it is necessary to form a "t ratio" and use the t distribution to calculate probabilities.[7] The t ratio is

$$t = \frac{b - E(b)}{s_b} = \frac{b - \beta}{s_b} \tag{13.19}$$

Computer programs calculate t ratios for an expected value of b equal to zero. For instance, in Table 13.2 under the column headed "T-ratio", the reported t ratio for the unemployment coefficient is

$$t = \frac{b - E(b)}{s_b} = \frac{-1.13456 - 0}{0.1922} = -5.903$$

↑ Assuming $E(b) = \beta = 0$

which indicates that $b = -1.13456$ is approximately 5.9 standard deviations below 0.

For the Phillips curve theory, we are interested in the closeness of $b = -1.13456$ to $\beta = -1.00$. The relevant t ratio cannot be obtained directly from a computer printout. It can be calculated using the standard error of b, which is reported on the printout.

$$t = \frac{b - E(b)}{s_b} = \frac{-1.13456 - (-1.00)}{0.1922} = -0.700$$

↑ Assuming $E(b) = \beta = -1.00$

Thus, $b = -1.13456$ is approximately 0.7 of a standard deviation below $\beta = -1.00$. To assess closeness we need the probability of being 0.7 of a standard deviation below the mean, with eight degrees of freedom. Using a computer program, such as MICROSTAT, we learn that

$$P(t \le -0.7 \mid \text{df} = 8) = 0.25$$

This probability and its associated area in the sampling distribution of b are shown in Figure 13.7. Since the shaded area for b values below $b = -1.13456$ is relatively large (25 percent of the entire distribution), we can say that $b = -1.13456$ is relatively close to the parameter value of $\beta = -1.0$. That is, our sample and estimated slope are not inconsistent with the Phillips curve theory.

FIGURE 13.7 A Sampling Distribution of b and Calculated t Value

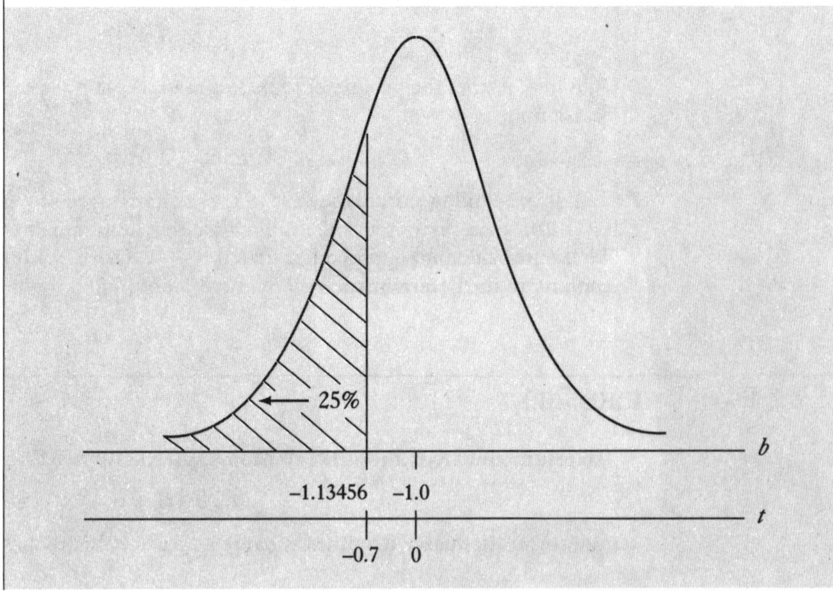

Notice that the denominator of the standard error of b is the square root of the sum of squared deviations in x. The more variability in the independent variable, the smaller the variability in the distribution of b. That is, greater variability in the independent variable makes the slope estimator more precise.

13.8 Testing Hypotheses About Individual Coefficients

Often a theory or someone's belief suggests the null and alternative hypotheses. The null hypothesis, designated as H_O, is the theory that is assumed true until contrary information is obtained. As discussed in Chapter 9 on hypothesis testing, the null hypothesis provides the value at which the sampling distribution is centered. In the case of the Phillips curve, we assumed that $E(b) = \beta = -1.0$; that is,

$$H_O\colon \beta = -1.0$$

The alternative hypothesis, designated H_A, is the challenging theory. It may involve a statement that allows the parameter to be any value other than that stated in the null hypothesis; for example,

$$H_A\colon \beta \neq -1.0$$

Or, it may restrict the parameter to be greater than the value stated in the null hypothesis; for example,

$$H_A\text{: } \beta > -1.0$$

Or, it may restrict the parameter to be less than the value stated in the null hypothesis; for example,

$$H_A\text{: } \beta < -1.0$$

For the Phillips curve, the first of these alternatives seems most appropriate (H_A: $\beta \neq -1.0$), since Fischer and Dornbusch's discussion implies that policymakers in the 1960s entertained no option other than $\beta = -1.0$. That is, either $\beta < -1.0$ or $\beta > -1.0$ is contrary to the deterministic Phillips curve presented in Figure 13.1.

13.9 Two-Tailed Test

To test the null hypothesis that β is some specific value β_O,

$$H_O\text{: } \beta = \beta_O$$

against the alternative hypothesis that β is a value other than β_O,

$$H_A\text{: } \beta \neq \beta_O$$

the ratio in Equation (13.19) is assumed to follow the t distribution, with $n - 2$ degrees of freedom. That is,

$$t = \frac{b - \beta_O}{s_b} \sim t(n-2) \tag{13.20}$$

where b is assumed to be distributed normally with mean β_O and variance σ_b^2.

As in any hypotheses testing, the probability of incorrectly rejecting the null hypothesis (Type I error) defines the calculated values of t that result in the rejection of H_O. Figure 13.8 shows the H_O: $\beta = -1.00$ and H_A: $\beta \neq -1.00$ critical rejection regions for a probability of a Type I error equal to 5 percent. According to the decision rule portrayed in Figure 13.8, if the absolute value of the calculated t ratio in Equation (13.19) exceeds 2.306, H_O: $\beta = -1.00$ is rejected in favor of H_A: $\beta \neq -1.00$. If the absolute value of the calculated t ratio does not exceed 2.306, H_O: $\beta = -1.00$ should not be rejected. In essence, this decision rule says that when the estimate of b is more than 2.306 estimated standard deviations away from the null hypothesized value of $\beta = -1.00$, we will no longer believe that β is equal to -1.00. In using this decision rule, however, we must acknowledge that 5 percent of the time we could get an estimate of b that is more than $2.306s_b$ away from $\beta = -1.00$, when in fact $\beta = -1.00$.

FIGURE 13.8 A Sampling Distribution of b and Critical t Values

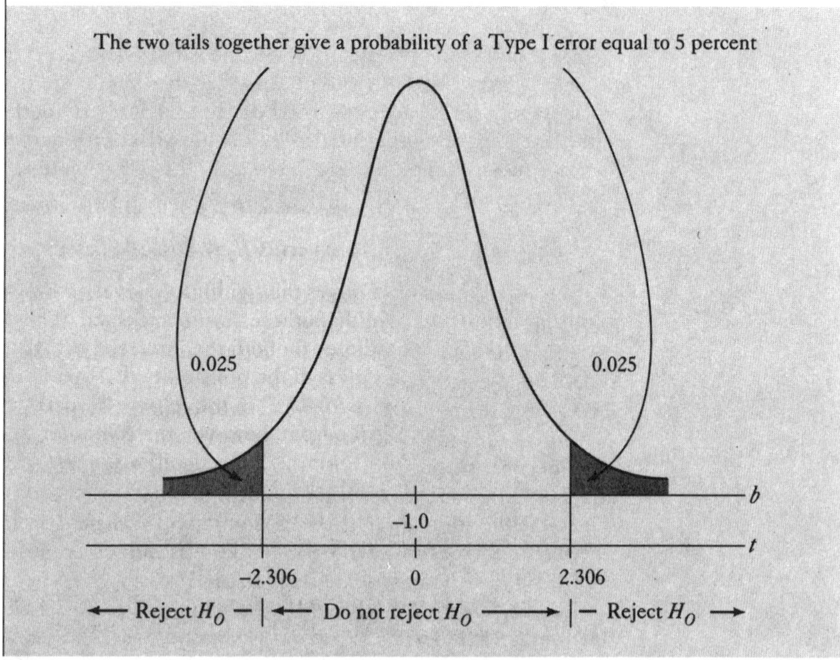

From Equation (13.20) and Figure 13.7, we know that the calculated t ratio for $b = -1.13456$ is $t = -0.7$.

$$t = \frac{b - E(b)}{s_b} = \frac{-1.13456 - (-1.00)}{0.1922} = -0.700$$

Since $b = -1.13456$ is only 0.7 estimated standard deviations below $\beta = -1.00$, while the critical t values in Figure 13.8 are minus and plus 2.306, H_0: $\beta = -1.00$ is not rejected.

We have not proven that the theoretical Phillips curve has a slope of −1.00. The sample evidence is simply not strong enough to reject this conclusion. We could be making a Type II error in not rejecting $\beta = -1.00$. In addition, any one of the other assumptions in our model (e.g., that the inflation rate is a linear function of the unemployment rate or that the disturbance term is independent of itself and the unemployment rate) could be wrong, implying that our test is biased. In the absence of any other information, however, the best we can say is that $\beta = -1.00$ cannot be rejected.

13.10 Two-Tailed Test and Computer Output

Computer printouts typically provide calculated t ratios for the test of a parameter value against zero. They also routinely provide the associated p-value for a two-tailed test. For instance, Table 13.3 provides the MINITAB output for the data in Table 13.1. As with the computer output in Table 13.2, the MINITAB output in the column headed "t-ratio" provides the calculated t ratios for the following tests

$$H_O\text{: } \alpha = 0 \text{ versus } H_A\text{: } \alpha \neq 0\text{; calculated } t = 8.45$$

$$H_O\text{: } \beta = 0 \text{ versus } H_A\text{: } \beta \neq 0\text{; calculated } t = -5.90$$

The next column "p" gives the significance level, or lowest probabilities of a Type I error for which the null hypotheses can be rejected. This MINITAB printout suggests that the null hypotheses for both the intercept (H_O: $\alpha = 0$) and slope (H_O: $\beta = 0$) should be rejected, regardless of the probability of Type I error, since the significance levels for both are given as "0.000," in the column headed "p" for p-value.

Unlike the MINITAB output, however, the computer output in Table 13.2 shows more decimal places. In Table 13.2, the significance level is 0.00003 for the intercept and 0.00036 for the slope. If the probability of a Type I error is set at 0.00002, for instance, neither the null hypothesis $\alpha = 0$ nor $\beta = 0$ could be rejected. This fine a distinction is not possible with the MINITAB output because significance levels are rounded to the thousandth decimal place.

Looking down the MINITAB printout in Table 13.3, at the bottom we can see that this computer program, as with most others, produces 95 percent confidence intervals for the expected value of y at the identified x values, and 95 percent prediction intervals for specific values of y at those x values. The reader can verify the correctness of the intervals shown using Formulas (13.16) and (13.17). (Notice in Table 13.3, with eight degrees of freedom, the critical t value that puts 0.025 in each tail for the 95 percent intervals is 2.306 instead of the 3.355 value used in the 99 percent intervals we calculated earlier. Discussions yet to come will address the remaining quantities in this and similar regression printouts.)

Finally, notice on the MINITAB printout that the "y-intercept" (7.9432) is called the "Constant." Computer programs use the words "intercept" and "constant" as synonyms in regression analysis.

TABLE 13.3 MINITAB Regression Output

```
MTB > read 'influnem.prn' cl-c3                  <----  to read ASCII file
      10 ROWS READ                                      "influnem.prn" which
                                                        contains the data on
  ROW    cl      c2     c3                              inflation and unemployment
                                                        rates in Table 13.1
    1    1960    1.6    5.5
    2    1961    0.9    6.7
    3    1962    1.8    5.5
    4    1963    1.5    5.7
  .  .  .

MTB> name c2 'infl'                              <----  to name columns
MTB> name c3 'unem'
MTB> regres c2 1 c3;                             <----  to regress inflation rate in
SUBC> predict 4.00;                                     column c2 on the unemployment
SUBC> predict 4.78;                                     rate in column c3
SUBC> predict 6.00.                              <----  to predict inflation rates at
                                                        unemployment rates of 4.00,
The regression equation is                              4.78, and 6.00 percent
infl = 7.94 – 1.13 unem

Predictor       Coef      Stdev     t-ratio      p
Constant       7.9432     0.9402      8.45     0.000
unem          –1.1346     0.1922     –5.90     0.000

s = 0.6310        R-sq = 81.3%      R-sq(adj) = 79.0%

Analysis of Variance

SOURCE         DF        SS        MS        F        p
Regression      1    13.871    13.871    34.84    0.000
Error           8     3.185     0.398
Total           9    17.056

Unusual Observations

Obs.    unem     infl     Fit     Stdev.Fit    Residual    St. Resid
 10     3.50    5.100    3.972      0.317       1.128        2.07R

R denotes an obs. with a large st. resid.

     Fit     Stdev. Fit      95% C.I.           95% P.I.
    3.405       0.250     ( 2.829, 3.981)    ( 1.840, 4.970)

    2.520       0.200     ( 2.060, 2.980)    ( 0.994, 4.046)

    1.136       0.308     ( 0.426, 1.846)    (–0.484, 2.755)
```

13.11 Two-Tailed Test and Confidence Intervals

As introduced in Chapter 9, reporting the significance level in hypothesis testing is helpful because it gives a sense of the strength of the evidence against the null hypothesis. Reporting a confidence interval estimate for coefficient estimates also is of value in demonstrating the sensitivity of results to sampling error. In the Phillips curve example, a 95 percent confidence interval for β is

$$b - t_{0.025}s_b < \beta < b + t_{0.025}s_b \tag{13.21}$$

$$-1.1346 - 2.306(0.1922) \leq \beta \leq -1.1346 + 2.306(0.1922)$$

$$-1.58 \leq \beta \leq -0.69$$

This 95 percent confidence interval $-1.58 \leq \beta \leq -0.69$ indicates that any null hypothesis value between −1.58 and −0.69 could not be rejected in a two-tailed test, for 0.05 Type I error level and this sample data. Both $\beta = -1.58$ and $\beta = -0.69$ are the end points for statistical significance at the 5 percent Type I error level—any null hypothesis value between −1.58 and −0.69 could not be rejected in a two-tailed test using this information. (Remember that probability is defined to be zero at a point for continuous probability density functions.)

Notice that once a null hypothesis of no difference has been rejected in a two-tailed test, we can do better than to simply say that a significant difference exists at the given Type I error level. From the corresponding confidence interval, we can say that β is in the direction of the sample mean. In the Phillips curve example, the 95 percent confidence interval suggests that β is negative, with −1.00 being a possible value.

Unlike confidence intervals for $E(y|x)$ and prediction intervals for y, EXCEL automatically produced 95 percent confidence intervals for the estimated β's. As seen in the last row of Table 13.2, the 95 percent confidence interval for the population slope, calculated in (13.21), as: Lower 95% = -1.577793 and Upper 95% = -0.691323.

13.12 One-Tailed Test

Often a theory will not restrict the value of β to a specific number, or an alternative theory might be consistent with values in only one direction. For instance, in the speed limit case introduced in Chapter 12, we might wish to test whether there is a positive relationship between death rate and speed limit. For this test, the null and alternative hypotheses are

H_O: $\beta = 0$, speed limit is not related to death rate

H_A: $\beta > 0$, speed limit and death rate are positively related

Setting the probability of a Type I error at 0.05, the critical value of t, and the H_O rejection and acceptance regions are shown in Figure 13.9. Because the alternative hypothesis only allows for β values greater than that specified in the null, the entire 0.05 probability of a Type I error is put in the upper tail. (If an alternative hypothesis allows only for β values less than that specified in the null, the entire probability of a Type I error is in the lower tail.)

FIGURE 13.9 A Sampling Distribution of b and Critical t Value

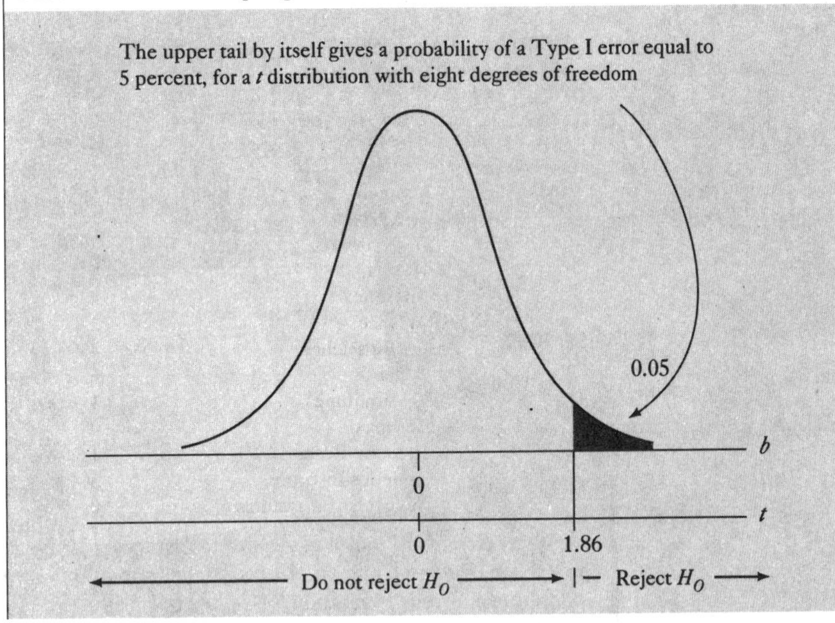

From the SAS computer printout in Table 13.4, or the MICROSTAT computer output in Table 12.7, the calculated t ratio is

$$t = \frac{b - \beta_0}{s_b} = \frac{0.075556 - 0}{0.04074} = 1.852$$

$t = 1.852$ is just short of the H_0 rejection region. The significance level or p value is 0.0504. This significance level is half the value reported in Table 13.4, because 0.1008 is the significance level for a two-tailed test where the alternative is $\beta \neq 0$. Most all computer programs report significance levels or p-values only for two-tailed tests. For our one-tailed test, we cannot reject H_0 unless the probability of a Type I error is raised to 0.0504 or higher.

As discussed in the previous chapters on hypothesis testing, raising the probability of a Type I error may allow the rejection of the null hypothesis, but at a higher likelihood of being wrong. The probability of a Type I error could be set at zero, but this would make it impossible to reject the null hypothesis when it is false and the probability of a Type II error would be at its maximum. As the probability of a Type I error is reduced, the probability of a Type II error increases. Holding the sample size fixed, the probability of a Type I error cannot be changed without inversely affecting the probability of a Type II error.

Table 13.4
SAS Regression Output

ANALYSIS OF VARIANCE

SOURCE	DF	SUM OF SQUARES	MEAN SQUARE	F-VALUE	PROB>F
MODEL	1	2.5689	2.5689	3.4395	0.1008
ERROR	8	5.9751	0.7469		
C TOTAL	9	8.5440			

ROOT MSE	0.8642	R-SQUARE	0.30067
DEP MEAN	4.2400	ADJ R-SQ	0.21325
C. V	0.2298		

PARAMETER ESTIMATES

VARIABLE	DF	PARAMETER ESTIMATE	STANDARD ERROR	T FOR HO: PARAMETER-O	PROB > |T|
INTERCEPT	1	–0.29333	2.460	–0.119	0.9080
SPEED	1	0.0755556	0.04074	1.852	0.1008

Query 13.4:
Use the information in Queries 12.4 and 12.6, concerning women with MBAs and management and administrative jobs, to test for a positive relationship between the proportion of women among MBAs and the proportion of women managers. Is there a difference in your conclusion for a probability of a Type I error of 1 percent versus 5 percent?

Answer:
The null and alternative hypotheses are

$$H_O\text{: } \beta = 0\text{, the two proportions are not related}$$

$$H_A\text{: } \beta > 0\text{, the two proportions are positively related}$$

With one degree of freedom, and a probability of a Type I error of 1 percent, the critical t is 31.821,

$$P(t > 31.821 \mid \text{df} = 1) = 0.01$$

With one degree of freedom, and a probability of a Type I error of 5 percent, the critical t is 6.314,

$$P(t > 6.314 \mid \text{df} = 1) = 0.05$$

The calculated t ratio is

$$t = \frac{b - \beta_O}{s_b} = \frac{0.5929 - 0}{.00545/\sqrt{.0449}} = 23$$

At the 1 percent Type I error level, the calculated t is less than the critical t, so H_O cannot be rejected. At the 5 percent Type I error level, the calculated t is greater than the critical t, so H_O can be rejected. Our conclusion is sensitive to the probability of a Type I error. Because the $P(t > 23 \mid df = 1) = 0.0276$, we can say that there is a statistically significant positive relationship between the proportion of women among MBAs and the proportion of women in management down to the 0.0276 Type I error level.

QUERY 13.5:
Using the EXCEL printout in Query 12.8, at what level of statistical significance is shoe lace length related to number of eyelets? Does it make a difference if the answer to this question is viewed as the outcome of a one-tailed or a two-tailed test?

ANSWER:
The EXCEL computer program and most other statistical programs automatically produce *p*-values for two-tailed tests. For the slope of the regression of lace length on number of eyelets in Query 12.8, the *p*-value is "6.3E-07" or 0.00000063, which is the p-value for a test of

$$H_O: \beta = 0 \text{ versus } H_A: \beta \neq 0$$

The one-tailed *p*-value for a test of

$$H_O: \beta = 0 \text{ versus } H_A: \beta > 0$$

is calculated from the reported two-tailed *p*-value to be 3.15E-07 or 0.000000315. In either a one or two-tailed test, the number of eyelets is a highly significant predictor of lace length.

EXERCISES

13.7 Use the data on subjective and objective probabilities given in Exercise 12.31 to answer the following questions.

a. Test the hypothesis that there is a one-for-one tradeoff between subjective and objective probabilities.

b. What are the practical implications of your test in part a?

13.8 Use the following computer printout in parts a through d.

INDEX	NAME	MEAN	STD.DEV
INDEP.VAR.:	x	13.5000	8.3832
DEP.VAR.:	y	21.0000	12.8668

VAR.	REGRESSION COEFFICIENT	STD. ERROR	T(DF= 8)	PROB.
x	.7747	.4685	1.654	.13678
CONSTANT	10.5415			

STD. ERROR OF EST. = 11.7813 r SQUARED = .2548 r = .5047

ANALYSIS OF VARIANCE TABLE

SOURCE	SUM OF SQUARES	D.F.
REGRESSION	379.6047	1
RESIDUAL	1110.3953	8
TOTAL	1490.0000	9

a. What is the magnitude of the standard error of estimation, and how was it calculated?
b. How was $t = 1.654$ calculated?
c. Explain the relationship between $t = 1.654$ and prob = .13678.
d. Test H_0: $\beta = 0$ versus H_A: $\beta > 0$, at the 0.01 significance level.

13.9 Use the following computer printout in parts a through d.

Dependent Variable is	y
Number of observations is	6
Mean of Dependent Variable . . .	2.00000
Std. Dev. of Dep.	.89443
Std. Error of Regression	.29277
Sum of Squared Residuals	.34286
R-Squared	.91429

Var.	Coefficient	Std.Error	T-ratio	(Sig.Lvl)	Mean of X	Std.Dev.of X
INTERCEPT	3.14286	.2119	14.832	(.00012)	1.0000	.00000
X	−.457143	.6999E-01	−6.532	(.00284)	2.5000	1.8708

a. What is the magnitude of the coefficient of determination, and how was it calculated?
b. How was the standard error of the coefficient of X calculated?
c. Explain the relationship between $t = 14.832$ and the significance level = .00012.
d. Test H_0: $\beta = 0$ versus H_A: $\beta < 0$, at $\alpha = 0.01$.

13.10 Articles in the business press periodically discuss the relationship between the percentage drop in industrial output and the peak in jobless rates. On the following page are data on this relationship for the past 12 slumps in business activity.

Period	% Drop Industrial Output	Peak Jobless Rate
1929 – 1933	53.4	24.9
1937 – 1938	32.4	20.0
1945 – 1945	38.3	4.3
1948 – 1949	9.9	7.9
1953 – 1954	10.0	6.1
1957 – 1958	14.3	7.5
1960 – 1961	7.2	7.1
1969 – 1970	8.1	6.1
1973 – 1975	14.7	9.0
1980 – 1980	8.7	7.8
1981 – 1982	12.3	10.7
1991 – 1992*	10.0	7.0

a. Calculate the least squares regression line for the jobless rate (y) as explained by the percentage drop in industrial output (x).

b. Is there a significant relationship between the jobless rate and the drop in industrial output?

13.11 Below are data on corporate sales and the amount spent on advertising (both measured in $1,000) by different firms. Can sales be explained by advertising in a significant way?

Sales	Advertising Expense
899	61
1354	71
957	62
910	61
890	59
1055	64
1111	77
1234	79

13.12 For the data on populations in the 25 cities reported in Exercise 12.35, is there a significant change in populations between the two years? How does your answer here differ from the test of differences in means in Chapter 10? How does it differ from your answer in Exercise 12.35?

13.13 An article in *The Wall Street Journal* (February 24, 1992) stated that "for Biotech (companies), pure genius isn't enough." The article quoted Dr. Wilkerson as saying that companies must show that "their technologies work and that they can successfully turn them into effective products." On the following page are data on the number of drugs companies have in clinical trials and the number of proprietary drugs for humans on the market.

a. What is the relationship between the number of drugs in trial and the number actually in the market?

b. Is this relationship statistically significant? At what level?

	Number of Drugs in	
	Clinical Trials	Market for Human Use
Amgen	8	2
Genentech	10	3
Chiron	14	3
Centocor	5	0
Synergen	3	0
Genzyme	1	1
Biogen	3	2
Gensia	1	0
Immunex	4	2
Alliance	2	0
US Bioscience	4	1
Zoma	6	0
Medimmune	1	1
Affymax	0	0
Immune Response	1	0
Genetics Institute	3	1
Molecular Biosystems	0	0
Cytogen	1	0
Immunomedics	2	0
Liposome Co.	3	0

13.14 Explain what happens to the magnitude of s_b and $t = (b - \beta)/s_b$ as n is increased. What are the implications of this for hypothesis testing?

13.13 Violations of the Assumptions

The least squares regression lines have desired properties for making inferences about the underlying population. If Assumptions (13.5) through (13.10) are true then the least squares estimators provide unbiased estimates of the population parameters, minimum variance estimates, and normally distributed sampling distributions of the estimators. The problem in assessing the correctness of these assumptions is that they deal primarily with the population error term ε_i, which we never observe. We only see the residuals from a least squares regression, e_i.

Serial Correlation
A situation in which the disturbance term in one time period is related to the disturbance term in another.

From the residuals we try to infer characteristics of the distribution of ε_i. For example, values of y do not occur randomly around the regression line in Figure 13.3. For higher and lower unemployment rates the inflation rates tend to be above the regression line (positive residuals). For mid-level unemployment rates the inflation rates tend to be below the regression line (negative residuals). If residuals occur randomly around the regression line, there is no sequence in the residuals. For data collected at fixed time intervals, it is not unusual for the residuals in one time period to be related to those in the next, **serial correlation**.

FIGURE 13.10 Scatterplots of Earning and Age

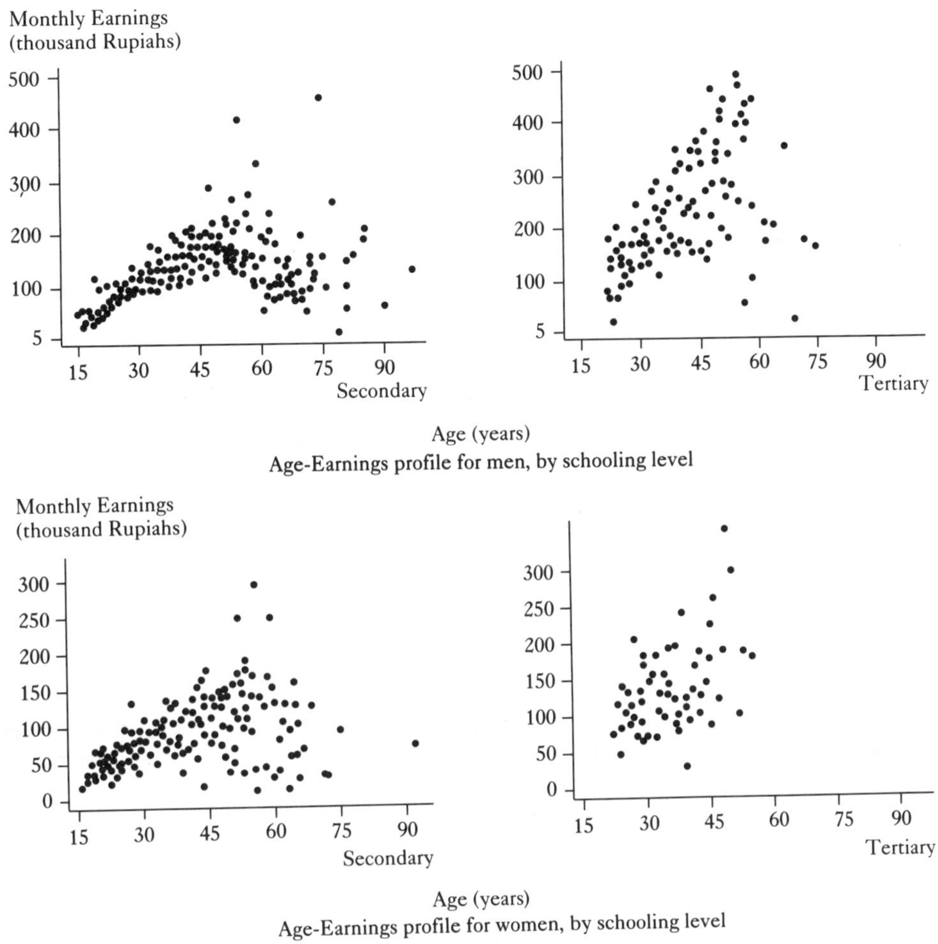

Source: Anil Deolalikar. "Gender Differences in the Return to Schooling and in School Enrollment Rates in Indonesia," *Journal of Human Resources,* Fall 1993, pp. 920-921.

As an example of residual analysis, consider the four scatterplots in Figure 13.10, reprinted from an article in the *Journal of Human Resources* (Fall 1993). Only the age-earnings plot in the lower right corner, for women with tertiary schooling, would produce random-looking residuals around a least squares regression line. [For this time denominated data, however, there may still be a question of whether the residuals for one period (the difference between actual and predicted earnings at age 30, for example) are related to residuals in subsequent periods (at age 31 for example), which would imply a violation of Assumption (13.8).] The other three plots all suggest that the variability in the errors increases with age, which is a violation of Assumption (13.7) and referred to as "**heteroscedasticity**." The top two scatterplots for men also show marked curvatures in the data that are not best represented by a straight regression line, which are violations of Assumptions (13.5) and (13.9). For all but the lower right scatterplot, the residuals suggest that the population error terms may not be normally distributed, Assumption (13.10).

Heteroscedasticity
A situation in which the variance of ε is not fixed.

Entire books are devoted to the identification of residual patterns, statistical tests for randomness, and alternative estimation methods when the least squares estimators are called into question. For now, it is sufficient to recognize that the appearance of patterns in the residuals can cast a shadow of doubt on the validity of least squares estimators. A violation of one of the (13.5) through (13.10) assumptions may imply that the least squares estimators are not measuring the desired population parameters or are measuring them with too much variability. On the other hand, a violation may not be severe and have little consequence. More detailed discussion of the issues surrounding the least squares assumptions are the focus of subsequent courses in econometrics.

EXERCISES

13.15 Use EXCEL to obtain a scatterplot of the data on school days and exam scores in Query 12.1. From your scatterplot can you infer anything about the correctness of Assumption (13.7)?

13.16 An economist states that a \$100 investment in a new type of portfolio can be expected to yield the following returns over a 10-year period. (Note: at the time of the investment, year 0, the investment is worth \$100; at the end of the first year, it is worth \$110; at the end of year 2, it is worth \$120, and so on.)

Year:	0	1	2	3	4	5	6	7	8	9	10
Return:	100	110	120	130	150	160	180	200	215	240	265

To calculate the rate of return, a financial analyst obtains the following regression results, where y = return and x = year.

Yr	Return
0	100
1	110
2	120
3	130
4	150
5	160
6	180
7	200
8	215
9	240
10	265

Regression Statistics	
Multiple R	0.9900
R Square	0.9802
Adjusted R Sq	0.9780
Standard Error	8.1340
Observations	11

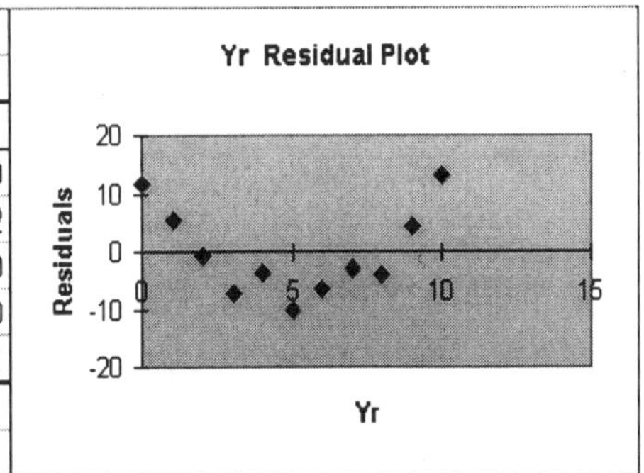

ANOVA

	df	*SS*	*MS*	*F*
Regression	1	29454.54545	29454.54545	445.1908397
Residual	9	595.4545455	66.16161616	
Total	10	30050		

	Coefficients	*Standard Error*	*t Stat*	*P-value*
Intercept	88.1818	4.588183009	19.21933323	1.28958E-08
Yr	16.3636	0.775544478	21.09954596	5.66043E-09

The financial analyst concludes that "this regression fits well, because the correlation coefficient is very high, and that for each additional year the investment will return a statistically significant $16.36." Comment on the validity of this statement.

13.17 The *1980 Census* suggests that electrical engineers could expect to earn the following amounts at the indicated ages.

Age:	30	40	50	60	70
Earnings:	$22,600	$28,284	$31,193	$31,505	$33,357

a. Fit a least squares regression to the dependent variable earnings and independent variable age; report the regression equation and all relevant statistics.

b. Construct a scatterplot of the data, and plot your regression line; show your five residuals.

c. Comment on the fit of your regression equation and the scatterplot's implications for the correctness of the least squares assumptions.

13.18 Draw the x-y scatterplot for the year (x) and return (y) in Exercise 13.16. How does the residual plot in Exercise 13.16 relate to your scatterplot here in Exercise 13.18?

13.19 Below is a relatively famous data set constructed by F.J. Anscombe, *American Statistician*, February 1973.

	x	y_1	y_2	y_3	x_4	y_4
1	10.0	8.04	9.14	7.46	8.0	6.58
2	8.0	6.95	8.14	6.77	8.0	5.76
3	13.0	7.58	8.74	12.74	8.0	7.71
4	9.0	8.81	8.77	7.11	8.0	8.84
5	11.0	8.33	9.26	7.81	8.0	8.47
6	14.0	9.96	8.10	8.84	8.0	7.04
7	6.0	7.24	6.13	6.08	8.0	5.25
8	4.0	4.26	3.10	5.39	19.0	12.50
9	12.0	10.84	9.13	8.15	8.0	5.56
10	7.0	4.82	7.26	6.42	8.0	7.91
11	5.0	5.68	4.74	5.73	8.0	6.89

a. Obtain the descriptive statistics for each of these six variables.

b. Estimate the intercept and slope for four simple regressions of y_1 on x, y_2 on x, y_3 on x, and y_4 on x_4.

c. What are the unique features of this data set?

13.20 Use a computer program and the Anscombe data set in Exercise 13.19 to get printouts of the scatterplots and fitted regression lines for the four regressions: y_1 on x, y_2 on x, y_3 on x, and y_4 on x_4. Which of the four scatterplots are consistent with the assumptions required to make an inference about the parameters in the population model $y = \beta_1 + \beta_2 x + \epsilon$? For each scatterplot, explain which, if any, of the assumptions may be violated.

13.21 For which, if any, of the scatterplots in Exercise 12.44 would Assumptions (13.5) through (13.10) hold?

13.15 Concluding Comments

Chapter 12 introduced least squares and correlation to represent and measure the strength of the relationship between paired observations in a sample. In this chapter, the techniques of classical regression analysis were extended to estimate and test population parameters. This process of statistical inference requires the building of a model to represent the population. The correctness of the assumptions that make up the model is critical to the internal validity of the inference process. As shown, analysis of the residuals of the regression provides a means for assessing the appropriateness of those assumptions.

The value of any statistical technique rests on its use in making correct inferences about the population. For predictive success, classical regression analysis involves more than just a determination of the statistical significance of an individual coefficient; consideration must be given to the overall fit of the regression, as well. The sample data and sample regression must conform to the assumptions of the population model.

The next chapter on regression analysis extends the simple regression model presented in this chapter to those involving multiple independent variables. An emphasis is placed on the building of models that are consistent with the underlying theory and sample data.

CHAPTER EXERCISES

13.22 Answer true or false to the following; if false state why.

a. The least squares estimator b is the most efficient estimator of β if the standard error of b is smaller than all alternative estimators of β.

b. If the $E(\varepsilon) = 0$ and x and ε are not related, then the least squares estimator b is an unbiased estimator of β.

c. As the standard error of b gets larger, the margin of error gets larger.

d. If a 95 percent confidence interval for the expected value of y, at $x = 20$, is $10 < E(y\,|\,x = 20) < 30$, then there is a 0.95 probability that the mean of y is between 10 and 30, for $x = 20$.

e. If a 95 percent prediction interval for an individual value of y is 20 ± 9, as given in the SAS computer printout

X	PREDICTED VALUE	LOWER 95% CL INDIVIDUAL	UPPER 95% CL INDIVIDUAL
4.0000	20.0000	11.0000	29.0000

then a 95 percent confidence interval for the expected value of y, at $x = 4$, could be $10 < E(y\,|\,x = 20) < 30$.

f. If a researcher states that there is a significant statistical relationship between x and y, then we know that the null hypothesis of no relationship is rejected irrespective of the α level specified.

g. The estimator b is a random variable for which $b = \beta$.

h. A 90 percent confidence interval for the expected value of y, at the mean of x, is more precise (narrower) than at extreme x values.

i. Hypotheses tests of the least squares slope are based on the t distribution, which requires that the sampling distribution of b be distributed normally.

j. The sampling distribution of b will be distributed normally if the population disturbance term ϵ is distributed normally.

k. The sole purpose of regression analysis is prediction of the dependent variable.

13.23 Query 12.1 provides data on the days spent in school per year and average math scores on exams administered to students around the world.

a. At the 0.05 Type I error level, is there a relationship between days in school (x) and math scores (y)?

b. Construct a 95 percent confidence interval for the slope.

c. How does the confidence interval in part b relate to the hypothesis test in part a?

13.24 For the data in Exercise 12.5, use your calculations from Exercise 12.17 to test if there is a relationship between the independent and dependent variables. State the null and alternative hypothesis, and test at the 0.05 Type I error level.

13.25 Use the computer printout and your answers in Exercise 12.30 to determine a 95 percent confidence interval for the expected value of y at the sample mean value of x. Construct a 95 percent confidence interval for the expected value of y at $x + 2s_x$; why is the second interval wider than the first?

13.26 Show how the "t Stat" and "P-value" for the coefficient of the X Variable were calculated in the EXCEL printout given in Exercise 13.16.

13.27 For the data set in Exercise 12.9, test if there is positive relationship between x and y, at the 0.01 Type I error level.

13.28 Use the information in Exercise 12.10 to calculate the standard error of the regression and the standard error of b. How could you use these two quantities?

13.29 Using the data set in Exercises 12.10, test whether the x and y relationship is significant at the 0.05 Type I error level.

13.30 Using the data in Exercise 12.14, for a candidate who receives 1,200 votes in the primary, construct a 95 percent confidence interval estimate of the expected number of votes this candidate will receive in the general election. State what this confidence interval says in a manner sufficiently clear that even the candidate can understand its interpretation.

13.31 Using the data on T-bill rates and price inflation and your computer output from Exercise 12.15, construct a 90 percent confidence interval for the expected inflation rate in the next year, if the T-bill rate this year is 7 percent?

13.32 Use the data on horse speed and jockey experience in Exercise 12.34 to answer the following questions.

a. Test the hypothesis that there is a significant relationship between horse speed and jockey experience, at the 10 percent Type I error level.

b. For a jockey with three years of experience, what is a 90 percent confidence interval for the mean horse speed?

c. For a jockey with three years of experience, what is a 90 percent prediction interval for an individual horse speed?

13.33 At the 0.05 Type I error level, is there a statistically significant relationship between excess returns and the book-to-market ratios in Exercise 12.40?

13.34 At what Type I error level is there a statistically significant relationship between portfolio returns and S&P market returns in Exercise 12.41?

13.35 Using the data in Exercise 12.53 on percentage of females in management positions and maximum weekly pay would you conclude that Publix Supermarkets is discriminating against women in salary determination? Explain.

13.36 Following are data on average annual percent changes in employment (employ) and industrial production (product), over the 1982–1988 period, for the United States and other G-7 nations. To assess the relationship between "employ" and "product," least squares regression results are also provided.

	employ	product
Canada	2.40%	5.90%
France	–.10	1.40
West Germany	.50	2.30
Italy	.50	2.40
Japan	1.10	4.70
United Kingdom	1.40	3.10
United States	2.40	4.90

Source: *Economic Report of the President*, February 1990, p. 45.

NAME	MEAN	STD.DEV.
product	3.5286	1.6520
employ	1.1714	.9656

VAR.	REGRESSION COEFFICIENT	STD. ERROR	T(DF= 5)	PROB.
product	.5317	.1086	4.895	.00449
CONSTANT	–.7046			

STD. ERROR OF EST. = .4395 r SQUARED = .8274 r = .9096

ANALYSIS OF VARIANCE TABLE

SOURCE	SUM OF SQUARES	D.F.	MEAN SQUARE	F RATIO	PROB.
REGRESSION	4.6286	1	4.6286	23.964	4.493E-03
RESIDUAL	.9657	5	.1931		

a. What does the slope of the regression line indicate?

b. What can be concluded about the population relationship from this slope coefficient?

13.37 For the regression in Exercise 13.36, if the percentage change in production is 3.10 percent, the predicted change in employment is approximately __________.

13.38 From this computer printout for Exercise 13.36 we know that the total sum of squared deviations (TSS) is__________________ and the Error sum of squares (ErrorSS) is ______________. The coefficient of determination is __________, which indicates what?

13.39 A *Wall Street Journal* (September 25, 1992) article, "Female Enrollment Falls in Many Top M.B.A. Programs," showed the percentage of women at these schools falling to an average of 25.3 percent. Use the information in Queries 12.4 and 12.6 about the percentage of women earning MBA degrees and the percentage of women in management and administrative jobs to obtain the point estimate and the 90 percent confidence intervals for the expected proportion of women in management and administrative jobs, if 25.3 percent of the graduating MBAs are women.

13.40 An article in *The Wall Street Journal* (October 12, 1992) reported the average compensation of CEOs in seven countries. Exercise 12.42 reported information on CEO compensation and number of headquartered companies in seven countries for the world's 100 largest public companies. Is there a statistically significant relationship between CEO compensation (y) and the number of headquartered companies in each country (x)?

13.41 Exercise 12.46 provides data on car weight and mileage. For a car of 2,910 pounds, what is the 95 percent prediction interval for gas mileage? Why is the reporting of this prediction interval superior to the point estimate calculated in Exercise 12.46?

13.42 Use a computer program and the data in the ASCII file "EX13-42.PRN," to estimate the relationship between time in the emergency room (Y) and the age of the 196 patients (X). Is there a significant relationship between these two variables? What are the practical implications of your findings?

13.43 Below are the data that accompanied a *Business Week* (June 7, 1993) article on economic growth. At the 5 percent Type I error level, is there a significant relationship between the inflation rate (y) and the unemployment rate (x)?

	Annual Average for 1982–1992			
	Inflation Rate %	Unemployment Rate %	Misery Index %	Index of Political Stability*
Spain	7.6	18.7	26.3	4
Greece	18.0	7.6	25.6	4
Portugal	14.9	6.6	21.5	4
Italy	7.4	10.1	17.5	4
Britain	5.5	9.6	15.0	2
Belgium	3.5	10.9	14.4	3
Australia	6.4	7.8	14.2	2
Canada	4.3	9.8	14.1	2
France	4.4	9.6	14.0	3
New Zealand	7.9	6.1	14.0	2
Denmark	4.2	9.4	13.6	3
Finland	5.3	5.8	11.0	2
United States	3.8	7.1	10.9	2
Netherlands	1.9	8.7	10.6	3
Norway	5.7	3.7	9.4	2
Sweden	6.7	2.4	9.1	2
Germany	2.2	6.0	8.2	2
Austria	3.0	3.5	6.5	2
Japan	1.8	2.5	4.3	1
Switzerland	3.1	0.9	4.0	1

*Index Value: 1(most stable) to 4(least stable) based on presence of coalition government, dictatorship, representation of extreme political parties, and political conflict.
Data: DRI/McGraw-Hill, OECD, Business Week, Alberto Alesina, Harvard University.

13.44 The *Business Week* article cited in the Exercise 13.43 stated that as political stability increased, the well-being of the country increased. Based on these *BW* data, is there a significant negative relationship between the misery index (y) and political stability (x)? At what Type I error level?

13.45 Based on the data in Exercise 12.47, if someone reports adjusted-gross income of \$100,000 and deducts \$20,000 for other taxes paid, would you suspect him or her of underreporting income or overreporting tax deductions? Explain, using a 95 percent prediction interval.

13.46 Use the income and tax data in Exercise 12.47 to determine if there is a statistically significant relationship between adjusted-gross income and deducted taxes. Test at the 0.01 Type I error level.

13.47 The data in the computer ASCII file "EX13-47.PRN," is from *Car and Driver* (April 1993). As described in Exercise 12.49, the first column identifies the car tested and the issue of *Car and Driver* in which the test appeared. The second column is the estimated price of the car tested. The third and fourth columns are 0 to 60 mph and 1/4 mile time in seconds. The fifth column is top speed. The sixth column is 70 to 0 braking distance in feet. EPA estimated fuel economy is in the seventh column. Finally, in column eight, road-holding ability (measured as g force) is provided as obtained from a 300-foot skid-pad. Which of the variables (which you might name TO60, quarter, top, braking, fuel, hold) has the highest significance level in explaining the car price?

13.48 Exercise 12.50 cited a *Wall Street Journal* article in which Song Won Sohn stated that there was a negative relationship between bond yield and the Dow. Use your monthly data and regression estimate to test whether this relationship exists at the 0.01 Type I error level.

13.49 An article in *The Wall Street Journal* (October 29, 1993), titled "Older Drivers Pose Growing Risk on Roads," provided the following data on the relationship between number of drivers, by approximate age, involved in fatal accidents for every 100 million miles driven. A representative of the American Association of Retired Persons (AARP) fit the following regression to these data using LOTUS 1-2-3 and concluded that there was not a significant relationship between age and involvement in fatal accidents. Comment on the appropriateness of this analysis and conclusion.

AGE	MIDPT	FATAL
15 TO	17.5	9.0
20 TO	22.5	3.7
25 TO	27.5	2.9
30 TO	32.5	2.1
35 TO	37.5	1.9
40 TO	42.5	1.7
45 TO	47.5	1.7
50 TO	52.5	1.8
55 TO	57.5	1.8
60 TO	62.5	2.2
65 TO	67.5	2.5
70 TO	72.5	3.3
75 TO	77.5	4.5
80 TO	82.5	7.9
85 +	87.5	14.0

Regression Output:

Constant	1.220416
Std Err of Y Est	3.457199
R Squared	0.116930
No. of Observations	15
Degrees of Freedom	13
X Coefficient(s)	0.054214
Std Err of Coef.	0.041321

Where X is MIDPT
Y is FATAL

13.50 Exercise 12.52 provided data for the analysis of the 1993 contested election in Pennsylvania's Second State Senatorial District in Philadelphia. Republican Marks received more votes in machine voting than his Democrat opponent, Stinson, but in absentee ballots Stinson received many more votes than Marks. Use the data and the analysis in Exercise 12.52 in the following questions.

a. At the 0.05 Type I error level, is there a significant relationship between the difference in absentee votes and machine votes?
b. Construct a 95 percent prediction interval for the absentee votes in the contested election of 1993.
c. Based on your result in parts a and b do you believe that there was fraud in this 1993 election?

(Note: Questions for analysis of the voting issue are continued in Exercise 14.49.)

13.51 Mark Kaiser, Paul Speckman, and John Jones, "Statistical Models for Limited Nutrient Relations in Inland Waters," *Journal of the American Statistical Association* (June 1994), p. 411, provided the following four scatterplots and ordinary least squares regression lines to describe the relationship between chlorophyll (y) and phosphorus (x) in two different samples. Each of the top panels are based on logarithmic transformations of the original data shown in the respective lower panels. What does the logarithmic transformation of each of the variables accomplish? Does the log transformation of both y and x appear to work better for either the left-hand or right-hand panels? Explain.

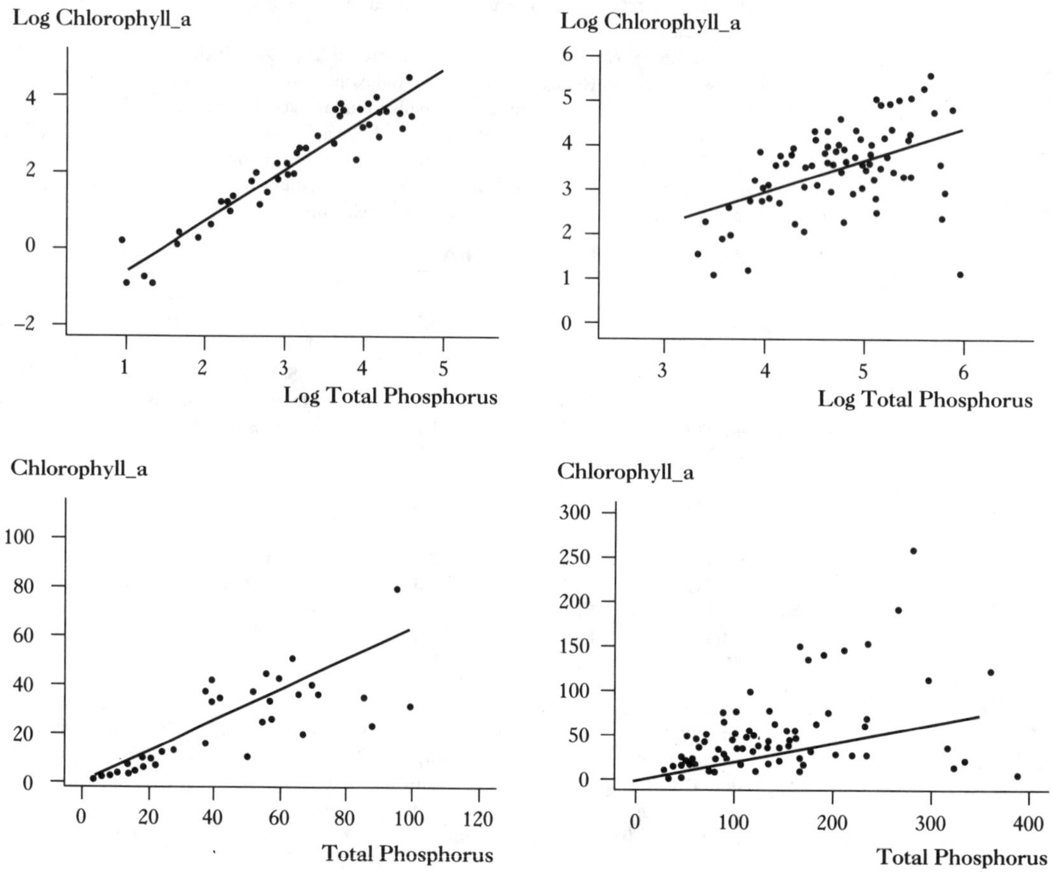

13.52 Citing the United States Bureau of Labor Statistics data shown in the scatterplot below, Dean Witter InterCapital Inc. in a 1997 "Money Talk" newsletter, stated that "a three percent CPI inflation rate would suggest a P/E of just under 17 percent ... Taking into account the 'standard deviation' of the relationship (a statistical range measuring variability), which in this case is a little over ±3, a P/E of 20 or of 14 would still not be unusual." Comment on whether the assumption required to make an inference from the least squares regression line to a population are fulfilled. Comment on using "the standard deviation of the relationship" (i.e., the standard error of the regression) as the soul measure of variability around the regression line in making predictions or forecasts about population relationships. How are forecasts of the P/E ratio influenced by the distance from the mean of the inflation rate?

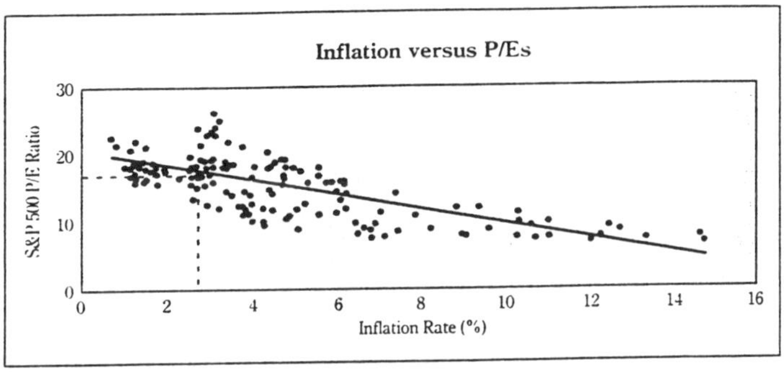

ACADEMIC REFERENCE

Fischer, Stanley and Rudiger Dornbusch. *Introduction to Microeconomics.* New York: McGraw-Hill, 1983.

FORMULAS

- Deterministic linear equation

$$y^* = \alpha + \beta x$$

where y^* is the dependent variable, and x is the independent variable

- Stochastic linear equation

$$y = \alpha + \beta x + \varepsilon$$

where y is the dependent variable,
x is the independent variable, and
ε is a random disturbance term

- Expected value of y, given x

$$E(y|x) = y^* = \alpha + \beta x$$

- Expected value of ε is zero

$$E(\varepsilon) = 0$$

- Expected value of sample intercept a

$$E(a) = \alpha$$

- Expected value of sample slope b

$$E(b) = \beta$$

- Variance of the residuals

$$s_e^2 = \frac{\sum_{i=1}^{n}\left(y_i - \hat{y}_i\right)^2}{n-2} = \frac{\sum_{i=1}^{n} e_i^2}{n-2}$$

- Variance of residuals

$$s_e^2 = \frac{\text{ErrorSS}}{n-2}$$

- $(1 - \alpha)$ percent confidence interval for $E\,(y|x)$

$$\hat{y} \pm t_{\alpha/2} s_e \sqrt{\frac{1}{n} + \frac{\left(x^* - \bar{x}\right)^2}{\sum_{i=1}^{n}\left(x - \bar{x}_i\right)^2}}$$

- $(1 - \alpha)$ percent prediction interval for an individual value of y

$$\hat{y} \pm t_{\alpha/2} s_e \sqrt{\frac{1}{n} + \frac{\left(x^* - \bar{x}\right)^2}{\sum_{i=1}^{n}\left(x - \bar{x}_i\right)^2} + 1}$$

- Standard error of the sampling distribution of b

$$s_b = \sqrt{\frac{s_e^2}{\sum_{i=1}^{n}\left(x_i - \bar{x}\right)^2}}$$

- t ratio for the slope of a regression line

$$t = \frac{b - E(b)}{s_b}$$

CHAPTER 14

MULTIPLE REGRESSION

*Figures speak
and when they do
courts listen.*

Brooks v. Beto 366 F.2d
(5th Cir. 1966)

14.1 Introduction

Applications of the two variable linear model are limited, if for no reason other than real world phenomena typically involve more than one explanatory factor. The two variable model must be extended to multiple regressors to handle problems of the following types.

- In part, a product's selling price is believed to be a function of research and development expenses, production costs, and advertising expense. The question: How important is each of these explanatory variables in determining selling price?
- The relationship between inflation and unemployment observed in the 1960s may have been affected by events in the early 1970s (e.g., Nixon's price controls, the Arab oil embargo, spread of unemployment benefits) and again in the early 1980s when interest rates skyrocketed. How might the long-term Phillips curve best be estimated over the past 35 years?
- Real estate appraisers claim that the selling price of a house depends on its location, square footage, age, construction material, and condition. How well do these factors jointly explain selling price?

Multiple Regression A method of regression analysis that uses more than one explanatory variable to predict values of a single dependent variable.

All of the statistical properties and assumptions developed in the previous two chapters may be transferred directly to applications of **multiple regression;** there are only a few new concepts to learn. Unfortunately, the computational formulas of the simple two variable model cannot be extended easily. Luckily, in this day of inexpensive computers and widely available regression programs, there is no need to burden students with these cumbersome hand-calculator routines.

Only the practical use of multiple regression analysis is emphasized here. Practical applications require that we have an awareness of how data are displayed for a multiple regression analysis, but a computer can do the calculations without our knowing the formulas employed. Thus, in this chapter we need emphasize only the

- specification of the population model and the sample regression used in a least squares estimation of the parameters of the multiple independent variables;
- testing of possible population relationship between the dependent variable and the independent variables;
- estimation of the expected values of the dependent variable at certain values of the independent variables;
- prediction of a certain value of the dependent variable for given values of the independent variables; and
- construction of confidence intervals for the expected value and the predicted value of the dependent variable based on the values of the independent variables.

14.2 The Case of Equal Pay

The United States Equal Pay Acts of 1964 and 1971 are based on the principle that a person's race or sex may not be used to establish merit, and that race or sex cannot be used to justify lack of performance and a lower salary. Remedies to sex and race discrimination have attempted to put the victim in the situation she or he would be in had there been no disparate treatment. Multiple regression has come to play an important part in assessing the fairness of the salary determination processes in both the private and public sectors of the economy. These regressions are used to detect the presence of discrimination and, if present, to estimate the magnitude of the remedy.

Although corporate executives in the United States talk about basing salaries on performance, in actual practice an employee's seniority and entry-level position may prove more important. Paul Regan, a senior vice president of Corning Inc., for example, in a *Wall Street Journal* (September 10, 1991) article on the lack of merit pay in private industry, said, "If you tell me the date someone joined a company and the starting pay, I'll tell you within $500 what (he or she) makes." This suggests that Regan had the following functional relationship in mind for the salary determination process.

$$\text{predicted salary} = \text{function(starting year, starting salary)}$$

Regan did not specify a functional form. It appears that he had in mind a multiple regression of salary on starting year and starting salary, with no explanatory variables needed for individual performance. He was confident that the error in his prediction would not exceed $500 of a person's current salary.

The use of regression analysis to study salary determination in the public sector has a slightly longer history than that in private industry. Mary Gray and Elizabeth Scott (*Academe,* May 1980, p. 180), for example, suggested a multiple regression equation to explain the salaries of college faculty. When updated for the current salaries of the men in an academic department, it corresponds to:

$$\hat{y} = 43000 + 1160x_2 + 250x_3$$

where $\hat{y}$ is the predicted salary (in dollars) of a man, x_2 is the number of years since he received the Ph.D. degree, and x_3 is the number of published books he has authored. As was the case with simple regression, the sample form fit by Gray and Scott indicates that at least implicitly they must have had the following population salary model in mind:

$$y = \beta_1 + \beta_2 x_2 + \beta_3 x_3 + \varepsilon$$

where y is a person's actual salary and ε is the population disturbance or error term that reflects the random chance factors in determining a person's salary. We do not know the population parameters β_1, β_2, and β_3. We only have the point estimates 43000, 1160, and 250.

According to Gray and Scott's sample regression, if a man in this department has a five-year-old Ph.D. and one publication, then he is predicted to receive $49,050.

$$\hat{y} = 43000 + 1160x_2 + 250x_3 = 43000 + 1160(5) + 250(1) = 49050 \qquad (14.1)$$

If a woman with like x_2 and x_3 values earned only $47,725, then, according to Gray and Scott's analysis, she is underpaid by $1,325. The question, however, is whether such a demonstration proves that a person's sex is being used in the determination of salaries. That is, is there a difference between the population models used to determine male and female salaries that is attributable solely to gender?

14.3 Interpretation of Coefficients and the Prediction of Y

The first term on the right-hand side of Equation (14.1) is the y intercept. This y intercept of 43000 is represented in Figure 14.1, panel a, as the point at which the regression line crosses the y axis. It indicates that a man who has just earned a Ph.D. degree ($x_2 = 0$) and has no publications ($x_3 = 0$) has a predicted salary of \$43,000.

The line in Figure 14.1, panel a, shows the relationship between the predicted salary of males and different vintage Ph.D.'s, given that the males have never published. A male who received his Ph.D. one year ago ($x_2 = 1$), but who has no publications ($x_3 = 0$), is predicted to have a salary of \$44,160. A male who received his Ph.D. two years ago ($x_2 = 2$), but has no publications ($x_3 = 0$), is predicted to have a salary of \$45,320, and so on. For each of these one-year increases in x_2, the predicted salary rises by \$1,160. Thus, the slope coefficient 1160 indicates that a one-unit increase in x_2 is associated with a \$1,160 increase in the predicted salary, holding x_3 constant.

An increase in publications (x_3) from 0 to 1 raises the predicted salary from \$44,160 to \$44,410 for a male who received his Ph.D. degree one year ago ($x_2 = 1$). For someone who received his Ph.D. two years ago ($x_2 = 2$), the predicted salary rises from \$45,320 to \$45,570 when he publishes a book (x_3 rises from 0 to 1). The implication for salaries of a change in x_3 from 0 to 1 for all values of x_2 is represented in Figure 14.1, panel b, by a move from the lower line to the higher line. At any value of x_2, increasing x_3 from 0 to 1 increases the predicted salary by \$250. Similarly, in panel c, an increase in x_3 from 1 to 2 shows predicted salary rising by \$250, at each value of x_2. Thus, the coefficient 250 indicates that a one-unit increase in x_3 is associated with a \$250 increase in the predicted salary, calculated at any specific value of x_2.

In general, any multiple linear regression that is fit to sample data can be represented as

$$\hat{y} = b_1x_1 + b_2x_2 + b_3x_3 + b_4x_4 + \ldots b_kx_k \tag{14.2}$$

where $\hat{y}$ is the predicted dependent variable,

x_j is the jth independent variable, $j = 1, 2, 3, \ldots k$, and

b_j is the jth coefficient, $j = 1, 2, 3, \ldots k$

Typically, but not always, x_1 is set equal to one so that b_1 is the y intercept. That is, if $x_2 = x_3 \ldots = x_k = 0$, and $x_1 = 1$, $\hat{y}$ is b_1, the regression Equation (14.2) can be written more succinctly as

$$\hat{y} = b_1 + b_2x_2 + b_3x_3 + b_4x_4 + \ldots b_kx_k \tag{14.3}$$

The remaining b's are the slope coefficients: b_2 gives the change in $\hat{y}$ for a one-unit change in x_2, holding all the other x's constant; $\hat{y}$ changes by b_3, for a one-unit change in x_3, holding all the other x's constant, and so on for each of the remaining slope coefficients.

FIGURE 14.1 Interpreting the Regression Line $\hat{y} = 43000 + 1160x_2 + 250x_3$

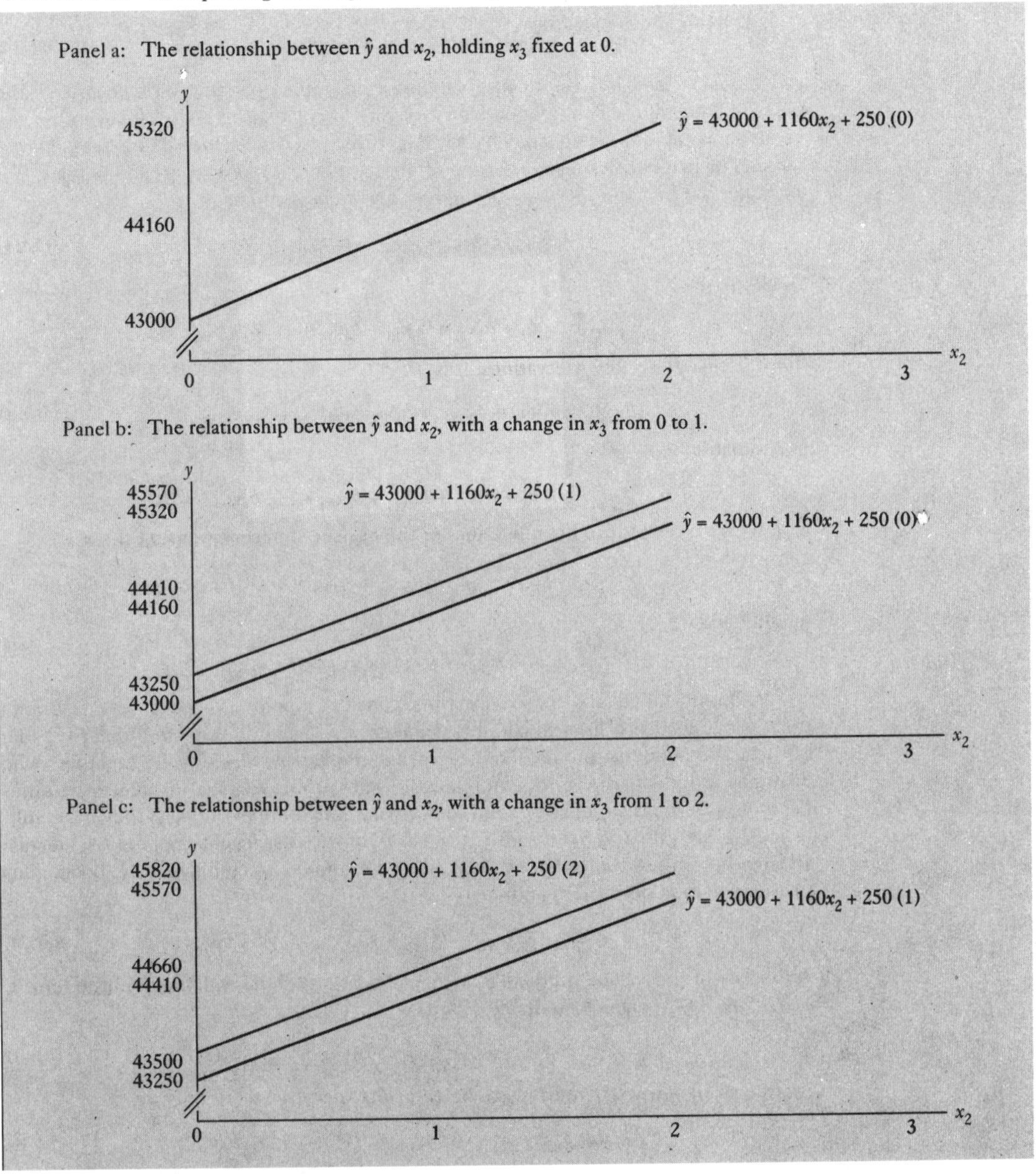

To identify specific observation values on each variable, an i subscript is added to each of the variables in Equation (14.2).

$$\hat{y}_i = b_1x_{i1} + b_2x_{i2} + b_3x_{i3} + b_4x_{i4} + \ldots b_kx_{ik} \tag{14.4}$$

where now x_{ik} indicates the ith observation on the kth independent variable and $\hat{y}_i$ is the ith predicted value of the dependent variable. The actual ith observation on the dependent variable is designated by $\hat{y}_i$. The subscript i is an index that runs from 1 through n. It identifies a set or group of observations on the identified variables. For example, the predicted y value for the first set of observations is

$$\hat{y}_1 = b_1(1) + b_2x_{12} + b_3x_{13} + b_4x_{14} + \ldots b_kx_{1k} \tag{14.5}$$

or alternatively

$$\hat{y}_1 = b_1 + b_2x_{12} + b_3x_{13} + b_4x_{14} + \ldots b_kx_{1k}$$

For the second set of observations, it is

$$\hat{y}_2 = b_1\,(1) + b_2x_{22} + b_3x_{23} + b_4x_{24} + \ldots b_kx_{2k} \tag{14.6}$$

or alternatively

$$\hat{y}_2 = b_1 + b_2x_{22} + b_3x_{23} + b_4x_{24} + \ldots b_kx_{2k}$$

and so on to the last predicted y value for the nth set of observations on the x's

$$\hat{y}_n = b_1(1) + b_2x_{n2} + b_3x_{n3} + b_4x_{n4} + \ldots b_kx_{nk} \tag{14.7}$$

or alternatively

$$\hat{y}_n = b_1 + b_2x_{n2} + b_3x_{n3} + b_4x_{n4} + \ldots b_kx_{nk}$$

To better understand these subscripts, consider a portion of updated data from a trial over alleged sex discrimination in a college at a large midwestern university. One of the academic departments involved in this trial had 10 male faculty members who were not administrators. These individuals, their current salary equivalents, the number of years since they received their Ph.D.'s, and the number of books they have published are identified in Table 14.1. The salary of the first faculty member is \$66,000; 19 years have passed since he received his Ph.D., and he has published one book. This first faculty member's predicted salary is

$$\hat{y}_1 = b_1x_{11} + b_2x_{12} + b_3x_{13} = b_1(1) + b_2(19) + b_3(1) \tag{14.8}$$

The salary of the second individual, with a 17-year-old Ph.D. and one published book, is \$63,500. This person's predicted salary is

$$\hat{y}_2 = b_1x_{21} + b_2x_{22} + b_3x_{23} = b_1(1) + b_2(17) + b_3(1) \tag{14.9}$$

and the predicted salary of the last (10th) faculty member is

$$\hat{y}_{10} = b_1x_{101} + b_2x_{102} + b_3x_{103} = b_1(1) + b_2\,(5) + b_3(2) \tag{14.10}$$

Without knowing the b values, however, no predictions can be made, which is one of the objectives of multiple regression.

Table 14.1 Male Faculty Salaries and Related Data

Individual i	Salary y_i	Constant x_{i1}	Years since Ph.D. x_{i2}	Number of Books x_{i3}
$i = 1$	$y_1 = 66000$	$x_{11} = 1$	$x_{12} = 19$	$x_{13} = 1$
$i = 2$	$y_2 = 63500$	$x_{21} = 1$	$x_{22} = 17$	$x_{23} = 1$
$i = 3$	$y_3 = 56700$	$x_{31} = 1$	$x_{32} = 11$	$x_{33} = 0$
$i = 4$	$y_4 = 56300$	$x_{41} = 1$	$x_{42} = 16$	$x_{43} = 0$
$i = 5$	$y_5 = 54900$	$x_{51} = 1$	$x_{52} = 12$	$x_{53} = 2$
$i = 6$	$y_6 = 52300$	$x_{61} = 1$	$x_{62} = 11$	$x_{63} = 0$
$i = 7$	$y_7 = 50650$	$x_{71} = 1$	$x_{72} = 7$	$x_{73} = 0$
$i = 8$	$y_8 = 50650$	$x_{81} = 1$	$x_{82} = 6$	$x_{83} = 1$
$i = 9$	$y_9 = 50500$	$x_{91} = 1$	$x_{92} = 10$	$x_{93} = 0$
$i = 10$	$y_{10} = 48000$	$x_{101} = 1$	$x_{102} = 5$	$x_{103} = 2$

Query 14.1:

Olson, Frieze and Good, in "The Effects of Job Type and Industry on the Income of Male and Female MBAs" (*Journal of Human Resources*, Fall 1987, p. 536), report the following regression of 1983 salary (y, measured in \$1,000) on the identified variables.

$$\hat{y} = 2.1114x_1 - 5.2544x_2 - 6.1665x_3 + 1.2517x_4 - 2.9075x_5$$

where x_1 is years of full-time work since receiving the MBA,
x_2 is years of part-time work since receiving the MBA degree,
x_3 is years of unemployment since receiving the MBA degree,
x_4 is years of prior full-time work, and
x_5 is one if female and zero if male.

What is the salary effect of unemployment after receipt of the MBA? What is the difference between the predicted salaries of men and women, with identical characteristics? What might be causing this difference?

Answer:

For both men and women, one additional year of unemployment (x_3) after receiving the MBA degree lowers the predicted salary by \$6,166.50. However, the predicted salary of a man is \$2,907.50 higher than for a like woman. This difference may be caused by sex discrimination in the markets for MBA's. Alternatively, it may be the result of differences in occupation selection (e.g., men tending to choose the higher-paying field of accounting), differences in industry selection (e.g., men tending to go into higher paying manufacturing industries), or the tendency of men to have line positions while females occupy staff positions. In addition to these possible systematic differences, the predicted salaries of men and women in this sample may reflect sampling errors (chance occurrences) that resulted in an unusual sample.

Query 14.2:

William Evans and W. Kip Viscusi in "Income Effects and the Value of Health" (*Journal of Human Resources*, Summer 1993), estimated and discussed the following regression (Note: $E - 2 = 10^{-2}$ and $E - 3 = 10^{-3}$):

$$\hat{y} = 246.53 + 2.3E{-}2x_1 - 2.7E - 3x_2$$

where: y is the amount of money an individual will desire as compensation to accept a risk of temporary injury (monetary loss equivalence)

x_1 is yearly income (in thousands of dollars)

x_2 is $x_1^2/10{,}000$

Draw the graph of this equation in the y-x plane. Why did the authors question the estimates of monetary loss for those with incomes above $45,000?

ANSWER:

Calculation of the monetary loss equivalence requires the creation of the x_2 variable as $(x_1)^2/10{,}000$. At $5,000 intervals, it is then calculated in a spreadsheet program as

$$\hat{y} = 246.53 + 0.023x_1 - 0.0027x_2$$

x_1	x_2	$\hat{y}$	x_1	x_2	$\hat{y}$
5000	2500	354.78	35000	122500	720.78
10000	10000	449.53	40000	160000	734.53
15000	22500	530.78	45000	202500	734.78
20000	40000	598.53	50000	250000	721.53
25000	62500	652.78	55000	302500	694.78
30000	90000	693.53	60000	360000	654.53

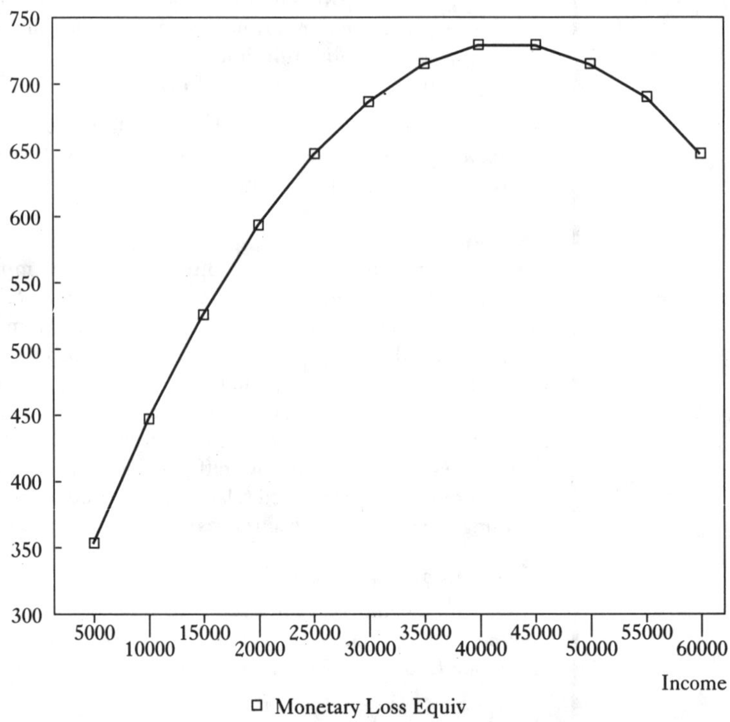

Monetary loss equivalence y is quadratic in income x; it rises with income at a decreasing rate, and then decreases, as most easily seen in the diagram on the previous page. It seems implausible that as incomes rise above $45,000, individuals would desire less compensation for additional risk of injury as their incomes grow. For this reason, predictions for individuals with incomes above $45,000 are not appropriate.

QUERY 14.3:

The lyrics to the theme song of the TV comedy "The Jeffersons" touted the up-scale Eastside addresses of New York City. A potential condominium purchaser is considering a 2,950 square foot Eastside unit. Using *WSJ* data in Query 13.1 and this information on location, what price can you predict for this condominium?

ANSWER:

Unlike Query 13.1, here we will make use of the distinction between Westside and Eastside addresses with a 0 - 1 dummy variable. For the 10 condominium sales (in millions) in New York City in *The Wall Street Journal* (February 28, 1997) we created the "East" variable shown in Chart 14.1, column B. To forecast (or predict) the price of an Eastside condominium the trend command "=TREND(D2:D11, B2:C11, B13:C13,1)" can be used. This command can be entered directly into a cell or accessed through the function wizard following the path "Insert" to "Function" to "Statistical" to "TREND," where the entries for the resulting dialog box appear in Chart 14.1. The predicted price for a 2,950 square foot Eastside condominium is $2,447,246.

CHART 14.1 The Trend Function Command for Forecasting

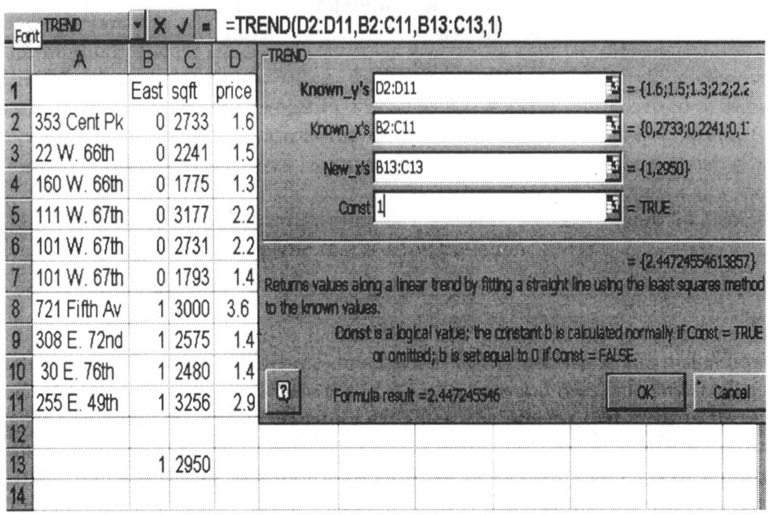

The general form for the TREND function command is

= TREND(y observations, x observations, x* values, constant)

where: "y observations" are the values of y in the sample (D2:D11 in Chart 14.1)

"x observations" are the sequentially ordered columns sample observations on each x to be included (B2:C11 in Chart 14.1)

"x* value" are the set of values for the x's for which the forecast of y is to be made (B13:C13 in Chart 14.1)

"constant" is the yes = 1 or no = 0 attribute for the inclusion of an intercept. As in Chart 14.1, it is typically set at "1 (TRUE)."

Unlike "=FORECAST()" command in Chapter 13, the "=TREND()" command enables forecasts with multiple regressors. Critical in the trend command is that the observations on the multiple regressors be in abutting columns.

14.4 Least Squares in Multiple Regression

In multiple regression, the prediction errors or residuals are formed exactly the same as in simple regression: the observed values of y minus the corresponding predicted values $\hat{y}$. The n errors or residuals associated with the differences between an actual value of y and its corresponding predicted value is written

$$e_i = y_i - \hat{y}_i, \text{ for } i = 1, 2, \ldots n \tag{14.11}$$

Substituting for $\hat{y}$ calculated from (14.2) gives

$$e_i = y_i - b_1x_{i1} - b_2x_{i2} \ldots - b_kx_{ik}, \text{ for } i = 1, 2 \ldots n \tag{14.12}$$

The idea behind the method of least squares here is the same as in Chapters 12 and 13. The only difference is that in multiple regression the multiple b's must be selected to minimize the sum of the squares of the errors, Σe_i^2, where again

$$\sum_{i=1}^{n} e_i^2 = e_1^2 + e_2^2 + \ldots + e_n^2 \tag{14.13}$$

The ErrorSS = Σe_i^2 continues to define the sum of the squares of the errors in multiple regression, but now the predicted value of the dependent variable is based on multiple independent variables.

Explanatory Variable
Variable that is used to account for the variability in a dependent variable.

The method of least squares in multiple regression requires the minimization of the ErrorSS, jointly selecting the values for b_1 through b_k. In the one independent variable case, where only one **explanatory variable** x and a constant are used to explain y, the regression line that minimizes the error sum of squares can be seen in a two-dimensional diagram, as in Figures 12.5 and 12.6. In the two independent variable case, where $x_1 = 1$ and x_2 and x_3 are the explanatory variables used to explain y, a three-dimensional scatterplot requires the fitting of a plane or surface. Figure 14.2 shows a scatterplot and the best fitting plane that has the equation

$$\hat{y}_i = b_1 + b_2x_{i2} + b_3x_{i3} \tag{14.14}$$

FIGURE 14.2 Three-Dimensional Scatterplot and Regression Plane

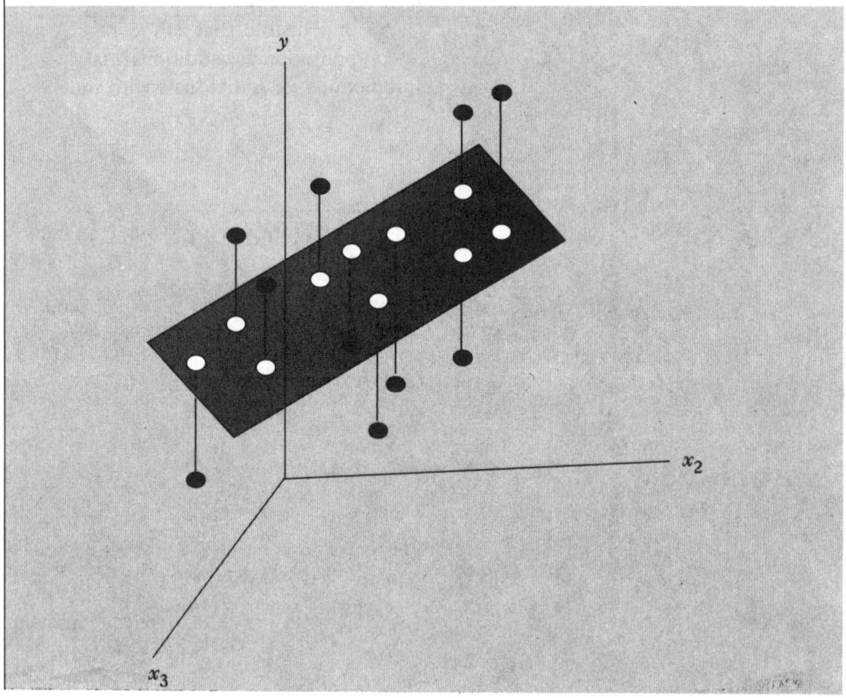

The unique feature of the equation for the plane in Figure 14.2 is that there is no other plane that could be drawn in this three-dimensional scatterplot that would make the sum of squared vertical distances between the (y, x_2, x_3) points and the plane any smaller.

As more x's are added as explanatory variables, the process that leads to the optimal values of the b's that minimize the error sum of squares cannot be visualized, since three dimensions is the most dimensions that can be drawn. The k coefficients in a multiple regression equation with $k - 1$ independent variables and one constant can be found by solving a system of k simultaneous linear equations in which $b_1, b_2, b_3, \ldots b_k$ are the unknowns. Determination of the resulting formulas and hand calculations of the b values are seldom done today.[1] The most common way to find the b coefficient is to use a computer program that has the least squares regression routine built in, as demonstrated in Query 14.3.

QUERY 14.4:
"A Scorecard on the B-Schools" (*Business Week*, January 11, 1988, pp. 164–165) provided three ratings on the top MBA programs in the United States. Michigan, the only public school among the five, had the lowest tuition but highest student/faculty ratio. Using a least squares regression of tuition (y) on the student/faculty ratio (x_2) and 0–1, public-private school variable (x_3), can you predict tuition for the five schools and show the residuals sum to zero.

	y: Annual Tuition	x_2: Student/ Faculty Ratio	x_3 = 1, if private
Chicago	$13,500	9/1	1
Harvard	13,300	9/1	1
Michigan	11,312	18/1	0
Northwestern	13,200	9/1	1
Pennsylvania	13,354	8/1	1

ANSWER:

Below is the MINITAB computer program and results used to estimate the equation that minimizes the error sum of squares.

```
MTB >  read   c1  c2   c3              <---- To read in the data into
DATA> 13500   9   1                          columns 1, 2, and 3.
DATA> 13300   9   1
DATA> 11312  18   0
DATA> 13200   9   1
DATA> 13354   8   1
DATA> end
      5 ROWS READ
MTB >  name c1 'y' c2 'x2' c3 'x3'     <---- To name columns 1, 2, and 3.
MTB >  regres c1 2 c2 c3               <---- To estimate a regression where
SUBC> predict 9  1;  --┐                     the data in column 1 is the dependent
SUBC> predict 8  1;    ├--┐                  variable and there are two independent
SUBC> predict 18  0. --┘  |                  variables in columns 2 and 3.
                          └-------------> To predict y for the pairs of x2 and x3
The regression equation is

y = 11684 - 21 x2 + 1835 x3

Predictor       Coef      Stdev     t-ratio        p
Constant       11684       3179        3.68    0.067
x2             -20.7      176.4       -0.12    0.917
x3              1835       1640        1.12    0.380

s = 152.8       R-sq = 98.6%      R-sq(adj) = 97.2%

Analysis of Variance

SOURCE        DF          SS          MS         F        p
Regression     2     3285682     1642841     70.41    0.014
Error          2       46667       23333
Total          4     3332349

SOURCE        DF      SEQ SS
x2             1     3256476
x3             1       29206

     Fit    Stdev.FIT         95% C.I.              95% P.I.
 13333.3         88.2   (12953.9,13712.8)    (12574.4,14092.2)
 13354.0        152.8   (12696.8,14011.2)    (12424.5,14283.5)
 11312.0        152.8   (10654.8,11969.2)    (10382.5,12241.5)
```

As an alternative to the MINITAB program, the EXCEL computer program could be used. Below are the relevant entries for the regression dialog box and resulting output:

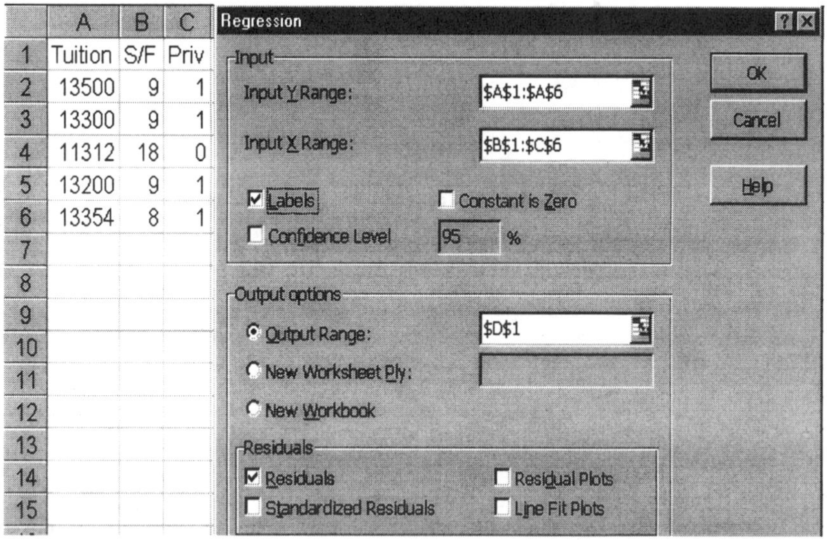

SUMMARY OUTPUT

Regression Statistics	
Multiple R	0.992973244
R Square	0.985995864
Adjusted R Sq	0.971991727
Standard Error	152.7525232
Observations	5

ANOVA	df	SS	MS	F	Sign. F
Regression	2	3285682.1333	1642841.067	70.4075	0.0140
Residual	2	46666.6667	23333.333		
Total	4	3332348.8000			

	Coefficients	StandardError	t Stat	P-value	Lower 95%	Upper 95%
Intercept	11684	3178.57410	3.67586	0.06669	-1992.31	25360.31
S/F	- 20.666667	176.38342	-0.11717	0.91743	-779.58	738.25
Priv	1835.3333	1640.46064	1.11879	0.37957	-5223.00	8893.67

RESIDUAL OUTPUT

Observation	Predicted Tuition	Residuals
1	13333.33333	166.6666667
2	13333.33333	-33.33333333
3	11312	5.45697E-12
4	13333.33333	-133.3333333
5	13354	7.27596E-11

From the preceding MINITAB or EXCEL results, the regression equation is

$$\hat{y} = 11684 - 20.7x_2 + 1835x_3$$

The predicted values (obtainable from the bottom of the printout) and calculated residuals are

	x_2	x_3	y	$\hat{y}$	e
Chicago	9	1	13500	13333.3	166.7
Harvard	9	1	13300	13333.3	−33.3
Michigan	18	0	11312	11312.0	00.0
Northwestern	9	1	13200	13333.3	−133.3
Pennsylvania	8	1	13354	13354.0	00.0
					000.1

As expected, with the exception of rounding error, the residuals sum to zero.

14.5 Assumptions, Estimation, and Hypotheses Testing

In the earlier example presented by Mary Gray and Elizabeth Scott, if a man in the department has five years of experience and one publication, then his predicted salary is \$49,050, by regression (14.1). If a woman with similar attributes has an actual salary of only \$47,725, then, relative to the salary predicted by the male regression, she is underpaid by \$1,325. The question to be raised, however, is whether this underpayment results from chance or sex discrimination. That is, from this sample, can we conclude that the expected salary of women is different from that of comparable men?

As another example of the need for estimation and hypothesis testing, consider the data in Query 14.4 where we might now ask: Are the student/faculty ratio and type of school (private or public) significant explanatory variables in predicting MBA tuition?

Attempts to answer questions of statistical significance start with the specification of a population model. In the Gray and Scott example, a population salary model to be considered is

$$y_i = \beta_1 + \beta_2 x_{i2} + \beta_3 x_{i3} + \beta_4 x_{i4} + \varepsilon_i \tag{14.15}$$

where y_i is ith person's salary, $i = 1, 2, 3, \ldots n$,
- x_{i2} is the years since the ith person completed his or her Ph.D.,
- x_{i3} is the number of books published by the ith person,
- x_{i4} is a 0-1 variable for the ith person's gender,
- β_1, β_2, β_3, and β_4 are parameters to be estimated by the least squares estimators b_1, b_2, b_3, and b_4, and
- ε_i is the population disturbance term, which reflects the random chance factors in determining the ith person's salary.

Now the variable x_{i4} is included to capture the effect of gender in the salary determination process. A person's sex is an attribute that can be represented by one of two

Dummy Variable An explanatory variable that represents a qualitative attribute with a 0 or 1 value.

arbitrary values. Typically, a one is assigned to represent one sex and a zero the other. An explanatory variable that represents a qualitative attribute with a 0 or 1 value is often called a **dummy variable.** Let $x_{i4} = 1$ if the ith person is female, and 0 if male. This definition of x_{i4} implies that β_4 is negative if the expected salary of females is less than that of comparable males (same vintage Ph.D. and same number of books published); it is positive if the expected salary of females is greater than that of comparable males. β_4 is zero if gender is irrelevant in the salary determination process. The hypotheses are thus

$$H_O: \beta_4 = 0 \text{ and } H_A: \beta_4 \neq 0$$

To test hypotheses and to construct confidence intervals, assumptions about the population model must be made.

First, as in Chapter 13, we assume the expected value of y, at any given set of values for the x's, is the deterministic part of the model; that is,

$$E(y_i|x_{i1},x_{i2}\ldots x_{ik}) = \beta_1 x_{i1} + \beta_2 x_{i2} \ldots + \beta_k x_{ik}, \text{ for } i = 1, 2 \ldots n \tag{14.16}$$

This requires that we assume that the expected value of each of the n population error terms is zero, that is,

$$E(\varepsilon_i|x_{i1},x_{i2}\ldots x_{ik}) = 0 \tag{14.17}$$

Second, now that there are more than one x, we must assume that each of these x's is independent of or linearly unrelated to the other x's. That is, the covariance between x's is zero:

$$\text{Cov}(x_{k-s},x_{k-t}) = 0, s \neq t \tag{14.18}$$

Multicollinearity Linear dependence of explanatory variables in a multiple regression analysis.

A violation of this second assumption is referred to as a problem of **multicollinearity,** which is discussed at the end of this chapter. The assumption of no multicollinearity is the only totally new assumption that is introduced in a movement from simple to multiple regression.

Third, the variance of each of the n disturbance terms is $\sigma_\varepsilon{}^2$, which was given as Assumption (13.7) in Chapter 13,

$$\text{Var}(\varepsilon_i) = \sigma^2_\varepsilon \tag{14.19}$$

In Chapter 13, it was also stated in Assumption (13.8) that the disturbance terms must be independent so their covariances will be zero:

$$\text{Cov}(\varepsilon_i, \varepsilon_{i-h}) = 0, \text{ for h} \neq 0 \tag{14.20}$$

Fourth, the population disturbance terms and each of the x variables must be independent so their covariances are zero. In the previous chapter, this was given by Assumption (13.9) and is now written

$$\text{Cov}(\varepsilon_i, x_{ij}) = 0 \tag{14.21}$$

Finally, as in Assumption (13.10), it is assumed that each of the n disturbance terms are distributed normally with zero mean and fixed variance σ^2_ε; i.e.,

$$\varepsilon_i \sim N(0, \sigma^2_\varepsilon) \tag{14.22}$$

If Assumptions (14.17) and (14.20) are correct, then the expected value of the least squares estimator b_4 is β_4 and $E(\hat{y}_i|x_{i1},x_{i2}\ldots x_{ik}) = E(y_i|x_{i1},x_{i2}\ldots x_{ik})$. As in the case of simple regression, the expected value of y, at the ith value of the x's, is estimated by $\hat{y}$, but now $\hat{y}$ is the multiple regression

$$\hat{y}_i = b_1x_{i1} + b_2x_{i2}\ldots + b_kx_{ik} \tag{14.23}$$

Assumptions (14.17) and (14.19) are required to define the standard error of b_4 and the other b's, as well. Assumption (14.22) implies that the least squares estimator b_4 and the other b's are each normally distributed, because they are linear combinations of ε. It is the normality of b_4 that will enable the use of the t statistic to test the hypotheses

$$H_O: \beta_4 = 0 \text{ and } H_A: \beta_4 \neq 0$$

Similarly, it is the normality of ε, and in turn the b's, that enables us to construct confidence intervals for $E(\hat{y}_i|x_{i1},x_{i2}\ldots x_{ik})$ and the β's.

Often, researchers start their analysis by simply assuming the above assumptions are true. As introduced at the end of Chapter 13, however, the correctness of these assumptions should be checked before relying on least squares estimators for predictions and hypothesis testing. The importance of these specification checks is not lessened by multiple regression.

EXERCISES

14.1 The following two data sets are based on the same observations, but the * superscript indicates that the variable is measured as a deviation from its mean. A regression fit to the second data set has the unique property that its intercept or constant term is zero. That is, only x_2^* and x_3^* are included on the right-hand side of the regression.

y	x_1	x_2	x_3	y^*	x_1^*	x_2^*	x_3^*
3	1	−2	4	2	0	−1	1
0	1	0	3	−1	0	1	0
1	1	−1	2	0	0	0	−1
2	1	−2	4	1	0	−1	1
−1	1	0	2	−2	0	1	−1

a. Use a computer program to estimate the regression

$$\hat{y}^* = b_2^*x_2^* + b_3^*x_3^*$$

b. Use a computer program to fit

$$\hat{y} = b_1 + b_2x_2 + b_3x_3$$

c. Is there a difference between b_2^* and b_2, and b_3^* and b_3? What is the difference between the y and y^* regressions?

14.2 Peter Asch and Richard Quandt, in *Racetrack Betting: The Professors' Guide to Strategies* (New York: Praeger 1991, p. 98), proposed the following regression to predict horse speed:

$$\text{predicted speed} = a + b(\text{jockey's experience}) + c(\text{jockey's sex}) + d(\text{weight carried on horse}) + e(\text{horse's condition})$$

a. If speed is measured in miles per hour and jockey's experience is measured in years, what is the meaning of b?

b. If the jockey's sex is equal to 1 if male and 0 if female, what is the meaning of c?

14.3 The following is the complete data set on a "A Scorecard on the B-Schools," from *Business Week* (January 11, 1988, pp. 164–165). Use the ranking on scale A and annual tuition to obtain an equation to predict starting salary. (Keep your computer printout for later use.)

School	Student/ Faculty Ratio	Annual Tuition	Appli- cations Accepted	1987 Grads	Average Starting Salary	Ranking on Scale A	B	C
Carnegie Mellon	4.6/1	$12,648	31%	134	$45,050	8	13	–
Chicago	9/1	13,500	30	692	46,000	5	5	3
Columbia	8/1	13,000	20	486	47,350	9	4	–
Dartmouth	8/1	13,000	19	165	49,100	11	11	–
Duke	12.5/1	12,500	27	241	42,000	18	10	–
Harvard	9/1	13,300	13	782	50,225	2	3	1
MIT	9/1	12,700	21	215	50,625	4	17	–
Michigan	18/1	11,312	39	400	42,750	7	6	7
Northwestern	9/1	13,200	17	480	48,550	6	1	4
North Carolina	12/1	4,533	26	156	39,625	17	18	–
Pennsylvania	8/1	13,354	18	772	48,350	3	2	5
Stanford	6.9/1	12,960	10	314	50,725	1	9	2
Texas	6.6/1	3,400	47	435	37,000	12	19	–
UCLA	9/1	5,902	21	450	44,150	13	12	–
Virginia	7.9/1	8,560	24	252	46,000	14	8	6

14.4 For the following data set, fit a first (x), second (x, x^2), and third (x, x^2, x^3) degree polynomial to the y data and comment on which best represents the sample relationship between x and y.

y	x
27.000	3.6660
28.000	3.6660
19.900	5.5830
28.000	1.5830
25.000	4.4170
25.000	4.2500
22.500	4.8330
23.500	4.8330
23.000	2.8330
19.000	2.5000

14.5 Below is an extension of Table 13.1. As in Chapter 13, fit a straight line regression to these data, but now include a dummy variable that equals 0, if the observations are from the 1960s, and 1, if from the 1970s. Write the equation for your fitted regression. Using a two-dimensional diagram, interpret the coefficient for the 0-1 dummy variable.

Year	Inflation Rate (%)	Unemployment Rate (%)	Year	Inflation Rate (%)	Unemployment Rate (%)
1960	1.6	5.5	1970	5.4	4.9
1961	0.9	6.7	1971	5.0	5.9
1962	1.8	5.5	1972	4.2	5.6
1963	1.5	5.7	1973	5.8	4.9
1964	1.5	5.2	1974	8.8	5.6
1965	2.2	4.5	1975	9.3	8.5
1966	3.2	3.8	1976	5.2	7.7
1967	3.0	3.8	1977	5.8	7.1
1968	4.4	3.6	1978	7.4	6.1
1969	5.1	3.5	1979	8.6	5.8

14.6 Labor economists assert that there is a relationship between earnings and age; as individuals age, their earnings tend to rise. Use the following data on real earnings to estimate this profile for males who are in the sales occupation under the conditions given below.

x = Age	y = Real Earnings
30	$ 8,495
45	10,517
60	9,949
30	7,756
40	10,068
50	10,467
60	10,021
70	8,957

a. Assume the "age/earnings profile" is linear.
   1. Write the equation of the regression for these data.
   2. Graph the regression equation on a scatterplot.
   3. Is the linear regression line a good representation of the "age/earnings profile"? Why or why not?

b. Assume the "age/earnings profile" is nonlinear.
   1. Write the equation of the regression fit to the above data for a third degree polynomial. (You have to create age-sq and age-cube.)
   2. Graph the regression equation on a scatterplot.
   3. Is this nonlinear regression line a good representation of the "age/earnings profile"? Why or why not?

14.7 The following regression is based on consumption (in $1,000), income (in $1,000), years of education, and age.

NAME	MEAN	STD.DEV.
income	25.3967	8.3428
ed	12.0833	3.3155
age	27.2500	9.8823
consump	22.6017	8.9233

DEPENDENT VARIABLE: consumption STD. ERROR OF EST. = 4.0027

VAR.	REGRESSION COEFFICIENT	STD. ERROR	T(DF= 8)	PROB.
income	.8463	.1712	4.943	.00113
ed	1.1606	.3792	3.061	.01556
age	–.0180	.1468	–.122	.90560
CONSTANT	–12.4259			

ANALYSIS OF VARIANCE TABLE

SOURCE	SUM OF SQUARES	D.F.
REGRESSION	747.7144	3
RESIDUAL	128.1726	8
TOTAL	875.8870	11

a. Write the regression equation in slope and intercept form.
b. What does the 0.8463 income coefficient indicate? Based on this estimate, could a $1 increase in income be associated with a $1 increase in expected consumption in the population? (Explain.)

14.8 The following data are from the Multiple Listing Service for a small midwestern college town. The prices are given in hundreds of dollars for 13 homes listed between $200,000 and $300,000. Rooms, Bedrooms, and Baths are simple room counts. Main Floor, Upper Floor, and Basement are square feet measures, with Fin Base being finished square feet in the basement. Age is the age of house in years, with zero representing a new house.

Price	2000	2050	2050	2090	2175	2175	2200	2235	2239	2295	2295	2299	2999
Rooms	12	7	6	10	7	10	10	9	8	9	10	9	8
Bedrooms	5	3	3	5	3	3	4	4	3	4	4	3	3
Baths	3.5	2.5	2.5	3	1.5	3.5	2.5	3.5	2.5	2	3.5	2.5	2
Main Fl	1478	1309	2100	1720	2050	2726	1371	1483	2850	1250	1457	2492	1898
Upper Fl	840	1064	0	1080	0	0	1079	1610	0	1000	2039	706	400
Basement	1188	1064	0	854	2050	328	1371	1443	0	1000	0	0	0
Fin Base	739	0	0	0	0	328	0	0	0	500	0	0	0
Age	5	50	3	0	27	14	0	3	1.5	71	0	1	0

a. Estimate a multiple regression of price on rooms, total square footage, and age.
b. For a new house of 2,500 square feet and eight rooms, what is the predicted price of the house?

14.9 In *Bazemore v. Friday* (1986), the U.S. Supreme Court reversed the Court of Appeals decision that rejected the petitioner's regression analyses because they did not include "all measurable variables thought to have an effect on salary levels." The Supreme Court stated that, "While the omission of variables from a regression analysis may render the analysis less probative than it otherwise might be, it can hardly be said, absent some other infirmity, that an analysis which accounts for the major factors 'must be considered unacceptable as evidence of discrimination.'"

a. Under what conditions would omitted variables bias the estimation of the included regressors? Does the U.S. Supreme Court's decision appear to address these conditions?

b. How does the omission of possible explanatory variables render the analysis less probative?

14.10 Economist Leonard Silk, in a *New York Times* (June 12, 1991) article, reported on an undergraduate's research paper aimed at explaining and predicting the relationship between a ball player's performance and pay. The paper was done by Joshua Engel in the University of Pennsylvania econometrics class of Professor Lawrence Klein, a Nobel laureate in economics. According to Silk,

> Mr. Engel found that when all other variables were held constant, every additional home run was worth \$9,000 in next year's salary, and every extra run created was worth \$6,000, for hitters. For pitchers, one more victory was worth \$38,000, one save, \$16,000, one more inning pitched, \$3,000 and every one-tenth of a point off the e.r.a. is worth \$12,000 on next year's pay.

a. Write the regression equation for batters; what magnitude didn't Silk supply?

b. Write the regression equation for pitchers; what magnitude didn't Silk supply?

14.11 A firm is interested in the relationship between net income Y (in \$10,000 units), the number of salespeople (SALES), and the number of products produced (PRODUCT). It calculated the following multiple regression equation using existing data:

Ordinary Least Squares			
Dependent Variable	Y	Number of Observations	5
Mean of Dep. Variable	16.8000	Std. Dev. of Dep. Var.	12.214745
Std. Error of Regr.	7.2827	Sum of Squared Residuals	106.075
R-squared	.82226	Adjusted R-squared	.64452
F(2, 2)	4.6262	Prob. Value of F	.17774

Variable	Coefficient	Std. Error	T-ratio	Prob |t|>x	Mean of X	Std. Dev. of X
Constant	−17.793	11.87	−1.500	.27247		
SALES	.9121	.7630	1.196	.35441	35.00000	11.18034
PRODUCT	.1589	1.408	.113	.92047	16.80000	6.05805

a. If the company were to employ 40 salespeople and to carry 20 products, what would you predict the net income to be?

b. What is the meaning of $b_2 = 0.9121$?

14.12 Below is a rough duplication of a plot that appeared in the 1964 Surgeon General's report, *Smoking and Health.* What does this graph show regarding death rates and smoking?

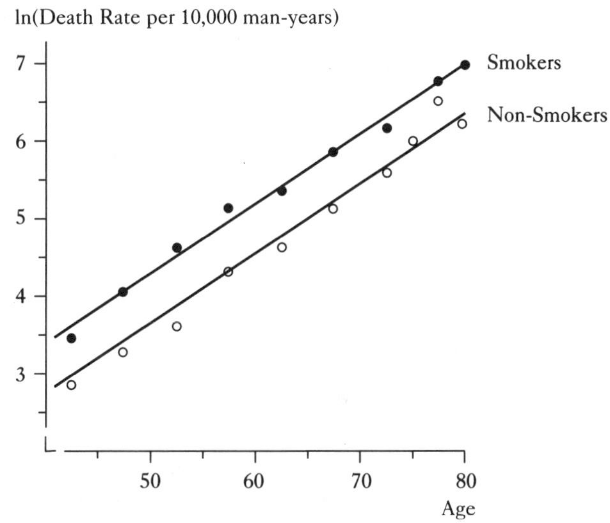

Source: Howard Wainer, "Graphical Visions from William Playfair to John Tukey," *Statistical Science*, August 1990, p. 342.

14.6 Estimation of a Conditional Expected Value of *Y*

As already stated, if the expected value of ε is zero, the expected value of y, conditional on a given set of values for the x's, is the deterministic part of the model:

$$E(y_i|x_{i1}, x_{i2} \ldots x_{ik}) = \beta_1 x_{i1} + \beta_2 x_{i2} \ldots + \beta_k x_{ik} \tag{14.24}$$

The least squares regression line

$$\hat{y}_i = b_1 x_{i1} + b_2 x_{i2} \ldots + b_k x_{ik} \tag{14.25}$$

provides the point estimate of the $E(y_i|x_{i1}, x_{i2} \ldots x_{ik})$. For any given sample, there is no reason to believe that $\hat{y}$ will be the same as the expected value of y, at the identified x values. If the population model is correct, the mean of $\hat{y}_i$, at the identified values of $x_{i1}, x_{i2} \ldots x_{ik}$, over a large (infinite) number of samples will equal $E(y_i|x_{i1}, x_{i2} \ldots x_{ik})$. That is,

$$E(y_i|x_{i1}, x_{i2} \ldots x_{ik}) = E(\hat{y}_i|x_{i1}, x_{i2} \ldots x_{ik}) \tag{14.26}$$

but randomness in sampling causes variability in $\hat{y}$, so $\hat{y}_i$, at the identified values of $x_{i1}, x_{i2} \ldots x_{ik}$, need not equal $E(y_i|x_{i1}, x_{i2} \ldots x_{ik})$.

As with simple regression involving only one explanatory variable, to reflect variability in estimation with multiple explanatory variables, a confidence interval estimate of $E(y_*|x_{*1},x_{*2}\ldots x_{*k})$ can be defined. A $(1-\alpha)$ percent confidence interval for this expected value of y_*, at the specified x_* values, is

$$\hat{y}_* \pm t_{\alpha/2,\mathrm{df}=n-k} s_{\hat{y}_*} \tag{14.27}$$

where $+t_{\alpha/2,\mathrm{df}=n-k}$ is the value of t for which $\alpha/2$ percent of the area is in the upper tail of the t distribution and $-t_{\alpha/2,\mathrm{df}=n-k}$ is the t value for which $\alpha/2$ percent of the area is in the lower tail. This t distribution has $n-k$ degrees of freedom, because k parameters are now estimated in the regression equation $(\beta_1, \beta_2, \ldots \beta_k)$. The rationale here is the same as in simple regression where two parameters were estimated and the degrees of freedom were $n-k=n-2$.

The quantity $s_{\hat{y}*}$ is the standard error for the $\hat{y}$ surface portrayed in Figure 14.2. As in simple regression, the standard error for the $\hat{y}$ surface gets larger the farther the value of the x's are from their respective means. Unlike simple regression, the standard errors for the $\hat{y}$ surface cannot be calculated easily by hand.[2]

The standard errors for the $\hat{y}$ surface are provided in computer printouts. For example, at the bottom of the MINITAB output in the answer to Query 14.4, we see that the standard errors for the sample regression tuition plane, where the student/faculty ratio and the public/private dummy are the explanatory variables, is given in the column headed "Stdev.Fit." That is,

x_{*2}	x_{*3}	y_*	$\hat{y}_*$	Stdev.Fit
9	1	13500	13333.3	$88.2 = s_{\hat{y}_{13333.3}}$
9	1	13300	13333.3	$88.2 = s_{\hat{y}_{13333.3}}$
9	1	13200	13333.3	$88.2 = s_{\hat{y}_{13333.3}}$
8	1	13354	13354.0	$152.8 = s_{\hat{y}_{13354.0}}$
18	0	11312	11312.0	$152.8 = s_{\hat{y}_{11312.0}}$

The 95 percent confidence interval for $E(Y)$ can now be calculated using the critical $t_{0.025}$ value found in Appendix Table A.4. The probability of a t value greater than or equal to 4.303, with $n-k=5-3=2$ degrees of freedom, is 0.025. That is,

$$P(t \geq 4.303 \mid \mathrm{df}=2) = 0.025$$

The 95 percent confidence interval for expected tuition at a private school with a nine to one student/faculty ratio is thus

$$\hat{y}_* \pm t_{\alpha/2,\mathrm{df}=n-k} s_{y*} = 13333.3 \pm 4.303(88.2)$$

$$\text{or} \quad 12953.9 \leq E(y_* \mid x_{*2}=9,\ x_{*3}=1) \leq 13712.8$$

and similarly for the other 95 percent confidence interval reported at the bottom of the MINITAB printout.

Whenever we use Formula (14.27), there is a 0.95 probability that the resulting confidence interval will contain the expected value of y. This *does not say* that there is a 95 percent chance that the expected tuition is between \$12,953.9 and \$13,712.8 when the student/faculty ratio is nine to one at a private school. Once numerical values are substituted into Formula (14.27), there are no random variables in the expression, and no probability statement can be made. The resulting confidence interval either does or does not contain the expected value of y. The expected tuition is \$12,953.9 to \$13,712.8 for a private school with a nine to one student/faculty ratio, but the probability of 0.95 applies to the theoretical interval (14.27) and not the values calculated from this single sample.

The quantity ±379.52 [= ±4.303(88.2)] is called the margin of error. As in simple regression, it reflects the imprecision in our estimate of the expected value of y. As the level of confidence increases (e.g., from a 95 to a 99 percent confidence level), the margin of error increases, because the t value gets larger.

14.7 Prediction of an Individual Value of Y

In addition to estimating the expected value of y at given x values, $\hat{y}$ can be interpreted as providing a prediction of an individual value of y. If so, then additional variability must be recognized, as discussed in the case of simple regression in Section 13.6. This additional variability can be seen in the prediction intervals provided at the bottom of the MINITAB printout in the answer to Query 14.4.

The 95 percent prediction interval for y_* based on the prediction $\hat{y}_* = 13333.3$ is \$12,574.4 to \$14,092.2, which is wider than the corresponding 95 percent confidence interval for $E(y_* | x_{*2} = 9, x_{*3} = 1)$.[3] Prediction intervals will always be wider than the corresponding confidence intervals because the confidence interval for $E(y | x_1, x_2 \ldots x_k)$ only involves variability of $\hat{y}$ around $E(y | x_1, x_2 \ldots x_k)$, as reflected in the difference $\hat{y} - E(y | x_1, x_2 \ldots x_k)$. Any individual value of y that might occur with x values, however, would involve the variability reflected in the difference $\hat{y} - E(y | x_1, x_2 \ldots x_k)$ plus the difference between $E(y | x_1, x_2 \ldots x_k)$ and the individual value of y that might be observed.

Exercises

14.13 What influences the width of the confidence interval for the expected value of y, conditional on x values? How do these factors influence the width of this confidence interval?

14.14 Why do the prediction interval and the confidence interval for the expected value of y, conditional on x values, get wider the farther the x values are from their respective means?

14.15 For the B-school data in Exercise 14.3, for a hypothetical school ranked eighth on the A scale, with annual tuition of \$13,000, would a 95 percent prediction interval for an individual student's starting salary be wider or narrower than a 95 percent confidence interval for the expected stating salary? Which interval should be of more interest to a prospective student considering an MBA program?

14.16 From your regression on the data in Exercise 14.8, for a new house of 2,500 square feet and eight rooms, what is the predicted price? Would a 95 percent prediction interval be wider or narrower than a 95 percent confidence interval for the expected price of all such houses? What is the difference between these two interval estimates?

14.17 For the firm in Exercise 14.11, for 40 salespeople and 20 products, would a 95 percent confidence interval for net income be at its narrowest width? What is the meaning of this confidence interval?

14.8 Hypotheses Testing

Returning to the case of possible sex discrimination in the salary determination of academic men and women, the question is whether the underpayment of women was the result of chance or sex discrimination. The data in Table 14.1 are for only the men in the academic department. This same information, along with that for the five women in the department, is in Table 14.2. Notice in panel a of Table 14.2 that x_{i4} is 1 if the ith person is female and 0 if male. Panel b shows the actual ASCII file that can be read into most computer programs, as shown in Table 14.3, which uses the SAS statistics package.

Once the data are entered into a computer program, users of statistical programs such as SAS, SPSS, MINITAB, RATS, SHAZAM, and the like need only give commands to regress y (salaries) on a constant (the column of ones created by the program), x_2 (a column containing years since receipt of the Ph.D.), x_3 (a column for number of books written), x_4 (a column of 0's and 1's for gender), or any other regressors to be included in the explanation of the dependent variable. Although the location of items differs slightly, all of these computer programs provide printouts with information similar to that in Table 14.3.

The columns titled "Variable" and "Parameter Estimate" in the lower part of this SAS printout show the estimated regression to be

$$\hat{y}_i = 43036.5 + 1025.35x_{i2} + 320.74x_{i3} + 56.36x_{i4}$$

In this sample, the coefficient on the gender variable is positive, indicating that a woman is predicted to receive \$56.36 more than a man with the same publications and Ph.D. vintage. Figure 14.3 illustrates the relationship between the predicted salary and time since earning the Ph.D. for men and women who have never published a book. Upon receipt of the Ph.D. degree, men are predicted to receive a salary of \$43,036.50; comparable women are predicted to receive \$43,092.86. Because salaries are assumed to be linearly related to time since receipt of the Ph.D., this predicted \$56.36 difference continues regardless of the Ph.D. vintage considered.

Given the variability in the sampling distribution of b_4 (as reflected in its standard error of 1489.659 and t of 0.038), there is a high probability of obtaining a coefficient estimate that is \$56.36 above or below the null hypothesis value of zero. This probability of 0.9705 is given in Table 14.3 under the column titled "(Prob>|T|)" and is shown in Figure 14.4 as the area beyond ± \$56.36. It is also the area beyond the calculated t values of ± 0.038 and it is the significance level or the p-value for $b_4 = 56.36$ in a two-tailed test. Because this p-value is extremely large, and well above the usual 0.05 Type I error level,

$$H_O\colon \beta_4 = 0$$

TABLE 14.2 Male and Female Faculty Salaries and Related Data

Panel a: Data in matrix notation

Individual i	Salary y_i	Constant x_{i1}	Years since Ph.D. x_{i2}	Number of Books x_{i3}	Sex x_{i4}
$i = 1$	$y_1 = 66000$	$x_{11} = 1$	$x_{12} = 19$	$x_{13} = 1$	$x_{14} = 0$
$i = 2$	$y_2 = 63500$	$x_{21} = 1$	$x_{22} = 17$	$x_{23} = 1$	$x_{24} = 0$
$i = 3$	$y_3 = 56700$	$x_{31} = 1$	$x_{32} = 11$	$x_{33} = 0$	$x_{34} = 0$
$i = 4$	$y_4 = 56300$	$x_{41} = 1$	$x_{42} = 16$	$x_{43} = 0$	$x_{44} = 0$
$i = 5$	$y_5 = 54900$	$x_{51} = 1$	$x_{52} = 12$	$x_{53} = 2$	$x_{54} = 0$
$i = 6$	$y_6 = 52300$	$x_{61} = 1$	$x_{62} = 11$	$x_{63} = 0$	$x_{64} = 0$
$i = 7$	$y_7 = 50650$	$x_{71} = 1$	$x_{72} = 7$	$x_{73} = 0$	$x_{74} = 0$
$i = 8$	$y_8 = 50650$	$x_{81} = 1$	$x_{82} = 6$	$x_{83} = 1$	$x_{84} = 0$
$i = 9$	$y_9 = 50500$	$x_{91} = 1$	$x_{92} = 10$	$x_{93} = 0$	$x_{94} = 0$
$i = 10$	$y_{10} = 48000$	$x_{101} = 1$	$x_{102} = 5$	$x_{103} = 2$	$x_{104} = 0$
$i = 11$	$y_{11} = 46000$	$x_{111} = 1$	$x_{112} = 2$	$x_{113} = 0$	$x_{114} = 1$
$i = 12$	$y_{12} = 45000$	$x_{121} = 1$	$x_{122} = 2$	$x_{123} = 0$	$x_{124} = 1$
$i = 13$	$y_{13} = 62200$	$x_{131} = 1$	$x_{132} = 17$	$x_{133} = 1$	$x_{134} = 1$
$i = 14$	$y_{14} = 61000$	$x_{141} = 1$	$x_{142} = 15$	$x_{143} = 0$	$x_{144} = 1$
$i = 15$	$y_{15} = 58300$	$x_{151} = 1$	$x_{152} = 19$	$x_{153} = 1$	$x_{154} = 1$

Panel b: Data in machine readable form

```
66000  19  1  0
63500  17  1  0
56700  11  0  0
56300  16  0  0
54900  12  2  0
52300  11  0  0
50650   7  0  0
50650   6  1  0
50500  10  0  0
48000   5  2  0
46000   2  0  0
45000   2  0  1
62200  17  1  1
61000  15  0  1
58300  19  1  1
```

cannot be rejected. Even at the 0.10 Type I error level, this null hypothesis cannot be rejected because the p-value = 0.9705 is just too large. Similarly, for standard Type I error levels, books published is not significant, because its p-value is extremely large.

The p-value or significance level gives the smallest probability of a Type I error for which the null hypothesis can be rejected and the alternative hypothesis can be accepted. At the typical 0.05 probability of a Type I error level,

$$H_0\text{: } \beta_2 = 0$$

TABLE 14.3 Least Squares Salary Regression Using SAS

```
DATA: TABLE142;                    ←— to read in file of data as presented
INFILE 'TABLE142.DAT';                 in Panel b of Table 14.2
INPUT salary yrs books sex;
PROC REG;                          ←— Request regression procedure
MODEL salary=yrs books sex;        ←— Regression model specification
RUN;
```

The SAS System

Dependent Variable: SALARY

Analysis of Variance

Source	DF	Sum of Squares	Mean Square	F Value	Prob>F
Model	3	513200598.39	171066866.13	24.077	0.0000
Error	11	78154401.61	7104945.6009		
C Total	14	591355000			

Root MSE	2665.51038	R-square	0.8678
Dep. Mean	54800.00000	Adj R-sq	0.8318
C.V.	4.86407		

Parameter Estimates

Variable	DF	Parameter Estimate	Standard Error	T for HO: Parameter=0	Prob>|T|
INTERCEPT	1	43036.5	1686.0941934	25.524	0.0000
YRS	1	1025.350585	123.45778801	8.305	0.0000
BOOKS	1	320.743018	1001.5175425	0.320	0.7548
SEX	1	56.363139	1489.6591912	0.038	0.9705

FIGURE 14.3 Sex Discrimination in the Salary Determination Process, as Reflected in the Regression $\hat{y} = 43036.5 + 1025.35x_2 + 320.74x_3 + 56.36x_4$

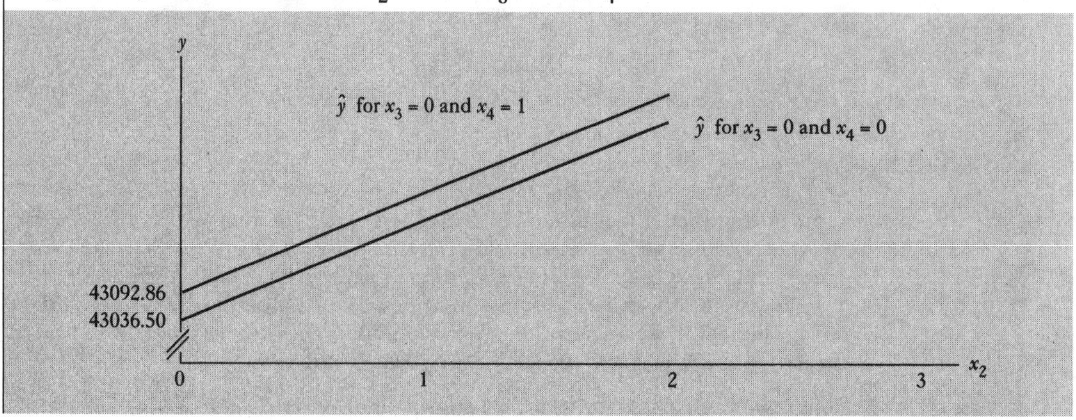

FIGURE 14.4 The Sampling Distribution of b_4 and Its p-values

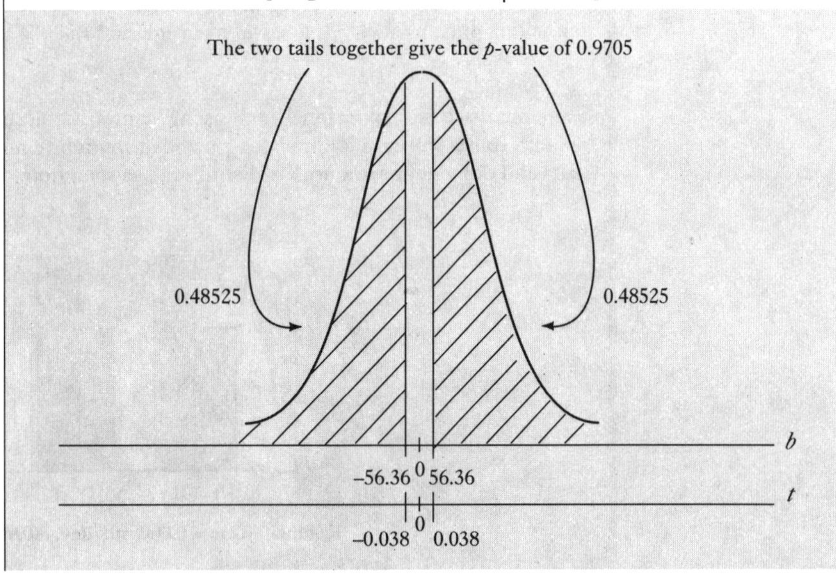

can be rejected because the p-value = 0.0000 is smaller than this 0.05 level. This p-value is so small that time since the receipt of the Ph.D. degree is a significant explanatory variable at any of the typical Type I error levels.

QUERY 14.5:

A yacht broker attempted to establish the relationship between the age of a class of racing boats and their selling prices. From sales records, she obtained information on

Variable	Coefficient	Std. Error	T-ratio	(Sig.Lvl)
CONSTANT	32.4348	1.272	25.502	(.00000)
AGE	–2.91528	.3584	–8.134	(.00004)

PLOT OF RESIDUALS

```
              -1.40                         0                         1.40
              ..........................................................
PRICE         :                             :                            :  Residual
19.0 17.86    :                             :                       *    :      1.14
19.5 18.59    :                             :                  *         :       .91
19.5 20.77    :  *                          :                            :     -1.27
20.0 20.77    :          *                  :                            :      -.77
22.5 22.96    :    *                        :                            :      -.46
22.5 23.69    :           *                 :                            :     -1.19
23.0 23.69    :                *            :                            :      -.69
25.0 24.42    :                             :            *               :       .58
25.5 25.15    :                             :        *                   :       .35
28.0 26.60    :                             :                           *:      1.40
```

10 boats sold through the brokerage. She ran the regression shown here and concluded that age was a significant explanatory variable, with each year predicted to lower the selling price by $2,915 (price was measured in $1,000). Comment on her analysis.

ANSWER:
From our discussion of residual analysis in Chapter 13, these residuals do not appear random (boats in the middle of the price distribution tend to have negative residuals) and do not appear normally distributed, as seen from their histogram:

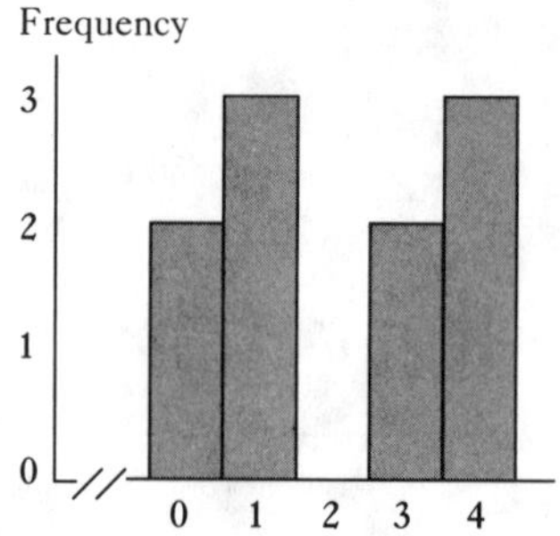

Residual Mean = 0.000, std. dev. = 0.992

			Frequency		Cumulative	
Class	Lower Limit	Upper Limit	Total	Relative	Total	Relative
0	−1.500	−.900	2	.2000	2	.2000
1	−.900	−.300	3	.3000	5	.5000
2	−.300	.300	0	.0000	5	.5000
3	.300	.900	2	.2000	7	.7000
4	.900	1.500	3	.3000	10	1.0000

Because these residuals suggest violations of the assumption required for hypothesis testing, her test of significance is questionable. As discussed in the optional sections at the end of Chapter 13, the "<" pattern in residuals suggests a nonlinear relationship that may be captured by a polynomial of the form PREDICTED PRICE = CONSTANT + b_1AGE + b_2AGE^2. The data set is now

PRICE	AGE	AGESQ
28.000	2.0000	4.0000
25.500	2.5000	6.2500
25.000	2.7500	7.5625
23.000	3.0000	9.0000
22.500	3.0000	9.0000
22.500	3.2500	10.563
20.000	4.0000	16.000
19.500	4.0000	16.000
19.500	4.7500	22.563
19.000	5.0000	25.000

The broker had data on only price and age. We created AGE^2 by squaring the age variable. Within the statistics package, we had to identify AGE^2 by the name AGESQ because the statistics program could not make superscripts. The AGESQ variable is then included as if it were just another regressor, and the new regression results are

Variable	Coefficient	Std. Error	T-ratio	(Sig.Lvl)
CONSTANT	44.9683	2.355	19.099	(.00000)
AGE	–10.4656	1.383	–7.566	(.00013)
AGESQ	1.05818	.1925	5.498	(.00091)

PLOT OF RESIDUALS

–0.810 0 0.810

PRICE		Residual
19.0	19.095	–.947E-01
19.5	19.132	.368
19.5	20.037	–.537
20.0	20.037	–.367E-01
22.5	22.132	.368
22.5	23.095	–.595
23.0	23.095	–.951E-01
25.0	24.190	.810
25.5	25.418	.821E-01
28.0	28.270	–.270

Now the residuals appear to be random, but the effect of age is no longer the same across all ages. For example, boats that are one, two, and three years old have the following respective predicted selling prices (in $1,000):

$$\text{Predicted price} = 44.9683 - 10.4656(1) + 1.0582(1) = 35.561$$
$$\text{Predicted price} = 44.9683 - 10.4656(2) + 1.0582(4) = 28.270$$
$$\text{Predicted price} = 44.9683 - 10.4656(3) + 1.0582(9) = 23.095$$

From one to two years of age, the change in predicted selling price is –$7,291. From two to three years of age, the change in predicted selling price is –$5,175. Students who know calculus realize that the effect of age on the predicted selling price is

$$\text{(CHANGE IN PRICE)/(CHANGE IN AGE)} = -10.4656 + 2(1.0582)\text{(AGE)}$$

Thus, the effect of age is negative for boats that are less than 4.95 years old, after which the effect of age turns positive. However, there are no boats in the sample that approach the 4.95-year turning point. Finally, note that both the AGE and AGESQ effects are highly significant, suggesting that they both belong in a population model of selling price.

14.9 Confidence Interval for β_j

An alternative to a hypothesis test of a specific value of β_j is the consideration of the values in the confidence interval for β_j. The 100(1–α) percent confidence interval for β_j is again given by the estimator minus or plus the margin of error:

$$b_j \pm t_{\alpha/s} s_{bj}, \text{ for df} = n - k$$

or

$$b_j - t_{\alpha/2} s_{b_j} \leq \beta_j \leq b_j + t_{\alpha/2} s_{b_j} \tag{14.28}$$

where $t_{\alpha/2}$ again is the value of t that puts $\alpha/2$ in the tail of a t distribution, with $n - k$ degrees of freedom.

In the case of the gender coefficient, the data in Table 14.3 yield a 95 percent confidence interval for β_4 of

$$56.36 \pm (2.201)\ 1489.659$$

or

$$-3222.38 \leq \beta_4 \leq 3335.10$$

From this 95 percent confidence interval, we know that any hypothesis value of β_4 between –\$3,222 and \$3,335 could not be rejected in a two-tailed test, at the 0.05 Type I error level. This is an extremely wide interval that includes the no discrimination value of zero but also includes a sizable discrimination and reverse discrimination dollar value.

EXCEL automatically produces 95 percent confidence intervals for the slope parameters. Users may also specify other levels of confidence by changing the "Confidence Level" in the EXCEL regression dialog box.

Historical Perspective

Although Sir Frances Galton receives credit for introducing the ideas of regression and correlation analysis to the social sciences, their use in economics is more closely tied to George Yule (1871–1951). Yule developed the idea of "net or partial regression" to represent the influence of one variable on another, holding other variables constant. He invented the multiple correlation coefficient R for the correlation of y with many x's. Yule's regressions looked much like those of today. In 1899, for instance, he published a study in which changes in the percentage of persons in poverty in England between 1871 and 1881 were explained by the change in the percentage of disabled relief recipients to total relief recipients (called the "out-relief ratio"), the percentage change in the proportion of old people, and the percentage change in the population.

Predicted change percent in pauperism
= –27.07 percent
+ 0.299(change percentage in out-relief ratio)
+ 0.271(change percentage in proportion of old)
+ 0.064(change percentage in population).

Stephen Stigler (1986, pp. 356–357) states that, although Yule's regression analysis of poverty was well known at the time, it did not have an immediate effect on social policy or statistical practices. In part, this lack of recognition was the result of the harsh criticism it received from the leading English economist, Arthur Pigou. In 1908, Pigou wrote that statistical reasoning could not be rightly used to establish the relationship between poverty and out-relief because even in a multiple regression (which Pigou called "triple correlation"), the most important influences, superior program management and restrictive practices, cannot be measured quantitatively.

Pigou identified the most enduring criticism of regression analysis; namely, the possibility that an unmeasured, but relevant, variable has been omitted from the regression and that it is this variable that is giving the appearance of a causal relationship between the dependent variable and the included regressors. As described by Michael Finkelstein and Bruce Levin (1990, pp. 363–364 and pp. 409–415), for example, defense attorneys continue to argue that the plaintiff's experts omit relevant market and productivity variables when they use regression analysis to demonstrate that women are paid less than men. Modern academic journals are packed with articles that argue for one specification of a regression equation versus another for everything from the demand for places in higher education to the demand for money.

Both Yule and Pigou recognized the difference between marginal and partial association, and the condensing of variables in contingency tables. Today, some statisticians try to give credit for this identification to E.H. Simpson (1951). The so-called "Simpson's paradox" says that marginal and partial association can differ even in direction so that what is true for parts of a sample need not be true for the entire sample. This is represented in the following figure, where the two separate regressions of y on the high values of x and the low values of x have positive slopes, but a single regression fit to all the data shows a negative slope. As in Pigou's criticism of Yule 90 years ago, this "paradox" may be caused by an omitted, but relevant, explanatory variable for y that is also related to x. It might be better named the "Yule-Pigou paradox" or "Yule-Pigou effect."

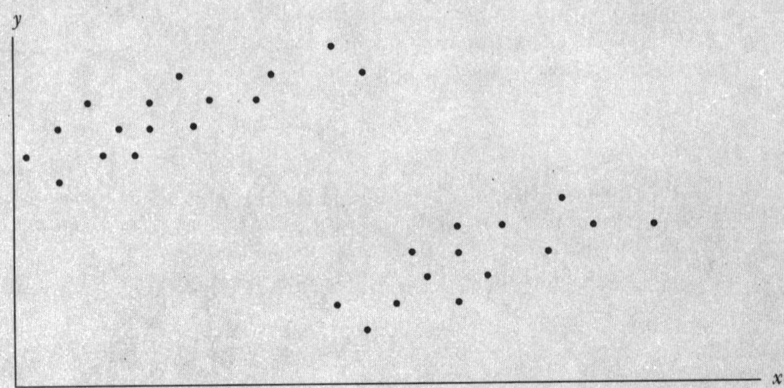

EXERCISES

14.18 In Exercise 14.5, was there a significant change in the Phillips curve relationship between the 1960s and 1980s? Why might you question the appropriateness of your test in this situation?

14.19 Redo Exercises 14.5 and 14.18, using a second degree polynomial to capture the curvature in the data. That is, for inflation and unemployment rates, estimate the following model.

$$\text{inflation} = \text{constant} + \beta_1 \text{ unemployment} + \beta_2(\text{unemployment})^2 + \beta_3 \text{ Dummy} + \varepsilon$$

Is $\beta_3 = 0$ or is $\beta_3 \neq 0$, at the 5 percent Type I error level?
How does this differ from your previous results?

14.20 For the consumption regression in Exercise 14.7, which, if any, of the individual regressors are significant at the 1 percent Type I error level?

14.21 For the B-school data in Exercise 14.3, what are the 95 percent confidence intervals for the A scale rank coefficient and the annual tuition coefficient in the starting salary regression? From these confidence intervals, can you tell if either of these coefficients would be significantly different from zero at the 0.05 Type I error level?

14.22 In Exercise 14.11, at what level is there a statistically significant positive relationship between net income and the number of salespeople?

14.23 For the consumption regression in Exercise 14.7, what is the largest and smallest hypothesized coefficient for education that could not be rejected, at the 0.01 Type I error level in a two-tailed test?

14.10 Multiple Coefficient of Determination

The relative amount of variability in the dependent variable explained by a multiple regression is defined the same as in simple regression; it is the ratio of the regression sum of squares (RegSS) to the total sum of squares (TSS). Now, however, the regression sum of squares, as well as the residual or error sum of squares (ErrorSS), is based on more than one independent variable.

Observed variability in the dependent variable y around its sample mean $\bar{y}$ was defined in previous chapters to be

$$\text{TSS} = \sum_{i=1}^{n}\left(y_i - \bar{y}\right)^2 \tag{14.29}$$

This total sum of squares continues to be that in Equation (12.12). Using the salary data from Table 14.2, the hand (or spreadsheet) calculation routine for TSS is demonstrated in Table 14.4, where TSS = 591,355,000. As reintroduced in this chapter, the residual or error sum of squares continues to be defined as

$$\text{ErrorSS} = \sum_{i=1}^{n} e_i^2 = \sum_{i=1}^{n}\left(y_i - \hat{y}_i\right)^2 \tag{14.30}$$

As defined in the previous chapters, the ErrorSS measures the amount of variability in sample observations on y around the regression plane, but in multiple regression $\hat{y}$ is calculated for each of the n sets of sample values on $x_2, x_3, \ldots x_k$. A hand (or spreadsheet) routine for calculating ErrorSS would start with the determination of the n values for the e vector followed by their individual squaring and summing. For the data set in Table 14.2 and the regression coefficients in Table 14.3, this process is shown in Table 14.5, where ErrorSS is calculated to be 78,154,401.

As discussed in the previous chapters, the total sum of squares is equal to the error sum of squares plus the regression sum of squares. Thus, the regression sum of squares can be obtained by subtracting ErrorSS from TSS, that is,

$$\text{RegSS} = \text{TSS} - \text{ErrorSS} \tag{14.31}$$

TABLE 14.4 Calculation of the Total Sum of Squares

y	$y-\bar{y}$	$(y-\bar{y})^2$
66000	11200	125440000
63500	8700	75690000
56700	1900	3610000
56300	1500	2250000
54900	100	10000
52300	–2500	6250000
50650	–4150	17222500
50650	–4150	17222500
50500	–4300	18490000
48000	–6800	46240000
46000	–8800	77440000
45000	–9800	96040000
62200	7400	54760000
61000	6200	38440000
58300	3500	12250000
822000	0	591355000 = TSS
$54800 = \bar{y}$		

From Tables 14.4 and 14.5, the regression sum of squares is

$$\text{RegSS} = 591{,}355{,}000 - 78{,}154{,}401 = 513{,}200{,}599$$

Hand or even spreadsheet calculations of TSS, ErrorSS, and RegSS are tedious. In addition, rounding errors tend to accumulate. For example, note in Table 14.5 that the sum of residuals is not exactly zero ($\Sigma e = -0.152$), as would be the case if there were no rounding error. A difference from zero of –0.152 is trivial, given the size of numbers with which we are working. A computer regression program written for statistical calculations in double precision, however, will not make an error even this small in the calculation of residuals and their squares.

Regression programs automatically provide sums of squares in an analysis of variance table. For the regression results in Table 14.3, an analysis of variance table is reproduced in Table 14.6. The measures of variability reported in Table 14.3 in the analysis of variance section of the SAS printout are large. As seen in Table 14.6, some computer programs report large numbers in scientific notation, where E+08 means multiply by 10^8. While all calculations are made in double precision, the number of digits displayed in the computer printout will be limited by the space available and the format specified by the programmer. Multiplying the values given for the sum of squares in Table 14.6 by 100,000,000 gives values extremely close to those obtained earlier in Tables 14.3, 14.4 and 14.5, namely

$$\text{TSS} = 591{,}355{,}000 \quad \text{RegSS} = 513{,}201{,}000 \quad \text{ErrorSS} = 78{,}154{,}000$$

TABLE 14.5 Calculation of the Error Sum of Squares

y_i	$\hat{y}_i = 43036.5 + 1025.35x_{i2} + 320.743x_{i3} + 56.3631x_{i4}$	$e_i = y_i - \hat{y}_i$
66000	43036.5 + 1025.35(19) + 320.743 (1) + 56.3631 (0) = 62838.893	3161.107
63500	43036.5 + 1025.35(17) + 320.743 (1) + 56.3631 (0) = 60788.193	2711.807
56700	43036.5 + 1025.35(11) + 320.743 (0) + 56.3631 (0) = 54315.350	2384.650
56300	43036.5 + 1025.35(16) + 320.743 (0) + 56.3631 (0) = 59442.100	−3142.100
54900	43036.5 + 1025.35(12) + 320.743 (2) + 56.3631 (0) = 55982.186	−1082.186
52300	43036.5 + 1025.35(11) + 320.743 (0) + 56.3631 (0) = 54315.350	−2015.350
50650	43036.5 + 1025.35(7) + 320.743 (0) + 56.3631 (0) = 50213.950	436.050
50650	43036.5 + 1025.35(6) + 320.743 (1) + 56.3631 (0) = 49509.343	1140.657
50500	43036.5 + 1025.35(10) + 320.743 (0) + 56.3631 (0) = 53290.000	−2790.000
48000	43036.5 + 1025.35(5) + 320.743 (2) + 56.3631 (0) = 48804.736	−804.736
46000	43036.5 + 1025.35(2) + 320.743 (0) + 56.3631 (1) = 45143.563	856.437
45000	43036.5 + 1025.35(2) + 320.743 (0) + 56.3631 (1) = 45143.563	−143.563
62200	43036.5 + 1025.35(17) + 320.743 (1) + 56.3631 (1) = 60844.556	1355.444
61000	43036.5 + 1025.35(15) + 320.743 (0) + 56.3631 (1) = 58473.113	2526.887
58300	43036.5 + 1025.35(19) + 320.743 (1) + 56.3631 (1) = 62895.256	−4595.256
		−0000.152

e_i^2
9992598
7353897
5686556
9872792
1171126
4061636
190140
1301098
7784100
647600
733484
20610
1837228
6385157
21116379
78154401

$\Sigma e_i^2 = 78154401$
ErrorSS = 78,154,401

TABLE 14.6 Analysis of Variance Information for Regression Results in Table 14.3

	Sum of Squares	d.f.
Total	5.91355E+08	14
Regression	5.13201E+08	3
Residuals	.78154E+08	11

Std. Error of Regression . .	2665.51038
R-Squared	.86784
Adjusted R-Square	.83179

Multiple Coefficient of Determination (R^2) The proportion of variability in y explained by a set of regressors.

A measure of the goodness-of-fit of the multiple regression equation is called the multiple coefficient of determination and is designated by R^2. As with the simple coefficient of determination, r^2 in Formula (12.15), the **multiple coefficient of determination (R^2)** is

$$R^2 = \frac{\text{RegSS}}{\text{TSS}} = 1 - \frac{\text{ErrorSS}}{\text{TSS}} \tag{14.32}$$

The R^2 is a number between zero and one that indicates the proportion of variability in the dependent variable explained by the independent variables. If $R^2 = 1.00$, then 100 percent of the variability in the sample y's is explained by the regression equation, and ErrorSS must be zero; all the y values are predicted perfectly. If $R^2 = 0$, then none of the variability in y is explained by x_2 through x_k, and ErrorSS = TSS. From Table 14.6, we see that 86.78 percent of the variability in salaries (y) is explained jointly by Ph.D. vintage (x_2), books published (x_3), and gender (x_4).

QUERY 14.6:
An article in *Newsweek* (January 22, 1996) stated that "Compared with real wine-drinking countries, the United States is practically dry. That may be a reason, scientists say, that our rate of heart disease is higher." Dr. Charles Fuchs is also quoted saying that drinking beer versus wine may produce extraordinary differences in life expectancy. Questions: 1) Does wine, beer or liquor consumption provide an explanation of death rates from heart disease? 2) Does wine consumption significantly lower death rates from heart disease? The following data on average country death rates and average country alcoholic beverage consumption, in liters per capita, were provided in the *Newsweek* article. "Heart Disease" is defined as the death rate per 100,000.

	Death Rate From	Consumption Per Capita		
	Heart Disease	Wine	Beer	Liquor
France	61.1	63.5	40.1	2.5
Italy	94.1	58.0	25.1	0.9
Switzerland	106.4	46.0	65.0	1.7
Australia	173.0	15.7	102.1	1.2
Britain	199.7	12.2	100.0	1.5
U.S.A	176.0	8.9	87.8	2.0
Russia	373.6	2.7	17.1	3.8
Czech Republic	283.7	1.7	140.0	1.0
Japan	34.7	1.0	55.0	2.1
Mexico	36.4	0.2	50.4	0.8

ANSWER:

Death rates from heart disease can be specified as a function of wine, beer and liquor consumption. The implied multiple regression can then be estimated in EXCEL via the path "Tools" to "Data Analysis" to "Regression." The regression dialog box is completed as shown in Chart 14.2. (Notice that the "Input X range" requires that the columns of explanatory variables abut.) The resulting regression output is shown in Chart 14.3. The "R Square 0.474945" indicates that 47.5 percent of the variability in death rates from heart disease, around the sample mean death rate from heart disease, is associated with wine, beer and liquor consumption. That is, the explanatory power of this regression is not great. In fact, as seen by the relatively small calculated "t Stat," none of the explanatory variables show much statistical significance. Each of the 95 percent confidence intervals for the respective population slope coefficients includes zero. More specifically, although the sample coefficient for wine is negative, its one-tail p-value is $0.31405 = P(t < -0.51024)$. Thus, at the typical Type I error levels, the null hypothesis $\beta = 0$ cannot be rejected in favor of the alternative $\beta < 0$ for wine consumption. The idea that death rates from heart disease are negatively related to wine consumption in the population of all countries is not supported.

CHART 14.2 EXCEL Dialog Box for Multiple Regression of the Death Rate from Heart Disease on Wine, Beer and Liquor Consumption

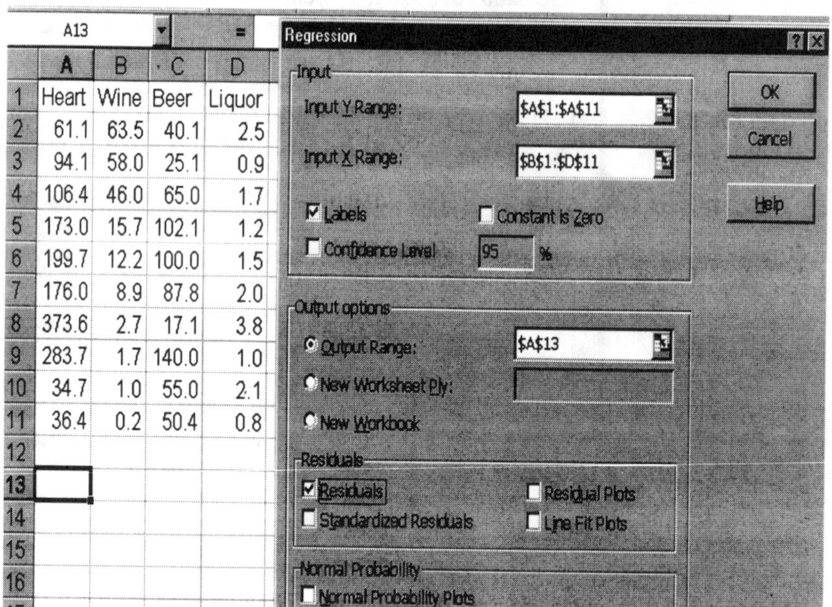

CHART 14.3 Summary Output for Regression of the Death Rate from Heart Disease on Wine, Beer and Liquor Consumption

Regression Statistics

Multiple R	0.689162
R Square	0.474945
Adjusted R Square	0.212417
Standard Error	98.346537
Observations	10

ANOVA

	df	SS	MS	F	Significance F
Regression	3	52493.7524	17497.9175	1.8091	0.2457
Residual	6	58032.2486	9672.0414		
Total	9	110526.0010			

	Coefficients	Standard Error	t Stat	P-value	Lower 95%	Upper 95%
Intercept	-68.02613	150.42307	-0.45223	0.66699	-436.09838	300.0461
Wine	-0.76033	1.49014	-0.51024	0.62810	-4.40657	2.8859
Beer	1.43092	1.09326	1.30886	0.23847	-1.24418	4.1060
Liquor	80.10335	42.67670	1.87698	0.10961	-24.32284	184.5295

RESIDUAL OUTPUT

Observation	Predict Heart	Residuals
1	141.3310	-80.2310
2	-4.1164	98.2164
3	126.1841	-19.7841
4	162.2577	10.7423
5	185.9449	13.7551
6	211.0485	-35.0485
7	258.7824	114.8176
8	211.1136	72.5864
9	178.1312	-143.4312
10	68.0229	-31.6229

HISTORICAL PERSPECTIVE

Milton Friedman (1912 –) won the 1976 Nobel Memorial Prize in Economic Science in part for his regression analysis of the relationship between personal consumption and income. In the appendix to an *American Economic Review* paper he wrote with Anna Schwartz (1991), Friedman tells an intriguing story about his early experience with regression analysis during World War II.

In 1945–1946 Friedman was a member of the staff of the Statistical Research Group at Columbia University, a brain trust providing consulting service to the U.S. Armed Forces. One of his assignments was to assist in the development of an improved alloy for high-temperature use in airplane turbo-supercharger blades. Experimental turbine blades were put in a furnace, heated, and timed until they fractured. At one point, Friedman combined the test data from all the separate experiments and built a regression model that expressed time to fracture as a function of stress, temperature, and variables describing the composition of the alloy. Because this was physics and not economics, Friedman took great care to make sure that his regression was consistent with the metallurgical theory of the day.

Although trivial now, a major problem for Friedman was the computation of the coefficients of the regression and the associated test statistics. Harvard University had the only large-scale computer in the country that could perform the calculations. It was built from a large number of IBM card-sorting machines housed in an enormous air-conditioned gymnasium. Friedman received time on the machine to perform calculations; they took 40 hours per regression. Had the calculations been done on a desktop calculator by skilled operators, Friedman estimated that it would have taken three months to obtain the estimates. Today the same calculations could be done on a desktop microcomputer in seconds.

Friedman reported that he "was delighted with the calculated regression. It had a high multiple correlation, low standard error of estimate, and high *t* values for all of the coefficients, and it satisfied every other test statistic . . ." Based on his regressions, he constructed two new alloys, which he named F-1 and F-2. According to his regression, each should have taken several hundred hours to rupture at high temperatures; yet, his two alloys showed fractures in something like one to four hours. According to Friedman "F-1 and F-2 were never heard of again." In conclusion, Friedman stated:

> Ever since, I have been extremely skeptical of relying on projections from a multiple regression, however well it performs on the body of data from which it is derived; and the more complex the regression, the more skeptical I am. In the course of decades, that skepticism has been justified time and again. In my view, regression analysis is a good tool for deriving hypotheses. But any hypothesis must be tested with data or non-quantitative evidence other than that used in deriving the regression or available when the regression was derived. Low standard errors of estimate, high *t* values, and the like are often tributes to the ingenuity and tenacity of the statistician rather than reliable evidence of the ability of the regression to predict data not used in constructing it.

EXERCISES

14.24 How strongly are condominium prices related to square footage and the Eastside location variable in the New York City data provided in Query 14.3?

14.25 Using your regression results from Exercise 14.24, are both size and location significantly related to condominium selling prices in New York?

14.26 How well do wine, beer, and liquor consumption in Query 14.6 explain variations in life expectancies? (Life expectance of France: 78 years, Italy: 78 yrs, Switzerland: 78 yrs, Australia: 78 yrs, Britain: 77 yrs, USA: 76 yrs, Russia: 69 yrs, Czech Republic: 73 yrs, Japan: 79 yrs, Mexico: 73 yrs)

14.27 Which if any of the beverages in Exercise 14.26 is significant (at the 0.05 Type I level) in explaining life expectancy?

14.28 Why is it true that if $R = 1.00$ then 100 percent of the points are correctly predicted, but if $R = 0.9$ we do not know that 90 percent of the points are correctly predicted?

14.29 What does an $R^2 = 0$ indicate?

14.30 How does R^2 relate to the standard error of the regression in Table 14.6?

14.31 How was the R^2 in 14.24 calculated?

14.32 How was the R in 14.26 calculated?

14.11 CONCLUDING COMMENTS

Multiple regression provides a powerful tool of analysis, which was recognized by Yule at the turn of the century. As cautioned by economist Pigou in an assessment of Yule and as reported by Milton Friedman, multiple regression also can produce parameter estimates that are statistically significant but meaningless in application. Computer programs make regression estimation easy, but only the researcher can assess the practical usefulness of the regression estimated. It is the application of the regression to real-world situations and problems that determines its value.

Historically, the extension from simple regression models (in which y is regressed on x) to multiple regression analysis (in which y is regressed on many x's) required researchers to have familiarity with advanced topics in algebra. Today, however, computer regression programs automatically make these complex calculations with little or no knowledge of the intricacies of matrix algebra required on the part of the user. To use these programs, it is only essential that you understand the assumptions and notation of multiple regression.

By now you should recognize that the assumptions for multiple regression are the same as those for simple regression with one addition: The multiple explanatory variables cannot be correlated with each other. That is, we assume no multicollinearity. You should be able to articulate why each of the assumptions is required for least squares estimation and testing. Finally, you should be competent at reading and interpreting computer printouts for the purposes of predicting the value of the dependent variable and testing hypotheses about individual coefficients.

CHAPTER EXERCISES

14.33 Answer true or false to the following. Give the reason for your answer.

a. Adding another explanatory variable to a regression will raise the error sum of squares.

b. Estimates that are precise (small standard errors) are also unbiased (expected value equals parameter value).

c. Unlike simple regression with one regressor, in multiple regression the regressors are always independent of the disturbance ε because no explanatory variables need be omitted.

d. Unlike simple regression, in multiple regression the residuals need not add to zero. For example, if the residuals add to zero for a regression of y on x_1, then they could not add to zero when another regressor is added.

e. As in simple regression, as the calculated t for a slope coefficient in multiple regression increases in absolute value, the p-value decreases.

f. The interpretation of TSS, RegSS, and ErrorSS is the same for simple and multiple regression. The only difference is that in multiple regression, TSS is based on more than one regressor.

g. The 95 percent confidence interval for the expected value of y, conditional on the x's, is just another name for the 95 percent prediction interval of y, conditional on the x's.

14.34 What is the difference between a simple r^2 and multiple R^2?

14.35 Below is the traffic death rate per 100 million vehicle miles traveled in the United States, for 1957 through 1984.

Year	Death Rate	Year	Death Rate	Year	Death Rate
57	5.71	67	5.25	77	3.26
58	5.32	68	5.17	78	3.25
59	5.17	69	5.02	79	3.35
60	5.06	70	4.72	80	3.30
61	4.92	71	4.44	81	3.20
62	5.08	72	4.32	82	2.80
63	5.18	73	4.11	83	2.60
64	5.39	74	3.52	84	2.60
65	5.30	75	3.35		
66	5.48	76	3.23		

In 1974, the 55 mph speed limit was imposed. Using the last two digits of the year as an explanatory variable (to control for any trend in the death rate) and a 0-1 dummy variable to reflect the 55 mph speed limit, test whether or not the enactment of this speed limit had an effect on the death rate. Do you feel that any of the least squares assumptions were violated in this regression?

14.36 If a human life is valued at \$2 million, and if this value is used as the dependent variable in Exercise 14.35, how would your estimate of the effect of the 55 mph speed limit change?

14.37 The following computer display is based on the useable records of the 182 faculty members of the college at the large midwestern university referenced in this chapter. The variables are defined as:

CURSAL = 1987-80 salary of person, the dependent variable
SEX = 1, if person is female and 0 if male
PROYR = last two digits of year of last promotion
ADMIN = 1, if person has been an administrator and 0 otherwise
SERV = 1, if person heavily involved in service activity; 0 otherwise
ART = number of articles written by person
BOOK = number of books written by person
DEPTi = 1, if person was a member of the ith department within the college (i = 2, 3, 4, 5, 6, 7) and 0 otherwise

Dependent Variable . . . . CURSAL   Number of Observations = 182
Mean of Dependent Var. = 54278.55495   Std. Dev. of Dep. Var. = 5500.86761
Std. Error of Regression = 3462.5369   R-square = 0.63006

Variable	Coefficient	Std. Error	T-ratio(Sig.Lvl)	Mean of X	Std.Dev.of X
INTERCEPT	53974.9	3979.	13.565 (.00000)		
SEX	−1030.45	680.8	−1.514 (.12776)	.20879	.40757
PROYR	−463.486	55.56	−8.342 (.00000)	70.775	5.2326
ADMIN	5025.02	785.1	6.400 (.00000)	.17033	.37696
SERV	2706.64	606.6	4.462 (.00003)	.29670	.45806
ART	166.006	73.71	2.252 (.02426)	3.7363	4.3642
BOOK	745.127	383.5	1.943 (.05082)	.35714	.77881
DEPT2	631.320	847.1	.745 (.46359)	.14286	.35089
DEPT3	−897.412	940.3	−.954 (.34363)	.10989	.31362
DEPT4	3175.07	1014.	3.132 (.00221)	.87912E-01	.28395
DEPT5	901.833	858.3	1.051 (.29528)	.13187	.33928
DEPT6	1347.50	814.5	1.654 (.09578)	.15385	.36180
DEPT7	2513.94	1088.	2.310 (.02097)	.71429E-01	.25825

a. Interpret the coefficient estimate on the SEX variable, and construct a 95 percent confidence interval for the population parameter it estimates.
b. Which of the coefficients are significant at the 10 percent Type I error level?
c. Calculate R.
d. What is the value of the error sum of squares?
e. What is the value of the total sum of squares?
f. There are seven departments in this college. Why isn't a dummy variable included for the department that is designated DEPT1?

14.38 The ASCII file "EX14-38.PRN" contains all 186 records on the faculty of a college at the large midwestern university. Every line contains a numerical value or missing observation (designated .). Observations on each of the 19 variables are separated by a space. In order, the variables are

CODE = Identification number (1 through 186)
CURSAL = 1988-89 salary of person
SEX = 1, if person is female and 0 if male
RANK = 0, 1, or 2 for assistant, associate, or full professor
PROYR = last two digits of year of last promotion
PHDYR = last two digits of year of receipt of Ph.D. degree
APPYR = last two digits of year of appointment

RYR = last two digits of year of regular appointment
STSAL = starting salary
ADMIN = 1, if person has been an administrator and 0 otherwise
SERV = 1, if person heavily involved in service activity; 0 otherwise
OFF = 1, if person received an outside offer in past three years
PIR = number of times person was principal investigator on a research grant
PIT = number of times person was principal investigator on a teaching grant
BOOK = number of books written by person
ART = number of articles written by person
ADV = number of Ph.D. advisees finished
DEPT = 1, 2, 3, 4, 5, 6, and 7 if person was a member of the ith department
BIRTH = last two digits of year of birth

a. Test for sex discrimination in department four for those 15 faculty members who are not administrators, using years since receiving the Ph.D., number of books published, and gender as explanatory variables of salary. Estimate a model in which you assume that raises are based on percentage increases and one in which you assume they are based on absolute increases. Which is the most appropriate for your test of discrimination in the salary determination process?
b. For all 182 useable records, estimate a semilog and a linear salary model that includes SEX, PROYR, ADMIN, SERV, ART, BOOK, and a zero-one dummy for the fourth department.
   1. Which model is better for testing hypotheses, and why?
   2. Is the fourth department significantly different from the others in explaining salary?
   3. Is the gender variable significant? What does this imply?

14.39 High school student learning of economics is of concern to economists and civic leaders. William Walstad and John Soper (*American Economic Review,* May 1988) report on a national study of student learning as measured by the *Test of Economic Literacy*. In a replication of their work, using a subset of their sample, the following results were obtained for the defined variables:

TELPOST, score on the test after the course is finished,
TELPRE, score on the test prior to the start of the course,
IQ, equals the ith student's score on the Quick Word Test,
MALE, equals 1 if the ith student is male and 0 otherwise,
SENIOR, equals 1 if the ith student is a senior and 0 otherwise,
BLACK, equals 1 if the ith student is black and 0 otherwise,
ECON, equal to 1, if course was economics and 0 otherwise,
CONECON, equals 1 if the ith student is in a consumer econ course,
SSECON, equals 1 if the ith student is in a social studies course with an economics component, and $i = 1, 2, \ldots n_1$.
TCOUR, equal to the number of economics credits taken by the teacher,
DEEP, equal to 1, if the school is participating in the Developmental Economic Education Program, and 0 otherwise,
SIZE, equal to the natural logarithm of school enrollment,
MIDINC and HIGHINC, equal 1 if the school is in a mid or high income SMSA district, respectively, and 0 otherwise,
SUBURB and URBAN, equal 1 if the school is in a suburb or urban community, respectively, and 0 otherwise,

NOREAST, SOUTH and WEST, equal 1 if the school is in the northeastern, southern, or western quadrant of the United States, respectively, and 0 otherwise.

Variable	Coefficient	Std. Error	T-ratio(Sig.Lvl)	Mean of X	Std.Dev.of X
INTERCEPT	-17.5855	1.951	-9.015 (.0000)		
TELPRE	.540466	.1868E-01	28.926 (.0000)	20.503	7.4713
IQ.	.170683	.9196E-02	18.561 (.0000)	59.870	15.198
MALE	.514706	.2299	2.239 (.0389)	.50886	.50003
SENIOR	.627319	.2679	2.341 (.0184)	.58228	.49329
BLACK	-.379560	.4001	-.949 (.3454)	.10549	.30724
ECON	5.15502	.3744	13.767 (.0000)	.55738	.49680
CONECON	1.41003	.4650	3.032 (.0026)	.15401	.36103
SSECON	2.53389	.5016	5.052 (.0000)	.12616	.33210
TCOUR	.514923	.6689E-01	7.698 (.0000)	4.4030	2.1498
DEEP	1.48799	.2914	5.107 (.0000)	.44599	.49718
SIZE	3.55161	.6239	5.693 (.0000)	3.0495	.22378
MIDINC	1.68947	.4180	4.042 (.0001)	.72489	.44666
HIGHINC	-.449207	.5039	-.891 (.3765)	.16793	.37389
SUBURB	.756856	.3441	2.199 (.0264)	.47679	.49957
URBAN	-.346618	.3685	-.941 (.3497)	.23207	.42224
NOREAST	.137861E-01	.3708	.037 (.9213)	.14388	.35104
SOUTH	-1.22757	.2888	-4.251 (.0001)	.37511	.48425
WEST	-.941348	.4989	-1.887 (.0561)	.11730	.32184

Number of Observations	2370
Mean of Dependent Variable	22.33418
Std. Dev. of Dep. Variable	9.04203
R-Squared	.63285
F-Statistic (18, 2351)	225.13248

a. What was the standard error of estimation for this regression?
b. What type of student, community, and region are represented by the constant term (that is, when all dummy variables equal 0)?
c. What is the effect of TELPRE on TELPOST? Is it significant?
d. What is the effect of the DEEP variable? Is it significant?

14.40 You are to analyze beverage sales in the Tri-city area. There are 22 records on three possible explanatory variables of SALES—the dollar value of advertising (abbreviated AD), the number of retailers in the area served by your outlets (NUM), and the number of competing wholesale distributors in the area (COMP), as given below. In the Tri-city area, there are 10 retailers, four competing wholesalers, and $16,500 is to be spent on advertising, which is the only variable at your control.

a. Estimate the linear relationship between SALES and the other three variables; write it as an equation.
b. Predict sales in the Tri-city area.
c. At the 1 percent Type I error level, is advertising expense a significant positive explanatory variable?

SALES (in thousands of dollars)	AD (in hundreds of dollars)	NUM (No. of Retailers in area)	COMP (No. of Competitors in area)
514	165	12	2
398	109	9	7
422	146	8	4
613	192	10	5
378	128	9	4
541	150	8	3
704	185	11	2
487	134	10	5
532	158	9	6
295	124	6	5
336	160	5	4
668	175	9	5
403	142	8	6
467	170	10	7
606	181	10	4
380	159	8	8
618	163	8	6
584	155	8	2
521	131	7	3
289	156	7	6
467	160	8	4
599	180	9	2

14.41 A study of bank teller efficiency yielded the following:

Observation Period	Average $ Amount Transacted During Observation Period	Average Minutes To Complete Transaction	Teller Type 1 If only human 0 If some automation
1	2,314	2.0	1
2	1,178	1.0	0
3	897	.9	0
4	987	1.1	1
5	2,037	2.5	1
6	1,987	2.3	0
7	1,005	2.1	1
8	1,764	2.2	0
9	987	1.2	1
10	1,741	2.0	1
11	1,200	.9	0
12	876	.9	1
13	1,435	1.7	1
14	1,143	1.1	0
15	1,998	2.0	1
16	2,345	1.9	0
17	1,067	1.1	0
18	958	.9	1
19	2,978	1.5	0
20	1,591	1.0	0

a. Estimate a least squares regression in which average time to complete a transaction is a function of the average dollar amount of the transactions and the type of teller. Write out the equation.
b. Does this regression provide a good fit?
c. Are the automatic tellers faster than the humans?

14.42 A *WSJ* (January 22, 1992) article gave the death rates of 12 in 368 bypass operations at Harrisburg Hospital, and six in 447 bypass operations at Lancaster General Hospital. A state health council predicted only 5.76 deaths for Harrisburg and 10.94 for Lancaster based on age, health, and the number of operations performed. Specify the multiple regression equation that the council might have used to make its predictions of death rates. Do you see any problems in fulfilling the assumptions for least squares estimation of this model?

14.43 The next table features a regression of profits that car dealers have made from each of their final offers given to "testers" who were sent into the dealerships as would-be buyers. It is from a study by Ian Ayers, "Fair Driving: Gender and Race Discrimination in Retail Car Negotiations," *Harvard Law Review* (February 1991).

a. What group is represented in the intercept term; that is, what group is not represented by a dummy variable?
b. Interpret each coefficient in terms of its influence on the profit.
c. Which variables are statistically significant at the 5 percent Type I error level?

Final Offer Profit Regression	Coefficients	t-ratio
Intercept	603.90	(1.17)
Tester-Salesperson Type:		
TWF (= 1 if tester white female, = 0 otherwise)	196.66	(1.37)
TBM (= 1 if tester black male, = 0 otherwise)	280.18	(1.84)
TBF (= 1 if tester black female, = 0 otherwise)	1029.67	(7.16)
SWF (= 1 if seller white female, = 0 otherwise)	83.21	(.41)
SBM (= 1 if seller black male, = 0 otherwise)	99.49	(.53)
Dealership Characteristics:		
SUB (= 1 if dealer in suburb,= 0 otherwise)	–84.59	(–.44)
WHITE (proportion of neighborhood white)	–271.53	(–.62)
RENT (average rent in neighborhood)	.83	(.42)
HOUSE (average house value in neighborhood)	–.002	(–.98)
INCOME (average income in neighborhood)	.013	(.97)
AGE (average age in neighborhood)	–10.6	(–.75)
Reliability Tests:		
PAIR (= 1 if the tester was the first member of the two testers to bargain at a particular dealership, = 0 otherwise)	–66.80	(–.67)
TEST (= number of tests that a tester completed)	.36	(.06)

R-squared	.388
Adjusted R-squared	.312
Standard Error	516.67
Degrees of Freedom	105

14.44 For Exercise 14.43 involving car dealership profits,

a. how many records (observations) were used in estimation?

b. what does the value of the coefficient of determination indicate?

14.45 Exercise 13.13 reported on an article in *The Wall Street Journal* (February 24, 1992) stating that "for Biotech (companies), pure genius isn't enough." The article suggested that both stock market capitalization and the number of drugs in clinical trial influence the number of drugs the company can bring to market. Listed with the data on capitalization were the number of drugs in clinical trials and the number of proprietary drugs for humans on the market. Fit the suggested multiple regression to these data.

a. What is the equation of your best fitting regression?

b. Are capitalization and the number of drugs in trial significant explanatory variables of the number of drugs on the market?

c. What is the explanatory power of your regression?

	Stock Market Capitalization ($ millions)	Number of Drugs in Clinical Trials	Number of Drugs in Market for Human Use
Amgen	$8,309.7	8	2
Genentech	3,080.2	10	3
Chiron	1,509.6	14	3
Centocor	1,296.8	5	0
Synergen	1,205.4	3	0
Genzyme	935.9	1	1
Biogen	879.8	3	2
Gensia	860.1	1	0
Immunex	791.8	4	2
Alliance	644.0	2	0
US Bioscience	570.8	4	1
Zoma	489.5	6	0
Medimmune	448.8	1	1
Affymax	409.6	0	0
Immune Response	395.2	1	0
Genetics Institute	379.6	3	1
Molecular Biosystems	373.8	0	0
Cytogen	352.3	1	0
Immunomedics	337.1	2	0
Liposome Co.	334.9	3	0

14.46 As discussed in this chapter, "Simpson's paradox," or more appropriately "Yule-Pigou effect," is a phenomenon in which matched pairs of y and x observations (say on salary and year of birth) from two groups (men and women) could show a negative slope for a regression within a group but a positive slope for a regression fit to the combined data. Would the inclusion of a dummy variable as an explanatory variable to reflect membership in a group cure the problem?

14.47 Frank's Poultry maintains a fleet of trucks. After reviewing the repair and maintenance bills for the trucks, the manager observed that the diesel trucks appeared to be more expensive to repair and maintain (R&M) than the gasoline-powered trucks; they also cost more to purchase. Frank's six diesel trucks averaged $1,400 and its eight gasoline-powered trucks averaged $1,374 in R&M expense, as shown below, along with the age and number of miles driven by each truck:

Truck	R&M Expenses (in dollars)	Mileage (in thousands of miles)	Age (in years, where 0 indicates not one year old)	Power Type (D = diesel, (G = gasoline)
1	1229	32.2	0	D
2	1550	34.8	1	D
3	1359	26.7	1	D
4	1350	24.8	2	D
5	1459	28.2	2	D
6	1480	27.5	2	D
7	1309	30.6	0	G
8	1310	29.4	0	G
9	1350	31.4	0	G
10	1360	28.3	1	G
11	1400	29.0	1	G
12	1310	26.2	1	G
13	1500	27.1	2	G
14	1460	25.8	2	G

The manager also found no relationship between a plot of R&M expenses and mileage driven, as seen in a scatter diagram. There appeared to be a negative correlation between R&M expenses and mileage, with the notable exception for the high expense observation for Truck 2. In previous years, there had always been a clear positive correlation between R&M expense and miles driven. The management at Frank's was disappointed that the diesel trucks had not produced savings in repair and maintenance expenses and it was puzzled by the breakdown in the relationship between R&M expense and mileage driven. As a consultant to Frank's management, write a memo explaining the problem, your analysis, and conclusions. Append printouts of your data set and the regression. Refer to these appendices by number in the body of your memo.

14.48 Using the six car characteristics in Exercises 12.49 and 13.47 to explain car prices, is the $471,375 Ferrari a good buy?

14.49 Exercises 12.52 and 13.50 provided Professor Ashenfelter's data for the analysis of the 1993 contested election in Pennsylvania's Second State Senatorial District in Philadel-phia. Fit a quadratic regression to these data and comment on why it might be more appropriate than the linear regression fit in Exercises 12.52 and 13.50. Does your quadratic regression change the conclusions reached in Exercise 13.50?

Academic References

Finkelstein, M., and Bruce Levin. *Statistics for Lawyers.* New York: Springer-Verlag, 1990, pp. 363–364 and pp. 409–415.

Friedman, M., and Anna Schwartz. "Alternative Approaches to Analyzing Economic Data: Appendix." *American Economic Review,* March 1991, pp. 48–49.

Simpson, E.H. "The Interpretation of Interaction in Contingency Tables." *Journal of the Royal Statistical Society,* 1951. B 13, pp. 238–241.

Stigler, S. *The History of Statistics: The Measurement of Uncertainty Before 1900.* Cambridge: The Belknap Press of Harvard University Press, 1986.

Formulas

- The population model is

$$y_i = \beta_1 + \beta_2 x_{i2} + \beta_3 x_{i3} + \ldots + \beta_k x_{ik} + \varepsilon_i$$

where y_i is ith value of the dependent variable
x_{ij} is the ith value of the jth independent variable
β_j is the jth parameter to be estimated
ε_i is the population disturbance term

- The sample multiple regression equation is

$$\hat{y}_i = b_1 x_{i1} + b_2 x_{i2} + b_3 x_{i3} + b_4 x_{i4} + \ldots b_k x_{ik}$$

where x_{ij} is the ith value of the jth independent variable
y_i is the ith value of the dependent variable
b_j is the jth coefficient

- The sample error term is

$$e_i = y_i - \hat{y}_i$$

where $i = 1, 2, \ldots n$, so that

$$\begin{aligned} e_1 &= y_1 - \hat{y}_1 \\ e_2 &= y_2 - \hat{y}_2 \\ &\vdots \\ e_{n-1} &= y_{n-1} - \hat{y}_{n-1} \\ e_n &= y_n - \hat{y}_n \end{aligned}$$

- The t statistic for any coefficient estimator b_j is

$$t_{\text{df}=n-k} = \frac{b_j - \beta_j}{s_{b_j}}$$

where s_{b_j} is the standard error of the least squares estimator b_j.

- A 100 $(1 - \alpha)$ percent confidence interval for $E(y_* | x_{*1}, x_{*2} \ldots x_{*k})$, at the specified x_* value, is

$$\hat{y}_* \pm t_{(1-\alpha)/2,\, \text{df}=n-k} s_{\hat{y}*}$$

where $+t_{(1-\alpha)/2, \text{df}=n-k}$ is the value of t for which α percent of the area is in the upper tail of the t distribution and $-t_{(1-\alpha)/2, \text{df}=n-k}$ is the t value for which α percent of the area is in the lower tail.

- The 100 $(1 - \alpha)$ percent confidence interval for β_j is

$$b_j \pm t_{\alpha/2} s_{b_j}, \text{ for df} = n - k$$

where s_{b_j} is the standard error of b_j.

APPENDICES

APPENDIX TABLE A.1 Binomial Distribution

The binomial mass function is $P(x) = \dfrac{n!}{x!(n-x)!}\pi^x (1-\pi)^{n-x}$

This is the probability of x successes in n independent trials, where the probability of success on each trial is π. The values of x in the left margin of each of the following sections are to be used in conjunction with the values of π at the top of that section. The values of x in the right margin of each section are to be used in conjunction with the values of π at the bottom of that section.

$n = 2$

x	π	01	02	03	04	05	06	07	08	09	10		
0		9801	9604	9409	9216	9025	8836	8649	8464	8281	8100		2
1		0198	0392	0582	0768	0950	1128	1302	1472	1638	1800		1
2		0001	0004	0009	0016	0025	0036	0049	0064	0081	0100		0
		99	98	97	96	95	94	93	92	91	90	π	x
x	π	11	12	13	14	15	16	17	18	19	20		
0		7921	7744	7569	7396	7225	7056	6889	6724	6561	6400		2
1		1958	2112	2262	2408	2550	2688	2822	2952	3078	3200		1
2		0121	0144	0169	0196	0225	0256	0289	0324	0361	0400		0
		89	88	87	86	85	84	83	82	81	80	π	x
x	π	21	22	23	24	25	26	27	28	29	30		
0		6241	6084	5929	5776	5625	5476	5329	5184	5041	4900		2
1		3318	3432	3542	3648	3750	3848	3942	4032	4118	4200		1
2		0441	0484	0529	0576	0625	0676	0729	0784	0841	0900		0
		79	78	77	76	75	74	73	72	71	70	π	x
x	π	31	32	33	34	35	36	37	38	39	40		
0		4761	4624	4489	4356	4225	4096	3969	3844	3721	3600		2
1		4278	4352	4422	4488	4550	4608	4662	4712	4758	4800		1
2		0961	1024	1089	1156	1225	1296	1369	1444	1521	1600		0
		69	68	67	66	65	64	63	62	61	60	π	x
x	π	41	42	43	44	45	46	47	48	49	50		
0		3481	3364	3249	3136	3025	2916	2809	2704	2601	2500		2
1		4838	4872	4902	4928	4950	4968	4982	4992	4998	5000		1
2		1681	1764	1849	1936	2025	2116	2209	2304	2401	2500		0
		59	58	57	56	55	54	53	52	51	50	π	x

Appendix Table A.2 Chi-Square Distribution

The cumulative chi-square distribution is defined by

$$F(\chi^2) = \int_0^{\chi^2} \frac{\chi^{(v-2)/2} e^{-\chi/2} d\chi}{2^{v/2}[(v-2)/2]!}$$

Example $P(\chi_9^2 \leq 16.9$ for df = 9
$P(\chi^2 \leq 30.1) = F(16.9) = 0.950$

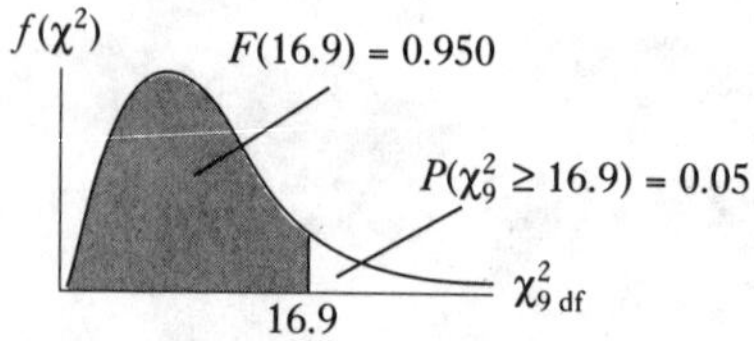

$F(\chi^2)$	.005	.010	.025	.050	.100	.900	.950	.975	.990	.995
1	$.0^4393$	$.0^3157$	$.0^3982$	$.0^2393$	0.158	2.71	3.84	5.02	6.63	7.88
2	.0100	.0201	.0506	.103	.211	4.61	5.99	7.38	9.21	10.6
3	.0717	.115	.216	.352	.584	6.25	7.81	9.35	11.3	12.8
4	.207	.297	.484	.711	1.06	7.78	9.49	11.1	13.3	14.9
5	.412	.554	.831	1.15	1.61	9.24	11.1	12.8	15.1	16.7
6	.676	.872	1.24	1.64	2.20	10.6	12.6	14.4	16.8	18.5
7	.989	1.24	1.69	2.17	2.83	12.0	14.1	16.0	18.5	20.3
8	1.34	1.65	2.18	2.73	3.49	13.4	15.5	17.5	20.1	22.0
9	1.73	2.09	2.70	3.33	4.17	14.7	16.9	19.0	21.7	23.6
10	2.16	2.56	3.25	3.94	4.87	16.0	18.3	20.5	23.2	25.2
11	2.60	3.05	3.82	4.57	5.58	17.3	19.7	21.9	24.7	26.8
12	3.07	3.57	4.40	5.23	6.30	18.5	21.0	23.3	26.2	28.3
13	3.57	4.11	5.01	5.89	7.04	19.8	22.4	24.7	27.7	29.8
14	4.07	4.66	5.63	6.57	7.79	21.1	23.7	26.1	29.1	31.3
15	4.60	5.23	6.26	7.26	8.55	22.3	25.0	27.5	30.6	32.8
16	5.14	5.81	6.91	7.96	9.31	23.5	26.3	28.8	32.0	34.3
17	5.70	6.41	7.56	8.67	10.1	24.8	27.6	30.2	33.4	35.7
18	6.26	7.01	8.23	9.39	10.9	26.0	28.9	31.5	34.8	37.2
19	6.84	7.63	8.91	10.1	11.7	27.2	30.1	32.9	36.2	38.6
20	7.43	8.26	9.59	10.9	12.4	28.4	31.4	34.2	37.6	40.0
21	8.03	8.90	10.3	11.6	13.2	29.6	32.7	35.5	38.9	41.4
22	8.64	9.54	11.0	12.3	14.0	30.8	33.9	36.8	40.3	42.8
23	9.26	10.2	11.7	13.1	14.8	32.0	35.2	38.1	41.6	44.2
24	9.89	10.9	12.4	13.8	15.7	33.2	36.4	39.4	43.0	45.6
25	10.5	11.5	13.1	14.6	16.5	34.4	37.7	40.6	44.3	46.9
26	11.2	12.2	13.8	15.4	17.3	35.6	38.9	41.9	45.6	48.3
27	11.8	12.9	14.6	16.2	18.1	36.7	40.1	43.2	47.0	49.6
28	12.5	13.6	15.3	16.9	18.9	37.9	41.3	44.5	48.3	51.0
29	13.1	14.3	16.0	17.7	19.8	39.1	42.6	45.7	49.6	52.3
30	13.8	15.0	16.8	18.5	20.6	40.3	43.8	47.0	50.9	53.7
z_α	−2.576	−2.326	−1.960	−1.645	−1.282	+1.282	+1.645	+1.960	+2.326	+2.576

APPENDIX TABLE A.3 Standard Normal Distribution

The cumulative standardized normal distribution $F(z)$ is defined by

Example $P(z \leq 1.75) = F(1.75) = 0.9599$ $P(z \geq 1.75) = 0.0401$

$$F(z) = \int_{-\infty}^{z} \frac{1}{\sqrt{2\pi}} e^{-z^2/2} dz$$

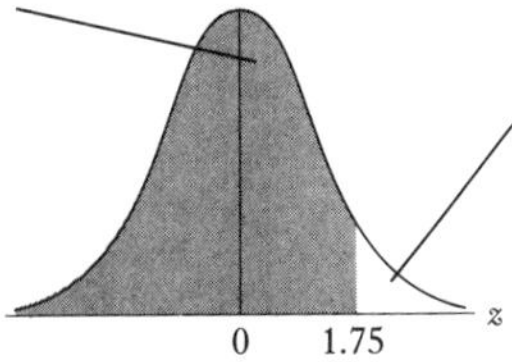

z	.00	.01	.02	.03	.04	.05	.06	.07	.08	.09
.0	.5000	.5040	.5080	.5120	.5160	.5199	.5239	.5279	.5319	.5359
.1	.5398	.5438	.5478	.5517	.5557	.5596	.5636	.5675	.5714	.5753
.2	.5793	.5832	.5871	.5910	.5948	.5987	.6026	.6064	.6103	.6141
.3	.6179	.6217	.6255	.6293	.6331	.6368	.6406	.6443	.6480	.6517
.4	.6554	.6591	.6628	.6664	.6700	.6736	.6772	.6808	.6844	.6879
.5	.6915	.6950	.6985	.7019	.7054	.7088	.7123	.7157	.7190	.7224
.6	.7257	.7291	.7324	.7357	.7389	.7422	.7454	.7486	.7517	.7549
.7	.7580	.7611	.7642	.7673	.7704	.7734	.7764	.7794	.7823	.7852
.8	.7881	.7910	.7939	.7967	.7995	.8023	.8051	.8078	.8106	.8133
.9	.8159	.8186	.8212	.8238	.8264	.8289	.8315	.8340	.8365	.8389
1.0	.8413	.8438	.8461	.8485	.8508	.8531	.8554	.8577	.8599	.8621
1.1	.8643	.8665	.8686	.8708	.8729	.8749	.8770	.8790	.8810	.8830
1.2	.8849	.8869	.8888	.8907	.8925	.8944	.8962	.8980	.8997	.9015
1.3	.9032	.9049	.9066	.9082	.9099	.9115	.9131	.9147	.9162	.9177
1.4	.9192	.9207	.9222	.9236	.9251	.9265	.9279	.9292	.9306	.9319
1.5	.9332	.9345	.9357	.9370	.9382	.9394	.9406	.9418	.9429	.9441
1.6	.9452	.9463	.9474	.9484	.9495	.9505	.9515	.9525	.9535	.9545
1.7	.9554	.9564	.9573	.9582	.9591	.9599	.9608	.9616	.9625	.9633
1.8	.9641	.9649	.9656	.9664	.9671	.9678	.9686	.9693	.9699	.9706
1.9	.9713	.9719	.9726	.9732	.9738	.9744	.9750	.9756	.9761	.9767
2.0	.9772	.9778	.9783	.9788	.9793	.9798	.9803	.9808	.9812	.9817
2.1	.9821	.9826	.9830	.9834	.9838	.9842	.9846	.9850	.9854	.9857
2.2	.9861	.9864	.9868	.9871	.9875	.9878	.9881	.9884	.9887	.9890
2.3	.9893	.9896	.9898	.9901	.9904	.9906	.9909	.9911	.9913	.9916
2.4	.9918	.9920	.9922	.9925	.9927	.9929	.9931	.9932	.9934	.9936
2.5	.9938	.9940	.9941	.9943	.9945	.9946	.9948	.9949	.9951	.9952
2.6	.9953	.9955	.9956	.9957	.9959	.9960	.9961	.9962	.9963	.9964
2.7	.9965	.9966	.9967	.9968	.9969	.9970	.9971	.9972	.9973	.9974
2.8	.9974	.9975	.9976	.9977	.9977	.9978	.9979	.9979	.9980	.9981
2.9	.9981	.9982	.9982	.9983	.9984	.9984	.9985	.9985	.9986	.9986
3.0	.9987	.9987	.9987	.9988	.9988	.9989	.9989	.9989	.9990	.9990
3.1	.9990	.9991	.9991	.9991	.9992	.9992	.9992	.9992	.9993	.9993
3.2	.9993	.9993	.9994	.9994	.9994	.9994	.9994	.9995	.9995	.9995
3.3	.9995	.9995	.9995	.9996	.9996	.9996	.9996	.9996	.9996	.9997
3.4	.9997	.9997	.9997	.9997	.9997	.9997	.9997	.9997	.9997	.9998

APPENDIX TABLE A.4 t Distribution

The cumulative t distribution is defined by

$$F(t) = \int_{-\infty}^{t} \frac{\left(\frac{v-1}{2}\right)!}{\left(\frac{v-2}{2}\right)!\sqrt{\pi n}\left(1+\frac{t^2}{v}\right)^{(v+1)/2}}\,dt$$

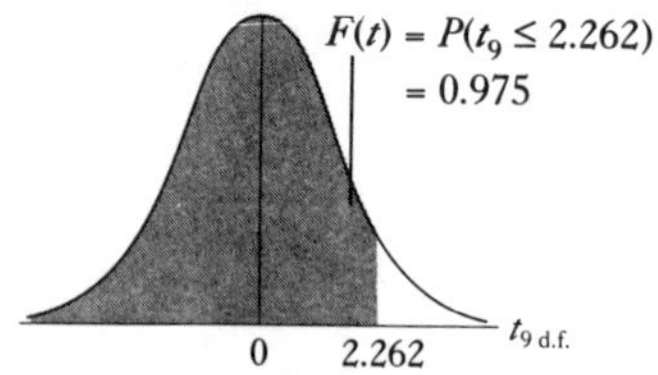

Example $n = 10$, df = 9

$F(t)$	.75	.90	.95	.975	.99	.995	.9995
1	1.000	3.078	6.314	12.706	31.821	63.657	636.619
2	.816	1.886	2.920	4.303	6.965	9.925	31.598
3	.765	1.638	2.353	3.182	4.541	5.841	12.941
4	.741	1.533	2.132	2.776	3.747	4.604	8.610
5	.727	1.476	2.015	2.571	3.365	4.032	6.859
6	.718	1.440	1.943	2.447	3.143	3.707	5.959
7	.711	1.415	1.895	2.365	2.998	3.499	5.405
8	.706	1.397	1.860	2.306	2.896	3.355	5.041
9	.703	1.383	1.833	2.262	2.821	3.250	4.781
10	.700	1.372	1.812	2.228	2.764	3.169	4.587
11	.697	1.363	1.796	2.201	2.718	3.106	4.437
12	.695	1.356	1.782	2.179	2.681	3.055	4.318
13	.694	1.350	1.771	2.160	2.650	3.012	4.221
14	.692	1.345	1.761	2.145	2.624	2.977	4.140
15	.691	1.341	1.753	2.131	2.602	2.947	4.073
16	.690	1.337	1.746	2.120	2.583	2.921	4.015
17	.689	1.333	1.740	2.110	2.567	2.898	3.965
18	.688	1.330	1.734	2.101	2.552	2.878	3.922
19	.688	1.328	1.729	2.093	2.539	2.861	3.883
20	.687	1.325	1.725	2.086	2.528	2.845	3.850
21	.686	1.323	1.721	2.080	2.518	2.831	3.819
22	.686	1.321	1.717	2.074	2.508	2.819	3.792
23	.685	1.319	1.714	2.069	2.500	2.807	3.767
24	.685	1.318	1.711	2.064	2.492	2.797	3.745
25	.684	1.316	1.708	2.060	2.485	2.787	3.725
26	.684	1.315	1.706	2.056	2.479	2.779	3.707
27	.684	1.314	1.703	2.052	2.473	2.771	3.690
28	.683	1.313	1.701	2.048	2.467	2.763	3.674
29	.683	1.311	1.699	2.045	2.462	2.756	3.659
30	.683	1.310	1.697	2.042	2.457	2.750	3.646
40	.681	1.303	1.684	2.021	2.423	2.704	3.551
60	.679	1.296	1.671	2.000	2.390	2.660	3.460
120	.677	1.289	1.658	1.980	2.358	2.617	3.373
$\infty(z_\alpha)$	.674	1.282	1.645	1.960	2.326	2.576	3.291

Appendix Table B.1 Most Valuable Companies

Rank	Company	Market Value ($ Mil.)	Rank	Company	Market Value ($ Mil.)
1	Exxon	69086	49	Intel	12699
2	Philip Morris	68770	50	Pacific Gas & Electric	12423
3	General Electric	66969	51	Sara Lee	12203
4	Wal-Mart Stores	60954	52	Emerson Electric	11911
5	Merck	57976	53	Schering-Plough	11452
6	Coca-Cola	52411	54	RJR Nabisco Holdings	11217
7	American Telephone & Telegraph	49426	55	General Mills	10964
8	IBM	49322	56	J.P. Morgan	10922
9	Bristol-Myers Squibb	41431	57	Syntex	10627
10	Procter & Gamble	33558	58	Gillette	10483
11	Johnson & Johnson	32019	59	Nationsbank	10319
12	Du Pont	29535	60	American Express	10152
13	GTE	26778	61	Kmart	10088
14	Abbott Laboratories	25410	62	Berkshire Hathaway	9970
15	Pepsico	25054	63	Motorola	9948
16	Pfizer	23941	64	Baxter International	9877
17	American Home Products	23828	65	Dun & Bradstreet	9859
18	Mobil	23699	66	Marion Merrell Dow	9843
19	General Motors	22792	67	Toys 'R' Us	9831
20	Bellsouth	21962	68	The Limited	9808
21	Amoco	21777	69	Southern	9627
22	Chevron	21367	70	Time Warner	9492
23	Eli Lilly	21105	71	Bankamerica	9467
24	Microsoft	21039	72	Union Pacific	9430
25	Waste Management	20916	73	H.J. Heinz	9392
26	Walt Disney	20229	74	Campbell Soup	9309
27	Minnesota Mining & Mfg.	19805	75	International Paper	9021
28	Hewlett-Packard	18690	76	Scecorp	8963
29	American International Group	18308	77	American Brands	8940
30	Southwestern Bell	17449	78	Archer Daniels Midland	8818
31	Ford Motor	17338	79	MCI Communications	8777
32	Federal National Mortgage Assn.	17062	80	Warner-Lambert	8715
33	Bell Atlantic	16731	81	Banc One	8324
34	Atlantic Richfield	16152	82	Monsanto	8311
35	Boeing	15828	83	Novell	8279
36	Ameritech	15798	84	Norfolk Southern	8273
37	Pacific Telesis Group	15790	85	Kimberly-Clark	8244
38	Sears, Roebuck	15785	86	General Re	8155
39	Anheuser-Busch	15619	87	Amgen	8043
40	Dow Chemical	15292	88	Texas Utilities	8007
41	Texaco	14734	89	Rhone-Poulenc Rorer	7929
42	Nynex	14671	90	Apple Computer	7583
43	McDonald's	14308	91	Commonwealth Edison	7523
44	Schlumberger	14308	92	Capital Cities/ABC	7320
45	Eastman Kodak	14084	93	ITT	7307
46	US West	13835	94	Digital Equipment	7287
47	Kellogg	13708	95	Loews	7237
48	Home Depot	12957	96	J.C. Penney	7225

Rank	Company	Market Value ($ Mil.)	Rank	Company	Market Value ($ Mil.)
97	Federal Home Loan Mortgage Assn.	7202	147	Marsh & McLennan	5370
98	May Department Stores	7202	148	Houston Industries	5296
99	Food Lion	7132	149	PNC Financial	5277
100	Xerox	7091	150	Philadelphia Electric	5253
101	Upjohn	7009	151	Melville	5162
102	Allied-Signal	6769	152	Pitney Bowes	5160
103	Westinghouse Electric	6742	153	AMR	5157
104	Gannett	6738	154	Rubbermaid	5083
105	Weyerhaeuser	6649	155	Unocal	5073
106	AMP	6508	156	Honeywell	5039
107	Duke Power	6474	157	Entergy	5001
108	The Gap	6409	158	Caterpillar	4995
109	Cooper Industries	6381	159	CNA Financial	4913
110	Conagra	6376	160	Wachovia	4853
111	Corning	6345	161	Tenneco	4845
112	Colgate-Palmolive	6332	162	Air Products & Chemicals	4840
113	American TV & Communications	6314	163	Bankers Trust New York	4832
114	CPC International	6302	164	Suntrust Banks	4809
115	PPG Industries	6291	165	Aetna Life & Casualty	4802
116	United Technologies	6232	166	Central & South West	4801
117	Raytheon	6047	167	Quaker Oats	4792
118	Automatic Data Processing	6043	168	Security Pacific	4788
119	Public Service Enterprise Group	6036	169	Sprint	4769
120	Tele-Communications	5929	170	Burlington Resources	4765
121	Rockwell International	5914	171	Borden	4738
122	Aluminum Co. of America	5913	172	Dayton Hudson	4737
123	Phillips Petroleum	5883	173	Chrysler	4709
124	American Cyanamid	5875	174	Dillard Department Stores	4691
125	CSX	5874	175	Medtronic	4685
126	Ralston Purina	5864	176	Carnival Cruise Lines	4604
127	Merrill Lynch	5855	177	American General	4598
128	USX-Marathon Group	5842	178	Norwest	4588
129	Student Loan Marketing Assn.	5796	179	Detroit Edison	4556
130	UST	5749	180	Times Mirror	4530
131	McCaw Cellular Communications	5739	181	Turner Broadcasting Svstem	4481
132	Consolidated Edison Co. of New York	5736	182	Walgreen	4446
133	Albertson's	5733	183	Newmont Gold	4431
134	Occidental Petroleum	5701	184	Primerica	4372
135	Chemical Banking	5679	185	Goodyear Tire & Rubber	4249
136	American Electric Power	5674	186	First Union	4222
137	Chubb	5673	187	Costco Wholesale	4204
138	Georgia-Pacific	5661	188	Morgan Stanley Group	4174
139	FPL Group	5656	189	Chemical Waste Management	4169
140	Reader's Digest Association	5650	190	Carolina Power & Light	4169
141	Pacificorp	5576	191	Sysco	4128
142	Citicorp	5535	192	Medco Containment Services	4105
143	Paramount Communications	5490	193	Viacom	4073
144	Dominion Resources	5480	194	Freeport-McMoran Copper & Gold	4052
145	U.S. Surgical	5383	195	Cigna	4016
146	Nike	5375	196	Masco	4002

Rank	Company	Market Value ($ Mil.)	Rank	Company	Market Value ($ Mil.)
197	International Flavors & Fragrances	3960	247	Knight-Ridder	3076
198	Deere	3916	248	Winn-Dixie Stores	3075
199	R.R. Donnelley & Sons	3913	249	Torchmark	3008
200	Humana	3881	250	Consolidated Natural Gas	2993
201	Lin Broadcasting	3881	251	Reebok International	2991
202	First Interstate Bancorp	3875	252	Sun Microsystems	2987
203	W.R. Grace	3799	253	Morton International	2971
204	Woolworth,	3746	254	Halliburton	2969
205	Genuine Parts	3737	255	Whirlpool	2967
206	Hershey Foods	3709	256	St. Paul	2966
207	Great Lakes Chemical	3688	257	Sun	2958
208	Pennsylvania Power & Light	3668	258	Bausch & Lomb	2950
209	Centel	3617	259	Ethyl	2943
210	H&R Block	3556	260	Safeco	2941
211	UAL	3555	261	Federal Express	2931
212	Arco Chemical	3548	262	Temple-Inland	2904
213	Browning-Ferris Industries	3547	263	Unocal Exploration	2892
214	Union Camp	3530	264	Newmont Mining	2881
215	Illinois Tool Works	3489	265	Ohio Edison	2861
216	NBD Bancorp	3463	266	Roadway Services	2851
217	Enron	3429	267	McGraw-Hill	2838
218	Liz Claiborne	3428	268	Texas Instruments	2834
219	Delta Air Lines	3422	269	Wm. Wrigley Jr.	2828
220	Fluor	3404	270	Newell	2821
221	Fleet/Norstar Financial Group	3376	271	Lockheed	2819
222	Deluxe	3366	272	Tribune	2815
223	Rohm & Haas	3354	273	W.W. Grainger	2804
224	Reynolds Metals	3353	274	Washington Post	2803
225	Consolidated Rail	3351	275	General Public Utilities	2798
226	Avon Products	3345	276	Phelps Dodge	2798
227	Union Electric	3345	277	Hillenbrand Industries	2788
228	Wells Fargo	3341	278	Wheelabrator Technologies	2777
229	Burlington Northern	3332	279	Dresser Industries	2763
230	U.S. Healthcare	3309	280	Northeast Utilities	2758
231	Salomon	3305	281	Fifth Third Bancorp	2721
232	Amerada Hess	3253	282	AON	2707
233	Transamerica	3252	283	Storage Technology	2706
234	Geico	3241	284	Bank of New York	2701
235	Dow Jones	3223	285	Oracle Systems	2697
236	Textron	3196	286	Computer Associates International	2680
237	Nordstrom	3192	287	Baker Hughes	2669
238	Scott Paper	3189	288	TRW	2666
239	Ingersoll-Rand	3183	289	Capital Holding	2654
240	Alza	3162	290	Potomac Electric Power	2653
241	Duracell International	3153	291	Martin Marietta	2646
242	Union Carbide	3142	292	Tambrands	2629
243	Genentech	3130	293	Crown Cork & Seal	2620
244	Alltel	3085	294	United Healthcare	2620
245	Freeport-McMoran	3081	295	Baltimore Gas & Electric	2608
246	Chase Manhattan	3077	296	Long Island Lighting	2575

Rank	Company	Market Value ($ Mil.)	Rank	Company	Market Value ($ Mil.)
297	National Medical Enterprises	2573	347	Sigma-Aldrich	2201
298	Gerber Products	2570	348	Pet	2190
299	Becton, Dickinson	2565	349	Keycorp	2176
300	Imcera Group	2564	350	Chambers Development	2155
301	Clorox	2547	351	Ivax	2148
302	Centerior Energy	2540	352	McCormick	2141
303	General Dynamics	2520	353	Teco Energy	2134
304	Autozone	2519	354	Household International	2118
305	Northern States Power	2517	355	Cooper Tire & Rubber	2116
306	Compaq Computer	2511	356	Mead	2115
307	McDonnell Douglas	2505	357	Republic New York	2108
308	Fruit of the Loom	2504	358	Stanley Works	2104
309	National City	2482	359	Hasbro	2097
310	National Health Laboratories	2480	360	Travelers	2083
311	Golden West Financial	2476	361	Cincinnati Gas & Electric	2082
312	Sherwin-Williams	2476	362	Santa Fe Pacific	2081
313	Wisconsin Energy	2475	363	Hilton Hotels	2078
314	Price	2469	364	U.S. Bancorp	2074
315	Circus Circus Enterprises	2462	365	Brown-Forman	2063
316	Biomet	2458	366	Interpublic Group	2054
317	Champion International	2451	367	St. Jude Medical	2054
318	Unum	2450	368	Comcast	2043
319	American Stores	2441	369	Citizens Utilities	2027
320	Niagara Mohawk Power	2433	370	H.F. Ahmanson	2020
321	Eaton	2432	371	Dole Food	2019
322	Nalco Chemical	2421	372	First Bank System	2019
323	Corestates Financial	2418	373	Pioneer Hi-Bred International	2017
324	VF	2409	374	Mattel	2001
325	San Diego Gas & Electric	2408	375	Mellon Bank	1995
326	Tyson Foods	2405	376	Dial	1990
327	Hercules	2376	377	First Chicago	1970
328	AFLAC	2360	378	Maytag	1967
329	Pall	2359	379	Bear Stearns	1965
330	Coastal	2359	380	MBIA	1963
331	Great Western Financial	2352	381	Stone Container	1962
332	Dover	2352	382	Willamette Industries	1962
333	Allegheny Power System	2339	383	Nucor	1959
334	Louisiana-Pacific	2337	384	Super Valu Stores	1952
335	Florida Progress	2336	385	Contel Cellular	1949
336	Lincoln National	2334	386	Amdahl	1929
337	Tandy	2321	387	New England Electric System	1925
338	State Street Boston	2317	388	Cincinnati Financial	1909
339	Barnett Banks	2311	389	Litton Industries	1902
340	Westvaco	2295	390	Franklin Resources	1900
341	First Fidelity Bancorporation	2286	391	Paccar	1885
342	New York Times	2263	392	Southern New England Telecomms.	1879
343	Cisco Systems	2250	393	MBNA	1863
344	CBS	2247	394	E.W. Scripps	1854
345	Lubrizol	2218	395	Ashland Oil	1849
346	Blockbuster Entertainment	2215	396	Pennzoil	1846

Rank	Company	Market Value ($ Mil.)	Rank	Company	Market Value ($ Mil.)
397	Society	1841	447	Panhandle Eastern	1582
398	Jefferson-Pilot	1838	448	BMC Software	1576
399	Rite Aid	1832	449	BHC Communications	1573
400	Lyondell Petrochemical	1830	450	Sundstrand	1570
401	Comerica	1815	451	First Financial Management	1563
402	Stryker	1807	452	Oklahoma Gas & Electric	1551
403	Amax	1804	453	Whitman	1549
404	New York State Electric & Gas	1799	454	Homestake Mining	1542
405	Mapco	1789	455	Johnson Controls	1539
406	Northern Trust	1768	456	Charming Shoppes	1536
407	Unitrin	1768	457	Murphy Oil	1534
408	Coca-Cola Enterprises	1767	458	Nipsco Industries	1533
409	CMS Energy	1766	459	Black & Decker	1531
410	Borland International	1757	460	Premark International	1523
411	Flightsafety International	1753	461	Unisys	1516
412	Molex	1743	462	Circuit City Stores	1516
413	Kerr-McGee	1742	463	Owens-Corning Fiberglas	1515
414	Ryder System	1741	464	Williams	1509
415	Consolidated Papers	1727	465	Union Texas Petroleum Holdings	1509
416	Premier Industrial	1723	466	Healthtrust	1507
417	Illinois Power	1715	467	T^2 Medical	1504
418	Sonoco Products	1708	468	Policy Management Systems	1503
419	Tyco Laboratories	1706	469	A. Schulman	1502
420	Chiquita Brands International	1692	470	Pinnacle West Capital	1501
421	Safeway	1685	471	Russell	1496
422	DPL	1682	472	Shaw Industries	1495
423	James River Corp. of Virginia	1681	473	DQE	1492
424	Hubbell	1680	474	Kroger	1490
425	Engelhard	1675	475	Dana	1490
426	Loctite	1669	476	Office Depot	1482
427	FMC	1667	477	Dreyfus	1480
428	Bandag	1664	478	Public Service Co. of Colorado	1478
429	Avery Dennison	1664	479	American Greetings	1474
430	Alco Standard	1663	480	Continental Corp.	1467
431	Oryx Energy	1643	481	Teledyne	1462
432	Allergan	1640	482	Stride Rite	1461
433	Snap-On Tools	1636	483	Giant Food	1459
434	Beneficial	1631	484	Vulcan Materials	1448
435	Marriott	1630	485	Lowe's	1447
436	Firstar	1628	486	Manufacturers National	1439
437	General Cinema	1625	487	Advanced Micro Devices	1439
438	Boatmen's Bancshares	1624	488	Safety-Kleen	1437
439	Betz Laboratories	1623	489	Mercantile Stores	1437
440	Scana	1616	490	CUC International	1435
441	Southwest Airlines	1615	491	Geo. A. Hormel	1427
442	Kemper	1599	492	Jostens	1425
443	Cabletron Systems	1599	493	EG&G	1423
444	International Game Technology	1597	494	AES	1420
445	Parker Hannifin	1592	495	Polaroid	1419
446	Carter-Wallace	1587	496	C.R. Bard	1412

Rank	Company	Market Value ($ Mil.)	Rank	Company	Market Value ($ Mil.)
497	Bancorp Hawaii	1411	547	Great Atlantic & Pacific Tea	1194
498	USX-U.S. Steel Group	1403	548	Armstrong World Industries	1183
499	Bank of Boston	1401	549	Computer Sciences	1182
500	Metro Mobile CTS	1392	550	Synergen	1170
501	Lotus Development	1388	551	Wendy's International	1169
502	Equifax	1386	552	Silicon Graphics	1159
503	Enron Oil & Gas	1385	553	Fina	1157
504	Raychem	1374	554	Vons	1157
505	Ameritrust	1368	555	Nicor	1156
506	Tandem Computers	1365	556	Conner Peripherals	1155
507	Service Corp. International	1361	557	Pep Boys-Manny, Moe & Jack	1150
508	Medical Care International	1354	558	Weis Markets	1145
509	Worthington Industries	1354	559	Marshall & Ilsley	1138
510	Pacific Enterprises	1351	560	Bemis	1134
511	Puget Sound Power & Light	1347	561	Fleming	1132
512	IMC Fertilizer Group	1340	562	Cincinnati Bell	1132
513	Gulf States Utilities	1340	563	Perkin-Elmer	1131
514	Bruno's	1331	564	Cracker Barrel Old Country Store	1130
515	Brunswick	1328	565	Stratus Computer	1130
516	Triton Energy	1318	566	Meridian Bancorp	1126
517	Sonat	1315	567	A.G. Edwards	1123
518	Charles Schwab	1314	568	Arkla	1121
519	Cintas	1310	569	U.S. Cellular	1117
520	Potlatch	1303	570	National Semiconductor	1117
521	Forest Laboratories	1294	571	MGIC Investment	1116
522	Telephone & Data Systems	1294	572	Adobe Systems	1115
523	Surgical Care Affiliates	1293	573	Bethlehem Steel	1113
524	Kansas City Power & Light	1288	574	E-Systems	1101
525	International Specialty Products	1286	575	Allegheny Ludlum	1101
526	Mylan Laboratories	1282	576	Unifi	1100
527	Alexander & Baldwin	1271	577	Century Telephone Enterprises	1096
528	McKesson	1271	578	Penn Central	1092
529	Southwestern Public Service	1268	579	McDermott International	1089
530	Centocor	1267	580	Thermo Electron	1084
531	Montana Power	1266	581	Asarco	1083
532	Destec Energy	1261	582	Wang Laboratories	1083
533	Huntington Bancshares	1260	583	Old Kent Financial	1081
534	CBI Industries	1259	584	Delmarva Power & Light	1080
535	National Service Industries	1257	585	General Signal	1076
536	TJX	1248	586	Critical Care America	1075
537	P.H. Glatfelter	1247	587	Perrigo	1074
538	Harris	1232	588	Anadarko Petroleum	1073
539	St. Joe Paper	1220	589	Kelly Services	1069
540	Valero Energy	1219	590	Thomas & Betts	1067
541	Smith's Food & Drug Centers	1217	591	Brinker International	1063
542	B.F. Goodrich	1216	592	American National Insurance	1058
543	Federal Paper Board	1210	593	Petrie Stores	1052
544	Ambac	1208	594	Cray Research	1046
545	Northrop	1201	595	First of America Bank	1045
546	Ipalco Enterprises	1197	596	Loral	1043

Rank	Company	Market Value ($ Mil.)	Rank	Company	Market Value ($ Mil.)
597	Mercury Finance	1041	647	Crompton & Knowles	940
598	Ecolab	1040	648	Navistar International	938
599	Scimed Life Systems	1036	649	Pacific Telecom	938
600	Rochester Telephone	1035	650	Painewebber Group	932
601	Shoney's	1034	651	Bowater	931
602	Hannaford Brothers	1029	652	New Plan Realty Trust	926
603	Family Dollar Stores	1026	653	Wellman	923
604	Atlantic Energy	1024	654	Cadence Design Systems	923
605	Kansas Gas & Electric	1023	655	Avnet	922
606	Harley-Davidson	1021	656	Universal	920
607	Seagate Technology	1020	657	Nordson	918
608	Duty Free International	1018	658	KU Energy	917
609	Dean Foods	1015	659	Fleetwood Enterprises	916
610	Block Drugs	1012	660	Harsco	908
611	Provident Life & Accident	1012	661	J.M. Smucker	908
612	Illinois Central	1010	662	Novacare	905
613	Witco	1010	663	Minnesota Power	903
614	Foster Wheeler	1009	664	Cipsco	900
615	Midwest Resources	994	665	Peoples Energy	899
616	Millipore	992	666	Symantec	897
617	King World Productions	991	667	First Alabama Bancshares	896
618	20th Century Industries	989	668	York International	896
619	Progressive	984	669	Old Republic International	894
620	Ogden	983	670	Wilmington Trust	890
621	Olin	982	671	PSI Resources	888
622	West Point-Pepperell	978	672	Intergraph	882
623	Multimedia	977	673	Idaho Power	879
624	Shawmut National	977	674	United Investors Management	879
625	Omnicon Group	976	675	Tosco	878
626	Genzyme	975	676	Service Merchandise	876
627	Ball	974	677	Yellow Freight System	874
628	Utilicorp United	973	678	Caesars World	868
629	LG&E Energy	968	679	Calgon Carbon	866
630	Countrywide Credit Industries	965	680	Georgia Gulf	864
631	Conseco	962	681	Boise Cascade	863
632	Legent	960	682	Integra Financial	862
633	Hartford Steam Boiler Inspection	959	683	Enquirer/Star Group	861
634	Chiron	958	684	Dell Computer	861
635	Amsouth Bancorporation	958	685	Hawaiian Electric Industries	859
636	Fund American	958	686	Alexander & Alexander Services	859
637	Boston Edison	957	687	Cyprus Minerals	859
638	Ohio Casualty	956	688	Universal Foods	856
639	Columbia Gas System	954	689	Biogen	854
640	Cummins Engine	952	690	John H. Harland	850
641	Promus	947	691	First Hawaiian	850
642	Southtrust	944	692	First Empire State	848
643	Echlin	942	693	Lafarge	843
644	Crawford	942	694	Washington Federal Savings & Loan	839
645	Kansas Power & Light	942	695	Star Banc	838
646	Manor Care	940	696	Stewart & Stevenson Services	832

Rank	Company	Market Value ($ Mil.)	Rank	Company	Market Value ($ Mil.)
697	First Virginia Banks	832	747	Continental Medical Systems	751
698	Ogden Projects	832	748	Century Communications	749
699	Marquette Electronics	829	749	Quality Food Centers	746
700	Transatlantic Holdings	829	750	IBP	745
701	Longview Fibre	827	751	Vanguard Cellular Systems	742
702	Crane	826	752	Wausau Paper Mills	742
703	Intelligent Electronics	822	753	Portland General	742
704	WPL Holdings	822	754	Ametek	742
705	Commerce Clearing House	819	755	Tootsie Roll Industries	741
706	Bob Evans Farms	818	756	Questar	741
707	Brooklyn Union Gas	817	757	Public Service Co. of New Hampshire	740
708	Keystone International	814	758	Briggs & Stratton	738
709	Continental Bank	813	759	Affiliated Publications	738
710	UJB Financial	809	760	Atlanta Gas Light	735
711	USAir Group	808	761	Fingerhut	733
712	Signet Banking	807	762	First Tennessee National	732
713	Rollins Environmental Services	805	763	Home Shopping Network	732
714	Communications Satellite	795	764	Cabot	731
715	Edison Brothers Stores	791	765	Rochester Gas & Electric	730
716	Central Fidelity Banks	791	766	Gensia Pharmaceuticals	730
717	Centex	790	767	Mirage Resorts	728
718	Crestar Financial	790	768	Spiegel	728
719	Healthcare Compare	790	769	Exabyte	727
720	Healthsouth Rehabilitation	789	770	JWP	723
721	Mercantile Bankshares	786	771	Valspar	723
722	Kansas City Southern Industries	785	772	Banponce	722
723	Louisiana Land & Exploration	785	773	Acuson	722
724	National Fuel Gas	785	774	Longs Drug Stores	721
725	Washington Water Power	784	775	Sensormatic Electronics	717
726	Mentor Graphics	783	776	Adolph Coors	716
727	Maxus Energy	783	777	Immunex	715
728	Ferro	782	778	Argonaut Group	715
729	Hanover Insurance	779	779	Tecumseh Products	711
730	Alleghany	777	780	Amax Gold	711
731	Varian Associates	774	781	Valley National	710
732	Lance	774	782	Jones Apparel Group	710
733	Enserch	774	783	Associated Communications	709
734	Applied Materials	773	784	Micron Technology	709
735	Equitable Resources	772	785	American Water Works	708
736	Diebold	771	786	American Power Conversion	708
737	Rouse	771	787	Federal Signal	707
738	USF&G	769	788	Rollins	705
739	Timken	766	789	Mercantile Bancorporation	704
740	Kaiser Aluminum	766	790	Puget Sound Bancorp	702
741	Sotheby's Holdings	766	791	MNC Financial	699
742	Leggett & Platt	759	792	Commerce Bancshares	698
743	Topps	757	793	Autodesk	694
744	First Security	756	794	J.B. Hunt Transport Services	694
745	Tiffany	753	795	RPM	692
746	Jacobs Engineering Group	752	796	Southland	692

Rank	Company	Market Value ($ Mil.)	Rank	Company	Market Value ($ Mil.)
797	Mitchell Energy & Development	691	848	Fred Meyer	620
798	Quantum	691	849	BWIP Holding	619
799	American Medical Holdings	690	850	CML Group	618
800	Bergen Brunswig	688	851	Beckman Instruments	618
801	Royal Appliance Mfg.	687	852	Nevada Power	617
802	USLife	686	853	Linear Technology	616
803	Vicor	684	854	OEA	616
804	Morrison Knudsen	683	855	Meditrust	614
805	Valhi	683	856	Atlantic Southeast Airlines	613
806	Consolidated Stores	682	857	T. Rowe Price Associates	613
807	Alberto-Culver	681	858	Clayton Homes	611
808	Springs Industries	681	859	Sbarro	611
809	U.S. Shoe	679	860	Cypress Semiconductor	610
810	Chris-Craft Industries	678	861	BB&T Financial	608
811	Inland Steel Industries	677	862	Heilig-Meyers	608
812	Waban	675	863	Ryan's Family Steak Houses	608
813	Jenny Craig	674	864	Ballard Medical Products	607
814	IES Industries	671	865	Filene's Basement	606
815	PHM	668	866	Central Maine Power	604
816	Watts Industries	668	867	Value City Department Stores	603
817	Cablevision Systems	668	868	Overseas Shipholding Group	603
818	Trinova	667	869	Calmat	602
819	Washington Gas Light	666	870	Wisconsin Public Service	601
820	Central Bancshares of the South	665	871	Teleflex	601
821	A.H. Belo	665	872	Apache	597
822	Iowa-Illinois Gas & Electric	665	873	Alliance Pharmaceutical	597
823	Union Bank	663	874	Itel	597
824	Merchants National	659	875	McClatchy Newspapers	595
825	Stanhome	658	876	Standard Federal Bank	595
826	U.S. Bioscience	655	877	Kaufman & Broad Home	593
827	Comdisco	654	878	W.R. Berkley	591
828	Beverly Enterprises	654	879	Harnischfeger Industries	589
829	INB Financial	651	880	M.A. Hanna	588
830	Consolidated Freightways	649	881	Pittston	588
831	Lee Enterprises	644	882	Foundation Health	587
832	Trinity Industries	644	883	MCN	587
833	Michigan National	639	884	Picturetel	586
834	Rockefeller Center Properties	638	885	Leucadia National	582
835	Hon Industries	638	886	Synovus Financial	581
836	Paging Network	636	887	Neutrogena	580
837	Danaher	636	888	PHH	580
838	Thermo Instrument Systems	633	889	Catellus Development	580
839	Community Psychiatric Centers	633	890	Verifone	579
840	Pacificare Health Systems	633	891	Wallace Computer Services	578
841	Diamond Shamrock	631	892	First Brands	577
842	Xilinx	629	893	Central Newspapers	576
843	Battle Mountain Gold	628	894	Octel Communications	575
844	Grumman	628	895	International Dairy Queen	575
845	Genetics Institute	627	896	Holnam	573
846	BP Prudhoe Bay Royalty Trust	626	897	Teradyne	572
847	AST Research	621	898	Church & Dwight	570

Rank	Company	Market Value ($ Mil.)
899	Marvel Entertainment Group	570
900	Pic 'N' Save	569
901	Merry-Go-Round Enterprises	567
902	Sierra Pacific Resources	565
903	National Presto Industries	564
904	Nerco	564
905	Media General	564
906	Broad	563
907	Westmark International	563
908	Morrison	562
909	Structural Dynamics Research	562
910	Fisher-Price	561
911	H.B. Fuller	560
912	Dominion Bankshares	559
913	Lawter International	559
914	Goulds Pumps	559
915	Lands' End	557
916	Mark IV Industries	554
917	Cardinal Distribution	554
918	Staples	551
919	Amsco International	549
920	Diagnostek	547
921	Dexter	543
922	Masco Industries	542
923	Eastern Enterprises	541
924	GATX	536
925	Transco Energy	533
926	Hechinger	531
927	United Missouri Bancshares	531
928	Armco	531
929	Flowers Industries	530
930	Santa Fe Energy Resources	529
931	Savannah Foods & Industries	529
932	Helmerich & Payne	527
933	Noble Affiliates	525
934	Henley Group	523
935	Airborne Freight	523
936	Weingarten Realty	522
937	Precision Castparts	522
938	Liberty National Bancorp	519
939	Artisoft	519
940	Green Tree Acceptance	518
941	Magma Power	516
942	Venture Stores	515
943	NCH	515
944	Home Beneficial	515
945	Delta Woodside Industries	514
946	Tokos Medical	514
947	Dollar General	513
948	Chesapeake	512
949	International Multifoods	512

Rank	Company	Market Value ($ Mil.)
950	Central Louisiana Electric	512
951	Control Data	510
952	Altera	510
953	American Health Properties	509
954	Standard Register	509
955	West One Bancorp	509
956	Handleman	507
957	Information Resources	507
958	Medimmune	505
959	Shopko Stores	504
960	Kimball International	502
961	Tektronix	502
962	Health Care Property Investors	501
963	Neiman Marcus Group	500
964	Wesco Financial	498
965	Lennar	498
966	Herman Miller	495
967	Advanta	494
968	SPI Pharmaceuticals	494
969	Albany International	493
970	Arvin Industries	492
971	System Software Associates	491
972	Mid-American Waste Systems	491
973	United Asset Management	491
974	Fisery	488
975	Sealed Air	487
976	Lancaster Colony	486
977	Anthem Electronics	485
978	Southern Indiana Gas & Electric	485
979	La-Z-Boy Chair	480
980	Buffets	478
981	Greif Bros.	477
982	United Illuminating	477
983	MGM Grand	477
984	Xoma	476
985	FHP International	476
986	Wellfleet Communications	476
987	Stop & Shop	476
988	Dauphin Deposit	476
989	Gibson Greetings	474
990	First American	474
991	Wetterau	473
992	Symbol Technologies	472
993	Public Service Co. of New Mexico	470
994	American President	470
995	Cilcorp	470
996	Pentair	469
997	MDU Resources Group	468
998	Dibrell Brothers	466
999	TCA Cable TV	466
1000	Paychex	465

Appendix Table B.2 CEO Compensations

Company	Executive	1991 Salary/Bonus (In thousands)	%Change From 1990	Long-Term Compensation (In thousands)	Total Direct Compensation (In thousands)
BASIC MATERIALS					
Air Products	Dexter F. Baker	$1161.4	6	0.0	1161.4
Alcoa	Paul H. O'Neill	562.4	-32	644.5	1206.9
Amax	Allen Born	900.0	-23	606.7	1506.7
American Cyanamid	George J. Sella Jr.	1309.4	6	1164.2	2473.6
Armco	Robert L. Purdum	654.0	N/A	19.8	673.8
Asarco	Richard de J. Osborne	850.9	-23	59.4	910.3
Avery Dennison	Charles D. Miller	1065.0	12	501.2	1566.2
Bethlehem Steel	Walter F. Williams	742.6	-8	10.1	752.7
Boise Cascade	John B. Fery	625.4	-10	0.0	625.4
Cabot	Samuel W. Bodman	500.0	-23	0.0	500.0
Champion Int'l	Andrew C. Sigler	1144.0	-8	0.0	1144.0
Consolidated Papers	George W. Mead	447.9	6	0.0	447.9
Dow Chemical	Frank P. Popoff	1069.0	15	256.3	1325.3
Du Pont	Edgar S. Woolard Jr.	1356.0	-10	20.7	1376.7
Ethyl	Floyd D. Gottwald Jr.	967.4	3	30.0	997.4
Georgia-Pacific	T. Marshall Hahn Jr.	1500.0	0	703.7	2203.7
Goodrich (B.F.)	John D. Ong	723.2	-28	805.5	1528.7
Hanna (M.A.)	Martin D. Walker	790.3	-9	349.0	1139.3
Hercules	Thomas L. Gossage	994.0	N/A	0.0	994.0
Imcera	George D. Kennedy	1325.0	17	3848.5	5173.5
Inland Steel	Frank W. Luerssen	523.6	6	0.0	523.6
International Paper	John A. Georges	1356.6	-6	1551.0	2907.6
James River	Robert C. Williams	768.1	N/A	434.9	1203.0
Kimberly-Clark	Darwin E. Smith	1428.0	4	0.0	1428.0
Louisiana-Pacific	Harry A. Merlo	750.0	15	586.7	1336.7
Lubrizol	L.E. Coleman	880.0	-5	442.4	1322.4
Lyondell Petrochem	Bob G. Gower	915.1	4	957.7	1872.8
Mead	Burnell R. Roberts	560.0	2	111.9	671.9
Monsanto	Richard J. Mahoney	1530.0	25	993.0	2523.0
Morton Int'l	Charles S. Locke	1164.2	8	468.0	1632.2
Olin	John W. Johnstone Jr.	787.6	6	91.4	879.0
Phelps Dodge	Douglas C. Yearley	1068.2	5	1482.7	2550.9
Quantum Chemical	John Hoyt Stookey	600.6	-25	0.0	600.6
Reynolds Metals	William O. Bourke	1090.0	-24	0.0	1090.0
Rohm & Haas	J. Lawrence Wilson	976.7	N/A	0.0	976.7
Scott Paper	Philip E. Lippincott	600.4	-1	121.9	722.3
Sherwin-Williams	John G. Breen	1077.7	0	417.4	1495.1
Stone Container	Roger W. Stone	803.5	N/A	1206.4	2009.9
Texas Industries	Robert D. Rogers	418.5	-21	0.0	418.5
Union Camp	Raymond E. Cartledge	939.3	N/A	195.0	1134.3
Union Carbide	Robert D. Kennedy	807.5	-43	0.0	807.5
Westvaco	John A. Luke	948.3	-4	286.9	1235.2
Weyerhaeuser	Geo. H. Weyerhaeuser	515.1	N/A	527.7	1042.8
Willamette	William Swindells	580.1	5	0.0	580.1

ENERGY					
Amerada Hess	Leon Hess	300.0	N/A	0.0	300.0
Amoco	H. Laurance Fuller	1302.2	N/A	236.3	1538.5
Ashland Oil	John R. Hall	1038.0	-6	0.0	1038.0
Atlantic Richfield	Lodwrick M. Cook	1673.9	-26	2008.9	3682.8
Baker Hughes	James D. Woods	916.0	-27	393.1	1309.1
Chevron	Kenneth T. Derr	1385.6	2	363.8	1749.4
Coastal	James R. Paul	813.8	N/A	913.4	1727.2
Dresser Industries	John J. Murphy	1070.6	-3	578.7	1649.3
Exxon	Lawrence G. Rawl	1812.8	17	7453.0	9265.8
FINA	Ron W. Haddock	476.3	N/A	0.0	476.3
Halliburton	Thomas H. Cruikshank	1200.0	9	401.5	1601.5
Kerr-McGee	F.A. McPherson	542.0	-32	129.4	671.4
Mobil	Allen E. Murray	2040.0	9	2624.9	4664.9
Occidental	Ray R. Irani	2324.0	N/A	147.1	2471.1
Pennzoil	James L. Pate	650.0	-2	0.0	650.0
Sun Co.	Robert McClements Jr.	1001.1	3	0.0	1001.1
Texaco	James W. Kinnear	1667.0	-14	1658.8	3325.8
USX	Charles A. Corry	1313.2	-18	840.2	2153.4
Unocal	Richard J. Stegemeier	1054.7	N/A	0.0	1054.7
Valero	William E. Greehey	1097.4	12	352.5	1449.9
INDUSTRIAL					
AMP	Harold A. McInnes	617.7	7	0.0	617.7
Allied-Signal	Lawrence A. Bossidy	809.1	N/A	0.0	809.1
Armstrong	William W. Adams	467.6	-25	23.8	491.4
Ball	Delmont A. Davis	815.0	N/A	22.0	837.0
Browning-Ferris	Wm. D. Ruckelshaus	806.0	0	0.0	806.0
Burlington Northern	Gerald Grinstein	1180.4	-8	0.0	1180.4
CSX	John W. Snow	1235.2	28	1832.4	3067.6
Caterpillar	Donald V. Fites	522.5	19	0.0	522.5
Conrail	James A. Hagen	1127.8	41	0.0	1127.8
Cooper Industries	Robert Cizik	1124.1	-16	5175.4	6299.5
Cummins Engine	Henry B. Schacht	450.0	2	1691.8	2141.8
Deere	Hans W. Becherer	654.0	N/A	162.7	816.7
Donnelley (R.R.)	John R. Walter	644.0	-16	99.6	743.6
Dover	Gary L. Roubos	765.0	-1	195.2	960.2
Dun & Bradstreet	Charles W. Moritz	1629.5	3	789.9	2419.4
Eaton	James R. Stover	693.8	-34	1015.8	1709.6
Emerson Electric	Charles F. Knight	1803.6	2	0.0	1803.6
Engelhard	Orin R. Smith	2119.3	32	3710.4	5829.7
FMC	Robert H. Malott	1238.1	N/A	3771.0	5009.1
Federal Express	Frederick W. Smith	662.5	14	0.0	662.5
Fluor	Leslie G. McCraw	1110.9	N/A	2191.3	3302.2
Harnischfeger	William W. Goessel	974.7	1	66.5	1041.2
Hillenbrand	W. August Hillenbrand	966.7	24	198.5	1165.2
Ingersoll-Rand	Theodore H. Black	1120.0	-6	278.6	1398.6
Morrison Knudsen	William M. Agee	2026.7	N/A	441.5	2468.2
Navistar	James C. Cotting	450.0	0	90.8	540.8
Norfolk Southern	Arnold B. McKinnon	1735.0	N/A	1208.4	2943.4
Owens-Corning	Max O. Weber	840.0	N/A	1164.1	2004.1

PPG Industries	Vincent A. Sarni	1038.9	-34	701.1	1740.0
Parker-Hannifin	Paul G. Schloemer	774.7	-21	46.2	820.9
Pentair	D. Eugene Nugent	979.3	47	487.9	1467.2
Premark	Warren L. Batts	1364.9	45	1593.8	2958.7
Raychem	Robert J. Saldich	448.8	N/A	447.9	N/A
Ryder System	M. Anthony Burns	764.2	-2	0.0	764.2
Santa Fe Pacific	Robert D. Krebs	977.1	78	294.4	1271.5
Stanley Works	Richard H. Ayers	678.9	-11	0.0	678.9
Tenneco	James L. Ketelsen	1469.6	N/A	21.1	1490.7
Trinova	Darryl F. Allen	504.6	3	0.0	504.6
Tyco	John F. Fort	1170.0	0	3150.0	4320.0
USG	Eugene B. Connolly	475.0	18	0.0	475.0
Union Pacific	Drew Lewis	2025.0	6	2131.3	4156.3
Waste Management	Dean L. Buntrock	1100.0	-30	2647.0	3747.0
Westinghouse	Paul E. Lego	677.1	-60	0.0	677.1
CYCLICAL					
AMR	Robert L. Crandall	600.0	0	3446.4	4046.4
Arvin	James K. Baker	488.8	-16	0.0	488.8
Bergen Brunswig	Robert E. Martini	676.4	N/A	0.0	676.4
Berkshire Hathaway	Warren E. Buffett	100.0	0	0.0	100.0
Black & Decker	Nolan D. Archibald	1300.5	2	269.5	1570.0
Brunswick	Jack F. Reichert	736.0	-34	189.0	925.0
CBS	Laurence A. Tisch	1382.9	2	0.0	1382.9
Capital Cities/ABC	Daniel B. Burke	842.0	-7	2839.1	3681.1
Chrysler	Lee A. Iacocca	976.4	-36	1904.0	2880.4
Claiborne (Liz)	Jerome A. Chazen	1185.0	-3	0.0	1185.0
Dana	Southwood J. Morcott	574.0	N/A	0.0	574.0
Delta Air Lines	Ronald W. Allen	475.0	-35	562.5	1037.5
Disney (Walt)	Michael D. Eisner	5441.5	-52	0.0	5441.5
Dow Jones	Peter R. Kann	730.0	N/A	0.0	730.0
Eagle-Picher	Thomas E. Petry	575.0	-2	0.0	575.0
Echlin	Frederick J. Mancheski	642.1	12	97.5	739.6
Ford Motor	Harold A. Poling	1140.8	N/A	0.0	1140.8
GM	Robert C. Stempel	1000.0	N/A	311.3	1311.3
Gannett	John J. Curley	1300.0	0	779.4	2079.4
General Cinema	Richard A. Smith	1275.0	3	0.0	1275.0
Goodyear	Stanley C. Gault	735.0	N/A	0.0	735.0
Hartmarx	Harvey A. Weinberg	557.0	-1	0.0	557.0
Hasbro	Alan G. Hassenfeld	1411.1	23	2740.6	4151.7
Home Depot	Bernard Marcus	1586.9	0	0.0	1586.9
Johnson Controls	James H. Keyes	659.2	8	182.8	842.0
Kmart	Joseph E. Antonini	1545.8	56	0.0	1545.8
Knight-Ridder	James K. Batten	605.0	-5	629.1	1234.1
Kodak	Kay R. Whitmore	1146.2	-19	49.2	1195.4
Marriott	J.W. Marriott Jr.	1304.4	71	0.0	1304.4
Mattel	John W. Amerman	1364.4	12	886.3	2250.7
Maytag	Daniel J. Krumm	982.6	N/A	0.0	982.6
McDonald's	Michael R. Quinlan	1335.0	7	0.0	1335.0
McGraw-Hill	Joseph L. Dionne	834.3	-19	506.8	1341.1
Melville	Stanley P. Goldstein	1297.0	7	601.6	1898.6
Miller (Herman)	Richard H. Ruch	405.0	-9	0.0	405.0
New York Times	Arthur Ochs Sulzberger	943.9	90	141.6	1085.5
Nike	Philip H. Knight	653.6	20	0.0	653.6

Outboard Marine	James C. Chapman	412.0	8	203.3	615.3
Paramount	Martin S. Davis	2750.0	-25	2280.8	5030.8
Penney (J.C.)	William R. Howell	937.2	-6	387.3	1324.5
Polaroid	I. MacAllister Booth	528.4	N/A	150.5	678.9
Price	Robert E. Price	270.0	12	0.0	270.0
Reebok	Paul B. Fireman	2007.2	-86	0.0	2007.2
Rubbermaid	Walter W. Williams	825.6	N/A	1594.1	2419.7
Sears Roebuck	Edward A. Brennan	979.8	0	1508.4	2488.2
Service Merchandise	Raymond Zimmerman	754.6	1	0.0	754.6
Shaw Industries	Robert E. Shaw	1334.0	9	0.0	1334.0
Smith (A.O.)	Robert J. O'Toole	442.4	-21	0.0	442.4
Springs Industries	Walter Y. Elisha	816.3	74	59.6	875.9
Tandy	John V. Roach	722.9	-17	0.0	722.9
Times Mirror	Robert F. Erburu	909.4	3	577.5	1486.9
Timken	Joseph F. Toot Jr.	536.0	-18	0.0	536.0
Tribune	Charles T. Brumback	869.2	N/A	1147.8	2017.0
UAL	Stephen M. Wolf	575.0	0	2235.0	2810.0
USAir	Seth E. Schofield	466.8	N/A	425.1	891.9
Vons	Roger E. Stangeland	1009.4	14	0.0	1009.4
Walgreen	Charles R. Walgreen III	858.8	8	207.3	1066.1
Washington Post	Donald E. Graham	375.0	N/A	0.0	375.0
Wendy's Int'l	James W. Near	947.4	30	147.0	1094.4
Whirlpool	David R. Whitwam	1590.4	60	0.0	1590.4
Zenith	Jerry K. Pearlman	523.7	16	0.0	523.7
NONCYCLICAL					
Abbott Labs	Duane L. Burnham	1340.5	15	2867.0	4207.5
Albertson's	Gary G. Michael	701.2	N/A	1710.0	2411.2
Alco Standard	Ray B. Mundt	742.9	-29	880.8	1623.7
American Brands	William J. Alley	1826.3	12	89.2	1915.5
American Home Prods	John R. Stafford	1840.0	8	3790.0	5630.0
Anheuser-Busch	August A. Busch III	1878.8	8	4776.1	6654.9
Archer-Daniels-Midland	D.O. Andreas	2000.0	3	0.0	2000.0
Avon	James E. Preston	1192.9	0	2230.5	3423.4
Bausch & Lomb	Daniel E. Gill	1777.0	N/A	3720.3	5497.3
Baxter	Vernon R. Loucks Jr.	1785.5	2	2517.1	4302.6
Becton Dickinson	Raymond V. Gilmartin	757.4	4	180.2	937.6
Borden	R.J. Ventres	1513.5	N/A	0.0	1513.5
Bristol-Myers Squibb	Richard L. Gelb	2051.1	-2	10126.9	12178.0
CPC International	Charles R. Shoemate	920.8	N/A	374.9	1295.7
Campbell Soup	David W. Johnson	1444.3	N/A	0.0	1444.3
Clorox	C.R. Weaver	869.5	N/A	240.3	1109.8
Coca-Cola Co.	Roberto C. Goizueta	2962.0	0	943.6	3905.6
Coca-Cola Enterprises	Brian G. Dyson	786.6	N/A	4224.5	5011.1
Colgate-Palmolive	Reuben Mark	1747.6	N/A	0.0	1747.6
ConAgra	Charles M. Harper	2463.0	33	4748.8	7211.8
Dean Foods	Howard M. Dean	779.0	18	211.8	990.8
Dial	John W. Teets	2160.6	6	1415.5	3576.1
Fleming	Dean Werries	763.9	12	314.3	1078.2
General Mills	H. Brewster Atwater Jr.	1786.9	8	3100.1	4887.0
Gillette	Alfred M. Zeien	1111.7	N/A	2724.4	3836.1
Heinz (H.J.)	Anthony J.F. O'Reilly	1075.8	4	73723.9	74799.7
Hershey Foods	Richard A. Zimmerman	815.0	6	562.5	1377.5
Hormel	Richard L. Knowlton	1662.3	4	2337.5	3999.8

Humana	David A. Jones	1366.4	20	5045.0	6411.4
Johnson & Johnson	Ralph S. Larsen	1253.0	N/A	1160.9	2413.9
Kellogg	W.E. LaMothe	1852.2	18	7873.7	9725.9
Kroger	Joseph A. Pichler	600.4	-21	91.4	691.8
Lilly (Eli)	Richard D. Wood	2217.9	N/A	3856.5	6074.4
McCormick	Charles P. McCormick Jr.	1035.7	4	1591.5	N/A
Merck	P. Roy Vagelos	3344.5	N/A	0.0	3344.5
National Medical	Richard K. Eamer	1397.6	5	15515.6	16913.2
National Service	Sidney Kirschner	756.9	-7	0.0	756.9
PepsiCo	D. Wayne Calloway	1911.9	1	0.0	1911.9
Pfizer	William C. Steere Jr.	1113.0	N/A	842.6	1955.6
Philip Morris	Hamish Maxwell	1740.8	N/A	13936.6	15677.4
Procter & Gamble	Edwin L. Artzt	2180.9	N/A	371.8	2552.7
Quaker Oats	William D. Smithburg	1404.6	30	2211.8	3616.4
Ralston Purina	William P. Stiritz	1197.8	3	12614.9	13812.7
Sara Lee	John H. Bryan Jr.	1750.8	25	0.0	1750.8
Schering-Plough	Robert P. Luciano	1674.0	12	1634.5	3308.5
Sysco	John F. Woodhouse	1067.4	-5	0.0	1067.4
Tyson Foods	Leland Tollett	886.8	N/A	0.0	886.8
U.S. Surgical	Leon C. Hirsch	1351.3	N/A	21211.9	22563.2
Universal	Henry H. Harrell	533.1	11	0.0	533.1
Warner-Lambert	Melvin R. Goodes	1286.7	N/A	1665.2	2951.9
Whitman	James W. Cozad	1209.6	24	2012.0	3221.6
Winn-Dixie	A. Dano Davis	646.4	8	1115.1	1761.5
Wrigley	William Wrigley	729.3	1	403.5	1132.8
TECHNOLOGY					
AM International	Merle H. Banta	450.0	-38	0.0	450.0
AT&T	Robert E. Allen	2061.2	2	788.8	2850.0
Amdahl	John C. Lewis	637.3	N/A	0.0	637.3
Apple	John Sculley	1338.0	-39	14531.0	N/A
Boeing	Frank A. Shrontz	1188.0	9	0.0	1188.0
Compaq Computer	Joseph R. Canion	737.3	N/A	1195.6	1932.9
Control Data	Lawrence Perlman	756.0	-16	168.7	924.7
Corning	James R. Houghton	981.6	7	690.7	1672.3
Data General	Ronald L. Skates	817.5	76	1225.0	2042.5
Digital Equipment	Kenneth H. Olsen	995.0	1	0.0	995.0
E-Systems	E. Gene Keiffer	957.9	8	91.9	1049.8
GenCorp	A. William Reynolds	870.0	6	0.0	870.0
General Dynamics	William A. Anders	1500.0	N/A	2950.0	4450.0
General Electric	John F. Welch Jr.	3207.0	8	1893.8	5100.8
General Signal	Edmund M. Carpenter	962.2	27	187.8	1150.0
Grumman	Renso L. Caporali	595.0	37	64.5	659.5
Harris	J.T. Hartley	868.8	-19	79.8	948.6
Hewlett-Packard	John A. Young	1519.4	2	1491.9	3011.3
Honeywell	James J. Renier	1276.3	-13	1291.9	2568.2
IBM	John F. Akers	1575.0	-40	921.1	2496.1
Intel	Andrew S. Grove	1115.4	36	0.0	1115.4
Litton	Orion L. Hoch	1406.5	N/A	0.0	1406.5
Lockheed	Daniel M. Tellep	1225.0	21	89.8	1314.8
Martin Marietta	Norman R. Augustine	1261.5	12	2981.5	4243.0
McDonnell Douglas	John F. McDonnell	850.8	47	0.0	850.8
Minn. Mining & Manuf.	Allen F. Jacobson	1300.9	N/A	1216.1	2517.0
Motorola	George M.C. Fisher	1118.4	20	0.0	1118.4

National Semiconductor	Charles E. Sporck	730.7	23	0.0	730.7
Northrop	Kent Kresa	1261.3	12	945.7	2207.0
Perkin-Elmer	Gaynor N. Kelley	389.6	N/A	0.0	389.6
Pitney Bowes	George B. Harvey	1166.3	51	0.0	1166.3
Rockwell Int'l	Donald R. Beall	1517.0	2	695.2	2212.2
Rohr Industries	Robert H. Goldsmith	625.2	94	384.1	N/A
Seagate	Alan F. Shugart	1179.4	-16	890.6	2070.0
Sun Microsystems	Scott G. McNealy	1571.6	12	0.0	1571.6
Sundstrand	Harry C. Stonecipher	945.8	2	0.0	945.8
TRW	Joseph T. Gorman	1098.8	7	141.1	1239.9
Tandem Computers	James G. Treybig	452.8	-17	0.0	452.8
Tektronix	Jerome J. Meyer	791.6	N/A	0.0	791.6
Teledyne	William P. Rutledge	683.0	N/A	0.0	683.0
Texas Instruments	Jerry R. Junkins	604.1	1	5.3	609.4
Textron	B.F. Dolan	2859.7	N/A	175.1	3034.8
Unisys	James A. Unruh	990.0	70	16.9	1006.9
United Technologies	Robert F. Daniell	1166.3	-15	0.0	1166.3
Varian	J. Tracy O'Rourke	1772.5	N/A	229.0	2001.5
Wang	Richard W. Miller	1000.0	N/A	0.0	1000.0
Western Digital	Roger W. Johnson	538.5	-8	0.0	538.5
Xerox	Paul A. Allaire	1083.4	-9	506.8	1590.2
FINANCIAL					
Aetna	James T. Lynn	1086.5	2	0.0	1086.5
Aflac	Daniel P. Amos	1108.9	N/A	1264.9	2373.8
Ahmanson (H.F.)	Richard H. Deihl	1214.4	-1	229.4	1443.8
Alleghany	F.M. Kirby	979.4	1	855.8	1835.2
American Express	James D. Robinson III	1625.0	-10	0.0	1625.0
American General	Harold S. Hook	1766.3	32	2182.9	3949.2
American Int'l Group	Maurice R. Greenberg	1950.0	11	0.0	1950.0
Anchor Bancorp	James M. Large Jr.	556.2	6	0.0	556.2
Banc One	John B. McCoy	1782.6	43	387.1	2169.7
Bank of Boston	Ira Stepanian	650.0	0	0.0	650.0
Bank of New York	J. Carter Bacot	809.6	-7	68.5	878.1
BankAmerica	Richard M. Rosenberg	1600.0	0	2350.0	3950.0
Bankers Trust	Charles S. Sanford Jr.	1850.0	23	2197.1	4047.1
Bear Stearns	Alan C. Greenberg	5299.1	26	0.0	5299.1
Beneficial	Finn M.W. Caspersen	1991.8	3	0.0	1991.8
Chase Manhattan	Thomas G. Labrecque	1180.0	N/A	0.0	1180.0
Chemical Banking	Walter V. Shipley	1715.8	132	762.0	2477.8
Chubb	Dean R. O'Hare	1241.3	8	997.9	2239.2
Cigna	Wilson H. Taylor	1058.0	3	510.4	1568.4
Citicorp	John S. Reed	1150.0	1	0.0	1150.0
Dime Savings	Richard D. Parsons	525.0	20	0.0	525.0
First Bank System	John F. Grundhofer	1009.5	N/A	0.0	1009.5
First Chicago	Barry F. Sullivan	770.1	5	0.0	770.1
First Interstate	Edward M. Carson	665.2	N/A	145.1	810.3
First Union	Edward E. Crutchfield Jr.	650.0	8	291.1	941.1
Fleet/Norstar Financial	Terrence Murray	1402.0	85	493.6	N/A
General Re	Ronald E. Ferguson	1257.3	N/A	540.4	1797.7
Glenfed	Norman M. Coulson	596.7	-12	0.0	596.7
Golden West	Herbert M. Sandler	774.6	7	0.0	774.6
	Marion O. Sandler	774.4	7	0.0	774.4
Great Western	James F. Montgomery	1719.4	27	0.0	1719.4

Household Int'l	Donald C. Clark	1094.6	-23	0.0	1094.6
ITT	Rand V. Araskog	2800.0	-27	1080.0	3880.0
Kemper	Joseph E. Luecke	685.7	-6	245.7	931.4
Loews	Laurence A. Tisch	339.3	N/A	0.0	339.3
	Preston R. Tisch	1324.2	6	0.0	1324.2
Mellon	Frank V. Cahouet	1176.8	N/A	1753.0	2929.8
Merrill Lynch	William A. Schreyer	5850.0	256	5586.2	11436.2
Midlantic	Garry J. Scheuring	574.4	N/A	0.0	574.4
Morgan (J.P.)	Dennis Weatherstone	2043.2	30	2069.1	4112.3
Morgan Stanley	Richard B. Fisher	7620.0	N/A	0.0	7620.0
NationsBank	Hugh L. McColl Jr.	2000.0	186	1353.0	3353.0
Norwest	Lloyd P. Johnson	1628.3	18	1439.3	3067.6
PNC Financial	Thomas H. O'Brien	1294.4	75	0.0	1294.4
PaineWebber	Donald B. Marron	3600.0	279	0.0	3600.0
Primerica	Stanford I. Weill	3106.6	21	13672.3	16778.9
Republic New York	Walter H. Weiner	1019.6	7	0.0	1019.6
Safeco	Bruce Maines	649.0	13	1068.0	1717.0
Schwab (Charles)	Charles R. Schwab	3176.2	73	0.0	3176.2
St. Paul	Douglas W. Leatherdale	954.5	0	238.7	1193.2
SunTrust	James B. Williams	601.7	37	5354.1	5955.8
Transamerica	Frank C. Herringer	1100.1	N/A	162.5	1262.6
Travelers	Edward H. Budd	923.1	32	0.0	923.1
U.S. Bancorp	Roger L. Breezley	623.3	5	0.0	623.3
USF&G	Norman P. Blake Jr.	1346.9	N/A	0.0	1346.9
Unum	James F. Orr III	1067.2	4	1377.4	2444.6
Wells Fargo	Carl E. Reichardt	775.0	-47	0.0	775.0
UTILITIES					
American Elec. Power	Richard E. Disbrow	618.0	N/A	0.0	618.0
Ameritech	William L. Weiss	1270.0.	-2	849.2	2119.2
Bell Atlantic	Raymond W. Smith	1457.2	14	1293.6	2750.8
Bell South	John L. Clendenin	1355.5	-1	39.6	1395.1
Centerior Energy	Richard A. Miller	504.6	8	41.7	546.3
Commonwealth Edison	James J. O'Connor	671.0	N/A	0.0	671.0
Con Edison	Eugene R. McGrath	802.7	N/A	0.0	802.7
Detroit Edison	John E. Lobbia	522.0	18	0.0	522.0
Duke Power	William S. Lee	624.9	4	0.0	624.9
Entergy	Edwin Lupberger	641.6	-15	38.9	680.5
FPL	James L. Broadhead	1120.5	29	0.0	1120.5
GPU	William G. Kuhns	537.4	N/A	0.0	537.4
GTE	James L. Johnson	2167.8	24	709.3	2877.1
Lilco	William J. Catacosinos	455.0	15	0.0	455.0
MCI Communications	William G. McGowan	1594.4	N/A	2594.4	4188.8
Nynex	William C. Ferguson	1214.5	16	338.7	1553.2
Ohio Edison	Justin T. Rogers Jr.	526.3	28	0.0	526.3
PacifiCorp	A.M. Gleason	1055.3	10	1279.2	2334.5
Pacific Enterprises	James R. Ukropina	594.0	N/A	440.0	1034.0
Pacific Telesis	Sam Ginn	1113.7	16	726.7	1840.4
Philadelphia Electric	Joseph F. Paquette Jr.	696.0	38	0.0	696.0
SCEcorp	John E. Bryson	810.0	N/A	125.6	935.6
Southern Co.	Edward L. Addison	971.8	N/A	0.0	971.8
Southwestern Bell	Edward E.Whitacre Jr.	1379.8	0	1088.2	2468.0
U S West	Richard D. McCormick	660.0	N/A	740.7	1400.7
Union Electric	William E. Cornelius	660.0	19	0.0	660.0

Appendix Table C.1 Random Numbers

53535	04260	77609	93799	92171	45524	10968	30231	70864	29908
41292	15201	66342	59155	46163	69248	31029	62034	21855	27863
07320	22682	09595	44805	54593	53350	61354	14029	10195	18644
77676	67772	45072	08940	02592	45976	82099	90739	77072	42081
43227	20568	16309	23841	53173	39475	27282	82699	00022	96419
90712	41695	67474	27567	93269	10163	94190	36188	41491	71217
88103	21514	60787	33170	58215	89951	01634	98155	05154	08971
72252	35791	84125	31962	81093	93068	41197	57779	88515	48002
51702	49516	69510	19678	47298	11355	68459	96360	13436	66314
63055	86998	22187	59898	96371	61370	35937	34292	00678	33505
32373	57889	85880	66515	37489	37854	72926	23437	62233	38651
71996	16525	25618	56577	69130	25035	93551	54394	81572	90624
26912	70619	22576	22780	99118	18487	58801	36063	32886	60453
74589	82677	13353	67658	17080	43212	34585	17179	86980	81899
56041	53072	19912	47466	32585	41414	07564	80712	27286	07966
09286	68067	84883	10023	78195	84711	85988	31545	39904	14984
33610	84843	07145	38437	06148	06094	89601	96751	49124	55092
14113	06396	59084	02534	09360	81918	77118	91640	92978	24815
56302	89765	63857	42747	28592	41784	00822	60356	96389	11728
06362	94540	29532	09994	55277	43897	63268	40481	00312	46039
48568	34412	84939	54850	84317	92032	60130	49071	68962	28953
65975	60965	77679	95782	67541	50654	09482	56111	98710	35803
66686	32977	48472	30226	54226	72490	18395	37338	88279	79089
51610	13000	73849	46654	30324	78000	72852	28934	83197	59003
47600	86103	25788	08774	72020	04543	25849	88887	41159	30131
34860	67572	83116	99579	81303	41889	56577	64142	51596	25329
76649	50908	67006	29332	29689	68786	98987	34815	53512	20620
78321	54309	85956	04976	37863	06711	72679	03405	28770	08515
35775	21295	39621	02339	16537	42246	06571	81193	94930	05376
06783	21338	89886	78826	02303	37886	70453	11021	62887	36855
25887	53024	71881	51208	95739	98572	01903	68043	62661	71273
37784	42100	70838	78963	10927	05448	25759	74051	47577	30196
02120	59536	82996	22671	89267	65924	46725	69179	15182	59158
55292	03836	28883	71134	08547	93204	09656	11671	29735	59573
66186	43648	97926	80469	66412	73647	36779	84688	96862	51937
55010	11479	55036	82146	37120	62328	56276	28906	45311	61818
02322	18679	18478	30052	05666	84405	47513	09244	78978	91819
78056	67836	82582	25809	20198	37222	62629	75733	77420	58746
69812	88260	83519	10062	60865	35038	14665	18163	59351	25794
84904	66864	26982	37928	32988	87652	81415	24416	93778	20391
83143	47631	79772	08576	10311	17597	71049	63326	47168	05737
44423	71197	91081	40781	72403	76245	31881	55716	89255	71997
59882	58479	59609	80115	91569	23152	51781	85744	78640	80172
74890	90405	75945	31645	61008	24448	42249	84909	29013	12529
52174	64334	77631	19855	17723	02897	80427	20700	92210	92091
41361	24347	53420	33639	83765	97935	83630	33765	21502	15589
94585	84798	98480	08335	08728	60428	22282	76784	37316	08624
36020	71966	61443	12554	67446	08676	46177	22422	87471	27283
08112	59807	28404	60316	49676	52901	90604	48379	85233	52060
05853	69681	52034	77617	78644	57321	14162	01849	94684	14628

Short Answers to Selected Exercises

Chapter 1

1.2 Yes. The set of all students taking a course in a given semester can be viewed as the population in research on those who take the course that semester. It can be viewed as a sample in a study where the population is the set of all students attending the university.

1.4

1.4	less than 25,000	0.033
	25,000–99,999	0.773
	100,000–199,999	0.168
	200,000–299,999	0.021
	300,000–399,999	0.004
	400,000+	0.002

1.6 Quarterbacks (1–19) tend to weigh less than running backs (20–49), who tend to weigh less than offensive linemen (50–79).

1.8 The former is a cross-sectional analysis; the latter is time series.

1.10 Depends on the data source.

1.12 The average age for deaths in a region in a given year tells us nothing about life expectancies at that age.

1.14 That more than 1 percent of those 30 percent who refused the interview may have had sex exclusively with other men in the past ten years.

Chapter 2

2.2 Consumer satisfaction is a qualitative variable. It is only meaningful to compare the order of the rankings and not the relative magnitudes.

2.4 $4.114 million

2.6 a. 1.85
b. 23,400

2.8 When a distribution is unimodal, continuous and symmetric.

2.10 a. 67.78
b. 70
c. Any value can be a mode.

2.12 a. The mean is 16.47; the median is 16.50.
b. The distribution is left skewed.

2.14 The medians for three years are approximately 15, 14.375, and 22.5 weeks, respectively.

Not all means can be calculated because the class 30+ is open.

2.16 The medians for three spreadsheets are 7.15, 5.825, and 6.34, respectively. The median is a better measure of central tendency because the values in this data set are qualitative.

2.18 He is probably referring to the median because he is comparing an average survival of 7.3 months with his own result that "half" of the patients have survived 23 months or longer.

2.20 Sample mean = 52.09(= 520.9/10 : sum of values divided by number of values). Sample standard deviation = 32.5438(= $\sqrt{1059.10}$: square root of sample variance). Sample variance = 1059.10(= 9531.9189/9: sum of squared deviations divided by degrees of freedom (n−1)). Standard error of the mean = 10.29125 = 32.5438/3.16 (the sample standard deviation divided by the square root of the sample size).

The other advertisers bought $1,069 million of commercial time.

2.22 The mean of data set B is 100 times larger than the mean of data set A. The variance is 10,000 times larger for data set B than for data set A. These relationships would hold even if these were population data.

2.24 The approximate sample mean is $9,520.

The approximate sample standard deviation is $190.595.

2.28 CEO compensation tends to deviate from its mean in the same direction as the number of headquartered companies deviates from its mean. This implies that the CEO compensation and the number of headquartered companies are positively related to each other.

2.30 The smallest fraction of calls that are handled within 25 and 85 seconds is about 0.95.

2.32 "At most" 44 percent of total students could have been paid above $140,000.

2.34 The mean delivery time is 156 minutes. The exact median and the mode cannot be calculated.

2.36 5th percentile = 3.90; 15th = 9.25; 25th = 11.70; 35th = 13.50; 45th = 15.35; 55th = 17.70; 65th = 20.65; 75th = 24.90; 85th = 33; 95th = 59.50.

2.40 An approximate median is 17.6 percent.

To calculate the median, we have to assume the observations are evenly spread within the median class.

2.42 The median numbers of times of play per year are 12 for skiers, 25 for tennis players, and 25 for golfers, respectively. The means and modes cannot be determined.

2.44 It would be possible to observe that 54.2 percent are above average if the distribution of the cost is left skewed.

2.46 The mean and median are not equal in each year because the distribution of automobile output is not symmetric. Mean in 1992 = 144524; mean in 1991 = 142188.6. Median in 1992 = 62000; median in 1991 = 49000.

2.48 The percentage change in average is a better measure of change than the percentage change in median.

2.50 a. No
b. No
c. Yes
d. Yes

2.52 For Austin-Los Angeles, Continental Airline has the median price of $258. For the remaining two cities, the medians cannot be clearly identified.

2.54 Mean = 41,914.8; median = 37,750; mode = 38,000 or 46,000; range =182,460; variance = 1,332,754,040; standard deviation = 36,506.904

2.56 a. The means cannot be calculated because the class 11+ is open. Approximate medians are 3.46 days and 5.63 days.
b. The data is not a proper form for a frequency distribution because there is an open class. It is not possible to calculate the mean with this data set.
c. The approximate median is a better measure because it can be determined without any trouble caused by the open class.

2.58 The sample mean is $21.618. The sample median is $18.42. The sample variance is 24.886 and hence the standard deviation is $4.989.

2.60 Average yearly production has increased with the introduction of new body styles, except for the last several years. Although the model average may show a trend in Corvette popularity, if the number of years that each model is produced is too different, then model average may not be comparable.

2.62 Average capital/asset ratio = 16.21 percent; the ratio of (average capital)/(average asset) = 14.64 percent

The average capital/asset ratio is the simple arithmetic average of capital/asset ratios of 100 banks while the ratio of (average capital)/(average asset) is nothing but the sum of 100 weighted capital/asset ratios(using the asset/(sum of asset) ratio as each weight).

2.64	Sales	Profit
U.S. firms:	6.77%	-7.73%
Netherlands/U.K. firms:	4.69%	2.94%
Japan firms:	6.43%	-12.22%
Germany firms:	12.75%	20.00%
France firms:	13.00%	6.00%
Italy firm:	16.00%	N.A.
Switzerland firms:	11.00%	26.00%
Australia firm:	16.00%	9.00%

2.66 Women are receiving less than the men. The median salaries are \$33,150 versus \$39,850. Even if the ten highest paid women each received \$50,000 raises, nothing changes in the median salary for women.

The mean is a better measure when assessing the cost of removing salary differences because both means would be exactly the same if a total of \$1,894,439.838(= (218)(43331.449 – 34641.358)) is raised for salaries for those 218 women.

2.68 Time of arrival seems to affect the range of wait time. Range of wait time tends to be small in early hours of the day with the exception of 0 – 2 hour time interval.

Chapter 3

3.2 An outcome is one of possible results in a statistical experiment. An event is a subset of the sample space that is formed by outcomes that share an attribute of interest.

3.4 Although the chance of failure is minuscule, we can observe it actually happens in less than 300 years, and we did. The Challenger accident could be understood as an event with a minuscule probability that was actually observed. The occurrence of an uncertain event is not tied to a fixed number of trials.

3.6 As long as there is a limited number of trials we cannot guarantee that the relative frequency of 0.2 will be actually realized.

3.8 They are different because one statement is referring to a fixed number of trials while the other is referring to an infinite number of trials.

3.12 720

3.14 1/3

3.16 3/10

3.20 a. False; if $P(A_1|A_2) = P(A_1)$, then they are independent.
b. True; $P(A_1|A_2) = 0$ implies $P(A_1|A_2) = P(A_1 \text{ and } A_2)/P(A_2) = 0$ and thus implies $P(A_1 \text{ and } A_2) = 0$.
c. False; two probability do not need to be the same for independent events.

3.22 0.0675

3.24 Letting P(A) be the probability that an institutional investor would favor the creation of a compensation committee, P(B) be the probability that an institutional investor would favor a compensation committee that has the power to hire and pay compensation consultants, P(A) = 0.66 and P(B) = 0.50 are given. P(B|A), however, is not given. Thus, we cannot calculate P(A and B), i.e., the probability that an institutional investor would favor the creation of a compensation committee that has the power to hire and pay compensation consultants.

3.26 0.0532

3.28 0.15

3.30 0.96

Chapter 4

4.2 Approximately 0.5

4.4 The expected value is calculated with probabilities. Thus, the expected value is not based on what has occurred but on what would occur over an infinite number of trials.

4.6 Because the expected payoff (\$50) is less than the cost of the policy (\$210), you would be better off not buying it.

4.8 The reason someone buys the service insurance policy might be that they calculate their expected payoff to be greater than the insurance cost (i.e., they subjectively estimate the probability of total destruction to be greater than 0.19192).

4.10 a. The profit to be made on sale of a 27-inch Schwinn.
b. \$40.50
c. 62.25 square dollars
d. \$4,050

4.12 a. 3.00
b. 1.24
c. 96 percent
d. The result is consistent with the "Rule of Thumb"

4.14 The risk neutral would prefer the investment C because it has the largest expected net return. The risk neutral does not care about the risk, but is only interested in the long run net return.

4.16 The risk neutral would prefer the investment B because it has a larger expected net return.

4.18 a. Marginal probabilities are calculated as follows:

	A_1	A_2	A_3	marginal
B_1	0.12	0.03	0.10	0.25
B_2	0.21	0.02	0.18	0.41
B_3	0.11	0.09	0.14	0.34
marginal	0.44	0.14	0.42	1.00

b. 0.12
c. 0.64
d. 0.48
e. not independent

4.20 $5,038.6

4.22 1500($)

4.24 478.71

4.26 a. 2.3
b. 2.3
c. 0

4.28 a. 1.41
b. 1.41
c. 0

4.30 –6.67($)

4.32 What is important to the insurance company is the amount of claim per accident. If the amount of claim is large, the expected loss could also be large, although the probability of accident is not high.

4.34 The word "expects" implies the expected value of Pepsi's market share.

4.36 He meant that the expected payoff for the lottery buyer is less than the cost to buy it.

4.38 a. Because of the increase in cost of administrating lotteries.
b. There would have been more educated people and thus an increase in numbers of those educated people who are not willing to buy lottery tickets might have led to future reduction in lottery revenues.

Chapter 5

5.2 0.0193

5.4 0.987

5.6 0.410. We have to assume that five mail friends should be a random sample from the large population of American men who use a hair dryer.

5.8 0.999967 ~ 1.0
We have to assume that each member independently decides to uphold a guilty verdict, which does not seem to be a reasonable assumption.

5.10 0.1536

5.12 a. 2; 1.26.
b. 8.5; 2.06.
c. 22.5; 2.37.

5.14 a. 2.1
b. 0.027

5.16 0.172. This probability could be viewed as "large." Thus, we might again question NordicTrack's ad.

5.18 a. fewer
b. 0.0036

5.20 0.049, for $\pi = .9$
0.375, for $\pi = .5$

5.24 approximately zero

5.26 $E(x) = 2.4$
$\text{var}(x) = 0.48$

5.28 0.096

5.30 0.3125

5.32 0.04

5.34 approximately zero

Chapter 6

6.2 The standard normal distribution is the normal distribution with zero mean and unit standard deviation. A normal random variable can take any value as its mean, and any positive value as its standard deviation. Once a distribution is normal, it can be easily converted into the standard normal distribution using the converting formula in calculating probabilities.

6.4 a. –2.55
b. 0.91
c. 3.43
d. 0.98
e. –2.00
f. 0.43

6.6 a. 53.8
b. 39.4
c. 48.04
d. 25.72
e. there is no such value of b
f. 17.8

6.8 0.9210

6.10 It does not seem to be reasonable to assume that the distribution is normal because the distribution is highly right skewed with a very large value pulling up the mean.

6.12 \$154.60

6.14 The probability that an agent is overcharged more than \$585 is less than 0.01, which is extremely unlikely. We typically do not observe unlikely events, so given the agent is truthful, either the assumption of normality or the assumed \$25 undercharge mean must be called into question.

6.16 62.47 percent

6.18 0.0001

6.20 The implied value of σ should lie between 3.8 and 4.4.

6.22 0.0287

6.24 0.2946

6.26 0.9216

Because the line speed is a continuous random variable that can be expected to vary symmetrically around its mean, with values closer to the mean occurring most often, it seems reasonable to assume that the average line speed (X) is normally distributed.

6.28 In order to satisfy the rule of normality, the distance between the mean and the upper end point and the distance between the mean and the lower end point should be the same. The distance between the mean and the upper end point is \$248,760(= 330000 – 81240) while the distance between the mean and the lower end point is \$61,240(= 81240 – 20000); the distribution cannot be symmetric, but is right skewed with a long right tail. It is reasonable to assume that the distribution is lognormal, because right skewed distributions can be transformed into lognormal distributions.

Chapter 7

7.2 Suppose the mean time devoted to prayer in the United States is to be estimated for Catholics, Jews, Muslims, and Protestants. Because these groups are not of equal size, simple random sampling might get none or too few of the smallest group. To avoid this, a number proportional to each group's representation in the population could be selected at random; thus, variability between the groups (strata) is controlled and precision is increased.

7.4 For a sample to be a random sample each and every element or set of elements in the population must have an equal chance to be selected into a sample. Those who valued their time at more than \$1.00 were less likely to respond.

7.6 Answer depends on the random numbers used.

7.8 Decreases; 1/2.

7.10 The standard error of the mean is the standard deviation of the sampling distribution of the mean, which Altman does not acknowledge. It is a measure of the average variability in the sample means around the population mean and it is equal to $\sigma/\sqrt{n}$, where σ is the standard deviation of the values in the population and n is the sample size. The standard error of the mean is estimated by $s/\sqrt{n}$, where s is the standard deviation of values in a sample. Altman's definition does not distinguish clearly between σ and s; his statement about the standard deviation pertains to s and not σ.

7.12 Yes. The standard error of an estimator varies inversely with the sample size but increasing the sample size does not result in proportional reductions in the standard error.

7.14 Whenever the sample size is large enough (i.e., $n \geq 30$), we can assert that the sampling distribution of the sample mean is approximately normally distributed according to the Central Limit Theorem.

7.16 a. 0.1587
b. 0.0228
c. The sample size is 1 in a and 4 in b. If n = 1, the sampling distribution of the sample mean is just the population distribution itself. With a larger size sample, sampling distribution of the sample mean has smaller standard deviation than that in the population.

7.18 0.1056

We need to assume that the population of time in household work is normally distributed in order to have a normally distributed sampling distribution of the sample mean of time. We don't need additional assumptions about the distribution of the mean time and about the sample of 4 families.

7.20 0.9332

7.22 a. False. There is no reason to believe that any one value of the sample proportion would equal to the population proportion.
b. False. The sample size has nothing to do with whether the population proportion is equal to a sample proportion.
c. Yes. See above.
d. False. The variance of the distribution of the sample proportion is $\pi(1 - \pi)/n$ where π is the population proportion, while the variance of X is σ^2.
e. False. s^2/n is an estimator of the variance of the sample mean. It has nothing to do with the variance of the sampling distribution of the sample proportion.
f. Yes. The variance of the sample proportion for samples of size n equals $\pi(1 - \pi)/n$ where π is the population proportion.

7.24 a. 0.206
b. 0.1446

7.26 Because division managers *handpicked* the 35 employees from the pool of 1,700 employees, it cannot be considered to be a random sample.

7.28 a. mean of 320 lbs.
b. 0.0013
c. 10 lbs.

7.30 Since the sample size n = 16 is not large, we need to assume that the population distribution is normal to answer the question. Under this assumption, the sample mean width will be normally distributed with a mean of 0.25 inches and a standard deviation of 0.0000025 inches. The probability that a sample mean is 0.25007 or larger will be 0.0000.

7.32 11.504

7.34 Even if the population mean (μ) is negative, we might observe a sample mean ($\bar{x}$) of 5.5 percent or greater. Thus, it could be possible to observe 5.5 percent or greater as a monthly change in sales of new homes when the sales in fact decreased.

7.36 $2.85 < \frac{\sigma}{\sqrt{4}} < 3.3$

7.38 Because the distribution of the time to be "up and running" is highly left skewed, it might be appropriate to use the binomial distribution instead of the normal distribution even though the sample size is relatively large. We can compare the following probabilities:

If the binomial random variable X denotes the number of "successes" with $\pi = 0.98$ when 30 days are randomly drawn, then the probability of getting 29 or fewer "successes" is

$$P(x \le 29 \mid n = 30, \pi = 0.98) =$$
$$\sum_{x=0}^{29} \binom{30}{x} 0.98^x (1-0.98)^{30-x} = 4.55$$

Or as an alternative method, we could try a calculation with the normal distribution. The sampling distribution of the sample proportion (p) is approximately normal with a mean of 0.98 and

$$0.0256 \left(= \sqrt{\frac{(0.98)(0.02)}{30}} \right) = \sigma/\sqrt{n}$$

Thus, the probability that the sample proportion (p) is 0.9667(= 29/30) or less will be

$$P(p \le 0.9667) = P\left(z \le \frac{0.9667 - 0.98}{0.0256} \right)$$
$$= P(z \le -0.52) = 0.3015$$

These two probabilities do not seem to agree with each other. The probability 0.455, calculated using the binomial distribution, can be regarded to be more accurate.

7.40 The probability of getting the mean difference 7.83 or greater is 0.0000.

Chapter 8

8.2 They are interchangeable before sampling, when a sample statistic has not yet been calculated. But once a confidence interval has been constructed based on a sample, the words are no longer interchangeable because the value of the random variable has been realized and thus there is no chance to which probability applies.

8.4 a. No, because they take their own samples independently, they are likely to have different samples and different sample means.
b. It depends on the situation. If σ is unknown and thus they must use their own sample standard deviations (s) instead of σ, then the margin of error will not be the same.

8.6 99.8 percent

8.8 2.58

8.10 The margin of error depends on the value of the sample proportion p. Thus, the margin of error for each question would not be the same as long as the sample proportion for each question differs.

8.12 a. 0.048 c. 2.11
b. 0.990 d. 1.71

8.14 Because the t distribution has more variability, the confidence interval using the t distribution is wider than the interval using the z distribution, other things being equal.

8.16 If the distribution of $\bar{x}$ is normal and the population standard deviation (σ) is known, the z distribution has to be used. But even in such a situation, t distribution can also be used instead of z, if the sample size is large enough.

8.18 0.242. Under the assumption of normality of the population of the car prices, the distribution of $\bar{x}$ is normal with a mean of 21,750 and a standard deviation of 849.618 ($= \sigma/\sqrt{n} = 2081.131/\sqrt{6}$)assuming $\sigma \sim s$.

8.20 a. 6.28 cents per dollar of sales.
b. 0.2794
c. $5.70 < \mu < 6.86$

8.22 $0.2286 < \pi < 0.4114$

8.24 $0.798 < \pi < 0.922$

8.26 $0.52 < \pi < 0.70$

8.28 a. n = 173 is required.
b. We need a sample size four times as large as what was originally required.
c. n = 40 is required.

8.30 139 or more.

8.32 a. Neither is appropriate.
b. z is appropriate.
c. Neither is appropriate.
d. t is appropriate.
e. Either may be used.
f. z is appropriate.

8.34 The pay distribution is usually highly right skewed with a few high paying jobs pulling up the mean.

8.36 This confidence interval does not say that chances are 95 percent that population average salary is within ± $410 of the survey result. We can say only that under repeated sampling, 95 percent of similarly constructed intervals would contain the true population average and the interval 29,700 ± 410 may (or may not) be one of those intervals.

8.38 984 or more.

8.40 a. 54.48
b. $46.26 < \mu < 62.70$
c. There is a truncation or censoring problem in the calculation of the mean and the confidence interval if there are bills that are never paid.

8.42 $339.961 < \mu < 2020.529$

8.44 2.7. We must consider a random sample of size 3 or more.

8.46 $0.61 < \pi < 0.69$

8.48 a. $0.62 < \pi < 1.04$

b. The interval constructed in part a is wrong because a proportion cannot exceed 1. We get this strange result because the sample size 12 is not large enough to assume that the sampling distribution of the sample proportion (p) is approximately normal.

8.50 The "unbiasedness" used in this quote implies that the opinion of a real estate appraiser is not biased for a specific interest. The "unbiasedness" in statistical estimation means that the mean of an estimator is equal to the corresponding population parameter.

8.52 The point estimate of the population proportion is the sample proportion, which is 0.07, and the point estimate of the standard deviation of the distribution of the sample proportion is 0.012.

8.54 a. 0.429

b. We need to assume that the population distribution is normal so that the sampling distribution of sample mean can be normal.

c. At a typical confidence level of 95 percent, a confidence interval for the population mean receipt is $465.88 < \mu < 576.52$. This interval includes the Healthy's claimed value \$517.40. This suggests the claimed value could be consistent with the true average receipt of the company and thus the IRS does not need to pursue the company.

8.56 95 percent.

8.58 $0.46 < \pi < 0.62$. This interval includes not only the majority (more than 50 percent) of judges but also 50 percent or less. This implies that the majority of judges does not necessarily think sexual bias is widespread in California state courts.

8.60 Because the distribution of the time to be "up and running" is highly left skewed, it would not be appropriate to use the normal distribution in a confidence interval construction even though the sample size (30) is relatively large.

8.62 The margin of error is 5 percentage points in either direction of the poll result. Using p as the sample proportion (poll result), a 95 percent (as implied by the statement "chances are 19 to 20") classical confidence interval for π is p ± 5%. This confidence interval of p ± 5%, however, does not say that chances are 19 to 20 (95 percent) that population proportion π (proportion of black-owned business with annual revenue of at least \$100,000) is within 5 percent of the poll result. We can say again that in classical statistics the population proportion is a parameter so there is no probability or chance associated with this interval estimate.

Chapter 9

9.2 A small p-value indicates an unlikely sample result when the null hypothesis is assumed to be correct. The observation of sample data that is highly unlikely casts doubt on the correctness of the null hypothesis.

9.4 To test the claim, we start by assuming $\mu = 1{,}000$ where μ is the average or expected life (hours) of the lightbulb. We have to randomly draw a sample of n packages ($n \geq 30$, so that we have an approximately normal distribution of sample mean). Using the sample mean x from this sample, we can calculate the test statistic to test the correctness of the claim.

$z = \dfrac{\bar{x} - \mu_0}{\sigma / \sqrt{n}} = \dfrac{\bar{x} - 1000}{50 / \sqrt{n}}$ where $\bar{x}$ and n are obtained from the sample.

If this calculated test statistic is "large" then we can reject the claim that $\mu = 1{,}000$.

9.6 a. H_0: $\mu = 87.4$ vs. H_A: $\mu \neq 87.4$, where μ is average number of applicants for a training program in sales at IBM.

b. H_0: $\mu = 0.05$ vs. H_A: $\mu \neq 0.05$, where μ is the inflation rate (%) in the area.

c. H_0: $\mu \geq 3$ vs. H_A: $\mu < 3$, where μ is the average sick days per employee per month at GM.

d. H_0: $\pi \leq 0.1$ vs. H_A: $\pi > 0.1$, where π is the defect rate (%) for the machine.

e. H_0: $\mu \leq .018$ vs. H_A: $\mu > .018$, where μ is the average stretch (%) of the new line at 15 percent of its working load.

f. H_0: $\mu = 378$ vs. H_A: $\mu \neq 378$, where μ is the average cost (\$) of piece work.

g. H_0: $\mu \leq 1000$ vs. H_A: $\mu > 1000$, where μ is the average breaking strength (lbs.) of the new composite per square inch.

h. H_0: $\pi \leq 0.07$ vs. H_A: $\pi > 0.07$, where π is the proportion (%) of unemployment in the next recession.

i. H_0: $\pi \geq 0.06$ vs. H_A: $\pi < 0.06$, where π is the proportion (%) of overdue accounts receivable.

9.8 a. $z_{critical} = \pm 2.33$
b. $t_{critical} = 1.753$
c. $z_{critical} = \pm 1.96$

9.10 A Type I error occurs if the null hypothesis is rejected in favor of the alternative when in fact the null hypothesis is true. Thus, 1 – P(Type I error) equals the probability of accepting the null hypothesis when it is correct. This does not equal the probability of making a Type II error.

9.14 If the hypothesized value of the population parameter in the null hypothesis is found to be inside the $(1 - \alpha)$ 100 percent confidence interval constructed based on a sample result, this implies that the null hypothesis value could not be rejected at a level of the probability of Type I error as high as α.

9.16 a. $H_O: \mu \geq 10{,}000$ vs. $H_A: \mu < 10{,}000$, where μ is the average mileage of the company's cars.
b. The null hypothesis cannot be rejected (i.e., the company's claim cannot be accepted as true) unless the level of α is set at 24 percent or higher, which is hardly usual.

9.18 We can conclude that the new process is better than the old.

9.20 To test the hypothesis $H_O: \mu \leq 1.0$ vs. $H_A: \mu > 1.0$, where μ is the average number of defects per car, we need to know the sample size and the sample standard deviation (or the population standard deviation) for the sample that produced a sample mean of 5.1 in order to conduct a z or t test.

9.22 a. $H_O: \pi = 0.5$ vs. $H_A: \pi \neq 0.5$, where π is the winners' chance of repeating their success.
c. 0.049
d. The value of the estimate could have been between 0.405 (40.5 percent) and 0.595 (59.5 percent). With any estimated value in this range, the p-value cannot be smaller than 0.05 and thus the null hypothesis cannot be rejected.

9.24 We need to test the following hypothesis:

$H_O: \pi \leq 1/3$ vs. $H_A: \pi > 1/3$, where π is the proportion of consumers who prefer bottle A. The p-value is 0.2843.

Because this p-value is greater than the α level 0.1, H_O cannot be rejected. Or equivalently, the test statistic $z = 0.65$ is not beyond the critical value $z_{0.1} = 1.28$ and thus H_O cannot be rejected. We cannot conclude that more than one third of the customers prefer bottle A.

9.26 We need to test the following hypothesis:

$H_O: \mu = \mu_O$ vs. $H_A: \mu \neq \mu_O$ where μ is the composition of vapors of the batch of alloys and μ_O is the norm.

Type I error would be rejecting the idea that composition of vapors does not deviate from the norm when in fact it does not deviate from the norm.

Type II error would be saying that the composition of vapors does not deviate from the norm and thus accept the batch when in fact it deviates from the norm.

9.28 a. Assuming the population distribution is normal, we have to use the t distribution for testing because the population standard deviation is unknown and the sample size is not large.
b. The p-value is 0.245 where the degrees of freedom of the t is 15. Since the p-value is greater than the α level 0.05, we cannot reject the null hypothesis. We cannot conclude that the average is more than six defects per car.

9.30 We need to test the following hypothesis:

$H_O: \pi = 0.5$ vs. $H_A: \pi \neq 0.5$, where π is the proportion of companies that showed a stock price falling after move.

The p-value is 0.4654. Because this p-value is greater than a typical α level 0.05, H_O cannot be rejected. The test result does not contradict the *WSJ*'s hypothesis.

9.32 We need to test the following hypothesis:

$H_O: \mu = 42$ vs. $H_A: \mu \neq 42$, where μ is the average passenger miles flown.

The p-value is 0.816 (=2(0.408)). Because this p-value is greater than a typical α level 0.05, H_O cannot be rejected. We can conclude that the regulators' claim has been realized.

9.34 a. We need to test the following hypothesis:

$H_O: \mu \leq 0.19$ vs. $H_A: \mu > 0.19$, where μ is Folger's average market share.

b. Using the t distribution, the p-value will be 0.146 where the degrees of freedom of the t is 9. Because this p-value is greater than a typical α level 0.05, H_O cannot be rejected. We cannot conclude that the market share exceeds 19 percent this year.

9.36 We need to test the following set of hypotheses: H_O: $\pi \leq 0.5$ vs. $H_A: \pi > 0.5$, where π is the proportion of GE 60-watt lightbulbs lasting longer than 1,000 hours. The p-value will be 0.0475.

Because this p-value is less than the given α level 0.05, H_O can be rejected. Or equivalently, the test statistic $z = 1.68$ is beyond the critical value $z_{0.05} = 1.645$ and thus H_O can be rejected.

9.40 a. If some consumers refuse to answer, the sample of those consumers who participate cannot be interpreted as random.

b. We need to test the following set of hypotheses:

H_O: $\pi = 0.36$ vs. H_A: $\pi \neq 0.36$, where π is the proportion of American consumers who would not respond to questions.

To test this, a large ($n \geq 30$) sample should be obtained to have a sample proportion and thus calculate the test statistic z. If the test statistic is beyond the critical value of z, then we can reject H_O in favor of H_A.

9.42 a. The following set of hypotheses needs to be tested:

H_O: $\mu \geq 500{,}000$ vs. H_A: $\mu < 500{,}000$ where μ is the average amount ($) of commission. The p-value will be 0.0000 where the degrees of freedom of the t is 24. Because this p-value is much smaller than a typical α level 0.05, H_O can be rejected. We can conclude that the average commission is smaller than the claimed $500,000.

b. The competitor's sample cannot be viewed to be random because the sample only included those brokers who applied for the competitor's fictitious position. This lack of randomness may have caused a lower sample average and thus a false conclusion in the test in part a.

9.44 We need to test the following hypothesis:

H_O: $\mu = 12$ vs. H_A: $\mu \neq 12$, where μ is the average percentage of health care cost.

Using the t distribution, the test statistic will be $t = -0.178$.

Because this calculated t statistic −0.178 is not beyond the critical value $-t_{(\alpha = 0.025, df = 9)} = -2.262$ at the given α level 0.05, the null hypothesis cannot be rejected.

9.46 We need to test the following set of hypotheses: H_O: $\pi = 0.5$ vs. H_A: $\pi \neq 0.5$, where π is the proportion of law firms having marketing specialists. The p-value will be 0.4238. Because this p-value is greater than a typical α level 0.05, H_O cannot be rejected. We can conclude that the observed 48 percent is not significantly different from the hypothesized 50 percent.

9.48 We need to test the following set of hypotheses: H_O: $\pi = 0.5$ vs. H_A: $\pi \neq 0.5$, where π is the proportion of decisions in favor of plaintiffs. The calculated z statistic will be 2.36. Because the test statistic $z = 2.36$ is beyond the critical value $z_{0.025} = 1.96$, H_O can be rejected at a typical α level 0.05. We can conclude that there is a significant difference between Han's sample and the national norm.

9.50 The observation that five (39 percent) of the 13 died implies nothing about the hypothesis that drinking prior to riding increases the risk of falling and dying. To test this hypothesis we need to know the proportion of those who drank and fell and the proportion of those who drank alcohol and did not fall.

Chapter 10

10.2 H_O: $\mu_2 - \mu_1 = 0$ vs. H_A: $\mu_2 - \mu_1 \neq 0$ where μ_1 is the average gas mileage of domestic cars and μ_2 is the average gas mileage of imported cars. The calculated $z = 0.995$ is smaller than the critical $z_{0.025} = 1.96$. Thus, H_O cannot be rejected.

10.4 a. H_O: $\mu_2 - \mu_1 = 0$ vs. H_A: $\mu_2 - \mu_1 \neq 0$ where μ_1 is the average reading time of older people and μ_2 is the average reading time of younger people. The calculated $z = -2.04$ is beyond the critical $-z_{0.025} = -1.96$. Thus, H_O can be rejected at $\alpha = 0.05$.

10.6 H_O: $\mu_2 - \mu_1 \geq 0$ vs. H_A: $\mu_2 - \mu_1 < 0$ where μ_1 is the average income ($) of academic engineers and μ_2 is the average income ($) of industry engineers. The calculated $t = -3.43$ is beyond the critical value of $-t_{(0.05, df = 23)} = -1.714$. Thus, H_O can be rejected in favor of H_A at the level of $\alpha = 0.05$.

Chapter 11

11.1 The expected frequency is 15 for a sample of 200.

11.3 We need to test the following hypothesis:

H_O: Days and type of worker are independent.

H_A: Days and type of worker are not independent.

The χ^2 test statistic is 2.96908. This is smaller than the critical value of 15.5073 at a level of $\alpha = 0.05$. Thus, we cannot reject H_O. We can conclude that days and type of worker are independent.

11.5 We need to test the following hypothesis:

H_O: Type of business and the period of observation are independent.

H_A: Type of business and the period of observation are not independent.

The χ^2 test statistic is calculated to be 2,095.698, which is much greater than the critical value of 21.0261 at $\alpha = 0.05$. Thus, we can reject H_O. We can conclude that type of business is related to the period of observation in which failures occurred.

Chapter 12

12.2 If r = +1 or –1, then $r^2 = 1$. If r = 0, then $r^2 = 0$.

12.4 b. The mean is 56.
d. The average change score for those who scored below the average (56) on the pretest is 4.41.
e. The average change score for those who scored above the average (56) on the pretest is 4.04.

12.6 For positive (negative) deviations from the mean of the pretest score, there tends to be positive (negative) deviations from the mean of the midtest score and vice versa.

12.8 $r^2 = 0.791$

12.10 r = –0.99752

12.12 r = 0.73321 for those selected for executive positions
r = 0.75903 for those not selected for executive positions
r = 0.88809 for the total group

The two correlation coefficients for the subsamples are less than the correlation for the entire sample. If we divide the entire data set into two subsamples, those wide ranged observations play crucial roles in determining the correlation coefficients for both subsamples and thus result in smaller correlation coefficients.

12.14 The correlation coefficient r is calculated to be 0.569. There exists a positive, but not strong linear relationship between the number of votes obtained by candidates in the primary and the general election.

12.16 a. True
b. False. The slope of the sample regression line indicates how the predicted value of y changes as x changes.
c. True
d. False. A residual can be positive or zero or negative. The sum of all residuals is zero.
e. False. The least square method minimizes the sum of squared residuals.
f. True
g. True
h. True
i. False. The residuals always sum to zero whether the y intercept is zero or not.

12.18 a. b = –1.06098, a = 0 and the regression is $\hat{y} = -1.06098$ x
b. Both the mean of x and mean of y are zero and thus the intercept is zero.
c. The slope coefficient –1.06098 means that a one unit increase in x is associated with a 1.06098 unit decrease in y.

12.20 a. The slope coefficient is 0.5019 and the intercept coefficient is 20.8247. As a result, we have the regression equation $\hat{y} = 20.8247 + 0.5019$ x
b. $\hat{y} = 20.8247 + 0.5019 (40) = 40.9007$

12.22 The slope coefficient is 0.4698 and the intercept coefficient is 4.2885. As a result, we have the regression equation $\hat{y} = 4.2885 + 0.4698$ x

12.24 The regression equation GENÊRAL = –375.634 + 1.45015 PRIMARY implies that each additional vote in the primary is associated with 1.45015 votes in the general election.

12.26 Considering a ~ 0 and b ~ 27, Fisher's regression can be written $\hat{y} = 0 + 27x$ where y is the TV station advertising revenue and x is the audience size. Using the relationship, a = $\bar{y}$ – b$\bar{x}$ the slope coefficient b can be calculated as

$$b = \frac{\bar{y}}{\bar{x}} - \frac{a}{\bar{x}} = \frac{\bar{y}}{\bar{x}} = \frac{\sum y/n}{\sum x/n} = \frac{\sum y}{\sum x} \quad \text{since a} \sim 0.$$

Σy is nothing but the sum of all television revenues and Σx is the total audience size. The total audience size equals the number of television households multiplied by the fraction (60 percent) of prime time that the average household watches television. Thus, the estimation of b should result in the same coefficient value, 27.

12.28 a. The slope coefficient is 1.0220 and the intercept coefficient is 2.9866.
b. The total sum of squares is 380. 905 and the residual sum of squares is 115.490.

12.30 a. \$17,546.6
b. \$103,670.4
c. 0.56047
d. 11584.0

12.32 $r^2 = 0.997$

12.34 b. The least-squares regression equation is

$\widehat{SPEED}$ = 33.713 + 0.727536 EXPERIENCE and r^2 is 0.93852

c. 35.90 mph

12.36 Approximately 83.9 percent.

12.38 b. $21,579,820

12.40 $r^2 = 0.729$

12.42 0.77044

12.46 The predicted MPG is 37.65. The regression equation gives a better prediction than just using the average mileage of the two cars because the regression makes use of relationship between the mileage and weight of all the cars.

12.48 The implied least-squares regression equation is

$\widehat{\text{CANCER-FACTOR}}$ = 2.5 CIGARETTE where $\widehat{\text{CANCER-FACTOR}}$ is the incidence of lung cancer and CIGARETTE is the number of cigarettes consumed by a smoker a day.

12.50 Answer will depend on data and years selected.

12.52 a. The least-squares regression equation is

$\widehat{ABSDIF}$ = –125.904 + 0.0127 MACHDIF

where ABSDIF is the difference in absentee votes and MACHDIF is the difference in machine votes.

The slope coefficient 0.0127 indicates that an additional machine vote is associated with 0.0127 additional absentee votes.

c. 0.699. There is a positive and somewhat strong relationship between the difference in absentee votes and the difference in machine votes.

Chapter 13

13.2 As shown in the confidence interval formula, when there exists a lot of variability in the independent variable x, the value of the denominator $\Sigma(x_i - \bar{x})^2$ tends to be large and thus the margin of error tends to be small.

13.4 $\hat{y} = 17.88$ at x = 5.

13.8 a. The standard error of regression (estimation) is 11.7813. This is the estimate of the standard deviation of population error term ε and is calculated to be

$$s_e = \sqrt{\frac{ESS}{n-2}} = \sqrt{\frac{1110.3953}{8}} = 11.7813$$

b. The t statistic is to test the hypothesis H_O: ß = 0 vs. H_A: ß ≠ 0 and is calculated as follows:

$$t = \frac{b - \beta_0}{s_b} = \frac{0.7747 - 0}{0.4685} = 1.654$$

where $s_b = 0.4685$

13.10 a. The least-squares regression equation is

$\widehat{\text{JOBLESS-RATE}}$ = 4.38196 + 0.300121 DROP-IN-OUTPUT

b. The p-value is 0.00805 for the slope coefficient. We can reject the null hypothesis of zero slope value at an α level as low as 0.00805; we can conclude that there is a significant relationship between the jobless rate and the drop in industrial output.

13.12 The least-squares regression equation is

$\widehat{\text{YEAR1988}}$ = –8488.10 + 1.01264 YEAR1986

13.14 As n is increased, s_b is decreased and thus t is increased. This implies that increasing the sample size results in an increase in the power of the test, because rejection of the null hypothesis becomes easier with a large t value.

13.16 Although the coefficient of determination ($r^2 = 0.9802$) is very high and the slope coefficient has a relatively large t ratio (21.1), the residual plot shows a "<" pattern and suggests that the year be not linearly related to the return.

13.22 a. True
b. True
c. True
d. False. This confidence interval of $10 < E(y|x = 20) < 30$ does not say that the mean of y is between 10 and 30 with a probability of 0.95. We can say only that under repeated sampling, 95 percent of similarly constructed intervals would contain the true mean of y and the interval 20 ± 10 may (or may not) be one of those correct intervals.
e. False. A 95 percent confidence interval for E(y|x) could not be wider than a 95 percent prediction interval for an individual value of y.
f. False. The decision to reject depends on the α level.
g. False. There is no reason to believe that an estimated b equals the parameter ß. We, however, can say that the mean of b equals ß, i.e., E(b) = ß.
h. True
i. True
j. True
k. False. The purpose of regression analysis is not necessarily limited to the prediction of the dependent variable.

13.24 To test the hypothesis H_O: ß = 0 vs. H_A: ß ≠ 0, the test statistic is –8.347. This t value is beyond the critical $-t_{(0.025, df = 8)} = -2.306$; H_O is rejected at $\alpha = 0.05$. We can conclude that there is a significant relationship between two variables.

13.28 The standard error of regression is 0.2226 and the standard error of b is 0.02588. We could use these quantities in the calculation of test statistic t.

13.30 A 95 percent confidence interval for the expected value of y (number of votes in general election) is 1365 ± 597. This interval means that, for a candidate who receives 1,200 votes in the primary, if we repeat the construction of a confidence interval for the mean number of votes that the candidate will receive in the general election, 95 percent of similarly constructed intervals would contain the true mean number of votes in the general election.

13.32 a. The slope coefficient estimate 0.727536 is significant at $\alpha = 0.1$. We can conclude that there is a significant relationship between horse speed and jockey experience.
b. 35.9 ± 0.49
c. 35.9 ± 1.16

13.36 a. The slope coefficient implies that a one percent increase in industrial production is associated with a 0.5317 percent increase in employment.
b. We can conclude that there is a significant relationship between a change in industrial production and change in employment in the population.

13.38 5.5943; 0.9657; 0.8274

13.40 The slope coefficient estimate 4902.26 is significant at $\alpha = 0.05$; we can conclude that there is a significant relationship between CEO compensation (y) and the number of headquartered companies (x).

13.42 The slope coefficient estimate 1.06059 is significant at a typical α level 0.05; we can conclude that there is a significant relationship between two variables.

13.44 The slope coefficient estimate 5.52941 is significant at an α level as low as 0.00000 (not zero, but very small), which means that there is a significant relationship between the misery index and political stability.

13.46 The t value for the slope coefficient is 85.762, which is significant at $\alpha = 0.01$. We can conclude that there is a statistically significant relationship between two variables.

13.48 Answer will depend on data selected.

13.50 a. The MACHDIF coefficient estimate is significant at an α level as low as 0.00042; we can conclude that there is a significant relationship between absentee votes and machine votes.
b. –133.07 ± 721.64
c. The observed absentee votes 1025 is not inside this 95 percent of prediction interval, which may suggest a fraud in the election.

Chapter 14

14.2 a. **If a jockey's experience increases by one year, then predicted speed increases by b miles per hour, holding all other things (jockey's sex, weight carried on horse and horse's condition) fixed.**
b. When a jockey is male (=1), then the horse speed is c miles per hour faster or slower (depending on the sign of c) than at a female jockey, holding all other things (jockey's experience, weight carried on horse and horse's condition) fixed.

14.4 The least-squares regression equation for a first degree polynomial is $\hat{y} = 27.1112 - 0.791624$ x, $r^2 = 0.09567$ and the slope coefficient estimate is not significant at $\alpha = 0.1$

The least-squares regression equation for a second degree polynomial is $\hat{y} = 21.2096 + 2.91584\,x - 0.51833\,x^2$, $R^2 = 0.15540$ and neither slope coefficient estimate is significant at $\alpha = 0.1$

The least-squares regression equation for a third degree polynomial is $\hat{y} = 62.2093 - 38.1160\,x + 11.7792\,x^2 - 1.13818\,x^3$, $R^2 = 0.54575$ and all three slope coefficient estimates are significant at $\alpha = 0.1$; this can be viewed to be the best regression equation to fit the given data set.

14.6 a. 1. $\hat{y} = 8130.65 + 29.0514$ x where y is real earnings and x is age.

3. This regression equation does not appear to be a good representation of the relationship between two variables. r^2 is only 0.017781 and the residual plot shows a ">" pattern in the following plot of residuals. We suspect that there is a nonlinear relationship between x and y.

b. 1.

$\hat{y} = -12103.3 + 1138.43\,x - 18.1007\,x^2 + 0.0876612\,x^3$

This regression equation appears to provide better representation of the relationship between two variables. R^2 is 0.96023 and the residual plot does not show any special pattern.

14.8 a. The least-squares regression equation is

$\widehat{\text{PRICE}}$ = 2719.54 – 4.94027 ROOMS – 0.125848 TOTAL –1.33721 AGE where TOTAL = MAIN-FL + UPPER-FL + BASEMENT

b. $236,540

14.10 a. For batters, the implied regression equation is

$\widehat{\text{SALARY}}$ = a + 9000 HOMERUN + 6000 RUN where SALARY is the batter's next year salary, HOMERUN is the number of homeruns and RUN is the number of runs. Silk did not supply the value of intercept coefficient.

b. For pitchers, the implied regression equation is

$\widehat{\text{SALARY}}$ = a + 38000 VICTORY + 16000 SAVE + 3000 INNING + 12000 ERA where SALARY is the pitcher's next year salary, VICTORY is the number of victories, SAVE is the number of saves, INNING is the number of additional innings pitched and ERA is the decrement in e.r.a. measured in the number of one-tenths of point. Silk did not supply the value of intercept coefficient.

14.12 The death rate of smokers is higher than that of nonsmokers of the same age, but since the dependent variable is measured in natural logarithm units (where the base is e = 2.71828) assessment of this difference requires the use of the antilog.

14.14 Those intervals get wider, because the standard error of $\hat{y}_\bullet$ in the formula $\hat{y}_\bullet \pm (\alpha/2, df = n-k)s_{y\bullet}$ becomes larger as the x values are farther from their respective means.

14.16 At ROOMS = 8, TOTAL = 2500 and AGE = 0, a 95 percent prediction interval for the individual price is (1695.6, 3035.2) and a 95 percent confidence interval for the expected price is (2075.9, 2654.9). The prediction interval is wider than the confidence interval.

14.18 In Exercise 14.5, the estimated least-squares regression equation was $\hat{y} = 3.84521 - 0.277241\,x + 4.42645$ DUMMY where y is inflation rate and x is unemployment rate. The dummy variable coefficient has the t value of 5.078, which is significant at an α level as low as 0.00009. The coefficient for inflation rate, however, has the t value –0.826, which is not significant at a typical α level. Further, a plot of residuals shows a "<" pattern, which suggests that the relationship between the inflation rate and the unemployment rate be adjusted.

14.20 Only the income coefficient is significant at $\alpha = 0.01$ because the p-value is 0.00113.

14.22 We need to test the hypothesis H_O: $\beta_2 \le 0$ vs. H_A: $\beta_2 > 0$, where β_2 is the SALES coefficient. We can reject H_O at an α level as low as 0.1772.

14.24 $R^2 = 0.5446$

14.26 $R^2 = 0.4242$

14.28 R and thus R^2 are not related to the percentage of correct predictions except the extreme case where R = 1. R = 0.9 and thus $R^2 = 0.81$ means that 81 percent of the total variation in y values is explained by the fitted regression line.

14.30 **Both depend on ErrorSS.**

14.32 $R = 0.424$

14.34 $R^2 = \frac{\text{RegSS}}{\text{TotSS}}$

14.36 The dummy coefficient estimate –0.987623 means that the enactment of 55 mph speed limit results in 0.987623 units decrease in death rate implying \$1,975,246 savings per 100 million vehicle miles (= 0.987623(2,000,000)).

14.40 a. $\widehat{SALES} = -30.5857 + 2.4199\ AD + 26.6538\ NUM - 18.2615\ COMP$

14.42 One example of a regression model that might be estimated is death = $\beta_1 + \beta_2(\text{age}) + \beta_3(\text{health}) + \beta_4(\text{operation}) + \varepsilon$, where age is the average age of those operated on in a year at each of the n hospitals in Pennsylvania; health is an average measure of a health index of those operated on in a year at each of the n hospitals in Pennsylvania; and operation is the number of operations per year performed at each of the n hospitals in Pennsylvania.

We assume that ε is distributed normally but death is a count (0, 1, 2, •••• 12, ••••); thus, it is not continuous as implied by the assumption that ε is normal.

14.44 a. n = 119

b. The multiple coefficient of determination (R^2) of 0.388 means that 38.8 percent of the total variability in the profit is explained by the fitted regression line.

14.46 Yes, the inclusion of a dummy variable would be able to cure the problem. If we use the dummy variable of DUMMY = 1 for women and 0 for men, we could separate the gender effect on salary.

Index